Also by Julie Nixon Eisenhower
Special People

PAT NIXON

The Untold Story

by
Julie Nixon Eisenhower

SIMON AND SCHUSTER
NEW YORK

Designed by Anne Scatto/Levavi & Levavi
Picture editor: Vincent Virga

Manufactured in the United States of America

1   3   5   7   9   10   8   6   4   2

Library of Congress Cataloging in Publication Data

Eisenhower, Julie Nixon.
Pat Nixon : the untold story.

Includes index.
1. Nixon, Pat, 1912–   .   2. Eisenhower,
Julie Nixon.   3. Nixon, Richard M. (Richard Milhous),
1913–   —Family.   4. Presidents—United States—
Wives—Biography.   I. Title.
E857.N58E35   1986   973.921′092′4   [B]   86-20209
ISBN: 0-671-24424-8

For permission to use the materials mentioned, grateful acknowledgment is made to the following:

Excerpt from lyrics of "Marie" by Irving Berlin on page 24, copyright 1928 Irving Berlin; copyright renewed © 1955 Irving Berlin. Reprinted by special permission of Irving Berlin Music Corporation.
Quotations from Marsha Elliot Wray and George Gortikov about Pat Nixon (then Thelma Ryan) used by permission of the Oral History Program at California State University, Fullerton.

(continued at the back of the book)

Acknowledgments

Many generous friends of Patricia Nixon gave of their time, letters, and diaries to help me tell my mother's story. To the eighty-two friends, family members, and government associates whom I interviewed and who are listed at the end of this book, I express gratitude. In particular, I want to acknowledge Alice Martin Rosenberger, who on her own initiative gathered comments from sixty people who knew my mother during the Whittier days; Jack Sherwood, Mrs. Wiley T. Buchanan, and Jack Carley, who allowed me to quote from their diaries; and two close friends, Cynthia Hardin Milligan and Betsy McCarthy Reimer, who read the manuscript at various stages and offered insightful comments and unwavering encouragement. Barbara Thompson Eisenhower, my mother-in-law, provided astute observations on the Eisenhower years. I found the Richard M. Nixon Oral History Project, California State University, Fullerton, to be helpful in reconstructing my mother's earliest years. I am grateful to my editors at Simon and Schuster, Michael Korda and Nancy Nicholas, who expertly guided me through the cuts and additions in the editing of this book.

Above all, I thank Helene and Jack Drown, whose memories, notes, and letters richly added to the fabric of the book; David, who believed in this project from the beginning, who reaffirmed throughout that my mother's story should be told, and who provided invaluable editorial assistance; and finally, my parents, for making available letters and diaries, for not looking over my shoulder once, and for the care and love they gave Jennie, Alex, and Melanie Eisenhower at crucial points in the writing of *Pat Nixon: The Untold Story*.

To David
and to Pat's grandchildren:
Jennie, Alex and Melanie Eisenhower
and Christopher Cox

Contents

Part I   1912–1945

1. "St. Patrick's Babe in the Morning"   17
2. "She Had Grit"   28
3. "Pat Will Be a Great Success"   34
4. "My Brainy Girl"   42
5. "To the Beautiful Teacher Who Wore a
   Red Geranium in Her Hair"   50
6. "Dearest Heart"   56
7. Patricia Ryan Nixon   65
8. On the Home Front   74

Part II   1945–1969

9. The First Campaign   84
10. "You Run Until You Can't Run Anymore"   93
11. The Senator   103

12. Checkers   113
13. Mrs. Vice President: The First Year   130
14. Second Thoughts   145
15. "No One Is Going to Push Us off the Ticket"   153
16. The Road to the Presidency   165
17. "Iron and Courage, Not Skin and Bones"   186
18. Home to California   203
19. Out of Defeat...   215
20. The Road to the Presidency II   224
21. The Campaign of 1968   235
Part III   1969–1976
22. The White House   250
23. A Real Pro   280
24. 1971: "The World's Hardest Job"   306
25. 1972: "Vive Madame Nixon"   329
26. 1973: "Fight, Fight, Fight"   359
27. 1974: The Last Year   399
Part IV   1976–1986
28. A Solitary Person   431
29. "A Shoulder to Everyone—
But Whose Shoulder Does She Lean On?"   444
30. "Onward and Upward"   455
Interviews   462
Index   463

PAT
NIXON

The Untold Story

Part 1

1912-1945

"St. Patrick's Babe in the Morning"

M y mother was born near midnight on March 16, 1912, in a miner's shack high in the mountains of eastern Nevada. Although it was almost spring, the nights in the copper boomtown of Ely were frosty, and one of her brothers, Bill Ryan, remembers being awakened by cold air seeping into the cabin. When he got out of bed, two-and-a-half-year-old Bill saw his father standing at the front door with a stranger. The man pocketed five dollars and then he was gone. Bill was round-eyed with questions. "You have a little sister now," his father, Will Ryan, explained. "That money was to pay the doctor."

At her mother's insistence the baby was called Thelma Catherine. But thoroughly Irish Will Ryan, whose parents came from County Mayo, circumvented the Thelma. His daughter was always "Babe" to him. He decided too that they would observe her birthday on March 17, the birth date of Ireland's patron saint. When Bill once asked why his sister's birthday was celebrated a day late, his father answered, "Well, she was there in the morning, my St. Patrick's Babe in the morning."

My mother's birthplace, Ely, had been named for one Ely Smith, a miner from Illinois who made his fortune in Montana, lost it in South Dakota, and died penniless. The town had a thirty-five-thousand-dollar school, a new water system, and two daily and three weekly newspapers, but the frontier was not far away. *The White Pines News* of East Ely headlined on March 17, 1912, the day after her birth, "Cherry Creek Barber Slashes Chinaman over Head with Hatchet Because He Objected to Being Shortchanged." There was not one item of national news on the front page, no hint that William Howard Taft was President of the United States, or that a former Princeton professor named Woodrow Wilson was talking about running for President.

The boomtown of Ely gave Will Ryan a steady job as a timekeeper in the Veteran mine, but little more. He was forty-six years old and had been a prospector intermittently for more than two decades. Shortly after little Thelma Ryan's first birthday, her mother, Kate, began to try to convince Will to leave Ely and settle in Southern California.

It was not easy for Will Ryan to give up his dream of striking it rich or to forgo the life of the adventurer that mining symbolized to him. For years he had willingly endured the hardships of prospecting, its steady diet of bacon, beans, and flapjacks, with only an occasional can of tomatoes; the unrelenting desert sun by day, and sleeping on sand under a cold sky of white stars; the physical test that made men lean and why so many of the miners earned the nickname "Slim." In 1913 he had had two careers already—sailor and miner. But now he was to try farming.

The Ryans traveled by train to Los Angeles, and for several weeks they looked for a small tract of land. Tom Ryan, then almost three years old, remembers the day his father drove them in a buckboard wagon to Artesia, a farming community of about four hundred people located eighteen miles southwest of Los Angeles. His mother and father sat in the front seat. In the back were Tom, Bill, Babe and their half-sister, Neva, Kate's daughter by her first husband who had been killed in a tragic flash-flood accident in South Dakota. When Will pulled up to a compact single-story ranch house on Pioneer Boulevard, Tom heard his mother exclaim: "That's the house I want!"

Their house, which had no electricity or running water, was on ten and a half acres of land as flat as a tabletop, indistinguishable in appearance from the neighboring "ranches," as the small farms in that area of Southern California were called. As a farmer, Will Ryan was in business for himself, as he had been throughout much of his life; he always told his children that "partnership is a hell of a ship to sail in." With only his wife and children helping him, Will Ryan ran a "truck farm." He could fit his yield of crops into a trailer that held forty boxes and then truck it into town behind his Model T. He taught himself how to run the farm by studying agricultural journals and reading articles on crop raising. Eventually his reputation was such that his neighbors regarded him as somewhat of a sage. They called the tall, angular Mr. Ryan the "cabbage king" because he raised the biggest and best cabbage for miles around. He was known too as a scrupulously honest man. When he borrowed farm equipment or hired extra help to harvest a particularly large crop, he formalized his agreements with a mere handshake—and a steady appraisal with his piercing blue eyes.

Although Will Ryan became a full-fledged farmer, he never looked upon himself as one. Unlike his neighbors, he did not wear a straw hat in the field; instead, winter or summer he wore his Danbury gray felt hat. Tom Ryan told me "my dad was always chasing rainbows." He invested in oil wells or mines whenever he could spare the cash. Among the few possessions he left his children was an old stock certificate dated 1921 for two thousand shares of Huntington Central Oil Company. And nightly, Will Ryan escaped the limiting boundaries of ten acres of plowing, planting, and fertilizing by drawing his rocking chair up to the kitchen table and reading by the light of a single kerosene lamp. He was a voracious reader, taking in the evening paper, farm journals, books that were traded from house to house among the neighbors, and, of course, everything he could about oil wells and mines. Invariably, his youngest child, his Babe, would crawl up on his lap for a story and then fall asleep while he rocked and read.

It was through his stories about his whaling and prospecting days that Will Ryan kept his dreams alive. He had been only seventeen when he left home. He boasted to his children that he had traveled to every state in the Union and well beyond and told them many times his tales of being lost on the Mojave Desert and almost dying of thirst; and of the exotic beauty of Borneo, and the strangeness of the pygmies of the Philippines. His stories made a particularly strong impression on Babe. The escape through books, the love of travel and adventure, and the fierce independence became as much a part of her as they were of her father.

Indeed, her first memory is not of the farm or of animals, but of traveling with her mother to Los Angeles on the "big red electric car" when she was only two or three years old. A nice couple sitting across the aisle on the electric car kept looking at her and finally gave her a small box of wintergreen candies. She had never had her own box of candy before. Thelma Ryan was noticed because she was an uncommonly pretty child. Her oldest brother, Bill, had strawberry-blond hair, Tom was a brunet, and she fell between the two with her shining red-gold hair. Both Bill and Tom had their father's deep-blue eyes, but Babe's were unique, her most unusual feature. Her eyes were almond-shaped and, most often, a luminous brown, though sometimes they appeared green or even gray-blue. The soft, pure color gave the impression of endless depth.

The trips into Los Angeles were important to both Kate Ryan and her youngest daughter. For Kate, they were a chance to see her firstborn child, Matthew Bender, who, since his father's death, had been raised by his well-to-do grandparents. In the immediate aftermath of the tragedy, they had convinced the young widow they could provide better for Matthew than she could.

But the excursions offered something else as well, as Thelma came to understand at an early age. "We lived in the country... my mother longed for something more," she told me. The rides on the big red electric car, the visits to Echo Park, the rare chance to shop were indelible memories for little Thelma Ryan, for they also gave her a sense that there was "something more."

My mother was five years old when the world beyond Artesia came closer. In April of 1917, President Woodrow Wilson, proclaiming that "the world must be made safe for democracy," asked Congress to align the United States with France and England by declaring war on Germany. The Ryan children and their schoolmates aided the drive for war materials by collecting walnut shells and bits of foil and metal and depositing them in big barrels on Main Street.

The war caused tension in the Ryan home. Kate, with her heart-shaped face and large, gentle brown eyes beneath a wide forehead and straight brows, made her children promise they would not tell anyone she was German-born. As a wave of anti-Hun hysteria swept the country, music by German composers was banned, even Strauss waltzes. No longer did Kate converse in her native tongue with Mrs. McCann, her German neighbor whose house was near the big red electric car stop. Thelma and her brothers were never told about their mother's family in Ober Rosbach where they had cultivated fruit trees for more than two hundred years, and heard only the barest details of her journey to America at the age of ten. More than fifty years after the war, when Tom Ryan wrote my mother describing his own son's army duty in Germany and his visits there with long-lost relatives, including Kate's brother who had been born after she emigrated to America, he would mention that "Mother's name was Halberstadt."

After Germany's defeat, when inflation was so severe that a hundred thousand German marks equaled one dollar and people needed wheelbarrows to hold their money when they shopped, Kate used her egg earnings to mail money and food secretly to her family. Those pitifully meager gifts saved the Halberstadts from destitution but were more than a financial burden to Kate. She lived in fear that Will, who was adamantly anti-German, would discover what she was doing.

Will and Kate did not discuss the war often in front of their children. In fact, my mother remembers that Christmas of 1917 was a particularly happy time. On Christmas Eve she heard noise in the family parlor, which was separated only by a curtain from the room she shared with her half sister, Neva. She got out of bed and discovered her parents filling the stockings with nuts, oranges, apples, and, at the bottom of each, a dime. They asked her to help them play Santa Claus. Together they hung the stockings and placed the homemade gifts around the tree—crochet-trimmed handkerchiefs for the girls, knit garments for the boys, and for each child one store-bought present.

Because the family had to struggle to make a living on the farm, the Ryan children learned early not to expect much and to be stoical in hiding their feelings. Their father in particular did not encourage open demonstrations of emotion. That is why my mother remembers so clearly the day he gave her a pair of shoes. New shoes were not an everyday occurrence, and my mother, slightly awed, accepted the present solemnly and wordlessly. Neva tugged at her sleeve and whispered that she should give her father a kiss. She hesitated, and then, shyly, slowly, went over to him. When he smiled with pleasure at her kiss she was happier than she had been the moment he gave her the shoes.

Will Ryan normally revealed his affection by teasing, which my mother often took literally. Although it was a treat to ride with him to town to see its bank, hardware store, barbershop, Scott and Frampton's for general goods, Neimes' Drugstore, and two blacksmith shops, she always dreaded the moment Will's friends would gather around the two-seater buggy to barter over a price for her. Amid much laughter, the men would bid, usually reaching the sizable sum of five dollars, a week's worth of groceries. My mother, sitting very straight, her red cape spread around her like a fan, her eyes straight ahead, never revealed even to her father that she was terrified he would sell her.

When the men finally drifted away, her father bought groceries and paid his bills while Babe waited in the buggy. Whenever Will had a few cents left over, he would bring his Babe a strawberry-ice-cream cone. And she always waited with tightly controlled anticipation, hoping against hope. If he was empty-handed, she did not let him know she was disappointed. "In our family, we held our disappointment," Mother remembers.

Perhaps because Will Ryan held himself so tightly in check, inevitably there were periodic explosions. My mother learned to watch carefully for her father's return from one of his infrequent trips to town. If she saw the buggy racing toward the house, she knew her dad probably had had too many whiskeys with his friends, and that once inside, he would pick fights with Kate until the children cried out, "Don't, Daddy, don't!"

My mother has resolutely buried the unpleasant memories of her childhood. Only once did she admit to me her father's temper and confrontations with Kate. Then firmly, so that I would know she was speaking her final words on the subject, she said: "I detest temper. I detest scenes. I just can't be that way. I saw it with my father." She paused for a moment and then added: "And so to avoid scenes or unhappiness, I suppose I accommodated to others." Unlike Will Ryan, whose moods shifted mercurially from quiet to bewilderingly angry, my mother as well as her two brothers would develop into even-tempered, gentle adults who preferred silence to confrontations.

Life on the truck farm was an all-consuming family effort. The day began early, at 6 A.M. Before leaving for school, there were animals to feed, and with several crops a year, always some field work. In the fall, the family planted pimiento peppers; in the winter, beets, cauliflower and cabbage; and in the summer, corn and tomatoes. And methodically, every three years, Will planted barley in order to build up the soil.

Harvesting had to be done quickly and efficiently. Will Ryan calculated that his family needed a thousand dollars to get through the winter and that at peak production his farm could provide just that. My mother often told me, "When we were growing up we didn't have money but we didn't lack things."

When she was six years old, she joined her brothers in the mile-and-a-quarter walk to the red-brick grammar school on Pioneer Boulevard, which was nothing more than packed dirt covered by a layer of rock shale. In the summer, it was oiled to prevent choking clouds of dust. Not until 1929, my mother's senior year of high school, did Artesia have a cement road and streetlights. Because my mother had learned to read by memorizing words in her brothers' books, she had an immediate reputation as a good student. Whenever the superintendent or an important visitor dropped in on the first-grade classroom, the teacher would demonstrate the success she was having with her students by asking Thelma Ryan to read.

With the start of school, Babe Ryan was officially listed as Thelma, though apart from her mother, teachers, and her parents' friends, few would ever call her that. To her brothers and father, she was Babe, and her classmates called her "Buddy." She encouraged the nicknames, because, even in grammar school, she had a well-defined sense of who she was, and Thelma did not seem to fit her.

Her teachers were impressed by her calm and maturity. Mary Bragg, who taught in Artesia for many years and eventually became principal of one of the town's primary schools, explained why: "She was quietly equal to anything. If something needed to be done, she did it. Life didn't bowl her over as a child." When she skipped second grade, her father delightedly boasted that she was "as smart as a whip." At home she heard him say over and over, "If it's worth doing, it's worth doing right." She very early became a perfectionist—whether it was in her schoolwork, keeping house, or her own appearance.

The school had an auditorium, and it was not unusual to see Thelma Ryan on stage, reciting a poem or prose piece. Since Artesia was a small town, it became known that Will Ryan's youngest did not lose her poise before an audience. "Doc" Neimes, owner of Neimes' Drugstore, and one of the leading figures in town, began asking her to recite for the local clubs. One of her triumphs was an oration on the merits of "Fighting Bob" La Follette, head of the Progressive Party. Though La Follette was considered a radical by his critics, Will Ryan—and therefore his daughter—supported him wholeheartedly because he was "for the workingman." Will, in fact, deserted the Democratic Party in 1924 to vote for La Follette.

Because she demanded much of herself and because others set such high standards for her, my mother came to value the rare moments of free time when she was without restrictions or expectations. Her brothers had built a tree house at the edge of the backyard, and whenever she could, she escaped to the protecting branches of the tree with a book and an apple. Reading became her favorite pastime and, as she told me years later, the "biggest influence on my life. It gave me a horizon beyond the small town we were living in. Somehow I always knew there was more in the world than what we were experiencing then. . . ."

My mother's first love was the outdoors. Even hard field work became a game as she raced her brothers to see who could get to the end of a vegetable row first. The only farm work she thoroughly disliked was picking bugs off the produce and dropping them into cans of kerosene. She was always planting, despite teasing from her brothers, and, occasionally, she had results. Behind the house, she planted the pit from an apricot and it grew into a rich, fruit-bearing tree. Her parents let her cultivate her own small flower garden along the front left corner of the house, and as she grew older, no matter how busy she became with increasing responsibilities, she tended her "English garden" of daffodils, narcissus, marigolds, and daisies. She loved particularly the red-orange of the India daisy, the larger marguerite, and the yellow-and-white English daisy because they blossomed most of the year. And, once cut, daisies lived in the house in a water jar for more than a week. Like my mother, they were tenacious and hardy survivors.

Myrtle and Louise Raine, who lived on the adjoining ten-acre ranch, were Buddy's most frequent playmates. The three beat a well-worn path back and forth through the Raines' sandy field of potatoes. When together, the girls were irrepressible. Will Ryan frequently teased, "What are you girls plotting now?" He had an uncanny ability to guess what was in their minds, so much so that Myrtle wondered sometimes if the distinctly deaf Mr. Ryan could indeed, as he claimed, hear them whispering.

The girls loved to walk on the railroad tracks across the bridge near their ranches, ignoring the danger of an oncoming train, which could kill them. They raided their neighbors' beehives, snitched a watermelon here and there, and became experts at pulling the heart out of select cabbages from Will's patch, leaving only the faintest teeth marks as evidence. The girls even penetrated Tom and Bill Ryan's all-male hideout, a long trench, deep enough to stand upright in, which the boys had boarded over and concealed with dirt. The favorite pastime in the trench was rolling cigarettes and smoking them. The girls gained admission when they proved themselves as adept at rolling cigarettes as the boys—and as capable of keeping quiet about it.

When Buddy, Myrtle, and Louise worked in the fields, they wore their brothers' jeans. The jeans were so comfortable that they finally got up their courage to go into Scott and Frampton's General Store and buy well-fitting boys' jeans for themselves. Although some of the neighbors were scandalized, the girls reasoned that it was more practical to wear the jeans during out-of-school hours, especially when horseback riding or climbing the two-story water tank in back of the Raines' house. The tank's platform was their stage for plays, and their audience, usually reluctant brothers, sat below.

Summer evenings provided the most fun. There were endless places to hide on the farm—tool sheds, icehouses, barns—and exciting twilight games of run, sheep, run. Will cultivated a peanut patch for the children so that on warm evenings they could sit outside and enjoy peanut roasts. Best of all was the special treat of a weeknight swim, followed by wieners and marshmallows cooked over an open fire. The Ryans most often drove their Model T over the dirt road to Seal Beach, since it had a bay side where those like Buddy, who did not know how to swim, could bob safely in inner tubes.

A half-dozen Saturdays a year my mother was able to spend the entire day at the beach stretched out on the warm sand until the last rays of sun had disappeared. She often took her Gramophone and small collection of records, which she and her friends played over and over. One of the records was "Marie" by Irving Berlin. To this day, whenever Louise and Myrtle Raine hear "Marie," they think of Buddy Ryan.

> Marie, the dawn is breaking.
> Marie, you'll soon be waking...
> The kiss, so very tender—
> The words "Will you surrender
> To me, Marie."*

In the summer of 1925, when she was thirteen, Thelma Catherine Ryan grew up. Neva had graduated from high school the year before and came into a small amount of money from her grandparents which enabled her to get her own apartment and attend Fullerton Junior College. Now Thelma was the only one at home to help Kate keep the five-room Ryan house "scrub clean."

With a seven-year age gap, Thelma and Neva had never been close. Neva was headstrong and vocal in her complaints, especially her feelings, not unfounded, that her brother, Matt, had had more advantages than she because he lived with their grandparents. She let her mother know that she missed the music lessons, the trips, and the city life, all things that Kate yearned for her daughter to have and could not provide. My mother, though still very young, sensed the pain Kate felt about Neva. The sadness created a special bond between Kate and her youngest child. "I tried to be especially good," my mother remembers. "So often my mother would put her arms around me

---

*Copyright 1928, Irving Berlin, Inc.

and hold me close and whisper, 'I don't know what I would do without you. ... You are the happiness in my life.'"

The summer Neva left home, Kate Ryan was ill, though neither she nor her family realized how seriously. Myrtle and Louise Raine remember coming to the house shortly after school had ended for the year and seeing Mrs. Ryan lying on the couch in the living room, her feet elevated against the wall. They were surprised to see their friend's mother, who was always carefully dressed, usually in slightly loose, feminine blouses, lying in such an unladylike pose.

Kate never complained of pain, but the children would know she had a headache if she was wearing a bandage tightly bound around her forehead. Only rarely now did she play the parlor's rosewood piano, which the Ryans had bought with the ranch. The music she most often chose was the plaintive song of the Indian maid Red Wing, who "... loved a warrior bold, this shy little maid of old. But brave and gay, he rode one day to battle far away."

Until her illness, without fail Kate had made cinnamon rolls for her children's arrival home from school. Even now, Tom and Bill Ryan's eyes light up when they describe the delicious, light rolls their mother miraculously baked in her old Perfection oil-burning stove. But now, as the children walked home, when they were within a quarter of a mile from the ranch they seldom smelled the fragrance of freshly baked bread.

Their mother's closest friend was Grace Coward, who lived across the street. She was a kind, well-read woman with impeccable manners. She also was a devout Christian Scientist, and during visits with Kate, she discussed her faith. Kate started attending Mrs. Coward's church. Whether because of her friend's influence or her own determination not to give in to her illness, for months Kate did not consult Doc Haskell, who cared for almost everyone in Artesia. When she finally did, there was little he could do to help her. She had both a kidney affliction called Bright's disease and cancer of the liver, an extremely fast-acting cancer.

After the diagnosis, Tom Ryan, then only fourteen years old, remembers going with his father to see the other doctor in town for a second opinion and hearing him say flatly that she was a very sick woman. The doctor did not mention the word "cancer," perhaps because in 1925 little was known about its causes and many regarded it as something shameful, in a class with venereal disease. And so the Ryan children were told only that their mother had Bright's disease.

Because the town did not have a hospital, Kate went to Doc Haskell's house where he boarded patients for three dollars a day. There she spent the last two months of her life, unable to go home although only a mile away. Thelma and her brothers grew closer than ever before. Not only was their mother frighteningly ill, but also during that freshman year at Excelsior High School in Norwalk, they were all in the same grade. My mother and Tom had been classmates ever since she skipped second grade. Now the school decided that

Bill, who had broken his right arm cranking the family's Model T Ford and had been unable to write for several months, would be better off repeating his grade.

With Kate at Doc Haskell's, thirteen-year-old Babe took over most of the responsibilities of the house. She was especially busy during harvesting time when she had to cook for extra hired help. The job of preparing huge quantities of food affected her own appetite. More and more often, long after she had sat through dinner barely touching her food, she would make a batch of fudge for herself and eat it for dinner.

Her brothers began to help her more. After supper they lowered the shade on the kitchen window so no one would see them doing "women's work" and helped her wash dishes. They also helped with the hard physical labor of the laundry, which required building a fire in the outdoor brick fireplace, lifting the clothes with long sticks from vats of boiling water into cold for the first rinse, and then a second rinse, and finally hanging the heavy, dripping wet wash on the line to dry.

There was less time than ever for play. Myrtle and Louise Raine found that Buddy had to go right home after school. She did not explain the changes in her life caused by her mother's illness. Not until a year after Kate Ryan's death, when their own mother was hospitalized, did Myrtle and Louise finally understand.

Every evening the family visited Kate at Doc Haskell's, and during the final weeks, Thelma often nursed her through the night. Only once could my mother bring herself to tell me about that time. "When I went to see my mother, every day I knew she would get better. After the boys left, I would change her nightie and feed her. But she could eat less and less. If she took half a teaspoon, I would be so happy. Toward the end they kept her sedated. I didn't like it when the doctors gave her so much medicine that she was dopey. I didn't realize that she needed it for the pain."

During one of Thelma's last visits, Kate, perhaps aware that she was dying, told her daughter that she had hidden a little money from selling eggs in the inner pocket of her old coat at home. Just Thelma was to know about it—it was for her.

Three days before Kate Ryan died, she called her son Bill back into the room as he was leaving and told him to get her clothes out of the closet so she could go home. "No, Mother," Bill answered. It almost broke his heart to leave her that night.

On January 18, 1926, when the children got up and went into the kitchen for breakfast, Will told them their mother was dead. Grace Coward kindly came to the house to gather clothes in order to dress Kate for burial. Later my mother went to the doctor's to pick up Kate's belongings. It was then that Haskell told her he put "cancer of the liver" on the death certificate. She remembers this vividly because the name of the disease was alien to her. When neighbors and friends started arriving at the Ryan ranch to offer condolences and to try to express how much Kate had meant to them, my mother thought she could not bear the pain any longer. The friends cried, and despite all her efforts, she cried with them.

Services for Kate were held at the Christian Science church in Norwalk, which she had attended occasionally with Grace Coward. Some of my mother's friends from school were there. They waited outside the church at the conclusion of the rites, uneasy about trying to comfort Buddy. But when she came down the church steps moments later, she walked directly over to her friends and said quickly, "Didn't she look beautiful?"

In the years that followed Kate's death, there were many questions that Thelma wished she had asked. She knew almost nothing about her mother's origins or family life. She did not know what Kate Ryan believed in or cared deeply about. She told me: "We were so busy on the farm. It was always a struggle. We didn't have much time to talk. And when you're thirteen you do not ask questions about philosophy or family."

Even the physical reminders of Kate were few: three photographs, a fat pewter cream and sugar set, and a small, dark rose-colored bud vase with a golden spider-web design. But Kate had left a legacy to her daughter, more apparent to others than to my mother herself. Tom Ryan, for one, saw his mother reflected in his sister, because she, like Kate, "had a big heart. She sacrificed and did things without complaining."

Kate's death made her youngest child old before her time. She told me matter-of-factly, "When my mother died I just took responsibility for my life." She became convinced she could do anything if she had to. One of the most pronounced results of Kate's death was her daughter's disciplined refusal to look back. Her unwillingness to discuss what had happened was self-preservation, for it took courage and willpower simply to go about her daily chores.

At the end of the school year, she went to the annual mother-daughter banquet, perhaps the biggest event on the school calendar, involving months of planning and decorating. The banquet, she confided to me, was one of the saddest nights of her life, for, in attending alone, she accepted undeniably the truth that her mother was gone.

CHAPTER 2

"She Had Grit"

With Kate's death, Thelma Ryan's life increasingly became a race against the clock. In the morning, after the farm chores, she prepared breakfast for the family—usually hot cereal, cocoa, and toast—and got ready for school. She memorized facts for tests and lines for school plays while she ironed her brothers' shirts. Sometimes she propped her textbook on the stove counter next to the steaming kettle so that no time would be wasted as she quickly hand-pressed waves into her short, thick bob.

She always left for last the task of ironing the box pleats of her school uniform. The serge skirt was difficult to care for, and some of her friends even pinned the pleats to the ironing board in order to get a perfect look. The uniform, which also included a white middy blouse with navy-blue collar and navy necktie, was required by the Excelsior High School faculty in an effort to eliminate competition over clothes among a student body from a six-mile rural area with widely varying degrees of prosperity. Only on Fridays could the girls wear what they wanted, and on that day rivalry was fierce. One of my mother's teachers remembers coming home from work and having to stay up until dawn in order to make a dress for her daughter, who had insisted tearfully that all the others would be wearing new outfits.

My mother was not always able to keep herself perfectly groomed, but as Marsha Elliott Wray, a member of the student council then, remembers: "She would never make excuses. She had too much pride and self-discipline. . . . Once Thelma had a blue slip for not being in uniform and I was one of the judges she appeared before. We gave her demerits and I have thought so many times since that we didn't stop to realize that she was getting clothes ready for three kids and cooking; and we had the nerve to give her demerits for not being in uniform one day!"

In high school, Thelma Ryan, at five feet five and a half inches tall, was sturdy and trim, a pretty girl whom one classmate described as having apricotlike cheeks—beautifully round, with just a touch of fresh freckling. Will Ryan did not allow his Babe to date unless her brothers were along in the group. He encouraged Bill and Tom to be protective of their sister. The boys hardly needed the encouragement. Ever since Kate's death, the children were a close-knit entity against the rest of the world—in Bill's memories, a "threesome." The Ryans were markedly self-contained and impressed their classmates as being slightly shy and "not commotion-causing." Tom explained their restraint as a habit that began at home: "I guess we were all quiet. My dad was hard-of-hearing and we had to talk loudly to him. And so among ourselves, we all just sort of quieted down."

There were, however, fights and brotherly competition between Bill and Tom, particularly over the use of the family car, "Liz." Will refused to arbitrate, sending his sons outside to settle their arguments with fistfights. He seemed proud of their athletic prowess. Bill, known to his teammates as "Wild Bill," was halfback on the football team, while Tom was its quarterback and captain. But my mother could not stay after school for athletics because it would have meant taking the five-o'clock bus home, not leaving her enough time to get the housework done. In later years, she often told Tricia and me that one of the few regrets of her childhood was that she never mastered a sport.

Since debate and drama activities did not require staying until five, Buddy Ryan was active in both. She was a member and eventually the secretary of Excelsior's Filibuster Club, founded "with the idea of promoting interest in parliamentary law and the fine art of oratory." My mother's sophomore yearbook reported: "You just ought to hear them [Thelma Ryan and her three fellow debaters] talk, why they could convince you that Chinamen walk on their heads and dig upwards for gold."

Her greatest pleasure at Excelsior was taking part in school plays. Acting represented the fantasy of leaving Artesia for a few hours during rehearsals and being part of another world. The plays provided an opportunity to dress up, the only touch of glamour she knew apart from infrequent summer visits with Grace Coward and her daughter to the "dance auditoriums" on the Pike in Long Beach. Excelsior's auditorium, which seated eight hundred, was almost as grand as the Pike's big halls.

Thelma Ryan had the female lead in her junior-year play, *The Romantic Age*, and the next year in the senior presentation of *The Rise of Silas Lapham*.

Excelsior Life, the student newspaper, reported on opening night: "Penelope Lapham, in all her girlish moods, gay or serious, was charmingly portrayed by Thelma Ryan." On the same front page, there was a smaller notice about a student-body convention being held at Orange High School; representing Excelsior was Thelma Ryan.

Throughout high school my mother was active in student government and popular enough to be elected to school-wide offices in both her junior and senior years. George Gortikov, who was president of the student body when she was its secretary, recalls that it was during those meetings he began to realize that pretty and reserved Thelma Ryan had a strong personality. He would be leading a discussion and by the end of it she would have skillfully and diplomatically taken over.

She was well liked—and remembered—by her classmates. In September of 1977, forty-eight years after graduation, more than thirty members of the Class of '29 sent her a card at San Clemente inscribed: "Dear Thelma: We are not sure just when your birthday is. But, when it arrives please get this card out and see you never lost any friends."

In her senior annual, the *Green and White,* many of those who wrote inscriptions to "Dear Buddy" or "Dear Thelma" refer to her as if she were an older person, someone to emulate. One girl, Marjorie Miyakawa, wrote: "Dear Thelma, I have always held you as my ideal. You whom I've always admired, I wish success and happiness in the future years to come."

When one of my mother's teachers, Dr. Ralph Burnight, later became principal of Excelsior, for years he encouraged innumerable students to work harder by telling them about one Thelma Ryan, a girl who was able to do the housework, keep a family united, and still be active in extracurricular activities and achieve high scholarship at school. For almost twenty of those years when Burnight talked about his model student, she was not yet the wife of a famous man.

But the competent, composed, smiling exterior was hard won. As a senior, her schoolwork had never been more demanding: English, modern history, civics, Latin, social problems, and chemistry. Eight years later, when she became a teacher, she was always sympathetic if a student dozed in class, at least until she had a chance to find out more about the student. She herself had only one instructor, Miss Watkins of the Spanish Department, who seemed to understand if she nodded off, and left her undisturbed when she did.

The finest tribute to Thelma Ryan during her high-school days is a senior-yearbook inscription written by her dramatics teacher, Madeline Thomas. Miss Thomas, one of whose legs was partially paralyzed from polio, had a philosophy of life that she shared with all her students: "Develop yourself—you can do anything." She had seen how my mother, when threatened with losing the lead in the senior play because she did not have all her gym credits,

difficult choice about which one would attend college. All three had scholarships, but they could afford to have only one go. Because Tom's future as an athlete seemed brighter than Bill's, he accepted a football scholarship to the University of Southern California. As the eldest, Bill took on the responsibility of the ranch. Tom and his sister made an agreement: if she stayed in Artesia and cared for her father, he would help her, someday, somehow, to get a college education. It was a promise he fulfilled five years later.

That summer she took a shorthand course at Woodbury College at night, trying to keep her eyes on the future. By day, she nursed her father. As he grew weaker and more wasted, barely able to move from his bed to his chair, one of his few pleasures was listening to baseball games on his crystal set with the volume at the maximum.

Tom remembers the crisp, beautiful fall day he took his dad on a long automobile trip to look at sanitoriums. Will Ryan ignored the reason for their mission and treated the trip almost as if it were a little outing, providing his son with the memory of a happy day. To Tom's surprise, Will showed the most interest in a Catholic sanitorium in Monrovia, at least an hour's drive from Artesia. On the way home, Will apparently felt he needed to explain his choice to his son: "It's all right to live without religion, but it's not all right to die without it."

In order to help pay for the hospitalization, my mother immediately got a job at Artesia's First National Bank on Pioneer Boulevard. Whenever she could, after work she made the long drive to Monrovia to see her father. After one visit, with sensitivity to the eastern Ryans' greatest wish, she wrote her Aunt Annie to tell her that as she left, Will had rosary beads in his hand. In May of 1930, four years after Kate's death, Will Ryan received the last rites from a priest. Following the Catholic service in Bellflower, he was buried in Whittier next to Kate.

Shortly before he died, Will had broken down in front of Bill and cried. He told his eldest son, "Take care of Babe." Bill took seriously his father's charge of watching over Babe, and yet at the same time he realized that she already knew her own course. "She wanted to make something of herself," Bill told me. "My dad was determined . . . to get things done and she had his determination—and grit, grit, grit." Bill spoke with passion. Then he repeated, as if I had not understood: "She had grit. Life didn't stop there; things went on." And, finally, almost as an afterthought, he said, "She fought for everything she got."

CHAPTER 3

"Pat Will Be
a Great Success"

In the fall of 1931, my mother enrolled at Fullerton Junior College as Patricia Ryan. The graceful-sounding name was a symbol of her new life.

When my father was running for the Presidency in 1960, my sister and I read in a magazine article that our mother's name as a child was Thelma. We showed her the article and asked, if it were true, why was she now Patricia? Her answer—"Patricia was my father's favorite name. . . . I was his 'St. Patrick's Babe in the morning'"—only partially satisfied us. Had she ever really been "Thelma"? We began a daily campaign of cajoling her to sign her name as she used to, Thelma Ryan. For days she resisted before finally giving in, but as she carefully framed a curl at the top of her T, she said firmly, "I'm not Thelma anymore, I'm Pat."

Although it was as Patricia Ryan that she registered at Fullerton Junior College, she still needed help from those who had known her as Thelma. In the year following Will's death, she had worked at several jobs in town in order to earn enough money to attend some classes at Fullerton in the fall. She had not been able to count on any income from the ranch. One of her carefully penned ledgers of the ranch's 1930 operating expenses still exists. For the period August 1930 to January 1931, she noted various costs: "Car greased $2.00; lumber $16.36; taxes $108.82." At the bottom of the page is the statement: "Total deposits: None made since a year ago January."

The stock-market crash in October of 1929 had plummeted America into a nationwide depression. As much as anyone, farmers felt the crisis of reduced income and joblessness. For Bill Ryan the last straw was the $15.30 they earned from the 1930 potato crop. He realized that he could make more money from the electrical work he did in town than he could if he spent full time on the ranch. With the approval of Babe and Tom, he arranged to rent most of their land to a Japanese farmer who wanted to grow strawberries. The rent money from the farmer just covered the cost of their taxes.

My mother's employers at the bank allowed her to arrange part-time hours. In the afternoons she did the bookkeeping. But her main job, for which she was paid thirty dollars a month, was as janitor. Daily at 6 A.M. she dusted, swept, and washed the floors and then returned home in time for her car-pool ride to college. It was hard, physical labor because most of the customers were farmers and dairymen and made their trips to the bank directly from the fields with dung and mud on their boots. Often Bill, who worried about Babe's trying to do too much, scrubbed the bank floor for her.

With a quarter of the nation unemployed, neither brother nor sister ever complained about the work, but when the bank hired someone else who had offered to do the job for less, my mother was secretly relieved. Being janitor had caused her some embarrassment among her friends. She still remembers with a sharp stab the morning when a carload of classmates from Fullerton drove past and hooted at her as she swept a pile of dust and refuse out the front door of the bank and down its steps.

The year at Fullerton was a drab one. Because of her part-time jobs and the commute from Artesia, Patricia Ryan did not enter much into life on the campus. Although her brothers helped her with the time-consuming house-work, the cooking and the laundry were still her responsibilities. A sign of her increasing independence, however, was her refusal to make dinner if she felt either Bill or Tom had not completed his share of the work on a given day.

The one bright note that freshman year was the school play, *Broken Dishes*, a comedy that had run on the New York stage in 1929 with Bette Davis in the starring role. At Fullerton the part was played by Patricia Ryan.

At the end of the academic year, the students were assessed by their teachers. Dr. Mabel Meyers stated on what was to be my mother's only record at college, "In any type of occupation requiring the meeting of the public, Pat will be a great success."

My mother did not return to Fullerton in the fall because she had the chance to leave California for the first time since coming to the state as a one-year-old. Her Aunt Annie had written with the news that elderly friends from Connecticut, Mr. and Mrs. Beers, who spent several months each year in California, needed someone to drive them back East since their chauffeur's wife was expecting a baby. Aunt Annie believed that her niece, though not quite twenty years old, would be able to convince the Beerses that she had the judgment and maturity to navigate a Packard over three thousand unfamiliar miles.

After one interview, Patricia Ryan was hired. For my mother the trip was a great adventure. She never forgot her first glimpse of life beyond the rolling breakers of the California coastline: the mountain peaks, the vastness of the deserts, the flat plains of the Midwest, and the little towns of the East. She became adept at reading maps and driving through mud and heavy rain. Her most difficult moments were two flat tires, which she changed unaided, and an incident at Pikes Peak when the car overheated and she had to roll large stones behind its front wheels in order to insure that the Beerses did not precipitously begin the steep fourteen-thousand-foot descent down the mountain.

The journey ended in Ridgefield, Connecticut, where my mother said goodbye to the Beerses. She was welcomed with open arms by aunts and uncles who had last seen Will Ryan almost fifty years before and by cousins who had never met him. Only with Aunt Annie did she find it difficult to explain that she had taken the name Patricia. Annie continued to call her Thelma, refusing to let go of the girl she had come to love as a sixteen-year-old in Artesia.

Annie's daughter, Jo Rockwell, then a student at Mount St. Mary's College, made a special trip from college in order to meet the California cousin with whom she had exchanged occasional letters since they were little girls. To Jo, Pat was a figure of romance, because she lived on a ranch and had written about riding horses and picking cauliflower for four cents a bushel. But when Jo actually saw her cousin, Pat was not dressed like a country girl. Not until later would Jo learn that Pat had made her dress herself, an elegant princess-style bouclé wool in a rich brown color that matched her eyes. Those eyes were beautiful. In fact, Pat Ryan was beautiful, with her thick shoulder-length red-gold hair, and fine, cream-colored complexion. She was as slender and quiet as Jo was large-boned and irrepressible. Though they were different in many ways, from that first day they became friends.

For her Aunt Kate, who was a nun, my mother felt much more than friendship. During almost two years in New York, Kate, who was known as Sister Thomas Anna, was the major influence in her life. My mother described her to me once as "witty, brilliant and very Irish." Like Will Ryan, she was tall and thin with angular features and, despite her black habit, strikingly beautiful. Though Kate was then seventy years old, my mother wrote home to her brothers that she was "loads of fun."

Young Patricia Ryan had intended to return to California after a short visit with her relatives. Her payment from the Beerses was a bus ticket home. But after spending a week with her Aunt Kate at Seton, a tuberculosis hospital run by the Catholic Sisters of Charity where Kate was head of the X-ray department and the pharmacy, she began to consider staying in New York longer. On November 11, she excitedly wrote her brother Bill from Seton. It was the nadir of the Great Depression and jobs were very scarce.

> Gosh!!!???** Bill! I just spoke to Sister Teresa about a job and she accepted me!! I am going to be the secretary of the whole works—do the typing, letters, be a companion for the nuns, do x-ray work, laboratory work, etc. etc. I have been visiting Aunt Kate here at the hospital and helping with all the work. Is extremely interesting as well as extremely difficult. The atmosphere is not just as I would choose, but then—I am to live here, eat here, etc. . . . But what an opportunity to learn—and then I have been wishing for a job because I have no spending money whatsoever and I hate to sponge on my relatives for more than a couple of weeks. They do not have too much by any means. I may not be good enough to keep my job or perhaps I won't like it—nevertheless I start on the 15th. I get room and board (which is a lot! and I don't suppose much salary). I'll let you know after the fifteenth. But in charitable organizations they can't afford to pay high wages. In these times, a job is a job!!! So I'm tickled pink!

She made no mention to Bill that most of those in the hospital were tubercular and would die as their father had. I asked her years later if she had worried that she might catch the disease. She replied matter-of-factly, as if surprised I had raised the question, "I had no fear."

At times Patricia Ryan seemed to forget that the young TB patients she befriended were ill, as if by denying their infirmities, they would become well. Medical opinion in the 1930s held that physical activity for the tubercular was detrimental, but when some of the young men, so pathetically eager to live, secretly left the hospital at night for sledding, Pat Ryan went with them. Thirty years later, she told an interviewer that those evenings were "among the most haunting of my life."

After she had been at the hospital a year, she uncharacteristically bragged a bit about her work in one of her frequent letters to Bill.

> I love to help others—and all day long I'm always trying to be cheerful to the unfortunates and to help them in every way possible. It's funny, but even a cheerful smile uplifts them. They call me "The White Sister," or if I go away for a few days they always say, "Oh, don't go and take all our sunshine away." Sometimes I feel that I should like to spend my life just working for the afflicted unfortunates—helping them to be more happy. Too, I enjoy hospital work.

The head of Seton's medical staff, Francis Vincent Duke, from Roscommon County, Ireland, was a thirty-five-year-old bachelor when he met Miss Ryan. Everyone liked him, from my mother's cousin Jo, who described him as a "beautifully spoken man," to Aunt Kate, who did all she could to protect the romance and thus keep it alive. The handsome doctor, with his reddish-blond hair and bright blue eyes, was a magnet for women and thus a prime topic of conversation among the nuns. But Kate realized that her niece's interest would wither if the nuns and members of the medical staff scrutinized her and Francis Duke too closely. Consequently, she kept the secret that they were dating, and playfully left cryptic notes for her niece whenever "His Royal Highness," or "Royalty," as she code named Dr. Duke, called.

With each date, Dr. Duke became more serious, much to Pat Ryan's discomfort. When he hinted about marriage, she responded by continuing to accept invitations from other men. She felt a need for the freedom to go where she liked, when she liked. In a lighthearted, half-teasing letter to her brother Bill at the end of two years in New York, she discussed her social life.

> Everyone here thinks I am so dumb because I can't "see" anyone except you and Tommy. My Aunts think the doctors and some of the fellows I go with are grand—but I don't care so much about even going out with them. They say I'll be a nun yet—what would you say to that?"

Her living arrangement with the nuns was hardly conducive to any blossoming romance. She had her own room on the top floor of the hospital, but all the rooms around her were occupied by the Sisters. They gave her permission to receive gentlemen guests in their own parlor. But, as my mother laughingly told me years later, "They were always hanging around!" In one letter to Bill she complained, underlining each of her words in exasperation: *"They restrict you so here!"*

Pat Ryan wanted to see as much of the East as she could, so at every opportunity she traveled. She wrote home to Bill about her first autumn in New England.

> One of the fellows I go with has a Chrysler 75 Coupe, and he has been leaving it here for me to drive. I took Aunt Mamie [one of Will Ryan's sisters] for a two-hundred-mile trip this last weekend. We had a good time, and the country is gorgeous aflame with autumn colors which were thrilling to see. It really is *beautiful* here.

In the summer of 1933 she went with two cousins to Washington. Most memorable was her tour of the White House, where Eleanor and Franklin Roosevelt had been in residence for just a few months. Then, in October, she wrote her brothers on Waldorf-Astoria Hotel stationery:

> ...I am attending a hospital conference here as a representative from Seton. There are representatives from every state and about twelve from all parts of California. Boy, it is fun and ever so interesting to meet so many doctors and heads of institutions, etc. The lectures are most interesting and the lunches—

wow!! Last night Al Smith, Mrs. and President Roosevelt, etc. attended the formal dinner and the latter gave the main speech of the evening. Perhaps you heard it on the radio as it was broadcast.

Remembering her first view of Franklin Roosevelt, my mother told me she was almost unaware that this man with the sure, strong gestures and vigorous voice was crippled by polio. Even when it came time for him to go to the podium, he had walked slowly and steadily, his leg braces barely noticeable.

Through her travels, Pat Ryan gradually was leaving the small-town girl behind. At Seton she took on more and more responsibility, explaining to Bill as her second year there ended:

Aunt Kate has been gone for the past two weeks and I've had *complete* charge of the pharmacy and the x-ray. And then the one in charge of the office has been gone so I've had to take all of that responsibility too. At night I just drop—I never could keep it up—not only is the work hard but it is mentally tiring for you have to be so sure of all details for just a drop too much in the pharmacy would be [drawing of cross, skull and bones]—same in the x-ray, and the office is so busy and so detailed—admitting of patients, etc. . . .

She was happy in New York and had no desire to return to Artesia, though she missed and worried about her brothers, particularly Bill when he started at Fullerton in the fall of 1932. After several years out of school, Bill found the adjustment to college difficult. With Tom in Los Angeles, then a senior at USC, and Babe three thousand miles away, Bill was lonely and often depressed. Pat wrote to encourage him: "I'm ever so glad you're enjoying life more for it is surprising the dumps we can let ourselves get in. I know you must have changed—and so have I! Just getting out of Artesia did me worlds of good. . . ." She was learning that activity and a sense of purpose were for her the roads away from sad memories. Shortly after her arrival in New York, she had written to Bill: "It must be lonesome [Bill was working in a mountain area for a while and missed their hometown] but Artesia is unbearable—so there you are."

She had no interest in a job that did not lead to a real future. In August 1933, while on a Hudson River Day Line trip to Bear Mountain, she was offered the opportunity to act in a Paramount Pictures movie. A professional scout from the studio, having spent all week on the boat searching for a girl to become "the glorious Miss Hudson River Day Line," spotted the brown-eyed, golden-haired Miss Ryan and asked her name and address. He explained grandly that Paramount was offering a trip to Hollywood and, in the words of the contest blurb, "fifty dollars a week for a guaranteed minimum of four weeks she plays in the picture *Eight Girls in a Boat*, with an option of renewal if she proves her ability."

On Monday, the nuns and patients and my mother perhaps most of all were surprised to read that "Thelma Patricia Ryan of 3221 Spuyten Duyvil Parkway, New York City" and two other girls had been selected for the contest from among the passengers on three boats that Sunday. My mother was summoned to the hospital administrator's office for what she feared would be a reprimand. Instead, Sister Teresa advised, "You may as well go and see what it is all about." She even gave her the day off to attend the judging. On September 6, my mother wrote Bill:

> Did Tommy tell you about me being chosen from all three hundred girls to compete in the contest? I went down to the Paramount Theatre (by request) and they photographed me, etc. etc., then offered me tryouts for stage dancing, etc. then modeling too. But that life is too tough, and unless you are featured the pay is low—one of the reasons why girls are tempted to accept presents and attentions—sheer necessity.

Paramount had guaranteed nothing beyond the four weeks of work on the film, while her fifty dollars a month at the hospital was a steady salary. But fifty dollars a month in New York did not go far. One drain on her pocketbook was the few dollars here and there she gave to the families of the poorer patients at Seton. At the end of almost two years she had saved very little. Increasingly, a college education seemed the answer if she wanted a job that would give her financial independence.

She had never really given up the hope that she could go back to school, but in letters home she was careful not to burden her brothers, who were barely making ends meet themselves, with reminders that her turn was coming. When Bill was most depressed at Fullerton in February of 1933, Pat had written a typically encouraging letter and, for the first time, hinted casually that she might like the opportunity herself.

> I'll be awfully mad if you play too much and don't get grades—There's no excuse because you have the brains and you must develop the willpower to concentrate and strive, to win. Maybe we could go somewhere to school together—that would be *swell*, and we'd practically be in the same grade. The world is just what we make it—so let's make ours a grand one. Too, it's fun to work and then enjoy the fruits of the success. I love to learn new things, no matter how difficult—also go to new places.

Neither Tom nor Bill had forgotten his obligation to his sister. In the spring of 1934, Tom was finally able to write Babe that he had saved enough money for her trip home and would help supplement whatever she earned from part-time jobs so that she could return to college. Her letter to Bill, half jubilation, half uncertainty, expresses how she felt about it.

Just received Tommy's letter and am so thrilled and excited that my heart just won't act sanely. Haven't seen any of the relations here (Aunt Kate is away) and they'll probably have fits. "What to do" is certainly the biggest decision I've ever had to make in my life. Of course I am learning so much here and doing technical things around professional people which will be a great let-down and a missed opportunity. But life is fleeting and . . . I want to finish my college education. Do you think I would be too great a burden to Tommy?— for it does take so much to *just live.*

Tom wrote reassuringly shortly afterward, proposing that the three Ryans share an apartment near the USC campus. His letter was the last good news she needed to make it easy to decide to leave the East.

In August, Patricia Ryan started home by bus, via Niagara Falls, one of the sites she wanted to see before she left the East. She was the only unmarried or unengaged person on a bus full of, in her recollection, "cuddlers." When they arrived at the falls, the driver asked her to remain behind for a moment. Puzzled, she agreed. Then, after the last passenger had gotten off, he asked her for a date! She politely declined and viewed the roaring water alone.

In February she had written Bill: "Write me some of the Artesia news now and again. Seems as though everyone I know is married and already has a family. I'm glad I'm not in their boots—especially in this 'Depression' weather." Those words explain, in part, why she refused Francis Duke when he had asked her a final time to marry him. When I questioned her forty years later, she expressed the reason for her decision in another way: "I didn't want to marry because I had been so busy all my life. I felt I had not lived yet. . . ."

"My Brainy Girl"

Patricia Ryan entered the University of Southern California in the fall of 1934 on a research fellowship, a new scholarship program the university was trying that year. For twenty hours of work per week grading psychology professor R. G. Watt's student papers and helping him research a book on orientation, her tuition of $270 was paid and she received a small stipend for living expenses.

But she needed part-time work to supplement her income. Tom had promised he would help her obtain a job. He took his sister to the office of the vice president of the university where job placements were arranged and introduced her to the secretary with the words: "This is my kid sister. She wants to work her way through college." Tom remembers that the secretary took one look at her and said, "Miss Ryan, I want you to work for me."

She managed to do the research and various part-time jobs (including typing term papers) by taking some of her classes at night, and she somehow maintained grades throughout that enabled her to graduate *cum laude*. Dr. Frank Baxter, a noted Shakespearean scholar and her English professor that first semester, told a reporter years later when my father ran for the Senate in 1950:

She was a quiet girl and pretty. And it always used to disturb me how tired her face was in repose. There seemed to have been plenty of reason for it. As I recall it, if you went into the cafeteria there was Pat Nixon at the serving counter. An hour later if you went to the library there was Pat Nixon checking out books. And if you came back to the campus that evening there was Pat Nixon working on some student research program. Yet with it all, she was a good student, alert and interested. She stood out from the empty-headed, overdressed little sorority girls of that era like a good piece of literature on a shelf of cheap paperbacks.

She lived with her brothers in a two-bedroom bungalow court apartment, but because of class schedules and different working hours, the three did not see very much of one another. Tom was studying for his master's degree in education, and to support himself he worked six days a week as foreman of the night crew in the prop department at Universal Studios. On Sundays he worked a twelve-hour day at his old high-school job as a soda jerk in Neimes' Drugstore in Artesia. Since Tom left for the studio around 4 P.M., he usually just missed Bill, who was arriving home from his lighting job at Twentieth Century-Fox where he had been employed since completing two years at Fullerton Junior College.

The only night of the week the three were home for dinner together was an occasional Sunday. Bill often took over in the kitchen much to his sister's relief, since she no longer enjoyed cooking. His specialty was "mock turtle," a concoction consisting of equal parts of beef, pork, rice, and zucchini in a tomato sauce. Bill and Tom, however, still depended upon Babe to do the ironing and the laundry and much of the cleaning. Her Aunt Kate, who knew her well, worried that she would try to do too much. On September 30, a few weeks after the start of classes, she wrote:

> Sunday afternoon, alone and lonely! My dear little girl:
> ... You have been exceptionally fortunate beyond a doubt if you do not work too hard. This is the one thing that causes me anxiety. I am sure the boys are willing to do the housework if you will let them, but I fear you will just do it all so generously that they may not realize just how much you have to do and thus they won't know that you are tired...

Two months later, Aunt Kate admitted in a letter that she wished she could hear more often from her niece, but added: "There are tasks for every minute now in your life and I realize letters take stamps and stamps take money and money is scarce these days." She continued, perhaps diffusing any nostalgia my mother may have felt for New York:

> Be grateful to God and do not forget, dearie, to pray for those less fortunate. Jobs on this side are as hard as ever to get and are not lasting. Where formerly employers would have to hire one for good, now with all these NRA, BVPS, etc. [government-sponsored public-work programs], they can get work done much cheaper by hiring a man and woman for a day at a time. Guess the rest!

The most significant news from the family in New York that first semester came not from Aunt Kate but from Aunt Mamie Ryan, who wrote: "Duke [Francis Duke] asked why you went without saying goodbye. Kate says he is moping around all the time, dying to say something but doesn't."

A year and a half later, when my mother sent her relatives a Los Angeles *Times* clipping of her and another of Dr. Watt's research assistants posing with a large sack of graduate survey questionnaires they had helped prepare, Cousin Catherine found an excuse to write about Dr. Duke. The photograph was a particularly flattering one of Miss Patricia Ryan. One sees a high-cheeked young woman, her hair becomingly parted in the center. Her stylish double-breasted suit, cinched at the waist with a thin black belt, is a sharp contrast to the casual sweater and skirt of the other coed.

> Dear Patricia:
> Such a riot as was at the hospital the day the front page edition arrived. It surely is a lovely picture of you and everyone was crazy about it. You never heard so many ohs and ahs and isn't she sweet in all your life. Auntie Sister [Aunt Kate] was right proud of her niece and scrutinized it to see if you were looking tired at all. She is forever worried that you will work too hard and ruin your health . . . and last but not least the Chief of Staff [Dr. Duke] lingered so long and thoughtfully with an oh-so-serious look on his face and it was not so much what he said as the sincere way in which he spoke of you that makes me believe that you are the girl he can't forget. Very quietly, he said, "My, she looks so lovely—so unusual for a newspaper picture to be so natural looking."

But Pat did not respond to the hints from Catherine or Aunt Kate, never mentioning in her letters the man who had wanted to marry her. She simply had no desire to become a wife yet. And, in fact, throughout her three years at USC, she did not have a steady boy friend. Her brother Tom belonged to a fraternity and she had many opportunities to meet men, but frequently she turned down dates, devoting most of her time to her jobs and studies. She was most likely to accept if it was an invitation to a football or basketball game or some other sporting event on the campus.

Perhaps in some ways her personality—the self-sufficiency and innate reserve—discouraged anything other than superficial contacts with college dates. A note from a beau that I found among some of my mother's old letters provides a clue: "I was just struck with the thought that I knew so damn little about you after being at your feet a whole lovely evening."

In 1955, one of my mother's classmates, Kay Nordquist, sent her a copy of a theme she had just submitted to a writing class. It is a perceptive, vivid portrait of the young Pat Ryan at the University of Southern California.

> She came to the door that first morning to borrow a newspaper, a scarf thrown over her head against the beating rain. She slipped quietly into the kitchen

and when she threw back the scarf, I thought she had the most beautiful hair I had ever seen. It was red and gold and curled around her face and down her back.

Her skin was clear and pale, her eyes amber. . . . The line of her cheeks and jaw was sharp, her body angular, but the feeling around her was all womanly softness and serenity and inner strength.

Pat, like my roommate and I, had just moved in with her two brothers into the court apartment next door to begin the fall semester at USC. We settled down to mugs of coffee and getting acquainted. Pat talked little, there was always a quietness about her. Stelle and I bubbled on about courses and professors, dates and parties. Her conversation was solicited. She was not distant, nor cold, but shy—and always listening.

We grew to love Pat. It distressed us that she lived in a world of hard work and responsibility contrasted to our frothy one of as little work and as much fun as possible. Money was not plentiful with any of us and the three Ryans next door had a hard time keeping even with the endless list of tuition, books, groceries and rent. Pat managed the purse, did the washing, ironing and mending. The apartment was spotless, and when one of the boys had a theme overdue, it was Pat who sat up late putting on the finishing touches and typing it.

Pat was pretty enough. We fretted about what we considered a dull and dreary life. We were anxious to bring some boys around, but we couldn't think of any "right" boys for Pat. So we just enjoyed her in the long walks in the rain when we needed advice, and the deep and warm understanding and tolerance of her. There was so much beneath the surface, and so few had the opportunity to find it. . . .

That first year at USC my mother began a lifelong friendship with Virginia Shugart. They were drawn together initially because Virginia was also on a tight budget and neither's social life centered around a sorority, which they could not afford. The two friends filled their free time with ice skating at the Polar Palace on Pan Pacific in Los Angeles and with trips in Virginia's little red Ford, all passengers contributing a dime to the kitty for gas. As often as possible, they went to their favorite movie theater, the Paramount. It was across the street from a See's candy store, where for ten cents each they could buy a third of a pound of candy to savor during the show.

Although my mother and Virginia enjoyed many of the same things, they were quite different. "I was so interested in boys and in getting as many dates as possible," Virginia remembers. "I think Pat liked me because I was carefree and loved to have fun, and was even a little silly." Virginia also recalled that my mother never mentioned the loss of her parents or any of her intimate feelings, and Virginia might have been surprised if she had, for to her "Pat was a person of incredible energy and capacity for work. . . . I know it's kind of strange for me to say this but, in a way, I always looked up to her to take care of me."

Perhaps one of the strongest links between Pat and Virginia was that both had to scramble for part-time jobs. They took almost anything, including signing on as amateur sleuths for Parker Herbex, the then-famous manufacturer of a wide variety of beauty aids. The company had discovered that some of the beauty salons in Los Angeles were advertising their products and then substituting less expensive ones. My mother and Virginia were hired to go to the suspect salons together. There, one would ask for the entire Parker Herbex treatment, and the other, under the guise of studying, would take notes on exactly what was done. At night they would help each other scrub out the treatments so they would be ready to investigate a new shop the next day.

By far their most lucrative part-time jobs were as movie extras for six dollars and fifty cents a day. Quite often they appeared in football scenes because of tips from their friends on the USC team who let them know the minute the studios requested athletes. Then Pat and Virginia would race down in the little red Ford, hoping to be ahead of all the other eager extras. Virginia always claimed that her car was the reason for their success. It seemed to be hired as often as they were. Its most noticeable appearance was in *Small Town Girl* with Robert Taylor and Janet Gaynor. My mother remembers this particular film for another reason: Robert Taylor was the handsomest man she had ever seen.

Patricia Ryan had a speaking role only once, in *Becky Sharp*, Hollywood's first full-length color movie, in 1935. But her one line was cut in the final edit. My mother liked certain aspects of movie work. The makeup sessions and fittings made her feel glamorous. Some of the costumes were beautiful enough to dream about later. She can still describe in detail today a hoop-skirted apple-green gown. But movie work was also boring and, most difficult for my mother to accept, time-wasting. "An entire day would go by," she remembers, "and the director would take and retake just one scene."

There was another unappealing aspect of Hollywood. The directors and producers acted as if they could have any woman and Pat Ryan had several brushes. The most serious one was with an assistant director of *Becky Sharp* who refused to recognize her cool lack of interest and finally showed up at her apartment one night drunk, demanding to see her. Tom and Bill were furious and closed the door in his face. Tom told Pat, his voice fierce with anger, "That kind of life..."—he was speechless for a second—"it's not for you."

During her senior year at USC, Patricia Ryan had one last opportunity to test her resolve about refusing an acting career. As a lark, she and Virginia Shugart entered a studio-sponsored contest on campus "to find a starlet." When my mother filled out the contest form she gave Dr. Watt's office phone number where she did her fellowship work.

It was Dr. Watt who answered the telephone when the studio called. Miss Patricia Ryan was to report immediately for contract-signing details. Normally

Watt was a reserved, even taciturn man. He had grown fond of his part-time assistant, however, and decided to offer some advice. To her surprise, he urged that she seriously consider the opportunity. My mother did talk to the studio executives and found out that the contract was for one film only and no future guarantees. She knew then that she would never accept it. But she was flattered enough to share the news with Aunt Kate. Kate responded immediately.

> While I hope that nothing will interfere with the completion of your college course, it would be great to see you taking some nice parts, but if it should be only one in a hundred kicking up heels, then it is not worthy of you. How does Bill feel about it?

Although the fast pace of an actress's life and the opportunity for travel appealed to my mother, she did not want to subject herself to the iron control or the whim of any film executive or studio. Later, when she explained her decision to Dr. Watt, she found herself expressing for the first time how much an education meant to her. In a word, it meant freedom.

Since her junior year Pat Ryan had worked at fashionable Bullock's Wilshire in Los Angeles during school holidays and on Saturdays. Positions were very hard to obtain, and when she was hired, the personnel director told her candidly he was giving her the job because he had noted in her application that she was carrying a full course load and yet already working almost full time.

My mother described her new Bullock's job to Aunt Annie in a Christmas letter dated December 22, 1935.

> As soon as school was out (12th) I started work at Bullock's—you remember the store you liked so well. It really is a beautiful store—but we have to work very hard during the Christmas rush—from eight in the morning until at least 6:30 at night. Then after standing up on the street car going home, cooking dinner, dishes, etc., I'm so exhausted (especially the *feet*) I could just collapse. I've been doing some modeling in the store and then was chosen for the gift service bureau. The moneyed class come in and ask us to do their shopping— or give them suggestions. We go to any department of the store with them— showing our suggested gifts—or else they sit in luxurious chairs while we go all over the store and gather things for them to choose from. So you see it is twice as much running than ordinary "sales gal" work. However, very *interesting* and we learn the merchandise from all the departments. The manager of our department is always telling or describing how I drape the lovely velvet robes, etc., around me, grin at the fat, rich customers and pff! they buy. But this is true—and I sell more than any of the other girls. Saturday I sold over $200.00— including a lovely velvet pajama and hostess gown to one gentleman. Really business is good—it makes one feel good to see people really *buying* instead

of *looking* as in the past few years. Our economics professor said that this Christmas sale is far exceeding the 1929 level which was the largest in history. That's something.

The most exciting aspect of the job was helping the movie stars. She saw the reclusive Greta Garbo just once. Marlene Dietrich was a frequent customer. She usually wore slacks, much to the disappointment of the salespeople at Bullock's, who complained, my mother told Aunt Kate, that they had been "denied a look at the beautiful limbs." My mother remembers particularly the day Walter Pidgeon brought his fifteen-year-old daughter into the store to buy her, in his words, "some smashing clothes." For two and a half hours, he sat and watched as Miss Ryan modeled, and his daughter chose her first grown-up wardrobe.

As much as my mother liked the work at Bullock's, as graduation neared she grew convinced the long apprenticeship as an assistant buyer at a very low salary was impractical. Her chosen alternative was teaching. In the past three years, she had carefully accumulated twenty-five hours in education and a semester of student training as well. The profession provided a good salary, and the long summer vacation would enable her to travel. Two months before graduation, Pat Ryan went to the Bureau of Teacher Placement at the university and filled out numerous school applications, noting on each that USC was accrediting her with a Special Credential, equivalent to a master's degree, because of her extensive business and job experience.

The college provided the schools that were considering hiring USC graduates with "frank estimates" of the applicants. The "Confidential Information on the Applicant Miss Patricia T. Ryan, not to be shown to the candidate" is an impressive collection of opinions. One of her professors lauded her "splendid attitude towards young people, with her buoyant enthusiasm for life in general." Another wrote that she was a "superior person in every detail." Her practice teacher reported, "Her students are very fond of her and she gets good results from them. . . . She is always animated." In the opinion of the director of student teaching at the university, Miss Ryan "is so resourceful she will be able to handle any class situation that may arise." Finally, Professor Watt was unrestrained in his praise: "I give her my highest and unqualified recommendation."

Her physical attractiveness did not escape the attention of any of the five men and women who gave opinions on Patricia Ryan. Their comments included: "Dresses most attractively and appropriately"; "Very pleasing appearance"; "A young woman of very attractive appearance."

Jobs were scarce, but the uniformly excellent recommendations undoubtedly helped. In June she was notified she had been selected to teach commercial subjects—typing, bookkeeping, business principles, and stenography—at Whittier Union High School for an annual salary of eighteen hundred dollars a year, to Pat Ryan a "fabulous sum!" Perhaps an equally important factor in her selection was that by a fortunate twist of fate her application had come to the attention of the newly appointed superintendent of the school district, David Stouffer, whose previous job had been as principal of Excelsior High School. He remembered Thelma Ryan, Class of 1929, well, for her good grades, her beauty, and her roles in the junior and senior plays. Stouffer gave her his highest recommendation when she appeared before Whittier's reputedly conservative Board of Trustees, and though she was then only twenty-five years old, a decade younger than most of the faculty members, they decided to hire her.

On Commencement Day, flanked by Tom and Bill, Patricia Ryan posed before the ceremony for a family snapshot. It was to be one of the last pictures of just the three together for many years. Tom, who had earned his master's degree and was teaching high school in Burbank, and Bill, in the lighting division at Twentieth Century-Fox, were both well launched in their careers.

She had the prayers and the pride of her family in New York with her on that day. They knew she was graduating with honors, and they knew too she had achieved the goal despite forty hours of extra work a week. Her Aunt Kate could not resist a touch of worldly pride when she wrote: "I am so happy that you made out so well in your exams but of course I would not expect anything else from my brainy girl."

She sent as a graduation gift a framed poem entitled "Someone Had Prayed." It ended with the inscription, "Congratulations and God Bless Thelma Patricia Ryan, Graduation, June 1937. Sister Thomas Anna."

"To the Beautiful Teacher Who Wore a Red Geranium in Her Hair"

In the fall of 1937 when Pat Ryan moved to Whittier, fifteen miles southeast of Los Angeles, the town was beautifully pastoral, with acres of citrus, avocado, and olive groves. In the spring, the scent of orange blossoms filled the air. By climbing to the highest of the gently rolling hills that surrounded the city, one could see the dazzling blue of the Pacific and on a clear day Catalina Island. The only signs of industry on the horizon were the Santa Fe Springs oil fields to the south.

Whittier is just eight miles from Artesia, but my mother found life in the Quaker city very different. Members of the Society of Friends, mostly from Indiana and Iowa, had come to the area in the 1880s and named their settlement for the antislavery Quaker poet John Greenleaf Whittier. By 1937, more than half the population of twenty-five thousand belonged to the Society of Friends. Its members gave Whittier a strong sense of community, which was absent in Artesia. To a large extent, Whittier College set the tone for all in town. It was a very straitlaced institution. My mother discovered that the college and the town's high schools had unwritten codes of dress and behavior. Faculty members did not smoke in public. Students and teachers were expected to dress modestly in accordance with the Quaker belief that what is inward is far more important than what is outward. Not until 1934 were dances allowed to be held on the college campus. The change in policy was due to the election campaign platform of one Richard Nixon, who ran successfully for student-body president that year. The college newspaper judged him to be "always progressive and with liberal attitudes..."

Young Miss Ryan found that in Whittier everyone seemed to know what everyone else was doing. One of her friends gave her a good piece of advice when she started her job: "Never talk about anybody in Whittier—they're all related to one another in some way or another." Quickly she learned that the most popular gathering place to hear the latest news was the Poinsettia Terrace for coffee in the morning and thick milk shakes in the afternoon. Though Prohibition had been repealed four years earlier, no hard liquor was served in Whittier. The Elks Club, which had a wine and beer bar, was disapproved of by many, as was the town's other bar, located in a small building across the street from the Bank of America Building on Greenleaf Avenue. When Miss Ryan started classes that fall, Whittier's twenty-four-year-old deputy city attorney, Richard Nixon—the same young man who had brought dancing to the college campus four years earlier—had to prosecute the bar for allegedly selling an early-morning breakfast of a bottle of beer and two hard-cooked eggs to the town's kindly, harmless drunk. According to one of Whittier's sharp-eyed citizens, the customer had left the bar weaving slightly, a bottle of beer still in his hand. The deputy city attorney, however, felt uncomfortable handling the case. Apparently the jury shared his feelings, for it acquitted the bar owner and Nixon gladly lost.

Some of the Whittier Union High faculty initially were skeptical of Miss Ryan because of her youth and beauty. There was much buzzing about a comment made by a member of the physical education department who had declared after his first glimpse of Pat Ryan: "Well, I can see that Stouffer [the superintendent] has not lost his eye yet." But by the end of the first semester, she had won full acceptance. One of the most respected English teachers at Whittier for thirty-five years, Beatrice Counsel Hawkins, would tell me years later, without qualification: "Everyone adored your mother. I don't think she had an enemy on the faculty or student body."

Because she was so youthful-looking, Miss Ryan's foremost challenge was to establish discipline in the five classes she taught daily and in her adult typing class at night. One of her students wrote later: "I have to laugh when I recall how all the boys thought Pat would be a cinch as a teacher. They thought here was a new teacher who was so attractive, full of enthusiasm and pep she couldn't be a hard teacher. But it didn't turn out that way as she was a real disciplinarian, and the course wasn't just fun and games."

Another student, Jean Lippiatt, described Miss Ryan vividly in an article published by *The Saturday Evening Post* in 1971.

She always arrived in the classroom well ahead of the time and stood at the door to greet us by name. By the same token she expected clock work punctuality from us and we absorbed the gentle hint that questions directed to her should be prefaced with her name. Tardy students were warned by a direct look which hurt more than any lecture she could have given. Miss Ryan followed the book. She allowed no compromises, no errors, no second-rate job. Perfection and high standards were the only thing she accepted.

She tried to instill pride in her students and in what they were doing. Jean Lippiatt remembered particularly Miss Ryan's words:

Don't just be a machine to be ruled by your typewriter. Use your brains and make your typewriter work for you. Type a letter or manuscript with proper spacing with the idea it must be pleasing to the eye—like a picture. Think of yourself as a person who is creating a piece of art.

The former student's most vivid physical image of Patricia Ryan was on test days, Fridays.

Usually she stood by the window and we could see her silhouetted against the sunlight. I was always fascinated by her marvelous posture. She was thin and stood so erectly. I can never remember her sitting down in class. She constantly went up and down the aisles and seemed somehow always to know what everyone was doing.

That fall, Whittier hired another young teacher, Margaret Mary O'Grady, as a substitute in the history department. Margaret, just graduated from UCLA, was pert and tiny with shoulder-length brown hair and dark-blue eyes. And she was Irish, so Irish that she confessed to Pat that she found it difficult to be fair to England in her history lessons. She also confided her "terrible problems" with discipline, which would plague her throughout the year.

Margaret O'Grady and Pat Ryan quickly became good friends. A weekday treat was dinner at Whittier's Green Arbor Restaurant. Margaret recalls: "It was quite a walk and it seems every step we took we laughed. But I can't remember now what we laughed about." When a second upstairs bedroom in the home of Mr. and Mrs. Raymond Collins on Terrace Place where Pat was renting became available, Margaret moved in. In the spring, the two young women got their own apartment, a bungalow court in the McNees Park area of Whittier. The greatest improvement was that they had their own kitchen. That luxury compensated for the apartment's major disadvantage: it was across the street from a bowling alley. Both Margaret and my mother have since described the noise that lasted until twelve each night as "deafening."

Several of my mother's students had part-time night jobs at the alley setting up pins, and she was understanding when they acted dazed or sluggish in class. She was sensitive to her other students as well, particularly the Mexican-Americans. Whittier was notably free of ethnic and racial prejudice, and, in fact, during one of my mother's years at the high school, the president of the student body was Mexican. But most of the Mexican students were at a disadvantage because of the long hours they had to work in order to supplement their families' incomes. During harvesting time, they were absent for days at a stretch. Though cases of truancy were to be reported promptly, my mother first always made the effort to speak privately to the parents. Many of them did not realize they were breaking the law by keeping their children out of school, and when the situation was explained, they were willing to make sacrifices so that their sons and daughters could remain in school.

Miss Ryan wanted close contact with her students and made it known that the door to her classroom would always be open between 3 and 5 P.M. while she graded tests and papers. One of the students who met with her during those open hours wrote a letter in 1970 to advice columnist Ann Landers.

As a gradeschooler I was overweight and had a million freckles. Homely would have been a kind description. Like "ugly duckling" [a previous letter printed in the column], I, too, had a saint of a teacher. She sensed I was miserable and asked me to stay after school so we could talk. She told me to stop thinking of freckles as disfiguring because many people considered them wholesome if not downright attractive. She encouraged me to lose weight. As for the boys who made cruel remarks, she said they were just trying to get my attention. "Smile and be pleasant," she advised. "Soon they'll be smiling back." I took her advice and I will never be able to repay her. She changed my life. . . . The teacher's name was Miss Thelma Ryan. Today she's known as Mrs. Richard Nixon. Signed C. L. of Whittier.

Always my mother's attitude as a teacher was to look for the positive and to ask her students to do the same. When the school newspaper invited her to share her first impression of Whittier High, she wrote:

Individuality, enthusiasm and pep! These are some of the fine traits in Whittier High School students which first impressed me. It is very stimulating and refreshing to see students "in action," for the same enthusiasm is employed regardless of whether the task be a difficult or a pleasurable one. Results are apparent: lessons are well done, games loyally supported, social events thoroughly enjoyed, encounters with others in all walks of life definitely successful and valuable. . . . Thus to you I say: never lose your enthusiasm—merely direct it—and that same enthusiasm will take you "where you want to go." Miss Ryan.

At the end of the year the tables turned and Miss Ryan's students had a chance to write their impressions of her, fulfilling Whittier's annual tradition of anonymous comments on teachers' abilities. Among my mother's souvenirs is a packet of odd-shaped slips of paper, some scrawled notes in pencil, others typed or carefully penned.

A swell teacher I like you a great deal. You always play fair with us, even when we sometimes fall down on our lessons.

Miss Ryan: You're a perfect shorthand teacher, very pretty, dressed nice, and swell figure.

Miss Ryan is a very nice teacher to everyone and she has no pets as some teachers do. She is very purty and she dresses well. She is easy on everyone and gives us time to do the things over that we've made a mistake on. Miss Ryan has very purty hair and eyes. She's not only purty but she's one of the youngest teachers in the school.

Perhaps inevitably because of her youth and friendliness, Miss Ryan captured the imagination of her students. Within weeks of the opening of school, a small gossip item had appeared in the student paper: "The boys of Miss Ryan's class say, 'We sure are lucky'—'Wonder where she lives?'—Flash!! Miss Ryan lives on Terrace Place next to a vacant lot! Wonder if it's for sale?" She also was a romantic figure to the girls in her classes. Forty years later a former student would inscribe her book of original poetry "To the beautiful teacher who wore a red geranium in her hair." Some of the girls went so far as to take up "Miss Ryan watching" as a sport. When they staked out her apartment, she began to rue the day she had moved across the street from the bowling alley where students had plenty of excuses for loitering. Several evenings one of the members of the group borrowed an older brother's car and then lay in wait for the moment Miss Ryan came home, maybe with a date, to shine the headlights on her.

Despite all their efforts, the students were successful in gathering only a small store of information. They detected that Miss Ryan wore lavender perfume, because when she stood over them to correct an error or to help with a problem, they could smell the faint scent. They were less certain whether or not she wore false eyelashes (she did not). And, according to a reliable report from an older brother of a classmate, they learned she had been a movie actress! Well, if not an actress, at least an extra. But what she did in her spare time, what her goals or struggles were, remained a mystery.

Every Friday afternoon, Miss Patricia Ryan left Whittier, often staying with her half sister, Neva, and brother-in-law, Marc Renter, in Los Angeles, where her dates would pick her up. Years later she would tell me, "I never spent a weekend in Whittier the entire time I taught there." She seemed proud to have thwarted those who tried to scrutinize her private life.

No matter how busy she or any of the members of the Whittier faculty were, however, they were expected to take part in community affairs. That is how, fatefully for Patricia Ryan, in February of 1938, at the start of her second semester at Whittier, she went to a Whittier Community Players tryout and met Richard Nixon.

The theater group was having difficulty finding someone to play Daphne Martin in its production of Alexander Woollcott and George Kaufman's mystery melodrama, *The Dark Tower*. The Cast of Characters described Daphne as a "tall, dark, sullen beauty of 20, wearing a dress of great chic and an air of permanent resentment." Whittier High's assistant superintendent heard of the little theater's plight and urged Miss Ryan to go to the tryouts being held in the Sunday-school room of St. Mathias Church. She went reluctantly and only because she found it difficult to say no to a school administrator. As she stood in the basement of the church, looking over the script, Pat Ryan realized there was no way out. A few days later, the Whittier High School newspaper announced:

> The community play *The Dark Tower* which is to be presented February 17 and 18 should hold added attraction for Whittier High students because of the fact that it features three very popular members of our faculty. Miss Dorothea Bell is starred and Miss Patricia Ryan and Miss Helen Mitchell play supporting parts.

At the end of the article, the names of the other members of the cast were noted: "Elizabeth Cloes, Grant Garman, D. D. Muncy, Richard Nixon, Charles Coffey, Donald Scheid, and Robert Jones."

Richard Nixon was in the church the evening Miss Ryan auditioned. He had just finished reading for the part of Barry Jones, who, according to the Cast of Characters, was a "faintly collegiate, eager, blushing youth of twenty-four." From the moment he saw Pat Ryan, he could not take his eyes away from her lithe, slender form and dazzling "titian-colored" hair, a phrase he and his relatives would use always to describe her red-gold hair. He thought she was beautiful and young, guessing her age to be twenty-one.

He fell in love with her that night. Although not usually impulsive, he said as they left the church, "You may not believe this but I am going to marry you someday." Since they had barely spoken to each other all evening, Pat Ryan was startled. She looked at him sharply to see if he was teasing and decided he was not. Virginia Shugart, who was at Pat's apartment when she returned from the audition, remembers distinctly that as Pat came through the door she said, "I met this guy tonight who says he is going to marry me."

CHAPTER 6

"Dearest Heart"

*A*t the rehearsals for *The Dark Tower*, Pat Ryan learned from the gossip of other cast members that the man she had referred to as "this guy" had been president of the Duke Law School Student Bar Association and elected to the Order of the Coif, the law equivalent of Phi Beta Kappa, just the year before. He was now a member of Whittier's Wingert and Bewley law firm. She discovered too that in the months he had been back in the community he had made a name for himself as a member (and future president) of the 20–30 Club, a service organization for young adults sponsored by the local Rotary, an active Kiwanian, and the town's deputy city attorney. As my mother described him to me years later, "He was considered a darling bachelor around town. All the mothers were getting in the act and asking him to dinner."

The "darling bachelor" had thick, curly black hair and very dark brown eyes that accentuated his fair, ivory-colored skin. At five feet eleven, he was almost six inches taller than Pat Ryan. Although both sides of Dick Nixon's family had settled in America before the Revolutionary War, he made a point of telling Miss Ryan that his mother's line had come from Timahoe, not far from County Mayo. They had far more in common than their Irish ancestry, however. Dick's description of his father Frank Nixon's hot temper reminded Pat Ryan sharply of Will. Indeed, one of the most striking similarities between

Dick Nixon growing up in Whittier and Thelma Ryan in Artesia was their dislike of scenes and an avoidance of them even at the cost at times of candor.

Both had been "orators" in grammar and high school. Both skipped second grade. Perhaps because their leisure time was so scarce, they both loved nothing more than to escape to a quiet hideaway to read and dream. My mother had her tree house. My father climbed the hills of Whittier. Often his favorite aunt, Beth Harrison, would ask, "Why is it you go up into the hills and lie down and look into the sky?" And always he gave her the same answer, "I just want to go up there and think." And Richard Nixon of Whittier, like Thelma Ryan of Artesia, had wanderlust. When he heard the train whistle as he lay in bed at night, he dreamed of traveling to far-off places.

They both knew tragedy. My mother was thirteen when Kate Ryan became ill, and my father a year younger when his seven-year-old brother, Arthur, died of tubercular encephalitis after a sudden two-week illness. Both my parents were considered old enough to help shoulder the family tragedy. They were old enough as well to be deeply affected by it. For my father, some of the bewilderment and pain over the loss of his brother would have been eased if Harold Nixon, the oldest son in the family, had not been ill as well. He had contracted incurable tuberculosis a few years before Arthur died, and his illness haunted him—and his family—for ten years.

Just as my mother and her brothers found their education and their financial survival on the ranch were vastly influenced by first their mother's and then their father's illness, the Nixon family's earnings from their small grocery store now went almost exclusively into the cost of trying to combat Harold's disease. Sadly, the family was separated for almost three years when Hannah Nixon cared for Harold in Prescott, Arizona, in the vain hope that the drier climate would help him. Harold died in March 1933, aged twenty-four.

By the end of the rehearsals for The Dark Tower, Patricia Ryan knew Dick Nixon well enough to care about the kind of impression she made on his parents. She was worried that when they saw the play, they would assume she was like the smart aleck, Daphne. A critique of the play in one of the town's newspapers, the Whittier Review, assessed her: "Patricia Ryan as Daphne Martin had a role which called for temperament—and did she have it? Plenty! She did some fine acting as she wheeled in and out of the room, always in a semi-rage." The Review had more subdued praise for Richard Nixon, who "had a small part and carried out his assignment well."

My mother need not have worried about the Nixons' reaction. A few weeks later, when she went to their home for Sunday-afternoon coffee and Hannah Nixon's strawberry shortcake, she sensed their acceptance immediately. Not until much time had elapsed, however, did she realize that she was somewhat of an enigma to Dick's parents and that her seemingly fragile beauty had made them underestimate her tenacity and energy.

Richard Nixon was a person of considerable tenacity himself. His courtship was determined. Only a month after the performance of *The Dark Tower*, he surprised Pat with flowers on her birthday. He sent her poems that had "the mysteriously wild beauty you would like."

The more she knew Dick Nixon the more she liked his sense of humor and his enthusiasm. She remembered for me, "He was handsome in a strong way. . . . He had a wonderful quality in his voice which I have never heard in another man." What appealed to her also was his "drive—he was going places and he always saw the possibilities. He believed that life could be good and that problems—well, if you could not solve them, you could make things a little better." When Margaret and Virginia, who were curious about the young lawyer who was pursuing Pat with such single-minded purpose, wanted to know more about him, she explained defensively who he was and what he did. Then she made a comment that neither of them ever forgot: "He's going to be President someday."

But the furthest thought from her mind was marriage. She tried gently to let him know that she could not yet return his love in equal measure, half joking, half warning that she was a vagabond, a gypsy at heart. But her disclaimers had no effect on him other than to give him the idea to refer to her from then on as "Miss Vagabond" or his "Irish Gypsy." Early in the courtship, he began one of his notes, "Hello Miss Vagabond," and enclosed a cornflower "placed here because it should go in a gypsy bowl—and because it's blue like Miss Pat's eyes are sometimes."

My mother carefully saved all his letters and notes, but because he was becoming serious so quickly, she hesitated to accept every invitation. Once she even arranged a date for him with Margaret, but he spent the entire evening talking about Pat. When she used work as an excuse, he offered to help her grade papers and more than once sat with her, a red pencil in hand, circling misspelled words and typing errors. A few times she tried pretending not to be at home. But when Dick saw that the door was bolted, he knew she was there, and once slipped a note to her describing a walk she had declined.

Miss Pat:

I took *the* walk tonight and it was swell because you were there all the time. Why?—because a star fell right in front of me, the wind blowing thru the tops of the palms making that strangely restless rustling, a train whistle sounded just as I got to the bridge. The Dipper was turned upside down right over where your house should be and was pouring down on you all the good things I've wished looking up at it in the past.

And because there was no moon the sky was full of stars—every one filled with good wishes for you.

Yes—I know I'm crazy and that this is old stuff and that I don't take hints, but you see, Miss Pat, I like you!

When she had a weekend date in Los Angeles, Dick Nixon often asked if he could have her company just for the drive into the city. On Friday night, he would take her to Neva's apartment and pick her up there Sunday afternoon. Sometimes those Sunday afternoons stretched into evening dates. But Pat Ryan did not like being put in the position of taking advantage, and the romance for the time being was too one-sided.

When Dick dropped by unexpectedly one evening, she circumlocutiously told him how she felt. A few days later he wrote her:

Dear Patricia:

Please forgive me for acting like a sorehead when you gently ushered me out the other night. You must have thought I was trying to put on the attitude that I really didn't give a darn—i.e., school boy bluff!

... may I say now what I should have said then: I appreciated immeasurably those little rides and chats with you. I hope that you survived them without too much mental worry over the problem "what shall I do to get rid of him before he falls." (And that isn't said in a sarcastic way either)—and may I tell you now what I really thought of you? You see I too live in a world of make believe—especially in this love business. And sometimes I fear I don't know when I'm serious and when not! But I can honestly say that Patricia is one fine girl, that I like her immensely, and that though she isn't going to give me a chance to propose to her for fear of hurting me! and though she insulted my ego just a bit by not being quite frank at times, I still remember her as combining the best traits of the Irish and the square-heads [Germans]—

Yours,
Dick

She decided to continue dating, but with the understanding that there would be no declarations of love or proposals of marriage. Dick neatly circumvented the agreement by being romantic in the notes he sent. During the remainder of the school year, they saw each other frequently. When classes ended for the summer, Dick Nixon gave his Irish Gypsy a gift.

You will note that it's kind of a masculine clock. But I just couldn't see you getting excited over one of those fancy pink things which "all the college girls just adore these days." And too, this kind of clock seemed rather to be like that vagabond within you that makes you want to go far places and see great things.

He continued his note with a gentle suggestion that she take better care of herself, revealing how well he had come to know her.

You know clocks are really not nearly as interesting as they seem to be. Now take this one for example—if you should get tolerant and decide to use it—

it should tell you that you should first of all this summer get a little sleep; that you shouldn't let the hours slip by without eating now and then; that you should rest, if such a thing is possible, and that you should do all these things because there are so many people who think so much of Miss Pat—they want her to stay around just as long as she possibly can in view of her irrepressible energy. And then it might also tell you that you will never grow old in spite of the many times it turns—because you, Miss Pat, will always be young— inside. And if you are honest with yourself you might hear people who feel a little warmer inside—who are a bit more tolerant—all because they have known Miss Pat. Because, despite your refusal to let me be much more than an acquaintance, by all that I hold sacred, Patricia, I say that you are a great lady—and now I think you know what I mean by that.

Pat responded:

I like it ever so much! Its new name is Sir Ric... I tried to think of one a bit dignified in keeping with it and yet a friendly one too—sort of needed your assistance so you be thinking of a better one if not approved...
See you soon.

Pat

P.S. Sir Ric has the nicest face—I like him so very much.

She was still reluctant to make any commitments, however. She had always made a practice of keeping her dates, including those with Richard Nixon, a secret from the townspeople of Whittier. For two years only a handful of close friends would know she was dating the deputy city attorney. Her secrecy gave her privacy, and it also made it easier for her to forget from time to time that she had any romantic entanglements at all.

In July, Pat took a bus to Michigan to buy a new car and then drove it by herself back to California. She did not get in touch with Dick Nixon when she returned to Whittier. Six weeks later, he sent her a note.

Patricia, I bet you're mad with me for pestering you with a letter sent to school. But after all since you don't tell me where you are what else can I do?
Yes you guessed it. I'd like so very much to see you again—after class, before breakfast, Sunday or any time you might be able to stand me! And of course it would have to be secret—you're protecting that reputation you know! It's been years since July and things have happened and I swear you'll not be bored if you'll give me a chance.

By Halloween, he was in good enough graces to convince Margaret to smuggle him and his eight-year-old brother, Eddie, into the apartment to leave a pumpkin he had carved glowing in the window. And at Christmas he again surprised Pat by decorating a small evergreen.

On January 9, 1939, he received a birthday clock from Miss Patricia Ryan. Two days later, from his law office on the second floor of the Bank of America Building, he wrote a thank-you and attached to it one of the office's "straight note" forms on which he promised to pay Patricia Ryan four billion dollars "when I'm fifty, or before if you'll let me."

That month Virginia Shugart introduced her fiancé, a young labor negotiator named Curtis Counts, to Pat Ryan and Dick Nixon. The four had a good time together and began to double-date whenever they could meet on weekends. Virginia recalls, "Dick was always fun . . . he was the one with the crazy ideas." One memorable evening he suggested that they go to a new nightclub, Topsy, in a town near Whittier to see whether or not its fan dancer lived up to her reputation. To play the madcap part, they decided to wear outlandish clothes, and raided Frank and Hannah Nixon's coat closet and attic. On a dare, Dick wore his mother's tight-fitting, old three-quarter-length raccoon coat.

Sometimes they went dancing. Pat, as faculty adviser for the Pep Committee, was eager to sample as many different dance casinos and auditoriums as she could in order to find good bands to play at school parties. She also loved to dance, and for Dick Nixon there were few greater pleasures than holding Pat Ryan in his arms as they moved to the rhythms of the Lambeth Walk, the tango, and the fox-trot.

Gradually, perhaps inadvertently, Pat Ryan's life was becoming more and more entwined with Richard Nixon's. The happiest times of all were long Sunday-afternoon drives, winter and summer, to the beach. They loved the solitude of the endless stretches of warm sand. The beach was the perfect place to read, the pastime both enjoyed more than any other. For hours they would sit with their books under the shade of a large beach umbrella, Dick's fair, sensitive skin protected as much as possible by a long-sleeved shirt. Almost always they took the Nixons' big Irish setter, King.

When my father was in the South Pacific during the war and Mother waited for him in San Francisco, the Frank Nixons gave King to a dairyman so that he would have a place to run. After the war, my parents tried to find the dog but, sadly, were unsuccessful because he had changed hands again and the new owners had moved away. For this reason they value more than most objects a silver paperweight of a setter my father chose as an end-of-school gift in 1939. He found the statue at a jeweler's in Los Angeles and splurged to buy it for twenty-five dollars. He then had the store oxidize the silver so that the dog's coat was the same rich red color as King's. Through the years the setter had aged gracefully as it moved back and forth between the West and East Coast numerous times. Today, his coat still a glistening red as it catches the sunlight, "King" stands proudly on my father's desk in his New York office.

My mother enjoyed playing with Eddie Nixon, and whenever Eddie thinks of young Patricia Ryan, she is running—running and laughing. He told me:

> As far as Dick and the family were concerned, I was a frail boy. I was very skinny, and, I guess, after Arthur's and Harold's deaths, they were overcautious. Dick was always challenging me to do things which would build me up physically. And Pat became part of this. She loved to run and she dared me to race her on the beach. She could always bring the spirit out in me and make me laugh. And she was patient. I loved math and mechanical things but I hated to read. She found adventure books for me and gave me savings stamps for reading a certain number of pages. They were the first books I ever read through.

My mother began to spend more time with Hannah Nixon also. During her 1939 summer vacation she got up several times at 5 A.M. to help her with one of the tasks she faced six mornings a week—baking the fifty pies sold in the store daily. Her pies were famous in Whittier, and my mother, after her marriage, never attempted to compete with pies of her own, but baked cakes and biscuits instead.

In getting to know the Nixons, Pat Ryan had her first chance as an adult to spend extended time with a married couple who could have been her parents. She discovered that Frank and Hannah were very different. When he was thirteen, Dick had described them aptly and timelessly in an eighth-grade "autobiography."

> My father has a rather light complexion. He is a middle-aged man of medium height. He is a very talkative man, liking to talk about politics, current events and the happenings of the day. He is a very ready debater on any subject.
>
> My mother, a middle-aged woman, was born in the state of Indiana. She likes to study foreign languages but she does not like to travel. She is rather dark-complected, medium in height. She is not very talkative.

With Frank Nixon, Pat teased, and he, in turn, teased her. Her relationship with the gentle, well-read woman who was to become her mother-in-law was more complex. She admired Hannah's capacity for hard work; her stoicism in the face of the loss of two sons; her gratitude for what life had to offer. And yet, in Hannah Milhous Nixon, Pat Ryan did not find someone with whom she could become close or share intimate thoughts. My mother explained to me once: "Nana and I were completely different. I admired her for what she was." My mother paused and thought for a few moments before continuing: "But, you know, she really wasn't a modern person. We did not have much in common."

Hannah's world revolved around her Quaker religion, her husband, three living sons, and her eight brothers and sisters. They met often for Wednesday devotionals, Thursday choir, church several times on Sunday. Most of all, they strived for awareness of the "inner light," which would enable them to draw closer to God. Hannah Nixon prayed throughout the day and often wrote her thoughts on whatever was at her fingertips: the backs of envelopes, in the margins of recipes torn from newspapers, and on little scraps of paper. But because of her deep reserve, she did not discuss her faith with many outsiders.

Nor did Pat respond to any of Dick's overtures to discuss the emotions she may have felt for her own mother. My father detected a sadness, and in one of his first love letters to Pat he wrote: "You with the strangely sad but lovely smile." But in time he came to realize that most of her past was a closed subject. He remembers that during their courtship she told him only three things about her childhood: that she had had a vegetable stand when she was a little girl; about waiting for the strawberry cone in her father's buggy; and how as little children she and her brothers would race one another to see who could get into bed first to sleep next to their mother, the boys always winning because they were quicker. Shortly after their marriage, she did mention briefly that Will Ryan had been sick for several years with what she called "miner's disease." My father did not realize until much later that he died of the same illness that killed Harold.

Richard Nixon thought often about his brothers' deaths. Most difficult to forget was his parents' pain at witnessing their firstborn's ten-year struggle. It may have helped him to talk about that pain, and yet he was joining his life with a woman for whom death was a taboo subject, a hurt so deep it was sacredly, privately her own. She pushed grief out of her consciousness, unwilling to open scars that had long since healed. Both were shy and both would find it difficult in the years ahead to break through their reserve and discuss their deepest feelings.

By August of 1939, Pat Ryan realized that she was falling in love. She found she missed Dick Nixon when she, Margaret, and Virginia took a car trip up the beautiful Pacific coastline to British Columbia. At certain stops along their carefully planned and budgeted route, they checked at local post offices to see if there was mail from their beaux, and to mail their own messages back to California.

From San Francisco, Pat wrote shyly, using the current slang:

Hi—

Just twelve and we have only now found hotel—very nice. The day has been fun: Pretty scenery (good talk!!); fiesta at Santa Barbara; stops; dog show at Salinas with beautiful Irish Red Setters—but not like King or his likeness.

I felt so sorta' lonesome—like Thursday because I didn't get to say a real goodbye—but anyhoo thanks for the hospitality. I do like my dog [the silver paperweight] muchly...

Lots of luck,
Pat

The girls went as far north as Vancouver. From there Pat, who was still keeping her romance a secret from most of Whittier, sent attorney Richard Nixon at the Bank of America Building a three-word postcard: "Love from mother."

By February, as Pat Ryan was well into her third year of teaching at Whittier, she had become Richard Nixon's "dearest heart." He wrote on the second anniversary of the day they met:

As I look out the windows at the clouds with the sun trying to break through, I'm thinking of how much you've meant to me the past two years. Do you remember that funny guy who asked you to go to a 20–30 ladies night just about two years ago? Well you know that though he still may be funny—he's changed since then. But you may not know—dear one—that he gets the same thrill when you say you'll go someplace with him, that he did when you said one time that he could take you for a ride in his car!

And did you know that he still looks out the windows towards wherever you are and sends you the best he has in love, admiration, respect and "Best of Luck"?

And when the winds blow and the rains fall and the sun shines through the clouds, as it is now, he still resolves as he did then, that nothing so fine ever happened to him or anyone else as falling in love with Thee—my dearest heart.

Love, Dick

CHAPTER 7

Patricia Ryan Nixon

*A*n hour and a half by car from Whittier is Dana Point, a promontory of land jutting into the blue Pacific. In 1940, with only a farmhouse or two within miles of the point, it had a wild, lonely beauty. A narrow dirt road led to the edge of the cliff, and from there one had a dazzling view of the white sands of Capistrano Beach and San Clemente curving for three miles to the south.

Pat Ryan and Dick Nixon loved to walk the beach at San Clemente. In a way it was their special beach, discovered one Sunday when they were on a drive with no destination in mind. They had stopped near Dana Point at a small inn for boysenberry pie à la mode and coffee, and then continued to drive south. At the top of a hill they had come upon San Clemente, a town of eight thousand then. The town had been founded only fourteen years before by a man named Ole Hanson, who decreed that all the houses be built in the fashion of Old Spain: white stucco with red tiled roofs. Below the hills of the town lay miles of light-colored sand and fine surf. They returned often to enjoy the palm-lined streets and constantly flowering hibiscus and geraniums.

Now in March of 1940, Richard Nixon took Patricia Ryan to Dana Point at sunset for a view of the San Clemente coastline. She remembers that they parked the Oldsmobile as close as possible to the edge of the cliff. Together they watched the last rays of color fade and the first stars gleam in the sky. Then Dick spoke of marriage and her answer this time was yes.

Impulsively and persistently in the last year, he had suggested that they elope and get married in Arizona. So insistent was he that Pat finally imposed a three-month moratorium on discussions of marriage. But in an exuberant note to his "Dearest One" he slipped in the Arizona ("Yuma") idea anyway.

> Would like to take you to
>   Bowl [Hollywood Bowl]
>   *Daughters Courageous*
>   Sonja Henie's latest
>   *Beau Geste*
>   *On Borrowed Time*
> Also to
>   Tahoe
>   S.F. (convention August 29)
>   Yuma(?!)
>   Mountains...
> And to take you to dance and to dinner like Sunday. And to write to you— and to learn things with you and to be with you more.

And in a letter dated October of 1939, he declared:

> Seriously, little one, let's go to Arizona (and if you don't want to go for the purpose just suggested, we could still have fun!). I just wanted to let you know again—since three months are gone.

When Pat Ryan finally said yes at the edge of Dana Point, sitting in an open car in the starlight with the sound of waves breaking below, she knew that she was in love. She loved Dick's romantic nature, which had brought them to Dana Point, and his visions of a great future. But even as she consented, she was not sure she wanted to marry. She was twenty-eight years old and had been independent for a long time.

My father, in winning his beloved at last, was elated. He insisted that they go directly from Dana Point to his parents' house so they could tell them the news. The Nixons already had gone to sleep and were groggy when Dick took Pat into their bedroom to announce his engagement. Hannah's natural reserve and shyness and Frank's blustery inarticulateness broke the romantic spell of the evening and gave my mother the impression that they were undecided. But later, both Nixons would tell her how glad they were to have at last their daughter "Patricia," explaining that as they awaited the birth of each of their five children, the name they had chosen for a much-wanted daughter was Patricia.

Mother decided to tell the members of her family individually. Neva was blunt and immediately asked: "What are you marrying him for? He's too quiet." Unlike Neva, Bill Ryan was not surprised that Pat was in love with Dick Nixon. His sister had visited the ranch on Sundays often when she first started teaching at Whittier, but in the past year Bill had seen less and less of her. On one visit she had explained that she often spent Sundays with Dick Nixon—and then suddenly asked, "Do you like him?" Bill guessed then that "she was hooked."

But suspecting something is not the same as confronting it as the truth. So when my mother drove to Artesia on a Sunday in April and told Bill that she had decided to marry Richard Nixon, for a few long moments he did not say anything. As tears sprang into his eyes, Bill felt not unhappiness, but the ache of losing his sister. He told me, "My dad had said, 'Take care of Babe,' and I thought that was forever."

Pat found it much easier to tell Tom the news. Of her family, he was most like her: a person with a can-do-anything attitude, almost cockily self-sufficient, and yet reserved about discussing intimate subjects. His reaction to the engagement was to laugh and give his sister a bear hug. His feelings toward Dick Nixon, expressed to me many years later, were "I thought he was fantastic. He could talk about any subject." And the subject he then liked to talk about most was football. Tom was coaching at three high schools, and Dick and Pat often went to his games.

Pat wrote to her family in New York of her engagement. To Aunt Annie she devoted four pages about Dick Nixon and his education and work, reassuring her that she would be in good hands. But she could not share her decision with Aunt Kate. In 1938, after more than fifty years as a nun, Sister Thomas Anna had died. Pat's last news of Aunt Kate was at Christmas, only a month before her death, when Cousin Catherine wrote:

Aunty Sister is mad at you for sending that money, she is afraid you are depriving yourself, also that you are working too hard. She has not decided whether to buy something she wants to eat or get a small electric stove. She says to tell you that she could not use a pad. God help her—I can see that she is weaker than last winter but mentally she keeps happy. We talk of you a lot.

With Aunt Kate's death, Pat lost the one person who had been close to her in a way her mother might have been had she lived. Now there was no one to whom she could confide her conflicting emotions of eagerness and doubt about her decision to marry.

In April, Dick took her to a jeweler in Los Angeles. He had his heart set on diamonds for his wife, although she actually preferred a wide gold band. But when she tried on an engagement diamond nestled between two smaller stones and a matching wedding band of diamond chips, she had to admit they sparkled beautifully. Their cost was also dazzling: $324.25.

On May 1, the jeweler called with the news that the bands had been sized and were ready. Dick arranged to pick them up and meet Pat at his parents' house where on school days he frequently prepared a quick lunch for them of sandwiches or bacon and eggs. They were always alone in the house at noon because Frank and Hannah Nixon were at work in the market.

On that May Day, my mother waited at the house her full lunch hour, and still no ring and no suitor. She returned to school and was at her desk grading papers after school when Tom Sulky, who worked in the Nixon Market, arrived carrying a small May basket. He set it down on her desk and explained it was something Dick had sent over. My mother looked inside. In the center, nestled among the flowers in a bed of straw so that it was almost covered, was the engagement ring. For a few seconds, she stared at it blankly. All morning she had anticipated her future husband's arrival, the unveiling of the ring, the romantic moment when he would put in on her finger. And, now, here it was, in a May basket. Impulsively, she shoved the offering a few inches away from her.

Alice Koch, who taught in the classroom next door, came into my mother's room a few minutes later. She noticed the basket and looked inside. Immediately, she squealed with excitement. When Pat remained silent, Alice picked up the basket and announced, "Look, you are going to put on that ring and right now." She proceeded to slip the ring onto her friend's finger, still having no idea to whom Pat was engaged. Then Alice went into the hall and called for the other teachers.

A few weeks later Dick wrote a serious formal letter, as if to remove any last lingering doubts.

11:35 P.M.

Dearest Heart,

From the first days I knew you, you were destined to be a great lady—you have always had that extra something which takes people out of the mediocre class. And now, dear heart, I want to work with you towards the destiny you are bound to fulfill.

As I have told you many times—living together will make us both grow—and by reason of it we shall realize our dreams. You are a great inspiration to me, and though you don't believe it yet, I someday shall return some of the benefit you have conferred upon me.

It is our job to go forth together and accomplish great ends and we shall do it too.

And, Dear One, through the years, whatever happens I shall always be with you—loving you more every hour and attempting to let you feel that love in your heart and life.

Pat Ryan and Dick Nixon decided to start their life together at a very small family ceremony. Dick, as deputy city attorney, was eager to avoid the pressure of having to invite people of casual acquaintance, and Pat did not want her brothers to have to bear a great expense. Already, Bill and Tom had touched her with their gift of a full set of sterling silver flatware in the Rosepoint pattern, the silver she uses to this day. Nor was she willing to have the Nixons take over what is traditionally the responsibility of the bride's family, and a Nixon family wedding would entail at least fifty members of the Milhous-Nixon clan, only a few of whom she knew well.

They chose to be married at the Mission Inn in Riverside. Dick had taken Pat there often to see the Italian frescoes, the medieval stained-glass windows, and the Oriental art, and to dine in the open-air courtyard where birds flew freely amid the lush variety of plants and flowers. They reserved the Presidential Suite for their June 21 ceremony. Theodore Roosevelt had stayed in the rooms in 1903, and two other Presidents, William Howard Taft and Herbert Hoover, had visited later. My parents, however, chose the suite not for its history or for the beauty of its Belgian paneling, but because it was the smallest, least expensive one to rent at the Mission.

On the wedding day, Don Nixon drove Pat from her apartment in Whittier to Riverside for the afternoon ceremony. At the inn, she changed into a short French-blue lace suit. Its dressy jacket had tiny crystal buttons and just skimmed the top of the graceful A-line skirt. Over her hair, she wore a close-fitting hat, which the eager saleslady at Robinson's Department Store in Los Angeles had described to her as an "ashes of rose" color. On one side of the hat was a small cluster of roses in the same blue as the suit. Pinned to the shoulder of her suit was her first orchid, white with delicately feathered petals, given to her by the groom. He remembers bumping into her in the hallway before the ceremony began and Neva saying, "Oh, Dick, you can't see Pat until the wedding." He laughed and said, "Okay, I've got my eyes closed."

At 3:30 P.M. Patricia Ryan walked alone into the room through a side door. Dick's parents and brothers and his Grandmother Milhous, the latter dressed in the red-velvet gown she wore for the family Christmas party each year, and my mother's brothers and half sister and a dozen friends remained seated while the president of Whittier College, who also was a minister in the Society of Friends, performed the short ceremony.

Both my parents remember how happy the reception was. It was held in the long Spanish art gallery and an organist played their favorite songs. The Nixons had baked a many-tiered wedding cake, its top layer crowned by a sprig of lily of the valley and a formally clad white-tailed groom and veiled bride. Before the reception ended, Don Nixon, Virginia Shugart Counts, and several other young friends slipped outside to work on the honeymooners' suitcases. Since the cost of the rings had depleted Dick's savings, he and Pat had pooled their resources for their auto trip to Mexico. Their friends knew that they had stocked up on canned goods. Quickly and efficiently, they tore the labels off the cans and then heavily loaded the contents of the suitcases with rice. For two weeks in Mexico, the honeymooners were destined to potluck meals of soup or canned beans for breakfast and sausages and grapefruit slices for lunch.

They spent the first night of their trip in Phoenix at the fine Westward Ho Hotel. The next morning they headed toward Laredo and the new Pan-American Highway. In Mexico City they splurged and spent one night at the city's most famous hotel, the Reforma, and then moved to a place recommended by friends, the Los Angeles Motel. Using the motel as a base, they took daily side trips to other cities—Taxco, Puebla, and Cuernavaca.

For two weeks they enjoyed the adventure of a foreign land—the new faces, sights, and smells. They stretched every penny, eating their canned goods for breakfast and lunch, and trying different restaurants at night. By the time they started back to Whittier, they were almost without money and had to drive nonstop, spelling each other every two hundred miles or so. The grand total spent on the trip was $178.

They came home to a one-bedroom furnished apartment in Long Beach, eventually moving twice more before settling into a small apartment on Whittier Boulevard across the street from where Dick had gone to grammar school. The first year of marriage was idyllic, perhaps best symbolized by Pat's birthday gift to her husband, a ceramic knight on a charger in subtle earth tones of pale green, tan, and deep gold.

Sunday was their day, the part of the week they reserved exclusively for each other. It became a ritual for Pat to bake biscuits and then set out little glass dishes containing strawberry and peach preserves, blueberry jam, and Dick's favorite, honeycomb. Carefully he would put a different jam or a spoonful of honey on each bit of biscuit. By late morning they would take their car for a long drive, heading most often to the coast for a walk along the beach.

Both had returned from Mexico determined to save their money so they could travel while they were young. They had seen too many older tourists unable to enjoy themselves because they had waited until the retirement years. So they decided to live as frugally as possible, with only occasional visits to their favorite Chinese restaurant in Long Beach. My mother cooked lots of meat loaf and spaghetti and, in my father's opinion, the best fresh vegetables he has ever tasted.

The school year 1940–1941 was Patricia Ryan Nixon's fourth and last year of teaching at Whittier. Her students had to adjust to sharing her with her husband. One of the members of her Pep Committee remembers:

My happiest memory was when we yell and song leaders were driven to the athletic events by Miss Ryan with all the fun and excitement she generated in all of us. My unhappiest memory is when she broke my heart by introducing the tall, dark and handsome young man who was to become her husband and our new chauffeur.

During that last year at Whittier, Pat Ryan Nixon met Helene Colesie Drown, who was to become her lifelong—and closest—friend. Helene was a graduate of USC's rival, the University of California at Los Angeles. After graduation, she received a coveted fellowship for her M.A. at the University of Ohio in the then-embryonic field of vocational guidance. A year later, she met her future husband, Jack Drown, a former football player at Stanford, who was now attending USC Law School.

Helene was just twenty-three when she came to Whittier, a vibrant, striking blonde with beautiful china-blue eyes. Her extracurricular assignment was as my mother's assistant on the Pep Committee. She was well suited for the job of creating "razzle-dazzle" at the games because of her zest for life and her contagious sense of humor. Helene Drown was as uninhibited as Pat Nixon was controlled. Nonetheless, Helene and Pat, both bright and spirited, found that they had much in common.

The Drowns' furnished apartment cost twenty-five dollars a month. Obviously, the furnishings left much to be desired. Particularly unattractive was the stained mohair couch in the living room. Pat took Helene to a Sears Catalog Store where they ordered an inexpensive cretonne cover. Pat ripped it apart and fitted it so well that the couch looked bright and new.

Dick Nixon and Jack Drown found that they too had interests in common. The two couples started going ice skating together and to football games. When they had some extra money from a birthday or Christmas gift, they bought second-balcony tickets for the Light Opera in Los Angeles. The music was great and the football field glasses gave them a fine view of the performers on stage.

Since both couples were on strict budgets, they often shared dinners at one or the other's apartment, but occasionally they splurged. When one of my father's classmates from Duke, Bill Perdue, and his wife came to California for a visit, the Nixons and the Drowns hosted an evening at a famous nightclub in Los Angeles, Earl Carroll's. The cover charge was two dollars and fifty cents, but the club's slogan, "Through these doors pass the most beautiful girls in the world," promised that the floor show would more than make up for what was then a stiff price. There was a contest that evening among the gentlemen diners to see who could throw the most garters onto the legs of the cancan dancers. To the joy of those at the Nixon table, my father was the most agile garter tosser in the nightclub, and they were able to end the evening in fine style with a bottle of champagne, the contest prize, at their table.

In June, when my parents drove east to New Orleans where they would embark on a cruise, their carefully saved for first-anniversary trip, the Drowns sent telegrams of good wishes. Helene also gave Mother a small brown-leather travel diary so she could record her impressions of her maiden ocean cruise and of the Caribbean ports where the ship docked. On June 16, Pat began her journal.

> Left home about seven in the evening and drove through the desert at night. . . . In morning discovered that we had forgotten Dick's draft board permission to leave the U.S. so put in a frantic long distance to Don to find it and send to New Orleans . . .

Most of Europe was already at war. Since September of 1939, when Nazi troops invaded Poland, Great Britain had stood virtually alone against Germany as country after country fell to Hitler. The United States was supplying Britain with much of its desperately needed war materials, but as Hitler continued his unrelenting air attacks, many Americans wondered how long England would survive and America would remain neutral.

On my parents' two-week-long trip, no one could forget that the voyage might be one of the last carefree times before America went to war. Shipboard camaraderie on the *Ulua* was instant. It did not take my parents' new group of friends long to realize that Dick Nixon had a pronounced tendency toward motion sickness. When the ship sailed between Panama and Honduras into the open seas, Pat commented lightheartedly in her diary: "Sail on and on! Bets on how long Dick would stay in the dining room!" He found little relief in his cabin, however. They had booked passage in the least expensive area of the ship, next to the engines, and the odor of the fumes intensified his misery. Choosing that room was the one mistake of the trip.

When the ship sponsored a vice-versa party, the men and women exchanging roles for the night, my mother recorded in her diary:

> Many laughs getting together costumes, trying stuff on, etc. Dick and I had a party for the gang first in the palm court. Then we paraded to the music room where the rest of the passengers roared at the costumes. Dick as a Grecian lady, draped costume—sheet, turban, brooch, bosom, etc.

For her, the most memorable part of the trip was the visit to the Canal Zone, in Panama.

> Colón is a short walk from here and it's at the Atlantic end of the Canal. Its law is that of the Republic of Panama and not of the Canal Zone which surrounds it—hence the playground of Americans away from their own laws. It is often called the most immoral spot in the world— Very easy to believe after an evening observing. Narrow, noisy hot streets loaded with bars, clip joints, cabarets, "women"—a horrid existence! The place was crowded with

handsome American soldiers—nothing to do and with so few Americans with whom to associate.

On July 8, the *Ulua* redocked at New Orleans and my parents started the long drive back across the country to Whittier. Two days later, at 3 A.M., my mother recorded her last entry:

> Could hardly believe there was a place left where a jacket felt good—*what wonderful coolness!*
> Always the letdown feeling at the end of a trip—just a gypsy at heart!

Before the cruise, she had made the decision not to teach at Whittier in the fall. My father was contemplating a change also, despite his success at Wingert, Bewley and Nixon, and his work as deputy city attorney, which kept him an up-and-coming young man in town. In October, he received a letter from David Ginsberg, the general counsel of the new Office of Price Administration in Washington, D.C. He explained that he was setting up a war-preparedness staff for price control and rationing, and that David Cavers, one of my father's professors at Duke, had suggested he contact attorney Richard Nixon. The salary was only thirty-two hundred dollars, half what they had earned jointly the year before. But money was not a major consideration. My mother believed that they would be limited staying in Whittier, and at her urging, my father told Ginsberg he was available.

During the next few weeks, as they waited for confirmation from the agency about the job, my mother grew more excited about the move. She could not know then that she would be leaving behind the town where she spent one of the busiest and happiest periods of her life.

On the Home Front

*I*n late November, still waiting to hear from the OPA, Pat and Richard
Nixon left Whittier for a long-planned trip to Michigan to buy a new car.
Pat's diary of the trip, recorded in shorthand notes, reads in part:

> Off on another jaunt, this time to Lansing to drive a new car home—and, of
> course, timed so that we could attend the U.S.C.-Notre Dame game at South
> Bend on the way home.
>
> Don and Eddie [Nixon] took us to Union Station where the Trojan team
> was getting a "send off" by the band and gangs of students cheering madly.
> What spirit and fun!
>
> En route, a telegram arrived from Tom Emerson requesting an interview
> with Dick about OPA position. Dick debated whether or not to turn back for
> the appointment and finally decided to continue ahead and phone Washington
> from Lansing.

They traveled east on the *Burlington Zephyr*, which Pat wrote was "the
most luxurious train as well as the fastest on the road." The candle-lit dining
car and the cozy hours in their own compartment, with the steady click of
the train a lulling companion, provided a romantic way to travel. In Lansing,
they picked up their new car, which they christened Ollie II, and then drove
immediately to South Bend to see USC play. In the morning they "woke up

to a transformed Indiana—a snowy fairyland," and skirted the storm by taking the southern route to San Francisco, where Dick had his OPA interview with Tom Emerson. The interview went well, he was hired, and within less than two weeks, the job took on a far greater significance. On December 7, as my parents came out of a movie theater in Los Angeles, they saw huge, bold headlines announcing a Japanese surprise bombing attack on Pearl Harbor, Hawaii. Within four days, America was at war with Japan as well as with Germany and Italy. Now the Nixons were only two out of thousands flocking to Washington to join the war effort.

On January 4, my mother began another shorthand diary, which she entitled "Moving to Washington, D.C., January 1942." The trip was rugged. From Tennessee to Virginia they took turns navigating through severe snow and ice storms, reaching Washington with great relief at 1:30 P.M. on January 9. It was Richard Nixon's twenty-ninth birthday.

> Parked near OPA building where Dick was sworn in and then on for apartment searching. Heard that it was impossible to find apartments in war-exploded and war-torn Washington. By luck drove to Alexandria and to the nearly completed Beverly Park apartments. The builder was a former Californian so favored us even though there was a waiting list. He rented us the apartment, called a friend who wanted to sell furniture, sent the truck to pick it up for us. So we moved in that evening. A miracle! Dick's birthday January 9, 1942 was a lucky day for us.

That night Pat called her cousin Jo Rockwell, who was working as a reviewing clerk in the office of the Secretary of State, and asked if she could show them the city. In the morning, the three set off on a driving tour of the capital's landmarks: the Lincoln and Jefferson memorials, the National Archives, the Capitol. When they reached the White House, Jo remembers how slowly my father drove her car down East Executive Avenue, "straining his neck all the while," to see the home of the President.

Until my mother was able to get a full-time job, she volunteered as a secretary at the Red Cross, working amidst the grandeur of the marble floors and gracefully curving staircases of their national headquarters on Connecticut Avenue. By summer she had a job in the same agency as my father, but in the Price Division, where she handled "hardship cases" brought by those who argued that the freeze on prices would drive them out of business. But she had been at OPA only two months when her husband was ready to leave Washington altogether. It had not taken him long to conclude he was merely one lawyer out of thousands in one of a dozen new bureaucracies in Washington, on the sidelines of the real war effort.

When Richard Nixon decided to apply for active duty as an officer in the Navy, he had his wife's complete support. Her acquiescence was important, because his Quaker family were troubled by his decision. They believed there were nonmilitary ways to serve, as the husband of Hannah's youngest sister had found when he left his business to become director of a conscientious objectors' camp in Oregon. But though my father's parents could not encourage him in his desire to fight for his country, they did not try to dissuade him.

My mother wrote her brothers, both of whom already were serving in the Navy, to tell them that Dick had now joined their ranks. A few weeks later, Bill responded.

Dearest Baby,
. . . I thought maybe Dick would stay out of this mess and leave it up to the single ones. You know after all he is doing valuable work there in Washington, D.C. Also he's married to the most wonderful girl in the whole world.

Shortly before entering the two-month naval officer training program at Quonset Point, Rhode Island, Dick took Pat to Cape Porpoise, a beautiful stretch of rocky Maine coastline. Their memories of the long weekend together at Cape Porpoise are almost as clear today as four decades before. The war and accompanying strict gas rationing had caused most of the hotels and restaurants to close. Pat and Dick Nixon were the only guests at a small clapboard hotel. It was not much different from the private homes in the area, and, in fact, at times they felt as if the house were their own, making it easy to establish a slow, peaceful rhythm to their stay. Each morning they went across the street to a gas station for a late breakfast of coffee and doughnuts, and around four o'clock they set off for their one full meal of the day at the nearest restaurant. It was a two-mile walk, and along the way they picked blueberries and ate their fill. At the Porpoise Restaurant, they usually had item No. 2 on the menu. For a dollar each they were served a small whole lobster, potato chips, bread, dessert, and coffee. There were no telephone calls or radios to distract them. Only the long, cool nights of reading and talking and sleeping beneath a warm comforter.

Almost ten years later, in 1951, my parents took Tricia and me to Kennebunkport, near Cape Porpoise, to recapture the unforgettable vacation. But the little hotel was gone, and the town had become a thriving tourist center. They still, however, have one tangible reminder of that long weekend. Near the Porpoise Restaurant they bought a painting of a small open boat beached along a curving coastline of azure-blue water. My mother has hung that painting in her bedroom everywhere we have lived, with the exception of the White House. She says simply, "I love it because we were so happy there."

On August 17, 1942, my father boarded the train for Quonset Point. A year later, on the anniversary of that day, he wrote from the South Pacific:

It is just one year ago that I left you at the Union Station and went off to Quonset. I shall never forget the day—Jake taking us to the station—saying goodbye to you—that lonely ride up to Providence—every mile reminding me of the time you and I had taken it together. Then the first night in the barracks—meeting Nimms, trying to sleep. That first week was the longest I've ever known—what with shots—marching—studying, etc. I thought of you so much...

To ease the separation, they wrote each other daily and a few times they were able to talk by telephone. After their first conversation, my mother wrote:

It's two o'clock but I just had to write you to say *how very much I love you!* It was clear all over again when talking to you on the phone. Also want to say that I hope I said nothing to worry you—when you are working so hard, etc. it would be awful to add to the load. In talking with you tonight it was the first time I really felt it was you...

Usually she tried to keep her letters light and yet let Dick know how much he was missed. Pat described her progress on the "plum-colored" suit she was making to wear on a visit to Quonset. She frequently wrote about going to the movies with Cousin Jo: "Saw *Crossroads* tonight—William Powell and Hedy Lamarr. It was a very good picture, with a good stage show. I missed Plum's hand very much." And she gently chided him about his weight loss, making it a contest between them to gain. "Have you gained any weight? You'd better, dern you! Last night I ate two baked potatoes—about killed me! Better hurry or I'll be the winner." To Margaret O'Grady in California she wrote, "Well, I'm on the widow list now—and dreadfully lonesome."

My father's letters from Quonset tended to be sentimental, reassuring his wife over and over of his love for her. "I may not say much when I'm with you—*but all of me loves all of you all the time....*" After a two-day leave together in New York, he wrote:

This weekend was wonderful. Coming back I looked at myself in the window and thought how very lucky I was to have you. I certainly am not the Romeo type and you are so beautiful. I was proud of you every minute I was with you....

When the two-month training period finally ended and duty assignments were announced, Lieutenant (j.g.) Richard Nixon, who had requested "ships and stations"—sea duty—was astounded and disappointed to learn that he was being sent to the Naval Air Station in landlocked Ottumwa, Iowa. There was one compensation: it would be a new experience to live in the Midwest.

My mother was not sorry to leave her Washington job. She too was frustrated by the OPA's inefficiency in carrying out wartime measures. In one of her last letters to my father at OCS she wrote in exasperation about having to use "kid glove" treatment with the regional offices when she reversed decisions in postaudit cases.

> Already I've put in some good digs on how the regional offices should be more helpful to applicants instead of dismissing cases because of formal inadequacies, etc., thus making it necessary for an entire re-filing which a lot of people won't go through again.

Her OPA experience helped her to get a job in Ottumwa. She was hired by a bank to set up the bookkeeping for the complicated stamp-rationing program the government had just instituted. Dick's job was as aide to the commander of the Naval Air Station, and one of his duties was talking to the recruits. As a result, he received a quick education on the Midwest. In one of his first interviews, he discovered that the Middle States have their own farming vocabulary. When a recruit responded "Pig sticker" to the question of occupation, Lieutenant Nixon faithfully recorded it, without knowing what he meant. Later he learned that the largest industry in town was meat-packing and that the recruit probably spent his time slitting the throats of pigs.

During their six months in Ottumwa, Dick Nixon chafed at his desk job. He was in the center of the United States, more than a thousand miles from the ocean on both sides, and thousands more miles away from where the war was being won or lost. He had begun to despair of ever attaining active duty until the afternoon he saw a notice on the bulletin board announcing that applications for sea duty would be accepted from officers twenty-nine years old and younger. My father was still twenty-nine and wrote immediately to request new duty. My mother admired what he had done. She had no doubt that it was the right decision.

My father's orders to go overseas did not specify where he would be sent or when he would return home, only that he report to San Francisco. In early June of 1943, Pat traveled with him to the Bay City and they said goodbye in a little hotel there. They wrote to each other every day. Almost thirty-five years later, in dictating a first draft of his memoirs, my father could recall effortlessly Mother's San Francisco address: 2829 Divisadero Street. More than two hundred of his letters, written on the thinnest of white onionskin paper, remain. They, along with my mother's letters to him, were packed in boxes and stored for years with Hannah Nixon. Unfortunately, when my grandmother died in 1967, it was discovered that mice had gotten into the boxes in the garage and had destroyed most of my mother's letters and about a hundred of my father's as well. But in reading the ones that are left, one can reconstruct vividly a marriage, a separation, and a war.

In one of her first letters Pat suggested:

Dear Plum,

Always write the day on your letters so I can picture it—also because the service seems to get all mixed up. I mail you a letter every day so I don't know how you get three at a time.

Thereafter, they both carefully dated their letters and even numbered the envelopes.

Pat, though she knew no one in San Francisco, had decided to stay in the city, reasoning that when Dick's ship came back it would probably dock there. He worried about her alone in a strange city, writing in an early letter:

Do you like your room any better? Have you considered moving in with somebody else? I know that isn't too advisable either unless you're very sure about the person. I'm anti-social, I guess, but except for you—I'd rather be by myself as a steady diet rather than with most any of the people I know. I like to do what I want, when I want. Only where you are concerned do I feel otherwise—Dear One.

Despite the severe housing shortage caused by the war, my mother had been able to find through a newspaper ad a bedroom and bath, formerly the chauffeur's quarters, in the garage of a private home at the top of one of the city's steep hills. The owners put a gas burner in the adjacent laundry room so that she could cook her own meals.

She obtained a good job at the OPA offices located on 10th and Market Streets. It paid two thousand dollars a year, and by the time my father returned home, she would be earning thirty-two hundred dollars and had been promoted to the position of price analyst. He was very proud of her and well aware that she was carving out an independent career. He stated frankly after her promotion: "Your job is far more important than mine was at OPA. I'm really very proud. I like to tell the gang how smart you are as well as being the most attractive person they'll ever see."

As a member of the South Pacific Air Transport Command (SCAT) on New Caledonia, he helped set up makeshift bases for bombers and other aircraft. The planes had to be unloaded and reloaded quickly so that they were not sitting targets for the Japanese. But when there were no flights scheduled, time hung heavily. Dick tried to keep busy studying Spanish and, as he wrote Pat, "reading everything out here." He also spent a considerable portion of his day thinking of ways to become more a part of the war. Only two months after arriving in the South Pacific, he balked at his noncombat job.

It just seems that every time I get into a place the damn central office wants to keep me there. This was supposed to be the better job—but I certainly wanted to get out and spend some time in a less civilized place where I would feel that I was doing more. I'm working on an angle and possibly before long something good may break for me. Keep your fingers crossed and wish hard.

In January of 1944 he moved a step closer to the fighting when he was assigned to Bougainville, an island that was the frequent target of Japanese bombers. He rarely mentioned any dangers to Pat, however, and did not tell her that in one month the island was under bombardment twenty-eight nights out of thirty. In March of 1944, he thought his request for frontline action had been granted at last when he received orders to Green Island. His new job was described in a letter that was published in *Life* magazine when he was President-elect. Marine Brigadier General Curl J. Felps, who served with him his entire fourteen months in the South Pacific, wrote:

As the Solomon Islands campaign progressed from Guadalcanal to Bougainville, Nixon became more restive in the rear areas. In the latter part of '43, about the time the battle for Bougainville was underway, he asked me to nominate him to head the SCAT contingent for the next advance, one which all of us felt sure would be a bloody invasion of Rabaul, Japan's "Gibraltar" in the South Pacific. I was glad to do so and he was picked for the job. As it turned out, the target was Green Island, the landing was unopposed and Nixon's desire to serve in an assault was frustrated.

He channeled his efforts to "do something" into other areas. On Green Island he opened a somewhat unorthodox hamburger stand for the fighter and bomber pilots. In order to provide free coffee, juice, and sandwiches, my father bargained with the Navy supply depot on the island and got his food by trading everything from Japanese rifles to introductions to base-camp nurses. *Life* magazine printed another letter in response to its story on Lieutenant Nixon, this one from a man who used to eat at Nick's Hamburger Stand.

Sirs:
   As a fighter pilot in the Air Force, I led several strikes against Rabaul in New Britain. We flew P-39s out of Bougainville and refueled at Green Island coming and going. We were also there on D-Day. How much we appreciated Lt. Nixon's hamburger stand on Green! As rushed as we were, I would never leave without those refreshments.
   It meant so much—just a few minutes' relaxation, good sandwiches, and the coldest pineapple juice in the islands. I didn't know then who our benefactor was. I'd like to thank him now on behalf of the 347th Fighter Group.

                                        Chandler P. Worley
                                        Indianola, Mississippi

My father wrote Mother about one of the get-togethers at the hamburger stand, and she responded:

I always like to hear of your get togethers too—you always make people have a good time. Our parties have always been your successes. Remember the time you even made the chop suey!! When I think of all the wonderfulnesses for me—didn't I take advantage?—but, dearest, it was appreciated then and now. I never shall forget how sweet you were the night Margaret and I had the teachers for a wiener roast—You carted, helped with the salad, bought the pies, went to LA for Mary's gift, etc.

They constantly reassured each other of their love. In August of 1943, my father wrote, "Please say it [I love you] always—because I always look for that first. . . . You are the only one for me, it's been that way from the first." For Dick, his wife was "part of everything beautiful I see." He described a Sunday jeep trip with several friends into the mountains of New Caledonia with its "beautiful bright, all blue butterflies," water rushing through the canyons, wild strawberries, and delicate ferns. He even enclosed some plant cuttings and a species of red berries he had never seen before. He ended the letter, "I do want to tell you you rode along with me all the way—*very close* because those jeeps are *very small*. I always think of you when I see beautiful things."

At times they both had an overwhelming physical sense of missing each other. In one letter Pat wrote about a friend's overnight visit: "Since we were both tired I slept on the studio couch so that she could have more room. I was cold and I snuggled under your top coat and felt so warm—even the coat seemed dear." In a letter scribbled from his barracks, Dick wrote: "Your letter of Sunday the twelfth had lipstick on it. Made me feel very lonesome—what a waste. You know I always liked whatever cosmetics you used. They were never offensive—always sweet—just like you."

For nine months he pestered my mother for a photograph. Finally, one afternoon after work she went to a portrait studio. In the picture taken that day one sees a smooth-faced young woman with a halo of downy, reddish gold hair agleam with light. The smile and shiny lipstick are irresistibly pretty. My father was jubilant when he wrote on April 29, 1944:

Dearest,
Today was the most wonderful day of all because the picture finally came. It's a swell shot—even though no picture can do justice as well as I tell everyone who sees it. You'll never know how proud I was to show it to all the fellows. Everybody raved—wondered how I happened to rate! (I do too.) Jimmy Stewart [a navy friend of RN's, not the film actor] said you were like a much younger and more beautiful Greer Garson and he's a real judge too. Several asked if you had any sisters! Dearest it's wonderful to see you again and even a picture brings you so very near to me.

Pat tried to lessen the distance between them with occasional gifts. On October 8, 1943, Dick wrote: "Two packages today. It seemed like Christmas to open them . . ." He called her selection of books perfect.

I have always wanted to read Karl Marx in order to be familiar with it. De Maupassant writes the best short stories the world has ever read. Van Loon's geography will be an education—a review of past learning and a preparation for our trips. Thanks for taking all the time and trouble to pick them for me. I'll bring them back as part of our collection.

In another letter he exclaimed over the soft "five-dollar pajamas . . . probably the most expensive I'll ever wear!"; so nice, in fact, that he told her he would save them for when they were together. "You see I just hate the idea of putting on anything so nice when you aren't here to see them."

There was not much he could send her from the South Pacific. Finally, however, in January of 1944 he was able to write her about a belated Christmas gift: "One of the enlisted men who had gone to Auckland remembered my request and brought back two very cute koala bears. These are much like your two raccoons. . . ." The raccoons he referred to were two fuzzy stuffed animals my mother had in her apartment in Whittier when they were first dating. Though the koala bears arrived long after December 25, at least she knew he had been thinking about her.

Christmas that year had been a particularly difficult day for my mother. She had not received a letter in almost a month and was worried that my father had been transferred to a more dangerous area. Though several friends had invited her for Christmas dinner, she simply did not feel like being the extra one in the family on that day. So she took a cable car to the ferry and rode around in the dusk, watching the lights come on in the city. When she got back to her apartment, she reread each letter from the South Pacific.

So often their letters were about hopes and dreams for the future—what life would be like once the war finally ended. In one letter my father wrote: "Do you still like San Francisco as well or better than L.A. or D.C.? Should we live there afterwards?" In another letter, dated April 1944, he asked: "So you are inclined to stay in California instead of trying Washington or something in the East?"

Neither of them had a desire to return to Whittier. My father wrote from Green Island: "Too many restrictions, etc. A little freedom is far more important than security, don't you agree?" In an earlier letter my mother had described an incident that perhaps reminded him of those restrictions. She and Gretchen King, her closest friend in San Francisco, "had one beer after work last evening—and of course reeking (but not staggering) I bumped into this ex-student from Whittier. I'm sure she whiffed it, but of course, nothing was said. . . ."

One of their hopes for the future was for a family of their own. Among my father's letters is a page of notes he took on various articles that he read while overseas. He had found a study on childbearing in the *Reader's Digest* and made notations: "No danger in first baby after thirty . . . more intelligent if older parents (only because of environment). Nursing better than bottles."

During the fourteen months of boredom and loneliness overseas, he had learned to play poker and accumulated a small nest egg from his winnings. A week before his return to the United States, he mentioned for the first time in a letter just how much money he had won: one thousand dollars. My mother during those months had tried to save also. She had lived frugally, taking the bus, making many of her own clothes, going out infrequently. My father worried constantly that she was denying herself. He urged:

> Dear one—I have nothing to spend money on here and for that reason I want you to make up for me there. Get good dinners, see lots of shows, buy nice clothes, have your hair fixed—and anything else you want or need. It will make me feel swell to think of you having some enjoyment...

In July my father received orders to return to the United States. My mother saw more clearly than he that there would be adjustments once they were reunited. In one of her last letters before he left for home, she wrote:

> Being with you, sweet, is all that matters and the thought of building a life without seems so dull. However, I will have to admit that I am pretty self-reliant and if I didn't love you I would feel very differently. In fact these many months you have been away have been full of interest, and had I not missed you so much and had I been foot loose, could have been extremely happy. So, sweet, you'll always have to love me lots and never let me change my feelings for you which has been so beautiful all these years. I love the story of Holmes' life [Supreme Court Justice Oliver Wendell Holmes] and want to buy you the book. I can't resist sending you a page of the condensation—it shows their fun and admiration at past eighty. They had a wonderful life and that is the way I always think of ours. Will you love me when I'm shriveled and ridiculous looking?!

When Lieutenant Nixon got orders in July to return to San Diego, Pat flew immediately from San Francisco to meet him. For months they had corresponded with each other, wondering what that first reunion would be like. In February he had written:

> You spoke of meeting in the lobby of the building. Hundreds of times I have pictured our first meeting again—wondered where it would be; what you would be wearing. Whether it's the lobby of the Grand Central or the St. Francis bar—I'm going to walk right up to you and kiss you—but good! Will you mind such a public demonstration?

The question was unnecessary. When she saw Dick at the airport gate, she ran to him and threw her arms around him in an all-encompassing embrace.

Part II

1945 - 1969

The First Campaign

Like many men who had spent time in the Pacific theater of war, Richard Nixon arrived home with a flourishing case of fungus caused by using rain- and seawater for bathing. It persisted for four months but eventually responded to the drier, cooler climate of San Francisco. Like others who had spent months overseas, he faced an adjustment when he became part of the noncombat navy at Alameda Naval Air Station near San Francisco. "My assignment was not particularly uplifting," he told me. "I was what is called the First Lieutenant, which, to put it bluntly, means I was the chief janitor."

His commander was exacting about cleanliness not only on the base but also in his personal office. One day he left a note: "Lieutenant Nixon, has my desk been dusted this morning?" My father was irritated enough to fold the paper into tight little squares, pocket it, and take it home to show Pat. But by the time he read it to her, he was able to see why she found the entire episode hilariously funny. She kept that piece of paper and has it today.

In January Lieutenant Nixon was ordered first to Philadelphia, then New York, and finally Baltimore to settle navy war contracts. Their stay in New York was a particularly happy one, for Pat learned she was expecting a baby. But they had no idea where they would be living when the baby was born. They simply had not yet made a decision about their future, although both agreed that Dick should not extend his navy duty and that, after the months in Philadelphia, New York, and Baltimore, they had little desire to return to life in a small town. In October my father wrote his Bougainville comrade Jimmy Stewart: "I'm eligible to get out now but have agreed to stay until January 1st—to clear up a few terminations. They offered me full commander to stay until April 17 but I've had enough." In the same letter he mentioned casually that he was planning a trip to California to meet with a group that was looking for a candidate to run for Congress from Whittier, adding: "I don't know if it will pan out. If it doesn't I believe I'll take a crack at business in the East."

My father's appointment was with the grass-roots Committee of 100, among them lawyers, businessmen, and housewives, who had banded together to replace their liberal congressman, Jerry Voorhis. In an ad placed in all the newspapers in the district, the Committee of 100 called for a candidate

> with no previous political experience to defeat a man who has represented the District in the House for ten years. Any young man, resident of the District, preferably a veteran, fair education, no political strings or obligations and possessed of a few ideas for betterment of country at large, may apply for the job. Applicants will be reviewed by one hundred interested citizens who will guarantee support but will not obligate the candidate in any way.

Dick Nixon learned about the ad and the congressional race through a letter from one of the "interested citizens," Herman Perry, an old Nixon family friend. Perry's brief note had included the postscript: "Are you a registered voter in California?" The answer was yes. My father had voted for Willkie in 1940 and for Dewey by absentee ballot in 1944 from the South Pacific. In contrast, Pat Nixon was originally a Democrat who had campaigned for Al Smith in high school. In 1937, as she was leaving work at Bullock's, she had been registered as an Independent by a member of the League of Women Voters.

The Nixons had spoken very casually in 1941 about Dick running for the state assembly. My mother remembers also that shortly after their wedding, "Dick told me one of the reasons he went back to Whittier after law school was that the professor he admired so much at Duke had advised him to return to his hometown in order to get into politics." Not until decades later, when my mother read Richard Nixon's eighth-grade autobiography, did she realize he had been interested in politics since he was a child. . . .

> My plans for the future if I could carry them out are to finish Whittier High School, and College and then to take post-graduate work at Columbia University, New York. I would also like to visit Europe. I would like to study law and enter politics for an occupation so that I might be of some good to the people.

With the arrival of Perry's letter, Pat and Richard Nixon spent two days talking about the novel, heady idea of serving in Washington. In some ways, it was half crazy even to dream that Lieutenant Commander Richard Nixon, an officer in the navy, three thousand miles away from Whittier, could return to his hometown, secure the Republican nomination, and then beat a five-term congressman. There were rumors, too, that General George Patton was thinking of the congressional seat himself, though there were many who felt old "Blood and Guts" did not have the discretion to last long in politics. Then there were the inescapable considerations of the coming baby and of finances. If my father declared himself a candidate, he could expect no monetary help from the party organization until after the June primary. My parents' entire savings of ten thousand dollars, painstakingly accumulated over five years from their joint salaries and Dick's poker earnings, would have to go into the campaign. They had planned to use the money, most of which was invested in war bonds, to buy a house.

But was a house so important? Their baby had not been born yet. They still felt like free-spirited adventurers. And, too, despite the years of Depression and war, they had not lost their curiosity and intense idealism. How could they say no to an opportunity for public service?

Forty-eight hours after receiving the letter, Richard Nixon called Herman Perry shortly after twelve midnight, Baltimore time, when the telephone rates were lowest. He told him he wanted the chance to outpoll Jerry Voorhis.

On November 2, he appeared before the Committee of 100 in Whittier along with five other prospective candidates. The Whittier *Daily News* reported that thirty-two-year-old Lieutenant Commander Nixon, dressed in his navy uniform, promised "an aggressive and vigorous campaign on a platform of 'practical liberalism' rather than the New Deal, which he characterized as 'government control in regulating our lives.'"

My father returned to Baltimore and for three weeks waited for the committee to make its decision. On November 29, at 2 A.M., the phone rang. Dick Nixon was the overwhelming selection. My parents, too excited to go back to sleep, talked until dawn. They had taken the first step down a long political road.

In January 1946, the Nixons returned to Whittier. It was not a carefree homecoming. The birth of their first child was a month away; they had a campaign to undertake and knew very little about politics; and, because of war shortages, they had not yet found a house or an apartment. On February 9, the date of Dick's first campaign speech, they were still living with Frank and Hannah Nixon. Twelve days later, on February 21, Pat's labor began. Ed Nixon, then fifteen years old, remembers Pat calling anxiously for Dick, who was in the kitchen having breakfast.

Pat and Dick were staying in the southeast corner bedroom, next to the back door. When I heard Pat call, I came from the kitchen and stood in the doorway to watch the happenings. Dick picked her up and carried her down the steps. He was very excited. They really hurried out that door and into the car.

By 9 A.M., my mother was at the hospital. The doctor examined her, and then concluded that because of her age, almost thirty-four, it would be a long labor and the baby might not even arrive until the next day. He assured candidate Nixon that there was no reason to postpone a campaign strategy luncheon in Los Angeles. The doctor, however, miscalculated. In the middle of the meeting, my father received word that a baby girl had been born at 1:26 P.M. He broke the speed limit driving back to Murphy Memorial Hospital. Although the labor was short, it had been a difficult one because the baby was in a breech position and her shoulder was broken as she emerged from the birth canal feet first. She weighed seven pounds, had "two double chins," according to her mother, and deep-blue eyes, which Pat would always say in the years to come were exactly like Will Ryan's.

That night Bill Ryan drove from Los Angeles to see his sister and the new baby. He remembers being surprised that an infant with such fair skin had a full head of black hair. It eventually would all fall out and grow in blond. When Tom Ryan and his wife, Dorothy, arrived a little later, they found my mother propped up in bed with papers and magazines spread out. Only six hours after the birth, she was doing research for the campaign.

In the next few days, some of the most enthusiastic Nixon supporters suggested that the baby be named Victoria, and my mother actually considered it, because she was at a loss for names. She had felt so certain the child she was carrying was a boy that she had crocheted a blue blanket in a shell pattern for Richard, whom she planned to call "Nic." At the end of her five-day stay in the hospital, the baby was still unnamed. Finally my father solved the dilemma by suggesting, "Let's call her Patricia. It's your favorite name."

Three weeks after Tricia's birth, Pat decided she was strong enough to start helping in the campaign and began leaving the baby with Hannah Nixon. The congressional race was being run on a shoestring, and almost the entire amount of their ten-thousand-dollar savings was at stake. She knew she was needed in the office and out meeting voters.

It took grit to work in the campaign by day and care for an infant at night. According to Hannah Nixon, Tricia was an "angel," sleeping peacefully most of the day. Too peacefully, in fact, for by the time Pat picked her up in the early evening, the baby was wide-awake and ready to play. The small, one-bedroom house they finally had been able to rent was less than ideal for a bone-weary congressional candidate, his equally, if not more, exhausted wife, and a restless infant.

My mother decided that the candidate had to get sleep. She put Tricia's crib in the living room, which was empty except for a couch and, in one corner, stacks of the *Congressional Quarterly* and newspapers. Nightly she rocked, fed, and crooned, but the minute she put Tricia in her crib, the child cried. The nights seemed especially long since there was no way to drown out the squeals of the minks their neighbors next door were raising to sell. The cages exuded a terrible stench, and each time my mother went into the yard to hang up Tricia's diapers, the animals let out piercing howls. At night their squeals and fighting crescendoed, tormenting her with visions of them killing their young, as minks will do unless prevented.

She was overjoyed when Dick came home one day with a secondhand radio. It seemed almost like a miracle that he had been able to find the radio, since so few had been made between 1942 and the end of the war. "He was so proud of it," she remembers. From then on, her radio kept her company during the long nights, making it much easier to face the day.

There were innumerable details to attend to in trying to launch the campaign, some of them minor, some important. For one thing, the candidate did not have a suit and was still wearing his uniform. Much to his irritation, Pat had given all his old suits to cousins while she was living in the small apartment in San Francisco. Because of postwar shortages, it was not until several months into the campaign that he was able to get a good-looking blue suit that fit him.

Pat did most of the work in setting up their one-room campaign office. A friend loaned them a typewriter, another contributed a throw rug, and they borrowed an old leather couch from Hannah Nixon. Then, assisted by one full-time secretary, Pat manned the office, typing letters, passing out literature, and accepting contributions "almost dollar by dollar," she remembers.

The Nixons were novices in political life. Neither had ever walked a precinct, prepared a mailing, or even observed someone who had run a campaign. But their rawness was perhaps more of an advantage than a disadvantage. It made them willing to undergo almost any sacrifice to insure a win, and it propelled them to prepare with a staggering thoroughness. My father described in his memoirs how he studied his opponent's voting record, carefully combing every *Congressional Record* until he was "confident that I knew Voorhis's record as well as he did himself. As it turned out, I knew it even better." And much of the research work was done by my mother.

Her part in the campaign went far beyond secretarial work. The year 1946 marked the beginning of the "Pat and Dick team," which would become so successful and famous. The team effort was not a conscious decision. My mother explained to me that her role simply evolved: "In 1946 not many wives were active in politics. But we were so anxious to win I just thought of ways I could be most helpful." Being helpful meant meeting as many people as possible. Since Dick Nixon was unknown in the 12th District except in his hometown of Whittier, he and his chief campaign adviser, Roy Day, devised a series of "house meetings." Republican supporters opened their homes to as many friends and neighbors as they could gather who wanted to meet the young Republican candidate. And Mrs. Richard Nixon began attending women's coffees. The candidate would appear first for half an hour and give a short talk, answer questions, and then leave his wife to socialize with the ladies.

With each house meeting and coffee, people had the opportunity to offer the candidate or his wife advice. Some of it was practical, all of it was well meant, but much of it was unusable. One lady on the Committee of 100 suggested, "You know what, Dick? I think you ought to do some work with a pick and shovel and get some calluses on your hands. You have a strong handshake but soft hands," and she added as an afterthought, "Get yourself photographed with a pick and shovel." My father did not take her advice, but he found that by the end of the campaign his hands were toughened simply by the thousands of hands he shook.

They key result of the house meetings and especially the coffees was that the Nixons were able to meet large numbers of women who had the time and could be persuaded to help the campaign. Mother told me unequivocally, "We just could not have made it without those volunteers. Our district was huge. In one day you couldn't travel the entire distance if you made any stops: Pomona, Arcadia, Glendora, San Marino, Alhambra." The musical-sounding names rolled effortlessly from her tongue though it had been more than thirty-two years since that campaign. It was the volunteers who canvassed door to door, informing others of the Nixon name and positions. They were the ones too who swelled the crowds at rallies and parades.

One of my mother's most important roles became sparking enthusiasm among these unpaid workers. Occasionally, she had to find jobs for those who had few skills. She remembers one half-blind man, probably in his late eighties, who lived in a home for the aged and came to the Whittier headquarters daily. He was proud that she sent him out to mail letters. At times it took a sense of humor to withstand the volunteers' close scrutiny. Campaign manager Roy Day recalled years later that though Pat Nixon made a good impression at the initial series of women's gatherings, some thought her nail polish was too dark! She decided that she would not smoke in public during the campaign. "It just wasn't acceptable in Whittier for women to smoke then. I was a very light smoker and felt why let something that's not that important to me become an issue."

My mother had an innate sense of what would or would not be politically appropriate for her. She knew that she would never be comfortable with a public speaking role, so she confined her remarks to brief "greetings" in which she thanked the volunteers for their efforts. She felt strongly also that there should be only one voice on issues in the campaign—the candidate's.

She learned during the first campaign that a political race can be a heartless game. Enough money to finance the campaign was my parents' biggest worry throughout. Several times, my mother remembers, they did not have funds to buy stamps for the mailings they had prepared. One of the most expensive items in their campaign budget was a four-page illustrated pamphlet designed to introduce Richard Nixon to the voters. When a local labor leader came into the Whittier office and requested fifty, my mother was elated. But my father cautioned her to question anyone who wanted such large numbers in order to be sure that they were not members of the opposition. A few days later, she refused a man who asked for a hundred pamphlets after getting him to admit he was a Democrat. That same week, the office was broken into and robbed of the remaining pamphlets that had not been mailed or distributed.

It was a major setback for the candidate whose chances of winning the election were slim at best, and for my mother, personally, a bitter blow. She had sold her share of the Artesia property to her brother Tom for three thousand dollars, her entire inheritance, and had invested most of it in the printing of the pamphlets.

When my mother first heard about the break-in at the Democratic National Committee headquarters at the Watergate in the summer of 1972, her immediate reaction was to tell Tricia and me the story of the theft of the pamphlets at the Nixon office in 1946. As the Watergate story mushroomed that election year, I heard her say more than once: "I wonder why it [the break-in] is played up so much. No one cared when it happened to us in '46!"

On June 4, 1946, Richard Nixon won the Republican nomination as had been expected and Jerry Voorhis was chosen by the Democrats. But in combined vote totals, seventy-five hundred more Democrats had voted for Voorhis than Republicans had voted for Nixon. The odds were heavily against a Nixon victory in November. My father promptly wrote a fighting note to his campaign manager in which he stated:

> I've decided to write personal letters to all the workers because I'm afraid the one we had in mind might not be too well received by some of our real helpers and justly so. It will take time but Pat can type them for me and I feel they deserve it. . . . All we need is a win complex and we'll take him in November.

The Nixon campaign was also in need of a breakthrough. It came in late August when my father was asked by a group called the Independent Voters of South Pasadena to participate in a debate with Voorhis. Most of the Nixon advisers were opposed to the idea, but as the underdog, my father felt he could not turn down the opportunity to meet the congressman face-to-face.

The first Nixon-Voorhis "debate" was actually a public meeting in which both candidates made opening remarks and then answered questions from the floor within a three-minute time limit. It was a resounding success for my father and he challenged Voorhis to repeat the encounter. In all, there were four more debates and Mother attended each one. She remembers: "They were like football games. Each side had a cheering section. All our volunteers would come. They yelled and clapped." At the end of the campaign, *Newsweek* magazine would report, "In five Lincoln-Douglas debates, [Nixon] bested his opponent, New Dealer Jerry Voorhis, who admitted 'This fellow has a silver tongue.'"

The central issue of the campaign, the one that became ever more apparent as the debates took place, was that the long-entrenched New Deal politics represented by Voorhis had grown stale. My father, echoing the nationwide Republican slogan that year of "Had Enough?," talked about meat and housing shortages, and the growing bureaucracy in Washington, which compounded rather than solved problems. In contrast, Voorhis, who had been a registered Socialist until the 1930s, defended the Truman Administration and his own long-standing beliefs in government programs.

Communism was a peripheral issue in the campaign. Voorhis had the endorsement of the Political Action Committee of the Congress of Industrial Organizations. The PAC was an arm of organized labor that had been created two years before to support FDR's re-election. It was known to be infiltrated by Communists, who, despite their comparatively small numbers, had a disproportionate amount of influence. The PAC had foreign Communist support as well. *Time* magazine reported in its October 28 issue, "This week the P.A.C. got a kiss of death. Moscow radio, speaking in English, urged U.S. voters to cast their ballots for P.A.C.-backed candidates." But not until my father made Voorhis's PAC endorsement an issue in the campaign did the congressman contact PAC national headquarters in New York and ask that its "qualified endorsement ... be withdrawn."

As far as my mother remembers, she did not miss one speech during the final six weeks until the election. Sometimes my father gave six or seven talks a day. He spoke without notes because he wanted to emphasize how well informed and prepared the "novice" in the race was. He deliberately varied each speech, thus saving himself from getting stale—and his number-one campaigner, his wife, from boredom. In the years ahead, my father would continue to speak without notes except when giving a major policy address. Nixon national security adviser Henry Kissinger accompanied my father on his first trip abroad as President and, after observing the speech giving, exclaimed to White House speech writer William Safire, "God, to stand up there without notes and to say the right things—do you have any idea what that takes?" My mother was also in awe of that ability to speak without notes. During every campaign, she would be asked how she could sit with an interested expression on her face and listen hourly to her husband. She told me frankly that if the talks had all been the same she could not have done it.

No polls were taken of the Nixon-Voorhis campaign. Consequently, the closing days of the race were a time of agonizing suspense. Even on Election Day itself, the Nixons were denied a swift, clean defeat or victory, because it took long into the night to hand-count all the ballots. Not until 4 A.M. did they finally know they had won: 65,586 for Nixon to 49,994 for Voorhis.

The Whittier *News*, noting proudly that Richard Nixon was "Whittier's first citizen ever elected to Congress," duly covered the victor's statement that "the vote of the people yesterday was a clear mandate for a program of action by the new Congress." Nixon also thanked his volunteers who had worked so hard. He saved his last words for his family: "I think today my greatest satisfaction over the results of this election is not for myself, but for my wife and my parents. Their happiness over this success is the best reward of all."

Richard Nixon was thirty-three years old; Pat Nixon, thirty-four. They had given every ounce of energy to fight for an uncertain win. It was a moment to savor. In his *Memoirs* my father recalls: "Nothing could equal the excitement and jubilation of winning the first campaign. Pat and I were happier on November 6, 1946, then we were ever to be again in my political career."

Neither the congressman-elect nor his wife could foresee that November day what changes, some dramatic, some subtle, political life would bring. The balance in their marriage shifted somewhat. From the first day he met her, Dick Nixon had respected and sought Pat Ryan's opinions. But politics was a harsh, even hurtful battle, a man's world, and he had difficulty thinking of women making political strategy and decisions. In the years ahead, Pat still had advice and criticisms, but her recommendations were no longer a matter exclusively between her and her husband. Rather, they were weighed along with the seasoned views of an entourage. And her advice was not always taken. In the race against Voorhis, for example, she saw that political consultant Murray Chotiner occasionally did not get press reports submitted in time for her husband's appearances. But when she voiced her disapproval, my father decided Chotiner's hard-line, street-smart political advice was more important to him than his wife's objections. So the subject of Murray became a nonsubject.

November 1946 marked the onset of a decade and a half of almost nonstop campaigning. Washington would provide a fast-paced existence and a life of adventure but also a life of constraints. Yearly, my mother would find that some of her fiercely won independence was chipped away. She had to consider how each action she took would affect her husband, and therefore herself. For a perfectionist, the careful scrutiny of her as a housewife, hostess, political figure, and mother was to be at times a formidable burden.

"You Run Until You Can't Run Anymore"

In December Patricia and Richard Nixon left Whittier for Washington, leaving ten-month-old Tricia with her grandparents, who would bring her East in time to witness the swearing in of the new members of Congress.

The three-thousand-mile car trip across the United States was almost like a vacation. The campaign was over; they were alone together and doing one of their favorite things—seeing new places. By driving until late each evening, they made time for several sight-seeing detours. Near Laredo, they crossed the Texas-Mexican border, planning to spend several hours in a small village friends had told them about. This innocent detour turned into a four-hour siege when the American border patrol required them to unload the entire contents of their car. Within minutes, the boxes of kitchen utensils and household goods and the suitcases that Frank Nixon had painstakingly and ingeniously fitted into the trunk and backseat of the car were dismantled. It took the Nixons two hours after the inspection to try to fit things back into place and they still ended up with several large boxes in the front seat with them. It never occurred to either that they probably could have avoided the search had they identified themselves as Congressman-elect and Mrs. Richard Nixon.

The housing shortage in Washington was very severe. Not until March did they find a two-bedroom unfurnished apartment in a new housing development in Park Fairfax, Virginia, a twenty-minute car ride to the Capitol. The apartment at 3538 Gunston Road was one in a row of identical low-cost duplexes teeming with small children and their pets. My parents lived there for four years until they were able to afford their first home.

Shortly after my parents moved into their new home, Hannah and Frank Nixon bought a dairy farm near Menges Mills, in York County, Pennsylvania. For Hannah, it was the fulfillment of a dream she had had since age twelve when her family left their acres of land in Butlerville, Indiana, where she was born. Though Frank Nixon had been reluctant at first to try farming, he soon entered into the venture with zest, naming his cows after his favorite movie stars. He delighted in telling visitors that they must excuse him; it was time to water and feed Loretta Young, Gary Cooper, and Dorothy Lamour. Now "Nana" and "Grandpa" were only a three-hour drive from Washington.

As my parents settled into life in the nation's capital, Mother began assisting with mail at the Nixon office during busy times, but generally she found that she was freer of work responsibilities than she had ever been before. She discovered also that congressional wives had few social obligations. In fact, it was difficult to know exactly what was expected, so haphazard and informal was the introduction to official Washington. There were no briefings offered wives of freshman congressmen, no "welcome to the nation's capital" kits. When my mother went to her first meeting of the Congressional Wives Club, she discovered that it was primarily a social organization offering such features as bridge lessons and a chance to work on an annual cookbook. It certainly provided no clues to the intricacies of Washington protocol.

To the frontispiece of her Congressional Wives Club address book for 1947, my mother Scotch-taped a now very yellow newspaper clipping entitled "Table of Precedence," which ranked the Cabinet, Supreme Court, and members of Congress. That clipping helped some in learning the Washington hierarchy, but she was unable to find a similar sheet of information on dress code. As a result, she and my father had one uncomfortable experience that first social season in Washington. Congressman Christian Herter of Massachusetts invited them to a dinner party, dress "informal." My mother bought a beautiful teal-blue cocktail dress for the occasion and my father wore his dark-blue suit. When they walked into the Herters' home the night of the party, however, they were stunned to see that they were the only two guests not dressed in black tie and long, formal gown. In Washington, "informal" meant black tie; "formal," white tie.

A favorite private outing for my parents became an evening of dancing at the Shoreham Hotel with their new friends, Louise and Roger Johnson. With Louise my mother indulged some of her creative interests, including attending a hat-making class where she learned the intricacies of how to braid, block, and retrim, and how to steam a silk rose. My mother wore one of her first handmade creations to her weekly hair-dressing appointment. Loretta Stuart, who did her hair from the time she arrived in Washington as a congressman's

Ely, Nevada, the copper boomtown where my mother was born in 1912. This was taken a few years earlier.

Kate Halberstadt, taken before her marriage.

My mother's parents' wedding picture. Widow Kate Halberstadt Bender shown here with her daughter, Neva, and forty-three-year-old bridegroom, miner William Ryan, standing in front of their cabin in Ely in 1909.

The five-room Ryan farmhouse in Artesia, California.

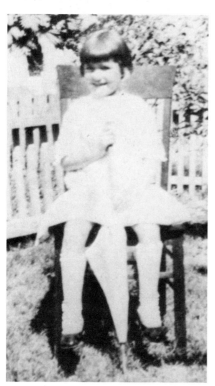

My mother, age four. At that time she was known to her friends as "Buddy," and to her family (except for her mother, who had insisted on the name Thelma), she was "Babe," a St. Patrick's Babe in the Morning.

Babe Ryan helped her father and brothers harvest the crops on their 10-acre truck farm.

My mother loved theatricals and had the lead in both the junior and senior high school plays. Here she is with Tom, made up for a performance of The Rise and Fall of Silas Lapham.

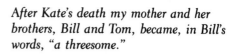

After Kate's death my mother and her brothers, Bill and Tom, became, in Bill's words, "a threesome."

◀ *Teenager Thelma Ryan at the beach with neighbors Myrtle and Louise Raine.*

▼ *Sixteen-year-old Thelma with her Aunt Annie in the Ryans' cornfield, 1929. Aunt Annie had come from Connecticut to visit her brother, Will, when he was dying of tuberculosis.*

Thelma Ryan's senior picture from the 1929 yearbook.

▼ *A page from the farm's account book at the bottom of the Depression. My mother carefully noted the expenses for the period January–June 1930; then, "Total deposits—none made since a year ago January."*

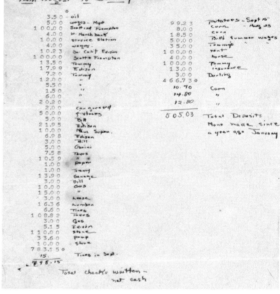

Pat Ryan (she changed her given name after her father's death) came east alone and worked for two years as a technician in New York's Seton Hospital for the Tubercular.

◄ *Pat with her Aunt Kate, Sister Thomas Anna, who ran Seton Hospital's pharmacy.*

THE GIRL SEARCH IS ON!

ON MONDAY THE FOLLOWING GIRLS WERE SELECTED:
MILDRED HOLLIS, 1000 NEILL AVENUE, THE BRONX
THELMA PATRICIA RYAN, 3221 SPUYTEN DUYVIL PARKWAY, N. Y. C.
HENRIA STONE, 1475 POPHAM AVENUE, THE BRONX

Yesterday three more Personality Girls
were picked by sharp-eyed scouts.

You may be among the lucky dozen to be
chosen Today, Thursday, Friday or Saturday

PARAMOUNT PICTURES

is choosing a beautiful passenger on one of the HUDSON RIVER
DAY LINERS for Charles R. Rogers' production—"EIGHT GIRLS
IN A BOAT." Professional scouts will find them.
One girl is selected on each trip—three girls a day—eighteen in
all. One of these will become the glorious "MISS HUDSON RIVER
DAY LINE."

READ THESE DETAILS

Miss Day Line's Award

A trip to Hollywood, first-class transportation there and back, paid
for by Paramount. Also, $50 a week for a guaranteed min-
imum of the four weeks she plays in the picture, with an option
of renewal as a Paramount player if she proves her ability.

Decision of Judges Is Final

No entry blanks—buy your ticket at the boat and you are a
candidate for a place in STARDOM!

*In 1934 Pat and two other girls were
"discovered" on a Hudson River Day
Liner, but Pat turned down her chance
for a movie career.*

▶ *At U.S.C., Pat worked an average of
40 hours a week to help finance her
education. One of her part-time jobs
was doing research for the University.*

So That Troy May Know

—Courtesy Los Angeles Times.

Pat Ryan and Mildred Simpson, U. S. C. coeds, are here seen stuff-
ing Uncle Sam's mail sack with a few of the 11,300 questionnaires
which have been sent out to Trojan alumni.

◀ *Pat Ryan with two women who
remained lifelong friends: Virginia
Shugart Counts and Margaret
O'Grady Theriault.*

*On Commencement Day, June
1937, just before graduation, Pat
and her brothers posed for a family
snapshot.*

Pat Ryan and Dick Nixon of Whittier at a wedding shower given by friends prior to their marriage in 1940.

Dick Nixon on Bougainville in 1944. During the thirteen months they were separated, my parents wrote each other every day.

The photograph Pat Nixon had taken to send to her husband in the South Pacific.

▼ Alone in San Francisco, waiting for her husband to return, Pat Nixon worked for the OPA regional office.

THE SAN FRANCISCO NEWS

READY TO GO.—Looking over a sweeping new order from national OPA headquarters, which delegates price-fixing authority to the San Francisco district office on many lines of civilian goods when permission to manufacture them is granted, are (left to right) Mrs. Patricia Nixon, price analyst; Robert B. Parks, district director, and

Lieutenant Commander Richard Nixon and his wife celebrate the war's end in Philadelphia with Navy friends, the Bill Garvers.

ELECT

RICHARD M.
NIXON
WORLD WAR II VETERAN

**YOUR
CONGRESSMAN**

The Nixons' first campaign brochure, financed by the sale of Pat Ryan's share in the Artesia farm.

My mother felt her most important contribution to the campaign was encouraging the volunteers. The Nixon campaign held a series of meetings in people's homes, and Mother attended them all.

Freshman Congressman and
Mrs. Richard Nixon with
year-old Tricia at the Tidal
Basin.

Freshman members of the
Eightieth Congress, January
1947, among them John F.
Kennedy and Richard
Nixon.

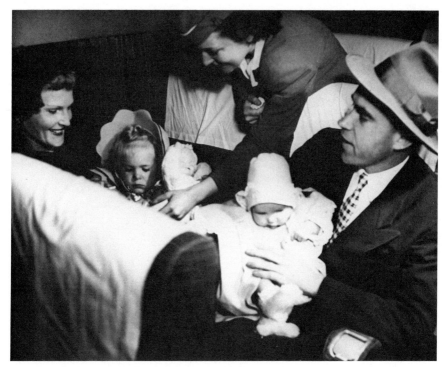

The airplane trip back to California's Twelfth District, an ordeal with six takeoffs and landings and a restless three-year-old Tricia and infant Julie to contend with.

During the 1950 Senate campaign, my parents traveled up and down the state in a station wagon. At each stop Mother, second from left, passed out thimbles stamped "Nixon for Senate."

By the time of the Senate race, the Pat and Dick team was well established.

Cracking the Hiss case brought Richard Nixon national prominence—and controversy. Shown here examining the "Pumpkin Papers" microfilm with Robert Stripling.

The Nixons with their lifelong friends Helene and Jack Drown. Pat and Helene met when they were both teaching school in Whittier in 1940.

At the Republican National Convention in 1952. Pat reacts to the news that Dwight Eisenhower has selected her thirty-nine-year-old husband to be his running mate. He calls her to be at his side on the platform.

A postconvention walk on the beach with
Checkers.

Mother and Mamie Eisenhower listen to
Eisenhower declaring that Nixon will
remain on the ticket.

▲ Mother appears serene as my father prepares
to explain his political expense fund, but the
unfairness of the charges changed her
idealistic view of politics forever.

▶ My father in Wheeling, moments after his
appearance with Eisenhower ended a
weeklong ordeal.

Helene Drown took this snapshot of my parents relaxing on one of their last carefree vacations.

The Nixon family gathered at our house in Washington for the 1953 Inauguration. Left to right: Don and Clara Jane, Frank and Hannah, and on the far right, Ed.

Pat Nixon begins her eight-year tenure as Second Lady. During those years, she was to visit 53 nations.

My parents in New Delhi on their first goodwill tour, fall of 1953.

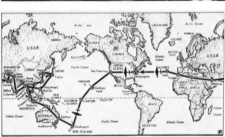

The route of my parents' 45,000-mile, ten-week goodwill trip to Asia and the Far East.

In Hanoi, Mother visits an orphanage run by French-trained nuns.

Dwight Eisenhower recognized and appreciated Pat Nixon's importance as a goodwill ambassador.

A kiss of welcome for Mrs. Nixon in Honduras during my parents' 1955 tour of Central America.

My father's personal secretary, Rose Mary Woods, and press secretary, Herb Klein, share a dogsled ride with Pat Nixon on the campaign trail.

wife until she left the city as the wife of the defeated presidential candidate in 1961, remembers that it was a "good-looking straw and tulle." She did not realize for a full year that her favorite client was married to a congressman, and only discovered it when the name "Nixon" began appearing in the newspapers during the Hiss case. "Pat was the most generous person I have ever known," Mrs. Stuart stated thirty-one years after first meeting my mother. "I loved her from the beginning. She never changed from the day I met her. She was always the same sweet person."

During my father's busy freshman year in Congress, he received a few notices in the newspapers that Mrs. Stuart, and most likely many others, missed. He was of interest to some Washington observers because of his unexpected victory over Voorhis, which *Time* magazine had characterized as a "grass roots campaign (dubbed 'hopeless' by Wheelhorse Republicans)." One newspaper profiled him as "the greenest congressman in town." An AP photographer felt the man who defeated Voorhis was enough of a "comer" to ask him to pose with his wife and fair-haired baby daughter in front of the beautiful, full-blooming cherry trees surrounding the Tidal Basin. The enterprising photographer rented bicycles, my father's with a basket seat for Tricia. Mother remembers how nervous she was throughout the picture-taking session. She was sure that Dick, who had not ridden a bike since high school, would dump Tricia into the water.

My father was assigned to the House Committee on Education and Labor (his first choice was Judiciary), and Speaker of the House Joe Martin asked him to sit also on the long-controversial House Committee on Un-American Activities, which was focusing on the problem of identifying and defining internal Communist subversion. His staff numbered three: administrative aide Bill Arnold and two secretaries. One of the secretaries, Dorothy Cox, remained for eight years and became close to "the boss" and especially to my mother. Dorothy remembers:

> At the office we were like a family. We all worked hard, though your father never asked us to stay and work longer hours. But because he worked such long hours, we did also. There was a good spirit in the office. Whenever I made a mistake on a letter, your father would call me in and speak privately about how it could be done differently. He never embarrassed us in front of the others. He won our respect and so we wanted to do our best and out of this developed an "esprit de corps" that is so important in a family. Your mother came down to help often. She usually drafted letters. We were really all in it together and pulling for the boss because he gave us the feeling he was going places.
>
> I felt close from the beginning to your mother because someone had told me about her childhood. My mother died when I was ten and my father was paralyzed three years later. I was the oldest and had to quit high school three times in order to make ends meet. I could understand some of your mother's

hardships and the more I knew her, the more I admired her. When my daughter was born in 1957 I named her Patricia. She's going to be a congresswoman...

It was not until July of 1947 that Dorothy Cox or the others on the staff had an inkling that their congressman was about to gain national recognition. My father was as surprised as anyone to learn that he had been chosen by Speaker Martin to be one of the nineteen members of a select committee headed by Congressman Christian Herter to go to Europe and prepare a report in connection with the foreign aid plan unveiled by Secretary of State George C. Marshall at a Harvard commencement speech in June.

It was a momentous trip for him. He saw Europe, something he and my mother had dreamed about doing together ever since they had first met, but a Europe devastated by war and threatened by Communism. Serving on the Herter Committee awakened him to the demoralization of Europe and to the danger of Communist expansion in the wake of pro-Soviet regimes imposed in Poland, Romania, Bulgaria, and East Germany within months of the war's end. Hungary moved into the Communist bloc just before the Herter delegation left Washington, and Czechoslovakia followed suit about a year later.

During the six-week trip the committee members were appalled by the conditions they found in every country they visited as they talked to farmers, shopkeepers, and workers. Millions of Europeans faced starvation or debilitating diseases caused by lack of food and medicine unless America provided economic aid. Equally troubling was the prospect of ever-increasing Communist-led strikes and riots. My father, in his frequent letters home, however, seemed purposely to dwell on the lighter side of the trip. Those letters from England, Germany, France, Italy, and Greece eased somewhat my mother's disappointment that she had to remain behind as summer recess for Congress began, and with it my parents' chance for a vacation together. In addition, Tricia was learning to talk and my father was missing so much of her development.

When he arrived home he brought small mementos from most of the cities he had visited. His major gift was Italian linen place mats for eight, each piece edged in exquisite lace. When my mother saw the beautiful workmanship she knew immediately the linen had been expensive. Without thinking, she blurted out, "Oh, Dick, why did you buy this?..." Her voice trailed off as she saw the hurt on his face. But she could not help what she had said. Ever since the campaign and its consumption of their nest egg, she had had to struggle with the budget to have adequate clothes for all, let alone luxuries. Through the years my mother has made amends for her first, hasty words. She has used the place mats countless times for entertaining, so often proudly telling Tricia and me, in our father's presence, "This is the linen Daddy brought back from the Herter Committee trip."

It was not until thirty years after the trip, when my mother went through some of the Nixon prepresidential papers, that she discovered exactly how much the linen cost: fifty-one dollars, a large sum for 1947. The record of that purchase still exists, because my father, always methodical, kept the bills not only of his business expenses on the trip but also of personal items. An intelligent, young, redheaded government secretary, Rose Mary Woods, was in charge of the bookkeeping details for the Herter Committee. She made a mental note then of the name Richard Nixon because he was one of only two or three congressmen who submitted itemized expenses on the correct voucher form, in contrast to the other incomplete, scrawled scraps of paper she had been handed. Some congressmen had just given a sum and said, "Work it out." In addition, the Nixon list was neatly typed, every date noted, and was, Rose noted, "the smallest one turned in." She was impressed by the congressman when she met him in person soon afterward. More than three years later, when asked to interview for a job in his office, Rose said yes without a moment's hesitation.

In traveling to Europe with the Herter Committee and during the weeks that followed when he crusaded for support in his district for the Marshall Plan, my father set a work pace that he did not abandon when he returned from California in late December. There was never any question that he would run for Congress again in 1948. When I asked my mother if they had even discussed the race, she answered matter-of-factly, without a pause, "Oh, no. You run until you can't run anymore."

Nonetheless, with her second child due in early July, my mother began to despair that the camaraderie and carefree times of her early married years were a thing of the past. There was so little free time now and much of it had to be spent with the Frank Nixons, who were increasingly plagued by poor health. Mother always had scorned complainers. Yet beneath her silent compliance she was feeling keenly, for perhaps the first time in her adult life, the need to be taken care of herself. Only in retrospect does she realize that she took charge of almost all the household responsibilities, oftentimes spending days alone with Tricia, with only the briefest glimpses of her husband. Her attitude was that "Dick had the capacity to do great things. I wanted to save his time. So I did all the chores so that he could use his energy for the problems at hand."

My father was stunned when she finally told him how deep her discontent was. Admittedly, he had been wrapped up in his new job, and when he did focus on his family, he saw not just his beautiful Irish Gypsy and his two-year-old daughter, but also his parents, who were lonely and struggling to keep their dream of a successful farm alive. He found it easier to compose a long letter than to express himself face-to-face. In the letter he wrote of his abiding love and promised to spend more time at home.

On the evening of July 4, Richard and Pat Nixon drove to Washington's

Columbia Hospital, located not more than a fifteen-minute walk from the White House. It was one of the hottest Independence Days in recent years, sweltering, airless, and humid, as only Washington—that low swampland that many argued in 1790 was unfit to be the nation's capital—can be in the summertime. Congressman Nixon was able to get a corner room for his wife so that at least she had some cross ventilation. I was born six hours later, at 4 A.M. My father, who was waiting in the lounge, remembers the obstetrician walking down the hall toward him, rivulets of sweat on his face and a huge grin as well: "You have a great big, beautiful baby girl." I weighed nine pounds six ounces, more than two pounds heavier than Tricia.

That afternoon my father called Roger and Louise Johnson to tell them the good news. The three had an early supper at the Shoreham Hotel and then my father went back to the hospital to visit. Before my birth, Mother had joked with Louise that if the baby was born on the Fourth of July, she was going to name her Independencia. Confidently, she had crocheted a pink blanket, sure the baby was a girl, just as she had been "sure" Tricia was a boy. And she considered only one name, Julie, chosen simply because she liked it.

When Mother was released from the hospital five days after my birth, she arrived home to find that Hannah Nixon, who had come down immediately from the farm to take care of Tricia, was so exhausted that she had become ill. The two bedrooms in the apartment were located upstairs, with the living room, kitchen, and dinette on the first level. Mother, against doctor's orders, began a marathon race of going up and down stairs dozens of times a day in order to care for her mother-in-law, a fretful infant suffering from heat rash caused by the unbearably hot, sticky weather, and a disoriented two-year-old who had greeted her upon her arrival home by pointing a finger at the camouflaged bundle in her arms and demanding, "What's that thing?"

Despite all the good intentions my father had expressed in his letter shortly before my birth, he was busier that summer than he had ever been before. His efforts were not given to his re-election campaign, because, in the June primary, he had resoundingly won both the Republican and Democratic nominations. Instead, he was caught up in two events: the Republican hope of capturing the White House in 1948, and the Hiss case.

On June 21, he had gone to Philadelphia to attend the Republican National Convention as an observer. While he liked both the front-runners for the nomination, Senator Robert Taft of Illinois and Governor Thomas Dewey of New York, he felt the Republicans needed a new face in order to beat Harry Truman. My father was for former Minnesota governor Harold Stassen, whom he had admired since first meeting him in February of 1944 in the South Pacific. He had written Mother then:

> Today Lt. Commander Stassen came in on one of our ships and I met him and furnished him transportation to his destination. He left this afternoon and

seemed appreciative. He is only thirty-five—a big, good-looking Swede—and I was very impressed by his quiet poise.

Two years later, when my father was running for Congress, Stassen endorsed him and was thoughtful enough to send an election-morning telegram wishing him good luck in the balloting.

At the convention, however, the Republican delegates nominated Tom Dewey, as they had four years earlier. My father campaigned for the national ticket all of October. But as he went from state to state, he sensed no eagerness to win among Republicans. Dewey's high-toned speeches did little to spark enthusiasm. Harry Truman in contrast waged a gutsy battle, and my father was not at all surprised when Truman was the upset victor on Election Day.

Almost in tandem with the presidential campaign was Congressman Nixon's involvement in what was to become famous as the Hiss case. Already the efforts of the Committee on Un-American Activities to expose Communist subversive activity in the United States had been denounced by some Washington liberals, including Washington *Post* cartoonist Herblock (Herbert Block), who in May of 1948 had portrayed my father and Congressmen Mundt and Thomas as Pilgrims burning a chained-to-the-stake Statue of Liberty. But in late summer, all of Washington began paying closer attention to the committee's hearings.

Former Communist Elizabeth Bentley, who said she had been a courier for a Washington spy ring during the war, testified at the end of July that thirty-two government officials had supplied her with classified documents. In trying to corroborate Miss Bentley's testimony, the committee subpoenaed a senior editor at *Time* magazine, Whittaker Chambers, who was known to have been a Communist Party member in the 1930s. Chambers testified on August 3. He described how he became a member of the American Communist Party in 1924 because he believed that Communism could fulfill its promise of equality for all. He told too of how his idealism was shattered a decade later when news of Stalin's massive purges of those who disagreed with him began to filter out of the Soviet Union. In 1937 he broke with the party, but not before he and other members of his cell, including a well-known New Deal diplomat, Alger Hiss, had infiltrated the U.S. government.

Immediately, President Truman came to the defense of Hiss, whose distinguished career had included service as assistant to the assistant secretary of state and as an adviser to President Roosevelt at Yalta. Truman called the investigation a "red herring" and reaffirmed his March order barring all federal agencies from providing the congressional committee with any information on government personnel. When Hiss, who was then president of the Carnegie Endowment for International Peace, appeared before the committee, he gave smooth, polished testimony. But it was too smooth in my father's opinion. Hiss denied he was or ever had been a Communist, but he never stated outright that he did not know Chambers. Always, my father noted, Hiss had qualified his answers, claiming that he had never known a man "by the name of Whittaker Chambers."

My father believed that Chambers, the rumpled, pudgy man who had admitted being a Communist and now feared and hated Communism, was telling the truth. After interrogating him privately several times, he became even more convinced and immersed himself in the case with an absorption that was almost frightening.

Those weeks in August when Chambers first declared he had known Alger Hiss as a Communist were difficult for my mother. Many influential journalists and government officials rallied around Hiss. Conversely, rumors were widespread in Washington about Whittaker Chambers: that he was an alcoholic, mentally unstable, even had been institutionalized. When my father questioned Chambers about the rumors, Chambers remained unruffled as he explained matter-of-factly that the attacks were typical of Communist smear campaigns.

Pat Nixon believed her husband when he said that he was convinced Hiss was lying about not knowing Chambers, but she became more discouraged daily with the newspaper coverage of the hearings. In her words, "Hiss was the press's fair-haired boy." The Un-American Activities Committee was widely denounced as an instrument of repression. As a result, her husband was placed "at target center," as James Keogh of *Time* magazine put it.

Finally, by the end of August, after Hiss and Chambers had confronted each other face-to-face before the committee, its members were able to establish beyond a doubt that the two men had known each other. When Hiss sued Chambers for libel a month later, the case was for a time out of committee hands and in the courts, where the skeptics thought it would die. But on November 17, during the pretrial hearing, Chambers turned over sixty-five pages of typewritten copies of stolen State Department documents and four memos in Alger Hiss's handwriting, and he testified that he had collected a similar number of documents from Hiss at least seventy other times. This "last haul," which Chambers had hidden away for so many years as a kind of life insurance against the possibility that the Communists might try to blackmail or even kill him, seemed to prove without a doubt that Alger Hiss was a Communist subversive.

Then, on December 1, a United Press story reported the incredible news that the Justice Department, which had intervened and impounded Chambers's evidence, was considering using the documents not against Hiss but against Chambers himself to indict him for perjury, because he had denied under oath his own involvement in espionage activities. When my father saw the news item, he and Robert Stripling, the committee's chief investigator, drove immediately to Chambers's farm in Maryland. Chambers told them that he had anticipated his first block of evidence might be suppressed and had thus kept back what he termed another "bombshell." The two men decided to subpoena the documents.

My father realized this latest turn might be a crucial development in the case. He was reluctant to leave Washington but even more reluctant to tell my mother that a vacation they had planned so carefully, booking cruise tickets months before, had to be canceled. Their August vacation had been canceled because of the Hiss case, just as the Herter trip and other events had postponed all their vacations since the campaign for Congress almost three years before.

My parents were at sea on December 3 en route to the Caribbean when a cable arrived from Robert Stripling requesting that Congressman Nixon return immediately because of "amazing" information in the Chambers documents. The next morning a second cable arrived, this one from Pulitzer Prize-winning columnist Bert Andrews, of the New York *Herald Tribune*, who initially had been an outspoken critic of the committee but who in the course of his careful reporting had come to the same conclusion as my father about Chambers's honesty. Andrews had signed his cable: "Love to Pat. Vacation-wrecker Andrews." My father quickly made arrangements to fly by seaplane to Miami where he would get a flight to Washington. Mother, hardly able to believe that their chance to get away had again been thwarted, made plans to fly home from the next port of call, Jamaica.

The "bombshell" was three small metal cylinders containing microfilm of hundreds of pages of stolen government documents that Hiss had given to Chambers in the months before the latter left the Communist Party. In his memoir, *Witness*, Chambers later explained why he had withheld as long as he did the damning evidence of espionage: he had not wanted to destroy Hiss and had acted only when it looked as if the Justice Department was going to gloss over the evidence of Communist underground activities in the United States. Thirteen months later, after one hung-jury trial—eight to four for conviction—a second jury unanimously found Alger Hiss guilty of perjury.

The repercussions of the Hiss case for my parents cannot be underestimated. On a hot summer day in San Clemente in 1978, my mother provided an epilogue to the Hiss case. We were sitting in her bedroom and her answers to the questions I posed on that period were brief and strained, indicating she had no desire to discuss it. But as we finished and I changed the subject, she interrupted me and said, with an edge of vehemence in her voice: "One thing I want to make clear to you. The reason people have gone after Daddy is that no one could control him—not the press, not the lobbyists, not the politicians. He did what he felt was right, and from the time this became apparent in the Hiss case, he was a target."

As my father wrote in 1962 in *Six Crises*, his memoir of his early political career, from 1948 on he was subjected to an ugly campaign of false charges, some whispered, others publicly aired: "Bigamy, forgery, drunkenness, insanity, thievery, anti-Semitism, perjury…" For my mother, the vindictiveness of some of the Hiss supporters in the years ahead caused an irreparable crack in her idealistic view of politics.

During the 1950s, my parents occasionally visited the Chamberses at their farm in Westminster, Maryland, usually when they were on their way to see my grandparents in nearby Menges Mills. During the visits, the two couples would sit around the dining-room table, or, if it was winter, gather in the only heated room in the farmhouse, the kitchen. From the windows in either room they could watch Tricia playing in the barnyard. The Chamberses worked very hard on the farm. Esther Chambers, a small, dark woman who wore her hair restrained in a tight bun, was invariably dressed in pants and boots, because she did her share of the manual labor on the farm. Its produce was their primary means of livelihood since Chambers had had to quit his job at *Time* after his public testimony. The first spring they visited the Chamberses, in 1949, my mother noticed that they still had their Christmas tree up in the living room. It was decorated with exquisite, handmade German ornaments. Over the next few years Mother observed the same phenomenon: several months after Christmas, the tree would still be standing in a corner of the room, a touch of beauty in a seemingly otherwise drab existence.

The year 1948 was a significant one for the Nixons. The Hiss case had given my father an unexpected early prominence. More important, his disappointment over the Republicans' lost presidential opportunity was keen. It propelled him to begin to consider, as he wrote in his *Memoirs*, "the possibility of trying to move up on my own instead of patiently waiting for seniority or party preferment in the House of Representatives." A move up on his own meant setting his sights on the Senate.

CHAPTER 11

The Senator

The Republicans' hold on Congress from 1947 to 1949, their first since 1933, had been all too brief. With Truman's victory, the Democrats once again had gained control of both the Senate and the House of Representatives, and my parents had to say some painful goodbyes to their defeated "Housemates," among them good friends Betty and George MacKinnon from Minnesota. My father and George MacKinnon had come to know each other the very first day that the Education and Labor Committee met and they were seated alphabetically along with another freshman congressman, John F. Kennedy.

My mother and Betty MacKinnon had become particularly close. Betty also had been a navy "widow" for part of the war, and had been active in her husband's campaign, still an unusual occurrence for political wives in the 1940s. Like Pat Nixon, she had a young daughter, Kitty. The second year in Washington, both she and Mother were pregnant again and shared maternity clothes.

The defeat in the '48 election left the MacKinnons reeling. As Betty told me, "We had to put our lives back together again." My parents were two friends who helped them do that. They encouraged George and Betty, who had just had their second child, to get away and, when it looked as if the trip would be postponed because of a baby-sitter's change of plans, volunteered to take care of the MacKinnon children on, of all nights, New Year's Eve. When Betty protested that she could not accept the offer, my mother told her, "Oh, Dick hates New Year's Eve parties. I'll come over and sit with your children and Dick can stay with ours." On the last day of 1948, she arrived at the MacKinnons' bearing an armload of her best clothes so that her friend would be able to supplement her wardrobe on vacation.

Betty MacKinnon best remembers that evening for the leave-taking. When she went into two-year-old Kitty's room to tell the little girl that she was going and that Mrs. Nixon would take care of her, Kitty became so upset that she was suddenly sick. Betty remembers:

> Pat just called out a cheery goodbye and waved me away. For a few seconds, I hesitated. Could I really leave my children? But Pat was blithely confident. There wasn't the slightest hint on her face that she found the mess on Kitty's bed unpleasant. So I went out the door and Pat stayed with my children. I could leave in peace . . . I just love her.

My father did not want to be retired involuntarily like George MacKinnon. He was well aware of the shifts in the mood of the voters every two years. A Senate seat meant a six-year term and the chance to accomplish more. But when he canvassed his advisers and good friends during the first months of 1949, most opposed the race because they feared he had no chance of defeating the incumbent, Democrat Sheridan Downey. In the midst of the negative voices, he had one vitally important backer who believed he could and should win, Pat Nixon. My father decided the Senate seat was worth the gamble. In August of 1949 he explained in a letter to his close political adviser Frank Jorgensen:

> . . . unless the Republicans do make substantial gains in both the House and Senate in 1950 . . . I seriously doubt if we can ever work our way back into power. Actually, . . . I do not see any great gain in remaining a member of the House, even from a relatively good district, if it means that we would be simply a vocal but ineffective minority.

My father knew that the decision was one of the most significant of his career. When Congress adjourned for recess a month later, my parents drove across country to spend time in his district so that my father could make the final decision on the Senate race. They asked Virginia Martin, the nineteen-year-old daughter of my grandparents' neighbors in Menges Mills, to help with Tricia and me on the long drive.

In an interview given during the 1960 campaign, when my father was a presidential candidate, she told her local newspaper what it was like to baby-sit for the Nixons. "The Nixons never raised their voices to the kiddies. Then again, Pat never had to. She can put on a look that reprimands. And even

in those days, the children could understand when Pat had had enough."
Tricia and I rarely did hear voices raised at home because both parents had
childhood memories of angry verbal clashes and they cherished harmony.

Virginia Martin recalled also: "They played games with the kiddies until
they were exhausted. The only time Pat wasn't up with the children for
breakfast was when she was out late the night before with her husband on the
campaign trail." The evenings my parents were home, we ate an early dinner
and then my father relaxed by reading or playing the piano, often "Some
Enchanted Evening," Virginia recalled, while Mother would "sew, bake vanilla
cakes, or read." She was making the draperies and slipcovers for a few of the
chairs in their Whittier residence.

On November 3, 1949, my father declared his candidacy for the Senate.
A month earlier, third-term Democratic congresswoman Helen Gahagan
Douglas had announced that she would oppose Senator Downey in the primary. With registration almost two to one against the Republicans, my father
realized that no matter whom the Democrats ran, the campaign was going to
be an uphill struggle. He promised his supporters a "fighting, rocking, socking
campaign" that would carry him "into every county, city, town, precinct, and
home in the state of California," and my mother was with him each step of
the way.

They canvassed up and down the state in a secondhand wood-paneled station
wagon with large signs reading "Nixon for Senate" attached to each side. By
June, the midpoint in the campaign, a Nixon for Senate press release boasted
that the candidate had "traveled, accompanied by Mrs. Nixon, close to ten
thousand miles to date . . . to carry his 'grass roots' campaign directly to the
people."

The wagon had a sound system on top, and as the vehicle came into a
town, music blared forth announcing candidate Nixon's arrival. Mother remembers that early in the campaign there would be only a handful of people
at each stop. My father would get out, lower the tailgate of the station wagon,
and stand on it to speak. Dorothy Cox came out from the Washington office
to help with the campaign and occasionally rode along in the station wagon.
She told me that between the ten to twelve stops a day there wasn't much
conversation.

Sometimes your mother's face would look so tired in repose. And I knew that
she was probably more tired than she even looked. I don't know how they
stood the pace day after day. If there was enough time, she would roll her hair
in the car and when we arrived at the next stop, she would get out, looking
just lovely. I noticed that she kept a record of the clothes she wore and at what
functions so she would not duplicate. She was meticulous.

In April, the Los Angeles *Times* described the Nixon campaign.

Nixon is a younger type of candidate with the frank manners and frank talk that gets right to the people. Looking over the audiences as he talks one can see them nodding their heads in agreement with what he says and bursting into applause from time to time. Nixon has been up and down the state traveling in a station wagon with Mrs. Nixon, making ten to twelve speeches a day. While he talks Mrs. Nixon distributes plastic thimbles to the crowd.

A typical two-day schedule, September 17–18, comprised a day of flying from San Diego to Glendale to Fresno to San Francisco to Los Angeles, with my parents landing at Burbank at 12:15 A.M. They were met in Burbank and driven in the station wagon to Whittier to spend the night. The schedule does not note bedtime, but they were lucky if they got to sleep that night before 2 A.M. The next morning a day equally hectic began.

7:30 A.M.	Breakfast meeting, SPEAKING ENGAGEMENT, Elks Club, 201 N. First St., Alhambra
9:00 A.M.	Leave Alhambra for San Gabriel
9:20 A.M.	San Gabriel, newspaper stop
9:50 A.M.	Rosemead, newspaper stop
10:20 A.M.	Temple City, newspaper stop
10:50 A.M.	Arcadia, newspaper stop
11:00 A.M.	STATION STOP—Outdoor meeting, Library Park, Monrovia. Congressman Nixon will speak from the bandstand in the center of the park over the station wagon PA system
12:00 Noon	SPEAKING ENGAGEMENT—Luncheon meeting, Civic Auditorium, 630 South Tyler Ave., El Monte
2:00 P.M.	Leave El Monte for Baldwin Park
2:30 P.M.	STATION STOP, front of Chamber of Commerce, East Ramona Blvd., Baldwin Park
3:20 P.M.	Puente, newspaper stop
3:45 P.M.	Covina, newspaper stop
5:00 P.M.	STATION STOP, center intersection of town, Azusa
5:30 to 7:00 P.M.	REST

7:00 P.M.   SPEAKING ENGAGEMENT—Dinner meeting,
             Ebell Club, 585 E. Holt, Pomona

REMAIN OVERNIGHT IN WHITTIER

The Nixons, driven by a desire to win, kept up the pace. My father's opponent, Helen Gahagan Douglas, was also working feverishly. After being bloodied by her own party during the primaries, she too had much to overcome. In May, Senator Downey had withdrawn from the race, citing ill health, but not before charging that Douglas was unqualified to be a senator because as a congresswoman "she has shown no inclination, in fact no ability, to dig in and do the hard and tedious work required to prepare legislation and push it through Congress." Downey further declared that she gave "comfort to the Soviet tyranny by voting against aid to both Greece and Turkey."

Even more damaging to the Douglas campaign were the attacks by her opponent in the primary race, Manchester Boddy. He circulated a document that compared her voting record with that of Vito Marcantonio, the only pro-Communist member of Congress. The two records were so strikingly similar that my father decided to use Boddy's campaign material in his own race and reproduced it on pink paper. Immediately, Douglas and her supporters alleged that this "pink sheet" was a smear.

In 1973, when Roscoe Drummond wrote a column about the 1950 Senate campaign, the charge "smear" had been repeated so many times in the intervening twenty-three years that it had become part of the Nixon legend. But Drummond challenged that image. "Did you ever hear of the 'sneaky, tricky, ruthless campaign' waged against Mrs. Douglas by her Democratic opponent? No, these are the descriptions repeatedly attributed to Nixon's pallid version of the same thing."

Forgotten too is that Helen Gahagan Douglas, determined to convince voters she was more anti-Communist than Nixon, charged throughout the campaign that the Nixon record of "blind stupidity on foreign policy gave aid and comfort to the Communists." In October, a month before the election, her staff circulated a flyer which read: "THE BIG LIE! HITLER INVENTED IT. STALIN PERFECTED IT. NIXON USES IT. . . . YOU PICK THE CONGRESSMAN THE KREMLIN LOVES!" At the same time, to cover all her bases, she flip-flopped to claim Nixon was a Red-baiter! And she predicted there would be another depression if Nixon was elected.

It was not a pleasant election to live through. The charges and counter-charges came fast and furious. My mother, in particular, recoiled from the shrillness of Helen Gahagan Douglas's personal characterizations of my father. She frequently referred to him as a "pip-squeak" and also called him a "peewee" and "tricky Dick," a label that would be resurrected time and again after the Senate race was history. My father's strategy was to scrupulously avoid responding to the personal attacks and, as he wrote in his *Memoirs,* to keep Mrs. Douglas "pinned to her extremist record": not only her vote against Truman on military aid to Greece and Turkey, but also the other votes that had, in all likelihood, caused the Communist newspaper *The Daily Worker* to call her "one of the heroes of the 80th Congress." He kept her pinned as well to her wild charges, some of them caused by sloppy research. When she issued a "yellow sheet" and accused Nixon of having voted five times with Marcantonio, he did not let her forget for the rest of the campaign that

> in two of the five votes in question, I had not done so—although she had. In the third there was no vote of record. In the other two cases, she had seized on procedural technicalities to distort the record. She accused me of opposing aid to Korea when I had actually supported it, and of voting to cut a Korean aid program in half when in fact I had voted for a one-year bill rather than a two-year bill.

As the campaign became more heated, hecklers organized by leftist labor and political groups routinely showed up at the Nixon station-wagon stops and rallies. Toward the end of the campaign Mother enjoyed seeing the tables turned when the Drowns and some of the other volunteers prepared a surprise for a small claque of demonstrators who came to a Nixon rally at the Long Beach Municipal Auditorium. The Drowns, then full-time volunteers in charge of the Long Beach office, were such enthusiastic boosters that they had painted both sides of their family car, a Plymouth sedan, with the slogan "Nixon for Senate," and had hooked up a loudspeaker on its roof for the campaign and other songs. The volunteers decided to park the Plymouth in front of the auditorium and play one of the popular records of the day, "If I Knew You Were Comin' I'd 'Ave Baked a Cake." When the Nixon supporters heard the song, their laughter diffused any points that the pickets may have hoped to gain.

Whenever Helene, who was striking with her pale-blond pageboy, drove the Plymouth, she attracted whistles and tooting horns. Before the election, my mother went on a last-minute shopping trip with her and had a taste of what it was like to drive the campaign car through downtown Los Angeles traffic. At every stoplight, she and Helene drew appreciative comments, and when Helene wheeled the top-heavy sedan up to the entrance of I. Magnin's, one of the most elegant stores in Beverly Hills, the white-gloved and capped parking attendant did a double take. Since the Plymouth was a bizarre contrast to the Rolls-Royces and other luxury cars he was accustomed to parking, he couldn't resist a comment, "I'm for your man, Nixon," and gave the car a prominent place in the parking lot.

Because Helene worked such long hours at the Long Beach campaign office, she could not afford to hire baby-sitters for her three children every day. Often the preschoolers, four-year-old Bruce and three-year-old Larry, wearing their everyday cowboy outfits and boots, helped at the office by passing out literature. One day a reporter for the Long Beach *Independent Press Telegram* happened to walk by the Nixon headquarters when Bruce was on the job. He quizzed the little boy: "Who is this man Nixon?" And Bruce unwittingly provided a small item for the newspaper the next morning by replying: "Why, he's Tricia's and Julie's daddy."

But not all the encounters with people off the street were as pleasant. One man who came into the Long Beach office asked Helene, "Does the Ryan name mean what I think it does?" She countered, "Mean what?" "Mean Pat Nixon's a Catholic," the man said. When Helene asked why that mattered, his next comment was predictable: "Well, I'd never vote for a man if he were married to a Catholic." Helene, in tight-lipped anger, told him, "Pat's not a Catholic, but I don't think Mr. Nixon would want your vote."

The Senate campaign was not the first time the question of my mother's Catholicism was raised. She was very sensitive to news stories that said she and her family were "fallen away" Catholics. One of the reasons she avoided discussing her childhood in interviews was her unwillingness to go into a subject as personal as Will Ryan's faith.

The support of friends like the Drowns and the other volunteers, many of whom were helping with the third Nixon campaign in five years, made the Senate race almost a family affair. A group of Whittier women my mother had known since the 1946 race even knit her some campaign dresses.

The Whittier supporters who did the knitting believed that Pat Nixon was the kind of person who would wear a homemade dress with flair and with appreciation. Her image was as much "at home" as it was that of a woman of accomplishment. During the campaign, the Congressman Richard Nixon for U.S. Senate Committee published an information sheet entitled "Meet Mrs. Pat Nixon." She was described as a "well-informed, intelligent and thoughtful young woman, seriously interested in national affairs and problems of government." The information sheet also portrays her as "a good house-keeper and a devoted mother... shopping for bargains," "planning budget menus," and "missing her little girls."

For my mother, the hardest aspect of campaigning indeed was worrying about Tricia, then four, and me, two years old. Since my grandparents were living on the East Coast, she had to depend on baby-sitters, some of whom she did not know well. If she was gone for the entire day, she would telephone several times. But it was impossible to keep abreast of everything, most notably the "surprise" that well-meaning supporters concocted toward the end of the campaign. They taught Tricia and me the Nixon campaign song so that we could sing it at the close of the television time that had been bought for a last-minute appeal. When my parents came home, they were presented with our carefully coached performance, sung to the tune of "Merrily We Roll Along":

On we go to Washington, Washington, Washington.
On we go to Washington . . .

And then, instead of "Vote for Nixon," I came forth with "Vote for Bunny," my favorite toy, a small rabbit with oversized ears and a face denuded of fur by constant rubbing and many washings.

Tricia and I did appear on the television broadcast, but instead of singing, we sat with Mother while my father delivered his election-eve talk. It was my mother's first experience with television, and she remembers it as a thirty-minute white-knuckle struggle to keep Tricia still, while holding me on her lap. We both squirmed, wanted to suck our thumbs, and, not surprising considering our ages, acted bored. It was twelve more years before we were included in another TV appeal.

The day after the broadcast, November 7, 1950, Richard Nixon won by 680,000 votes, the biggest plurality achieved by any Republican that fall.

After my father had been in the Senate for a month, he hired a private secretary who was to become a mainstay of his life and my mother's: Rose Mary Woods, who had handled the bookkeeping chores for the Herter Committee. My mother and Rose, a woman of verve and keen intelligence, became friends immediately, a friendship based on mutual respect. My mother frequently spent several days a week volunteering at the Senate office whenever there was a heavy volume of mail. Rose saw that the boss's wife was quietly efficient. Without having to ask, she found ways she could help, whether it was running the duplicating machine, sorting mail, or drafting responses.

Rose came from an Irish Catholic family hit hard by the Depression. Like Pat and Dick Nixon, she had struggled since her teen years to earn a living and help her parents. She was very close to them and to her two sisters and brother, supporting them through difficulties and sharing in their happinesses. She particularly admired my mother for the way she cared for Tricia and me. She knew Pat took her turn twice a week as an aide at my cooperative nursery school. Rose saw too that Mother was always there when we needed her. Since Rose's family lived in the small town of Sebring, Ohio, the Nixons and the office staff became her family away from home.

In the first four years of the Vice Presidency, Rose was usually the only other woman on the long, grueling foreign trips. When my father took work with him on vacations, Rose occasionally went along as well. Often when she had free time on those trips she spent it with my mother, usually reading side by side in quiet companionship. They enjoyed each other's company and remained friends throughout the pressures and disappointments of twenty-five years of political life because, as my mother explained to me once, they were careful never to cross each other or to second-guess a decision. As a teen-ager, I saw another reason for their enduring friendship: in times of difficulty, both put on cheerful faces and in that way sustained each other.

In February of 1951, only a month into the term, my mother wrote Helene: "We bought a house!...we hope we can stand the crowded quarters here until then [moving-in-day]! (My clothes are even hanging on doors—we're bursting at the seams.)" The two-story white-brick house was located in a new residential section of Washington called Spring Valley. Although its cost, forty-one thousand dollars, stretched them to the limit, they felt they needed the seven-room house for the family and the increasing social obligations the next six years in the Senate would bring.

At 4801 Tilden Street, Mother for the first time enlisted the help of a decorator. The results were pleasing. A reporter for the *Christian Science Monitor* who interviewed her shortly after the home was furnished wrote that the living room had a "bright California look with its cheerful aqua walls, peacock blue draperies and a touch of spring green in furniture covering. . . . It all reflects the good taste of the slim, attractive woman who sat opposite me. . . ." The reporter was particularly impressed by Pat Nixon's idea of mir-roring one wall of the living room in order to create the illusion of spaciousness.

My mother was most daring in decorating the master bedroom. She chose a dull-silver tea paper for the wall behind the bed and asked a local artist to paint a graceful, free-floating tree in shades of green and blue. Tricia and I shared the second bedroom, leaving the third free for Hannah and Frank Nixon, who visited often.

The spring that we moved into the new house my father was bothered for the first time by severe back and neck pains. He consulted several doctors and finally was diagnosed as being too tense. When I was doing research for this book, my father told me that during the initial years in Washington, as he worked long hours at his job, there were many times he did not get home for dinner. There were other times when he was too busy to play with Tricia and me. We do not recall those early years as being fatherless, however. It seemed to us he was there at the important times. During the Senate race, as often as he could he walked Tricia across the field at Hugheston Meadows and put her on the bus for kindergarten. We had picnics on weekends in his office, and we played together on long summer evenings in our backyard. We always knew he cared. As Mother wrote Helene in one letter: "Dick went to a luncheon and the magician sent the rabbit home to the children. Oh, boy, it was just what we needed!"

The Senate years did mean more travel for my father, however, since immediately after his big win in November, the Republican National Committee decided to use the young senator from the second-most-populous state for fund raising. But Mother never complained about his absences, talking instead of how much we had to look forward to when he came home. Occasionally she was able to go with him on the more interesting trips. When Senator Nixon was invited in April 1952 to give a series of speeches in Hawaii, he decided not to worry about the family budget this time and invited his wife to go with him. Then to surprise her, he telephoned Jack and Helene Drown, who arranged to borrow money from Jack's parents in order to make the trip.

The days in Honolulu were a second honeymoon for both couples. Each morning they had breakfast of fresh pineapple on the balcony of their hotel, and, with the exception of the night my father gave his speech, they danced every evening after dinner at the Royal Hawaiian, even taking one hula lesson at the Queen Surf Hotel. Their hotel entrance to the beach was locked after dark, but when they felt like a midnight swim, they thought nothing of going through the staid, formal lobby swathed in towels. Looking back, my mother recalls, "It was the last carefree vacation I ever had." Within eighteen months, Richard and Patricia Nixon would have public faces, Secret Service protection, telephones that must always be able to contact them, and the position of the Vice Presidency to uphold.

CHAPTER 12

Checkers

In the spring of 1952, a few months before the opening gavel of the Republican National Convention, there were occasional squibs in the newspapers that Richard Nixon, the youngest Republican member of the Senate, was a potential vice-presidential candidate. Neither of my parents took the rumors seriously, but Alice Roosevelt Longworth, whose father, Teddy Roosevelt, had despised the "boring" job of being Vice President under William McKinley, did. Alice Longworth had taken an interest in up-and-coming young Senator Nixon and she counseled him that if there was any truth to the stories, he'd better think twice before accepting. ". . . You should talk to Pat about it so that just in case it does happen you aren't caught with your drawers down! If you ask me, and since you did I'll tell you again, if you're thinking of your own good and your own career you are probably better off to stay in the Senate and not go down in history as another nonentity who served as Vice President."

One always paid attention to Alice Longworth. She had been a legend since 1902 when she was the White House's "Princess Alice." Frank Nixon had often told his sons of the thrill and shock of seeing the President's daring daughter smoke a cigarette on the streetcar he was operating in Columbus, Ohio. But when Alice Longworth spoke of the Vice Presidency, my father barely heard the warning, so "impossibly remote" did the opportunity seem.

113

His attention was on the emerging battle between those Republicans supporting World War II hero General Dwight David Eisenhower and the forces behind Senator Robert Taft of Ohio. There were many lifelong party members who felt the general was an interloper and that Taft, known as "Mr. Republican," deserved the nomination. My father, however, was going to support Eisenhower at the convention in Chicago because he considered him a genuine statesman who could deal with the Cold War.

Like most of the Republicans who went to Chicago that hot, steamy July, my mother was intrigued by the legend of General Eisenhower, the Supreme Allied Commander who had led America to victory in Europe, and had been president of Columbia University and the head of NATO forces. When Ike's supporters hosted a reception for delegates to meet the general, she was eager to attend—until she heard that there would be at least an hour's wait in line. But Helene, whose husband was a California delegate, insisted they go, telling Pat, "We may never get to meet him again." They did wait in line for more than an hour. But meeting Eisenhower was worth it. He was warm and friendly, especially so when his aide, who recognized the name Nixon, made a point of telling him that Mrs. Nixon was "the wife of *Senator* Dick Nixon." As Mother openly scrutinized the general, she found him looking at her just as closely with eyes that she would remember all her life as "round, baby-blue and mesmerizing."

Pat Nixon found everything about her first convention exciting. Sometimes it was hard to believe how far her husband had come in just six years. When the Chicago *Daily News* predicted in a headline on page one that the GOP ticket would be Eisenhower-Nixon, my father sent an aide out to buy half a dozen copies so that he could show his grandchildren one day. He was convinced, he told my mother, that the newspaper was "only guessing." But the Chicago *Daily News* apparently felt it was betting on the right man. One of its reporters was sent to the Knickerbocker Hotel to interview Mrs. Nixon. In the short profile that appeared in the paper the next day, Pat Nixon was described as "Senator Nixon's Man Friday"—a homemaker and her husband's secretary while in Chicago, taking care of his mail, phone calls, and other business chores.

That evening, Pat Nixon and Helene Drown attended the convention session together. When Pat returned from a late supper, she found her husband waiting for her and anxious to talk. Though only twenty-four hours had elapsed, this time he was taking the possibility of the Vice Presidency seriously. They talked for an hour, and then a second and then a third. My mother was wary—and realistic. She resisted being swept away by the surface glamour of the idea. The grueling work of the Senate campaign with its heated rhetoric was still a vivid memory, and she dreaded the prospect of having to leave Tricia and me, then six and four years old, for another long campaign.

Finally, at 4 A.M., they woke up Murray Chotiner, now a full-time Nixon aide, and asked him if he would mind coming down to their room. Chotiner said later in an interview that when he saw the Nixons he "could tell Pat had been talking against it." Nevertheless, he gave his usual blunt appraisal: "There comes a time when you have to go up or get out." He argued that if my father won and did not like the job he could quit after four years. "Any man who quits political life as Vice President as young as you are certainly hasn't lost a thing."

Murray left around 5 A.M. and my parents talked a while longer. In the dawn, sitting in the hotel room at the Knickerbocker, too excited to sleep, and too weary to get in bed, they found Murray's arguments powerful. My mother finally said, "I guess I can make it through another campaign." But neither she nor my father truly believed it would happen.

Less than nine hours later, at 1:50 P.M. on July 11, Dwight D. Eisenhower was nominated on the first ballot. The convention recessed in order to give the nominee time to make a decision on his running mate. At 4 P.M., playwright and former congresswoman Clare Boothe Luce, whose husband was head of Time Inc., was standing near the press boxes when the news was announced that Richard Nixon was Eisenhower's choice. In an interview with me almost thirty years later, she recalled vividly that as a throaty cheer went up from the delegates, she heard "shouts of rage and disbelief" from the journalists standing near her.

My mother was not even in the Convention Hall at that moment. She was having a late lunch with Helene and Murray Chotiner's wife at the Stock Yard Inn. As they ate, they watched a grade-B movie on the restaurant's large screen. Abruptly, a bulletin interrupted the film, "Ike chooses Nixon." My mother opened her mouth in astonishment and her bite of ham sandwich fell out. Helene exclaimed, "Oh, Pat, you're going to be in the history books!" Suddenly, Mother felt a tremendous sense of elation. She and Helene, though in high heels, literally ran back to the Convention Hall. They stopped in the ladies' room in order to comb their hair and adjust their hats, and Mother had the strange experience of hearing everyone buzzing about the choice of Senator Nixon, not realizing his wife was within pinching distance.

My father learned the news of his selection in an even less formal setting. He had gone back to the hotel to try to rest. Since the temperature in his room was, he guessed, at least a hundred degrees, he undressed to his underwear and flopped on top of the bed. He was semiconscious when the telephone rang. It was Herbert Brownell, who headed the group of advisers Eisenhower had entrusted with helping him choose a vice-presidental candidate. He heard Brownell say Nixon was the unanimous choice. For a moment he was speechless in disbelief.

Brownell asked him to come as quickly as possible to meet with the general at the Blackstone Hotel. There was no time to shower or shave. My father put on the only suit he had brought to Chicago—light gray in color, and by that time very wrinkled. When he arrived at the Blackstone and saw Eisenhower standing in the doorway of his suite waiting for him, he was visibly, boyishly excited. "Congratulations, Chief," he exclaimed exuberantly, assuming Eisenhower would like the title intimates used affectionately when speaking to former President Hoover. But he sensed immediately that the general was displeased. For my father, it was the first hint that beneath the engaging, disarmingly wide smile, Eisenhower was reserved and protocol-conscious, and frankly uncomfortable with informality from his staff and working associates. At the meeting, the general did most of the talking. He told Senator Nixon that the campaign would be a crusade against the corruption of the Truman Administration and Democratic complacency about the Communist threat. The general made it clear that his running mate would be expected to lead the attack while the presidential nominee remained above the battle.

After conferring with Eisenhower, my father and Chotiner went directly to the Convention Hall. By 6:33, he had been nominated by acclamation. When Congressman Joe Martin asked Senator Nixon to leave the California delegation and come to the rostrum, Mother immediately started to make her way from the Distinguished Visitors Gallery to join him on the floor. Friends and strangers slapped her on the back, grabbed her arm, squeezed her hand. As soon as she reached her husband, she gave him a kiss in the intense excitement of the moment. She agreed to repeat the kiss at the insistence of the photographers who were not quick enough to capture that moment of joy. Then, together, they pushed their way to the platform.

In his acceptance speech, General Eisenhower told the delegates about his "great crusade for freedom in America and freedom in the world." My father promised a "fighting campaign," and made an attempt in his speech to begin the process of healing party wounds by praising not just Dwight Eisenhower but Bob Taft as well.

Mamie Eisenhower, sitting next to Mother on the stage, had been given a sedative to dull the throbbing of a toothache. Mamie had never met Pat Nixon before. She did not expect someone so young and greeted her with the exclamation: "You're the prettiest thing." My mother remembers Mamie's comment because those words at that moment, in that place, surprised her so much. She learned that evening, however, that Mamie Doud Eisenhower was a woman who spoke the first thing that was on her mind. Thus, on a night of triumph and consequence for the future, as Mamie and my mother sat together while their husbands, following their speeches, shook hands with the delegates, Mamie wanted to talk about the ordeal she had suffered with her tooth.

The papers the following morning were full of profiles of Senator Richard Nixon and articles on his family. The Associated Press quoted Frank Nixon as saying, "I really didn't want Dick to get into this job . . . I felt that he'd do a good job as a Senator and then later he could be a candidate for President."

In postnomination interviews, Pat Nixon stated she would campaign with her husband because "we always work as a team." Already millions of people watching the convention on television had had a good glimpse of her. She made a memorable impression: she was young, she was beautiful, and she happened to be wearing a dress with a bold, very busy print.

Helene had come into her room early that morning, wanting to know what she planned to wear to the day's session. When Mother had shown her her coolest voile shirtwaist dress, Helene had suggested impulsively, "Oh, why don't you wear this," pointing to a pretty, full-skirted silk dress dotted with black and white coins and trimmed with black-velvet cuffs and collar. As soon as Mother returned to Washington, she received a phone call from her half sister, Neva, who asked characteristically without preliminaries, "When are you going to send me that black-and-white dress? You can't wear it again—it's been pictured in every newspaper and on TV." But she did continue to wear the dress during the campaign and, later, at my father's request, packed it away to save.

Mother had arrived home just forty-eight hours after the acceptance speech, anxious to see Tricia and me. She was worried by Hannah Nixon's call on nomination night describing how reporters had descended upon the house on Tilden Street demanding that Tricia and I be awakened to pose for photographs. One of the secretaries from my father's Senate office met her at the airport and Mother admitted then she was too tired to cook. She took Tricia and me to a Hot Shoppe, a short-order restaurant where they served what we thought were the best hot dogs in the world. Mother did not get much sleep after our early supper, however. Until dawn, Western Union delivered telegrams. She ruefully told an interviewer later, "Next time I'll know to call them up and ask them to hold the telegrams until morning."

My parents' first presidential campaign became a blur of new experiences. Mother discovered that the reporters assigned to write about the Nixons tried hard to come up with different "angles" so that their stories would not all sound alike. One enterprising writer revealed the "romance" between six-year-old Tricia and five-year-old David Kefauver, son of the Democratic senator who happened to live at the end of our block. When Jacqueline Bouvier (later Kennedy), the "Inquiring Photographer" for the *Times-Herald*, encountered me playing outside our house, she asked, "Do you play with Democrats?" My response was "What's a Democrat?" My mother also was introduced to the "as told to" articles in which the celebrity who has neither the time nor the expertise tells his first-person story to an assigned writer.

Although Tricia and I were too young to take part in the campaign, my parents did take us with them to California for the kickoff event of the campaign on September 16—a rally on the Whittier College football field. I sat on the lap of Mrs. Earl Warren, the governor's wife, and slept through my father's speech. The next morning, the travel began in earnest in Pomona, where my parents had launched their campaigns for both the House and Senate. From the back platform of the *Nixon Special* they waved to the crowd as the train slowly inched down the tracks. My mother's red-gold hair glistened in the sunlight, a vivid contrast to the coal black of my father's. They were young, attractive, full of fight, and, in the opinion of those watching the scene, headed for victory. But within twenty-four hours their world came apart.

On September 18, newspapers across the country printed a long story by syndicated columnist Peter Edson about an eighteen-thousand-dollar political expense fund established for Senator Nixon following his defeat of Helen Gahagan Douglas almost two years earlier. Edson reported the purpose of the fund: to enable the senator to campaign continuously for Republican candidates and for himself. The money raised was to pay for printing and mailing political materials to supporters and, since the senatorial allowance provided only one round-trip ticket between California and Washington per session, for more frequent trips home. Contributions were limited to individuals—no corporate money allowed—and to maximum amounts of five hundred dollars so that no one could be accused of buying favors. A letter describing the fund and soliciting the money openly had been sent to several hundred people by a local lawyer, Dana Smith. Edson included in his story Smith's suggestion that other states adopt the plan so that senators who had no independent income would not be tempted to bow to outside pressures.

The same day as the Edson story, Smith's suggestion was brushed aside when the New York *Post*, long a partisan Democratic paper, launched a fierce personal attack on my father's integrity. The banner headline read: "Secret Nixon Fund!" Inside, the story was captioned: "Secret Rich Men's Trust Fund Keeps Nixon in Style Far Beyond His Salary." In the days ahead, the Democrats cynically ignored Edson's story and pounced on the *Post* version, especially since the Eisenhower-Nixon ticket had made the campaign promise to drive the "crooks and cronies" from power.

With the election only six weeks away, as the *Nixon Special* traveled up through the central California valley to Oregon, the story of "the fund" mushroomed amid rumors of mounting newspaper investigations and silence in the Eisenhower camp. Pat Hillings, a twenty-eight-year-old congressman who had won the seat my father vacated to run for the Senate, remembers:

> The tension on the train became unbearable. We were so isolated. Here we were rolling along, no telephones, no newspapers, no radios. At each stop hecklers came out. They held up signs. That was the way we got our news. It was like reading Chinese wall posters.

When the train came into a station, the press on board rushed to telephones, sometimes even knocking on strangers' doors, in order to call their editors back East to find out what was happening. Pat Hillings also would race for a phone to call the Eisenhower train. But too often the lines on the *Look Ahead, Neighbor Special* were busy or the train had just departed or had not yet come into a station.

For more than two days, my parents lived a surrealistic existence. On one plane, they were candidate and wife, meeting the local press, entertaining the local politicos between stops, giving speeches, and shaking hands. On the other level, they were almost frantic for news of what was happening and utterly frustrated that there were still no statements of support from the Eisenhower train. My father, the thrice-elected politician, at first had doubted that Eisenhower would confess an error in judgment and push him off the ticket in the face of flimsy charges, but he began to wonder late on Friday night when he learned that the Washington *Post* and the New York *Herald Tribune* were calling for his resignation. The news stunned him. Especially ominous was the action of the New York *Herald Tribune*, since it was so closely aligned with the Eisenhower candidacy and presumably reflected the Eisenhower campaign's point of view.

He met immediately with Murray Chotiner and William Rogers, a Washington lawyer and friend since the Hiss case. It was not until 2 A.M. that he returned to his compartment on the train. My mother woke up immediately when he came in. He told her then about the newspaper editorials, concluding with the words: "If the judgment of more objective people around Eisenhower is that my resignation would help him win, maybe I ought to resign." Her response was an unqualified "No." Stepping aside would hurt Eisenhower, she insisted, because Nixon supporters would desert the ticket. They would just have to see it through.

And yet, although she insisted my father keep fighting, by evening, when the *Nixon Special* reached Portland, Oregon, the strain had become almost unbearable for her. As my parents walked from their car to the entrance to the Benson Hotel, they had to run a gauntlet of shoving hecklers from local Democratic headquarters who threw pennies and shook tin cups labeled "Nickels for poor Nixon." The suddenness and ferocity of the attack had come as a shock to my mother. To the Drowns she repeated over and over, unbelievingly: "It can't be happening. How can they do this? It is so unfair. They know the accusations are untrue." Helene recalls, "We were sitting in her room. It almost killed me to look at her—she was like a bruised little kitten. And what could we do to counteract what was being said? The oppression was so thick that you could cut it with a knife. I decided we just had to get out of the room." They went for a car ride out to the falls near Portland. Mother took her shoes off, put her feet in the water, and, for the first day in days, she laughed. But it was a laugh of one who wakes up only momentarily from a nightmare and then goes back to the same vicious cycle of dreams.

All day Sunday at the Benson Hotel the press kept hinting at additional "revelations," and it looked as if my father's political career was over. For hours he held informal meetings with his staff, vainly trying to find a way to halt the distortions and innuendos that were bound to grow until the Price Waterhouse accountants commissioned by the chairman of Citizens for Eisenhower could render an opinion. Jack Drown cannot talk about that day in which my father seemed to age a lifetime without his voice cracking with emotion. He saw his friend sit limply in an armchair, his arms dangling over the sides. Halfheartedly, my father discussed a television broadcast in order to take his case to the people. Finally, Bill Rogers voiced the unspeakable: perhaps the only solution was for him to publicly renounce his vice-presidential candidacy, especially since Eisenhower had not come to his defense or even telephoned privately. Then others spoke up. They questioned how long the Republican ticket could take the beating from the fund story. But Murray Chotiner quieted them all when he broke in: "You can't quit, Dick. Too many people believe in you. You can't let them down. And you have a wife across the hall who believes in you."

My father was still talking to his staff when Governor Thomas Dewey called from New York to offer crucial advice. He reported that though most of the advisers with Eisenhower on his campaign train wanted Nixon off the ticket, Ike himself was still undecided. Dewey urged a Nixon TV broadcast: "I don't think Eisenhower *should* make this decision. Make the American people wire their verdict to you."

At 10:00 P.M. that night, Eisenhower finally called. He endorsed Dewey's suggestion but cautioned, "We'll have to wait three or four days after the television show to see what the effect of the program is." My father knew now he would be staking everything on the television speech. He remembers that as the conversation trailed off, Eisenhower's last words were "Keep your chin up."

In the bedroom, a few feet away, my mother was waiting for news, any news, aware now that she and her husband were in the political battle of their lives, with the 1952 national election in the balance. She was lying down because of a painful stiff neck when her husband told her about the phone call. Then, revealing the pressure, he asked, did he owe it to Eisenhower to offer publicly to resign? Without a moment's hesitation, she answered: "We both know what you have to do, Dick. You have to fight it all the way to the end, no matter what happens." My father told me years later that those words were what he "desperately" needed to hear. "From that time on I never had any doubt but that I would fight the thing through to the finish, win or lose."

The next morning, they flew from Portland to Los Angeles. Mother watched as my father jotted down speech notes on the backs of some postcards from the seat pocket directly in front of him. When he told her he was going to lay bare their private financial situation, she burst out: "Why do we have to tell people how little we have and how much we owe? Aren't we entitled to have at least some privacy?" But she argued fruitlessly because the issue had passed beyond the technical legality of the fund to whether my parents had been enriched by public service. Only public disclosure of all their finances would quiet the storm now.

They arrived in Los Angeles at 2:45 P.M. Fewer than twenty-eight hours remained before the Tuesday evening broadcast. Both Bill and Tom Ryan were at the airport in a silent, unquestioning show of support. My father sequestered himself in the Ambassador Hotel to write the speech that would determine his political future, and Mother went home with Helene Drown to the white-picket-fence horse country of Rolling Hills, high in the hills above Los Angeles. She was in excruciating pain from her stiff neck. Helene put her to bed in the Drown bedroom, and she remained there until it was time to drive to Los Angeles for the broadcast.

That Monday night before the broadcast, our neighbor Margaret Fuller had come across the street to be with my grandmother, Tricia, and me. She was amazed by Hannah Nixon's calmness and serenity, the product of constant prayer and an unshakable faith in her son. Hannah told Margaret Fuller, "I know Richard would never do anything like what his accusers charge." Earlier she had sent her son and daughter-in-law a telegram: "Girls are okay. This is to tell you we are thinking of you and know everything will be fine. Love always, Mother."

In my grandmother's family, the phrase "we are thinking of you" means "we are praying for you." The telegram had arrived while my parents were still in Portland, and Pat Hillings took it to my father, hoping it would cheer him.

By now, both my parents, Mother in the isolated beauty of Rolling Hills, my father in his hotel room at the Ambassador, felt very much alone. They had no idea that already thousands of telegrams and letters of support were arriving at his Senate office and at our Tilden Street home.

At the Ambassador Hotel, my father worked feverishly throughout the evening. There was so much information to gather for the speech, including a detailed account of his personal financial history, much of which had to be dictated over the phone from the senatorial office in Washington, that Rose Woods and her assistant, Marje Acker, after an hour or so of sleep, worked steadily through the night and next day until right before the speech Tuesday evening. In fact, they were so pressed for time that they were still in their nightgowns and robes when the broadcast began.

The results of the Price Waterhouse audit of the fund were available shortly before the broadcast, as well as an opinion of the fund's legality by a respected Los Angeles law firm, Gibson, Dunn, and Crutcher. Both groups confirmed there was nothing illegal or unethical about the fund. Ironically, only the day before, my father had heard the news report that the Democratic nominee, Adlai Stevenson, had a fund also. But Stevenson was refusing to meet with reporters. All he would say was that his fund existed for the purpose of supplementing the income of his appointees to state jobs.

For one week, Stevenson stalled off reporters and finally, instead of answering questions at a news conference, released incomplete information about his fund, claiming it totaled $21,644.96, most of it money left over from his 1948 race. The story quickly died, and, as Johnson Kanady of the Chicago *Tribune* later wrote, "No newspaper was ever able to get details of the 1950 and 1951 Stevenson funds, and so far as I know no newspaperman with Stevenson, except me, tried very hard." Not until twenty-five years later, with the publication of Stevenson's official biography by John Bartlow Martin, did the public learn that the governor's explanation of his fund failed to include additional sums totaling almost sixty-five thousand dollars, and that some of the money was used for other than political purposes, including a band to play at a dance for his sons and gifts to newsmen.

But in September of 1952, it was the Nixon fund that was big news. Only an hour before my father was scheduled to begin his nationwide address, he was shaken by a phone call from Tom Dewey. Dewey reported that Eisenhower's top advisers had just met and recommended my father announce his resignation from the ticket at the end of the broadcast. My father was dumbfounded—and then angry. He knew that though the suggestion had not been directly endorsed by Eisenhower, he suspected it was the general's thinking as well. He told Dewey he did not know what he would say at the end of the speech, adding defiantly, "Tell them [Eisenhower's advisers] I know something about politics too."

On the drive to the El Capitan Theater, an NBC studio, my father sat in the front seat of the car; Mother, who had arrived at the hotel a half hour earlier, sat in the back. Purposely she did not talk in the car. She knew instinctively, even though she was unaware of the phone call, that my father was laboring to maintain his composure during the last-minute review of his notes.

NBC had converted the stage of its 750-seat theater into a simple, makeshift "living room" for the broadcast: a desk, a chair for Mother, and a bookcase against the wall. After a brief lighting and sound check, the Nixons were escorted to a small room just off the stage. When they were given the three-minute time warning, as my father described in his *Memoirs*, "I was suddenly overwhelmed by despair. My voice almost broke as I said, 'I just don't think I can go through with this one.' 'Of course you can,' Pat said matter-of-factly. She took my hand and we walked back onto the stage together."

Except for the technical crew, they were alone now. Before them were hundreds of empty seats. Out of sight in the control booth, Bill Rogers, Pat Hillings, and Murray Chotiner watched on a monitor, and across the country, millions of people stopped what they were doing to listen to the thirty-nine-year-old candidate for the Vice Presidency.

Mother listened more intently than anyone else, steeling herself, not knowing what was coming next. She was wearing the toast-colored dress knit for her by the Whittier women during the Senate campaign. A soft leopard-print scarf was at her throat and her hair was tightly curled—ready for a week of travel. Some of those who watched the broadcast spoke of Pat Nixon's frozen expression, her face a mask. But others saw more. The Long Beach *Independent Press Telegram* editorialized the next day:

> Mrs. Nixon said not a word. She was shown only briefly on four or five occasions during the broadcast. One could hardly detect a movement in her face, as she sat on a divan near the Senator's table, her eyes on him.
>
> But the character in her face, the picture of a loyal wife backing up her husband in the greatest test of his life, the feeling of emotion held in restraint which the views of Mrs. Nixon conveyed, made her a vital factor in the success of the appeal.

She was, in fact, unaware of any role she might be playing. She did not even know when the camera was trained on her. She was conscious only of her husband's words. Without once looking at his notes, he laid bare the facts of the charges, and then attacked the hypocrisy of his Democratic accusers who failed to demand that Adlai Stevenson disclose the details of his fund. She heard him tell the public that Pat Nixon, unlike many other congressional wives, was not on the government payroll; and she listened as he praised Dwight David Eisenhower. But most of all she heard the words as he listed, point by excruciating point, everything they owned and owed, from their 1950 Oldsmobile to four thousand dollars in life insurance. "Pat and I have the satisfaction that every dime we have is ours..." he declared, adding a dig at the Truman Administration's scandal over a nine-thousand-dollar mink coat given to a White House secretary, "Pat doesn't have a mink coat. But she does have a respectable Republican cloth coat."

In the speech he did mention one gift the family had accepted, a black-and-white cocker spaniel Tricia had named Checkers, sent to us from a Texan who heard my mother say during a convention radio interview that she wanted to get a dog for her daughters when she returned home. In mentioning our new pet, my father handed the media a name for his talk—the Checkers Speech, they would dub it.

The conclusion of his broadcast was high drama. Richard Nixon appealed to his audience to "wire or write the Republican National Committee whether you think I should stay on or whether I should get off. And whatever their decision is, I will abide by it. ... And remember, folks, Eisenhower's a great man ... and a vote for Eisenhower is a vote for what is good for America."

That was his last full sentence. Time ran out just when he intended to tell the people the committee's address. It was all over. The TV cameras were dead. He could only mutter, "I'm sorry... I should have timed it better." In his dressing room he said, "Pat, I was a failure." Emphatically, she answered, "Dick, I thought it was great."

An estimated sixty million people watched the broadcast. Even before it was over, Pat Hillings ran to the NBC switchboard and found that the operators were inundated with calls. As my parents left the studio, clusters of people emptying the bars on Hollywood Boulevard cheered and shouted. At a red light an Irish setter came lumbering up to the car. My father looked down at the dog and said dryly, "Well, at least we got the dog vote."

Although a tumultuous mob of well-wishers greeted the Nixons in the lobby of the Ambassador Hotel, when my father reached his suite he threw his speech notes into the wastebasket. Helene Drown and Rose Woods quickly retrieved them. Both had been taking phone calls and realized already that the speech was an extraordinary success. But the full magnitude would not be known for several weeks. In all, somewhere between one and two million telegrams were received. An exact count was never made because messages were sent to five locations—the Ambassador Hotel, the Eisenhower train, the Republican National Committee, my parents' home, and the Nixon office. Three million other people wrote letters, many of them addressed to Mrs. Richard Nixon. They wrote because for thirty minutes they felt they had endured the same ordeal.

General and Mrs. Eisenhower and thirty or so key aides listened to the broadcast in Cleveland in a room above the hall where Eisenhower was scheduled to speak that night. Thirty minutes later he told his audience, "I happen to be one of those people who, when they get in a fight, would rather have a courageous and honest man by my side than a whole boxcar of pussyfooters. I have seen brave men in tough situations, I have never seen anyone come through in better fashion than Senator Nixon did tonight."

But my father had no idea Ike had reacted positively. He never saw the general's telegram, which began "YOUR PRESENTATION WAS MAGNIFICENT..." It got lost in the deluge of wires sent to the hotel that night. Instead, he heard only about the wire-service bulletin which reported that Eisenhower had declared in Cleveland at the end of his speech that he could not make a decision based on the broadcast alone, and that he wanted to meet with his vice-presidential candidate the next day in Wheeling, West Virginia. My father felt despair, then anger. He decided he would not go to Wheeling. Instead he would fly to his scheduled campaign stop in Missoula, Montana, and wait there for Eisenhower to announce that he had withdrawn from the ticket. He called Rose Woods to his room and dictated his resignation. Rose took the dictation, but she knew she would never send it. In the hallway, she showed the statement to Murray Chotiner, who tore it to shreds.

Just before taking off for Missoula, my father received a phone call from columnist Bert Andrews, a devoted friend since the days of the Alger Hiss case, who talked stern common sense: "Eisenhower . . . is the boss of this outfit. He will make this decision, and he will make the right decision. But he has the right to make it in his own way, and you must come to Wheeling to meet him and give him the opportunity to do just that." Realizing Andrews was right, my father gave orders for refueling after the rally in Missoula, so that they could proceed to Wheeling.

Jack Drown was waiting for the plane in Missoula where he had gone to do the advance work, certain that my father would resume his tour. Alone in a small hotel room he had heard the Checkers Speech on the radio. At the end, he was so overcome with emotion that he felt he had to get out for some air. As he walked down the main street of town, a young man wearing a Stetson hat and boots stopped him. Jack had a "Nixon Staff" button on his coat, and the cowboy asked, "You're with Nixon?" Jack nodded, not trusting himself to speak. "Here's a hundred dollars. That's the best speech I ever heard."

People were coming out of saloons where they had gathered to hear the talk on radio, and Jack heard their comments: "Is Nixon coming?" "Hell of a speech." "What time is the plane landing?" At 1:00 A.M., what he guessed to be three-quarters of the townspeople of Missoula were waiting at the airport in the bitter cold.

The reception in Missoula was only a prelude to Wheeling, West Virginia. The plane doors had just opened and my parents were still putting on their coats when Jack Drown felt someone jostle him from behind. Instinctively, he jabbed back with his elbow and then turned around to come face-to-face with General Dwight David Eisenhower. Jack was stunned only for a second. Then he recovered with a snappy "Yes, sir!" Eisenhower had bounded up the steps of the plane the minute they were in place. My mother remembers, "He was grinning all over" as he extended his hand and declared, "You're my boy."

My mother rode with Mamie to the football field for the Eisenhower-Nixon rally. It was a cold, starless night and at one point, among the rolling hills shrouded in fog, she and Mamie got separated from the motorcade. For several minutes they searched for a glimmer of light from the other cars. The two women were quiet during the ride. My mother was still numb from the strain of the ordeal. Mamie broke the silence to complain that the Nixon story had hurt the campaign and added plaintively, "I don't know why all this happened when we were getting along so well." The emotion Mother had felt all week burst forth and she told her, "But you just don't realize what *we've* been through." The tone of her voice, much more than her words, ended the conversation.

In the bitter cold of the football stadium, Mamie and Pat huddled shoulder to shoulder, the future First Lady's warm white-fox fur draped protectively over both. Together they heard the general praise his running mate and then read a telegram from Hannah Nixon:

DEAR GENERAL:
    I AM TRUSTING THAT THE ABSOLUTE TRUTH MAY COME OUT CONCERNING THIS ATTACK ON RICHARD, AND WHEN IT DOES I AM SURE YOU WILL BE GUIDED RIGHT IN YOUR DECISION TO PLACE IMPLICIT FAITH IN HIS INTEGRITY AND HONESTY. BEST WISHES FROM ONE WHO HAS KNOWN RICHARD LONGER THAN ANYONE ELSE. HIS MOTHER.

The climax of the speech was a telegram from the chairman of the Republican National Committee stating that its members wanted Richard Nixon to stay on the ticket. A tremendous cheer went up from the crowd. When my father stood to acknowledge the ovation, he said emotionally, "I want you to know that this is probably the greatest moment of my life."

But the moment had been bought at a terrible price for both my parents. As my father admitted in his *Memoirs*, they were "scarred for life," yet they each reacted differently to the crisis. My father's response was to go on the attack, to fight back, to win. He came to think of the fund ordeal as a personal victory. As a teen-ager I remember him saying each year, "Did you know today is the anniversary of the fund speech?" In 1977, he invited Rose Woods, who was in San Clemente helping him research his *Memoirs*, to dinner to commemorate the twenty-fifth anniversary of the speech. But he did not mention to my mother the reason Rose came on that particular night, for she is the one person of whom my father never asks, "Do you remember?"

The public questioning of my father's integrity, and thus her own, is a nightmare to her still, a subject that she can barely bring herself to discuss. In the spring of 1978, I asked her about those weeks in September, twenty-six years before. We were sitting in her bedroom. Mother was at her desk, her chair facing me. But she turned away and toward the wall when I raised the subject of the fund. Now I could see only the back of her head as she spoke. "Do we have to talk about this? It kills me. . . ." She paused for several moments and then faced me. There was so much pain in her eyes that I could not bear to look at her. I started to riffle through my notes and heard her say, with a rare but unmistakable tone of defeat in her voice, "It makes me so exasperated, so tired—the unfairness. . . . Ours was probably the only honest expense fund."

My mother realized even in 1952 that, though vindicated in the eyes of millions of voters after the speech, the fund irreparably hurt their reputation. As Earl Mazo and Stephen Hess wrote succinctly in their 1968 biography of Richard Nixon, "Much of the 'I don't like Nixon, but don't know why' talk stems from the incident."

If the accusations about the fund had been isolated, perhaps my mother's disillusionment with politics might have been passing. But only hours after the Ike and Dick team was reunited in Wheeling, Bert Andrews would tell Jack Drown, "That broadcast [the fund speech] was one of the greatest speeches I've ever heard, but they'll never quit. They'll never quit." Even as Drown and Andrews talked, Eisenhower was meeting privately with Nixon on his train to ask about new rumors, including the story that Pat Nixon had paid ten thousand dollars in cash for interior decorating at the Spring Valley house. My father denied the rumors and warned the general that there probably would be more charges. His prediction was confirmed as Richard Wilson, who first began covering presidential campaigns in 1933, stated a few months later in an article for *Look* magazine entitled provocatively "Is Nixon Fit to Be President?": "No charge of wrong-doing has been sustained against Nixon, though he has been, and continues to be, subjected to a smear campaign without parallel." Among the false charges was that my father had accompanied Dana Smith, the trustee of the fund, to a Havana gambling casino; that the oil industry had bought Nixon off for fifty-two thousand dollars a year; and that the "Nixon family" owned real estate valued at more than one-quarter of a million dollars.

My mother hated living with the smears. She urged a libel suit against syndicated columnist Drew Pearson, who had charged strategically just five days before the election that a Mr. and Mrs. Richard Nixon had sworn falsely to a joint property value of less than ten thousand dollars in order to qualify for a veteran's exemption on their California taxes. The story received wide-spread coverage, but not until three weeks after the election did Pearson print the truth, namely that a different couple, who coincidentally had the same names, had filed for the exemption.

It was not Pearson's first lie, and my mother knew there would be more. She felt so strongly about the suit that she talked with Bill Rogers and urged him to take her side in persuading my father. Rogers, however, advised that the suit would involve many months of preparation, testimony, and publicity, and that they would probably lose in the end because it is almost impossible to prove malice as required under libel laws.

The issue of a lawsuit was closed, but not in my mother's mind. Pearson's reckless stories continued until his death, and then his heir apparent, Jack Anderson, who first came to public prominence when he was caught electronically eavesdropping on a Washington hotel room, took over the column. My mother has always regretted that a suit was not filed in 1953, for perhaps then Pat and Dick Nixon would not have had to endure as many false charges in the years to come.

For my parents, the '52 campaign did not start and end with the fund speech, though in later years it almost seemed as if it did. In reality, they had another six weeks of hard campaigning ahead of them.

From Wheeling, the Nixon party flew to Nashville, Tennessee, for a rally in the town square. *Time* reporter Jim Murray whistled low under his breath when he saw the square packed with people shoulder to shoulder. He turned to Jack Drown and exclaimed, "My God! I can't believe this. It looks like they think Nixon is running for President." Until Election Day the crowds continued to be enormous. In New York, at Eisenhower headquarters, as the campaign momentum built, Herbert Brownell heard more and more reports about Pat Nixon's crowd appeal. Repeatedly Republican officials told him, "Send Pat" and "She's the best one on the whole ticket." Years later Herb Brownell tried to analyze why Mother had such an impact on people. "She had a graciousness about her and yet she was spontaneous," he told me. "It's an unusual combination and hard to define. The crowds just loved her. She was *simpatico*."

Train travel resumed and, once again, the candidate and his staff and the traveling press corps were in their own insulated world. For Betty MacKinnon, whose husband, George, was the research director for the campaign, life was confined to a small stateroom that contained two berths, each holding three trunks full of research material. At night, so that they could get in bed, the MacKinnons hauled the trunks to the floor and stacked them one on top of another until they reached the ceiling. By day, Betty would get off the train at various stops. Those towns were

> the unreal world where people gathered—I would float among them and then go back to my own encapsulated world of books and telephones and papers. The press was isolated also. When I went into the press car, I found reporters who were so jaded that they'd knock out their stories without even getting off the train to hear the speeches. Without even seeming to look out the windows at the crowds they were estimating. It was so disillusioning to me. But I found it hard to remain in touch with the outside world and I guess they did too.

Strangely, the campaign, with its brief contacts with hundreds of thousands of people, brought my mother close to her parents for a few moments. In Ely, Nevada, an old prospector worked his way through a crowd and pressed a gold nugget into her hand. He told her that he had known Will Ryan and then he pointed to some shacks on the hillside. That hill, he said, was where she had been born.

In all, my father spoke at 143 whistle-stop appearances and visited 214 cities. Daily he hammered away at the Truman-Acheson policies that had "lost us China, much of Eastern Europe, and had invited the Communists to begin the Korean war." President Truman accused Eisenhower and the Republicans of having a program of "anti-Semitism, anti-Catholicism, and anti-foreignism."

The last two weeks of the campaign, my parents were so tired they were almost like zombis. By now it was a familiar, numbing fatigue, which they recognized from previous campaigns, and which made the end of the campaign hazardous because it became easy to misstep. They almost had a minor mishap in Boston when they encountered Massachusetts senatorial candidate John F. Kennedy seated in an open car in front of their hotel. Kennedy waved enthusiastically to his fellow 1947 House member. When my father waved back, Mother nudged him sharply and whispered, "Remember, he's running against Lodge for the Senate." Lodge and Kennedy were in a very close, hard-fought race, with every vote important. My mother could imagine how annoyed the Lodge campaign people would be if the newspapers carried a photograph of Nixon hailing Kennedy.

My father and Kennedy were more than casual acquaintances, however. Only two years before, Kennedy personally had delivered a thousand-dollar check signed by his father and made out to the Nixon Senate campaign. Even after the Republican convention, when Richard Nixon had become a national figure in the opposition party, Kennedy wrote him a congratulatory note stating he was "the ideal selection . . . I was always convinced that you would rise to the top—but I never thought this quickly. . . . Please give my best to your wife and all kinds of good luck to you."

On Election Day, Eisenhower-Nixon won a landslide victory, carrying thirty-nine states and 55.1 percent of the vote. In Washington, the day after the election, one of the secretaries from the Nixon Senate office came out to our house on Tilden Street to help answer the telephone and the door. She remembers: "Your grandfather was so proud I thought the buttons would burst on his shirt. He said really to no one but himself, 'I'm the father of the Vice President.' Your grandmother heard him and said quietly, 'I'm the mother of Richard Nixon.'"

CHAPTER 13

Mrs. Vice President:
The First Year

As Inauguration Day, January 20, approached, my mother's anticipation increased tenfold. Neither she nor my father knew what to expect of the Vice Presidency. Its duties, other than presiding over the Senate, were ill defined. John Adams, who first held the position, called the office "the most insignificant that ever the invention of man contrived or his imagination conceived." A century later when President Theodore Roosevelt had the crystal chandeliers removed from the East Room because he did not like the tinkling sounds, he sent one of them to his Vice President, reportedly to "keep him awake." Calvin Coolidge's Vice President, Charles G. Dawes, had declared that his office held but two duties: to listen to the senators give speeches and to check the papers daily for news of the President's health. The office had changed, but not much, in the intervening years.

My mother's role as wife of the Vice President was even more vague. No books had been written on the nation's Second Ladies, and few observers of the Washington scene that winter of 1953 gave much thought to the idea of the Vice President's wife making a significant contribution, let alone capturing the imagination of the public. In a preinaugural profile of Mrs. Richard Nixon and her new position, the Washington *Star* stated:

> The only thing that is clearly expected is to preside over the Senate Ladies Luncheon Club, a group of wives, daughters and other assorted relatives of

present and past members of the Senate who meet every Tuesday in the Senate office building to roll bandages and perform other chores for the American Red Cross.

Almost as an afterthought, the article mentioned one other duty: "The Vice President's wife also acts as a stand-in for the Chief Executive's wife from time to time." The *Star* profile concluded with the observation that "Mrs. Nixon is not widely known in Washington social circles . . . they do little entertaining and go out seldom. Washington society is eager to know this attractive couple better."

Assorted aunts, uncles, and cousins made the long trip from California to Washington for the inauguration. Tom Ryan remembers being surprised that the house on Tilden Street was so small and, at that point, chaotic. He noticed my father worked at a folding table in the upstairs hallway until Tricia and I went to bed, because until then it was simply too noisy and congested to use any room downstairs.

Secret Service agent Jack Sherwood, who arrived at our house at 7 A.M. the morning of the inauguration, noticed immediately that Mrs. Nixon was prepared. Remembering those first hours with my family, he wrote:

> I approached cautiously . . . children up, the press assembled, neighbors arriving. Mrs. Nixon offered coffee and juice and sweet rolls and I helped her set it out on the side porch. She was a very attractive strawberry blond, physically very active and attentive to others around her. She was full of hope and great expectancy. . . . Getting ready for this big day.

Jack Sherwood was a ten-year veteran of the Secret Service whose previous assignments were on the White House detail of Franklin Delano Roosevelt and Harry S Truman. He had called on Senator Nixon at the Capitol a week before the inauguration and explained that the protection law covered the President and members of his immediate family and "the Vice President of the United States at his request." Sherwood remembers that Senator Nixon "wasn't much interested" in protection but agreed to try it at his public events for a few months.

My parents had decided that Tricia and I, though only six and four years old, should witness our father taking the oath of office. We had to be seated in the Capitol stands an hour before the start of the ceremonies. Tom Ryan and Don Nixon took turns watching us and for the first half hour allowed us to run up and down the row of Nixon family seats. Near us were several members of my father's secretarial staff wearing white corsages that "the boss" sentimentally had sent them for the grand occasion. Texas Senator Lyndon Johnson had a seat directly behind us and told my parents later that he had to restrain me when the wives of the President-elect and Vice President-elect made their entrances, followed within minutes by their husbands. Fortunately, my exclamations of "There's Mommy," "There's my daddy" were unnoticed by most because we were seated far at the back of the platform. Once the ceremonies began, I fell asleep in my uncle Tom's arms, and though he says he awakened me to witness the oaths of office, I remember nothing about the day and did not hear Dwight Eisenhower's Inaugural Address or the brief, eloquent prayer he delivered beforehand.

The new President, his Vice President, and their immediate families had luncheon in the Law Library at the Capitol, while their more distant relatives and special guests ate box lunches of coleslaw and fried chicken on the buses that took them to the parade reviewing stands. Then the slow, stately procession by car down Pennsylvania Avenue began. Jack Sherwood, who sat in the front seat of my parents' limousine, remembers the massive crowds and the Nixons' reaction: "The look on their faces . . . you just couldn't duplicate it—the tremendous excitement and exaltation."

For my parents, the Washington whirlwind was just beginning. After the inaugural parade, which stretched out to an unexpected four and a half hours, they were driven home for the first time in the official black Cadillac of the Vice President of the United States. The use of a government car and driver was the most dramatic change in their life-style. Jack Sherwood, the only agent assigned full time to the Vice President that first year, was rarely seen on Tilden Street. He met my father at his office each morning and said good night to him there as well, unless there was a public evening event. Jack was introduced to Tricia and me as a "friend." We did not question his identity because my parents rarely discussed the Vice Presidency. There was only one tangible sign of the White House in our home, the new "alert" telephone in our parents' bedroom, but Tricia and I were unaware of its significance. That emergency phone rang only once during the entire eight years my father served as Vice President—and that call was a check to see if the phone was functioning!

Because my father did not always remember to carry a house key, Mother left the front door unlocked whenever he had to be out late. And, of course, the door was open during the day for Tricia and me. The mailman and the cleaner's routeman continued to step inside our house to leave deliveries. My parents had no fear of walking in the neighborhood late at night, as they often did with Checkers and our two cats. Tilden Street did become the object of some tourist interest, however, particularly on weekends. Since the house was set back only a few yards from the curb, one could see directly into the living room by driving slowly past number 4801.

Despite his elevation to the Vice Presidency, my father's new office suite, number 363, in the Old Senate Office Building, had exactly the same space as he had had when he was a senator: an anteroom, secretary's office, bathroom, and the Vice President's office. And his staff of eleven was equal to that given a senator from California. Today, senators have from 20 to 60 employees, the Vice President around 70, and his wife 8; and the vice-presidential Secret Service detail numbers around 150.

The Nixon staff learned to double up on duties, whether it was handling press inquiries, mail, congressional requests, or driving the Vice President home when his wife needed the official car for an important event. In one of her early letters to Helene soon after the inauguration, my mother wrote:

> By the way, about the nicest luxury is a chauffeur. I feel a little embarrassed at times to be slinking along in a big black car...but it is wonderful not to have the parking problem or the discomfort of getting wet by the constant rain here when trying to look "natty" for meetings.

But when there was a schedule conflict and my father could not spare the car, Mother drove herself and hoped for good luck with parking spots. Mrs. John Stennis, the wife of the senator who chaired the Armed Services Committee, told me years later, a hint of disbelief still in her voice, how Pat Nixon arrived at her house for a tea one afternoon carrying her shoes in a little bag. She had walked in boots for several blocks in the snow past a steady stream of limousines bearing military and diplomatic wives.

Mother also drove herself to one of the first luncheons at the White House. Mamie Eisenhower, as the wife of an army general, had been accustomed to staff cars for years. Consequently, she recalled that otherwise unmemorable luncheon: "One of my most vivid memories of your mother was at a Cabinet Wives Luncheon. We had eaten and were sitting around just chatting girl talk when finally Pat said, 'Mrs. Eisenhower, I hope you don't mind but I have to leave to pick up my children at school.'"

By asking permission to leave, my mother undoubtedly was conscious that she was departing from protocol, since Mamie had not yet signaled the party's end. In 1953, official Washington was rigidly protocol-conscious. During the first six months of the Vice Presidency, my parents dined out at least four nights a week because all seventy-six foreign missions in Washington were expected to entertain the new Vice President. The chairman of the Foreign Relations Committee had to attend all those receptions and dinners as well. He was an older man, in his seventies, and, after too many years in Washington, his main goal at a diplomatic party was to see how soon he could slip away. Since protocol prohibited him from leaving before the Vice President, almost nightly he prodded my mother in the ribs as soon as the after-dinner cigars had been passed, half whispering, half growling, "I wish you and Dick would go home so that my wife and I can go home, get up in the morning, and get to the office on time."

The much-consulted *Green Book* on Washington etiquette devoted fourteen pages of its 1953 edition to the ritual of the official call. As the "Second Lady,"

Pat Nixon received scores of courtesy calls from Administration as well as foreign wives. Tricia and I were unaware of the importance of some of the people who rang our doorbell, and my mother never restricted us or our friends from almost constant use of the front door.

That first busy year of the Vice Presidency, my mother found that after 8 P.M., when Tricia and I were in bed, was the only time of day she could catch up on work. Very frequently, when neighbor Margaret Fuller got up in the night, she would see the Nixons' bedroom illuminated at 2 or 3 A.M. More often than not, Mother was going through the two hundred or more letters that arrived at our house weekly.

In February, Mother had written Helene, "I'm starting a diary—do not be alarmed—just a harmless one! It will aid me in the book I shall write later— besides I'll send it to you for laughs in the meantime." But not until July, when the hot, buggy dog days of the Washington summer slowed the hectic pace, did my mother find the time to write in that diary. Her July entries, though brief, provide a vivid glimpse of her social and political life in 1953. On July 4, after an official visit to Independence Hall, she wrote:

> We rode in our campaign car to Philadelphia. As I stepped in and saw it unchanged even to the blue and white striped slip covers (which Dick reminded me had at least been dry-cleaned!) it brought back memories of the busy and difficult campaign days. I could almost hear the recording of "The Sunshine of Your Smile," which blared forth at every campaign stop, and I fully expected to see the candidates file in, the flags put in their stands, and the whistle stop proceed.

Almost every party she described that month was "business," i.e., political, with one notable exception. On July 8, she wrote:

> 7:15
>
> We went to Lorraine Shevlin's [later married to Senator John Sherman Cooper] interesting Georgetown home for a buffet on the terrace. Later went to National Theatre to see *Guys and Dolls*. A humorous and gay show. It was one of the few fun evenings of the year. Met Senator Kennedy's fiancée, a darling girl.

By the time summer ended my mother was no longer writing in her diary. The pace had quickened as she prepared for a ten-week, 45,000-mile trip to Asia and the Far East.

My parents and the Drowns had talked for years of a vacation in Europe, and in April my mother had written to Helene after seeing Jack in New York.

> Jack reported that you are interested in the European trip. We'll probably go in August or September so save your dimes until then. If we run short in Europe perhaps we could get a few bookings doing the hula.

But in June she had to explain to Helene:

> The President asked Dick what his plans were for the summer and when Dick said he hadn't any definite ones yet, he was told "I want you to go on a goodwill trip and take Pat with you." The following day the President announced at a Cabinet meeting that Dick was going to give up his vacation to go on a goodwill tour! He then mentioned the Far East as the sore spot—so I guess that's where we will go and it will be work—though interesting.

The Far East was a sore spot to the United States because Soviet pressure and the formidable presence of more than half a billion Communist Chinese neighbors were forcing many Asian countries to adopt the position of neutrality or, in some cases, become openly anti-West. Eisenhower wanted his Vice President to remind the Third World countries of the benefits of friendship with America, as well as get a firsthand look at Vietnam and Korea, two countries on the front lines of the anti-Communist struggles in Asia. For weeks my parents prepared for the trip by studying State Department briefings and reading newspaper and magazine articles about the nineteen countries on the itinerary.

For my mother, the trip would be the fulfillment of her fantasy dream of seeing the world: Angkor Wat, the Taj Mahal, emperors, kings, and queens. But it also would be a test of every ounce of strength and discipline she possessed as she endured extremes in temperature ranging from below freezing to more than a hundred degrees, experienced punishing time changes that turned night and day upside down, and for more than sixty nights, dressed in long gowns and elbow-length white gloves. None of the countries on the schedule had ever received an official visit from a President or a Vice President of the United States before. Their hosts did not know what to expect of the young Americans, and, in turn, my parents underwent an instant education in diplomacy. The group traveling with them was small: Phil Watts, who had been executive secretary of the Herter Committee and who was serving without pay as my father's chief of staff for the trip; my father's administrative assistant, Chris Herter, Jr.; a navy doctor; a military aide to handle protocol; and Rose Mary Woods, the only other woman on the goodwill mission.

On departure day, October 5, my mother started a journal in a small black loose-leaf notebook. Her first sentence read: "Today the excitement was high— the anticipation great but the thought of leaving Julie and Tricia dominated and saddened the day." She had never been separated from us for more than two weeks before.

> I read the girls stories and Tricia in turn read a complete book—her first book other than one at school. I kissed them goodnight knowing it would be the last time in over two months that I would see them. The hour was black with

sad thoughts because the love for them made any thoughts of the thrill of traveling seem as a mere nothing. But a job had to be done—so full force ahead.

At the start of the journey, everything was new and exciting. On a visit to Honolulu's Fort Shafter, Mother wrote in her journal, "I heard the firing of a cannon and was somewhat startled until I realized it was the first shot of a nineteen-gun salute [honors rendered a Vice President]!" Even the drastic time changes and the long flights were an adventure. When they flew eight hours from Honolulu to Canton Island and then 2,950 miles across the International Date Line to Wellington, New Zealand, Mother, very much the first-time traveler, noted: "What an interesting experience to gain twenty-one hours in one flight."

In New Zealand she had her first glimpse of the sometimes grand life-style of the British nobility. The staff at Government House included a butler, underbutler, two footmen, a lady-in-waiting, two aides-de-camp, plus cooks, chauffeurs, and maids. She wrote in her diary:

> Very amused at the daily list of engagements which were placed in our room enumerating the schedule for the Governor General and Lady Norrie [her hosts]—from the time "their Excellencies are to be called" and even including "barber arrives at Government House to cut his Excellency's hair."

Aware of the British strict adherence to protocol, she was mortified when misinformed about dress for a dinner: "I had inquired about white gloves and was told that they were worn at white-tie dinners only. But much to my horror all the women were wearing them except me."

At Government House elaborate plans were being made for the visit in two months of the recently crowned twenty-seven-year-old Queen Elizabeth II. The Nixons were shown the suite the queen would occupy, its furniture freshly upholstered in peach-colored satin and covered by sheets for protection. When Mother was told that the queen would be traveling with her own "dresser," she realized Elizabeth would be spared the agonizing experience she had just endured. By mistake, all four pieces of her luggage had been unloaded from the plane and sent ahead to Government House and everything had been unpacked: hats, gloves, and bags placed on shelves in the closet; tissue paper she had so meticulously folded into pleats and between each dress set aside; winter clothes for the cold of Iran, Korea, and Japan, which she had segregated into a separate suitcase, hung up indiscriminately with her cooler dresses.

Despite such minor setbacks, Pat Nixon adjusted well to the role of diplomat abroad. As the official party flew from Australia to Indonesia, INS News Service reporter William Theis, one of three members of the press on the trip, filed an initial, breezy report:

Perhaps the smartest assignment of President Eisenhower to date was his insistence that Pat Nixon accompany the Vice President on his current Far Eastern global tour. Blonde, attractive Mrs. Nixon is a hit overseas.

In Hawaii, New Zealand, and Australia, local newspapers have splashed the Nixon party. Photographers had a field day in each place shooting the photogenic Pat. A good trouper, she posed with Koala Bears, Kangaroos, a platypus—and, of course, hundreds of people. As a mother absent from her own two children, she particularly enjoyed visits to children's homes and hospitals.

Before their trip began my parents had decided that they would try to break through the cocoon of formal lunches and dinners that usually encase the foreign visitor. My mother in particular departed from the normal course of events by asking to visit schools and institutions rather than fill her time with the customary teas and shopping expeditions. Her activities were all the more remarkable because in many of the countries, especially the Moslem nations, wives rarely accompanied their husbands in public.

Some State Department officials were unenthusiastic about the Nixons' desire for such an unorthodox schedule. Jack Sherwood remembers:

> ... some resentment arose vs the Nixons in U.S. Missions abroad because of their "tactics." The very idea of stopping along the roads and streets and talking with and hugging and shaking hands with the poor. The very idea of Mrs. Nixon visiting schools, including "untouchables," lepers, etc. What could the Vice President have in mind by inviting to and holding meetings with persons, labor leaders, communists, etc., whom our Chiefs of Mission had never included and would not consider including?

The traditionalists' reservations were unfounded, as U.S. News & World Report pointed out.

> The folksy handshaking part of the tour is strictly Mr. Nixon's own idea—an idea not encouraged by Embassy people. Some diplomats told him Asians would laugh at such conduct, but it hasn't worked out that way. ... It's too early for the diplomats in Asia to measure the full impact of the Nixon trip. But one thing is certain already. Thousands of Asians—workers, store keepers, school children—will remember for a long time the sight of an American Vice President who was neither afraid nor reluctant to make the simple gesture of shaking hands with them.

At times, however, it proved impossible to meet the people. During a tour of a factory in Pakistan, whenever one of the workers tried to peer around an aisle for a closer look at the American Vice President, he was whacked on the head by guards who carried bamboo sticks. Secret Service agent Rex Scouten told me that in Iran when a little boy started to run toward the car to shake hands, a policeman picked him up by his shirt and threw him over the heads of the crowd.

The most important part of the journey in 1953, certainly in terms of the future, was the six days in Cambodia, Laos, and Vietnam. For the next twenty-five years, the world would hear the names of those countries often, but at that time few Americans could even find them on a map. One of my mother's most vivid memories of Indochina, as alien to her as to most Americans, was a little girl Tricia's age, whom she met in Cambodia the day she toured the ancient ruins of Angkor Wat. The child, introduced to her simply as Princess, had taken her hand and held it tightly. Together the woman in spike heels and the girl in black American Mary Janes climbed the steep steps of the temples. Princess did not let go of Mrs. Nixon's hand until my mother got in her car to return to the American Embassy. At the welcoming banquet that night, she learned that the child was King Sihanouk's daughter.

Until reaching Vietnam, Mother had scrupulously sent separate letters to Tricia and me. But now she wrote:

Dear Tricia and Julie:
    This is a letter for both of you because it is now late since we are just getting back from a meeting. However, I did want to write you a few lines before going to bed just to tell you we are thinking of you constantly and loving you every minute.

She was in a country at war, but to her young daughters she mentioned nothing about her harrowing visits to the hospitals to see the wounded or to the orphanages where pathetic, homeless children were cared for by French-trained Vietnamese nuns. Instead she wrote:

I saw lots of children today because I visited some homes where they lived. They send greetings to you both.
    Please write us a nice long letter and let us know what you are doing and how you are feeling. Do you ever brush Checkers? Give her a pat "hello" for me. Tomorrow we go to Hong Kong—see if you can find it on your map.

                                                    Lots of love to all of you,
                                                    Mommy and Daddy

Vietnam then was still not completely independent from France, and the troops fighting the Vietminh Communist guerrillas were French-trained and led by French officers. In Hanoi, a "beautiful city" with wide boulevards that reminded Mother of a small Paris, she was taken to a French Foreign Legion hospital. Throughout her visit, a succession of ambulances arrived with wounded and departed quickly to gather more. Many of the men, who had come from all parts of Europe to join the famed service because of dreams of gallantry, were hideously wounded. She also visited a Vietnamese hospital in the refugee camp of Sontay, an appalling contrast to the quarters afforded the French officers. Six hammocks were stacked one on top of another, row after row, with only a foot of space between the rows. The smell of disease and death was overpowering.

Both my parents left Hanoi depressed, convinced that the French, if not losing the war, did not know how to win it. They segregated themselves from the Vietnamese, whom they considered inferior. After six years of fighting side by side, there were no Vietnamese leaders who had risen to power in the French-sponsored system. The Vietnamese chief of state, Emperor Bao Dai, who spent much of his time on the shores of the Mediterranean, was also held in little esteem.

When they reached Korea, they saw the devastation caused by another war between a Communist north and a non-Communist south. It was the middle of winter and many people were homeless. My mother wrote to me from the American Embassy:

> The Korean children are still in need of clothes so when I get home we'll send them a bundle. The last clothes you and Tricia sent them were very appreciated. The schools here are not heated so the children wear slack suits to school and keep them on all of the time. The children had made Korean and American flags out of paper before we arrived. They were dismissed from school and gathered along the streets to wave their flags in greeting to us...

In Burma, my parents witnessed again the specter of Communism. The Burmese, like many newly independent Asians, wanted to be free of European colonialism and independent of the West. My parents' guide in Burma was a young man from the Foreign Office named U Thant, who eight years later was to serve as Secretary-General of the United Nations. He wore the native dress of his country throughout the visit and did not conceal his skepticism about America, frequently comparing American culture unfavorably with Burmese.

Although U Thant did not speak of unrest, pro-Communist insurgents were the force trying to move into the vacuum created by the departure of the Europeans. On November 26, Thanksgiving Day in the United States, my parents left Rangoon, the capital, at 8:30 A.M. to drive fifty miles into the jungle to see the famous reclining Buddha. The week before, Communist guerrillas had murdered some government officials on the same road. Consequently, Burmese security was tight. Secret Service agent Jack Sherwood noted in the abbreviated diary he kept sporadically during the trip: "Communist guerilla infested jungle... two open-top armored trucks. Soldiers every one hundred yards facing the woods and at some sections of the road." Sherwood fully expected an attack either along the road or at the luncheon in Pegu where the Communists had organized a demonstration. Yet he had only one agent with him, because the other two men on the detail had leapfrogged ahead to the next country to make advance arrangements.

The trip to Pegu was uneventful, but during the luncheon, my father was informed that the mood of the crowd was increasingly ugly and that the local police wanted him to ride to the Shwemawdaw Pagoda to see the Buddha rather than attempt walking amongst the demonstrators. Nonetheless, he told the police he would proceed on foot, ordering that no security flank him. With the words, "Come on, Pat, you walk with me," he steered Mother toward the sign carriers.

She remembers vividly how surprised and disarmed they were to see the American Vice President and his wife stroll up to them so casually. My father talked to the demonstrators, "tactfully on a humorous plane," as American ambassador William Sebald noted later in his diary. He also asked some pointed questions, including where the money came from for the signs and the sound truck. By the time my parents had toured the temple, abandoned signs on the ground were all that was left of the demonstration.

Upon her return to the United States, my mother admitted in an interview that the incident at the pagoda was "the only time I was a little frightened during the trip." But on her schedule that day, which included visits to two mass-education centers, a rehabilitation and health training center, and the Dayebo village, she had noted coolly in the margin next to the stop at Pegu, "Communists with public address system, signs. Dick shook hands with them and completely demoralized them."

The Nixons returned to Rangoon immediately after the demonstration in order to attend at the American Embassy a Thanksgiving Day dinner that consisted of Chinese food. Throughout the trip there were many unidentifiable ·dishes, as well as other foods that were unmistakably what they were, such as the unplucked baked snipe served at one banquet whose beady-eyed head rolled off when my mother touched it with her fork. More and more my parents and those in their official party looked forward to canned soup and saltines on the flights between countries and began to dream of the simple luxuries at home like a glass of cold milk.

Miraculously, my mother did not once need the military doctor who traveled with them. But others on the trip, including the physician himself, did not fare as well. The one time that my father became ill, the doctor was too sick to attend him, and he had to sit through a marathon thirty-course dinner, given by the Hong Kong Chamber of Commerce, barely able to keep down a bite of rice. Upon his return home, my father was diagnosed as having amoebic dysentery. He was also ten pounds lighter.

Sleeplessness was a greater concern to my parents than illness. It became such an obsession that, once home, for months they would continue to find it impossible to fall asleep easily. For ten weeks they had had to adjust to different beds every two or three nights, hoping each time their body clocks, often set to the day before, would not rebel. And all too frequently they had been sleepless because of the active insect population, the heat, and the humidity. Mother's hair often did not dry by morning when she shampooed it at bedtime. Only once, in Saigon, where the American ambassador gallantly gave them his room, did they have air conditioning.

But their only totally sleepless night on the trip was in Pakistan where they were assigned personal guards whose lives were at stake if they failed to protect the American Vice President and his wife. When Mother's guard insisted he sleep at the foot of her bed, repeating in broken English, "Oh, but my life, I must," she finally had to enlist the help of Jack Sherwood. He settled the discussion by pointing to the Vice President and saying, "No! Man says no!" So instead of occupying a post at the foot of the bed, the guard lay across the threshold of the door. And hour after hour until dawn, my parents were kept awake by his consumptive hacking.

My parents were at times overwhelmed and humbled by the efforts of their hosts to welcome them, and never more so than in the remote kingdom of Afghanistan. The Secret Service agent who flew to Kabul to do the advance arrived on the only scheduled flight of the week, an Indian Airways prop plane that landed on a dirt runway. Since transportation into the city was by bullock cart, he felt fortunate to be able to get a ride with the airline crew in their car.

Once in the capital, the Afghan officials questioned him closely on how to give the Vice President a proper welcome. As a result, when the Constellation touched down and my parents appeared in the doorway, a hastily organized band played a barely recognizable "Star-Spangled Banner" and soldiers rendered a hesitant nineteen-gun salute—bang, long pause, a burst of three explosive bangs, long pause, bang. And when the official cars started the journey into Kabul along sparsely populated streets, there was a police bicycle escort in lieu of motorcycles. My parents were upset later when they learned why the streets were so empty. The government had rounded up the homeless and the beggars and put them in makeshift barbed-wire camps, certainly a blow to potential friendship between America and Afghanistan. The Afghans had read that Americans liked heated rooms. Consequently, that placed a small, red-hot stove in the suite of honor. To insure security, they had nailed the windows shut, so that even when the temperature in the room reached what Mother guessed was more than a hundred degrees, they were unable to get any relief.

By the time my parents reached India, the seventh week of the trip, they had not had one free evening. At last there was an unscheduled night in New Delhi, with no need to dress in black tie and long gown. Their hosts, upon discovering that the Vice President and his wife were unoccupied, had tried hurriedly to arrange an informal dinner, but my parents for once ignored their pangs of conscience and politely declined. They ate K rations from the airplane and then packed the empty tin cans in their suitcases so they would not hurt their hosts' feelings.

It was not easy to deceive the servants who hovered over them at Government House and entered their room at all times of the day without knocking. My mother had started doing her own laundry early in the trip after one of her dresses was destroyed when it was beaten clean in the traditional Asian manner of washing clothes, but at Government House, her self-sufficiency caused her embarrassment. On the second morning of her stay, even before she was out of bed, the housekeeper arrived to inquire if all was satisfactory, and looked pointedly toward the bathroom where assorted clothes were drying. My mother, perhaps a trifle too quick and enthusiastic, spoke up, "Oh, I always do my own laundry—I enjoy it."

She had packed only dresses that would withstand more than two months of constant travel, and very few of them needed ironing. But in India, she decided to wear the one chiffon evening gown she had brought with her and, eager to reassure the housekeeper that she was pleased with the servants, gave the dress to a maid to press. Unfortunately, the young Indian did not realize that chiffon stretches easily. That night, as my mother hurriedly dressed for the state dinner, she discovered her hem had grown by several inches! There was not enough time to get another gown and accessories ready. Somehow she managed to twist the skirt around her body so that she could walk. In the receiving line, she stood motionless and elegant, a swirl of chiffon at her feet. Mother laughed when she told that a new style, "the statue," was born that night.

It was in India that Jack Sherwood saw my mother get upset for the only time on the long trip. The danger of a Communist-controlled road in Burma had not unnerved her, nor deprivation of rest or food. But now in tears, she explained to Jack that the American officials who were in charge of preparing her New Delhi schedule had frustrated her at every turn by arranging formal teas and events with Indian officials instead of trips to schools, outlying villages, and especially the visits with women's groups that she had requested. She took seriously her mission of highlighting the problems and achievements of women, especially in countries where they had been nonentities for centuries. When she returned to the United States she would tell reporters, "Everywhere I went it helped women."

The display of emotion in India was an aberration. My mother's sense of humor invariably sustained her and the others throughout the long trip. When I asked agent Rex Scouten, who was part of the traveling party from start to finish, for his most vivid memory of that journey, he answered,

Your mother. She could always think of something to laugh about no matter how much she had to do—taking care of herself, your father's packing, the awful schedule. She never seemed to eat anything, but she had so much energy. Every time I think of your mother, she's laughing—with her hands raised and spread out.

On December 14, the Nixons arrived back at National Airport in Washington. At the White House, President Eisenhower praised them publicly: "Dick, I've heard some pretty good reports on you." Then he turned to the "Second Lady" and smiled his widest grin. "But the reports on you, Pat, have been wonderful."

The President was not alone in his praise. Neil Stanford of the *Christian Science Monitor* wrote:

The success of this goodwill tour, it need hardly be added, should rightly be divided between the Vice President and his young, active, and gracious wife. While the Vice President officially represented the President on this ten-week tour and constantly was greeting and speaking to the leaders of the countries visited, his wife found time to visit more than two hundred schools, hospitals and other public institutions looking into social and educational conditions.

Gracefully, seemingly effortlessly, she had carried out her duties. My father told me years later, "There were many times when she was tired—even possibly sick. But she prided herself on always keeping her commitments. She had the characteristics of a great actress—always being at her best when on stage."

It would take months to wind down from the trip, let alone sort out all the impressions. Overriding all, the trip would ignite a lifelong interest in and concern for the fate of the peoples of the Far East.

In June of 1954, more than six months after her visit to Indonesia, she wrote Helene Drown:

I am wondering if you could do me a favor?! —buy a cowboy outfit for the son of the President of Indonesia. He is a great Roy Rogers fan and sees the movies at the Palace. I promised to send him a cowboy outfit. The only ones here are to be found in the toy department and are of such poor quality I didn't feel I could send one. It is hot in Indonesia so the texture should not be too heavy. Expense is no item so perhaps you could find a nice one at a Beverly Hills shop or some department store. If you send it airmail to me I'll reimburse you "by return post!" —and bless you too!

Two months later, Madame Sukarno thanked her for "the impressive Roy Rogers cowboy dress which Gunter immediately tried on." It had been the moments like meeting Gunter—the flash of understanding between a child and a mother far from her own children—that gave the trip particular significance for Pat Nixon. And, too, she really believed what she wrote in the outline of the remarks she gave to women's groups upon her return: "People can sense when another person is friendly and genuinely interested. A smile is the universal language."

Second Thoughts

As the second year of the Eisenhower Administration began, my mother gave an interview to *Collier's* magazine. The writer, Helen Erskine, pointed out that the Nixons were extremely energetic with a capacity for hard work. She then quoted my mother's analysis of how she and her husband were alike: orderly in their thinking, meticulously organized, slow to anger, and even-tempered. The most remarkable statement in the article was her assertion, "We've never quarreled. Dick and I are too much alike. We don't even differ in our opinions." That response, one of many she tossed off quickly, even glibly, during the course of the long and chatty interview, became part of the written record. She would be asked about the statement many times.

When I questioned my mother about this, she explained, "Reporters were always asking me what Dick and I argued about. I didn't want to air differences publicly, and so in self-defense, and to turn them off quickly, I gave that answer." Certainly her statement, if not the literal truth, was a reflection of what she valued most in marriage, namely harmony; but in her attempt to protect her private life, she exposed herself to the charge that she was not "real."

My mother did not enjoy interviews, nor did she enjoy reading about herself. Very early in the Vice Presidency, she was typecast as wifely, and for the next eight years, those who wrote about her viewed her primarily through that prism. She continued to give occasional interviews only because she believed they were part of her job, something to be gotten over with quickly and forgotten. But the duty she felt to meet with members of the press did not include exposing Tricia or me. We were photographed only on major occasions—an election, buying Easter Seals, or an occasional family portrait. In a memorandum dated February 1954, Rose Woods, after talking to my mother, noted on a letter from the National Symphony Drive requesting a photograph of Mother with Tricia and me: "P.N. says no pictures of children/too many."

Virginia Shugart Counts, who visited us in 1954 with her children, was surprised how unaware we were of our father's position. Her daughter Carol was at our house the afternoon I came home from school innocently and proudly singing a ditty I had just learned. Carol today remembers all the words of the ditty except the first: "*Something* tastes sour just like Eisenhower." My mother had gently explained that it was not a nice song. Our parents were "famous," but that had only one meaning, which Tricia expressed to a reporter in 1954: "If he's famous why can't he stay at home? Why is he gone all the time?"

I realize now my mother constantly felt torn between having to leave us and her desire to do the best job possible as wife of the Vice President. Perhaps some of the anxiety she felt in having to be separated from us would have been relieved if she had been able to find a motherly housekeeper. Instead, she was frequently in a position of firing and hiring help. One woman was too old and would not play with us; another was an alcoholic.

Unfortunately, many times Mother had to leave on a trip feeling unhappy about the arrangements at home. There were small worries—a cat had kittens in the furnace vent on the eve of one departure—and the larger problems of whether Tricia and I would adjust to a new housekeeper's rules, cooking, and routine—and whether the housekeeper would adjust to us.

Margaret and George Fuller, along with Louise and Roger Johnson, very often went out to National Airport or Andrews for my parents' departures and arrivals even if they knew they would not have a chance to speak personally to them. Sometimes the Fullers took Tricia and me. Margaret Fuller remembers particularly one farewell when I was protesting, "You can't go, you can't go." Margaret said, "I could see tears in your mother's eyes . . . I know it broke her heart."

It was the way she cared about her daughters that made Margaret Fuller tell me: "I admire Pat more than anyone I have ever known. She never left you girls in the lurch." My mother made arrangements for us when she had to be away. George Fuller took us to Brownie meetings; Bessie Newton or P. J. Everts, two secretaries from my father's office whom Tricia and I adored, filled in for other events; Louise Johnson made our Halloween costumes one year. If my mother could not be home at lunch, someone else always was there when Tricia and I arrived from Horace Mann Public School.

Whenever there was a state visitor, we knew Mother would not be home for lunch most of the week. Each official visit took three or four full days of my parents' time. They would meet the head of state at the airport, and then escort him or her in a motorcade to the White House where the Eisenhowers served tea. In the evening there would be a state dinner, and the next day sight-seeing, and then a luncheon or dinner hosted by the Vice President. The third night there was the return dinner at the visitor's embassy, and on the fourth day, the trip back to the airport.

Strict protocol governed all events, including the seating of guests. My mother was always on the President's left and the wife of the chief of state on his right. Mother thoroughly enjoyed sitting with President Eisenhower. He was a good conversationalist and kept the seating diagram of all his guests in front of his water glass, so he could point out the more interesting people to Mother, casually providing a chatty background on each.

There were many nondiplomatic parties to attend as well, including informal dinners my parents themselves gave in their effort to establish friendships with political figures, members of the press, and out-of-town guests. Since the dining room in our house on Tilden Street seated only eight, my parents entertained most often at hotels or private clubs. When foreign guests did visit us on Tilden Street, they frequently expressed surprise that the home of the Vice President was a compact two-story white-brick house on a street of almost identical houses, each separated from the next by about fifty feet.

Since Washington social life was so busy, my mother looked forward to summer when the majority of the diplomatic corps and many political figures as well escaped the heat of Washington and entertaining came to a standstill. In July of 1954, Tricia left for Vermont and her first camp experience. Mother realized I felt left behind and made a special effort to be home for lunch each day. By the end of the summer, we had established a ritual: sandwiches in the clammy coolness of the basement, its walls wet with condensed humidity, and then "The Cisco Kid," "The Howdy Doody Show," or another television favorite.

In August my parents rented a house in Ogunquit, Maine, for fourteen days with the idea that my father would commute for long weekends. On August 13, a Friday, Mother wrote Helene Drown:

> As you know from the news, Dick has not joined us yet so we are again enjoying (?) a manless vacation . . .
> The Lundquists [friends from Washington] were here a few days so at least I saw a play at the summer theater while they were here. Otherwise, I've stayed "close to home." There seems to be no happy medium: If I accept one invitation life would be on the Washington scale, consequently, I'm a hermit reading my books faithfully. Actually, I have enjoyed it, but right this minute feel like a little heel-kicking. "Wish you were near"—a constant cry—anyway our love,
>
> Pat

My mother's note to Helene illustrates the dilemma the Nixons faced as vacationing celebrities. That is why increasingly we went to Key Biscayne, Florida, where my parents could have a social life without society obligations. Its slow pace was a welcome change from Washington. The palm-tree-lined downtown consisted of one hotel, one service station, one semicircle of shops. Most of all, Key Biscayne was a magnet for us because it was the home of Charles G. "Bebe" Rebozo.

My father had met Bebe in 1951 through his Senate colleague George Smathers. Bebe quickly became an unofficial member of our family. Jack Sherwood, who observed the friendship for eight years during the Vice Presidency, told me,

> He was kind and gentle with you and Tricia. You adored him, and with your parents, he was someone with whom they both felt relaxed. He had a special sense of knowing when to be present and when not. He could be detached when he felt it was necessary to be that way. And he knew when to come in and lift spirits. Most of all he loved to laugh. He was a good raconteur—I just liked him at first sight.

The son of Cuban immigrants and the youngest of eleven children, Bebe was a self-made, successful businessman. His house on the calm waters of Biscayne Bay was a typical bachelor's quarters with lots of big easy chairs, and rugs that could stand constant running back and forth from the beach by two little girls. Often when my parents went out for dinner and dancing with Bebe and one of his dates, Tricia and I were included. Those nights on the dance floor, whirling around with Bebe and my father, were the highlights of our stay. Other nights, however, Jack Sherwood would volunteer to baby-sit for us, simply because "I wanted your parents to be able to go out and relax." And so he convinced them that he felt like spending his evenings with Tricia and me. We did have fun playing our games of "wolf," with Jack slowly climbing the stairs of the villa, his usually soft, calm voice becoming more frenzied with each step, while Tricia and I retreated from room to room.

From the beginning, Bebe tried to provide my family with as much privacy as possible. On one visit an angry reporter for the Miami *Herald* berated my father for trying to "sneak into town . . . with all the planning and precision of a major war campaign . . . a team of Secret Service agents, airline employees, sheriff deputies, and port authority officials shielded the Vice President from curious taxpayers and the single 'unwashed' press." Because Bebe had refused to answer any questions about the vacation, the newsman portrayed him in the article as sloppily eating a hot dog and "wiping a smattering of mustard from his lips" as he talked. We have all laughed about that story ever since because, while he was indeed caught by the reporter having a late hot-dog lunch while waiting for the plane, Bebe doesn't eat mustard! In those busy vice-presidential years, Bebe was a constant—someone to depend on, someone who never broke confidences, someone who understood the pressures.

The pressures were particularly intense during the latter part of 1954 when my father was involved in two painful and frustrating events—the rampage of Senator Joe McCarthy and the 1954 congressional elections. Joe McCarthy's pursuit of Communists in the government had begun four years earlier, in February of 1950, when he announced he had a list of individuals employed by the State Department who were known to the secretary of state to be members of the Communist Party. McCarthy's campaign tempted other Republicans to support him because they saw great potential in gaining votes. But Eisenhower was wary of McCarthy, whom he considered a demagogue. He particularly was angered by the senator's attacks on General George Marshall and some of Eisenhower's other wartime associates. Yet he was reluctant to denounce publicly a member of his own party, fearing that he might split the Republicans down the middle. My father, because of his desire for party unity, decided he would act as the go-between.

My mother wanted to believe that Joe McCarthy had his facts straight and that those he charged as being Communists would soon be out of government. The experience of the Hiss case had convinced her that the issue of Communist infiltration was a real one. Moreover, during her 1953 world trip, she had been disturbed by the number of State Department officials, most of them long-term careerists, who seemed to be lukewarm advocates of our own government and apologists for local insurgencies and, occasionally, Communism. Some had gone so far as to tell her outright that the people of the country where they served would be better off under Communism. Even as growing numbers of Americans questioned McCarthy's sincerity, my mother resolved not to do so, but she soon recognized that with his reckless charges, sloppy research, and insatiable desire for headlines, he was his own worst enemy.

In 1954, when McCarthy decided to investigate the Army as a likely place for Communist infiltrators, reasoning that Julius Rosenberg, who with his wife Ethel had been convicted for stealing atomic secrets, had worked at an army base, his congressional investigation was televised. At its conclusion McCarthy was no nearer to exposing Communists in the military than he had been when the sessions began. Public opinion now shifted dramatically against him, with 51 percent disapproving.

My father had broken with McCarthy a few months before when the senator started lumping the Eisenhower Administration with Roosevelt and Truman in his "twenty-one years of treason" attacks. At Eisenhower's specific request, Vice President Nixon had delivered a half-hour televised speech in March in which he did not mention McCarthy by name but called for "an end to reckless talk and questionable methods" that divert "attention from the dangers of Communism." The speech, which my father impressively delivered without notes, covering all his points within the allotted twenty-eight minutes as if he had an automatic timer in his head, was widely regarded, and rightly so, as the Administration's position on McCarthy.

Because the McCarthy issue hung over the congressional elections, leaving the Republican Party vulnerable, it was with very little enthusiasm that my father embarked on a forty-eight-day, thirty-state barnstorming campaign. In fact, he was one of only a handful in the Administration on the road that fall trying to convince voters that their popular President needed a Republican Congress in order to accomplish his goals. In its November 15 edition, *Newsweek* would call him "the sparkplug of the entire Republican campaign . . . it was Nixon who kicked them [complacent Republicans] awake. He went from one group of party workers to another, saying, 'Let's face it, we can lose this election.'"

My mother traveled with him for only part of the campaign because she did not want to leave Tricia and me. In fact, a reporter who covered my parents on one of their joint campaign swings later told a writer for a women's feature magazine that the only time he saw my mother lose her composure on the busy trip was when he mentioned to her that he had spoken to his children by phone the night before. Involuntarily, tears welled up in her eyes.

The campaign was hard fought. Stevenson had put the Administration on the defensive by repeatedly challenging Eisenhower to denounce McCarthy. In response, the Nixon strategy was to go on the offensive, to hammer home to voters that Republicans, unlike the Democrats, were not blind to the "Communist conspiracy." Aroused by the Vice President's plea to "vote for an Eisenhower Congress [because] we recognize the Communist menace and this Administration is determined to crush that menace," the Democrats made alleged Nixon "smears" an issue in the campaign.

Five days before the election, Eisenhower, who had made very few campaign appearances and was well aware that his Vice President was the Democrats' target, wrote a warm note of encouragement:

Whenever my burdens tend to feel unduly heavy, I admire all the more the tremendous job you have done since the opening of the present campaign. You have personally carried a back-breaking load of hard, tedious, day-by-day and state-by-state campaigning. And in doing so you have been undismayed by problems of time, distance, and physical effort.

He ended his letter with a gallant reference to my mother: "Please tell Pat, too, that she has aroused my admiration as an able campaigner; there is no question but that she is the most charming of the lot."

Praise from the boss was welcome, but more than once that year my parents were wondering where the Vice Presidency was leading. The McCarthy problem still festered. Stevenson had succeeded in making Nixon a campaign issue and in exploiting questions that persisted from the Hiss days and the fund. The travels and hard work had been interesting but now seemed to be nullified by the looming off-year election losses. Indeed, during the last week of the campaign, my father, as he wrote in his *Memoirs,* was "so tired that I could hardly remember what it felt like to be rested... By the time I made a nationally televised broadcast on election eve, I had decided not to run again in 1956 unless exceptional circumstances intervened to change my mind." The next morning, as he flew back to Washington to watch the returns at our house on Tilden Street, he took his election-eve broadcast notes out of his briefcase and handed them to Murray Chotiner, who was sitting next to him. "Here's my last campaign speech, Murray. You might like to keep it as a souvenir. It's the last one, because after this I am through with politics."

On November 2, the Republicans lost sixteen House seats and two Senate seats. Though this off-year loss was substantially less than usual for the party in power, Eisenhower was downcast as were many in his Administration. Their disappointment appeared to be a reflection on the effectiveness of the man who had worked hardest in the campaign, the Vice President.

Although *Life* magazine in November 1954 had credited my father with making the Vice Presidency, "heretofore the butt of ridicule, an important office..." and for establishing himself as "assistant president," the article apparently did not alter my mother's belief that the Vice Presidency was a dead end for them. She feared that as Tricia and I grew old enough to read the newspapers and listen to the news, inevitably we would be affected. She spoke too about the consuming nature of the job. It seemed as if their time was not their own.

A few weeks after the election my parents had a talk about their future. Mother worried that her husband would always be called upon to undertake the hard tasks; she knew inevitably that if things happened to turn out well, they had to expect the credit to go to the President; that if things did not turn out well, as with the '54 election, Nixon would get the blame. The nub of what she was saying was that although she still believed my father had much to give the country, she chafed at an existence in which they were not in control and in which their relationship with their boss, Dwight David Eisenhower, remained so delicate and tenuous.

As early as February of 1954, months before the Army-McCarthy hearings and the off-year elections, my father himself, with a premonition of a hard year ahead, had begun to rethink his future. On February 19, he had scribbled some notes on a sheet of a yellow legal pad and put the paper in his suit pocket, forgotten. When my mother was getting his clothes ready to send to the cleaner, she found the paper and kept it. "He has no idea I have it even today," she told me.

At the top of the page he had written "Reasons to get out," and then divided his reasons into two categories, "Personal" and "Political." Among the four personal reasons, he listed "Wife—(columns, personal, staff hurts)." His political reasons were:

1. Politician must be able not to take issues to heart—fight and forget—twist and turn—I live each one—and hard ones—
2. Don't like social life, the prestige.
3. Some convince selves [they are] indispensable—but not the case.
4. Therefore—no reason to stay in—unless—you
   a. Enjoy it—personal
   b. Need the job (economic, money)
   c. Job needs you—

Now, in November of 1954, the Nixons were wondering if their friend Alice Longworth had been right all along about the Vice Presidency. It might have been wiser to remain in the Senate where they would have retained a certain amount of independence instead of taking on all the frustrations and uncertainties of being the President's deputy. But in the months ahead, Pat and Dick Nixon would realize that there was no retreat from the Vice Presidency without abandoning politics altogether.

CHAPTER 15

"No One Is Going to
Push Us off the Ticket"

On February 6, 1955, two and a half months after their sober post-election conversation about the future, my parents were caught up in the whirlwind again as they embarked on their second goodwill trip, this time to Central America. The correspondent for *Time* magazine who traveled with them reported that the journey

> ... brought reams of enthusiastic newspaper stories, and snapshots of Dick and Pat Nixon getting keys to cities, eating bananas in banana Republics, shaking hands with grinning laborers, sipping coconut milk, greeting hospital patients and—finally—getting the big welcome home hug from their kids after landing in Washington last weekend. But between the scrapbook pages there was another story—the story of grueling, eighteen hour days, of hard cramming that would stagger a Phi Beta Kappa, of life out of suitcases, and schedules regulated right down to an item reading "rest—ten minutes."

The reception in Central America was uniformly warm, and as with the Far East trip, my mother had her own schedule in each of the countries they visited. Peter Lisagor of the Washington *Daily News* reported from Havana, "Nixon believes his wife's work is almost as important as his own on these goodwill missions." In describing Pat Nixon's visits to public housing projects, orphanages, and anywhere else she could "earn friends for the U.S.," Lisagor stated that the only thing she had declined so far was an offer at a Cuban hospital to witness an autopsy. In Panama, she was the first foreign dignitary ever to visit a leper colony.

With the exception of the hectic trip to Central America, 1955 was a relatively peaceful year until Saturday, September 24. President Eisenhower was on vacation in Denver and Congress was in recess. For a change, my father was spending the weekend at home with no speeches scheduled. The only event on the calendar was the marriage of Drusilla Nelson, a secretary in his office, to the son of Senator Henry Dworshak of Idaho.

At five-thirty Saturday afternoon, shortly after their return from the wedding reception, Mother was upstairs changing her dress when my father heard the phone ring. It was Jim Hagerty, the White House press secretary. Without preamble, he said, "I have some bad news. The President has had a coronary." My father was stunned. He wrote later in *Six Crises* that he sat alone in the living room for "fully ten minutes." Finally, he called Bill Rogers, who was acting attorney general while Herbert Brownell was in Spain, and asked him to come over.

Hagerty had been able to give him only the barest details. The President had been stricken at 2:30 A.M. while in his mother-in-law's home and had been taken to Fitzsimmons Army Hospital; the doctors were sure it was a heart attack. My father decided that the wisest course of action was to avoid any public statements until he knew how serious the illness was and to what degree the President was incapacitated. No public comments meant that he needed to avoid the press, some of whose members already had started to gather in front of our house. It would be best if he were not home. So when Bill Rogers arrived, he called his wife, Adele, almost immediately and asked her to drive to Tilden Street and park in a side street behind the house. As soon as Adele Rogers pulled up, my father and Bill dashed out the kitchen door, crossed our neighbors' yard, and got into Adele's car.

My father spent a sleepless night at the Rogerses' awaiting any word of the President's condition and trying to ignore the sound from the bedroom above him of fifteen-year-old Tony Rogers's all-night ham-radio communications. When he returned home the next morning, he took the family to services at the Westmoreland Congregational Church, about a mile from 4801 Tilden Street. Accompanying us was a large contingent of the press corps. At the church, my father was joined by Jack Sherwood and the Secret Service reinforcements who would stand watch for weeks.

For several days, as the President's condition remained guarded, about a dozen members of the press kept their vigil in our basement playroom, at my parents' invitation, so that they could avoid the late-September chill. During those long weeks, Richard and Pat Nixon were on guard against any appearance of assuming President or First Lady roles. When the Vice President presided at Cabinet and National Security Council meetings, he sat always at his own place, not the President's. He met with Cabinet members and others in his office, not the President's, and was ever careful to "act more as a moderator than director," as he wrote in his *Memoirs*. My parents also took over the entertaining of foreign dignitaries, and their days lengthened to an average fourteen to sixteen hours. Slowly Eisenhower improved, and finally, in early November, returned to Washington.

But the increase in social activity was to become permanent. By late October, my mother was taking the intensified schedule in stride. A clipping from the Whittier *Daily News* noted that Washington correspondents "are marveling at the way Pat Nixon, wife of the Vice President, manages to stretch an already crammed schedule to take on extra duties and yet stay unruffled and serene." One reporter, Alicia Hearst of NEA, quoted an official at the State Department who told her, "We have called her at the last minute to help out, and she always does a wonderful job even though it has been inconvenient at times." Hannah Nixon sent her daughter-in-law the article and wrote across the top, "Pat, this is very good! We are so proud of you and love you—Mother and Dad."

At the end of the tense period of the President's illness, my parents had a respite. With Louise and Roger Johnson, they spent a weekend in New York going to the theater, dining out, and enjoying the city at Christmastime. Christmas dinner was with our neighbors George and Margaret Fuller and their college-age son, Bill, as it had been since 1951 when we had moved to Tilden Street. Mother prepared a simple menu of turkey and dressing, mashed potatoes, peas, and pumpkin pie; "all things," in Margaret Fuller's words, "you girls would like." After dinner Tricia and I performed an "original" ballet, and then my father played the piano, George Fuller the clarinet, and Bill, who was in a singing group at school, led the Christmas carols in a deep bass voice. It was an especially happy Christmas and would be a memory to cling to as 1956 began, the most difficult year for my parents since the campaign-fund incident of 1952.

My father's conduct during the President's illness and convalescence had increased his stature. James MacGregor Burns, in analyzing the Vice Presidency in October of 1955, wrote that after Dwight Eisenhower vowed in Chicago in 1952 that he did not want his Vice President to be a "Throttle-bottom," the mythical do-nothing Vice President, "he had thoroughly . . . built up the Vice Presidential office" by sending Nixon on goodwill trips, using him to present the Administration's case to the public, and by asking him to take over Cabinet meetings during his absence. Eisenhower also decided to have his Vice President preside over National Security Council meetings, which in previous Administrations had been the domain of the secretary of state. In all, my father would preside over nineteen Cabinet meetings and twenty-six meetings of the National Security Council, heavy responsibility for someone who had been in politics less than ten years. Moreover, his rising stature suggested to many that he would be around for a long time. Political writer Richard Rovere acknowledged in *The New Yorker*: "Almost as far as one can see down the corridors of time—1956, 1960, 1964, 1968, 1972, 1976, 1980 and even 1984—Nixon will be available."

Yet at the very time Rovere wrote those words, and certainly when my father least expected it, his political future was in doubt. In his *Memoirs*, my father tells the story of a private meeting with Eisenhower at the White House the day after Christmas, when the President suggested that perhaps it would be wise for him to accept a Cabinet position, which would give him "administrative experience." For a moment, my father reflected that the advice meant he should start considering the Presidency one day, since he had often heard Eisenhower say that administrative experience was crucial to being a good President. But when Eisenhower in the next breath referred to a poll showing Stevenson beating Nixon by a wide margin, my father concluded, as he wrote in his *Memoirs*, that

> Eisenhower's staff or his friends had evidently been sowing doubts in his mind, suggesting not only that I might lose if I ran on my own, but that I might be a drag on the ticket if I were his running mate again. It was hard not to feel that I was being set up, since more recent polls than the ones he was referring to showed me doing considerably better.

That meeting with the President hardly seemed real until Eisenhower restated his suggestion a few weeks later, reminding my father that no one since Martin Van Buren in 1836 had been elected President from the office of Vice President. My father decided to accept Eisenhower's advice as well meant, but then, on February 29, a "Dump Nixon" movement, as the press came to call it, became public knowledge. On that day Eisenhower ended months of speculation by declaring at a news conference that he would seek a second term. Republican leaders were elated. The President was enormously popular and sure to be re-elected despite Democrats' charges that ill health was hindering his performance. At the same press conference, Eisenhower expressed "unbounded" admiration for his Vice President, but stated that the decision on a second term for Nixon would have to wait until the delegates to the Republican National Convention convened and made their choice known. Hadn't the President used almost exactly the same words in Cleveland after the Checkers broadcast? My father was now on notice that his nomination was being questioned by some of Eisenhower's powerful backers and advisers, and that his staying on the ticket depended in part on how determined he was to stick it out as Eisenhower's running mate and his success in demonstrating his political strength in the months ahead.

But what were the President's wishes? Over the course of the next seven days the media wrote hundreds of articles speculating on just exactly what the President meant. By the end of the week, Eisenhower felt compelled to denounce those who would have "the effrontery to come in and urge me to dump somebody that I respect as I do Vice President Nixon." He then confirmed press reports that he had discussed a Cabinet post with Nixon and asked him to "chart out his own course, and tell me what he would like to do." When my father heard about the press conference, he remarked wryly to Republican National Chairman Len Hall, "Everyone in politics knows that a Vice President cannot chart his own course."

Mother says that during the long weeks of uncertainty that followed, my father was more depressed than she ever remembered. There was little to cheer him. He found some solace when Secretary of State John Foster Dulles, whom he regarded as a devoted friend, suggested that he should consider a Cabinet job seriously, perhaps secretary of defense, because it would be far better for his career than the Vice Presidency. But my father knew the public did not perceive a Cabinet position as a step up, and would interpret it instead as a flagrant demotion.

Having reassessed politics in 1954, my parents were doing so again, but not by choice this time. Inevitably, Dwight Eisenhower's request that his Vice President "chart out his own course" changed my mother's feeling toward the President somewhat. While there remained warmth between the two, and while she still greatly admired Eisenhower, she was hurt that her husband's efforts were not more appreciated at the White House.

There were increasing signs that her husband was an effective politician. Indeed, my mother wondered whether the President's staff and backers were underestimating the Nixon vote-getting appeal. On March 13, the day of the New Hampshire primary, her conviction that the Nixon name was independently popular within the Republican Party was unexpectedly and dramatically confirmed. When she and my father arrived at Alice Longworth's for dinner, they were greeted at the door by their hostess with news of radio reports of a big write-in vote for Nixon. The Vice President's name was not even on the ballot, but twenty-three thousand Republican voters decided to add it. The next morning, when Eisenhower was asked his reaction he responded warmly, "Apparently there are lots of people in New Hampshire that agree with what I have told you about Dick Nixon. . . . Anyone who attempts to drive a wedge of any kind between Dick Nixon and me has just as much chance as if he tried to drive it between my brother and me. . . ." But still Eisenhower stopped short of an outright formal endorsement. For six more weeks my parents were in a state of limbo.

Pat Nixon's idealistic, unshakable view of her husband as a man with unique talents and her refusal to be a quitter explain why she did not urge him during that period to bow out of the Vice Presidency and abandon politics. Although only a year earlier, as Bebe Rebozo remembers, on a drive from Fort Lauderdale to Key Biscayne after a boat trip, my mother had remarked that she hoped Dick would serve only one term, adding half in jest and half in earnest, "I'm not going to do it [campaign again]," being forced out of politics was another matter. Jack Drown once put it, "Any time you pressured Pat, her Irish came out... thank God." And so, as she told the Drowns when they were together at Easter, "No one is going to push us off the ticket."

Gradually the decision was being made for them as Republican leaders paused to consider the implications of breaking up a ticket that was running two points ahead of all Democrats in sight. The episode was all but resolved on April 25 when President Eisenhower confirmed at a press conference that his Vice President had not "reported back" his decision yet, which made it clear that Nixon would have to be the one to come to him. A day later my father seized his chance to halt the speculation and went to the White House to tell the President he would be honored to continue as Vice President. The sequel has been told many times. It was then that Eisenhower called James Hagerty into the Oval Office and said, "Dick has just told me he'll stay on the ticket. Why don't you take him out right now and let him tell the reporters himself? And you can tell them that I'm delighted by the news."

The unspoken aspect of the Dump Nixon episode was that it marked the onset of the succession battle for 1960. For this reason it was not surprising that Harold Stassen, the President's adviser on disarmament, labored in vain until the Republican Convention in San Francisco in late August to keep the Dump Nixon movement alive. On July 23, he launched a formal campaign to replace my father with Christian Herter, the governor of Massachusetts. Herter would be embarrassed by what he later termed the "comic opera," but Eisenhower's silence, because he had vowed in February he would not "dictate a choice" to the Republican Convention, lent the Herter for Vice President movement a certain credibility. Not until August 16 did Herter announce categorically that he would not allow his name to be placed in nomination. But still Stassen did not give up until the eleventh hour, even trying to see the President on August 22, the day the convention was to announce its nominee for Vice President. When Eisenhower refused to talk to Stassen until he agreed to second my father's nomination, the last shred of uncertainty about the next four years was finally removed.

The Republican Convention of 1956 in San Francisco should have been an exciting and triumphant time for my parents, with Harold Stassen and the preceding months of uncertainty finally behind them. Almost without my parents' noticing it, my father, the all but unanimous choice for Vice President, had become the consensus front runner for 1960. But Frank Nixon was seriously ill. Since breaking his arm in a tractor accident in 1950, Grandpa had been hit by a series of physical ailments, and he and Nana had returned to Whittier in 1954. He suffered so much agonizing pain from gout and arthritis that any movement was torture. My grandmother asked Mother to send Tricia and me to Whittier during the convention in the hopes that her husband's spirits would be lifted. We were with him on the morning of August 22 when he suffered a ruptured abdominal artery. It was the day his son was to receive the vice-presidential nomination for the second time.

The convention had begun on a high note for my mother. The Associated Press reported that when she took her seat in the mezzanine section, she received a "roaring ovation, the loudest thus far of the convention, one more indication that Nixon is on his way to easy renomination despite Harold E. Stassen's effort to stop him." That morning she had held a press conference and visited six state delegations. The *Washington Post* correspondent wrote, "Reporters who watch her... could not help reminding themselves that Patricia Nixon seems to be a woman without enemies." In fact, in reading all the accounts of the convention, it was a personal triumph. But the political pageantry came to an abrupt halt with news of Frank Nixon's illness.

My parents hurriedly arranged to fly to Whittier. Rose Woods was with them in the car on their way to the airport. She sat on a jump seat and took shorthand notes as my father dictated the acceptance speech he did not expect to be able to deliver in person. Tricia and I were waiting anxiously when they arrived. Mother remembers how confused and upset we were by our grandfather's illness and by the Dump Nixon talk that our grandmother had been unable to explain.

That evening my parents watched on television as my father was renominated by a vote of 1,323 to 1. Frank Nixon was ecstatic and seemed to regain some of his old fight. By morning, he had rallied enough to insist my parents return to the convention for the acceptance speech. They did go back to San Francisco where my father made his speech to the delegates, and then they flew back to Whittier. During the next few days my grandfather improved slightly and we were able to return to Washington. But he did not live to see his son re-elected; he died on September 4.

Fourteen days later, my parents were again on the campaign trail, this time with an Eisenhower victory and four more years in the Vice Presidency an almost certain bet. On September 18, Dwight Eisenhower, who planned very few campaign appearances himself, had driven to National Airport to see them off on the first of three concentrated trips. In the next sixteen days, their chartered plane would take them to thirty-two states. When I asked my mother how they did it, she replied with a wry smile, "We killed ourselves." Yet, hand in hand with the frenzy of traveling to two states in a day, there was the dead time of waiting: waiting for a plane to land, waiting in a hotel room to go to a speech, waiting for my father to finish a strategy meeting.

In the 1956 election, the Democrats once again made Nixon an issue. *Newsweek* magazine described the Democratic National Convention: "From the opening crack of the gavel in Chicago until the last lusty cheer echoed and died, Nixon was the target." Adlai Stevenson charged that the Eisenhower Administration was "ruthless" and a "gang of marketeers and rascals," and emphasized Eisenhower's precarious health, describing the Vice Presidency as "this nation's life insurance policy." Time and time again he asserted that an Eisenhower-Nixon victory would mean that the nation would "go for four years uninsured."

Stevenson's remarks received wide coverage, but my parents, and Mother in particular, offset the negative press with excellent notices of their own. A camaraderie developed between my parents and the reporters assigned to travel with them on their chartered plane. It was a closeness born of shared discomforts—long hours in the sky, little sleep, food grabbed on the run, and, in the words of correspondent George Dixon, "snow in the morning and subtropical heat by noon." Dixon wrote a tongue-in-cheek yet admiring column about my mother's ability to survive the rigors of the campaign.

ON TOUR WITH NIXON—Most of us on this flying filibuster are getting pretty rumpled because we don't stay on the ground long enough to press a duck, much less a suit. But Pat Nixon continues to look immaculate. The other morning, desperation gave one of the more crumbled of our covey the courage to ask her how she did it. The Vice-President's gracious lady smiled mysteriously and said she had a secret.

We were standing in a snow-storm in Medford, Ore., just then, and shivering local ladies were heaping Mrs. Nixon's arms with frostbitten roses. We recognized that the time was not propitious for trying to worm a secret out of a lady, so we waited until we were headed for Santa Rosa, Calif., and Pat came down the plane. She sat on the floor, as usual, and we clustered around. Again one of our ruffled grouses asked her how she managed to stay so dainty.

Mrs. Nixon replied she had brought five dresses, four suits, two pairs of shoes, and eight hats on this trip.

"In one bag?" gasped a newspaperwoman. "All the rest of us were told we're limited to one bag!"

"And a briefcase,"amended the second lady. "I don't have a briefcase so I felt I was entitled to substitute a hatbox."

"But one bag?" persisted the reporter, who feels qualified for Miss Weatherbeaten of 1956. "Please—please, Mrs. Nixon. Tell us your secret!"

After more coaxing, Pat finally told her secret. It was a secret all right—but one every wife knows.

"I do the packing for these trips," she grinned, "and I pack at least two of my suits in Dick's bag when he isn't looking."

During the 1956 campaign, Tricia and I were now old enough to realize that our father's work was different from that of most of our friends. And we were becoming aware of the antagonism that exists between Republicans and Democrats at election time. I remember a night shortly after the Eisenhower-Nixon victory. I was sitting in the den with my father, glad to be close to him after he had been gone so long. While he relaxed listening to music, I looked at a book on the Presidency. Under the photograph of Lincoln, the caption read "The first Republican President." In distress I asked, "Daddy, was George Washington a Democrat?" I couldn't imagine that the Father of Our Country was a member of the party that opposed my father.

The three children of Stevenson's running mate, Senator Estes Kefauver, attended Horace Mann Public School with us. They also lived at the end of the same block and were included in our various neighborhood parties, the most memorable of which was a birthday for Checkers one year. They had brought their dog to the party, and while he enjoyed a slice of my mother's meat-loaf "cake" with the other pets, they ate angel food with us. But by 1956 we were aware that the Kefauver girls and their brother were Democrats. There had been lots of campaign talk at school, and a mock election had been held in each classroom. The morning after the election, Tricia and I begged Mother to make a special exception and let us skip school that day. She did, and later we felt slightly ashamed that we had stayed home while the Kefauver children bravely had gone to school.

Mother realized that Tricia's and my new awareness of my father's political prominence complicated our lives. We were going to need both reassurance and attention. Because she was so busy, she already felt at times as if she were shortchanging us. That may have been a reason why in December of 1956 when my father returned from his trip to Austria where he had met with hundreds of Hungarian refugees who had fled over the border after failing to overthrow their Soviet-dominated government, my mother said no to his suggestion that they adopt one of the parentless children. My parents had considered the adoption seriously enough, however, to raise the possibility of a new brother or sister with Tricia and me. We heard too about my father's 3 A.M. visit to the border where he saw some of the bleak terrain the Hungarians had had to cross in order to reach the freedom of Austria. For my mother it was not an easy decision to say no to the adoption when her heart said yes, but she knew that she could not give enough time to an uprooted child who did not speak English and who would face difficult adjustments if he became a member of one of America's most famous political families.

As my mother anticipated the second term, she knew she would be increasingly on call to substitute for the First Lady, who was not robust. Mamie told me in 1978, "Your mother was my helpmate. I never hesitated to ask her to substitute. She was always gracious and she never put on any airs." Then, from her perspective of a quarter century of friendship, Mamie added, "She's been the rock of Gibraltar. A good, thoroughly dependable person all her life."

Loie Gaunt, who had joined the staff in 1951, and who has worked for my father in one capacity or another for more than thirty years, remembers:

> The one thing I disliked about my work was the assignment of calling your mother and asking her if she could be somewhere in one or two hours. So often your father would be called unexpectedly to the White House or some other meeting and your mother would be tapped to substitute. I knew how difficult it was for her, and yet she was always so nice and she always tried to arrange to go.

Surely one of the greatest strains of the vice-presidential years was the daily need to be ready to go—hair looking nice, nails groomed, something suitable in the closet to slip on for a luncheon, tea, or a formal evening. At times my mother felt the urge to get off what had become a nonstop merry-go-round of parties. In February of 1956, she had written frankly to Helene, "I would like to do part-time work rather than all the useless gadding I am expected to do."

Since January 20, 1957, Inauguration Day, fell on a Sunday, and it was considered inappropriate to attend a parade and balls on the Sabbath, the oaths of office were administered in a private three-minute ceremony in the East Room. Only the Eisenhower family, including one-month-old granddaughter Mary Jean, my mother and grandmother, Tricia and me, the Cabinet, and a handful of White House officials witnessed the President and Vice President officially begin their second terms of office. No members of the press were present and only one navy photographer. Bob Hartmann of the Los Angeles *Times* reported: "The scene, as reconstructed by Hagerty, was typical of the two men, both humbly born, both with strong family loyalties, both essentially lovers of privacy despite their demonstrated political appeal."

The next day, my mother rose at dawn. She dressed Tricia and me, helped her mother-in-law get ready, dressed herself, prepared breakfast, and made the house presentable before the 10 A.M. arrival of the reporters who wanted a preinaugural interview with the Vice President. Breakfast was simple and quick—orange juice and shredded wheat for the family, coffee and a piece of toast for herself. The only snag during the morning was that for ten minutes my aqua-blue velveteen hat was lost, and Mother had to search for it through the press conference being held in our dining room so we would be able to depart for the Capitol on time.

Twenty-five thousand people gathered on the Capitol plaza to witness the public ceremony. They applauded only once during the President's somber fourteen-minute speech. In the aftermath of the crises concerning Hungary and the Suez Canal, he dedicated his second four years of service to "our hope and our belief that we can help to heal this divided world." Some analysts wrote later that it was the most internationalist Inaugural Address ever given, a harbinger of the turbulent decade ahead.

The inaugural parade lasted three and a half hours, mercifully an hour less than in 1953. It was cold and windy, and throughout the parade, the wispy feathers of Mother's American-Beauty-rose-red hat danced in the wind. At one point in the afternoon, the President called David and Anne Eisenhower and Tricia and me to the front of the reviewing stand. I had a dramatic black eye and skinned nose because of a sledding accident the week before. When photographers began snapping pictures, the President said, "Turn this way, Julie, so they won't see your black eye." So I looked toward the President, David, and Anne. David, in turn, stared in open admiration at my black eye. Ten years later, when David and I became engaged, the picture was resurrected to show that he was interested in me even then. In truth, it was the black eye.

It was dark by the time we arrived home at six. My mother had arranged for the wife of John Wardlaw, my father's official driver, to come to the house to cook dinner so that she would have time to get Tricia and me and herself ready for the balls. But Mrs. Wardlaw never reached Tilden Street. She was trapped in a snarl of traffic from the three-quarters of a million people who had gathered to watch the parade.

A friend, Austine Hearst, wife of the publisher William Randolph Hearst, managed to get to our house with the dresses for Tricia and me that Mother had asked her to shop for in New York. We were excited about our first "ball gowns." For several weeks, we had opened Mother's closet door at least two or three times daily to look at her ice-blue Elizabeth Arden gown with its dazzling bodice of pearls and crystal. We had visions that our dresses would be similar. But when we opened the box from New York that night we were crushed. Inside were short, ordinary party dresses. I started to cry. We both refused to try them on.

Mother, exhausted and with dinner to cook, lost her patience and became angry for one of the few times I can remember. She had agreed to let us attend one of the four inaugural balls only because my father had urged her so persuasively. Now, in a severe tone of voice, she said that we could not go. Tricia and I ran to our father in tears. He tried to comfort us. Then we heard him say gently, "Pat, we have to let them go. It's a big moment."

Mother did not say anything as she left the room to go upstairs. In a few minutes she returned with some silk flowers that she pinned to our dresses. George Fuller, our beloved "Uncle Nibs," arrived at the house shortly thereafter to exclaim over the beauty of our short pink dresses. My father had telephoned an SOS to him. So Tricia and I have the memory of going with our parents to one of the balls, and waving from the Vice President's box to the ladies in their beautiful evening gowns before being whisked home with our grandmother in one of the big, black White House limousines.

The Road to the Presidency

As the second term began, my father's staff numbered eleven. They were a weary group, having just survived the backbreaking campaign and the influx of friends and constituents in town for the inauguration. As early as 1953 Jack Sherwood had made some notes about what it was like to be on the Vice President's staff.

> V.P. : analytical, coldly critical mind, quick to size up an opportunity and turn an event to his advantage:
>
> 1. Staff's devotion to V.P. Very long hours at work—resulting in sacrifice of rest and pursuit of normal pleasures and necessities.
> 2. His unorthodoxy of thinking and doing things keeps self and staff moving from crisis to crisis.

In 1957, the staff pressures were eased thanks to the intervention of the chairman of the Joint Chiefs of Staff, Admiral Radford, who had been aware for quite some time that my father was understaffed. He had sent his executive officer as an observer on an eighteen-day around-the-world vice-presidential trip in July of 1956. During one of the flights between countries, Radford's executive officer sat with Rose Woods and questioned her on how a military aide could be of assistance to the Vice President. Rose began talking and, within fifteen minutes, the aide had a list of data three pages long. But he did not really need the list. He had seen how Miss Woods often worked until one or two in the morning. He realized too that she and my father's administrative aide were helping with all manner of trip logistics, even directing baggage when necessary. What Rose Woods had stressed, however, was the need for someone to take custody of the National Security Council reports.

By March 1957, two military aides had joined the staff and were members of the first vice-presidential party to visit the continent of Africa. The eight-nation tour came at a historic time as Ghana celebrated its independence, the first country in black Africa to shed colonial rule.

One of the new aides, thirty-two-year-old Major James "Don" Hughes, fortified as were the others on the trip by several weeks of ingesting yellow-fever tablets, was amazed by what was required of both my parents in the next twenty-one days. Hughes met Mrs. Nixon for the first time when they boarded an Air Force DC-6 in Washington for the departure to Africa, but did not anticipate that she would be more of a factor in his new job than someone simply to be courteous to because she was the wife of the Vice President.

Several days into the trip he changed his mind after escorting her to a Liberian produce market on a wharf in Monrovia where she charmed hundreds in weather he described as "a hundred and forty degrees in the shade." That day she earned the respect as well of New York *Herald Tribune* reporter Earl Mazo. Suffering as Don Hughes was from the overpowering heat, Mazo was touched by my mother's sensitivity to her hosts. The Liberians proudly had provided her with a new Fleetwood Cadillac for her trip to the marketplace. The driver, however, was unfamiliar with the car. During the tour of the produce stands, he kept the air conditioning running. When it came time to depart, the car battery was dead. As the driver frantically turned the ignition key and heard an alien "click, click," my mother led the way out of the car with a breezy comment, "Oh, this always happens to President Eisenhower's car too," and then got into a beat-up Chevy for the trip back to town.

Mazo had also reported from Liberia that "several women political leaders" who acted as my mother's hostesses on her visits to schools, markets, and orphanages "wondered at first why she wouldn't talk politics." But, he continued, after an afternoon of "handshaking and baby kissing," the women leaders realized that she was much more effective than if she had ventured opinions on African or American politics. Mazo quoted them as saying, "'She's shrewd, also sweet.'"

Part of her diplomatic success was her conscientious effort to learn local customs and to conform to her hosts' plans, whether they included sampling warm goat's milk and honey or visiting a snake farm. But it was difficult sometimes to keep abreast of what was expected for each event. In Liberia, the schedule called for my father and the men in the party to be dressed in morning coats and striped pants upon arrival at the airport, and my mother wore her dressiest short lace evening gown. When they arrived at the guest quarters, they had to change immediately for a formal dinner. My father discovered to his dismay that white tie was required and that the Air Force steward, Sergeant Flukus, another new addition to his entourage for the trip, had left his trousers on board the plane. Don Hughes was summoned. In his most assured military voice, Hughes told his boss, "We'll handle it, sir." Then he turned crisply and left. In a few minutes, my father and mother heard Hughes's voice through the thin wall of the next room: "Somebody's got to go back to the plane. Flukus forgot the Old Man's pants." Resourceful Flukus somehow was able to get the United States Embassy's air attaché to commandeer a small plane for the fifty-mile hop back to the airport. Flukus arrived at the guest quarters with the pants—and ten minutes to spare.

The high point of the trip, the Ghanian independence celebration, was a mixture of British formality and joyous exultation. The new prime minister, Kwame Nkrumah, wept as he proclaimed at the stroke of midnight on March 6: "The battle is ended. Ghana, our beloved country, is free forever." Coretta and Martin Luther King, Jr., attended the independence celebration at the invitation of Nkrumah. By inviting King, the prime minister was giving worldwide recognition to the man who had protested segregation by leading the Montgomery, Alabama, bus boycott. Thus, five thousand miles away from their own country, America's Vice President and the civil rights pioneer met for the first time and made arrangements for another visit together once they returned home.

At the end of the grueling three weeks, Peter Lisagor filed a story from Tripoli, Libya, entitled "Pat's Stamina Shames Males." Lisagor related how even Vice President Nixon finally yielded for a few hours to a cold, but not Pat. "This frail-looking but remarkably durable woman has smilingly ignored the hazards of a brutal sun, rain, dust and itinerant bugs." He ended his report:

She says she loves to meet people and she gives every evidence of it. She has the rare knack of making people feel she has known them for a long time when she first meets them, usually by putting her arms around them casually in a friendly gesture.

The average woman on this routine would yield up to weariness by this time. But not Pat Nixon. She's as dedicated as her husband on the goodwill circuit. And from all the signs she is as indestructible.

When my parents returned from Africa, Tricia and I were there to greet them at the plane with two very important news items. First, Tricia's cat, Puff Ball, had given birth to three kittens in my doll buggy, a step up, since her last litter had been born in a trash can. Reporters covering the welcome overheard us ask our parents where we could find homes for the kittens and reported the inquiry the next morning in the newspapers. Within days, Mother received a letter from the Humane Society requesting that she "prevent further breeding of surplus animals in your home."

The other good news we gave our parents was that we had moved. Shortly before leaving for Africa, my mother and father had bought an older, larger house in the quiet, residential section of Wesley Heights, seven miles from Tilden Street. Three of Mother's friends decided that the last thing she needed upon her return from a strenuous foreign trip was to have to face a move. And so Louise Johnson, Margaret Fuller, and the wife of the director of the Republican Senatorial Campaign Committee, Mrs. Vic Johnston, oversaw the packing and unpacking.

When we walked into the lovely English Tudor house, music was playing on the stereo, and all the furniture was in place, exactly as Mother had diagramed it before she left for Africa. She found, in fact, that the only thing her friends had overlooked was to bring the pots and pans, so she made a quick trip back to the old house in order to be able to start dinner.

Forest Lane became my mother's favorite of all our homes. She had fallen in love with the thirty-year-old stone house the first time she saw it, even though it needed extensive remodeling and redecorating. When my parents took Alice Roosevelt Longworth to their new home just a few days after the purchase, the outspoken lady surveyed the dingy walls, the heavy furniture, and the dismal colors and declared, "Pat, if you can make this place livable, you'll accomplish a miracle."

She did make it beautifully livable and alive with warm beige carpets throughout the first floor and a restful, soft French blue for the walls. For the dining room she chose a Karastan rug in an oriental pattern. Mother called it her "cookie rug," because Tricia and I and our friends could snack all day without the patterned rug showing crumbs or dirt. The old kitchen became especially bright and cheerful with new cabinets of sunny fruitwood and walls papered with a fresh design of lemons and green vines. Our kitchen was the focal point for Tricia and me, our favorite place to talk to Mother when she was home. She usually fixed an after-school snack for us of cinnamon toast and cocoa, or biscuits and honey. As a very special treat, one which she seemed to enjoy as much as we did, sometimes she made fudge.

Mother spent much of her time in the master bedroom. Her desk was there in front of a window that overlooked the beautiful oaks, maples, and elms of Rock Creek Park, but placed facing the room, because Mother wanted as much natural light behind her as possible while she worked. I remember my parents' bedroom as being peaceful and restful. It was painted a cool celadon green and was simply, almost starkly, furnished, with two unframed Chinese wall scrolls over the beds.

Mother let Tricia and me decorate our own rooms. Tricia went through several evolutions on her pink walls: from a collection of baseball caps and autographed balls and bats to numerous horse pictures and even pink-and-black jockey silks, given to her by John Hay Whitney, which she mounted on one wall. My room was painted blue and had fluffy white curtains at the windows which Mother had made for me herself. Two parakeets, goldfish, and several dollhouses with miniature furniture were my prize possessions.

With the larger house, my mother began entertaining more at home, but it was still necessary to hold larger formal dinners in hotels or at the F Street Club. The Vice President's annual salary, which had been raised in 1955 from thirty thousand dollars to thirty-five thousand dollars, did not include an allowance for household help or housing. The entertainment allotment of ten thousand dollars a year had to be stringently budgeted to cover the costs of the expensive hotel ballrooms and elaborate menus. My parents' luncheon for Queen Elizabeth II in 1957, for example, consisted of Crenshaw melon, breast of guinea hen on Kentucky ham and wild rice, stuffed tomato with French peas, alligator pear, romaine and endive salad, and almond blanc-mange—all accompanied by appropriate wines. At times my parents simply exceeded their budget and dipped into their savings in order to entertain graciously.

Because they had to attend so many official functions, evenings at home were precious, especially to my father. Mother told me, "Daddy liked to come home and enjoy you and his house during a happy dinnertime. He didn't want any dissension. The minute he got home he'd turn on the stereo. Checkers would start barking. You girls would rush to him."

Because my father wanted the few hours he did have with his family to be harmonious, he left by default all the disciplining to Mother. His severest reprimand was "I wouldn't do that, honey." Mother's disciplining technique was "the look," as Tricia and I called her freezing, reproachful glance. She did not spank, raise her voice, or whine. If we failed to heed "the look," we had to endure the most dreaded treatment for major offenses: her silence. And because the silence was so impenetrable and such a contrast to the usually loving woman, we avoided provoking it.

To Mother as well went the task of explaining why she, and more often my father, had to be away during a holiday or miss a school or Girl Scout event. Consequently, when she was home, she tried to give us almost one hundred percent of her time. She took us on many outings—the zoo, museums, movies, ice skating. Mother gave us allowances, but we rarely needed to use the money since she was always there to take care of tickets or to buy things for us. Rose Woods once mentioned how surprised she was that Tricia, then thirteen, did not carry any money with her even for a phone call.

Mother was protective of us because she had seen how easily aroused we were by other children's comments about our father. Since politics were not often discussed at home, we had little comprehension of the political passions and disagreements that would make a schoolmate say, "I hate your father."

My parents wanted us to have a "normal" life. They did not dwell on meetings with the world figures, like Charles de Gaulle, Queen Elizabeth, or Nikita Khrushchev, who came to Washington. With a few exceptions—among them Israel's Ben-Gurion and German chancellor Konrad Adenauer who came to our home—Tricia and I in eight years did not meet heads of state.

Imposing yet grandfatherly Adenauer made the biggest impression on us. He was particularly interested in our yard, and upon his return to Germany would send Mother dozens of rosebushes. Although more than eighty years old, he had an eye for beauty. He asked my father what Mother's background was. When he learned that it was German and Irish, the chancellor had snapped his fingers. "His Sphinx-like face broke into a broad smile," my father recalls, "and he told me, 'I would have guessed it; the Irish-German combination makes the strongest and most beautiful women in the world.'"

When Tricia graduated from public Horace Mann in 1958, my parents debated whether or not she should be enrolled in private school. Politically it was important that the Nixon children be in public school so that no one could accuse the Vice President of not believing in Washington's integrated institutions. But in fact the Washington public school system was inadequate. At Horace Mann there was no gym supervision and only minimal art and music instruction. Only the year before, a photograph had appeared in the Washington *Star* of a group of children crowded into a school hallway. The caption told the story:

> Children of VIPs, including Vice President Richard M. Nixon's daughters, attend Horace Mann Elementary School, Norwalk and 44th Street North West. Some three hundred pupils jam a second floor hallway for assemblies because funds have never been provided for construction of an auditorium.

Mother was adamant about changing schools, so in the fall of 1958, Tricia and I were enrolled at Sidwell Friends, a coeducational private Quaker school, which not only was integrated but also highly respected academically. Horace Mann had not prepared us well for the competition of private school. When Mother witnessed our academic struggle that first year, she regretted even more that she had not insisted earlier on taking us out of Horace Mann. Though she helped us with our homework almost daily, Tricia, then in the seventh grade, and I, in the fifth, often had to stay up until ten or eleven to complete our work. Frequently Mother would arrive home at midnight or later from a formal dinner and find a note asking for help: "Mommy—Please make holes for this project. It is in the right order—I love you. Julie." On a Mother's Day card we sent her when she was on one of her trips, Tricia wrote: "I hope you are having a good time. Everybody is fine here." My message read: "Dear Mother, Come home soon and help me with my report on Norway."

In the spring of 1958, the pressures on Pat Nixon were building and almost became too much. She was making preparations to go on yet another goodwill trip, this time to South America. Tricia and I needed more of her time for help with our schoolwork. President Eisenhower had suffered a mild stroke in November and, increasingly, he and Mamie cut down their schedules, leaving more entertaining responsibilities to my parents. The Nixons had never been more in the public eye.

Then in March, Mother sprained her back lifting me up to see a bird's nest. The injury was painful, and for several days she lay in her darkened bedroom. Finally, my father called Helene Drown, who flew to Washington to stay with us as Mother entered the hospital for the first time since my birth almost ten years before. The physicians gave her sonar heat treatments for her back and eased her discomfort somewhat. But, uncharacteristically, she left the hospital feeling as weighed down as she had when she entered. Loretta Stuart remembers that Pat telephoned shortly after she got home, admitted that her back was "killing her," and asked Mrs. Stuart if there were some way for her to enter Woodward and Lothrop's beauty salon without having to use the busy front doors of the department store. She just did not feel she could face the usual handshaking and autographing from people who recognized her.

Even so, she did not let Tricia and me know just how much discomfort she felt, and this was typical. I asked Helene Drown once why Mother resisted admitting illness. Helene responded that Pat did not want her children to have to worry about her. It was this self-sacrifice and good-soldier attitude that prevented her from blowing off steam with her children, or even with her husband. She was ever conscious that he was under pressure far greater than hers. Had she talked candidly then, the answer to the pressures might have been to bow out of public life. But public service was the life they had built together the past eleven years. She could see that her husband was making tremendous contributions to his country, and, in addition, she was awakening to the fact that his nomination for President was inevitable.

When Helene Drown returned to California after spending a week with us, she typed my father a note, urging him to clear the air with Pat about looming political questions.

Have a talk about the future—what are the roads—

    I. Quit now and enter a law firm somewhere

   II. Refuse to run in 1960 and leave the country in a mess, because who else is there? Not fair to you or Pat when you have put so much in and others have worked for you because they believe in you both— but if you decide not to run you *must* resign now! So that someone else may be trained.

III. Go ahead and try for the nomination.

You may get it
You may not

IV. If you do get it you may win or you may not.

If you win you are Pres.
If you don't win you're set for any job you want.
What have you lost really—not everyone wins and there certainly is no disgrace in losing a public office so singular as the presidency.

In April my parents departed, with little enthusiasm, on a goodwill journey to South America. Mother still was not completely recovered from her sprained back, and my father had his mind on other things, primarily the congressional elections that lay ahead that fall. He admitted in *Six Crises* that of all the trips he made abroad as Vice President, the one that he least wanted to take was that visit to South America, "not because I thought it would be difficult but because I thought it would be relatively unimportant and uninteresting compared to the assignments I had in Washington at that time." The itinerary, in fact, was routine: an inauguration to attend (Argentina had its first democratically elected president in twenty years) and stops in every country in South America except Brazil and Chile. The White House had received a report, again fairly routine, that there might be several leftist or Communist demonstrations. Anti-American sentiment was on the rise not only in South America but worldwide.

When my parents reached Peru, after stops in Uruguay, Argentina, Paraguay, and Bolivia, the first open hostility against the American Vice President became evident. Jack Sherwood, in reflecting on the trip, feels now that "the trouble was like a tidal wave, slowly but steadily building until it reached a terrible crescendo." The Peruvian Communists had boasted that they would prevent the Nixons from visiting San Marcos University. The city's chief of police, as well as most of the American Embassy staff, took the threats seriously and urged that the visit be canceled. The rector of the university also quietly made it known that he hoped the Vice President would not visit. Unfortunately, however, the rector refused to withdraw the invitation. My father's only recourse was to go to San Marcos in order to avoid the charge that an American Vice President had been intimidated by demonstrators. The night before the scheduled visit, when my parents went to bed, they fell asleep to the ugly sound of anti-American, anti-Nixon chants in the streets below the Grand Hotel Bolivar.

In the morning, my father asked Mother to stay behind. It was the first time the possibility of danger had canceled one of their joint appearances. Two blocks before his car reached San Marcos, he could hear the mob chanting

"*Muerte a Nixon*" ("Death to Nixon"). Two thousand demonstrators, many of them too old to be students, blocked the entrance to the university. When my father got out of the car, he requested that only his interpreter, Colonel Vernon Walters, and Jack Sherwood walk with him toward the mob. He reached out and shook a few hands. For several moments, the crowd was stunned. Then others began to move forward to meet him.

Suddenly, from the edges of the crowd, the chants "*Fuera* [out] *Nixon, muerte a Nixon*" began again. Fruit and rocks flew. As they returned to the car, Jack Sherwood was hit in the mouth, a stone breaking a tooth. As the car pulled away from the university, my father stood up in the convertible, Jack Sherwood holding his legs, and yelled, "You are cowards. You are afraid of the truth!"

The Vice President and his party did not realize how much danger they were in as they drove directly to the next stop, Catholic University. For thirty minutes my father took questions from the students until Jack Sherwood interrupted him with a whispered warning: "We better get out of here; the gang from San Marcos is on its way." By the time the Vice President and his aides reached the hotel, a large part of the mob, which apparently had split up to cover both Catholic University and the Grand Hotel Bolivar, was waiting for him at the front entrance. From her fourth-story window, Mother watched as a protective wedge of Secret Service and local security surrounding the Vice President tried to push their way through the demonstrators.

Tricia and I learned about the incident at San Marcos even before my father's office got word. We were home from school for lunch and eating sandwiches in front of the television when our program was interrupted by a bulletin announcing that Vice President and Mrs. Nixon had been attacked in Lima, Peru, by a mob. There were no further details. Almost hysterical, Tricia ran into our parents' bedroom and telephoned the office. Though it was the first Loie Gaunt had heard of the incident, she calmed us, promising everything was all right, and by our three o'clock dismissal time, the principal had received a call from Loie and was able to tell us that our parents were safe.

The purpose of the trip to South America was goodwill, and consequently they tried to minimize the encounter with the mob. At a reception at the American Embassy several hours after the San Marcos episode, my mother was able to reignite some of the spirit that had prompted the visit. An American priest from New Bedford, Massachusetts, whose parishioners were now the people of Lima who lived in the *Carrolon*, a warren of mud-thatched huts, remarked that there seemed to be a great deal of party food left over. Immediately, Mother suggested to the ambassador's wife that the food be given to the priest to take back to the *Carrolon*. He left the embassy laden with food.

In Quito, Ecuador, the next stop on the trip, Jack Sherwood got a tip from an adviser to the president of Nicaragua. He warned that since the Communist demonstrators had gotten away with San Marcos, hostile groups probably would launch an all-out attack in Caracas, Venezuela. By the time the vice-presidential party reached Bogotá, Colombia, the CIA officially had informed the Secret Service of rumors of a plot to assassinate the Vice President in Venezuela. Already there were widespread rumors in Washington about the danger. When Vernon Walters spoke from the Nixon plane via the single-band radio to his mother in Washington and told her that they were en route to Venezuela, she cried, "Oh, my God, that's where the assassins are waiting."

Meanwhile, Jack Sherwood had radioed an SOS to the eight Secret Service agents who were leapfrogging ahead to other countries to make arrangements for the final stops on the schedule. Thus, when my parents landed in Venezuela, their security force had increased to a dozen. But the band of twelve was no match for the raucus demonstrators waiting on the observation deck and behind fences at the edge of the runway. They cursed, screamed, and whistled throughout the playing of both the American and Venezuelan national anthems. The angry sound so frightened Jack Sherwood that while my parents shook hands with the welcoming party at the ramp of the plane, and the Venezuelan chief of security assured my father, "They are just kids. They are harmless," Jack hurriedly ordered that the waiting convertibles be switched to closed cars.

Even before the airport ceremonies had ended, it was apparent that the demonstrators felt nothing but hate for the Americans—and for their own military rulers. When the Venezuelan national anthem was unexpectedly played again at the entrance to the terminal, causing my parents to stand immobile in respect for their host country, the screaming crowd on the observation deck directly above them showered them with a sustained rain of spit and some garbage. At first the spit looked like giant snowflakes, but it turned to foul, dark blotches when it hit my mother's red suit and the clothes of those standing with her. Then, with the aid of the Secret Service, my parents walked through a shouting, spitting mob to the motorcade. At the car, Don Hughes hurriedly rolled up the windows and then pulled out his handkerchief and wiped the saliva off the seat my mother would occupy. And yet, as Americans read in their newspapers the next day, reporters saw Pat Nixon ignore the final onslaught and stop to hug a child who had given her flowers. They also saw her lean across a barricade to pat the shoulder of a young girl who had just cursed and spit at her. The girl turned away in shame.

When the driver started the engine of Mother's car, there was so much spit on the windshield he had to use the wipers. During the twelve-mile drive into the city, there was not much conversation between Mother and the wife of the foreign minister. Their car followed closely behind my father's black limousine until, just as they reached the outskirts of Caracas, they found the highway blocked by a solid mass of cars, trucks, and buses. As soon as the motorcade halted, a group of demonstrators surrounded the cars and ripped the Venezuelan and United States flags from the vehicles as they spat and shouted. Secret Service agents who were in cars behind rushed forward and were able to clear enough of a path for the motorcade to start again. But the ordeal was far from over. Just four blocks from the city's Panteón Nacional, they again were stopped, this time by a man-made barricade of empty cars.

Mother looked out and saw that the high curb and oncoming traffic on the other side of the divided highway made it impossible for them to escape. She noticed too that the shop windows were closed and their metal protectors down. Then suddenly from both sides of the road she saw hundreds of men and women running toward them armed with lead pipes, stones, and baseball bats. Before the attackers even reached the cars, most of the Venezuelan motorcycle police escorts roared off. Mother knew they were alone except for the Secret Service agents. All twelve would later be commended by President Eisenhower for heroism.

A mob of more than five hundred descended on my father's car, beating on the windows with clubs and pipes, increasingly frenzied because it was a closed, locked limousine, not the open car that he had used on his six previous stops in South America. Slivers of glass flew through the air in the Vice President's car. Some shards hit Vernon Walters in the mouth, and the foreign minister bled profusely from cuts around one eye. My father watched as one of the gang, using a baseball bat, ferociously hit the window near his side of the car, hitting the glass ten times before it smashed. Soon all but two of the windows were smashed.

The driver of Mother's limousine had had the sense to pull up bumper to bumper with the Vice President's car, thus preventing the mob from totally surrounding the lead car. When one thug holding a huge stone came running up to Mother's car, he shouted through the window, pointing at Don Hughes, who was in the jump seat in front of her, "You Mr. Nixon?" Quickly, he realized he had the wrong car and ran forward to join the others. When the mob started to rock my father's car in an effort to overturn it and set it on fire, the wife of the foreign minister became hysterical. She uncontrollably jerked forward and then fell back in her seat, crying, "Oh, my God, my husband will be killed, we'll all be killed." Mother comfortingly put her arm on the woman's shoulder, trying to restrain her.

Then several rocks struck Pat Nixon's car. Don Hughes remembers vividly the first one that smashed within a few inches of his face: "It looked small but it kept getting bigger and bigger. Then it impacted with a terrible sound. I see that rock again and again in my mind, almost like a motion picture. But your mother was serene." Hughes, who had survived combat in World War II and in Korea, told reporters later that Pat Nixon had "more guts than any man I've ever seen."

I asked my mother how she felt during the twelve long minutes the mob attacked, pulling repeatedly at the door of my father's car in an effort to haul him out. She told me she was more angry than frightened: "I kept thinking that here we were on a trip that was supposed to be goodwill and we wanted it to be a success. Over and over I thought, 'Why did these Communist-inspired hoodlums have to do this?'" Not until she was inside the American Embassy, and part of the mob had surrounded it, did she have time to think about what had happened and what might have happened. She told me it was then that she was most frightened.

The nightmare ended when the big press truck immediately in front of my father's car was able to break out of the jam and cross the dividing island, blocking oncoming traffic. Within seconds, my father's limousine, with my mother's close behind it, screeched and swerved into the opposite lane of traffic. At the next intersection my father told his driver to make an abrupt U-turn and stop. He sent Vernon Walters back to see if Mother was all right. When Walters came running up to the car he saw that every window was smashed. Yet Pat Nixon was composed, her hands folded in her lap. "She looked up at me and quietly said, 'Tell him I'm all right too, but it was quite a sight to watch from back here.'"

Walters then gave her the message that my father had decided they would proceed directly to the American Embassy. Not taking the planned route to the wreath-laying ceremony probably saved their lives for the second time that day. When the Secret Service investigated before nightfall, they found several hundred Molotov cocktails and other explosives under the porches surrounding the park where the ceremony was to have taken place. Investigation eventually revealed that the mob had intended to hang Nixon's body ignominiously by the feet.

Rose Woods was in the fifteenth and last car of the motorcade. Since she was so far behind, she could not tell what was happening to her boss. Then, when the press truck and my parents' cars finally broke away, the frustrated mob vented its fury on the vehicles that remained behind. Finally, a Venezuelan policeman fired a tear-gas shell, thus clearing a path. As Rose's car screeched away from the mob, she was choking. A few minutes after she arrived at her hotel, she got a call from Don Hughes: "The boss and Mrs. Nixon want to know if you're all right." She could barely answer because she was swallowing back tears of relief. They were all safe.

At the American Embassy, reporter Bob Hartmann, who had watched the attack from the press truck, was one of the first to talk to my parents and to file a dispatch back to the United States. Part of his report read, "Pat Nixon was magnificent today"; at the end of her ordeal, "she still had a stiff upper lip, but when newsmen cheered her, tears welled in her eyes." On the embassy steps, my father told the reporters, "Those incidents are against Venezuela. No patriotic Venezuelan would have torn down his country's flag as the mob did to the Venezuelan and also to ours." And to a group of university students who had gathered to apologize, he said, "As far as I'm concerned the incident is closed."

It was all over, but the White House did not know if the Vice President and his wife were safe or not. The State Department had received only an initial flash report that the Nixons were under attack by anti-American mobs and that the Venezuelan security system had failed completely. They could establish no more communications with Caracas: even the Air Force radio network was not functioning. President Eisenhower, in a precautionary move, dispatched two companies of marines and two of airborne infantry to the Caribbean on a standby basis. The Venezuelan government professed to be outraged by the decision, and it was reported on Venezuelan radio that the dispatch of troops from the United States was a full-scale invasion. Immediately, my father issued a statement from the American Embassy affirming his confidence in the Venezuelan government to protect him and emphasizing that the U.S. troops would not be called upon.

My parents spent the night at the embassy, by then heavily guarded, and the next day bowed to pressure to make one last official appearance at a luncheon at the military club, the Círculo Militar, which was a citadel of wealth and militarism so resented by the poor. The junta had guaranteed the Nixons' safety on the drive to the club, and Mother found that when she tried to get into her limousine the floor was covered by submachine guns and hand grenades. She firmly asked Don Hughes to remove all the military hardware. He did so, but when she was not looking he hid two of the grenades under his jacket. In my father's car, the Venezuelan security chief declared that order had been restored in Caracas, but he held a pistol in one hand and a tear-gas gun in the other throughout the drive.

To my mother, the luncheon seemed to last forever. It was an empty charade of small talk, course after course of food she did not feel like eating, and fine wines she did not touch. Afterward, they were taken on a long tour of the building. It was evident that their military hosts were stalling. Finally, an aide whispered to the provisional president, "All is ready." On the drive to the airport, my parents discovered what the aide had meant. Along the route, the streets were empty. Tear-gas bombs had sent everyone inside. Policemen stationed on street corners wore gas masks. The airport too was eerily deserted. At the top of the plane ramp, however, the Vice President and his wife turned and waved to the handful of Venezuelan officials below, their last official gesture on the goodwill trip.

Tricia and I were waiting at National Airport when my parents returned home to Washington. A secretary from my father's office kept a restraining hand on our shoulders for what seemed like a long time as the plane slowly taxied to a stop, the stairs were rolled out and secured, and finally the doors opened. The next two hours were a blur of excitement as we were ushered into President Eisenhower's open-top car for a ceremonial ride with him and my parents to the White House. One hundred thousand of Washington's usually blasé citizens cheered us along our route. At the Executive Mansion, Tricia and I sat with the President and my parents in the family living quarters and were served Coca-Colas.

We had no idea of the trauma my mother and father had endured. Venezuela was a country far away. Nor did they talk to us later about what had happened. It was not until researching this book that I realized how close to death they had come—and the immediate impact Caracas had on my father's career as many praised his conduct under fire. As for my mother, Washington columnist Betty Beale wrote:

> Mrs. Richard M. Nixon is even more remarkable than Capitol newswomen thought... they knew she was so well organized she could accomplish most anything, and that her lean frame was no drawback to her endurance. But they did not suspect just how much mettle was behind the fragile blonde. You probably have never seen a more exhausted woman than Pat Nixon when she and the Vice President showed up at the Women's National Press Club pre-dinner reception the evening they returned from South America. Usually responsive and keen, Pat stood on a platform beside her husband as he spoke, with her arms hanging limp beside her, her face so numb with fatigue it couldn't smile... She seemed to move like an automaton. She and the Vice President came because they promised to... Washington press women take their hats off to Mrs. Richard M. Nixon.

Despite many accolades after my parents' return from South America, correspondents were mindful that my father was emerging step by step as the certain nominee two years hence and that his presidential prospects would be affected by the state and national races that election year of 1958. The New York *Post*, a flagrantly anti-Nixon newspaper, simply rewrote the Caracas story, describing my mother as a "silent wax-like doll" who had "sobbed when stoned in Caracas." The *Post* dismissed the significance of the welcoming crowd that greeted the Nixons' return to Washington: "A whole lot of wisecracks were being circulated about the enforced government march to the airport to receive Nixon. A sample: When asked whether he had gone, one man's reply had been: 'No, I haven't got a black shirt!'"

The 1958 off-year elections were an inauspicious start to the 1960 presidential race. My mother traveled less with my father on behalf of the candidates that year than during any previous campaign. When queried by the press, she gave as her reason not wanting to leave Tricia and me. An unspoken reason for her limited participation was that my father, seeing so little chance for Republican success, wanted to insulate her from what would be a long and draining experience and thus did not urge her to join him. As he journeyed to twenty-five states, he decided that even if the Republicans had fielded better candidates, they were handicapped by a sluggish economy and two events: the Soviet Union's launching of the first outer-space satellite, Sputnik, in October of 1957; and the resignation of Eisenhower's chief of staff, Sherman Adams, shortly before the election.

In June, Adams had been charged with accepting favors, including the payment of some three thousand dollars of hotel bills and a vicuña coat, from Bernard Goldfine, an industrialist being investigated by the Securities and Exchange Commission. During the next three and a half months, while the Democrats kept the story alive in the newspapers, Eisenhower vacillated over whether or not to request Adams's resignation. He did not believe his chief of staff had used his position to gain profit, but it was becoming increasingly clear that the Democrats would continue to charge "influence peddling" in the White House until Election Day.

As soon as Congress adjourned on August 24, as my father wrote in his *Memoirs*, "I kept a long-standing promise to Pat and the girls and took them by train to The Greenbrier in West Virginia. Every vacation we had planned since coming to Congress in 1947 had been cut short, but this time I really thought it would be different."

The morning of our arrival in West Virginia, however, the President called my father back to Washington and asked that he gently suggest to Adams that his presence in the government was hurting Republican chances in the congressional elections. My father carried out the President's request, but it was a fruitless conversation. Adams was not ready to accept such a suggestion from anyone except his boss.

My mother would remember always that particular episode, not only because the vacation plans were ruined, but also because she foresaw that for her husband it was a no-win proposition: Adams would resist, and the President would be disappointed. For four more weeks, Adams hung on until Republican National Committee chairman Meade Alcorn was authorized to tell Adams that Eisenhower himself felt it was time he tendered his resignation.

On Election Day, the Republicans suffered the worst defeat in the history of a party having control of the White House. The Democrats emerged with 34 of the 48 statehouses, 13 more Senate seats, and with 282 House seats to only 153 held by the Republicans. Tom Dewey had warned my father not to get involved in the campaign at all, saying, "You've already done enough, and 1960 is what counts now." In his *Memoirs*, my father wrote from the perspective of twenty years, "Perhaps Dewey had been right: I should have sat it out."

After the election, my parents went to Key Biscayne. It was there that my father began discussions for 1960. Everyone conceded that the Republican defeat was not a good sign and that the Democrats somehow had gained the initiative. Leonard Hall, the former chairman of the Republican National Committee, put the odds against Nixon being elected in 1960 at five to one.

He would have to win all of his party's votes, more than half those of the Independents, and those of five or six million registered Democrats as well. Offsetting these numbers was my father's steadily rising popularity.

My mother sat in on a few of the strategy sessions. After surviving the Dump Nixon talk in 1956, it was understood tacitly that my father would be in line for the Presidency in 1960 and would run. Patricia Ryan Nixon may have grown to dislike politics, but she believed wholeheartedly that her husband was the best man for the job, and she had sensed as well for some time that they were being carried along by a momentum that she could not stop. Only eight months after Helene suggested my parents talk candidly about the future, my mother would find herself swept up in the passions of the campaign of 1960.

Meanwhile, shortly after returning from Florida, and still smarting from the sting of the election results, my parents flew to London for the dedication of the American Memorial Chapel in St. Paul's Cathedral honoring the twenty-eight thousand GIs based on British soil who died in the Second World War. The English press and some of the liberal British leadership had not expected to warm to the Vice President. The London *Times* profile of Pat Nixon, which appeared just prior to the visit, had stated flatly, "There is no more controversial character in American politics than Richard Milhous Nixon, Vice President of the United States, and that one of his greatest assets is his wife is perhaps the only point about which all are agreed." But after my father's Guildhall speech, on November 27, in which he asked England and America to help the developing nations, many of them former British colonies, by adopting "as our primary objective not the defeat of Communism, but the victory of plenty over want, of health over disease, of freedom over tyranny," the trip became an unexpected "triumph," as seen by *Newsweek* magazine.

For my mother, one of the most memorable events on the four-day schedule was the Thanksgiving dinner at the American Embassy for the queen. The evening began on a frantic note for my parents. My father had assumed that the dinner would be white tie. But in London he learned that the queen had specifically requested less formal attire. He had to come up with a dinner jacket in a hurry. He arranged to borrow one from Jim Bassett, who was on leave from the Los Angeles *Times*, acting as my father's press aide on the trip. Bassett in turn commandeered a suit from a Scotland Yard detective. *Punch* magazine later ran a cartoon that depicted a trouserless London bobby on guard outside the embassy wistfully commenting that he hoped it wouldn't be a long evening.

Unfortunately for the mythical bobby, the party lasted until after midnight, a good hour later than the queen usually stayed at official functions. Mother had never seen Elizabeth more relaxed. When my father, self-conscious in Bassett's jacket, which was too short in the arms and looked as if it had come from a local rental agency, explained his predicament to the queen, she laughed heartily. She seemed to enjoy the relatively small group of guests, fifty-six in all, and the traditional American Thanksgiving dinner of roast turkey with sweet potatoes, and pumpkin and mince pies for dessert.

My parents' visit to London ended at midnight the following day. On the flight to Washington, my father remarked to Ruth Buchanan, wife of Chief of Protocol Wiley Buchanan, that he was sick of formal trips and the press coverage on these trips. He said that he and Pat knocked themselves out and then got criticized. But although there were some negative comments, much of the press coverage of the London trip was favorable. The Birmingham *Post* correspondent could fault Nixon solely for his perfection at his press conference: "If only he made a *faux pas* to match his forgetting to pack a dinner suit. This man, one felt, would not forget even his toothbrush." My father's comments to Ruth Buchanan were the impulsive reaction of one whose party has just sustained a defeat and who was slightly weary after six years of being expected to come forth with the correct words, the correct actions, and the correct appearance, especially when representing his country abroad.

As 1959 opened, however, my parents were looking ahead. That July my father's travels assumed even greater significance as the vice-presidential party visited the Union of Soviet Socialist Republics. In the words of the President's brother Dr. Milton Eisenhower, who was part of the official party, it was a journey of "hope, mystery and fear." The trip symbolized hope since it was the first visit by an American Vice President; mystery because so little was known about life behind the Iron Curtain and even less about its leaders; and fear because of Nikita Khrushchev's bellicose, unpredictable flaunting of his power. His open testing of nuclear weapons, his saber rattling over Berlin, and his refusal to respond to overtures from the West about disarmament struck many as irrational.

Appropriately enough for a pioneering journey, my parents flew for the first time on the President's new Air Force Boeing 707 jet. As they neared the Soviet Union, there was only one confirmed event on their Moscow schedule: the official opening of the American National Exhibition. Mother's role on the trip was especially vague since Mrs. Khrushchev and the wives of other Soviet officials did not accompany their husbands in public. In fact, Nina Khrushchev's photograph had never appeared in the Communist newspapers. But *The New York Times*, in its profile of Pat Nixon written on the eve of the trip, had stated that Mrs. Nixon, in her three-inch spike heels, which had clicked across the world, would have no difficulties in the Soviet Union because "she is self-possessed, self-made, the right word at the right time, orderly, precise... yet she can banter with the heads of government, Ambassadors, the man-in-the-street, or newsmen."

When Vice President and Mrs. Nixon landed in Moscow, they received a sobering welcome: no flowers, no band playing the national anthems, no crowds. The American ambassador, Llewellyn Thompson, told them that for weeks the Soviet press had ridiculed the exhibit of "typical American life," which my parents had come to open. The following day my father and Khrushchev toured its model home and sparred in the kitchen. It was an incongruous scene. The rotund but muscular sixty-five-year-old premier stood face-to-face with the serious-looking forty-six-year-old American Vice President in front of an automatic washing machine and dryer and debated foreign policy, missile strength, and which country cared more about peace.

Khrushchev boasted, "We are strong, we can beat you."

My father responded in turn, "In some ways you are stronger than we are. In others we are stronger. But to me it seems that in this day and age to argue who is the stronger completely misses the point. . . . No one should ever use his strength to put another in the position where he in effect has an ultimatum. . . . If war comes we both lose."

The debate continued later that day at the welcoming luncheon hosted by Khrushchev in the Kremlin. My mother and Mrs. Thompson were the only women present, but their attendance did not seem to inhibit the Soviet leaders' vodka consumption and loud toasting. The noise in the room was so overwhelming that Mother felt her ears buzzing. Repeatedly, the Soviets asked her to join in the drinking. She demurred with the explanation, "Oh, no, I don't care for it." Finally Deputy Premier Mikoyan leaned heavily across the table, his head almost touching his outstretched arm, and said, "Ah, I know, we'll drink to peace." She answered, "For peace, I'll do anything." The luncheon ended with the jarring sound of shattering glass as Khrushchev and his entourage smashed their beautiful crystal vodka glasses against the fireplace.

That afternoon and the next day, the Soviets took Mother on unannounced visits to a market, a hospital, and a school. To her hosts' relief, she was the soul of tact and diplomacy. When she toured Moscow's eight-hundred-bed Children's Hospital and was asked what she would like to "inspect," she relieved her guides with a quick reply: "I'm not here to see the medical equipment but just to visit with the children because I know at home how much they enjoy visitors." With those words, a slight thaw began.

The thaw increased that evening when my parents hosted at the American Embassy a traditional Midwestern dinner of Iowa beef and corn on the cob, which they had brought with them on their jet. Khrushchev, Mikoyan, and several others in their entourage stunned the Americans by arriving for dinner with their wives in tow. No one at the embassy had dreamed that Mother's comment to Khrushchev at the welcoming luncheon about wanting to meet the wives would be heeded, at least not that night. Dinner was only slightly delayed while the embassy staff set more places at the table, but the delay was enough to ring the last ounce of tenderness out of the corn. The Russian chef, despite careful instructions from Mrs. Thompson, already had boiled the corn for more than an hour. The beef also was shriveled and tough. The

Soviet guests politely pushed the food around on their plates, as did their American hosts.

Before my parents left Moscow, Khrushchev unexpectedly insisted that they spend a night at his country dacha in Usovo, a half-hour drive from the Kremlin. Dimly lighted and dwarfed by 150-foot trees, some of which had been planted during the reign of Catherine the Great, the dacha seemed strangely forbidding. The "manager," who greeted them at the door, refused to admit Jack Sherwood, forcing him to spend the night in an outlying building. My mother remembers how uneasy she felt not knowing who else was on the premises or how she would call for help if necessary. Not surprisingly, she hardly slept the entire night in the guest suite with its king-size bed, ten-foot-high windows, and bathroom equipped with a massage table and whirlpool equipment. Nor was she ever able to learn if Khrushchev or other Kremlin leaders regularly used the suite. In the morning the dacha seemed less imposing, though my mother and father were served breakfast at a dining-room table large enough to seat sixty people. The by-now-familiar menu was one she had come to enjoy: thick, black Russian bread, caviar, smoked salmon, and oranges.

They had no idea how soon Khrushchev would arrive for more conferences. My father used the time to work on the unprecedented thirty-minute television speech the Soviets had given him permission to deliver to the Russian people at the end of the journey. Mother decided to take a walk through the gardens and forest paths on the edge of the gently sloping banks of the Moskva River. It was very beautiful, but everywhere she looked, there was a man behind a tree. Being followed so overtly was embarrassing and she decided to return to the dacha where she sat in the living room and enjoyed the view from there. Jack Sherwood told her later that listening devices were planted openly on many of the trees and shrubs along the dacha's crooked paths.

At noon, Khrushchev, Mikoyan, and Koslov arrived, accompanied by their wives. The entire party went out on the river in motorboats so that the premier could show the Vice President the "captive people"—a sarcastic reference to the recent American Congress's Captive Nations resolution, which had condemned the Soviets for their domination of Eastern Europe. Almost as if they were giving a performance on cue, hundreds of bathers swarmed about the little boats.

Luncheon was served after the boat trip, but it was more than just a pleasant Sunday afternoon under the shade of the towering birch and pine trees. It evolved into a five-hour marathon debate about missiles, bombers, terrorism, exporting revolution, and Berlin. While the vodka flowed freely, no one excused himself from the table. Mrs. Khrushchev passed chocolates and offered coffee and fruit, but otherwise the women were silent—with one exception. When my father asked Khrushchev about the development of solid fuels for missile production and the premier refused to answer, Mother interjected,

"I'm surprised there is a subject that you're not prepared to discuss, Mr. Chairman. I thought that with your one-man government you had to have everything firmly in your own hands."

Quickly, Mikoyan answered for his premier, "Even Chairman Khrushchev does not have enough hands for all he has to do, so that is why we are here to help him."

After the luncheon Jack Sherwood watched as my mother and Mesdames Khrushchev, Mikoyan, and Koslov chatted and then embraced. He told me:

> It was nice to know that these women were concerned about the same things. They worried that their husbands worked too long, cared about the welfare of their children and grandchildren, and what peace would mean to all of them. There was a down-to-earth, honest quality in that exchange between your mother and those Russian women. The Soviet wives didn't know how to be devious or coy. They weren't acquainted with diplomacy.

My parents returned home via Poland, one of the "captive nations." The Polish government, mindful that the population of Warsaw had received Khrushchev coolly only a few weeks earlier, did not make a public announcement of the Nixon visit. But Radio Free Europe beamed the news, and the Poles, by watching police preparations carefully, determined which route the Americans would travel from the airport. Mainly thanks to word of mouth, a quarter of a million people gathered along the fifteen miles leading to Warsaw to cheer two people who symbolized America and freedom. Men, women, and children threw bouquets of roses, bunches of wild flowers, sometimes just a single bud, into the cars in the motorcade. Many wept and many in the American press buses and official limousines wept as well. Several times my father got out of his car to shake hands with the people. Jack Sherwood used those moments to unload the knee-deep mounds of flowers.

My mother never forgot the outpouring of emotion from the Polish people. Her already intense patriotism was deepened. She found it impossible to be casual about her country and what it meant to the world.

Only six weeks after the journey to Moscow, Nina and Nikita Khrushchev visited the United States. It was the first time Nina Khrushchev had accompanied her husband on an official trip, indicating that the Russians were pleased with the exposure Mrs. Khrushchev had received as a result of my mother's presence in Moscow in July.

My mother hosted a luncheon for Mrs. Khrushchev while her husband was at Camp David with the President. Mamie Eisenhower decided to present Madame Khrushchev with a hat made by her favorite milliner, Sally Victor. Contrary to current fashion, the Soviet leader's wife had been hatless throughout most of her visit with the exception of a small net veil worn once or twice, and, on occasion, a tiny bowler placed at the back of her steel-gray hair. When Mother and Ruth Buchanan learned about Mamie's gift, they made a private bet that Mrs. Khrushchev would never wear the hat.

Shortly before Nina Khrushchev was scheduled to leave Blair House for the luncheon, Ruth Buchanan ceremoniously presented Mrs. Eisenhower's gift. Ceremoniously Mrs. Khrushchev unwrapped it, looked at the hat, and then said, politely and diplomatically, "Well, I don't think it will fit me because I have a very big head." Immediately Ruth said, "Oh, yes it will. Sally Victor made it extra large." Despite Ruth Buchanan's enthusiasm, however, Nina Khrushchev firmly resisted the daring idea of wearing an American capitalistic hat. Her final words on the subject to Ruth were "I'll just take it back to Russia so the millions can copy it."

When Ruth arrived at the luncheon with Nina Khrushchev at her side, she caught my mother's eye; they looked at each other, looked back toward the hatless guest of honor, her hair as usual tightly drawn back in a bun, and they winked.

CHAPTER 17

"Iron and Courage,
Not Skin and Bones"

In January my mother began her last full year as the Second Lady of the land. *Time* magazine profiled her in a cover story in February and stated unequivocally that her "stamina and courage, her drive and control have made her into one of the U.S.'s most remarkable women—not just a showpiece Second Lady, not merely a part of the best-known team in contemporary politics, but a public figure in her own right." The profile noted also that her critics found her "too serene, too tightly controlled...."; one who "smothers her personality with a thick smile and a mask of dignity." There was much truth in the praise and some in the criticism as well.

In order to survive public life, my mother had learned that she could never be too careful about what she said or did. By the time the 1960 campaign was launched, her instinct for caution, even in fashion, had become deeply ingrained. With her excellent political judgment, for years she had dressed for the "Pat and Dick" constituency. In January of 1959, the Washington *Daily News* analyzed her style:

Mrs. Nixon knows the first, and hardest, principle of "best dressing"—her type. She consistently chooses clothes to emphasize her fragile Patrician look, yet subtly de-emphasize what could be a too thin look. . . . She never looks too fluffy, too dramatic, too fussy, too casual. Her clothes never shriek the name of the designer. She has a fine eye for good lines and subtle colors.

A year later, in responding to a reporter's question about her wardrobe, my mother revealed just a hint of weariness as she explained:

> Everything I buy, I think of the life I live. I never choose something just because I like it. I think: Will it pack? Is it conservative enough? Can I wear it a long time? Can I doll it up with accessories?
>
> Always before it was sort of fun to get some one thing that was completely different, high style. But this is not appropriate now. I avoid the spectacular. I don't go overboard anymore. I used to. Maybe it's age.

For so long newspaper profiles had highlighted her domestic tasks that, perhaps inevitably, her super-self-sufficiency was now suspect. Thus, when the Detroit *Free Press* did a series of prepresidential interviews with her, Mother declined to be photographed in the kitchen, saying, "I think we've had enough of this kitchen thing, don't you?" She was still stung by several widely syndicated stories in 1958 and 1959 skeptical of her "domestic martyrdom." Particularly irritating to the general public, according to one article, was the information that Mrs. Nixon pressed her husband's pants, since one could only conclude that GOP publicists were trying to imply that the wife of the Vice President did not have household help. The only humorous note in the brouhaha was an offer from an Illinois cleaner for "an unlimited number of P.O. (press only) on your husband's trousers."

Gradually, as the presidential nominating conventions neared, the emphasis on Pat Nixon's domesticity dimmed somewhat as questions about the future became more important. How did Mrs. Nixon feel about becoming First Lady? To all she refused comment, explaining feelingly to Hazel Markel of the *Ladies' Home Journal*, "We like to think of now. I can't project into the future. We are trying to let the girls grow up happily in a good home. I want that more than anything else."

No matter how hard she tried, however, Pat Nixon could not ignore the intense interest in the campaign that lay ahead. In June, at the last Ladies of the Senate meeting until the fall, she was given a crystal bowl in appreciation of her leadership of the group for almost eight years. Lillian Tobey, the widow of the senator from New Hampshire, spoke for herself and for the other women, Democrats and Republicans alike, with whom Mother had spent so many Tuesdays rolling bandages:

> Pat Nixon, we have a gift for you. It is a crystal bowl. We chose this because it was crystal clear eight years ago when you became the president of our group here, we liked you. Later on it was crystal clear we loved you, and we still do. You are *friendly*, *faithful*, and *fair*.
>
> You are *friendly*, irrespective of party or age. You are *faithful*, far beyond the call of duty. You are *fair*, adding beauty to our interior decoration!

You have a rare and heartwarming quality of making everyone you greet seem more important than yourself.

Our gift is a crystal bowl, not a crystal ball. You won't be able to see into the future, but we hope you can see clearly into the past, and how much happiness you have brought us. Great happiness to you, Pat Nixon, and God bless you.

On July 2, 1960, with the Democratic and Republican conventions only weeks away, my parents enjoyed the unexpected treat of a weekend at Camp David. President Eisenhower had called early on Saturday morning and offered the camp. My father, in turn, telephoned Ruth and Wiley Buchanan to see if they would like to drive up to the mountains for the night.

It was a relaxed Sunday. Mother and Ruth sat in the sun on the flagstone terrace of Aspen Lodge and looked out over the expanse of green, leafy woods that tapered off into the sunlit valley beyond. Their quiet companionship was broken when they noticed a large black snake slither by. The snake curled up in the sun in a corner of the terrace, only a few feet from their chaise longues. After a few minutes Ruth said, rather nonchalantly, "Shouldn't we tell our husbands?" They did and both men became very excited. They summoned the marine guard on duty near Aspen's kitchen door and he alerted some of his comrades. The reinforcements arrived quickly in a big truck. One of them picked up the snake, and the whole contingent departed, with Mother's words echoing behind them, "Don't hurt the snake."

That Sunday, politics had been very much on everyone's mind as Ruth recorded in her diary: "Dick really is worried about K [John F. Kennedy] winning the Democratic nomination. He's sure that's who he'll have to beat and he doesn't feel too easy about it." In Los Angeles, less than two weeks later, the Democrats did nominate Senator John F. Kennedy of Massachusetts as their presidential standard-bearer. He selected as his running mate Senator Lyndon B. Johnson of Texas. My father considered the ticket, as he wrote later in his Memoirs, the "strongest the Democrats could possibly put in the field."

The Republican Convention was held in Chicago, beginning on July 25. Tricia and I had spent most of the month at camp in Montecito, California. A few weeks before we were to fly to Chicago, Mother wrote me and included in her note the injunction, "Keep this letter for instructions." She explained how "a Secret Service friend" would pick up Tricia and me and drive us to our grandmother's house; and when we arrived at our hotel in Chicago, we would find new dresses that she had hemmed, hoping we had not grown two inches in the past few weeks. She also gave me some advice, which reflected her own philosophy of life:

In regard to the girls in your cabin [I had complained that some were not friendly]: Just remember that some people are not as friendly and sweet as others. The main thing is to treat them in a friendly fashion and stay your own sweet self rather than becoming like them. When you think kind thoughts about them they will change for the better. That is true all through life.

I love you very, very much!

When Tricia and I arrived in Chicago twenty-four hours before our parents, Mother saw a television newsclip of us getting off the plane, wearing white gloves and the dresses she had suggested in her last letter—and chewing gum! In my diary, I described the triumphant welcome to Chicago: "Mommy and Daddy arrived today. We rode in the parade. All the people wanted to see Daddy and so they were just about squeezing us to death...."

When my father stood before the delegates as their nominee, it had been almost fifteen years since his selection by the Committee of 100, eleven years since the Hiss case, and less than five years since the Dump Nixon ordeal. Despite the controversy that had followed him during those years, he had become indispensable to the party and to the Administration he served—and represented—that night. In his acceptance speech he reminded the delegates that he knew Khrushchev and had seen the world. "What we must do is wage the battles for peace and freedom with the same... dedication with which we wage battles in war.... When Mr. Khrushchev says our grandchildren will live under Communism, let us say his grandchildren will live in freedom." To many, including my mother, the most memorable words of the forty-eight-minute speech were "I believe in the American dream because I have seen it come true in my own lifetime." The words were as true of Pat Nixon as they were of the man who spoke them.

As the long-awaited campaign commenced, the importance of my mother's role was undisputed. Ruth Montgomery wrote in her syndicated column that in the opinion of the top strategists in the Nixon campaign, "for the first time in American history one woman could conceivably swing a presidential election." Another reporter evoked historical precedent when she pointed out that Pat Nixon was the first woman around whom a separate campaign was being built. The Republican National Committee's women's division decided to sponsor a Pat Week beginning October 3, during which Mother would attend coffees and mini-rallies in her honor, and precinct workers would canvass the neighborhoods. The committee also stated in a news release:

When you elect a President, you are also electing a First Lady whose job is more than glamour. The First Lady has a working assignment. She represents America to all the world. Pat Nixon is part of the experienced Nixon team. She's uniquely qualified for the position of First Lady.

The committee's Pat Week, including a Pat for First Lady button, had caught my mother unawares. In studying the 1960 campaign, when I questioned Mother about the activities, she explained that the committee had not consulted her before unveiling its plan: "They had the best intentions, but they got carried away... it was pretty embarrassing but I was caught in it. The teas and coffees had all been announced." My mother was uncomfortable with the focus of the women's division; the nation was electing a President, not a First Lady.

In the course of the campaign, there would be criticism that Pat Nixon was too active. In response, she explained to one reporter that her role as a campaigner was "reflective of women all over America taking an active part, not only in political life, but all activities. There was a day when they [women] stayed at home... but they have emerged as volunteers for a cause they believe in." For almost eight years in Washington my mother had had an unofficial full-time job. In fact, in Leningrad, the year before, when a little girl asked what work Mrs. Nixon did, my father had interjected, "Being the wife of a Vice President is a working job."

In contrast, Jacqueline Kennedy, who was expecting her second child at the end of November, was unable to make more than a few campaign appearances. Neither the public nor my mother, for that matter, knew Jacqueline Kennedy very well. Jackie had not attended the Senate Ladies' Red Cross meetings, and rarely appeared at political events in Washington. During the campaign, her most widely quoted comment would be on the subject of clothes. She denied the allegation that she spent thousands of dollars a year on her wardrobe—adding humorously, "I would have to wear sable underwear"—and countered that Mrs. Nixon probably spent more.

But the fashion asides were soon overtaken by the inherent drama of the closest election in this century. The campaign officially began for my parents on August 17 with an ill-fated trip to North Carolina that had wide-ranging repercussions. In Greensboro, my father bumped his knee getting into a car. By Saturday, August 27, he was experiencing such intense pain and swelling that he went to Walter Reed Army Hospital for tests. The results came back on Monday, August 29, and assistant White House physician Dr. Walter Tkach called immediately to say that the knee was badly infected and required hospitalization and massive dosages of antibiotics. When my father protested that he could not possibly take the time for the treatment, Tkach brusquely informed him that he would be campaigning on one leg if he delayed any longer.

In severe pain because of injections underneath his infected kneecap, my father lay in bed for two weeks while Kennedy campaigned. The hospitalization meant that he could not visit the seven states that had been scheduled during that period. His advisers, many of whom originally had doubted the wisdom of his nomination-night promise to visit all fifty states, urged him to issue a statement explaining that illness now made the pledge impossible to keep. My mother felt torn; she agreed with the hard-nosed advice that the double-time schedule would exhaust them all, and yet she felt that they were bound by the public promise. And too, there were 50 million Democratic voters to only 33 million Republicans. In all the polls taken in the past year, Nixon had led Kennedy just once. Maybe visiting all the states would give the Nixon campaign the edge it needed. Mother decided not to side with those urging my father to withdraw from the fifty-state commitment and with her concurrence, he went forward with his nomination-night pledge.

An already full campaign schedule now became a whirlwind. My parents covered twenty-five states in two weeks before my father headed for Chicago late Sunday night, September 25, for the first televised presidential debate in history. He had not yet recovered his strength from the knee infection, and by this time, though he did not realize it, was ten pounds underweight. With the tight schedule, he had left himself no time to rest and only Monday afternoon to prepare for the evening's debate.

He had agreed to the four debates reluctantly, knowing that the exposure might benefit Kennedy, who was less well known. Kennedy already had the advantage of being on the offensive, promising to "get the country moving again," and warning that Americans were in danger of becoming "second-raters," while my father found himself defending the Administration in the hope that he would prevail on the substantive issues of peace and prosperity.

An estimated eighty million people watched the verbal confrontation on September 26, and my father, for the first time in his career, emerged from a debate running behind. Though the majority of editorial writers called the debate a draw on substance, polls taken of the television audience indicated significantly that Kennedy was the winner by a slight edge. What made the difference was not so much what was discussed but rather the physical appearance of the two candidates. Watching at his home in California, Bill Ryan, now a lighting expert with Universal Studios, was surprised by the contrast between his brother-in-law, who had refused pancake makeup and wore only a thin "beard stick" over his five-o'clock shadow, and the fit, deeply tanned Kennedy. All too clearly Bill Ryan saw how unflattering the contrast was: "Dick looked so haggard, so strangely dark."

Rose Woods recalls being shocked by the image on the screen. Her boss looked exhausted. Because of his weight loss his collar gapped at the neck, giving him, in Rose's words, a "sloppy" appearance. Immediately after the program ended, Rose received a call from Hannah Nixon, who asked her, "Is Richard ill?"

Since my mother had been home for only half a day in the past two weeks, she had arranged to be in Washington to watch the debate with Tricia and me. She noticed that my father looked worn but was concentrating on what the two men said and was confident Nixon had emerged the winner. But one question rankled her, and she worried about it that night on her flight to Chicago to rejoin my father. The question had been asked by John Kennedy's friend Sander Vanocur of NBC, who brought up an August 24 news conference during which the President had been asked, "What major decision of your Administration did the Vice President participate in?" It was the last question of the conference and the President was already preparing to walk away from the podium. He had responded quickly, "If you give me a week, I might think of one." Eisenhower had realized immediately that the remark would be misconstrued, and instead of being taken as "Ask me at next week's conference," it would be used against the Vice President. He had called my father that afternoon, reaching him on the golf course at Burning Tree Country Club, to say contritely, "I've been trying to get this damned thing explained." But, as Vanocur's question indicated, ultimately it was Nixon who would have to do the explaining.

In the next three debates, the majority of editorial writers decided Nixon's performance excelled Kennedy's each time. In polls of radio listeners, Nixon consistently was given the edge. But the television audience that had watched the first debate was 20 million more than for the following ones. It became vitally important now for the Nixon campaign to reach great numbers of voters through personal appearances.

The next four weeks were a blur. Teddy White, in *The Making of the President 1960*, wrote that the competition between Kennedy and Nixon "flung them, by senseless ritual and tradition, into such physical exertion day after day, night after night as would sap the energies of a trained athlete." Bob Finch, my father's campaign director, believes, "We will never see a campaign like it again—two such young men, forty-seven and forty-three, fighting with every ounce of strength."

My father told me the only way he and Mother could sustain the pace during the entire campaign was to live like Spartans—little food, tempers under control, no alcohol. Sometimes the entourage had to fly all night. The only way many could keep awake during the daytime was by taking mild pep pills. Bob Finch was expected to travel with my father as well as coordinate efforts with the Republican National Committee in Washington. He felt split in half. He now realizes that the strain of ceaseless flying between Washington and wherever the candidate might be was too much and that by November he could not have stood another week. One of his most vivid memories of those days is of walking into the hotel where my parents were staying and Mother commenting, "Oh, Bob, you're exhausted. You have to slow down and take care of yourself." He told me, "And there she was, having been hauled and pushed and exhausted by the schedule herself."

In the final weeks of the campaign, when the pollsters said the election was too close to call, the fight to win intensified. Writer Fletcher Knebel had stated in a preconvention article on the Nixons that "no politician has been more vigorously attacked than Vice President Nixon. Pat took it hard at first but since then has learned to live with criticism she deems unfair." One way she lived with the criticism was by reading as little of it as possible. But she was aware of it, and also frightened by the ruthlessness of what *Newsweek* called Kennedy's "win or else" campaign.

Although the polls were deadlocked, the Kennedys skillfully exploited sensitive issues to gain the initiative. For instance, Kennedy's brother and his running mate turned the question of his Catholicism into a powerful asset: "Jack's Brother Says Religion Top Issue" (Columbia [South Carolina] *State*), "Johnson Blasts 'Haters' Attacks on Catholics" (Washington *Post*), "Bob Kennedy Scores Stress on Religion" (Cleveland *Plain Dealer*). Repeatedly, Bobby Kennedy asked audiences, "Did they ask my brother Joe if he was a Catholic before he was shot down [in World War II]?" On Election Day, my father would receive only 22 percent of the Catholic vote, the lowest of any Republican presidential candidate in history, and with no corresponding shift of Protestants away from Kennedy.

Then, just twenty days before the election, Martin Luther King, Jr., was arrested for his part in an Atlanta sit-in demonstration, and was given a four-month sentence based on a former charge of driving without a valid license. Robert Kennedy, realizing the tremendous political impact if his brother became Dr. King's champion, set aside legal propriety and called the judge in the case. Praise by Martin Luther King, Sr., and other black leaders for Bobby Kennedy's action implied at the same time that Richard Nixon's silence signified indifference, a point that was made by Kennedy campaigners in the black communities.

But my father had not been inactive. Privately, and without publicity, he had asked the Justice Department to investigate whether there had been an infringement of Dr. King's constitutional rights. An added frustration for the Nixon campaign was that some Democrats were playing both sides of the race issue and, according to Bruce L. Felknor of the Fair Campaign Practices Committee, circulated in white communities a "flier displaying three photographs of Nixon in various poses of affection and affinity with Negroes." Black leaders knew that as Vice President my father had made key rulings in the Senate that were essential in getting the Eisenhower Administration's civil rights legislation to the floor, and that it had been southern Democrats, including Lyndon Johnson, who had blocked it. Yet on Election Day, blacks would vote for Kennedy 64 percent to 34 percent for Nixon.

Once during the course of the campaign, Loretta Stuart came to our house to do Mother's hair before a trip. She asked my mother why the Nixon campaign was not exposing some of the shady tactics of the powerfully financed

Kennedy camp. An example was the anti-Catholic mailers sent out during the Wisconsin primary to heavily Catholic precincts—all postmarked Minnesota, to look as if they were from Hubert H. Humphrey, Kennedy's main opponent in Wisconsin—but which in truth were the work of a friend of Robert Kennedy's. The demolition of Humphrey in West Virginia also had included the innuendo that he was a draft dodger. Humphrey was so angered by the Kennedy tactics that he publicly accused the candidate and his brother of "cheap, low-down, gutter politics." In a 1976 autobiography, Humphrey would express his unhappiness with the Kennedy organization in this way: "Underneath the beautiful exterior there was an element of ruthlessness and toughness that I had trouble either accepting or forgetting."

Bryce Harlow, an Eisenhower speech writer who was helping in the Nixon campaign, told me that two weeks before the election he saw my mother get upset for the first time. It was late at night in a motel in California and Bryce was waiting for my father to finish taking a shower so they could go over some notes for a speech. Mother was distraught by polls that showed Kennedy and Nixon neck and neck. With anguish, she asked Bryce, "How can we let the American people know in time what kind of man Kennedy is?"

Repeatedly in the last weeks, my father had tried to focus public attention on the government spending programs Kennedy was advocating, which would cost billions and lead to inflation. But my father's attempt to point out the differences between his economic policy of emphasis on individual initiative and a highly productive private sector, and Kennedy's focus on government activism, was overshadowed just seven crucial days before the election when government statistics were released showing that the country was in an economic slowdown. It was this latter news that triggered Eisenhower to invite the Republican leaders to the White House on October 31 to discuss giving the Nixon campaign a boost. The popular incumbent's involvement was a sensitive question, since both my father and the President had agreed previously that Eisenhower's appearances would be kept to a minimum, lest Nixon be seen as trying to ride Ike's coattails into the White House. But the appearance of unity had become more important now.

The night before the meeting, however, my mother received a rare phone call from Mamie Eisenhower. The First Lady sounded distraught. She reminded Pat that Ike was seventy years old. He was not well, Mamie said, and his blood pressure simply could not withstand the pressure of campaigning. She urged that my father must not ask Ike to undertake any additional campaigning—and not to let him know that she had called. My mother said very little in response, only that she would convey the message, and she did.

In the morning, when my father received a second warning about Eisenhower's health from the President's physician, Major General Howard Snyder, he concluded that Mamie was speaking for her husband. Consequently, at the meeting an hour later with Eisenhower and the assembled Republican

Party leaders, he stunned them all by rejecting the President's offer to add three states to the two already scheduled. He asked instead that the President fulfill only the already-planned trips to Cleveland and Pittsburgh and his election-eve broadcast. The President was angry—and confused, as were the political strategists, who were baffled by Nixon's abruptness. Since New York, Michigan, and Illinois were crucial states, appearances there by Ike could tip the scales in what the polls were still showing was a whisper-close campaign. But it was a classic misunderstanding. From Nixon's point of view, Eisenhower was not being forthcoming; from Eisenhower's viewpoint, Nixon was throwing it all away. Because Mamie did not tell her husband about the phone call until several years later, the misunderstanding was destined to persist and would heal only partially with time.

Within ten days of the meeting with Ike, the campaign of 1960 was all over. November 7, 8, and 9 are one endless day in Mother's mind, because during those seventy-two hours she slept for only a few hours. The seventh started with an 8 A.M. speech in Madison, Wisconsin, then a flight to Detroit for a four-hour telethon during which my father answered viewers' questions phoned in from all over the country. From Detroit, the Nixon party flew to Chicago, where my father broadcast the traditional election-night speech, and, finally, on to Los Angeles.

At 2 A.M., in Ontario, California, Richard Nixon spoke at the closing rally of the 1960 campaign. Despite the hour, more than ten thousand people had gathered. Tricia and I had joined our parents for the final leg of the campaign and Mother did not get us to bed in the Ambassador Hotel in Los Angeles until four. She never completely undressed since she had only an hour and a half before the early-morning drive to Whittier, where she and my father planned to cast their votes.

After the traditional photograph at the voting booths, Mother returned to the hotel to rest, and my father and Don Hughes set off on a drive down the beautiful California coast, eventually lunching in Tijuana. At the Ambassador, Mother washed her hair, caught up on some mail, and waited. As she waited, she was not thinking of defeat. She told me in 1978, "I knew it would be close, but I thought we would win. I knew Kennedy too well to think that the country would elect him."

Like Mother, Tricia and I had never contemplated defeat, nor had our parents prepared us fully for the possibility. We were too young to be deeply involved in the issues of the campaign, or even to follow the polls closely. What little we gleaned of the contest between my father and Kennedy came from snatches of information from our friends or random newspaper and magazine articles like the movie magazine in the grocery store with the split cover, "The Love Story of Pat and Dick" and "The Love Story of Jack and Jackie." The stories were pure Hollywood fantasy, a mishmash of fact and fiction. My mother was portrayed as the starlet who never made it. The

Kennedy story was even more farfetched: Jackie having a miscarriage on the beach, and other such "facts" that the magazine made up out of whole cloth.

Tricia and I spent Election Day with the Drown family in Rolling Hills. During the drive back to the hotel late that afternoon, Helene turned on the car radio. It was seven-thirty back East and we heard the first early returns from Connecticut and New Hampshire, which gave Kennedy the lead. It was inconceivable! Then Helene began to talk to us gently about the possibility that our father might not win.

Our room at the Ambassador was on the fifth floor, next to Mother's. The campaign headquarters and my father's suite were on the floor below. There was much running up and down stairs during the early evening, as Bill and Tom Ryan, Rose Woods, Bob Finch, Bebe Rebozo, and Jack Drown popped in on us from time to time. Then, by eight-thirty, despite the closeness of the vote, the commentators were predicting a Kennedy victory. When CBS reported that Kennedy would carry California "by a very considerable margin," and 92 percent of the California precincts had yet to report, with none of the absentee ballots counted, Mother became visibly upset. As time went on, she was less able to hide her agitation from Tricia and me. By ten-thirty, I wanted to go to bed. Mother tucked me in and kissed me good night, telling me that everything would be all right in the morning.

Tricia, who was holding up very well, spent an hour with the Nixons and the Ryans, who had gathered in a guest suite down the hall. At 11 P.M., 2 A.M. Eastern time, the big eastern states' results were in. The early projections of a Kennedy landslide now were called inaccurate, but Kennedy held the lead by a slim margin. Don Hughes whispered to secretary Bessie Newton, who was acting as an unofficial hostess in the family suite, that "the boss" was going to make a statement and wanted my mother and Tricia with him. As Bessie walked Tricia down the hall, only then did she realize how much strain the fourteen-year-old was enduring despite her outward composure. Tricia asked anxiously what was going to happen, and admitted that if she met anyone just then, she feared she would break down.

A few minutes later, Tricia, closely followed by Mother and Helene Drown, went into my father's suite. Tricia managed a smile and asked as casually as possible, "Hi, Daddy, how's the election coming?" He answered truthfully, "I'm afraid we've lost, honey." She could not help crying. Through her tears she said, "I'm not crying because of myself but for you and Mommy. You have worked so long and so hard."

For a few minutes my father was at a loss for words. Then he told Tricia and my mother that he thought it was time to go down to the ballroom to thank the people who had gathered for what they hoped would be a victory celebration. Mother reacted sharply. Exactly what would he tell their supporters? When he explained that he planned to say that if the trend continued,

Kennedy was the victor, she adamantly refused to go with him. They had not lost yet. Also, she had heard the reports from Texas and Illinois of ballot-box "irregularities" and voting machines unaccountably breaking down in key districts.

When Mother turned and left for her room, Helene followed her. As soon as the bedroom door was closed, Helene spoke frankly, "You've got to go with him." Reluctantly, Mother conceded Helene was right. But her emotions were barely in check. Just before she went back downstairs to my father's suite, she burst into the room where a three-man Secret Service contingent was waiting, men who had been with them through campaigns, Caracas, and the Soviet Union. She kissed the agents on their cheeks, and said, "I love you all." Then, as lightheartedly as possible, she added, "I guess I'll have to get a job teaching again."

At a quarter past midnight, my parents walked onto the stage of the Ambassador Hotel's ballroom. For two minutes the crowd cheered, two of the longest minutes my parents ever remember. Finally, the room was quiet and my father spoke. Pat Nixon looked out over the faces and saw people who had supported and believed in them for fourteen years. Some had given up time with their families, others had sacrificed to make a twenty-five-dollar contribution or a thousand. Friends were calling out: "Don't give up!" "Don't give up!" "You're still going to win." Many were crying.

Bob Finch was in the ballroom that night. Like Pat Nixon he had opposed making any kind of statement, because with every report he received in the last hour, the popular vote had narrowed. When my father began to speak, Bob cried openly. Mother caught his glance at the moment. Her face contorted as she tried to hold back tears. When Bob Finch told me about my mother's struggle to remain in control that evening, though it had been eighteen years before, he choked up when he said, ". . . your mom and I sort of set each other off, I think." My mother was always to dislike intensely the photographs taken of her during those moments of grief. The day after the election, the film clips were televised several times, and the reaction of many was that the cameras had exposed too much pain, pain my mother had not intended others to see.

Leaving the ballroom was a further ordeal. As the Nixons came down off the stage, friends and supporters grabbed and hugged them. My father spotted Beatrice Counsel Hawkins, his English teacher at Whittier who had taught later with Mother. She remembers he "had tears in his voice" as he patted her shoulder and told her, "You go home now and go to bed because that's where we're going."

I woke up at 6 A.M. feeling panicked. I called to Tricia in the twin bed next to me: What had happened? Who had won? Where were our parents? But she refused to open her eyes. A Secret Service agent in the hall told me my father was in his room on the floor below. Still in my pajamas, I ran down the flight of stairs and into my father's bedroom. I shook him awake, asking, "Did we win?" As gently as he could he explained that Kennedy was the victor.

He ordered breakfast for us, and we were joined shortly by Rose Woods, and then by Mother and Tricia. During the meal, my father went into the bedroom to take a phone call from Everett Dirksen of Illinois, the Republican leader of the Senate. Dirksen urged him not to concede the election and to demand a recount on the basis of massive vote fraud in Illinois and Texas. My father thanked the senator, but even as he hung up, he knew he could not keep the country in limbo, without a leader possibly for months, no matter how good his case. Although many more calls came in reporting cheating and irregularities, at 11 A.M. Richard Nixon sent a telegram of congratulations to John Fitzgerald Kennedy at the Kennedy family compound in Hyannis Port. The ordeal of 1960 was over, but the postmortems were ahead.

We left the Ambassador at noon to return to Washington. My grandmother, aunts, uncles, and family friends stood in the hallway outside our rooms to say goodbye. Mutely they hugged us. Then my uncle Don said, "Dick," faltering for a moment, "Dick, I hope I haven't been responsible for your losing the election." In the last weeks of the campaign, the Democrats had publicized widely a Drew Pearson story that falsely charged my father had used his influence to get Don a $205,000 loan in 1956 from the Hughes Tool Company for his restaurant business. Hannah Nixon had provided as security for the loan her one asset, a valuable piece of property that she subsequently lost when Don went bankrupt. Though my father had no part in negotiating the loan, or in his brother's restaurant business, for that matter, the story would continue to dog him politically until after his last campaign in 1972.

Tears came to my eyes and I put the book I was carrying over my face to hide the tears from the cameramen who were waiting in the lobby to film our departure. During the flight to Washington, my mother and father walked through the chartered plane to thank everyone for the magnificent effort they had made. Then the defeated candidate and his wife tried to rest. Jack Sherwood, who had been with them every step of the way during the campaigns of '54, '56, '58 and, finally, 1960, told me: "A campaign takes everything out of you and the loss is the final drain of energy, both mentally and physically. You're just empty, almost devoid of feeling, zombi-like . . ." Jack spoke of how my mother was perhaps even more exhausted than the candidate.

I could almost predict when your father would snap when the campaign pressures became too much and let off steam. But your mother did not show tensions at all. When you talk about a campaigner, she was it, taking everything, even the people at the stops who turn you inside out with their local problems, with the petty and innocuous. But not to reveal tension is harder, because when you come to the end, you are totally spent.

It was drizzling in Washington when we arrived. A loyal group of several hundred friends and Cabinet members, headed by John Eisenhower representing his father, let out a loud cheer when they saw my parents in the doorway of the aircraft. Not many words were spoken at the airport. Adele Rogers softly folded Tricia and me in her arms while my father, with Mother at his side, stood on a small platform in the rain and thanked their friends "from deep in our hearts."

Two days later, we went to Key Biscayne for a short vacation. Jack and Helene Drown joined us there. Rose Woods, Herb Klein, and Don Hughes were part of the group as well. Don remembers that everyone was numb with fatigue. Years later, as a three-star general, when one of his aides asked him what the 1960 campaign was like, he replied, "I've been through three combat tours and I've never been so tired—so mentally and physically drained."

The day after our arrival in Key Biscayne, my father told Don to go to the airport to meet a passenger. When Don asked whom he was to meet, my father would say only, "You will know." Don was stunned when he saw his wife, Betty, get off the plane and realized "the boss" had arranged the surprise. Marge Klein had also flown to Key Biscayne to be with her husband. The friends fell into a relaxed daily routine. Around noon they met for a swim, followed by hamburgers at my parents' villa. In the evening they tried different restaurants in Key Biscayne or Coral Gables. In Don Hughes's opinion, "It was not a wake. We were good friends, and together we licked our wounds and we had a good time doing it, and together we went back to Washington."

The day after Thanksgiving, Helene Drown wrote Mother:

> I do want you to know how very much it meant to us to come to Florida and even though we left so many things unsaid—we hope that the radar was working between us as it so frequently does. . . .
>
> Just because we won't be campaigning for the next eighteen years doesn't mean, I hope, that we will be far removed for too long. You know I've always been proud of you in success, but I don't think that we've ever been prouder of you than on November 8. . . . You've taught me a lot—not just about hanging up my clothes ready to wear from the closet, but about courage and unselfishness and loyalty. . . . So I guess that on the day after Thanksgiving, I'm thankful along with Jack for the friendship we've been privileged to have with a few "real" people—people like you and Dick . . .

Although my mother tried to make the best of what had happened, her spirit had been badly bruised by the election. Even the news that they had finally won their home state after California's absentee ballots had been counted brought Mother little joy. Officially, my father had lost by a paper-thin two-tenths of 1 percent out of a total vote of nearly 69 million, and he had lost in the face of unmistakable evidence of vote fraud. He had resisted the urgings of many, including President Eisenhower, who even offered to help raise the necessary money, for recounts in the disputed precincts. Mother also had spoken strongly for challenging the results, "just on principle." But my father rejected a recount. More than that, he tried to silence the divisive talk and articles about one. The first week in December he spoke to Earl Mazo, who had just published in the *Herald Tribune* the first four in a planned series of twelve investigative articles on the vote fraud in Texas and Chicago. Mazo's investigation revealed that in Texas, which Kennedy carried by 46,000 votes, a minimum of 100,000 votes officially tallied for the Kennedy-Johnson ticket were "nonexistent," and in Chicago, "mountains of sworn affidavits by poll watchers and disgruntled voters" in Wards 4, 5, and 6 were testimony to the cheating. Kennedy had carried Illinois by 8,858 votes out of 4,757,409. Mother has wondered ever since whether my father's early concession caused the loss of Illinois, since Republican poll watchers abandoned their vigil downstate, where returns might have offset the Cook County cheating.

But when my father met with Mazo he told him: "Earl, those are interesting articles you are writing—but no one steals the Presidency of the United States." Mazo recalls:

> I thought he might be kidding. But never was a man more deadly serious. We chatted for an hour or two about the campaign, the odd vote patterns in various places, and this and that. Then, continent by continent, he enumerated potential international crises that could be dealt with only by the President of a united country, and not a nation torn by the kind of partisan bitterness and chaos that inevitably would result from an official challenge of the election result.

My father had concluded that it would take up to a year in Cook County to examine the balloting; and in Texas, since there was no provision for a defeated candidate to obtain a recount, he would have to undergo months of partisan wrangling in the Democratic-controlled state legislature before the process even could begin. When Mazo heard the arguments, he realized Nixon was right and he informed the *Tribune* he was scuttling his remaining eight articles.

With the new year, plans for the transition from the oldest President to the youngest in history went forward. On January 6, Richard Nixon as President of the Senate presided over a joint session of Congress for the official counting of the electoral votes. A Vice President had announced his own defeat only once before, a century ago, in 1861, when John C. Breckinridge formally declared the election of Abraham Lincoln. The Washington *Star*, in a farewell profile of a woman whose activities it had covered meticulously for eight years, wrote: "Mrs. Nixon has been practical and a perfectionist and at times an extension of the Vice President himself. It has been said 'her greatest fault is faultlessness.'" The *Star* quoted a "close friend's" comment: "I think she is put together with iron and courage, not skin and bones."

On January 19, the day before the inauguration, even though Rose Woods and the other staff members had worked eighteen-hour days for two weeks trying to sort through hundreds of thousands of letters and organize eight years of files and memorabilia, they still were not completely packed and ready to vacate the offices. When Bob Finch arrived at our house with some important papers at nine o'clock that night, he was so tired he was "punch-drunk." My mother greeted him with the news that he must stay for dinner. "We're going to have some stew, and I have some bottles of red wine from Doug Dillon," she said with a wink. Eisenhower's under secretary of state, Douglas Dillon, now Kennedy's treasury secretary—designate, had not conspicuously supported the Nixon campaign. Bob remembers:

> It was a great evening. Pat was in a funny mood, joking about what the next day would be like, what an outrageous outfit she was going to wear, what she would say to Dirksen and Johnson, imitating their individual drawls, of course. It could have been a dour, sad evening, but it wasn't.

The next day, Tricia wrote succinctly in her diary:

> D Day 1961 January 20.
>
> Dear Diary,
>   Mommy and Daddy left at ten thirty for the Inauguration. They had a police escort. First they stopped at the White House for coffee. Then they drove down Pennsylvania Avenue to the Capitol where JFK was inaugurated President at 12:20. (Daddy should have been; he won the popular vote!)* Next they went to a private luncheon at the F Street Club. Julie and I watched the ceremony on TV. Bad day.

That evening, as Mother packed for a holiday in the Bahamas, my father decided to return to Capitol Hill for one last visit. In his *Memoirs* he described how he stood on the balcony that looks out across the west grounds.

---

*Tricia was discounting the allegedly fraudulent votes for Kennedy in Texas, Illinois, and Missouri.

The mall was covered with fresh snow. The Washington Monument stood out stark and clear against the luminous gray sky, and in the distance I could see the Lincoln Memorial. I stood looking at the scene for at least five minutes. I thought about the great experiences of the past fourteen years. Now all that was over, and I would be leaving Washington, which had been my home since I arrived as a young congressman in 1947.

As I turned to go inside, I suddenly stopped short, struck by the thought that this was not the end—that someday I would be back here. I walked as fast as I could back to the car.

CHAPTER 18

Home to California

The day after the inauguration, my parents flew with Roger and Louise Johnson to the Bahamas. Bebe Robozo was waiting at the airport when they landed. Louise Johnson remembers, "It was a time for regrouping. As your dad walked, you could almost see the wheels going around and around in his mind." But after so many years of schedules and not enough hours, the languid Bahama weather and the slow rhythm of life in the islands were almost too big a change, and after two weeks, half the time they had set aside, they flew home.

For my mother, the pace did not quicken much upon her return to Washington. She had decided that it would be too difficult for Tricia and me to change schools in the middle of the year, and so, while my father went on to Los Angeles to begin work in the law firm of an old friend, Earl Adams, Mother remained behind. She believes that in retrospect it was a mistake: "We waited seven months to make our new start—seven months in limbo."

Because my father was away, Mother turned down the few party invitations she received. Washington was different now; a new Administration was in power. Tricia and I were aware of the change even at school as children of Kennedy Administration officials enrolled in our classes for the spring semester. It was especially difficult for Tricia, then a freshman, who had to sit through high-school assemblies and hear speakers discuss the new President and, occasionally, our father.

In a sense, those months in Washington marked another turning point in my mother's attitude toward politics. Nineteen sixty disillusioned her beyond redemption. She saw a stolen election and could not understand why so many were indifferent. Gradually she resolved to channel her energy into the new life awaiting us in California and to reassure Tricia, who had left Whittier as a baby, and me, who had never lived in the West, that we would like our new state. She also had important decisions to make on our new home. Prior to her first house-hunting trip, she had joined my father for a weekend at a ranch in Arizona and wrote to us from there about horseback riding and their plan to go to Los Angeles to find our "dream house." But the dream house eluded them, and finally they decided to build their own in a new section of Beverly Hills called Truesdale Estates. The contractors promised a finished house in six months and plans were made to rent the home of movie producer Walter Lang in Brentwood until then.

We moved in June, and by the time we arrived, the pace had quickened. For one, my father signed a book contract to write his political memoirs, *Six Crises*, in his words, "probably the hardest work I had ever done in my life up to that time." Looking at his schedule for the six and one-half months before his deadline, it is apparent why the book writing was so hard: he was busy as "of counsel" (rather than member, so that he could undertake political work) with the Adams, Duque, and Hazeltine law firm, author of a syndicated column and several magazine articles, and major fund raiser for the Republicans, responsible for raising more than $2 million by December. At the close of the year he was "more tired than I had been at the end of the 1960 campaign." The one compensation was that all of his law and writing efforts the first year out of office brought him more income than his total earnings during the fourteen years he had served as congressman, senator, and Vice President.

Earl Mazo came out that summer for a few weeks to assist my father with recollections and research for *Six Crises*. "I had never seen Pat Nixon so happy," he told me. "She was so glad to be out of politics." That impression was confirmed as well by TV producer Paul Keyes, who became a close friend after the move to California. When he met my mother that summer he discovered she was "softer than I had expected. My image of her was from the angular, even harsh photographs in Caracas and during the presidential campaign. She was warm and relaxed and very unlike a woman who had known the highest echelons of power."

For my mother, it was a family summer. She gardened, enjoyed the California weather, and entertained a nonstop succession of houseguests for Tricia and me. In fact, the day we arrived in California, my best friend came to stay for a month since her family was going through a difficult time with the unexpected death of her grandmother.

My mother must be part child at heart for she always encouraged our exuberance and fun, even allowing us from time to time to subject her friends to small doses of home entertainment. When J. Edgar Hoover, who had been a frequent dinner guest of my parents in Washington, visited us at the Lang house, Mother sanctioned the performance of an "original" water ballet. Unfortunately, she had forgotten that the director had told her when they were in La Jolla in 1956 that he was desperately uneasy around water. At the announcement that we would all go to the pool for Julie's program, Hoover turned pale and began to fidget. Perhaps on his mind were the widely reported stories in Washington then of the Kennedy Administration parties where guests were thrown fully clothed into swimming pools. He asked nervously, "Now they don't have a trick like pushing you in the water, do they? You know I told you that water's the only thing I'm afraid of." The water ballet was performed without incident, however, and promptly the next day the director wrote me to say how much he had enjoyed the performance.

Despite the relaxed summer, it was obvious my father was not out of politics. By August, those urging him to declare himself a candidate for governor of California redoubled their efforts. Dwight Eisenhower asked him to run for the sake of the Republican Party in the state, cautioning that if he did not run, GOP leaders might blame him if the Democrats won California in November. Barry Goldwater warned that if he did not hold a public office his influence in the party would diminish greatly. And Len Hall went so far as to say, "Either you run or you're finished in national politics."

My father was torn. Whittaker Chambers had written him in February of 1961, only three months after his loss to Kennedy, "You have years in which to serve. Service is your life. You must serve..." But becoming involved in state politics was another matter. His tried to bide his time, to talk to more friends. J. Edgar Hoover voted "run." My father conferred at the Waldorf Towers with former president Herbert Hoover, who advised him to run for the House of Representatives, as John Quincy Adams had done successfully after leaving the Presidency; then, still in the Waldorf, with General Douglas MacArthur, who gave him the exact same advice. Rose Woods, Bob Finch, and several other trusted friends thought the race would be a mistake—and so did Mother. When others brought up the subject, however, she carefully expressed her opposition in a hypothetical, lighthearted way. Tom Ryan remembers, "Pat told me that if Dick ran for governor she was going to take her shoe to him."

Completely apart from her determination to spare Tricia and me the trials of another campaign, she had sound political reasons for opposing the race.

Although polls then indicated Nixon would beat incumbent governor Pat Brown, registration in California was two to one in favor of the Democrats. Most significantly, the Republicans in the state were deeply divided, with the ultraconservative John Birch wing of the party in favor of a state assemblyman, Joe Shell. She had no doubt that my father could beat Shell but feared the party would remain divided and that enough Shell supporters would sit out the election to deny a Nixon victory in November.

My father knew how she felt and delayed discussing the final decision with the family until two days before a scheduled press conference to announce whether or not he would be a candidate. My mother remembers:

> We talked about it for a while. Then we took a vote. You voted for running. Tricia and I voted no. Then Daddy said, very softly, "Well . . . that is life. You don't always win." He got up from the table and went to his room. You girls left too. But in a few minutes Tricia came back. She knew how dejected he was. She said to me, "If it means so much to Daddy, maybe we should change our votes, Mother."

When Tricia spoke, the image of my father walking out of the room slowly, and with such disappointment, flashed through Mother's mind. "All right," she said to Tricia, "you run upstairs and tell Daddy."

Tricia found him in his study, writing a statement for the press conference that would explain why he had decided not to become a candidate. When Mother came upstairs a little later, my father described in his *Memoirs* what happened.

> She sat down on the sofa, outside the pool of light cast by my desk lamp. Her face was in the shadows, but I could tell from her voice that she was fighting not to show her tremendous disappointment. "I've thought about it some more," she said, "and I am more convinced than ever that if you run it will be a terrible mistake. But if you weigh everything and still decide to run, I will support your decision. I'll be there campaigning with you just as I always have."
>
> "I'm making notes to announce that I won't be running," I said, pointing to the yellow pad before me on the desk.
>
> "No," she said firmly, "you must do whatever you think is right. If you think this is right for you, then you must do it."
>
> We sat for some time in silence. Then she came over to me, put her hand on my shoulder, kissed me, and left the room. After she had gone, I tore off the top sheet of paper and threw it into the wastebasket. On a fresh page I began making notes for an announcement that I had decided to run.

In her diary that night Tricia explained why she had changed her vote: "Tricia wanted Daddy to run because she thought that was what he wanted and that it was the best thing for the people of California and the world."

On September 27, at the Statler Hilton Hotel in Los Angeles, my father, with Mother, Tricia, and me at his side, publicly announced that he was a candidate for governor: "I have often heard it said that it is a sacrifice for men or women to serve in public life. For me, I have found it to be the other way around. . . . I find that my heart is not there [in private life]—it is in public service." What he said that day was true. But it is equally true that his heart was not in the race for the governorship. A few years before, he had told a Republican campaign audience, "Show me a reluctant candidate and I'll show you a lousy candidate." He would concede much later, "In 1962 I was not a good candidate. I had no fire in my belly."

Rose Woods, and Herb Klein and Bob Finch, with their wives, had dinner with my parents that night. Mother and Carol Finch ended up sitting side by side. Carol remembers the evening vividly because it was one of the few times Pat Nixon let down her guard. They were talking about the campaign ahead when, unexpectedly, my mother sighed deeply. "Carol, I'm trapped. Which way can I go?" She spoke for a few minutes about all the pressures on Dick to run. Then she said, "One of my big regrets is that in this kind of life, where people think you have everything and all the opportunities, the girls have not had more music and dancing lessons. I haven't had time to supervise or encourage them . . ." Before she could finish, the others at the table intervened and brought them back to the supposedly gay reason that they had all gathered for dinner.

I asked my mother once about her return to politics so soon after the presidential defeat. She explained to me that when a person feels there is something he must do, there is no other choice for him or for his family. Strangely, I found that a ghostwritten article that appeared in the *Ladies' Home Journal* that campaign year expresses her reasons best of all: "Well, Checkers, here we go again"—the voice of reluctance. "I'm once more a candidate's wife—and proud to be too"—the good soldier speaking. "How else can a wife and children feel if their husband and father is a dedicated man who desires to go on serving his country?"—overriding all, always the belief in her husband.

Before the campaign got under way in earnest, my mother remembers happy moments as a private citizen. In January there was an outing to Palm Springs to visit with President and Mrs. Eisenhower. We stayed at a cottage near the Eisenhowers' on the grounds of the Eldorado Country Club. While my father and President Eisenhower played golf, Mamie took us for our first look at fashionable Palm Springs with its small, elegant one-story boutiques, and, what seemed to us, endless blocks of hedges and trees shielding homes and golf clubs from prying eyes. Toward the end of our tour, the former First Lady suggested we stop for ice cream. Mamie, in a hot-pink dress and matching short cashmere sweater, slightly tottering on her two-inch spike-heeled pink pumps, led the way into a drugstore. The boy behind the counter had to take our ice cream order several times when he saw the customers at the counter were Mamie Eisenhower and Pat Nixon. At dinner, when my mother told the President about her day, he wanted to know if she had gone to a grocery store. He said boyishly, "I just go crazy in a supermarket. I have to hide the green stamps from Mamie so she won't know what I've spent."

On a previous visit a few months before, Mother had seen Ike's easel, which was set up in a corner of the living room. Mamie told her that he rarely kept the finished paintings: "Oh, he just gives them away. If the postman comes by and says, 'I like that,' Ike will say, 'Take it.'"

"Well," my mother had responded, "save the next one for me." So Sunday morning when we stopped by the Eisenhowers' to say goodbye, the President took my mother over to the easel and showed her two landscapes, one a lush, green meadow with a cloudless blue sky behind. The other painting, which Ike explained he had completed when "it was a hundred degrees in the shade," was of a white church nestled in the midst of some dark-red A-frame houses. Mounds of snow covered the rooftops and ground. She chose the peaceful snow scene, thinking we might never live in the East again.

Shortly afterward, we moved into our four-bedroom "dream house," as my parents always referred to it. It was all on one level, with white carpeting and large picture windows and sliding doors throughout so that the rooms were light and sunny. We have one particularly happy memory of the house high in the hills of Beverly Hills in which we lived so briefly: Manolo and Fina Sanchez, a Spanish-born couple who had escaped from Castro's Cuba only a few months before, came to work for us. At first they were in awe of the former Vice President and his wife, but the awe changed quickly into mutual affection and friendship. As the campaign commenced, it was a relief to my mother to know that she had two dependable people at home with Tricia and me during what she correctly predicted would be a bitter primary fight with Joe Shell.

For the first time my father was heckled by the right wing, and even after Shell's defeat on June 5, members of the John Birch Society, whose founder had declared Dwight Eisenhower to be a "conscious agent of the Communist conspiracy," attended Nixon rallies and did the Democrats' job for them by asking the difficult questions. My father publicly repudiated the John Birch Society during the campaign, overruling his advisers, who warned, correctly it proved, that the society's members would never forgive him and would not help him in the fall. Indeed, after the primary, Beatrice Counsel Hawkins, who had been active in all the campaigns of her former English student, found that the Republican headquarters in Montebello would not even allow my father's portrait to be hung because of their loyalty to Shell. She had to open her own Nixon for Governor office on Whittier Boulevard in a small real-estate building.

In our own way, Tricia and I felt the Shell candidacy almost as keenly as our parents. The majority of our classmates at the private girls' school we attended in Los Angeles came from conservative, wealthy California families who supported and, in many cases, were personal friends of Joe Shell, and when he was defeated, they were unhappy. Tricia and I might as well have been attending a school with an entirely Democratic student body, and we were not very successful in concealing from our parents how uncomfortable we felt.

Yet my mother campaigned throughout the election year as if she never questioned the wisdom of the decision to run. In 1962 she was scheduled separately for more events than in any previous campaign. The Nixon for Governor Committee had discovered that an appearance by Pat Nixon usually could outdraw one by my father's opponent, Governor Brown. Local Republicans throughout the state hosted Community Receptions to meet Mrs. Richard Nixon. My mother chose the title "Community Receptions" herself because she realized that her constituency included Independents and Democrats as well as Republicans, and she did not want them to be scared away by the idea of attending a partisan event.

Some of the receptions were held in private homes where the hostesses never dreamed that several thousand women would line up patiently for blocks to shake hands with Pat Nixon and have a cup of coffee. A Sacramento reporter, Mae Belle Pendergast, described my mother's visit to her city.

> Despite a chilly wind and a trip from Los Angeles in an unheated plane, Mrs. Richard Nixon could not help but be warmed by the Community Reception given for her Tuesday in Hotel Eldorado. Overexceeding the committee's dreams or even hopes, nearly four thousand women jammed the reception.

Mrs. Pendergast also described the kind of women who waited to meet Pat Nixon.

> There were young women, just becoming intensely interested in politics. There were older women, long the mainstays of their party. There were women from the Democratic party, there were Independents. All came to view a very gracious lady, and to pay tribute to her.

In the last weeks of the campaign, she averaged three Community Receptions a day and a rendezvous with my father in the evening for a rally and speech. Because of her predominantly independent schedule, however, she had very little contact with my father's staff. An advertising executive from J.

Walter Thompson named Bob Haldeman was campaign manager. Mother had met him when he did advance work in the 1956 campaign and saw him occasionally in 1960 when he headed up advance work for the presidential race, but by the end of the '62 campaign, she knew him only slightly better.

Her principal aide was twenty-one-year-old New Jerseyite Jack Carley, who had never been involved in a political campaign before and had never even been to California. In early September he had driven across the country and arrived unannounced at Nixon headquarters at 3950 Wilshire Boulevard. After explaining that he wanted to help, Jack was hired at seventy-five dollars per week and was told to go to the airport to pick up the candidate. "Of course, I said yes," Jack remembers, "but I didn't even know where the airport was."

By the end of September, Jack was spending most of his time chauffeuring for my mother and acting as her aide at meetings. Working so closely with her, Jack Carley came to know well my mother's political rules and her idiosyncrasies. He observed that Mrs. Nixon was very meticulous about her appearance. On one occasion when she wanted to change her gloves and the only fresh pair was in her luggage in the trunk of the car, "We pulled off the side of the freeway, with traffic careening by at sixty-five miles an hour. . . . I managed to break into the trunk with a screwdriver, since it would not open . . ." He learned that she liked to count political bumper stickers and was unhappy if she did not see many during the day, and that she always waved at the driver with a Nixon sticker. Mrs. Nixon did not like to arrive too early at any of her functions, because she knew that most people habitually arrived late. Jack frequently had to circle the neighborhood in order to kill time, and once he and my mother were caught. Their hostess was standing out on her front lawn waiting when she saw the car go by. She ran after them, trying to save Mrs. Nixon from getting lost.

Because of the fast pace of the campaign, Jack did not have many opportunities to talk to my mother at length. That is why he remembers so clearly the one time they did discuss her early life. On October 11, during a drive from Long Beach to a rally in Downey, Mother told Jack a little about her childhood on the ranch, about driving the Beerses across the country to New York, and how she had wanted a college education. She told him also that the greatest trauma had been the 1952 fund incident, and Jack remembers:

Her voice tightened as she spoke of the continuing personal attacks on her and her husband's integrity. She mentioned the frequency with which their personal affairs were reviewed and I recall a comment to the effect that the government was then examining their tax returns. As to why did they continue to run, my diary merely said, "Why run: belief in cause, in husband, his devotion . . ." Indeed, I became so engrossed in what she was saying during that trip that I drove right by the place where we were to meet her husband.

In 1962, Pat Nixon's role was to remind the voters of California that she was a California girl at heart, interested in the state, as was her husband. But many could not forget, or wanted to remind voters, that Richard Nixon—and his wife—were national political figures with perhaps national ambitions. As hard as my father tried to make "waste-free, low-tax state government" and more jobs the central issues of the campaign, "there was no morning, afternoon, or evening," as he wrote in his *Memoirs*, "that I did not deny that I was planning to use the governorship as a stepping-stone to a presidential candidacy in 1964." And every press conference brought questions about the personal attacks being launched against him, particularly questions on the Hughes loan to Don Nixon.

There also had been numerous stories about our supposed "palatial" new home, and when the *Herald Examiner* interviewed Mother just before the June primary, the reporter asked if it was partially financed by the Teamsters Union boss, Jimmy Hoffa. Mother had responded in dismay:

> I've never heard of a man in public life who's been attacked more than Dick. People have investigated him for years and years—to the point where our entire life is an open book. . . . That Hoffa story is just another part of the whispering campaign. Everybody knows that the Teamsters Union has endorsed Brown. How could they endorse Dick too? It's ridiculous. . . . In a way, it's kind of pathetic the way they've combed and combed his activities and turned up nothing. It's heartbreaking too because it's done with such an evil purpose.

She seemed to be giving herself a pep talk with her concluding comments: "If you know in your heart that you are right and you believe in the power of truth, you cannot be eternally upset by the things you hear every day. You just get on with the business at hand."

But the campaign was doomed. Pat Brown was well entrenched as governor, and on top of this, the voters perceived my father as running against Kennedy, whose popularity was on a steep rise. Then, suddenly, on October 22, what little chance my father had of winning the election evaporated. In his room at the Edgewater Inn at Oakland where he was campaigning, he watched President John Kennedy announce that the U.S.S.R. had deployed medium-range nuclear missiles ninety miles off our shore in Cuba. In response, the President called for a naval blockade of the island and the immediate removal of the missiles.

With that stunning diplomatic news, my father turned to Rose Woods and said, "Well, I just lost the election." He knew all attention would be focused now on the tense international crisis rather than on the state issues he had built his campaign upon. At the time, many Republicans, including Eisenhower, wondered whether Kennedy's response to the Soviets was politically timed. Almost two months before the President's dramatic speech, New York

Senator Kenneth Keating had warned publicly of the arms buildup, stating on August 31 that the influx of war material was "deliberately designed" to enable the Soviets to construct missile sites on the island. By October 10, Keating was warning from the floor of the Senate that he had confirmation of six IRBM launching pads under construction in Cuba. Yet Kennedy's action did not come until almost two weeks later.

There was no denying, however, the gravity of the situation Kennedy found himself in, and Mother was as aware as my father of the impact the Cuban missile crisis would have on the election. But the charade of campaigning had to go on. The morning after the speech, Jack Carley drove her to Long Beach. They were scheduled to spend from 11 A.M. to 1 P.M. at a coffee hour and then return to Los Angeles for an interview with Eric Sevareid at the Biltmore Hotel. Jack remembers:

> Without warning, Mrs. Nixon asked me in the presence of her hostess to remind her to leave at a certain time so as to allow enough time to make the Sevareid interview. I was baffled because there was ample time. I merely nodded assent dumbly. But I soon realized the reason for her request because, as I recorded in my diary, "Coffee hour was dismal and a waste of time." I noted also, "Mrs. Nixon looked awful, frail and thin today . . . my God, she could use twenty pounds." We made the Sevareid interview easily. In fact, we parked on the street and spent some time talking. The interview itself went well and I was surprised by the amount of work required to film it and later by how only a thirty-second spot of it was ever used.

When my father returned from Oakland that night, he and Mother discussed the probability of defeat, for they both knew there was no way to build enough momentum to catch Brown in the polls. My father felt Tricia and I should be prepared. But Mother was adamantly opposed: "The girls have to go to school. They have to live through the next two weeks. We can't tell them now."

On November 3, when we went with my mother to the last telethon, a recent poll had just been released showing Brown leading 48 percent to 41 percent. Jack Carley remembers that I asked him if we were going to win, and, as he confided to his diary, "Mrs. Nixon rescued me by saying that I had bet five dollars we would, which I had, but no longer believed in."

The day before the election, Paul Keyes, who had taken leave from his work as producer of *The Jack Paar Show* to help in the campaign, met my father at his law office for a lunch of carry-out Chinese food. Paul remembers his astonishment when his friend told him that he was so certain he would lose the election that, as soon as lunch was over, he was going home to prepare Tricia and me. In her diary, Tricia recorded what happened.

November 6 Tuesday

Today was the second saddest day of my life. The first being the 1960 Presidential election. . . . Last night, election eve, the greatest man in the United States of America told his family that it would be a miracle if he won the election for Governor of California . . .

Since early on the morning after the election the press corps had been clamoring for the defeated candidate. They were not satisfied when Press Secretary Klein came into the ballroom to read the Nixon concession statement. Klein went back upstairs to see if my father would reconsider appearing. He refused, and when Klein returned alone, there was an undercurrent of rumbling. Then Bill Stout of CBS called out, "What's the matter, Herb, is he afraid to come down here?"

My father, watching the scene on television, was furious. Impulsively, he decided to talk to them himself right then and there. When he strode to the podium, as he wrote in his *Memoirs*, "I had not had time to shave. I felt terrible, and I looked worse." He began his remarks by thanking those who had worked so hard for him. Then he congratulated Brown. But his memorable words were his closing comments on the press coverage of his campaign.

I leave you gentlemen now and you will now write it. You will interpret it. That's your right. But as I leave you I want you to know—just think how much you're going to be missing.

You won't have Nixon to kick around anymore, because, gentlemen, this is my last press conference, and it will be one in which I have welcomed the opportunity to test wits with you. I have always respected you. I have sometimes disagreed with you. . . .

I believe in reading what my opponents say, and I hope that what I have said today will at least make television, radio, and the press first recognize the great responsibility they have to report all the news and, second, recognize that they have a right and a responsibility, if they're against a candidate, to give him the shaft, but also recognize if they give him the shaft, put one lonely reporter on the campaign who will report what the candidate says now and then.

Thank you, gentlemen, and good day.

Watching my father on television in the den at home, Mother shouted "Bravo" at the conclusion. To this day, she does not believe that he made a mistake in expressing his frustration with the biased reporting.

We were waiting tearfully for my father in the hallway at the front door when he arrived. Mother spoke first. She said brokenly, "Oh, Dick." He was so overcome with emotion that he brushed past and went outside to the backyard. That afternoon was the first, and the only, time my parents gave way to their emotions simultaneously, and it bewildered Tricia and me. Mother lay on her bed, the room darkened by closed shutters, and cried in front of us for the first time we could remember. Tricia and I sat on the floor by the bed and cried also.

That evening Helene and Jack Drown took us to their home for a few days. When we returned, my parents seemed fine. My father told us he would like to drive us to school for our first day back since the election. There was not much conversation in the car as we clipped along the freeway on that dazzlingly beautiful sky-blue November day, the sun so bright it made us squint. When we stopped in front of the school and I started to open the car door, my father reached out and put his hand on Tricia's arm. There was something he wanted to say. "In life, you don't always win and it's difficult to lose, but you just go on. You go on with your head high."

Out of Defeat . . .

Time magazine's November 16 postelection issue declared, "Barring a miracle, his [Nixon's] political career ended last week." Just five days after the election, ABC had a special program entitled "The Political Obituary of Richard Nixon." Despite my father's request that we not watch, Mother, Tricia, and I sat through the entire painful thirty minutes. The panel of guests comprised Nixon friends Congressman Jerry Ford and Murray Chotiner; and on the other side, Jerry Voorhis, whom he had defeated for Congress sixteen years before, and convicted perjurer Alger Hiss, whose presence would evoke eighty thousand letters and telegrams of protest once the program ended. The tone of the broadcast was captured in host Howard K. Smith's coldly clever comment at the end: "Mr. Nixon has been referred to in the past tense so much in this report that we may forget that this is a political obituary and not a biological one."

My parents tried to make the best of what had happened. As soon as Tricia and I were out of school for the Thanksgiving break, they took us to the Bahamas for a holiday. Although our spirits rallied some, everyone was subdued. Tricia and I dreaded the return to California and school. And, though we did not realize it then, our parents must have dreaded it even more.

As far as my mother was concerned, the '62 campaign was best forgotten. My father, in dictating notes for his *Memoirs*, recorded, "After the loss in

1962, Pat never once said, I told you so." But the humiliating defeat, coming so soon after the narrow presidential loss, left scars. Once Tricia, in talking about the gubernatorial race, wondered whether our parents made too much of losing. I asked her what she meant, since they rarely had discussed it with us. She answered, "There was a sadness and the sadness went on for years."

Nineteen sixty-two brought the greatest change in my parents' lives since their marriage. No longer was Richard Nixon a viable member of his chosen profession of politics. He would practice law, but where? Tricia's and my immediate reaction was anywhere but California. My father kept turning over in his mind the idea of New York, where the preeminent law firms were located. Mother was enthusiastic about a move to New York, since it would be a clean break with politics. There my father would be without a political base and, in fact, in foreign territory, since his longtime rival Nelson Rockefeller controlled the state party.

In March 1963, they flew to the city to house hunt, and Ned Sullivan, the son of Mother's beloved Cousin Catherine, in whose home she had met Dr. Duke for dates, met their plane. Although the flight was delayed until 2 A.M., Ned sensed no fatigue in the Nixons, only elation to be back in New York. My father took him aside at the baggage area and confided that he had decided to join the old, established law firm of Mudge, Stern, Baldwin, and Todd at 20 Broad Street, which would become Nixon, Mudge, Rose, Guthrie, and Alexander after he was admitted to the New York bar in December.

In the morning, Ned drove them to Westchester to look at houses, but they did not see anything they liked, and Mother was not sure she wanted to be a forty-minute commute from the city. The following day they looked at a dozen apartments on Manhattan's Upper East Side. They were discouraged until the broker took them to the last one on her list, a ten-room cooperative at 62nd Street and Fifth Avenue. The apartment had a view of Central Park and of the Plaza Hotel. It was just the right size—four bedrooms plus a study for my father, a large living room, and a separate dining room. But it was in very poor condition. The previous owner had done nothing during her long tenure. Naked light bulbs hung from many of the ceilings, every room needed to be painted, and the kitchen would have to be redone completely. As they walked from room to room, the broker apologized several times, admitting that she had hesitated even to show them the apartment. But each time my father brushed off her apologies with the same comment: "Pat can make anything look good."

In fact, both he and my mother were jubilant that they had found something they liked. My father suggested that they walk the fourteen blocks from 810 Fifth Avenue back to their suite at the Waldorf where they would make plans for their bid. That morning he had been stopped numerous times on the street by friendly people and wanted my mother to know that when they moved to the city the welcome would be warm. Ned Sullivan remembers that they talked nonstop all the way about how they would change the apartment. At the Waldorf, Mother kicked off her shoes and sat down on the sofa to tell two friends who had come for a visit all about 810 Fifth Avenue. My father interrupted every few sentences to add more details. Ned could not help thinking, "They were just like two newlyweds getting their first apartment. Your mother sounded exactly like a brand-new bride."

After submitting a bid on the apartment, they flew back to Los Angeles that night. By the time they arrived home, a telegram reading simply "It's yours" was waiting for them. The broker had telephoned all eleven families in the cooperative that evening, even reaching two who were out of the city. Only later would my parents learn that among the tenants of 810 Fifth Avenue was Governor Nelson Rockefeller.

In early June 1963, we were ready to leave California. One of the most complicated parts of the move had been finding a home for our two cats. Tricia and I wanted them with people we knew, and when a former neighbor in Washington said she would take them, Mother happily made the arrangements to ship Nicky and Puff Ball back East. Two years later, when it was necessary to find another home for the cats, again Mother willingly arranged for a cross-country journey, this time to the Drowns', where Nicky and Puff lived to be nineteen and twenty-two, respectively.

When we said goodbye to California, I do not think any of us expected ever to live there again. We flew to New York for a few days before embarking on a six-week journey through Europe with Jack and Helene Drown and their twenty-year-old daughter, Maureen. It was the long-talked-about trip my parents and the Drowns had dreamed of ever since their days in Whittier. Together we explored the museums and palaces of Europe and Egypt and had plenty of chances to pause and enjoy what we were seeing.

In a diary I started on the trip, I described our exciting arrival in Cairo and how "Daddy, Mommy, and I spent a wonderful few minutes on the balcony at 1:00 in the morning and listened to the music and watched the Nile." It was the longest unbroken period my father had spent with us in many years and he learned quite a bit about his teen-age daughters. On my birthday in Florence, the Drowns teasingly had given me several Italian movie magazines. I noted in my diary the next morning, "I walked into the sitting room and found Daddy scowling and reading a movie magazine. He read one-half of it!!"

During one of the last flights, Mother and Maureen Drown sat together. Maureen remembers their conversation clearly, because, although she had known my mother all her life, it was one of the first times she and Pat had talked on an adult level. Mother told Maureen that the trip was a dream come true—she was with her family, traveling to far-off places. She also said that without parents, her early life had been difficult, and that now, on this trip, she appreciated every moment. She chose her words carefully and Maureen sensed no regret, only gratitude for the chance to have happy family times.

With our arrival back in America at the end of July, we settled easily into life in New York. Mother had planned most of the changes in the apartment before we took the trip, so we returned to rooms that were freshly painted and decorated. There were only a few details to complete, like the floor-length blue swag draperies my mother made for my room, and the identical ones in pink for Tricia's.

My mother relished being able to explore the city with Tricia and me. She did not seem to mind the necessary chore of transporting us around Manhattan, since even in the daylight many areas of the city were not safe. Indeed, I can remember that when Tricia went to the bus depot for a trip to Princeton to see a beau named Ed Cox, my mother and I took her by taxi to the terminal. Coming out of the building at Thirty-ninth Street and Eighth Avenue, we saw two big teen-agers beating up another boy half their size. When one grabbed the boy around the neck, he screamed in fear. At least seven cabdrivers sat in their taxis and watched. I wrote in my diary, "I was very proud of Mother when she told the boys to stop hurting the little one. She yelled at them and they let go. I was afraid they would attack us."

My mother, though still recognized occasionally, enjoyed more anonymity in New York than she had experienced since before the vice-presidential campaign in 1952. I described in my diary that fall how Mother and I had come home from lunch at Schrafft's, one of the nicer coffee shops in Manhattan, still laughing because "a woman came up to us and said, 'I'm sorry to bother you but I just wanted to tell you that thanks to you I've had three free cups of coffee.'" The waitress, anxious to get a good look at Pat Nixon, had kept refilling her cup.

From time to time, Mother joined friends for luncheon or tea, usually at the Plaza Hotel's turn-of-the-century Palm Court where violinists played. But more often than not, she avoided the round of ladies' social gatherings. She much preferred spending time with a small circle of friends, which included Kathleen Stans, whom she had known since 1958 when her husband, Maurice, became Eisenhower's director of the budget. Kathleen, vibrant and intelligent, was always taking a college course, enjoyed her amateur painting, and was an avid museumgoer. Most of all she had a delightful sense of humor.

At the end of the Eisenhower Administration, the Stanses had moved to New York, and in 1963 lived only two blocks from 810 Fifth Avenue. Kathleen Stans told me: "I had the feeling New York was a happy release for your mother. We never talked politics." But Maurice Stans had become convinced a comeback was possible for Richard Nixon the night he and Kathleen went with my parents to the 1964 New York World's Fair. At the Johnson Wax Pavilion, my father was so mobbed by the audience that not only was the next showing of the film delayed but my parents and the Stanses never got to two other scheduled exhibits and were one hour late for their dinner reservation. Maurice Stans told Kathleen when they got home that my father would be the next President. Ironically, earlier in the day, Stans had received a telephone call from an associate in the Nixon law office who asked that he and Kathleen not bring up politics in my mother's presence.

On Friday, November 22, 1963, Tricia and I were just home from the Chapin School, a private girls' school near Carl Schurz Park, and eating lunch in front of the television when we heard a bulletin that President Kennedy had been shot as his motorcade moved through the streets of Dallas, Texas. Within a half hour of that first sketchy report, my father burst into our apartment, just back from a business trip to the very city where the President had been attacked.

At 1 P.M. Dallas time, the President was pronounced dead. More than fifty reporters and TV cameramen surrounded our apartment and began a vigil. Who knows what they were waiting for. Ned Sullivan came to handle phone calls, and, finally, at 10 P.M. he took Tricia and me outside through the tradesmen's entrance in the back for a breath of air. In my diary the next day I recorded how Tricia and I sat immobile for hours in front of the television witnessing the tragedy of the mourning Kennedy family.

My parents flew to Washington for the funeral Mass and the burial at Arlington National Cemetery. Several weeks later, Jacqueline Kennedy, in response to a letter of sympathy from my father, wrote in part that she knew how he must feel, "so long on the path—so closely missing the greatest prize—and now for you, all the question comes up again—and you must commit all your and your family's hopes and efforts again—" And if the Presidency did elude him again, it was her hope he would "be consoled by what you already have—your life and your family—"

As the year ended my parents gave an open-house Christmas party. A friend carefully studied the guest list of a hundred and then dressed as Santa Claus to greet by their first names many of those invited. My father played Christmas carols on the piano, and former governor Tom Dewey and Monsignor Ahearn, Cardinal Spellman's assistant, blended their baritone and sweet tenor. The party was such fun that it became an annual ritual, repeated the next five Christmases in New York. Tricia and I also had Christmas parties for our classmates, and my father joined us the last ten or fifteen minutes to play carols by ear, always in the key of G. He tried also to play our friends' modern requests, and although he never mastered The Beatles' songs, which were popular then, he got everyone to join him in singing spiritedly the Christmas carols and old standards like "Hail, Hail, the Gang's All Here" and "Home on the Range."

That winter, my father was home for dinner more frequently than ever before. Rose Woods, who had become our unofficial aunt since all our family was in California and hers in Ohio, often accompanied him, coming straight home from the office. For her, those family evenings are her most vivid memory of our five and a half years in New York. The minute the elevator doors opened and they walked through the front door, my father would turn on any lights that were not already on in the living room and in his study. He always put a record on the stereo, and, in winter, lighted a fire. Within minutes the rooms would be warm and bright and filled with happy voices and the music from *Carousel* or *The King and I*, or Strauss waltzes.

On the last page of my diary for 1963 I wrote briefly about each member of the family.

Tricia... Seems happy and more cooperative and is interested in Germany, the Allies and World War II—especially the book *The Rise and Fall of the Third Reich*.

Mommy is pretty, sweet, unselfish, kind, understanding and her same self—if not better than ever—which is near perfect.

Daddy is nice and busy and seems happy. He tries hard to have a fun "family life."

With the new year, my father was involved in his law practice. The national political focus was on Barry Goldwater, who was systematically and successfully garnering delegates for a victory at the Republican Convention in San Francisco in July. The New York triumverate of Governor Nelson Rockefeller, Senator Jacob Javits, and Congressman John Lindsay showed no signs of softening their policy of excluding my father from Republican events in the state. He had told Roscoe Drummond in an interview given at his law office shortly after coming to New York,

I can say categorically I have no contemplation at all being a candidate for anything in 1964, 1966, 1968, or 1972. Let's look at the facts. I have no staff, I am not answering any political mail. I am only making an occasional speech, writing an occasional magazine article. I have no political base. Anyone who thinks I could be a candidate for anything in any year is off his rocker.

In July my parents, Tricia, and I watched the pre–Republican Convention special on television. The memories of the closeness of the election in 1960 and the ballot-box irregularities were strong, and at first my mother did not want to go to the convention; but something, perhaps her strong sense of duty to the Republican Party, changed her mind. On July 11, I recorded in my diary: "Mother now is going to the Convention. It is hard to say 'no' and explain. Anyway, I don't blame her for feeling a little reluctant to go—such memories."

In San Francisco my father introduced the party's nominee, Barry Goldwater, to the convention on the night he delivered his acceptance address. The Nixon talk was an attempt to unify the party in the aftermath of last-minute Stop Goldwater efforts by Governors George Romney of Michigan and William Scranton of Pennsylvania. The speech was one of the best of my father's career, an attempt to lay the groundwork for a conciliatory address by Barry Goldwater.

But the mood of the convention was combative. Nineteen sixty-four was the year of civil rights, but it also was the year of white backlash and unpredictable emotions aroused partly by the Kennedy assassination. Unfortunately, Goldwater's remarks that night confirmed the worst fears of the moderates in the party. Divisive and strident, he told the convention, "Extremism in the defense of liberty is no vice!... Moderation in the pursuit of justice is no virtue." My father remembers: "Pat and I were sitting together on the platform and almost automatically she began to stand up, but I had been listening carefully. I reached over and put my hand on her arm and we both sat there, not applauding. Goldwater had won the battle [for the nomination] and lost the war."

The 1964 campaign was the first since my parents had entered politics in which they did not have a direct stake in the election. Mother's limited participation in the campaign would not begin until Tricia and I returned to school in the fall. As my father went on the road for Goldwater and dozens of Senate and House candidates, Mother took Tricia and me to Europe for a vacation with Louise Johnson, who for the past two years had been living in England, where her husband had been assigned to the London office of Superior Oil. Europe was a good place for Republicans to be that summer, because it looked as if President Lyndon Johnson, not yet bogged down in Vietnam, was headed for a landslide victory. For four weeks we traveled, a good part of it via bus, through Ireland, Scotland, Belgium, Holland, and Scandinavia, all countries we had been unable to visit the year before. The trip was completely carefree and, happily, the combination of two adults and two teen-agers worked. My most lasting memory of the vacation is of Louise and Mother giggling.

The combination of a Mrs. R. Nixon and a Mrs. L. Johnson traveling together raised eyebrows at ticket and hotel reservation counters, and, in Edinburgh, Scotland, nearly panicked the American counselor. His driver had been at the airport on an errand and heard the rumor that Mrs. Richard Nixon and Mrs. Lyndon Johnson were arriving later that afternoon. When informed of this news, the counselor, accompanied by a military aide and a plainclothes detective, rushed to meet our plane. We were mystified by the official reception until, as we walked to our car, the counselor whispered anxiously in Mother's ear, "That isn't really Mrs. Lyndon B. Johnson, is it?" Mother could not resist the teasing reply, "No, it's the President's sister." The counselor's interest began to flag at once, but he did not know how to exit gracefully. Finally, he asked whether there was anything he could do for us while we were in Scotland. Again, Mother could not resist a little teasing and responded in a low, confidential voice, "Why, yes. We would love to have tea with the queen." The counselor hesitated and then offered three or four oracular explanations of why he could not possibly arrange such a meeting with Queen Elizabeth, who was vacationing at Balmoral Castle. For the rest of the trip we called Louise Johnson "Louise Bird."

That fall Tricia started college. After attending three high schools in four years, with her senior year as the only new girl in a close-knit class of thirty, Tricia was not anxious to move again. She chose Finch College in Manhattan, which offered a four-year liberal arts program, and daily commuted the sixteen blocks to college. She enjoyed Finch, was elected class president her junior year, and, as a modern European history major, was a member of the academic honor society.

As soon as Tricia began classes and I returned to Chapin, Mother went almost daily to the Nixon, Mudge law office. In answering the mail and the telephone, which rang incessantly at the office, Mother used her maiden name, Miss Ryan, and she did not reveal her identity, even to the insistent caller who demanded, "Well, Miss Ryan, I want to talk to someone close to the former Vice President." She worked long hours toward the end of the campaign, occasionally staying until ten or eleven o'clock. Some Saturdays, Tricia and I helped as well, and as I recorded wearily in my diary, even worked until six o'clock one evening. My father, meanwhile, undertook a final five-week swing through thirty-six states. Although my parents realized Goldwater had little chance of winning, they had both devoted years of effort to the Republican Party and neither had given up hope that my father's aid would help local candidates survive the Johnson landslide.

To the surprise of no one at 20 Broad Street or in the nation, on November 3, Lyndon B. Johnson became "Landslide Lyndon" with his overwhelming victory. His sweep caused the Republicans to lose thirty-seven seats in the House of Representatives, two in the Senate, and more than five hundred in the state legislatures. But in the midst of the massive defeat, my father was on the road to a comeback. Party workers would long remember his strenuous efforts on behalf of Barry Goldwater and hundreds of state candidates. No one could deny he had worked hard, as hard, in Rose Woods's view, as he had worked for himself in 1960.

The long hours in the air took a toll. In late November, on a business trip for the law firm to Japan, my father's left leg became very swollen toward the end of the exhausting twenty-six-hour flight. By the time he landed in Tokyo, he had to call a doctor. The physician diagnosed phlebitis, a severe inflammation of the veins probably caused by the preceding weeks of extensive airplane travel with his legs stationary and no regular exercise once he was on the ground. My father arrived home from Japan at 5 A.M. on Thanksgiving Day. He had been wearing an elastic stocking and the swelling had almost disappeared. He mentioned the attack only briefly to Mother and was so casual about it that they both put the incident out of their minds.

The Road to
the Presidency II

In January of 1965, my father for the first time since the defeat in 1962 rethought his political future and even began to hope that he might run for the Presidency again. He started accepting more speaking engagements. Between the Goldwater defeat in November of 1964 and the start of the 1966 off-year congressional campaign, my father would appear before four hundred groups in forty states and raise more than $4 million for the party. He also authorized Maurice Stans to set up a committee called Congress '66 to raise funds for travel so that he could campaign full time for Republicans in that important election. So much traveling and speaking were necessary because my father realized that without a home-state political base his constituency was the country. But the increased political activity, on top of his already demanding duties as a partner in a law firm of more than one hundred lawyers, inevitably meant there was less time for the family.

He began to urge Mother to go with him on his shorter trips to Canada or Europe, making it clear that he could afford to pay privately for the extra ticket. But as often as not she turned down the chance because she felt she should be home with Tricia and me. My high school was very demanding academically, and I spent four or five hours on homework nightly. Mother frequently typed my long term papers for me, checked out research books at the library, and made snacks of cocoa and cinnamon toast when I studied late. That winter, when I had a very high fever and flu, after seven days of lying in bed in a darkened room, I made an entry in my diary: "Yesterday evening M went for a walk with D. She hasn't been out of the house for a week because she's been taking care of me." During that illness, my mother read to me so I would not fall so far behind in my schoolwork. Because of my raging headache, we kept only one light on in the room, a high-intensity Tensor lamp. I can still see Mother's profile in the shadows cast by its harsh glare, and I can still hear her voice as she read so beautifully and movingly Tennessee Williams's play *The Glass Menagerie*.

With my father traveling so much, Mother had fewer social obligations and thus more time on her hands than ever before in her life. It was a void not easy to fill. When Carol Finch visited her in New York in 1965, she remembers that Mother took her to the Frick Collection, a small, exquisite gem of a museum with paintings, sculpture, and furniture all harmoniously displayed. Afterward, they talked briefly at lunch about life in New York. "After you've been in political life," Mother confided to Carol, "at first you try your hand at charity work, but it's not the commitment of politics. You know, I do get restless..."

That summer, the Nixons—all of us—were on the road. To celebrate their twenty-fifth wedding anniversary, my parents took Tricia and me with them on a sentimental return to Mexico. Bebe Rebozo—and a sizable contingent of the Mexican press—were waiting for us at the airport in Mexico City when we landed.

We stayed at the Reforma, the elegant hotel at which my parents' honeymoon budget had allowed only a one-night splurge, and my father planned the entire anniversary day, from breakfast in the hotel's beautiful Jardin Restaurant to taking my mother downtown to buy an anniversary gift. Lunch was at Sanborn's, a famous restaurant my parents also remembered from their honeymoon. For dinner, my father chose the Normandie, which had an orchestra, because he knew Mother loved music at restaurants. Bebe had ordered a cake with twenty-five candles. It was a festive evening, and when the orchestra played "More," my parents joined the other couples on the dance floor.

Later that summer we again left New York for a weekend in Massachusetts in the course of which my father unwittingly started a chain reaction that led to my decision to go to Smith College. Our destination was the home of my parents' friend William Bullitt, FDR's ambassador to Russia and later to France. As we neared Northampton, Massachusetts, my father, who was at the wheel of our rented car, pointed out that Smith was located in the town. My diary entry for July 16 records the rest.

We decided to drive to the Smith campus to see what it was like. . . . As we were driving out the gate, a secretary called out the window and invited us to come in! She recognized Daddy. I didn't want to and this was the general feeling of T, M, and me. D insisted that we go in and I am so glad that we did. (D says that we are all—including himself—sensitive and shy about doing things—one must force oneself or one will miss many opportunities.)

The tour that day included an interview for me with the admissions director. Soon, I began to consider the college seriously, and as I debated the decision, I discovered my parents were unenthusiastic about Smith. As with Tricia, Mother hoped I would go to a coeducational college like Stanford and "have some fun" after the dateless, one-school-dance-a-year life at Chapin. When I did receive word in November of admission to Smith on the early-decision plan, which meant I could escape the intense pressure of waiting for word of college acceptances six months before most of my classmates, I reported in my diary: "D had already left on a trip when I came home but M said he was happy I got in but not surprised. His other comment was 'fine. Now she can turn it down and go to Stanford or Northwestern!!!'"

At the end of the year, we flew to Key Biscayne for a week in the sun. Increasingly my father was depending on our stays in one of the villas at the Key Biscayne Hotel to restore his energy and spirits, and we all looked forward to the visits with Bebe with his sense of fun and eagerness to try new things. We particularly enjoyed going to Bebe's two-bedroom house on Biscayne Bay. A perfect day was reading in deck chairs on his lawn, occasionally looking out over the glassy calm toward the city of Miami, five miles in the distance, its skyscrapers just tiny white boxes. If it was warm enough, we took a morning and afternoon swim, always a walk on the beach, and finished the day with one of Bebe's delicious steak and Cuban black-bean dinners.

On Key Biscayne, life still moved at a snail's pace. By 1965, it had a second resort hotel, but that was all. The island remained half wild mango groves, half modest one-story homes, each with its yard of thick emerald-green grass. Though my parents did not drive in New York, they enjoyed renting a car when they were in Key Biscayne to go to the small shopping center for groceries or to look for beach clothes. And Bebe and my father particularly delighted in combing the drugstore for funny cards for birthdays and anniversaries.

When we arrived home from that Christmas trip, my mother caught up on her holiday mail. One letter was a thank-you to Bessie Newton: "We just returned home from a week in Key Biscayne where we went the day after Christmas. It was wonderful to escape the constant pressure which follows us no matter where! Of course, life would be dull otherwise." But the pressure was only about to begin. In 1966 my father would set his course, inexorably, on the road to the Presidency.

By January of 1966 my father had hired twenty-seven-year-old Pat Buchanan to help him with political speech writing and research. Buchanan, more conservative than his boss, had made a reputation for himself as a quick-witted, versatile editorial writer for the St. Louis *Globe-Democrat*. At 20 Broad Street, he crowded into the same office room with Rose, Shelley Scarney, who had helped with the 1960 campaign, and, quite frequently, "Miss Ryan." As befitted her shadowy background, Miss Ryan's desk was inconspicuously situated in a corner against the wall as one entered the office. Rose's was a few feet beyond, and on the opposite wall, near my father's office door, were Pat's and Shelley's desks. The din of typewriters and voices was constant, especially since Pat Buchanan, in his own words, "cursed and mumbled" in a nonstop, one-way conversation as he typed, and Rose spent more time on the telephone than off.

The four shared a camaraderie of hard work and friendship but had little time for small talk. Lunch was always eaten at the desks. As the afternoons wore on, Pat Buchanan, who was trying to quit smoking, bummed cigarettes from my mother, and Rose would occasionally describe her most recent conversation with an "old bat," her favorite description for the pest telephone caller.

As my father accepted more political invitations, he tended to gloss over Mother's reluctance to go with him on political trips. In a diary entry dated January 27, 1966, I described how my father and I "took a long walk along Madison Avenue" and agreed that Mother needed something to do. "... D said that we all have to contribute and try if we want to be happy. You must learn to accept things as they are and forge ahead."

Although Tricia and I were tremendously proud of our father's activities, we also had mixed feelings about politics. In April, when my father was scheduled to speak at Tulane University before a Republican fund-raising dinner, my parents invited Tricia and me to go along for our first visit to New Orleans. After a hectic two days of teas and dinners, under the scrutiny of the local press, I wrote:

> Tricia and I have secretly decided never to go on another political trip. It is a strain to be on show and entertain (so to speak) so many people. Yet next time D suggests a trip to an interesting city that we've never seen—I guess T and I will want to go. Anyway M worked very hard on the trip for us—she wanted us to have a good time.

As the 1966 congressional elections neared, my mother began to feel guilty about her frequent decisions not to go along on the political trips, actually wondering aloud at one point to Tricia and me during a vacation in Key Biscayne over the Fourth of July whether she was "a failure to Daddy." He must have been aware of the conflict she felt of wanting to help him but disliking politics. When he left Florida a few days before us in order to begin a business trip to Europe, he called every day, and when we arrived home in New York, there were bouquets of flowers waiting in my mother's, Tricia's, and my bedrooms.

A few days later, we all met in England, as planned, for the last part of the trip. His meetings with most of the European leaders reminded us that political life opened many doors. Before leaving England we had an eerie visit with billionaire Jean Paul Getty at his sixteenth-century estate, Sutton Place, thirty-five miles from London. My father was late arriving from a private meeting with Edward Heath. While we waited for him, Tricia, Mother, Bebe Rebozo, who was traveling as my father's unofficial aide, and I enjoyed a tour of some of Getty's extraordinary art collection, including works by Tintoretto, Titian, Rubens, and Renoir. Then we visited with our host in a cozy sitting room. Getty was seventy-three years old when we met him, a small, quick-minded man who was slightly stooped, as if burdened by his vast wealth. In the sitting room, Getty confided to Mother how tortured he was by what he termed "begging letters," which arrived for him by the hundreds every day. While my mother listened sympathetically, Getty became more animated and asked her if she would like to see the form letter he sent in response to requests for financial assistance.

He went to fetch one of the form letters, and when he returned, handed it to me and asked if I would read it aloud. It was a two-page, single-spaced typed explanation of how much of his income already went to charity, and of how, even if he liquidated all his assets and gave money to those who asked, he still could not afford to comply with every request. Reading the letter was painful, because it was so obvious that the man who spent hours composing it could not erase the guilt of dealing mechanically with those who appealed for help.

After visits to two countries my parents had missed on their world travels, Israel and Jordan, my father flew directly to Pakistan on business, and Mother, Tricia, and I branched off to visit Istanbul, Zurich, and the Black Forest of Germany. During the two-day drive through the beautiful German countryside, Mother made no mention that Kate Halberstadt had been born within a few miles of Frankfurt, the city from which we flew home.

That fall my father campaigned intensively on behalf of the eighty-six Republican congressional candidates who had asked for his help. Before Election Day in November, he would barnstorm thirty-five states. The killing pace seemed worth it. Lyndon Johnson's conduct of the growing war in Vietnam was beginning to arouse questions. During the campaign against Goldwater, Johnson reassuringly had promised he was "not about to send American boys nine thousand or ten thousand miles away from home to do what Asian boys ought to be doing themselves." Yet the President was committing American aid piecemeal to the war. In 1966, there were more than 300,000 men in Vietnam; two years later, there would be more than 500,000.

As early as January 1965, my father, long an advocate of United States involvement in Southeast Asia, had said in a speech in New York that the United States was losing the war because Johnson's limited-war policy left the initiative to the Communists. Following a visit to Saigon eight months later, he called for stepped-up air and sea bombardment against the North, convinced now that Johnson's emphasis on gradualism and negotiation in the face of bad news from the battlefield was just prolonging the conflict. My father realized that although most Americans supported the President's aim of helping South Vietnam, they demanded a quick resolution of the conflict.

In March 1966, at a hastily arranged meeting with Johnson at the White House the morning after the annual Gridiron Dinner, which both had attended, my father told the President privately that he felt stronger measures were needed against the North Vietnamese. But he also assured Johnson that on his recent trips abroad he had defended the foreign policy of the Administration and would continue to do so because America at war, even an undeclared war, had to be united in the eyes of the world.

It was his first time back in the private quarters of the White House since 1960. The two men talked in the President's bedroom. Johnson remained in bed throughout the visit. When Mrs. Johnson came in to say hello, wearing a bright-red kimonolike dressing gown, she simply got into bed next to her husband. Lady Bird inquired warmly about my mother and expressed the hope she would see her that year at the annual Senate Ladies Luncheon. (For eight years, however, Mother always sent her regrets to that invitation.) She also asked where Tricia and I were in college. In my diary, I wrote: "D said we were both in girls' colleges but that he'd preferred coeducation. Mrs. J. said that she had gone to a junior women's college for two years and that when she went to the University of Texas, 'It was like the whole world opening up to me.'"

At Smith a whole new world did open up to me that fall because of a political invitation from the Hadley, Massachusetts, Republican Women's Club. When the ladies learned that David Eisenhower, grandson of Ike, was a freshman at Amherst, and that Julie Nixon, daughter of Ike's Vice President, was a freshman at Smith, they proceeded to invite us both to speak at one of their meetings. Although I had not seen David since his grandfather's second inauguration in 1957, he called me to ask if I was planning to attend. He sounded relieved when I said no and admitted he was going to decline the invitation as well.

He must have liked the sound of my voice, because he dropped by my dorm a few days later with his roommate and we went out for ice cream. Two days later he unexpectedly came again. The girl on "watch"—the rotating job of signing in visitors—called my floor to give me the message that "some guy" was in the living room. I was in the midst of washing my hair and, since I was not expecting anyone, told her to explain why I couldn't come down. The tone of the brief note David left behind convinced me he was sure I had given him the brush-off. I did not even read the note until an hour after he had left, and when I learned he was the "guy" downstairs, I panicked. I wanted to see him again, but how? I called my mother for advice: "What should I do?" She answered immediately, "Call him up and explain." The phone call made amends. Within a week, on election night, 1966, he was back. We spent most of the evening listening to the returns and rejoicing. With my father's help, Republicans had won forty-seven House seats, three Senate seats, eight governorships, and 540 seats in state legislatures.

From that night on, we dated frequently. At Thanksgiving, David drove to New York to stay at our apartment and escort me to some holiday dances. We both came home again at Christmastime. Waiting for us was a Blum's chocolate cake, which on the last visit David had pronounced to be "the best in the world" because of its thick, chewy fudge icing. From then on, Mother made a point of having Blum's on hand and teases me to this day that I had a successful courtship because of the cakes.

After David's visit and Christmas at home, the family flew to Key Biscayne for a few days in the sun. My father did not discuss the possibility of a presidential race with us, perhaps because, despite the excitement he had generated by his successful role in the congressional campaign and the partial dispelling of his "loser" image, he himself still was not completely sure. The day before Thanksgiving he had authorized Maurice Stans to begin forming a low-key campaign organization but he told Stans that he would wait six more months to make a final decision on the race. Simultaneously, my father went forward with plans for four "foreign study trips" to Europe and the U.S.S.R., Asia, Latin America, and Africa and the Middle East.

Presidential politics was on our minds nonetheless that Christmas in Florida. One afternoon Mother, Tricia, and I sat together on the beach. It was a bleak day, the wind was cold, and we had on sweaters and beach towels tucked around our legs. My mother said flatly, almost tonelessly, that she could not face another presidential race. She spoke of the "humiliation" of defeat. It was apparent to us that she simply no longer had the heart to fight the battle that Churchill memorably described as "as exciting as war and quite as dangerous. In war you can be killed only once but in politics many times."

In December of 1966, only a handful of people believed that it was possible for Richard Nixon to win the 1968 Republican nomination, let alone the Presidency. And some of those who believed he could win did not want him to go through the effort. Bebe Rebozo privately offered his opinion that Christmas at the conclusion of a meeting in New York of potential Nixon campaign advisers: "I told him, 'Hell, no, I wouldn't get involved.' I felt it strongly. To me it was a personal thing. I didn't want him or the family to get hurt again. I'd seen what had happened in 1960 and especially in 1962. It just wasn't worth it."

As the countdown began in the election year 1968, overwhelming frustrations were building up nationwide over the war and the release of long-smothered demands by black Americans to be treated as first-class citizens. Johnson continued to escalate American involvement in Vietnam, yet at the same time he pressed forward with the Great Society, his massive domestic spending programs, in part to keep pace with the rising demands of the civil rights movement. Overlying all was a nationwide fear of crime, which had risen by 89 percent since 1960. The President was caught in a dangerous balancing act, and as the Johnson Administration unraveled, Republican hopes were astonishingly resurrected. Mother must have realized that slowly, irretrievably, my father was moving toward a second try for the Presidency.

As early as the summer of 1967, unspoken questions about the future lay between my parents. Although still the loving and concerned parent I had always known, busy making plans for Tricia and me and our college friends, who were in and out of the apartment, Mother was unmistakably troubled as she faced the prospect of another political race. At the same time, she was confronting the reality that her children were growing up and would be out on their own.

In August my mother flew alone to California to spend three weeks with Helene and Jack Drown. They talked several times about my father's evident determination to seek the Presidency, Mother always returning to the same questions: How could he possibly win? Wouldn't the fight for the nomination be a long and bitter one? Could the family stand another defeat?

From afar in California, Jack and Helene Drown had witnessed the gradual rebirth of my father's political career, which they could document in polls and news items. By the summer of 1967, eight months after his triumph in the off-year elections, my father had emerged as the leading choice among Republicans and abreast of Lyndon Johnson in the polls. Unbelievable, maybe, but the fact was that Dick Nixon was going to have a chance to redeem 1960 after all. How could Pat oppose him? They gently turned aside her protests that she wanted "peace of mind" and to "lead a normal life." They pointed out that she had left Whittier because she knew there was so much more in the world. Now that she was a public figure, could she deny that she was a woman who thrived on challenges?

In reconstructing those conversations for me years later, Helene explained why she and Jack were so uncompromising in advocating a second try: "I sensed strongly that Pat still had a deep belief in your father's unique talent.

She was sure that he alone was capable of solving some of the problems we were facing in the country then."

Only unforeseen changes in the nation could have accounted for my father's political rebirth. For the family there were significant changes as well that fall. In September of 1967 Hannah Nixon died. She had been in a nursing home in California for more than two years, the victim of a series of strokes. Even when she had visited us in New York in 1964 to attend Tricia's graduation from high school, she had been quite frail. Services were held at East Whittier Friends Church and burial was next to Frank Nixon in the Milhous family plot in Whittier. After the last prayer, as Tricia and I stood numbly in front of the grave and people started coming up to squeeze our hands or silently hug us, my uncle Tom called us aside. Without speaking he led us several yards from the gently sloping hill and stopped in front of two simple slab markers, almost buried in the lush grass. They read: "Kate Ryan 1879 to 1926" and "William Ryan 1866 to 1930." Tom said little except to explain that as he had walked up the hill to Nana's grave site a half hour before, he had realized suddenly that the area was familiar. After a few minutes of searching he had found his parents' graves. Before we rejoined the others, Tom said quietly, "Tell Pat."

Happier changes were in the wind. By Thanksgiving David and I had decided we would confide in all the members of our families that we wanted to marry before graduation from college. The Eisenhowers had gathered at the Gettysburg farm for the holiday. David simply confirmed what his parents, sisters, and grandparents already had guessed. Mamie Eisenhower's reaction to the engagement was uncomplicated excitement. She immediately produced the ring her mother had worn through sixty-three years of marriage and gave it to David. When he telephoned me from the farm to describe the diamond, he said it looked "like an old silver dollar." I had no idea what to expect. My mother cautioned, "You can't hurt his feelings. No matter what it looks like you'll have to pretend you like it." When David arrived in New York a few days later, I saw with unexpected pleasure that the old-fashioned setting of tiny diamond chips surrounding a larger "miner's cut" stone was exquisite.

My task of informing the family consisted solely of talking to my father since Tricia now knew as well as Mother. Daddy was in his den working to the soft sounds of a classical record and a fire crackled on the hearth as it always did in winter. I explained that in a few days David would bring me his great-grandmother's engagement ring. In his shy way my father seemed pleased, but he did not say much. Though I realize now he was at a loss for words, at that moment I felt let down by the subdued conversation and told my mother so. Sensitively she acted as a bridge between us. In the morning, I found a note slipped under my door.

Dear Julie,
I suppose no father believes any boy is good enough for his daughter.
But I believe both David and you are lucky to have found each other.
Fina often says, "Miss Julie always brings life into the home."
In the many years ahead you will have your ups and downs but I know you
will always "bring life into your home" wherever it is.

Love, Daddy

As 1967 drew to a close, my father faced a decision on the presidential race. On December 22, the day he later described as one of the longest of his life, he had lunch with his law partners, followed by a meeting with some of his still unofficial campaign advisers and then the annual Christmas party at 810 Fifth Avenue for more than one hundred friends.

His newest partner, John Mitchell, brought his wife, Martha, to the party. She had just been released from a private sanitorium where she had undergone psychiatric care and treatment for alcoholism. John had explained to my mother before the party that since this would be Martha's first outing since her hospitalization, he was very anxious that all go well. Shelley Scarney's initial glimpse of Mrs. Mitchell that night was unforgettable.

Martha was flying all over the place. I had never met her before, and I just couldn't get over her erratic behavior. The only time I saw her quiet was just as we were leaving. The elevator doors were closing and she was sitting in the living room on the sofa next to your mother, and your mother was talking quietly to her.

After the last guests had left, my father went into his den and wrote on a yellow legal pad, "I have decided personally against becoming a candidate." He gave as his reasons, first, he did not want the Presidency in order to *be* someone; and second, that losing again could be "an emotional disaster for the family" since the memories of 1960 and 1962 were still very painful. He wrote too that a good candidate must have five qualities: brains, heart, judgment, guts, and experience. He felt that he measured up to four of them, but he was not sure anymore whether he still had the heart.

In a diary I began a few weeks later, I summarized the turmoil my father was undergoing then.

Christmas vacation this year Daddy called Tricia and me in separately and told us that he had decided—almost definitely—not to run. He was very depressed. I had never known him to be depressed before—not even after 1962. He said that there was small chance of his winning. Furthermore he wondered if it were worth the "hell" of campaigning. He spoke of the incompetence, yet goodwill, of his organization. He spoke of the overwhelming obstacles against him: unfavorable news media, Rockefeller's money, the labor vote ...

On Christmas Day itself my father talked to all three of us about the race. Mother could not bring herself to urge him to run, but she told him she would help if he felt he had to make the race. Tricia and I, however, had decided finally that he should meet the challenge. I told him, "You have to do it for the country," and Tricia said, "If you don't run, Daddy, you really have nothing to live for." I wrote in my diary:

It was an awful decision for Tricia and me—and most of all Mother. I became reconciled to the idea over the summer. For a while, I just could not believe that it was really happening. I hate being pointed out. It really bothers me that people can't accept me as I am until I go through the sometimes long process of convincing them that I really am for real—and not a snob. David and I want to get married this summer. Since Daddy has decided to run, we can't. It would look politically contrived. The question of what Daddy would do with his life has been on my mind for quite a while. Tricia has been unable to sleep. I've gone through similar periods when I have just felt I had to know what was going to become of our future.

On December 28, my father went to Key Biscayne where he debated with himself "the most important decision of my life." By the time he returned to New York, he had decided he would seek the Presidency a second time. But not until January 15, when I was able to come home from college for a weekend, did we commit ourselves as a family, for it was as a family that we were undertaking the race. It would affect us all irrevocably. I wrote in my diary:

Rose was at the house when I arrived home. I'll never forget dinner. Daddy called Fina and Manolo in, since they are part of the family too, and asked Fina why she thought he must "do this terrible thing." She said that in the world there are few men that are born to do something and that D was one of them. It brought tears to his eyes and to Mother's too. Tricia said something very wise also. She said that no matter if we win or lose, it is still a victory for us all. I keep using "we" but, really, it was a decision we all had to make. Deep in my heart, I still think Mother is opposed to running but at least she is reconciled now ...

The Campaign of 1968

The mood of the country as 1968 was ushered in was volatile, with anger so close to the surface that it exploded into violence not once but many times before Election Day: two political assassinations; race riots engulfing the major cities; obscenity-shouting antiwar student protesters; and a President who was finding it all but impossible to command enough support and respect to deal with the problems at home or the war abroad. Lyndon Johnson could now go few places without confronting demonstrators frustrated by the endless war who chanted: "Hey, hey, LBJ, how many kids did you kill today?" By all reports, the Secret Service kept packed suitcases in the basement of the White House because the President often would give no more than an hour's advance notice of a trip. Someone had to bring direction and order out of the chaos as the 1960s were drawing to an end. Pat Nixon believed her husband was the man.

It took courage to re-enter public life as spiritedly as she did. She had no illusions about campaigns or Washington; no confidence that success lay at the end of the rainbow. She knew her husband was bucking history by running. If he won, he would be the only presidential candidate to have been defeated, denied renomination four years later, and then succeeded in recovering sufficient political strength to win on the second bid. His strategy had to be to nullify his "loser" image, and that meant capturing the majority of votes in every Republican primary that spring. In the months ahead, my mother would be at his side as they campaigned, and won decisively, in New Hampshire, Nebraska, Wisconsin, and Oregon.

On January 31, my father announced his candidacy by mailing a letter to every registered voter in New Hampshire: ". . . For these critical years, America needs new leadership." The announcement was a minor item on the front page of *The New York Times*, overshadowed by bold headlines about the opening of the North Vietnamese Tet offensive, which would further shatter domestic support for Johnson's war policy.

On February 2, my father made his first appearance in New Hampshire at a press conference at the Holiday Inn in Manchester. That day an unusually dense fog throughout New England closed all the airports. Mother and Tricia were supposed to be in New Hampshire at 5 P.M. for a press reception but arrived hours late. They had left Manhattan at noon in a rented limousine with Ned Sullivan and Bebe Rebozo, who had flown up from Florida for the campaign kickoff. Even as they pulled away from 810 Fifth Avenue, a light rain mixed with snow was falling.

At eleven o'clock that morning, I had received word from my father's aide Dwight Chapin that because of the fog my flight to New Hampshire was grounded. Since he knew I did not have a license, he asked if David or another friend could drive me there. Fortunately, I was able to reach David at noon; he picked me up and we arrived in Manchester with less than a half hour to spare.

David's unscheduled presence raised a small problem. His grandfather, as he had in 1964, was maintaining a preconvention policy of neutrality. My father was worried that the press would write that David, by attending the reception, was trying to imply the general's support. But if the media learned David had driven me to Manchester and then not stayed for the Nixon party, it would imply a lack of support on Eisenhower's part. So he went to the press gathering and was quietly baptized into the presidential campaign. The reception was well attended by representatives of the national and local press and went smoothly. When Mother and Tricia arrived at the tail end of the reception, the family all had dinner together. That night at the New Hampshire Highway Inn, which was almost completely taken over by Nixon campaign staff, the Nixon advance man gave David a room a respectable twelve-minute walk from mine. (When David came to pick me up in the morning for breakfast, he timed it.)

The race was under way, and until Election Day we campaigned with barely a pause. Mother, as she had in 1960, planned to travel almost exclusively with my father. Tricia, about to turn twenty-two, and David and I, both nineteen, would have our own schedules, which took us to many of the smaller towns and cities in more than thirty states. The issue of David's grandfather's support, however, would remain a prickly one until July 18, just a few weeks before the Republican nominating convention, when he broke his own rule of preconvention neutrality by endorsing my father. Eisenhower was biding his time because, in the wake of the Goldwater debacle, he desperately wanted a candidate who could win; the primaries would be a test not only of my father but also of the other contenders.

Mamie Eisenhower, like David, was an avowed Nixon partisan from the beginning. After Ike suffered his third major heart attack in April of 1968, she campaigned from her tiny bedroom next to his suite at Walter Reed Army Hospital. Doctors, nurses, orderlies, and all visitors were handed a Nixon for President button from a glass bowl Mamie kept by her favorite chair. She herself habitually wore a large button on her dress. Her warmhearted personal campaign touched my mother, and during the next few years their friendship flourished and deepened as never before.

Early endorsement or not from the general, both he and Mamie welcomed me as a prospective member of the family. In February Mamie had sent me a Valentine's Day card with the message, "Please call me 'Mimi' like David does for we consider you one of our family." She kept reminding me that she was heartily in favor of an early marriage, and by summer, each time I saw the general, he would ask, always with a smile, "Well, when are you going to become an Eisenhower?" David kept his grandfather informed of his campaign activities and the former President offered sound, old-fashioned advice— "Always take your subject but never yourself seriously"—and political commentary. On February 21 he wrote David:

Of course I have been listening over the past twelve years to some of those whiners saying "I don't like Nixon" or "Dick can't win." Most of these same people will concede that Dick is the best-prepared man for the Presidency of anyone in the United States. When they express this sort of ambivalent attitude to me, I answer, "Well, if you are convinced that he is the best qualified then why don't you take off your coat, roll up your sleeves, and go to work for what you believe is best for the U.S.A." . . .

Just one week later, my father was denied the opportunity in New Hampshire to beat his only declared opponent, Governor George Romney of Michigan. Romney's sudden withdrawal from the race because of his low standing in the polls was a disappointment for my parents, who had wanted a clear-cut victory. But they pressed on, visiting factories, schools, and shopping centers. For Pat Nixon, 1968 was her eighth campaign. The political pace was so much a part of her blood that occasionally she forgot that it was a challenge for us to keep up the stride. She had spent so many years on the road that she was relaxed even during the deadliest hour in politics: the one between 6:30 and 7:30 A.M. in a nondescript hotel room when all the luggage has been picked up to be preloaded on the plane and when you wish you could go back to bed but instead have to be dressed, with makeup on, and have to sit carefully to preserve the "well-groomed look" for the remainder of what will surely be a long day.

At age fifty-six, my mother's energy seemed undiminished. During the rare weekends off, which periodically dotted the campaign, she thought nothing of working when it was necessary. I noted in my diary during a three-day stay in Key Biscayne after the New Hampshire primary: "M got out about fifty-five letters today. [All handwritten.] She really worked hard."

Because campaigning involves giving so much of oneself—meeting people, listening to them, responding to them, with most of the exchanges in the spotlight of the press—my mother sought increasingly to preserve a core of privacy when interviewed. She kept the focus on the Nixon programs and on the volunteers. When she was asked about her childhood, invariably she recited two or three unchanging stories: her father bringing her a strawberry ice cream cone, raising a prizewinning 4-H pig. Only occasionally in her carefully phrased answers did she reveal glimpses of herself, perhaps most poignantly when she told a reporter, "Life was sort of sad, so I tried to cheer everybody up. I learned to be that kind of a person." And one of the most candid comments among the thousands she made that year was her response to the question, "What is your greatest contribution to your husband?" She had answered simply, "I don't nag him. The best I can [do] is cheer him up."

On March 12, New Hampshire primary day, the Democratic race for the Presidency changed dramatically. Senator Eugene McCarthy, running as an anti–Vietnam War candidate, surprised Lyndon Johnson and many political observers by winning 42.4 percent of the Democratic vote. Four days after McCarthy's strong showing, Robert Kennedy, assured now that Johnson was vulnerable, entered the race. We heard the Kennedy news in Portland, Oregon, where we were spending the weekend campaigning. Years later, Pat Buchanan told me that as soon as Bobby Kennedy declared, he noticed fear among the Nixon staff members who remembered the 1960 campaign. He personally felt that Kennedy would be the easiest to beat, but those who had lived through the election eight years before had memories too vivid to be able to look at the situation rationally.

Despite their unease in the next few weeks, the Nixon staffers could not deny that my father's campaign was going well with large, enthusiastic crowds at every meeting. The crucial Oregon primary was not until the end of May, and my parents were dividing their time between that state and Wisconsin, where on April 2 voters would go to the polls. The entire family was in Milwaukee for a large handshaking reception on March 31, David's twentieth birthday. On board the flight back East, we ate sandwiches and a birthday cake.

The plane landed first at Bradley International Airport, in Connecticut, so that David and I could pick up his car for the drive back to Massachusetts and college. My parents and Tricia then went on to New York. At La Guardia Airport, Pat Buchanan rushed on board the Lear jet before anyone could deplane. He had astonishing news: President Johnson had announced at the end of his scheduled speech on Vietnam that he would not be a candidate for the Presidency in November. He had given as his reason the need to devote every ounce of energy to his job and particularly to the war in Vietnam. But it was a fair assumption that Johnson feared he could not win his own party's nomination.

Overnight it appeared Robert Kennedy would be my father's opponent after all. We soon crossed paths with Kennedy staffers in the lobby of Portland's Benson Hotel, where, despite political persuasions, all the candidates stayed. We took it for granted as well that at the airport the Nixon and McCarthy chartered prop Electras would be lined up next to the lone, sleek Kennedy jet.

But, as would be true throughout the election year, our focus on the political competition was abruptly overshadowed by a new shock. Only four days after Lyndon Johnson's bombshell announcement, Martin Luther King, Jr., was assassinated in Memphis, Tennessee. In the aftermath, there was rioting in more than one hundred cities, and in Washington, there were fires and violence at times as close as six blocks from the White House. Nationwide the disturbances left more than thirty dead.

On April 30, within a month of Johnson's surprise announcement and Dr. King's death, the complexion of the presidential race changed again as Nelson Rockefeller declared his candidacy. For three months, Rockefeller had carefully avoided subjecting himself to possible defeat in the primaries, all the while openly planning strategy with his supporters. Simply by looking out our fifth-floor windows we could observe some of his "noncampaign" efforts. I remember particularly a meeting at the Rockefeller apartment a month before his announcement. A few of my father's supporters had put Nixon signs on the trees across the street from 810 and 812 Fifth Avenue. When the police removed the signs, Manolo and Fina decided to take action. My mother found some Nixon buttons and we decorated an umbrella in red, white and blue. Fina held it aloft and paraded with Manolo and our two dogs in front of the entrance to 812, while Mother, Tricia, and I observed the scene from our fifth-floor vantage point.

A sense of humor was an important ingredient in the scramble of the primary campaigns. Because the staff was small and the budget tight, duties overlapped and everyone helped one another. We shared a sense of adventure and many inside jokes. The staff, and Mother as well, occasionally referred to the candidate as Mr. Warshank, a title dating from early in the campaign when an inexperienced advance man booked my father into a hotel under the name of one of the Nixon, Mudge law partners. At the next airport arrival, several staff members had rushed off the plane first and begun to chant, "We want

Warshank, we want Warshank." The intimacy and personal excitement of the goal everyone was working toward was captured by one of the stewardesses on my parents' chartered plane in Madison, Wisconsin. She had greeted the passengers with the words, "On behalf of your crew and North Central Airlines, I would like to welcome you to the next portion of your flight to the White House."

But what had been an adventure shared by a small, intimate staff was evolving into a serious bid for the Presidency of the United States. The night of the Oregon primary victory, Bob Haldeman joined the Nixon staff and rapidly the hectic but intimate atmosphere of the primaries acquired a businesslike, no-nonsense tempo. Hobart Lewis, a personal friend of the family who traveled with the Nixon campaign whenever he could squeeze time from his job as an executive editor of the *Reader's Digest*, spent three days with the staff shortly after Haldeman became chief of staff. Once home, he brooded for forty-eight hours before finally telephoning Rose Woods to ask bluntly, "What's happened? The fun's gone."

At forty-one, trim, highly intelligent, and a practicing Christian Scientist, Bob Haldeman demanded much of people. Shelley Scarney remembers that "though he was terribly good at organization, Bob lacked the human quality of making people want to work for him. The abrupt, threatening phone calls if things were not done quickly were a matter of course, even for unimportant reasons." In Pat Buchanan's opinion, "We became sort of a corporate structure, and access to the boss and senior staff members was denied." The change that Buchanan worried about more than any other was that the easy relations with the press ceased.

Haldeman had specific ideas on how to wage a successful campaign. He rejected the 1960 strategy of trying to reach people by making hundreds of speeches and shaking thousands of hands, contending that such efforts were exhausting and ineffective. He had advocated instead in a June 1967 memo a schedule that allowed the candidate "time to think, to study his opponent's strategy and statements, to develop his own strategy and statements." Television coverage of the 1968 campaign was unprecedented in presidential politics, and my father's schedule accordingly placed heavy emphasis on getting the most effective television exposure.

My father had been stung by all the postmortems criticizing his campaign strategy in the 1960 race against Kennedy. In *Six Crises* he reflected: "A candidate must save himself for the major events and his staff must never forget this." Saving himself meant keeping free from petty concerns and stress, free from unnecessary intrusions from his staff. Bob Haldeman would provide the right atmosphere for thinking and planning.

When my mother and Bob Haldeman met again in June 1968, they were little more than casual acquaintances due to Mother's almost entirely separate schedule during the gubernatorial campaign. Apart from his advance work in

1956 and 1960, Haldeman had been on the periphery during the vice-presidential days, and thus underestimated my mother as a political asset. At a rally soon after he became chief of staff, she was not introduced, and at the next rally, the same thing happened. Since Bob provided the local Republican organizations with exacting details on how to run a Nixon rally, Mother could only assume the oversight was Haldeman's. My father noticed also and gave orders that it not happen again.

In early June, fast on the heels of Bob Haldeman's arrival, the campaign underwent another major change when my parents were assigned round-the-clock Secret Service protection. The family had gathered at our New York apartment on June 4 to watch the televised results of the California Democratic primary battle between Senators Robert Kennedy and Eugene McCarthy. At 2:30 A.M., when it was clear Kennedy had won a modest victory, everyone went to bed except David. About forty-five minutes later he woke us up with the incredible news that Kennedy had been shot as he left the ballroom of the Ambassador Hotel where he had just delivered his victory speech. First reports indicated a thigh wound, but as the early-morning hours wore on, news bulletins revealed that a bullet was lodged in his brain and that Robert Kennedy's life was ebbing away. On June 6, a little more than twenty-four hours after the attack, he died.

From June 5 on, the Secret Service protection ordered immediately for all candidates and their wives by Lyndon Johnson was a constant reminder of the madness of the year. When my father kept a commitment to speak at Tricia's graduation from Finch College shortly after Robert Kennedy's death, he walked down the main aisle of the church garbed in black cap and gown like the others in the procession, but with an agent within touching distance of him.

One of the agents, Chuck Rochner, who was destined to remain on the Nixon detail the next six years assigned to various members of the family, remembers that security for my father "was as tight as what you'd find at the White House. Crowds were unlike anything we had experienced before. No matter where we went, we had demonstrators. It was a very tense time for us because of the unpredictability of the groups, particularly the splinter groups."

Because Tricia and I were so active in the campaign, protection was extended to us as well when on political trips. Spur-of-the-moment activities became almost impossible since we were expected to let the agents know our plans in advance. An all-seeing presence could not help but note what we ate, who we saw, and what we did and said except in the privacy of our own home or in the homes of friends. Tricia's first date to arrive at the apartment after the Secret Service began its vigil was the friend of a friend, a blind date. Unfortunately, before he took the elevator upstairs, he was frisked. The agents so unnerved him he could barely speak the entire evening, and it was not until years later Tricia learned the cause. For Tricia and me, Secret Service protection set us apart from others. Suddenly, I was more glad than I had ever thought possible that I had decided to take the fall semester off from Smith where I already was an oddity on the overwhelmingly—and passionately—pro-McCarthy campus.

In the spring both David and I had juggled full course loads and campaigning. By summer, I found the political pace so fast it was difficult for me to keep up even my diary. I stopped writing just before the Republican Convention and did not resume until a week before the election. July was the last full month of political work before the convention. On July 18, from his bed at Walter Reed, President Eisenhower issued his statement endorsing my father: "The issues are so great, the times so confusing, that I have decided to break personal precedent and speak out to endorse a presidential candidate prior to the national convention. . . ." He sent a copy of the statement to my father, and wrote with a thick, black felt-tip pen across the top: "Dear Dick—This was something I truly enjoyed doing—DE."

The endorsement was extremely well timed and helped burst the bubble of Nelson Rockefeller's well-financed postprimary blitz. But there was still the possibility that if Ronald Reagan also declared himself a candidate, as many expected him to do, he and Rockefeller could deadlock the convention and prevent a Nixon first-ballot victory. And on August 5, the day of the opening gavel of the Republican National Convention in Miami Beach, Reagan announced his bid.

My parents had arrived at the resort city the same day and were lodged in the penthouse of one of the city's skyscraper hotels where the air conditioning would not budge from below sixty degrees despite the efforts of the management. Because room service was overtaxed, our food orders usually arrived *after* we had left for one of our events. By the end of the four days in Miami, I had a hundred-and-three-degree fever and strep throat.

On the eve of a narrow victory, we were existing on three levels: the daily battle to stay alive in the hotel; our forays into the dazzlingly hot sun of Miami Beach with its tourists in loud shirts and the shortest of mini-skirts, the yachts and other boats shimmering on the bright-blue water; and the world far removed from Miami—the reason we were there—the world of urban decay and violence, and of Americans fighting a war in Southeast Asia thousands of miles away.

On nomination night, August 7, the family, joined by Rose Woods, Bob Haldeman, Pat Buchanan, and staffers Ray Price, Dwight Chapin, and Len Garment, placed bets on how many votes Rockefeller and Reagan would get. Most of us in the room were jubilant when the past six months of hard work brought a first-ballot victory. In contrast, Mother was subdued. Burned by her overconfidence in 1960, she was taking each day of the campaign as one simply to get through until the final test—and that August, she saw many,

many days ahead. And she saw as well the enormous problems my father would be dealing with if elected.

My father accepted the Republican presidential nomination for the second time on August 8, and the following morning the family flew to California. Tricia and I had agreed to a full schedule of appearances on local talk shows and at press interviews in the northern part of the state immediately following the convention. Since I still had a fever from the strep throat, Mother gave up a rest with my father in San Diego in order to substitute for me. The trip went well, but my mother did not enjoy going from station to station for the television interviews and being asked virtually identical questions. She felt artificial when she gave the same responses, and thus had the self-imposed pressure of trying to answer in a fresh way each time. Nor did she have enough "show biz" inside her to try to use the camera to her advantage rather than react to it. Throughout the campaign and indeed to the end of the White House years, she would never feel completely at ease during television interviews, and for this reason few filmed interviews with her exist. My father was not a full-fledged television-era politician either. As President, he did not try to master the then relatively new Tele-Promp-Ter, explaining to me, "I just wouldn't have felt comfortable with it."

My mother much preferred her old tried-and-true campaign methods of encouraging volunteers and talking directly to people. To one reporter she explained that she was a volunteer, the eyes and ears of the women voters— "I fill him in on what women think. They are thinking peace at home and peace abroad." She avoided policy statements, telling correspondent Vera Glaser of the North American Newspaper Alliance, "I don't think one person can speak for another. The candidate should speak for himself." Repeatedly, she declared that individuals could make a difference:

> Get involved. Instead of complaining, go to work. People should participate in local political groups. Each community has some kind of organization in which it is possible to become active. Work for a candidate whom you believe to be qualified—they are the ones who can take a problem to the top. Indicate interest to your Congressman or Senator.

That philosophy—the individual can change the quality of life—would be the theme of her White House years.

A few weeks after the Republican Convention, the Democrats met in Chicago and, in an atmosphere of violence, nominated Hubert H. Humphrey, Johnson's Vice President, as their standard-bearer. In his memoir of the Presidency, Lyndon Johnson wrote starkly about that week in Chicago.

... Fighting between police and students at the Democratic National Convention in Chicago proved to every television viewer in America how deep the cleavage was in our society, how intense the hatreds, and how wide the gulf between law enforcers and those who had nothing but contempt for the law. These conflicts also exposed the ugly side of the so-called new politics, in spite of its claim of idealism.

Johnson was one of those who saw the proceedings and scenes of street fighting on television, because he was unable to attend his own party's convention for fear of even greater disruption. All week the major antiwar group in the country, the National Mobilization Committee to End the War in Vietnam, staged demonstrations for peace, at times provoking violent confrontations with the police. Although many of the twenty to thirty thousand predominantly young people who gathered in Chicago were idealistic "innocents," as journalist Theodore White described them, they fell under the overall direction of the Mobilization organizers, who were bent on disrupting the convention proceedings. In the glare of television lights, the protesters waved Vietcong flags and red revolutionary banners and chanted "The whole world is watching," and the mocking "Sieg Heil," made famous by Hitler's followers.

The scenes of sporadic violence amazed the worldwide viewing audience. The confrontations peaked on August 28, the night Humphrey was nominated. The worst confrontation was at Balboa Drive and Michigan Avenue where the police set up barricades to prevent the demonstrators from reaching the Conrad Hilton Hotel, only a hundred yards away, which was the headquarters of the Democratic Party and provided lodgings for both Humphrey and McCarthy. When the police were bombarded by packets of leaflets and cellophane bags of bathroom waste hurled from the Hilton's windows by some demonstrators, they reacted by forming a flying wedge and wading into the shouting mob of demonstrators, brutally clubbing and removing anyone in their path. The networks repeatedly juxtaposed the startling images of fighting in the streets, the hurly-burly of the convention hall, and the hotel suite of the Vice President, who was smiling broadly, waving, and kissing his wife's image on the television screen.

A week after the unsettling violence at the Democratic Convention, a half million Chicagoans cheered my parents as they motorcaded through the city. The tremendous success of the visit not only was an undeniable contrast to the Democrats' week in Chicago, but also it was evidence that many regarded Nixon as capable of breaking with the Great Society and the piecemeal efforts to end the war. Sensing this, Humphrey himself became more determined than ever to appear independent of the President, especially on the issue of the war. On September 30 he announced in a nationally televised speech that if elected he would stop the bombing of North Vietnam in an effort to bring about successful peace negotiations.

His speech not only reassured the "doves" but also reminded voters of Nixon's hawkish past, spurring fears that Nixon might drive America deeper into the war. The obscenity-chanting demonstrators who had plagued Humphrey's campaign, at times refusing him the right to be heard and even bringing him to tears of frustration, now concentrated increasingly on my father. The tactics of the demonstrators had caught both campaigns unaware, and they had to improvise ways of isolating those who tried to disrupt meetings. For instance, Jack Carley, who six years before had been Mother's aide in the gubernatorial race, did the advance work for a rally in Akron, Ohio. Unfortunately, the gathering was infiltrated by fifty members of the Students for a Democratic Society. Throughout my father's speech they shouted, "Fuck the flag," "Tell the truth," "Eat grapes," barely pausing for breath between their mindless chants so that the words became one long string of noise. My father was speaking without notes and the yelling made him lose his train of thought. Finally, he cut his talk short.

Afterward, John Ehrlichman, a Seattle attorney who was second in command to Bob Haldeman, wanted some answers from Jack. Why didn't he implement the new "reserve rally plan"—namely, finding twenty-five to fifty large, muscular Nixon supporters who, armed with campaign signs, would surround the demonstrators and try to outyell them, all the while carefully avoiding physical contact. Jack answered truthfully that he had been taken by surprise to find demonstrators in the hall. Then Ehrlichman countered with the question: "Why was anyone with long hair allowed to enter?" By now, Carley was angry himself and he snapped back, "Well, John, why are we running for the Presidency if that's what it's all about?"

Looking back on that incident, Jack Carley has a different perspective.

> Nineteen sixty-eight was a whole new political world. All the rules were being broken. There were no standards. The radicals were yelling down speakers, students were taking over universities, violence was, in the words of Black Panther Huey Newton, "as American as apple pie." And, when the senses are assaulted and brutal obscenities are hurled, it is difficult for those being attacked not to develop a mentality of "them versus us."

Haunting the Nixon campaign in the closing days were rumors that Lyndon Johnson might attempt a dramatic action in Vietnam, such as a last-minute bombing halt that might swing the election to Hubert Humphrey. He did so on October 31. The family was in New York that night to attend a huge rally at Madison Square Garden, and in my diary I described our reaction to his speech.

Johnson wants peace—he has two sons-in-law in Vietnam. Yet he came across to us over television as reeking insincerity. I truly do not believe that the American people will accept this more than four days before the election. [Neither did South Vietnamese President Thieu, who announced his government would not take part in the negotiations Johnson was proposing.] It would be a different story if Johnson had received word from Hanoi—he would have to jump at that chance if Hanoi offered to honor the principles of the bombing pause.

My last comment in the October 31 entry was: "If D is elected I dread his future task of ending the war. It will be hell on earth for him to resolve the war."

Five days later, on Election Day, as we flew from California to New York, the polls showed Nixon and Humphrey neck and neck, with pollster Lou Harris predicting Humphrey would be the victor by three points. From 7:30 P.M. until shortly after noon the next day, in our suite at the Waldorf Astoria Hotel. Mother, Tricia and I watched the seesaw returns in an excruciatingly long vigil. Down the hall, my father was in constant meetings with Bob Haldeman, John Mitchell, his campaign director, and other staff members who brought him reports throughout the night. We had very little communication with him during those hours of suspense. In fact, apart from Jack Drown, who was in contact with John Mitchell and by phone with some of the state chairmen, we spoke to no one who was in authority in the campaign and who might have brought us up to date on any information that was not being reported on television. Though both Jack and Helene Drown, who stayed with us throughout, were rocklike in their assurances that my father would win, we were extremely tense and uneasy.

By 10 P.M. some of the television commentators began to speculate that Hubert Humphrey would win, and by midnight he actually had a lead in the popular vote. At 2 A.M. David could not stand the suspense any longer. On the pretext that he was going to his room to try to sleep, he left our suite and went down a floor to the staff headquarters to try to get an honest appraisal. Mother, Tricia, and I, and Jack and Helene Drown, continued to hear over and over the phrase "too close to call." No one went to bed, though my mother dozed on the couch for half an hour at one point. At 6 A.M., when the television commentators reported that Mayor Richard Daley of Chicago was holding back precinct votes in Cook County, my mother experienced a wave of agonizing memories of 1960: the vote fraud in Chicago; the suspect returns in Texas. She got up from the couch without a word and went into the bathroom. We could hear that she was sick to her stomach.

Just doors away, my father was unaware of what the tension was doing to us. Although by 3 A.M. he was 99 percent sure he would be the next President, he hesitated to come to our suite to say we had won, because 1960 had been so close. What if he were wrong? And so my parents, though only yards apart that night, separately relived election night 1960.

At 7:45 A.M. on November 6, David woke up in the staff room. He had fallen asleep on the floor in front of the television an hour before. The voice that woke him was John Mitchell's. He heard the next attorney general speak to a Democratic official in Illinois. "We know we've won. We've got the votes." The message was for Mayor Richard Daley: release the Cook County votes, and Republicans would release Lake County; Republicans could count too, and there was no point in further delay. Thirty minutes later, Daley's precincts reported, and ABC declared Illinois in the Nixon column.

When Dwight Chapin saw the ABC board, he immediately hurried to my father's bedroom. The President-elect was lying down, dressed in his robe, talking to Haldeman and Mitchell. When Dwight exclaimed, "ABC has just declared you the winner," my father jumped up and rushed into the sitting room, where there was a television.

Then, still dressed in his bathrobe, he came down the hall to our suite to tell us that the long night was over. We were all overcome with a tremendous sense of relief, an emotion so strong we felt little else. I went into my bedroom and came back with a gift for my father, an embroidery of the Great Seal of the United States that I had worked on secretly during the long campaign flights. Later, my father said publicly that he felt the gift meant that I never had doubts about the election outcome, but, as I admitted in my diary on November 6, "I did have doubts but I never doubted him—I always had faith in him."

For a few minutes my parents spoke alone. Mother still could not believe that it was over. She asked, "But, Dick, are we sure of Illinois? Are we completely sure?" When he assured her that the victory was won, she cried with relief and happiness. It was only then that she allowed herself to feel elated. She told me later, "I felt at last that Daddy was where he could really be of value to the country and to the world." She was buoyant enough to keep a pre-election promise to telephone our friend Priscilla Kidder, the designer who was then hard at work on my wedding dress. Even before Priscilla could offer congratulations, Mother exclaimed, "We won!"

Hubert Humphrey made his concession statement at noon. He had lost by half a million votes. At twelve-thirty, just before we entered the elevator to go down to the Grand Ballroom of the Waldorf where my father would speak to the American people for the first time as President-elect, the family stood close around Billy Graham in the hallway for a moment of prayer. Waiting below were the supporters who had suffered and worried with us through a sleepless night. When they saw my father step onto the platform, they let out a prolonged, overwhelming volley of cheers. Then the cheering stopped. There was a deep hush. As I looked out at the faces, I saw that people were not smiling anymore. Their faces were troubled and they were straining to catch every word of the new President.

Abruptly, the stillness in the room was broken by a sound so thunderous I jumped. For a moment I was disoriented. Then I realized that my father had opened his mouth to speak and that as many as four hundred cameras had clicked in unison. His first sentences were almost drowned out as the clicking continued, only gradually tapering off as he talked about his phone call an hour before from Hubert Humphrey, who had lost so narrowly, and of his belief that no matter if one won or lost, "what is important is that a man or a woman engage in battle, be in the arena." His closing remarks were per-sonal—a thank-you to his family and future son-in-law: "Surrounding me are four people who have meant much to this campaign and to my life."

At a small reception upstairs we hugged and grasped hands with friends and members of the Nixon and Ryan families who had traveled from California to wait out the election. Almost everyone tried out the sound of "Mr. Presi-dent." Then, under heavy New York City police escort, their sirens blaring, and with double the number of Secret Service agents from the day before, we drove back to our apartment at 810 Fifth Avenue. All the rooms were dark, the living-room drapes drawn and the shutters closed in the bedrooms and my father's study. Manolo and Fina were downtown taking their oaths of citizenship. They never dreamed that the election would take so long to resolve or that we would return to the apartment that afternoon.

None of us had had anything to eat for a long time, but there was almost nothing in the refrigerator. We opened some cans of tomato soup and ate crackers and toast with it. The two eggs went to the President-elect. After the snack, while the rest of us packed for the postelection rest in Key Biscayne, my father sat in his study. He turned up his *Victory at Sea* recording so loud that we could hear it despite the closed double doors. It blared triumphantly throughout the apartment.

From New York we traveled in a windowless Air Force jet provided by President Johnson. It was eerie to fly in a skyless, groundless vacuum. If it had not been for the "Fasten Seat Belt" signs and the pressure in our ears, we would never have known when we were going to touch earth. But despite the strangeness of the airplane, even to step aboard one of the presidential aircraft was an exhilarating experience. Press assistant Ron Ziegler was waiting at the cabin door as my parents climbed the steps in the cold and dark. He watched as Mother crossed the threshold first, the new President right behind her. Once under the shelter of the plane, they turned to each other. Simultaneously they embraced, and my father swung Mother around in a pirouette.

The jet stopped first in Washington so that my father could pay his respects to former President Eisenhower in Walter Reed's Ward 8. Mamie was at the elevator door when we stepped off at the third floor. She had champagne waiting on a silver tray. She told us that she had not slept all night, and that when Ike went to bed on doctor's orders around 11 P.M., he had been extremely upset and worried. In the morning, when she could tell him that everything had turned out all right, the joy had been intense.

During the drive back to Andrews Air Force Base in the new half-million-dollar presidential limousine, the reality of what had happened and what lay ahead began to intensify. The hordes of Secret Service men who had surrounded my father in New York had increased once we reached Washington. They moved in syncopation with my parents—five or six surrounding each, turning when they did, pausing when they did. Only then did I grasp how complete a change had come over our lives.

For the next few days in Key Biscayne we gave way to the fatigue we all had denied for so many months. But even though there were no planes to meet, no speeches to give, those days were not completely carefree. Already my father was planning his inauguration, structuring his Administration, and filling Cabinet and other high-level positions. Mother had important choices to make as well on her own staff, especially a press secretary and a social secretary. Ahead of her she faced my wedding on December 22, then Christmas, the inauguration, not to mention a watchful media whose members, after January 20, expected a smooth-running White House and, of course, an active First Lady. Much less visible to the public were her personal needs: to choose clothes appropriate for all these events—and to help Tricia and me with ours as well; to close down our New York apartment, deciding which furniture should go to storage, which to Washington; and to furnish the two small houses on Biscayne Bay, next to Bebe's, which my parents had just bought.

At times during those five days in Key Biscayne, I felt that Mother was putting her mind in neutral. Perhaps it was the only way she could cope with everything that had descended upon her. Carol Finch sensed something of the same thing. She and Bob Haldeman's wife, Jo, came over to the houses on Bay Lane to spend an afternoon a few days after the election. The three sat in deck chairs on the lawn and looked out over the tranquil bay, so tranquil that there was barely a ripple on the surface. Carol remembers: "We mused about the election. . . . Your mother was in a quiet, philosophical mood. I felt as if she were storing up her energy for what lay ahead."

Part III

1969–1976

The White House

Inauguration morning, January 20, 1969, was gray and penetratingly cold. At 11 A.M., as the presidential limousine neared the North Portico of the White House, my parents saw Lyndon and Lady Bird Johnson waiting at the top of the steps. A few feet away were our French poodle, Vicky, dressed in a new white jacket trimmed in red, white, and blue, and Pasha, our Yorkshire terrier, his thin hair pulled back from his face by a ribbon. President Johnson sentimentally had arranged for the dogs to be the first to greet us in our new home. They were frisky after their first night's sleep in the White House kennel. Vicky strained at her leash, trying to jump up on Mother's cherry-red double-breasted coat. The dogs seemed to know instinctively to ham it up for the hundreds of cameras banking the steps of the portico.

The Johnsons hosted a preinaugural coffee in the Red Room and could not have been more cordial. In contrast, outgoing Vice President Hubert Humphrey, who had lost so narrowly in November and who usually was quick-moving and -speaking, was in a somber, quiet mood. The President's daughters, Lynda and Luci, did not try to conceal the tremendous sadness they felt. We were later told by Billy Graham that when he spent the night before the inauguration at the White House he had never known the President to be more melancholy and thought then that Johnson's black mood would not lift once he returned to his ranch in Stonewall, Texas. Here was a heartbroken man, a theme that biographers and columnists would repeat in the next four years, until Johnson died of a heart attack in January 1973 at the age of sixty-four.

During the drive down Pennsylvania Avenue to the Capitol for the inaugural ceremony, my mother and Lady Bird Johnson sat side by side in the second official limousine, separated from their husbands' car by a station wagon tightly packed with Secret Service agents. Eight years before, they had taken the same ride together, but on that day my mother was leaving Washington and Mrs. Johnson was beginning her tenure as Second Lady that would lead in a thousand days to the White House. There was not much talk in the car. My mother's stomach was knotted with excitement. She tried to keep the conversation light, sensing that behind Lady Bird Johnson's detached smile and soft answers in her carefully modulated southern voice she too was concentrating on keeping her emotions in check. Mrs. Johnson remained composed, but when she reached the LBJ Ranch that evening, she would remark, "The chariot has turned into a pumpkin and all the mice have run away."

At the Capitol, the First Ladies and their children were escorted to a small sitting room to wait for the ceremony to begin. My father was nearby in another room with his official congressional escorts. Now both Lynda and Luci cried openly. Finally they retreated into a bathroom for a few moments of privacy. During the last year in the White House, with both their husbands serving on active duty in Vietnam, the sisters had been drawn much closer. Luci had taken me aside at the coffee to offer heartfelt advice: don't let all the attention drive a wedge between you and Tricia.

Shortly after noon, my mother, as she had at the 1953 and 1957 inaugurations, held high the two Nixon family Bibles, printed in 1828 and 1873, which had been handed down from generation to generation. They were opened to the second chapter of Isaiah, the fourth verse: "They shall beat their swords into plowshares, and their spears into pruning hooks: nation shall not lift up sword against nation, neither shall they learn war any more." My father placed his left hand on the Bibles as Chief Justice Earl Warren administered the oath of office.

There was a brief silence after the last solemn words of the oath, "So help me God." Then my father gently guided Mother to her place of honor in the front row, bowing low to her as she took her seat. From the north came the roar of cannons, the first volley of the twenty-one-gun salute.

In a restrained but strong voice, my father began his Inaugural Address. His theme was peace—among nations and in our sorely divided country: "... We cannot learn from one another until we stop shouting at one another—until we speak quietly enough so that our words can be heard as well as our voices." And he solemnly made "... this sacred commitment: I shall consecrate my office, my energies, and all the wisdom I can summon to the cause of peace among nations."

Less than two hours later, following a luncheon in the Capitol hosted by the leaders of Congress, the ceremonial parade down Pennsylvania Avenue was marred by hundreds of New Left demonstrators screaming obscenities. They pelted the presidential limousine with sticks, small rocks, empty beer cans, and homemade smoke bombs. None of the debris hit my parents because the Secret Service had insisted that the bubble top of their limousine be closed until the car passed the corner of 13½ Street and Pennsylvania Avenue, where most of the protesters had massed. On one side of the parade route was a shouting, fist-clenched mob; on the other side, District of Columbia police and paratroopers of the 82d Airborne Division, their arms linked. Only ten minutes after the presidential car was bombarded, several protesters shouted "Into the streets" and, according to the Washington *Post* report, hundreds of demonstrators rampaged through downtown Washington "stoning police, breaking store windows and blocking traffic." A "pitched battle" occurred between police and demonstrators at H and Lafayette Streets, and by day's end, eighty-one had been arrested.

There were 250,000 cheering people along the parade route that day, but their enthusiasm did not soften the frightening intensity of the demonstrations. Those first hours of the Presidency were a sobering reminder of the deep discontent in the country and of the urgent need for action. Although my family entered the White House with great hopes that my father could help with the healing process, we never underestimated the divisions caused by the war and by decades of racial injustice, nor forgot that the President who had lived in the White House before us had been broken by the bitterness and unrest.

Yet the excitement of the moment was tremendous. Mamie Eisenhower stood next to my parents in the reviewing stand for part of the inaugural parade. The night before, my father had placed a call to Ike, who still lay in Walter Reed Army Hospital, daily more wasted and thin, his heart attached to monitors. Mamie had been sitting next to him when the phone call came. She heard her husband's voice choke with emotion as he told the man who had served him for eight years as Vice President, "This is the last time I can ever call you Dick. From now on you'll be Mr. President."

Because Mamie was anxious to return to her vigil at the hospital, she left midway through the parade. It lasted longer than expected, and we were all chilled to the bone by the time the last unit marched by the reviewing stand at 5:25 P.M. In the dark, a light rain falling, we left the inaugural reviewing platform on foot for the short walk to the White House. A planked pathway had been built to guard against snow or mud, but despite the wood beneath our feet, we could still feel the intense cold of the former swampland that is Washington. Then, suddenly, in front of us was the most breathtakingly beautiful sight: the White House softly illuminated by the lights of the television crews.

When my parents walked through the double glass doors of the North Portico, it was the first time in eight years that they had been in the White House for a party. Awaiting them in the East Room were several hundred relatives and close friends. There was much hugging and kissing and exclamations of "Can you believe it . . . it's a dream come true!" Bill Ryan exclaimed to a friend, "Did you ever think my little sister would end up in the White House?" By the time we had whirled from one friend to another and still not talked to a third of the guests, there was barely time left to eat and get ready for the six inaugural balls.

My mother was so excited she did not want any dinner. When my father protested, saying, "You've got to eat something, Pat," she decided to have a bowl of cottage cheese in her bedroom. She learned later that what she thought was a simple request had thrown the kitchen into a tizzy. There was no cottage cheese on hand, but someone was dispatched immediately to a nearby twenty-four-hour delicatessen and Mrs. Nixon was none the wiser.

The staff had set the dinner table in the Family Dining Room and, guessing that the new First Family might enjoy steak, had prepared sirloins for everyone. With the candelabra lighted and the table beautifully set with silver flatware engraved "The President's House," Tricia and I felt shy about asking for dinner on trays in our rooms. And so, for our first dinner in the White House, we hurriedly ate in the dining room with our hair in electric curlers.

Fortunately, the experienced White House staff had unpacked and hung up our evening clothes so that we could quickly slip them on. They had also cleared away most traces of the Johnsons. Lynda had told Tricia that she left some bath salts for her, but when Tricia opened what had been Lynda's medicine cabinet, she found that the salts too had vanished.

Hours later, at about 1:20 A.M., my parents, Tricia, David, and I stood on our sixth ballroom platform, this time at the Statler Hilton Hotel where we had started out that morning. Below us, three thousand people were jammed shoulder to shoulder with no room to dance. In fact, none of us had danced at any of the inaugural balls. Everyone was in a happy mood, however, and my father joked with the crowd: "This is our seventh [he had lost count] and last ball—I mean the last for this inauguration!"

When we returned to the White House shortly before 2 A.M., we walked slowly through the long, dark corridor of the second-floor family quarters, turning on lights in each room as we went. David led the way. Eight years before he had stuffed a note under a rug on the third floor proclaiming, "I will return." Now he showed us the tiny room next to the second-floor elevator that had been his grandfather's painting studio; the hidden door to the passageway linking the second floor with the third; and even took us to the storage rooms on the third floor where he recognized a few pieces of his grandmother's wicker furniture, which had been removed from the Solarium.

After our tour, we sat together for a few minutes in the West Hall at the end of the corridor. My father decided to try out the piano in the center of the grand hall facing us. He played first Sindling's "Rustle of Spring," which his Aunt Jane had taught him as a young boy and which remained a favorite. Then, a soft melodic song he had composed when courting Miss Patricia Ryan. As the music faded we became aware of how very quiet it was in the great house. Below us the state rooms where we had visited with our friends and family in the late afternoon were empty and dark. Suddenly Mother said, "Dick, let's turn on all the lights in the White House and make it cheery." "It's done," he responded. He picked up the phone, asked for the usher's office, and made the request.

During the first weeks in the White House, my mother was very much aware that the role of First Lady had changed dramatically since the Eisenhower Administration. For eight years the newspaper coverage of Mamie Eisenhower was no more weighty than what she wore, her menus, and the stir she caused when she decided to receive guests with her right glove off.

But now the Washington-based newswomen my mother saw virtually every day during the five and a half years of the Nixon Presidency wanted a First Lady "project" and a news maker in her own right. In the first months, as Mother considered the various suggestions for projects, she was aware that any First Lady's influence must be wielded cautiously and responsibly. She continued to emphasize what she called her "personal diplomacy," telling United Press International reporter Helen Thomas that it was her "only claim to fame both at home and abroad... it's [politics] Dick's life."

During the Eisenhower years, she had demonstrated her personal diplomacy crisscrossing America and traveling to fifty-three nations. By the end of the White House years she had journeyed to seventy-eight countries, making her the most widely traveled First Lady in history.

Now, as the media began to ponder her style and image anew, Mother took the scrutiny in stride. In 1969, after more than twenty years in political life, she cared little about press notices. When she left Washington in 1961, she had been hailed as the most popular, effective, and active Second Lady. Yet less than a decade later *Time* would describe her pre–White House image as "the matron in the Republican cloth coat, the silent partner in the Nixon marriage who never appeared quite comfortable as a wife of a public man...."

Mother would keep no written record of her White House years other than a few jotted notes on her monthly calendars. No diaries exist for several reasons. Events moved very fast, with much to learn and plan for and very little time for reflection. My mother, with her love of order and harmony, at times felt inundated by too many functions, coming too closely together, one after another. And so she concentrated on the present, not the past or the distant future. It had been her way of dealing with pressure for years. She told me once, "I looked at each day in the White House as a new day. I didn't think about the day before. I just accomplished what needed to be done. So instead of thinking of the past, I concentrated on the present, and on the days to come." Finally, although by fate a public person, she was a woman of private thoughts that she did not care to commit to paper.

For those White House observers who were searching for clues to what kind of First Lady Mrs. Nixon would be, a good source would have been Roy Day, my father's first campaign manager back in Whittier in 1946. In an interview on November 6, the day after the 1968 election, Day had given his assessment of what Americans could expect of Pat Nixon as First Lady: "Well, she'll never be traipsing along behind the President, she'll never be in front of him, but she'll always be at his side."

Likewise during those first months in the White House, a question that periodically interested the writers of what were then still called the society or women's pages was my sister Tricia's "image." With the press on the outside wanting to know what she was doing inside, even when Tricia was "at home" there was little privacy. The Secret Service was not with us on the mansion's second and third floors, the family quarters, but the minute we stepped onto the public floors below our rooms, we were guarded, as Tricia discovered the first hour in her new home. Following the inaugural parade and family reception, Tricia had decided to walk from the first floor up to her new room on the second. When she reached the top of the Grand Staircase and put her hand on the doorknob, she heard a voice, as if coming from outer space, "Do not try to open the doors. They are locked." An agent had followed her up the stairs. Her reaction was "Good grief! We're going to try to live here?"

The White House, the world's only official residence of a chief executive open to the public, is not, in fact, an easy place in which to live. Tricia's bedroom, whose most recent previous occupants had been Lynda Bird Robb and Caroline Kennedy, was, I believe, the least desirable in the house because it is located over the Grand Entrance Hall, where, five days a week, twelve months of the year, more than 1.5 million tourists enter. At 7 A.M. on visiting mornings, Tricia was awakened by the loud clanking of chains and the clash of metal as the guards set up the restraining aisles for the day's visitors. Her room had the further disadvantage of being directly across the hall from the Yellow Oval Room where my parents met with guests before formal dinners and which Mother also frequently used for teas. If Tricia was not attending an event, she was trapped in her room until the guests were gone.

From the beginning, there were occasional rumblings among White House watchers about Tricia's absences. Once when I was cornered at a reception by a group of reporters who wanted to know where my sister was and what she was doing, I finally joked in desperation, "Tricia is the Howard Hughes of the White House." Yet Mother rarely tried to persuade Tricia to attend an event if she had indicated she was not interested. She understood that Tricia and I, but particularly Tricia, because she lived in the White House, needed as much freedom as possible. Within the first few weeks of my father's Administration, Tricia had received dozens of requests and invitations as well as literally hundreds of phone calls from people offering jobs, children eager to talk to the President's daughter, and young men who claimed to be boy friends.

At the Republican Convention in August, my family already had a foretaste of the dating problems Tricia would encounter if my father was elected President. Tricia, David, and I had met at a reception a young man who excitedly told us that he knew "John Doe," one of Tricia's "steady boy friends." When Tricia responded that she had never even heard his name before, our new friend's mouth dropped in astonishment. He blurted, "But he showed me teeth marks where you'd bitten him!"

In Washington, it was not hard to get Tricia's phone number. The President's home is listed in the District of Columbia phone book under "White House." Tricia finally had to provide a list of names to the White House operators so that people who actually knew her would be able to get through. Fortunately, the operators were a group of remarkable, quick-thinking women with uncanny ability to recognize voices and remember names. They also were amateur sleuths who frequently were called upon by the President and his staff to reach people at the most unlikely times in the most unlikely places. One soon got the feeling the operators were omniscient. Since there were no direct-dial phones, the operators knew whether or not you were up (had you called the kitchen yet to order breakfast?); whether or not you were making plans to go out (did a call go to the Secret Service?); even whether or not your boy friend had called you!

Although Tricia did not attend every White House function, she hosted quite a few events on her own, and occasionally substituted for my mother when she had to be away from Washington, earning at one point from *Newsweek* magazine the title "Assistant First Lady." But more meaningful to Tricia than the public events at the White House was her tutoring under the auspices of the Urban Service Corps. For a year, beginning in the summer of 1969, two students from one of Washington's inner-city schools came to the White House for help with reading, writing, and arithmetic. Because they met with Tricia in her "own house," she was able to avoid the disruption at the school inevitably caused by the comings and goings of the President's daughter, who was accompanied, to the thrill of children everywhere, by armed secret agents.

As the unmarried daughter of the President living in the big White House, surrounded by handsome bodyguards, Tricia was a romantic figure to some. Physically, she was right for the role, with her long blond hair and dark-blue eyes fringed by black lashes. One whom she captivated was President Dwight David Eisenhower. During the summer of 1968, Tricia had accompanied

David and me several times to the hospital to visit his grandfather. She continued the visits that winter from the White House, always telephoning David and me at college afterward to give us a health report. She told the general how much she and friends enjoyed using the small kitchen on the third floor installed for him while he was President. But she also admitted that more frequently than not she ordered in pizza and Chinese food, because when she cooked in the kitchen, five-foot-three-inch Tricia had to use a stepladder to reach the cupboards that had been built to accommodate the five-foot-eleven-inch general.

On February 21, Tricia's twenty-third birthday, she and my mother had made plans to visit General Eisenhower, but that morning he was not well enough and the visit was canceled. Eisenhower summoned his military aide, General Robert Schulz, and asked him to deliver personally an old-fashioned nosegay to Miss Patricia Nixon at the White House. He also asked to see the flowers before they were sent. Schulz ordered a nosegay from a local florist and confidently bore the flowers into his commanding officer's bedroom. But Eisenhower was displeased; the nosegay was all wrong; it wasn't "dainty enough"; there weren't enough ribbons on it; the flowers should have been pink and white instead of red and white. Schulz telephoned the florist and a new nosegay was rushed to Walter Reed. Schulz reported to Eisenhower, but once again, the general was displeased. Only on the third try was Schulz given permission to deliver the bouquet to Miss Nixon.

Although immediately after the inauguration David and I returned to our new apartment in Northampton for the start of second-semester classes at Amherst and Smith, our adjustment to the presidential spotlight was no less abrupt than Tricia's. Our wedding, on December 22, 1968, twenty-nine days before my father took the oath of office, was the last major family event we could keep private before the omnivorous publicity of the next five and a half years. We had set the date twelve months before, choosing Dr. Norman Vincent Peale's church where we had attended services together so many times during our courtship. We knew that regardless of whether or not my father became President we wanted to be married in a church over our Christmas vacation from college, with only family and friends present.

Mother and I had snatched time to plan the wedding when we were on the same campaign flights. Helene Drown has Mother's copy of the campaign schedule for the third week in September. On it Mother had jotted notes of what needed to be done for the wedding reception. She encouraged David and me to have just the kind of wedding we wanted. Our decision not to allow press coverage of the ceremony seemed heretical. One Washington columnist took us to task by pointing out that in recent years Margaret Truman, David's own mother, Barbara Eisenhower, and the Johnson girls all had allowed reporters and photographers at their ceremonies. Despite many press appeals to us to change our minds, my parents never questioned our decision, nor did they try to make the wedding a political thank-you party. They had been friends with members of Congress for more than twenty-one years, but David and I barely knew most of these men and their wives. Consequently there were few congressional faces at our wedding.

December 22 was a completely joyous day. David and I, both twenty years old, were very much in love. The future seemed bright as my father and I drove the thirty-three blocks down Fifth Avenue from our apartment to the church. Large crowds in a holiday mood stood along the streets waving and calling greetings. The only sadness for us on December 22 was that David's grandparents were both hospitalized at Walter Reed since Mamie had developed a severe respiratory infection the week before. NBC generously had arranged a close-circuit television hookup so that the Eisenhowers could view the ceremony from their bedrooms. Not until seven years later did Mamie finally admit, however, that the broadcast reception had failed that day and all they had was sound.

As guests left the church, fragrant with swags of pine boughs and hundreds of red and white poinsettias, they were transported in buses to the reception at the Plaza Hotel. This was my mother's idea so that they would not have to worry about parking or New York traffic. Each bus was decorated with small wedding bells and sprigs of mistletoe.

After the reception, the family went upstairs to a suite in the hotel so that we could say goodbye privately. We knew that waiting outside the Plaza were hundreds of members of the press. But it would not be goodbye for long. On Christmas Day, David and I decided to surprise my parents by driving the short distance from our borrowed honeymoon house in North Palm Beach, Florida, to Key Biscayne, arriving in time for Christmas dinner.

The new houses on Bay Lane were at the time sparsely furnished and my parents and Tricia were practically camping out. My father had decided that an after-Christmas-dinner fire would end the day in a fitting manner. Manolo somehow scrounged up wood, crumpled newspapers, and struck a match. The fire blazed up nicely. Then smoke slowly, steadily started to fill the room. We were watching a movie on television, and my father kept repeating, as if to reassure himself, "Isn't this wonderful? Isn't this fun having a fire and being here together?" Meanwhile, our eyes were killing us, and it was getting harder and harder to breathe. The flue was open, but I do not think the fireplace had ever been used and it obviously didn't work.

Mother was the first to slip quietly out. As the smoke got worse my father, only slightly less enthusiastic, repeated again, "Isn't it fun to have a fire?" David lay down on the floor next to the dogs, who had stretched out very low in order to breathe more easily, but within minutes, Pasha and Vicky got up and staggered out of the room. Finally my father was the only one left. Manolo and several Secret Service agents moved in and put out the fire.

We saw my parents again on January 9 when they, Tricia, and Bebe flew to Northampton to celebrate my father's fifty-sixth birthday at our off-campus apartment in one of Smith's oldest former dorms. In order to prepare the birthday dinner I had had to spend an hour and fifteen minutes on the telephone with Helene Drown in California getting step-by-step instructions on how to make Chicken Divan, a broccoli, chicken, and cheese casserole. First the chicken had to be simmered. "How do you simmer chicken?" I had asked.

January 9 was a bitterly cold day and everyone had arrived bundled in heavy coats. When we sat down to dinner and Bebe kept on his overcoat, I hardly noticed. But as soon as I brought out the casserole and the molded Jell-O salad, I realized that the coat was part of a grand scheme my father and Bebe had dreamed up. From out of mammoth pockets, Bebe pulled two tuna-fish sandwiches and a bag of carrot sticks.

Although David and I were happy to be together at last in our own apartment starting a new life, the constant presence of the Secret Service brought us far too much attention on campus. Shortly after the election, the agents had submitted half a dozen code names for me to choose from, all beginning with S. I selected Sunbonnet. Among the other names offered, the worst was Student Princess.

From the beginning, I had found being guarded twenty-four hours a day almost more than I could endure, and each day it was harder to accept, not easier. Yet all of us in the family liked the agents assigned to us and realized that not only were they willing to risk their lives to protect us but also that they tried hard to provide at least a modicum of privacy when we were in restaurants or other public places on nonofficial occasions. My father was the only one who seemed to be able to detach himself mentally from the Secret Service most of the time.

Being considered symbols of the new Administration set David and me apart as well. In the preceding six months we had traveled across the country to thirty-three states and talked to thousands of Americans, and now we were back in an academic community that had a rigid view of America's problems and fiercely opposed our involvement in Vietnam. The overwhelming majority of the faculties at both Smith and Amherst had supported first Eugene McCarthy and then Hubert Humphrey, or, in protest against Humphrey's Johnsonian taint, had not voted at all. Most of the students reflected their professors' views, and the atmosphere on campus was far from tolerant. During the primaries, I had noted that many of the students who supported my father were quiet about it because they had tired of being constantly challenged, even badgered, by the ones who opposed him. Nor was there a willingness at Smith to give the new Administration a chance. On November 7, the Smith newspaper, the Sophian, had printed a full-page photograph of President-elect Richard Nixon. The only words beneath the smiling face, floating shoulderless on an ink-black page, was a quotation from Ibsen: "A lie, turned topsy-turvy, can be prinked and tinseled out, decked in plumage new and fine, till none knows its lean old carcass." Inside, an editorial questioned the "crisis in legitimacy" presented by the Nixon election.

That winter, with yet another graduating class facing draft calls, there continued to be little discussion on campus of Administration programs other than ending our involvement in Vietnam. When I shared the frustration I felt with my mother, she always had time to listen and to offer quiet encouragement. In retrospect, I regret that I let her know how upset I was by what was happening at college. She had so many concerns and adjustments of her own, and to see her daughter under stress was surely the greatest strain of all. Although when questioned by the press about my role in my father's Presidency, I emphasized the excitement and great opportunities, in my heart I knew from that first year that any opportunities I had as the daughter of the President could not compensate for the loss of privacy and a normal married life.

When my family moved into the White House on January 20, Mother already had begun planning the changes she would make in the 132-room mansion. Two floors had been added since Abigail Adams's day when she had described the White House to her daughter as a drafty and cold "castle" of twenty rooms but only six inhabitable. Mother had met with Mrs. Johnson and toured the private quarters on December 12. At the same time my father had conferred in the Oval Office with the President, who, seated in his favorite king-size rocking chair, had towered over him. Lady Bird Johnson had taken Mother and Tricia from room to room, opening closet doors in each bedroom. She apologized for the numerous dog spots on the once-white carpeting in the family quarters and explained that she had not replaced it during their last year in the White House because, typically thoughtful, she felt the new occupants, be they Republicans or Democrats, would want to choose their own.

The formal rooms also needed to be redecorated. They had been untouched since Jacqueline Kennedy had moved out, and five years of visits by seven million tourists, and literally hundreds of parties, had taken a toll on the furnishings. The draperies were faded and frayed around the edges, most dramatically in the Yellow Oval Room where one badly shredded panel had been moved to the center window and hidden by a sofa. Fabrics on the walls were worn through to the plaster from the touch of curious fingers. In the Blue Room, the white silk wall covering was peeling from the walls.

After her tour, Mother had the distinct feeling that the White House of the Johnsons was still haunted by the Kennedys. She had read about Lyndon Johnson's reluctance to replace Kennedy aides. In fact, Johnson would write in his memoirs several years later that not having a staff personally loyal to him was one of the major mistakes of his Presidency. Lady Bird Johnson apparently was unwilling to change anything that Jacqueline Kennedy had done in her acclaimed decoration of the Red, Blue, and Green rooms. Even on the second floor where the family entertained, with the exception of some of the artwork and their own personal photographs and objects, the Johnsons lived with many of the colors and fabrics Mrs. Kennedy had chosen.

Although the state rooms would have to be tackled, Mother's first priority was to make the family quarters homelike and to redecorate the Oval Office where, as of January 20, my father would hold all his formal meetings. She contacted her New York friend and decorator Sarah Jackson Doyle and immediately they made plans to replace the off-white carpeting and muted green sofas of John Kennedy's and Lyndon Johnson's days with the California state colors: brilliant yellow-gold fabric for the chairs and sofas, and a deep-blue carpet with the Presidential Seal woven in gold in the center.

The character of the room had been transformed even before the new fabrics and carpeting arrived. My father had the AP and UPI tickers with their incessant all-day clattering removed and a specially designed three-set color-television console removed also. President Johnson had kept the sets on night and day, although with the sound off, so that whenever he pressed the remote-control button at his desk to open the doors to the console, he could see the three networks simultaneously without a moment's delay.

From what had been Lyndon Johnson's bedroom, a smaller console containing three televisions was taken out. Mother also removed his elaborate telephone with its taping capability and dozens of buttons. There were telephones everywhere in the family quarters, three in the West Hall alone. Within days of moving in, Mother requested that two be taken out of the West Hall and the phone in the Family Dining Room removed as well. Four sets of ceiling lights installed in the Family Dining Room by President Johnson so that TV cameras could film events were also taken down.

Removing excess telephones and TVs was part of my mother's efforts to make the living quarters less official and more serene. The center hallway that ran the length of the second floor was a dark moss-green. On the walls hung portraits by Charles Bird King of Indian emissaries from the Oto tribe who had visited the White House in 1821. Many of the chiefs wore war paint and their expressions were severe. My mother chose a sunny yellow for the long corridor and replaced the Indians with two beautiful Monets and other paintings borrowed from New York's Metropolitan Museum of Art.

She made the fewest changes in the First Lady's bedroom, which opens directly onto the West Hall sitting area and faces the doors to the second-floor kitchen installed by Jacqueline Kennedy. Only a year before, Lady Bird Johnson had chosen draperies and a matching silk spread patterned with soft gold, coral, and green flowers for the four-poster bed. Mother liked the fabric and decided to add only the gold-and-white French chairs from our New York living room and favorite art objects and paintings, including the snow scene given her by Dwight Eisenhower in 1961. It was a formal room and uninvitingly dark because of the white sheer curtains in both windows, needed to prevent people from seeing into the room. Mother spent most of her waking hours in a small adjacent dressing room that was dominated by two large corner windows facing southwest which despite their sheer curtains provided plenty of light. The delicate blue flowers and birds of the French wallpaper that Jacqueline Kennedy had chosen several years before were still fresh. Mrs. Johnson had installed a wall of closets and now there was room only for a chaise longue, covered in French blue by my mother, a single armchair, and Mother's mahogany tabletop working desk. She placed a utilitarian black padded typing chair behind the desk despite Tricia's and my protests about its appearance. Because of the long hours she spent at her desk, she insisted on having a comfortable chair.

Mother's decision not to redecorate the rooms where she spent most of her time in the White House was a simple matter of priorities. Because she did not want her days dominated by time-consuming decorating, she had decided to confine her main efforts to the rooms where visitors were entertained and which needed immediate attention. Privately, she confided to Tricia and me that the task seemed monumental, adding she wished Lady Bird Johnson had tackled at least one of the major rooms and that not all of them had shown their wear and tear so dramatically and at the same time. She was reluctant as well to undertake the decorating because she knew the news media, riding the first wave of the women's movement, were eager to focus on issues more substantial than decorating.

Within five months of moving into the White House, Mother saw more clearly why Mrs. Johnson had avoided changing anything Jacqueline Kennedy had done. In the last month of the Johnson Administration, with Lady Bird presiding, the Committee on the Preservation of the White House, whose responsibility is to approve changes on the state floors, made the decision to remove a wooden mantel from the First Lady's bedroom and replace it with a historic late-eighteenth-century marble mantel by Benjamin Latrobe, who had been appointed by Jefferson to survey Washington. The wooden mantel, which was placed in the government warehouse where all former White House furnishings are preserved by law, was the newest in the White House and therefore the least historical. But it had an inscription on it that immediately caught the attention of the press. Underneath a brief carved statement that Abraham Lincoln had occupied the room, Mrs. Kennedy had added, "In this room lived John Fitzgerald Kennedy and his wife Jacqueline during the two years, ten months, and two days he was President of the United States." When the committee's decision was carried out in early 1969, there was a disagreeable uproar, and one Washington newspaper entitled its story "Erasing White House History." In the privacy of the family, my mother threw up her hands in frustration over the stories that implied the Nixons were trying to eliminate all traces of the Kennedys from the White House.

Mother was meticulous about any changes she made at the White House. With the new curator, Clement Conger, whom my mother had brought over from the State Department where he had masterfully transformed the reception area into historic Federal period rooms, she studied each fabric, wall color, rug, or drapery choice in the morning, afternoon, and again at night in order to see how the light changed the colors. Conger remembers "the quiet Sunday afternoon" in January 1969 when he and Mrs. Nixon "went through every room in the White House beginning on the third floor and ended up in the basement below... without a note for three hours. It was all in her head; Mrs. Nixon told me what needed to be done."

Only one-third of the furnishings in the White House were antiques at the start of the Nixon Administration, but by the end, two-thirds were historic. Mother and Clem Conger, virtually unnoticed, added more than five hundred eighteenth- and nineteenth-century pieces of American furniture, artwork, chandeliers, and rugs to the collection. In addition, beautiful window moldings and cornices were created for the state rooms by Edward Vason Jones of Albany, Georgia, the nation's foremost restoration architect of the Federal era. In order to accomplish a restoration of this magnitude, Mother and Clem Conger had to become major fund raisers, since the United States government does not furnish monies for decorating the White House. Mother frequently entertained potential contributors at lunch or tea.

Several of the new acquisitions originally had been in the White House. One of the most exciting discoveries Clem Conger made was when he visited the Pennsylvania Academy of Fine Arts looking for paintings to be loaned to the White House. The academy had a Gilbert Stuart portrait of Dolley Madison that, research revealed, had hung during the Madison Presidency in "Mrs. Madison's sitting room," now the Red Room. It was removed on August 23, 1814, as the British marched on Washington. Dolley Madison had written her sister, "Our kind friend, Mr. Carroll, has come to hasten my departure and in a very bad humor with me because I insist on waiting until the large picture of General Washington is secured." The portrait was screwed to the wall and there was not time to unfasten it. Dolley ordered the frame torn apart and the canvas rolled up. The footnote to this story of patriotism is that Dolley also saved her own portrait from the British fires. And in 1970, one hundred and fifty-six years later, the portrait was returned to the red parlor and the room was painted, at the request of Pat Nixon, the Dolley Madison red of the velvet draperies in the portrait.

After my parents left the White House, Clem Conger would tell longtime Washington reporter Nick Thimmesch that Mrs. Nixon was "always regrettably modest" about transforming what he characterized as the "average" White House collection into the "preeminent collection in the country." The reason

Clem Conger gave for the modesty was that Mrs. Nixon "never wished her work to be compared to that of other First Ladies." She wanted Jacqueline Kennedy "to have all the credit due her for having made the nation aware that it was time we stopped treating the White House like a stepchild and that a national collection of Americana furnishings for the White House had to be assembled..."

ABC correspondent Virginia Sherwood, who covered the Nixon White House for four years, also noted Mother's reluctance to claim undue credit. "Whenever I asked your mother, 'Why aren't you telling the American people more about what you are doing in the restoration of the White House?' she would say that she did not want to draw comparisons. She had tremendous respect for other people and for their places in history and their accomplishments."

As the months passed, the White House became a home. When a poster child, one of the dozens of afflicted children who came to the White House to pose with the First Lady, visited, he stared at my mother and said, "This isn't your house." "Why don't you think this is my house?" Mother asked. The frightened boy answered, "Because I don't see your washing machine." So Mother took him up in the elevator to the third floor, walked halfway down the red-carpeted hallway, left through the double doors and into the laundry rooms. When she returned to the White House Library, the little boy's hand in hers, his parents told her that it was the first time their son had gone anywhere with a stranger. But he was happy now. The big house did belong to the nice lady. He had seen her washing machine.

Louise Johnson told me once, "Your parents were so proud of the White House. They wanted it to be beautiful for everyone who saw it." John Davies, who was chosen to head the Office of White House Visitors, remembers meeting with Mrs. Nixon in Florida immediately after the election. "She knew exactly what she wanted for the mansion: a warm house which was more accessible to the public." She did not think it was appropriate for the Executive Protective Service officers who led the White House tours to wear police uniforms with exposed pistols. Within the first three or four months of my father's Presidency, they were wearing gray trousers, their guns concealed beneath navy blazers.

When I volunteered the summer of 1969 as a White House guide, taking random groups of tourists from the long line waiting outside the gate, I also escorted many groups of blind and deaf people through the state rooms. Mother had arranged for the White House to be open in the afternoon for these special tours. At her suggestion, all the guide officers were instructed how to face the deaf groups and speak slowly enough for lip-reading and interpretation. Mother also arranged for blind visitors to be allowed for the first time to touch furniture and objects. Children and adults felt the scaled serpent legs of the wooden

Empire sofa in the Red Room, enjoyed the smoothness of the silk tassels on the draperies in the Green Room, and touched the cool silver of the two-hundred-year-old coffee urn that had belonged to John and Abigail Adams.

The incredibly busy social schedule of breakfasts, luncheons, teas, dinners, and after-dinner entertainments meant that my mother had to learn to delegate a great deal of responsibility to staff members, not an easy adjustment for a woman who enjoyed being self-sufficient. She had a ten-woman staff, including a social secretary, press secretary, and assistants who made arrangements for trips and handled correspondence and special projects. An executive housekeeper and the chief usher directed the White House domestic and maintenance staff of seventy-five: ushers, doormen, maids, three chefs, florists, electricians, even engineers to check and repair equipment and lay fires. Running the White House in 1969 was a far cry from the days of Benjamin Harrison when the First Lady personally fired her French cook because of his "extravagant" salary of fifty dollars per month and hired an American cook for fifteen dollars.

During the first weeks in the White House my mother had to determine whether or not to become personally involved in a wide variety of decisions. For example, state gifts were exchanged with foreign visitors, the State Department allotting one thousand dollars for each. Although they were given in the name of President, in some Administrations the chief of protocol had chosen the gifts. Mother's solution was to select two or three types of gifts— Boehm porcelain bird sculptures or enameled vermeil flowers, for example— and let the protocol chief and his wife decide which would be most appropriate for the visitor.

The attitude of the President's aides toward the First Lady—and her East Wing staff—was divided into two groups: on one hand, her presence has little to do with us; on the other hand, a keen interest in her activities. Those who did take an interest in the First Lady's role in the Administration were agreed that she should, as the press inquiries mounted, focus on one project above all others.

When one looks at my mother's full schedule for the first five months in the White House, it is difficult to imagine how she could have carved out the time to devote to one particular project. In May, for example, she had meetings, dinners, or receptions—sometimes all three—on twenty-three days that month. The official calendar for May contains Mother's jotted additions of private appointments (such as tea with Princess Muna, wife of Jordan's King Hussein, on May 22), last-minute scheduling (the luncheon for the king and queen of the Belgians on the twentieth), and her notations of dresses worn (to avoid rewearing them too soon). Her schedule included the annual Senate Ladies' luncheon, a meeting with the chairman of the Commission on the Status of Women, and a state dinner for the prime minister of Australia. In between these official functions she had to oversee the decorating, answer her mail, and engage in the time-consuming planning for the events that took place at the White House.

Sometime during that busy month, Mother began to prepare for a June trip to the West Coast to spotlight volunteerism. My mother had been a volunteer all her adult life. In an interview during the 1960 campaign, she had recalled a George Bernard Shaw quotation she had read first as a high-school student: "The worst sin toward our fellow creatures is not to hate them, but to be indifferent to them." Already, she had applauded as the Cabinet and Administration wives, among them Adele Rogers, wife of the secretary of state, who was an aide in a Washington public school, got involved in their own volunteer activities.

On June 16, Pat Nixon embarked on a visit to ten Vest Pockets of Volunteerism in California and Oregon. At her request, it was a working journey with no governors or mayors at the airports, no political rallies or crowds, no bouquets. America was at war and the mood of the country was sharply questioning and worried. Mother was sensitive to the mood of unease and wanted her trip to be without frills or pageantry. Forty members of the press corps traveled with her as she visited, among other sites, an adult literacy center, a community garden project in a black slum area, a day-care center for children of migrant workers, and a volunteer Braille operation at a Jewish temple.

At several different stops, the First Lady was picketed by demonstrators, some against the war, others advocating various social issues. The Associated Press correspondent noted at one stop that Mrs. Nixon "took little notice during the tour of demonstrators who carried banners reading 'How many people will be fed by your visit today?'" But the majority of reports filed from California and Oregon emphasized that the cause of promoting volunteerism had been well served. *U.S. News & World Report* summarized the tour as "a quiet trip, a working trip, and a trip with a purpose. That seems to be Pat Nixon's style."

My mother truly believed in the power of individuals to help one another and to change society. The Vest Pockets of Volunteerism trip gave her a quiet satisfaction, but at the same time she was not blind to the resistance among feminists and some in the media to her focus on volunteerism, with its reputation of being the preserve of those with time on their hands (although statistics show that more than half of those who volunteer also work full time). In addition, in refusing to allow volunteerism to be labeled her sole project, as beautification was Lady Bird Johnson's, she knew she was disappointing those who wanted a neat label for her.

She continued to believe that what she was doing for the White House in acquiring American antiques and in opening the mansion to more people, as well as her meetings with those from foreign nations and with citizens from across the country whom she helped honor for their achievements, was as important as a news-making trip to promote volunteerism. "People are my project," she told one interviewer.

The first Sunday after the inauguration, my parents held a worship service in the East Room of the White House with Billy Graham as the speaker. Over the next five and a half years, services were conducted from time to time by ministers of every faith, from all parts of the United States, including Terence Cardinal Cooke, Rabbi Louis Finkelstein, lay minister Bobby Richardson, the former baseball player, and Dr. Norman Vincent Peale.

Since their marriage, my mother and father had not attached themselves to a particular denomination, choosing in each place they lived a church which provided a happy medium between my father's Quaker upbringing and the Methodist services Mother had attended as a child. The White House church services provided an opportunity to hear outstanding speakers. And worshiping in their own home enabled my parents to avoid the disruption that occurred each time they visited a public building with their huge security entourage. The services also gave them the pleasure of opening the White House to families. Children were infrequent guests in the Executive Mansion and, until Amy Carter, were never included in state dinners or luncheons. My parents welcomed the worship services as a way for diplomats, congressmen, and senators, whose sons and daughters are often among the most neglected in the political city of Washington, to bring their children. At any given church service one might meet the Chief Justice of the Supreme Court and Mrs. Burger, one of the White House telephone operators who worked out of a basement office in the Executive Office Building (EOB), a congressional staff member, or the butlers, maids, and other invaluable men and women who made the White House run.

Kathleen Stans, whose husband, Maurice, was secretary of commerce, came to almost all twenty-six of the services held in the first two years. She told me:

> They were one of the greatest forms of bringing people together, and for Maury and me personally, they were especially meaningful. We are both Catholic and at that time we were studying other religions. And suddenly, in the White House, we had a chance to experience ecumenism. There it was, unfolding in front of our eyes—one world, just as it should be.

As newspaper articles about the worship services appeared, some of them sharply critical of the White House for blurring the separation between church and state, social secretary Lucy Winchester was deluged with hundreds of letters from people wanting invitations, as well as by those who wrote to suggest choirs and ministers. The volume of letters surprised Lucy; people rarely wrote her to ask to come to state dinners. At Mother's suggestion she began keeping on file all letters that gave dates for expected visits to Washington, and when a service was scheduled, she would check the file and try to contact the families. In this way, at least a hundred people from across the country as well as several choral groups came to a White House worship service.

On July 20, 1969, the day man first set foot on the moon, there was a worship service with Colonel Frank Borman, an Apollo 8 astronaut, reading the first lesson from Genesis. In the beauty of the East Room, we sang with special fervor the words of the Navy hymn, "Lord, guard and guide the men who fly, Through the great spaces in the sky."

A few days after Neil Armstrong's moon walk, my parents undertook a goodwill trip to Asia and Europe code named Moonglow. Many of the hundreds of thousands who came out to see them in Asia could not believe that the Americans had put a man on the moon. The acting president of India explained that the majority of his countrymen thought the moon walk was a Hollywood production.

My parents were gone only eleven days but in that time visited eight countries. In addition to India and the Philippines, they went to Indonesia, Thailand, South Vietnam, Pakistan, Romania, and Great Britain. Mother told Helene Drown that she felt like a "dress extra" because she had changed her clothes so often for different climates and events. Her stage analogy was an apt one. The First Lady abroad is literally on camera most of the time.

Some of the events on my mother's schedule had been suggested by the host countries, such as her visit to a children's hospital in Indonesia, which Mrs. Suharto, the president's wife, was anxious for her to see. Bill Codus, who since 1966 had taken periodic leaves of absence from CBS in order to help in my father's political work and who was now with the State Department, had been sent ahead to make arrangements. My mother thoroughly enjoyed Bill and always felt at ease when he was involved in planning a trip. He was at her side during the hospital tour and watched helplessly while a huge American and Indonesian press entourage engulfed her as she attempted to chat with the children. She spent most of her time trying to calm crying youngsters who were terrified by the cameras and glaring lights. As soon as she left the hospital, Mother caught Bill's eye and, not trying to hide how upset she was, whispered that she never would visit another children's hospital with a large press contingent.

One of the correspondents covering the Nixon journey, Robert Donovan, described the First Lady's visits to hospitals and schools while "the Statesmen on the trip had long ago settled down in air conditioning and relaxed over a good chat about Red China." Donovan, whose daughter had been my fifth- and sixth-grade classmate, wrote that Mrs. Nixon

has a distinctly motherly way with them [children], returning their gestures and patting them on the head. When her daughters, Tricia and Julie, were teen-agers attending the Sidwell Friends School in Washington, Mrs. Nixon would wind up their slumber parties by tucking their guests into bed and kissing them good night to make them feel at home. This manner with children she carries around the world with her.

Pat Mosbacher, the wife of the chief of protocol, discovered on the trip that the First Lady was "a self-contained unit capable of taking care of her clothes, her hair, her schedule. She never wanted anything special at all." Mother's two-person staff on the trip, press secretary Gerry Vander Heuvel and her assistant Pat Gates, was remarkable given the full schedule the First Lady had in the nine countries, and more remarkable when one considers that a modern presidential trip can consist of between six hundred and eight hundred people. The traveling party includes numerous White House staff members and their secretaries, communications experts and baggage handlers, at least fifty Secret Service agents, and a press contingent of three hundred or more. But throughout the Nixon Presidency, Mother would choose to travel, both at home and abroad, with the fewest number of aides possible, because she felt that a personal entourage was not appropriate for America's First Lady. Being surrounded by staff was a barrier to talking informally with others and enabling them to feel at ease with her.

The purpose of the trip that took the presidential party around the world was to search for a solution to Vietnam and to explain to our Asian allies what became known as the Nixon Doctrine: the United States would keep all existing treaty commitments in the Pacific but would not make new commitments that might lead to another Vietnam involvement. An unannounced visit to South Vietnam was the most important day of the journey. President Thieu was uneasy about the withdrawal of American troops announced several months earlier. In Saigon, my father reassured him that, although the withdrawals would continue, military and economic assistance would still be provided. He emphasized that the American public would no longer tolerate an increase in the number of fighting men in Vietnam. Vietnamization, the process of training the South Vietnamese to defend themselves, was to begin.

The Secret Service had strongly opposed the trip to South Vietnam and insisted it be secret from all except a handful of senior agents and presidential aides. When the news became public, however, not many among the press corps and the White House staff were totally surprised since all had noted the President's schedule for Thailand had one relatively unscheduled day—certainly a rarity on a foreign trip. But the head of my mother's Secret Service detail, Vern Copeland, a relaxed, kindly man who often bent the rules to give the First Lady more freedom by allowing her to walk far in front of him, was shaken and pale when he learned the news that they were to depart Bangkok within the hour for Vietnam. Fervently he warned, "Mrs. Nixon, this is one day you're not going to get away from me!"

The trip marked the first time that a First Lady had been in a combat zone, although another First Lady, Eleanor Roosevelt, had also visited troops on her numerous travels to England and throughout the South Pacific, Australia, and New Zealand during World War II. National Security Adviser Henry Kissinger later described how the President and his party were "whisked from the airport to the Presidential Palace in a helicopter that seemed to go straight up out of range of possible sniper fire and then plummeted like a stone between the trees of Thieu's offices. I never learned how often the pilots had rehearsed this maneuver or," he added ruefully, "how its risk compared with that of sniper fire." While my father met with President Thieu, Madame Thieu hosted a formal tea for Mother in the Presidential Palace. The palace was an armed fortress, with sandbags in every entrance to douse fires from shelling and bombing attacks. Mrs. Thieu told Mother she had sent her children to the country, out of danger of the war zone, and how much she missed them.

Precautions for Mrs. Nixon's security made her contacts with the Vietnamese during the one-day visit very difficult. At the Thuduc orphanage, where 774 children were housed, the hordes of Secret Service agents, reporters, military guards, and the din of the army helicopters whirring overhead all but drowned out any words spoken inside the buildings constructed years before by the French. As Mother emerged from the hospital, she saw fighter jets above the thick shield of circling helicopters. Their shrill whine added to the overpowering noise.

Soon she was in an open-door military helicopter flying eighteen miles north of Saigon to visit the Twenty-fourth Evacuation Hospital at Long Binh. Occasionally she caught glimpses of scattered U.S. troops on the ground below. The agents who traveled with her were armed with machine guns and bandoliers loaded with cartridges slung across their shoulders. In the news dispatches filed from Saigon on July 30, one correspondent wrote:

> Mrs. Richard Nixon risked her safety and possibly her good relations with some diplomats, brass and bureaucrats in Vietnam today. In trips to an orphanage, to a GI field hospital, and her exchanges with high-ranking officials, she made it clear she had little time for high-level formalities and wanted to see more of the men who were hurt and the children who had suffered. . . . At the hospital, officials tried to tell her all about what they do. She brushed them aside. "I don't really want to learn about the hospital, I came to see the boys," Mrs. Nixon said.

She spent more than two hours there, visiting personally with each man, sometimes jotting down names and addresses so that she could let families at home know their sons were all right. Pat Gates remembers how Mother several times got down on her knees next to the wounded men in order to talk privately with them.

Before returning home via Great Britain, my parents visited Romania, which had been included in the hectic round-the-world journey because it was hoped that face-to-face meetings between my father and President Nicolae Ceauşescu would aid the Vietnam peace negotiations. Ceauşescu was both a neighbor of the U.S.S.R. and known to have excellent relations with the isolated People's Republic of China—and the North Vietnamese.

Romania was the only country on the itinerary my parents had not visited before. It was also the first time that a President of the United States had visited a Communist country since the Iron Curtain fell in the spring of 1945. On August 2, 1969, nearly a million people lined the streets from the airport to the capital city of Bucharest, many of them hopeful that a new era was beginning.

My parents were buoyed by the apparent success of the round-the-world trip. Less than a week after their return, they began a three-week "working vacation" in San Clemente, California, at what the press called "the Western White House." The house had been built in 1926 by Hamilton Cotton, a onetime national finance chairman for the Democratic Party. FDR's campaign train once had stopped directly below Cotton Point, and pulleys had hoisted the crippled President up the steep cliff so that he could play poker with his friend.

The white stucco-walled house with red-tiled roof, had not changed much since Cotton had first moved in. Tricia remembers that when she first saw the house, "It was something out of the past. If there were ghosts, they would live at San Clemente." The rooms were dark and musty, with Spanish-style furniture, heavy damask drapes, and wrought-iron bars on the windows. Tall, thick hedges and canvas awnings at the windows reduced the sunlight and blocked most of the view. "The house had such a strong personality," Tricia told me, "that I wondered if we could ever make it our own."

That August was the first time David and I had visited San Clemente. I had been with Mother and Tricia a few months before, however, when in one long, incredibly busy day Mother had worked with decorators in Los Angeles and chosen carpeting, draperies, furniture, wallpaper, even accessories. Now, miraculously, each room was light and beautiful. My father chose the name La Casa Pacifica, the peaceful house. And it was peaceful, with its vista of the deep-blue Pacific and the towering, gently swaying royal palms and sheltering eucalyptus trees.

Every day that summer it seemed we discovered a different kind of flower or plant as we walked along the paths of small, round inlaid stones, themselves works of art. With delight Mother pointed out to her city-bred daughters the vegetation, including a mulberry bush of the nursery rhyme. The weather in mid-August was beautiful: soothingly warm days and cool, crisp nights. Tricia remembers that although my father went daily to his office, which was located in one of the temporary one-story structures erected on the grounds of the adjoining Coast Guard LORAN station, those weeks in San Clemente were "the last calm period in the Presidency." And yet there were undercurrents. Nightly, along with the steady pound of waves, we could hear clearly the sound of gunfire and shelling from Camp Pendleton where marines were being trained, many of them destined for Vietnam.

My parents broke their vacation numerous times to attend special events. For several months my father, with Mother's enthusiastic support, had talked to the family and staff about wanting to "take the White House to the people." One way to do that was to hold state dinners outside of Washington. On August 13, a few days after arriving in San Clemente, my parents honored the Apollo 11 astronauts at a spectacular dinner in Los Angeles attended by 1,440 guests, among whom were forty-four governors, fifty members of the House and Senate, fourteen Cabinet officers, and eighty-three foreign representatives.

A state dinner eight days later in honor of President Chung Hee Park of Korea was held in San Francisco, the city known as "The Gateway to the Orient." Unfortunately, six thousand protesters against the war in Vietnam used the opportunity of the visit of one of America's staunchest Asian allies to gather in Union Square, across the street from the St. Francis Hotel, where the dinner was being held, and set up powerful microphones that blared out rock music, protest songs, and four-letter-word obscene chants. During the dinner, the orchestra muted the sound, but at my father's meeting with President Park that afternoon and the simultaneous tea Mother held for Mrs. Park, most of the words were clearly discernible. Tricia, Adele Rogers, and I were present at the tea and tried to shout above the nerve-jangling din. Each time the protesters paused to organize the next chant, we would fall silent, resting and waiting. Then when the chants began again, Mother or Adele Rogers, or Tricia and I, would start up the conversation with Mrs. Park again.

A dinner for President Díaz Ordaz of Mexico a year later, in September of 1970, would be the last held outside the White House. The idea was abandoned not because the evenings were unsuccessful but rather because the logistics of setting up a state dinner away from Washington were a nightmare. Social secretary Lucy Winchester, who had unlimited energy in spite of weighing less than a hundred pounds, remembers that the Díaz Ordaz dinner— one she almost missed—aged her "about thirty-five years." Bob Haldeman, firmly convinced as was my father that holding dinners outside of Washington not only was a good idea but could be achieved quickly and efficiently, had sent word to Lucy that she was not needed in San Diego. But when it developed that the elegant old Hotel del Coronado did not have enough waiters and that the waitresses, once they felt the weight of the tray for each table, decided to picket because they did not want to have to do such heavy work, the television cameras minutely covered the story. Then there was the problem of not enough matching silver, china, and crystal. Finally, Bob Haldeman had to send an SOS to Lucy. She quickly arranged for the Century Plaza Hotel to send extra waiters, china, uniforms, and even salt shakers.

On September 5, at the end of the vacation, Mother drove forty miles from San Clemente to Artesia for the dedication of the Pat Nixon Park. Her childhood home and four of the acres she and her family had farmed were now city property. In February, her brother Tom had written:

Just want to warn you—Artesia-Cerritos (our old home is in the city of Cerritos now) are to have a Pat Nixon Day on May 10th. Boy did I stay clear of this one—I do everything known to keep people from bothering you—but now you belong to all the people.

Not only did Artesia have a new name but also the familiar character of the town had changed. Many of the citizens of the now busy city of Cerritos were Mexican-Americans. The park would be a welcome island of green in the midst of the low-cost tract housing where once there had been farms. The Ryan home was destined to be used as a center for community activities for Girl Scouts, Camp Fire Girls, and other gatherings for teen-agers.

Myrtle and Louise Raine were in the crowd of one thousand and heard their old friend Buddy Ryan deliver one of her rare public talks. "I remember so well living here. It was just a wilderness then with rows of trees there," Pat recalled, making a sweeping motion toward South Street. "But we felt we had a good education and we made progress, and I know those who live here now will continue that spirit."

After the dedication, the Whittier *Daily News* editorialized:

It was the simplicity of the Cerritos event that was impressive. Mrs. Nixon put on no airs. She spoke of her joys of childhood. Her remarks were unadorned and straight from the heart. The sum total of what she said reflected the early lives of millions of other Americans. And it is this quality of understanding similarity, of life experiences, that binds the middle-class Nixons to so many other Americans.

Almost twenty years have passed since my parents moved into the White House. Writing about those years now, with Ronald Reagan in the White House, the cities and campuses quiet, an all-volunteer army in place, and America no longer at war, it is difficult for me to convey the fierceness of the dissatisfaction with the Presidency and our institutions in the late sixties. My father had won the election on November 6, 1968, but the sense one got in the White House that first year was that we were still running. In a national call to action, many in the peace movement demanded a less impersonal, uncaring government and institutions. On the campuses, students wanted parietal privileges, ungraded courses, a greater say in governing their schools— and peace in Vietnam, *now*. Two small, fanatical militant groups, the Weather Underground and the Black Panthers, demanded an end to racial and social injustice, *now*.

Increasingly, violent rhetoric ("Off the pigs [police]" was the most widespread graffito of the day) and violent actions were considered acceptable means of drawing attention to the ills of society. In the words of Tom Hayden of Students for a Democratic Society (SDS), when students succeeded in destroying social institutions, the universities would be caught in the middle: "What we are seeking is instability"; the protesters "want a new independent university standing against the mainstream of American society or they want no university at all." Nationwide, from January of 1969 to April of 1970, there were more than forty thousand bombings, attempted bombings, and bomb threats. On the campuses alone during the school year of 1969–1970, David's and my senior year, there were 174 major bombings and bomb attempts and 274 arsons. The FBI would report for the same academic period 1,792 campus demonstrations, 8 people killed and 462 injured, of which 299 were police.

In the fall of 1969, with the return of students from summer vacation, the demonstrating resumed with unparalleled intensity. Antiwar activists planned a nationwide day of protest, the Vietnam Moratorium, in Washington on October 15, declaring that they would hold similar demonstrations in different cities on the fifteenth of each month until the war ended. My father feared, correctly it developed, that because of the demonstrations, his private warnings to North Vietnam to end the impasse at the conference table or face "measures of greatest consequence" would have little effect on the Communists. How could the President ignore the overwhelming national attention that was being focused on the moratorium? And how much longer would it take before more Americans, shocked by the sight of death and violence as television for the first time brought scenes of war into their homes nightly, decided any way out of the war was better than staying in Southeast Asia? The North also realized the bombing halt was vastly popular. It was far from certain the President would be able to muster enough domestic support in the increasingly likely event he decided to resume the bombing in order to bring Hanoi to the negotiating table.

As the national media focused on the college teach-ins and plans for the Vietnam Moratorium, Washington *Post* columnist David Broder wrote on October 7, "It is becoming more obvious with every passing day that the men and the movement that broke Lyndon Johnson's authority in 1968 are out to break Richard Nixon in 1969. The likelihood is great that they will succeed again." Former secretary of state Dean Acheson echoed Broder a few days later in his comments to *The New York Times* about "the attempt being made from so many sources to destroy Nixon. . . . I think we're going to have a major constitutional crisis if we make a habit of destroying Presidents."

Although outwardly serene, behind the walls of the White House my mother felt a tenseness in the air so sharp it was almost tangible. On Moratorium Day, October 15, as a quarter of a million people converged peacefully on Washington, Mother kept her originally planned schedule, presenting awards at a luncheon given by the American Association of Nurserymen, a tea for members of the Soroptimists, a service club, and a meeting with Señora Aurora Juárez de Oporta, mayor of Uyuni, Bolivia. That evening, as the news was blanketed with reports on the demonstrations, my father began work on a speech he would deliver November 3. He was now convinced, as he wrote in his *Memoirs*, that the "protest for peace" ironically had "destroyed whatever small possibility may still have existed of ending the war in 1969." Across the top of his yellow legal pad he noted: "Don't get rattled—don't waver—don't react."

The night of November 3, my father had his last chance to heed the advice of those in Congress who warned him not to let Vietnam become "Nixon's war." Instead, the Americans heard their President announce that the United States would not desert the South Vietnamese until an equitable peace had been achieved and the South could defend itself. Vietnamization would continue, as would troop withdrawals depending upon the level of fighting. As the President spoke, there was no mistaking his refusal to be swayed by the demonstrations. Just as thousands of those who had marched peacefully in Washington three weeks before sincerely believed America should leave Vietnam with no conditions, my father believed the United States must honor its commitment to help a small—and to some, unimportant—country retain its independence.

The address had tremendous impact. At the conclusion, my father had appealed "to you, the great silent majority of my fellow Americans —I ask for your support . . . North Vietnam cannot defeat or humiliate the United States. Only Americans can do that." Thus, the Silent Majority was born. The White House mailroom received more than fifty thousand telegrams and thirty thousand letters in support of the President, the largest response ever to a presidential address.

The speech also led to a celebrated confrontation between the press and the White House. In his address my father had used the medium of television to appeal directly to the people. Immediately following the address, however, correspondents for CBS, NBC, and ABC had launched into what can best be described as rebuttals of the speech. They carried no reactions from the viewing audience or from political leaders who supported the speech.

Although traditionally there is an adversarial relationship between the President and the press, during the Nixon Administration, advocacy journalism reached new heights. In a landmark study financed by the Historical Research Foundation and published in 1971, Edith Efron, a staff writer for *TV Guide*, documented television's resistance to a Nixon victory. Efron analyzed the transcripts of all nightly network news broadcasts for the seven weeks prior to the 1968 election, and then flatly concluded:

> All three networks clearly tried to defeat Mr. Nixon in his campaign for the Presidency. . . . If Richard Nixon is President of the United States today, it is in spite of ABC-TV, CBS-TV, and NBC-TV. Together they broadcast the quantitative equivalent of a *New York Times* lead editorial against him every day—for five days a week for the seven weeks of his campaign period.

Critics were quick to challenge Efron's methods, but candid insider accounts of the campaign bore out the conclusions. For example, Gloria Steinem, in an article for *New York* magazine, had written:

> . . . The reporters don't like Nixon. As far as I've been able to find out, only two members of the ninety-odd press corps are likely to vote for him: the *U.S. News & World Report* man, who was also for Nixon in 1960, and the Voice of America correspondent, who is thought to be Republican because he doesn't join in anti-Nixon bull sessions and smokes an unlit pipe.

Although my mother did not watch much television, she read avidly and of course was aware of anti-Administration stories. Whenever she had an opportunity, she urged my father to hold televised news conferences because she felt the question-and-answer format was an excellent way of communicating his views to the public. In a press conference, he could answer questions directly and not have his views "interpreted" or a point ignored or distorted. But my father, because he was so busy, did not always want to set aside the full forty-eight hours with no interruptions that he felt were needed to be prepared for a minimum of a hundred and fifty to two hundred potential questions. In addition, he did not relish the confrontational atmosphere of most of the press conferences. They tended to underscore that the Nixon Administration from the beginning was fighting for its life and could not afford a mistake. Consequently, he did not hold as many press conferences as Mother and some of his advisers urged.

The Administration's frustration with the media's coverage of the war peaked a few days after the November 3 speech when Pat Buchanan sent my father the draft of a speech criticizing the network commentators' "instant analysis" following presidential addresses. Vice President Spiro Agnew agreed with my father and Buchanan that the issue of media influence and bias needed to be aired. Agnew refined the speech, and on November 13, ten days after the Silent Majority address, he directly challenged the networks by charging that their "endless pursuit of controversy" had resulted in "a narrow and distorted picture of America." For too long in 1968 and 1969, a majority of news coverage had gone to demonstrators and protesters while the views of those who supported the President's actions in conducting the war or in other areas went unrecorded. Making it clear that he was "not asking for government censorship or any kind of censorship," Agnew called on the public to "let the networks know that they want their news straight and objective."

Agnew's speech was the impetus to more Americans to begin to look critically, carefully at what they read in the newspapers or saw on television. As with the November 3 speech, an onslaught of favorable telegrams and mail descended upon the White House. My mother was pleased and not at all surprised by the public's response, but privately she questioned the wisdom of speaking out so bluntly through Agnew. In her role as First Lady she tried to ignore the controversies, deliberately proceeding as if the dangerous polarization in the country did not exist. It worried her that the networks were so clearly stung by the unprecedented criticism of their objectivity by a high-level government official. Their official reaction was to charge "repression" and "intimidation" and vigorously to defend their practice of immediate commentary after a presidential speech, even a speech through which the President was trying to rally the nation. Not until four years later did they substitute the more balanced approach of airing the views of those who agreed and disagreed with a speech. It concerned Mother also that while Agnew's point had been to warn the public about the bias in television news, in the months ahead some in the broadcast industry would change the focus of the debate and insist that the speech represented instead an assault on freedom of the press.

On November 15, the November Vietnam Moratorium, known as the New Mobe, staged demonstrations in San Francisco and Washington, marked by shrill rhetoric and sporadic violence. In San Francisco, Black Panther leader David Hilliard told a crowd of 125,000, "We will kill Richard Nixon. We will kill any[one] that stands in the way of our freedom." And comedian–peace activist Dick Gregory told the 250,000 demonstrators who had massed at the Washington Monument, "The President says nothing you kids do will have any effect on him. Well, I suggest he make one long-distance call to the LBJ Ranch."

Tragically, the lines were drawn.

Less than two weeks after the New Mobe, my parents enthusiastically celebrated their first Thanksgiving in the White House with 280 Washington-area senior citizens. Both my mother and father were always very sentimental about holidays. Each one was to be savored and made special. Dinner with those in the old-age homes, who otherwise might have a cheerless, lonely holiday, would be a Thanksgiving to remember.

Cabinet officers, my mother, Tricia, David, and I, and three members of

David's family—his grandmother Mamie, Mamie's ninety-year-old Uncle Joel Carlson from Boone, Iowa, who was our houseguest over the holiday, and David's seventeen-year-old sister, Susan—hosted tables set up in the State Dining Room and, for the first time, in the East Room. Apart from some deafness, Uncle Joel was in better health than many of the guests. Mamie, at seventy-three, looked remarkably youthful, her face unlined, her complexion still creamy. With her big china-blue eyes twinkling, she did not hesitate to tell her tablemates her age and succeeded in charming all completely.

My parents frequently invited the recently widowed Mamie to stay with them at the White House. No matter how busy my mother's schedule, when Mamie visited, she always set aside time for what Mamie relished most, "girl talk." My mother welcomed such moments with Mamie, especially the visits that coincided with a state dinner. The hours following a stimulating state dinner were often an anticlimax. My parents usually chatted in the West Hall for a few minutes, exchanging views about the evening. But afterward my father would go immediately to his small study in the Lincoln Sitting Room, across from the Queen's Room, where, still in his evening clothes, he smoked a cigar as he read the last war reports of the day and briefed himself for the morning events. He often worked late, placing phone calls once he felt his Administration officials had arrived home from the party.

Sometimes it seemed as if the White House were designed to keep husband and wife separated in the midst of their own activities and responsibilities. Both had busy schedules with more individual than joint events. In the vice-presidential days, Mother had often been intimately involved in negotiations and decisions simply because of her proximity when meetings were held in our home on Forest Lane, and because there were not unlimited staff members available. During the steel strike in 1959, for example, for nine days and nights all parties met secretly at our home. While my father acted as mediator, Mother had provided coffee, greeted both sides, and made all feel welcome. But she would never play that kind of role in the White House, especially since my father tried increasingly to separate his political and personal life.

At the end of a glittering evening of entertainment, the President and First Lady did not leave and go home to relax. Home was upstairs, and even had they been eager for bed, it was too noisy to sleep. Into the early-morning hours, they heard the sounds of the dismantling of the party. First, the monotonous, even-pitched voice of the military aide who announced the guests' cars. Next the scrapes and thuds as men removed the spindly gold-and-white chairs from the East Room, where the entertainment had been held, so that in the morning, when the tourists filed through the White House, the room would be impressive in its vast emptiness. Then the whir of vacuum cleaners.

The night I attended one of my first state dinners, after the party ended I came down from my third-floor bedroom to get something to eat from the family kitchen on the second floor. As I stepped off the elevator into the long, wide hallway, only one lamp was lighted on a table a few feet from where I stood. Thirty yards away, at the entrance to the Grand Staircase, I saw my mother, still dressed in her evening gown. She was swaying to the faint sound of music coming from the Grand Foyer where some of the guests were still enjoying the dancing. On tiptoes, she moved gracefully across the gleaming parquet floor. I did not intrude but rather turned and went on to the kitchen.

CHAPTER 23

"A Real Pro"

The morning of February 13, 1970, Mother arose around her accustomed time of seven o'clock, rang for some coffee, dressed, and then opened her sitting-room door to pick up the Washington *Post*, *The New York Times*, and the "Presidential News Summary," all of which lay on the round coffee table a few steps from her room. The summary, usually forty-plus pages, was a compendium of television, newspaper, and magazine news prepared each night for the President and distributed to senior staff as well. Attached to the summary that morning was a special fourteen-page section entitled "The Administration's First Year—Editorial and Column Reaction." My mother read the fourteen pages, marking passages as she went. She starred a single item: columnist David Broder, who four months earlier had described the anti-Nixon coalition, wrote that the President's major achievement in 1969 had been to demonstrate that the "violence-wracked America of the late 1960's was capable of being governed"; the "breaking of the President" had failed.

But enormous problems remained, and the most intractable was Vietnam. The young protesters were increasingly active. At the first White House church service, in January of 1969, Billy Graham had spoken of the spiritual emptiness of Americans, particularly the young, and of their search for meaning in life. Some were finding meaning in volunteer efforts to help those in need, and my mother wanted to draw attention to their idealism and good works. On

March 2 she began a week-long trip to visit college volunteer programs in Michigan, Kentucky, Ohio, Colorado, and Missouri.

I remember that my mother's mood as she embarked on the trip was subdued. She knew that by reaching out to the student volunteers, she inevitably would be accused of ignoring the voices of the Vietnam activists. Her trip would not change substantially how young people viewed the Administration; the war would continue to be the great divider. Yet my mother had always been a doer, driven by a sense of duty; she was not going to pass up an opportunity to do something positive.

That first week in March 1970, student volunteers were in the news as Pat Nixon, in the words of *Time* magazine,"... filled her fourteen-hour days with visits to the poor, the blind, the retarded, the aged and the outcast...." She held four stand-up press conferences, each time sharing the microphone with the volunteer students, some of whom wore "peace" buttons. The Washington *Post* reacted to the press conferences by commenting on an emerging "facet of Mrs. Nixon's personality that reporters had not heretofore seen... that is her ability to face with poise and assurance a roomful of reporters and to express with ease and articulateness her interest in and concern for people." Although my mother would be criticized later by *The New York Times Magazine* for avoiding all the "demonstration-prone campuses," she nonetheless encountered antiwar demonstrators and heckling at some of her stops. When asked pointedly just how useful volunteerism was in combating poverty, she replied, "Government is impersonal and to really get our problems solved we have to have people too. We need the personal touch."

As more news items appeared about the First Lady and the students who were ignoring the "generation gap," interest in her trip grew. At the last stop, in Missouri, several thousand people were waiting for Mrs. Nixon at the Springfield airport. *The New York Times* reporter wrote that a crowd of enthusiastic adults pressed forward so heavily on the children in the front row that a Secret Service agent shouted, "Don't squash the Brownies."

My mother's college trip had been conducted "under extraordinary security precautions," according to *The New York Times*, including the use of a four-engine military jet. And despite the publicity about the increased security, while in Boulder the Secret Service learned of a death threat against the First Lady by an individual in nearby Denver. The first Mother heard of the threat was when the correspondent for *Women's Wear Daily*, who had overheard the Secret Service radio traffic, asked her how she felt about her life being in danger. Mother had responded, "I don't know anything about that," and quickly changed the subject. Later, when she was alone with her agents, she got some details, but she characteristically dismissed the danger. When she returned home she never mentioned the incident to Tricia or me. She recognized that the President and the First Lady were vulnerable whenever they were in public, but she had a kind of courage that I frankly was in awe of.

Nineteen seventy was promising to be as volatile a year as 1969 had been, especially on the campuses, where, increasingly, protests against school policies and the war were marred by violence. A six-hour pitched fight with police occurred in April at Ohio State University when angry students demanded the admission of greater numbers of black students and an end to ROTC on campus. Later that month at Stanford, fires set by student protesters destroyed the work of ten visiting scholars and caused $100,000 in damage. And in August, when a bomb set off at the University of Wisconsin killed a graduate student and did $6 million of damage, underground newspapers from coast to coast heralded this blow against the "pig nation."

The domestic terrorism was unprecedented. In 1969, three hundred forty-eight Black Panthers, whose "Minister of Communication," Eldridge Cleaver, had called on the masses to "kidnap American ambassadors, hijack American airplanes, blow up American pipelines and buildings, and shoot anyone who uses guns and other weapons in the bloodstained service of imperialism against the people," had been arrested because of criminal activity, including murder. On March 6, 1970, a town house in New York's Greenwich Village where the Weathermen had secretly operated a bomb factory exploded, killing three who were in the makeshift factory at the time. Twice during my father's Presidency, when I felt I could no longer tolerate being guarded, the Secret Service conferred with me and showed me dozens of threats to kidnap or kill me. Of course there were many more threats against the President and the First Lady. So concerned was the Secret Service about the safety of the President's family that it strongly urged that my mother, sister, and I not travel on commercial aircraft. Because of the escalating airplane hijackings in the United States, seventeen in 1968, thirty-three in 1969, the Secret Service felt the risks were simply too great. How, it argued, could the President answer a terrorist who held captive a member of his family? President Johnson had raised the same issue with my father at their last meeting before the inauguration. Twice in December he had called Don Hughes, who was now a general and slated to head up the White House Military Aide's Office, into the Oval Office for forty-five-minute sessions on the security of the First Family. Consequently, particularly during the first four years of my father's Presidency, Mother, Tricia, and I together with our agents traveled in the United States on government aircraft, usually small military jets.

Despite the certainty of encountering protests and sometimes violence, my parents refused to become trapped in Washington. My father's personal aide during the Presidency, Steve Bull, who usually walked next to him in public to be able to hand him autograph cards to sign and pens to give out, told me that he and many other staff members always wore their oldest suits on domestic trips. They simply could not predict when or where an egg or worse would fly.

Although the Washington newspapers focused heavily on the war and the unrest in the country, they were writing also about the "style" of the occupants of the White House. As a result, I think my mother often felt as if she were living two lives. On one hand, there was much buzzing in Washington about the "breaking of the President"; and on the other, there was talk about whether the Nixons would be pacesetters in entertaining and fashion and whether or not they were "with it." On Inauguration Day itself, *New York Times* columnist Tom Wicker had complained about the Marine Band "playing such square music as 'This Is My Country' and 'God Bless America,'" as well as criticizing the President for offering only "the old values and the old assumptions and even the old rhetoric."

Two of the more widely quoted slogans of the day were "Whatever turns you on" and "Let it all hang out." White House press aide Julie Robinson watched the First Lady quietly resist all the transient changes, and told me:

> I have tremendous regard for your mother because of the times she served in, and "served in" is the only phrase for it. Perhaps because she is a completely self-made woman she had that strong sense of herself and could step back and sort out a society which was going through a self-indulgent adolescence. She was, above all, always a gentlewoman, an old-fashioned way of saying lady.

In entertaining, my parents gave the press much to write about. *U.S. News & World Report* declared in an end-of-the-first-year report that the number of functions President and Mrs. Nixon held in the White House was "unprecedented; one would have to go back to Andrew Jackson who opened the mansion indiscriminately to the general public on important occasions." By January of 1970, my parents had entertained 45,313 people as compared to the previous record of 28,000 in the Johnsons' final year in office. There had been 64 state and official dinners and 116 receptions. *U.S. News & World Report* also pointed out that Mrs. Nixon entertained guests at tea at the rate of 26,000 a year.

One of my mother's priorities in 1969 had been to meet privately with the wives of all the ambassadors in small groups of ten or twelve. The gatherings, which never appeared on the official schedule, were small because Mother wanted her guests to feel at ease and really have an opportunity to converse. Because of her extensive travel overseas, she knew how important a personal meeting was to members of the diplomatic community. It was vitally important to our American Foreign Service (AFS) wives also, many of whom had never met a President or a First Lady and who were embarrassed when questioned by citizens of their host countries about when they had last seen the chief executive or his wife. So Mother hosted several hundred AFS wives at a White House tea.

She made a point never to let guests be rushed through a receiving line, and she had the ability to make people feel at ease. Susan Porter, who would join her staff in 1971 as appointments secretary to handle the hundreds of invitations a First Lady receives, particularly recalls a White House reception when Mother received a cherry-tree quilt from the Appalachian Fireside Crafts, a self-help group located in one of the nation's most poverty-stricken areas. The quilt makers were very simple hill people, in Washington for the first time, and so nervous at the thought of meeting the First Lady that most of them were weeping. When Mother walked into the Diplomatic Reception Room to greet the quilt makers and heard the sobbing, she simply went around the room and wordlessly gave each of her guests a hug. Susan remembers that as the tension eased she was so moved that she felt tears spring into her own eyes.

In the words of Penny Adams, who was on Mother's staff for four and a half years,

> Your mother was a great equalizer. She did not have much use for phonies. She showed interest in everyone she met and found that something special in each. We all want to be loved and that's what she looked for. You never felt she was two people, waiting for the cameras and then turning it on and turning it off. She was always Patricia Nixon, always true.

Above all else, my parents wanted their guests to feel at ease in the White House and yet remember the evening as something out of the ordinary. They both carefully studied the guest lists, jogging their memories for the names of the children of their guests or when they had seen them last. Because my father is shy, he took particular care with such details. Of course there were times when my parents had entertained three nights in a row or were too preoccupied with problems to feel much like a party. I have seen them also when they were simply not rested enough for a long evening. The formal dinners took the most effort. The receiving line formed at seven-thirty sharp, followed by a four-course dinner, coffee and brandy in the parlors, and the entertainment. But I heard my parents tell each other so many times as a party was about to begin that it might be someone's first, and only, evening in the White House. That thought brought the host and hostess to life once they stepped below to the state floors.

Inexorably, however, in the spring of 1970, my father was drawn back after the festivities to deal with problems, not only about the war but also about the threat of renewed racial tension. At the time of my mother's visit with the college volunteers, *Time* magazine's story on the trip had been preceded by an article about a riot in Lamar, South Carolina, caused by a federal court order requiring busing to achieve school desegregation. An angry mob had overturned a school bus. The violence was symptomatic of what the President's assistant for urban affairs, Daniel Patrick Moynihan, had called "an ominous new racial division . . . and with it also a new sectional division, unattended and underappreciated, but not less threatening . . ." There had been no major race riots since the summer of 1968, but could this last? In addition, emotions were running high over "forced busing," a result of the Supreme Court's unanimous ruling on October 29, 1969, that segregated schools be integrated or closed *at once*.

As a former teacher, Mother hoped that the long-cherished system of the neighborhood school could be preserved whenever possible, and she heartily supported the Administration strategy of creating a climate of cooperation in the South toward integration so that the lower courts would not be compelled to resort to rulings such as busing to carry out the higher court's decree. Acting upon the advice of his informal Cabinet Committee on Education, my father encouraged the formation of State Advisory Committees made up of a cross section of blacks and whites in each of the seven southern states that were still in noncompliance with school desegregation. Skillfully, the debate was shifted from whether desegregation would take place to how it would be achieved. By the time my father left office, the number of black children in all-black schools would drop from 68 percent in 1968 to 8 percent in 1974.

On April 29, only nine days after the announcement that 150,000 more troops would be withdrawn from Vietnam over the next twelve months, Rose Woods telephoned David and me at our apartment in Northampton to tell us my father was preparing a major speech on the war. Earlier in the month, the North Vietnamese had launched an assault against Cambodia's new government under Lon Nol and had reached within twenty miles of the capital, Phnom Penh. The Communists now controlled more than one-quarter of the country and, from their military bases on Cambodian territory bordering South Vietnam, were staging large-scale attacks on American and South Vietnamese troops. My father had decided to back a joint U.S.–South Vietnamese "incursion" into Cambodia's Fishhook and Parrot's Beak, two of the key North Vietnamese–controlled areas of the country. The troops, staying a maximum of sixty days, would destroy enemy military supplies, drive out the North's troops, and then withdraw. In presenting this decision, the White House would carefully use the word "incursion," not "invasion." But, Rose explained, my father feared the reaction to the speech, especially on the campuses. Already that month there had been some two hundred antiwar protests. So as not to worry him when he had his mind on the speech, she continued, would we come down to the White House that evening?

Twenty-four hours later, my father told the nation that the time had come "to protect our men who are in Vietnam and to guarantee the continued success of our withdrawal and Vietnamization programs." Appealing for patience, he said he was resolved that America not become a "pitiful, helpless giant" that stood by while its men were slaughtered by Communist weapons stored in Cambodia and by Communist troops billeted there. He said the purpose of the incursion was to end the war more quickly, and defiantly declared the action was necessary even if it meant he would be a one-term President.

I remember that after the address to the nation my father sat with us for a while in the Solarium while he ate a light supper. He was still keyed up from the speech. Mother, with unmistakable intensity, led the way in reassuring him of the rightness of the decision. In a little while he went down to the second floor and sequestered himself in his favorite room for thinking and working, the small Lincoln Sitting Room where Mother had placed his old brown-velvet easy chair and ottoman from our New York apartment.

We all felt drained. The family talked a little longer, Mother admitting finally that she did not know how Daddy could hold up under such continual strain day after day. Then around ten-thirty, Mother got up and went into her bedroom. In a few minutes we were surprised to hear the elevator. A heavyset, compact figure emerged; it was the chief justice of the Supreme Court, Warren Burger, his shock of thick white hair neatly combed back. Briefly he glanced toward Tricia, David, and me at the far end of the West Hall, then turned and started walking down the long center hall. We whispered to each other: Was he expected? Did he know how to find my father in the Lincoln Sitting Room? Later my father told us that a Secret Service agent had telephoned with news that Burger was at the northwest gate with a personal note. My father had asked that the chief justice meet him in the Lincoln Sitting Room. Warren Burger had been moved by the speech, telling my father, "I think anyone who really listened to what you said will appreciate the guts it took to make the decision."

My father would remember the chief justice's words in the next few days as a fire storm of criticism and protest against the "invasion" of Cambodia engulfed his Administration. Critics who charged the United States had "invaded" a neutral nation overlooked, in the words of Britain's *The Economist*, the reality that it was

not the Americans who have brought the war to Cambodia, but the Communists. For years, North Vietnam has violated the neutrality of this country—with barely a chirp of protest from the rest of the world. . . . To condemn the United States for "invading" neutral Cambodia is about as rational as to condemn Britain for "invading" formally neutral Holland in 1944.

In part, the frantic reaction to the Cambodian incursion was a result of the strong tone of my father's speech. Another reason for the outcry was that many of the war opponents simply did not believe there was a Communist buildup in Cambodia. Not until more than eight years later, when two Western reporters, Elizabeth Becker of the Washington *Post* and Richard Dudman of the St. Louis *Post-Dispatch*, were allowed into Cambodia in 1978 were the facts established by an unlikely source: the Cambodian Communists themselves. In a ninety-four-page document, the Cambodians angrily detailed the aggression of the Vietnamese: in 1970 there were 1.5 to 2 million Vietcong in the Fishhook area. When Nixon ordered troops into the region, there were some 200,000 to 300,000 Vietcong, including the long-elusive COSVN (the Central Office of South Vietnam), the Communists' military headquarters for operations in Vietnam, which the Cambodian document stated had been able to elude capture at the time of the incursion.

The morning after the speech, my father went to the Pentagon for a briefing from the Joint Chiefs on the Cambodian operation. As he left the Pentagon lobby he was mobbed by an excited, friendly group. One woman thanked him for what he had done, saying that her husband was serving in Vietnam. "I have seen them [the soldiers in Vietnam]," my father responded. "They're the greatest." Then his thoughts went immediately to those student protesters who, with their draft deferments and the privilege of being in some of the finest universities and colleges in the free world, used violence to express themselves not only about the war but also about social issues. He lashed out, calling those who burned books and blew up the campuses "bums." By evening, the "bums" statement was a sensation. Tragically, within a few days my father's singling out of campus *radicals* who burned books and set off bombs was distorted and Nixon was accused of believing that all students were bums. Eleven major eastern college newspapers endorsed an editorial calling for a nationwide academic strike to protest the Cambodian "invasion." The National Student Association called for impeachment of the President. At Kent State University, in Ohio, on May 2, an Army ROTC building was burned as hundreds of demonstrators watched. Two days later there was a confrontation between the National Guard and a large group of students protesting the action in Cambodia. Some of the students began throwing pieces of concrete and rocks the size of baseballs at the guardsmen, forcing them to move backward up a hill. The soldiers panicked and shots were fired. Four young people lay dead, two demonstrators and two bystanders; eleven were wounded.

When the news reached the White House, my mother's reaction was disbelief. She was appalled by the tragic deaths, and tremendously upset that my father's "bums" statement had been so distorted and so indelibly linked to Kent State that the father of one of the victims would tell a reporter, "My child was not a bum." My father would admit later that those few days after Kent State were among the darkest of his Presidency. What made the period so bleak was the seemingly unbridgeable gulf between those who opposed the war for what they believed were all the right reasons and the President who wanted to end it "honorably" for what he believed were all the right reasons.

In response to Kent State, the peace movement called for a National Day of Protest on Saturday, May 9, in Washington. On the eve of the protest, my father held a press conference in an effort to ease the tension somewhat. Afterward, perhaps dreading the next day and obviously distressed by all that had happened, he had been unable to sleep except fitfully for an hour and a half. Between 9:22 P.M. and 4:22 A.M. he spoke to almost forty people by phone. By 4:00 A.M. he was up for the day. In his bedroom on the third floor, Manolo heard music coming from the Lincoln Sitting Room and went downstairs to offer his boss coffee or cocoa. Impulsively, my father suggested that they take a ride to the Lincoln Memorial. Secret Service agents were, in my father's words, "petrified with apprehension" when he told them he was going on a drive and that they were not to notify any staff members. But Egil ("Bud") Krogh, who worked for John Ehrlichman's Domestic Council, happened to be at the Secret Service Command Post in the Peace Corps Building that night and overheard on the loudspeaker the White House agent's report: "Searchlight [the President] has asked for a car," and the other communications about the President's destination. Krogh ordered a car and followed the President to the Lincoln Memorial. There he heard my father talk for thirty minutes or more to a group of eight young people. The gathering grew to thirty or forty before the sun was up. No press representatives were present, but reporters the next day wrote stories based upon what several students told them after my father had left. One said, "He wasn't really concerned with why we were here," and another stated that he had aimlessly discussed sports and surfing. Stung by that account of the meeting, my father dictated a lengthy memorandum to Bob Haldeman describing what "actually took place at the Lincoln Memorial."

Bud Krogh also wrote a memo about the President's impromptu talk with the young demonstrators. "It was very quiet, even hushed, and the President was speaking in a very low, conversational tone to the students, really in with them, not out in front talking to them." First, he told the students that the reason for the Cambodian action was to get out of Vietnam more quickly. As my father recalled in his memorandum to Haldeman, he expressed the hope that

they would not allow their disagreement on this issue to lead them to fail to give us a hearing on some other issues where we might agree. And also particularly I hoped that their hatred of the war, which I could well understand, would not turn into a bitter hatred of our whole system, our country, and everything that it stood for.

When one of the students said, "I hope you realize we are willing to die for what we believe in," my father pointed out that "many of us when we were your age were also willing to die for what we believed in." The point was that "we are trying to build a world in which you will not have to die for what you believe in . . ."

A soft pink light was beginning to illuminate the Lincoln Memorial, and the Secret Service agents were becoming increasingly anxious that the President start back to the White House. But the President had a more basic point to make. He agreed that there was currently a great deal of emphasis on the environment. "Those are material problems. They must be solved." But what was really important, why they were all gathered at the monument, were

> those elements of the spirit... I said candidly and honestly that I didn't have the answer, but I knew that young people today were searching, as I was searching forty years ago, for an answer to this problem. I just wanted to be sure that all of them realized that ending the war, and cleaning up the streets and the air and the water, was not going to solve spiritual hunger which all of us have and which, of course, has been the great mystery of life from the beginning of time....

By the time my father was back at the White House, Mother, Tricia, David, and I were just waking up at Camp David. Mother had agreed to go to the camp because my father had seemed so worried about the thought of us in the White House during the demonstration. But that morning she decided that we should return to the White House to be with my father. The Secret Service was not happy when the First Lady said she was determined to go back to Washington, but within an hour the agents had devised an elaborate security plan. When we opened the front door of Aspen, awaiting us was a plain sedan and several yards behind was a black presidential limousine. An agent ushered us into the smaller car and quickly closed the door, making it clear there was no room for questions.

Down the mountain we wound, the black armored car with Fina and the two dogs in the backseat following us closely. At the foot of the mountain, a Red Cross ambulance joined us to head the procession. Now it was clear what the security plan was. A police car escorting us would have been like waving a red flag. But the ambulance with siren blaring just might help us clear an intersection if students surged at the car. The black limousine was obviously the decoy.

When we reached the city, the streets were crowded with demonstrators, many of them carrying Vietcong flags and dressed in what had become almost the required uniform of the day—long hair and jeans for both men and women. A few blocks from the White House, we recognized several agents at street corners, standing amidst groups of milling students, ready to clear a path if necessary. Until we reached the northeast gate, the car ride was like a play, removed from reality. But at the gate we came face-to-face with helmeted soldiers and at least a dozen policemen. I had a sick, hollow feeling in my stomach when I saw that the White House was solidly ringed by military buses parked fender to fender. The last time buses had been used was in 1968 following Martin Luther King's death and the ensuing riots and fires within blocks of the White House.

When we walked up the steps of the North Portico and entered the White House, it was like entering a tomb. All the window shades were drawn; no lights were burning. But as if nothing were out of the ordinary, the usher led the way to the stairs with a courtly gesture of his hand. We assumed the elevator was being held on the second floor in case it was needed by the troops housed in the bomb shelter under the East Wing of the mansion. Later we learned that the bomb shelter was the official command post, and from there close contact was being kept with the military in case there was a need for reinforcements from the EOB where National Guardsmen were bivouacked.

All day we heard the orchestrated chants of the protesters and the high-pitched whine of their sound equipment. It was extremely difficult to concentrate on anything or anyone else. I marveled at Mother's discipline when she went to her room and spent several hours catching up on her mail. She also joined Tricia, David, and me to watch some of the demonstration on television. Twice we went into Tricia's second-floor closet and through the sheer lace curtains looked out on the crowd massed at the north façade of the house. My father spent most of the day working in the Oval Office. By nightfall, as the groups dispersed, we inside the White House felt the numbness that comes after an intense assault on the senses.

Four hundred fifty colleges and universities were now on strike, among them Smith and Amherst, and classes and study were suspended. Several weeks before our graduation, the head of my Secret Service detail had asked if he could talk to David and me. Formally he told us what we already had heard as campus scuttlebutt: if we or my parents or any of David's family attended either the Smith or Amherst graduation at the end of the month, the campus organizers were boasting they could swell protester ranks to 200,000 people by busing students from the enclave of colleges around Boston and other points in the East. College officials at Smith and Amherst had made it clear to both the Eisenhower family and my Secret Service detail that they could not guarantee our safety at graduation ceremonies. Emotions were running high. The demonstrators' usual chants were "Hell, no, we won't go," "Peace now," "One, two, three, four, we don't want your fuckin' war." But recently the Northampton *Hampshire Gazette* had reported that at an antiwar rally the crowd had screamed a new chant, "Fuck Julie, fuck David."

At Camp David on June 6, the twenty-sixth anniversary of D-Day (and of John Eisenhower's graduation from West Point), my parents hosted a family party for David and me, and for Susan Eisenhower, who was graduating from high school. It was good to be with David's parents, who were home on leave from Belgium where John was United States ambassador. Mamie and her brother-in-law Dr. Milton Eisenhower joined us as did Bebe Rebozo, Rose Woods, David's godfather, George Horkan, and White House doctor Walter

Tkach and his wife, who were special friends of mine. My father seemed particularly anxious that it be a relaxed, fun time. He had had a meeting with Secretary of Labor George Shultz earlier that day and impulsively asked the secretary if he could borrow the robes he had just worn at Notre Dame graduation ceremonies.

At dinner Bebe, wearing the Notre Dame robes, read a funny graduation speech coauthored by Pat Buchanan. The gigantic chocolate cake read "Happy Graduation, John, Julie, David, and Susie." My father offered several toasts and then called on the others at the table to speak. But despite all his attempts to make the party a gala celebration, most of us were unable to forget why we were not in Massachusetts. My mother was quieter than usual. She got down on the floor at one point to play with Tricia's little Yorkie, showing him off for Mamie. But otherwise she did not seem to be part of the party. I knew she had looked forward to celebrating the conclusion of my years of study at Smith and of David's at Amherst. She told me later that she was finding it difficult to accept that the mood of the country had changed so little since the 1968 campaign when screaming demonstrators had reduced Hubert Humphrey to tears.

The events of spring of 1970 seemed cataclysmic at the time to my mother and to all of us. The students continued their protests, but then the onset of summer vacation slowed the momentum, and on June 30, as my father had promised, the last American troops left Cambodia. But for two and a half years more, the frustrating, tragic war in Vietnam would continue to be the center of all things.

On May 31, the awesome twenty-two-thousand-foot-high Huascarán Mountain in Peru became a deadly force when an earthquake triggered an avalanche of ice and debris. Reports of the extent of the damage filtered out slowly because the areas that were struck were remote, inaccessible villages. As the news accumulated, it became apparent that the earthquake was one of the most devastating in history.

Three weeks after the disaster my parents helicoptered to Camp David where they quietly celebrated their thirtieth wedding anniversary. Mother had become increasingly distressed by news reports from Peru: 50,000 dead, an estimated 800,000 homeless. She knew the U.S. government already had provided substantial aid, but before dinner on Saturday night she remarked to my father, "I just wish there were something I could do to help." He suggested she go herself to Peru. Mother remembers how he then picked up the phone and started making calls: Would a trip to Peru by Mrs. Nixon be welcomed? How soon could she go? How fast could more supplies be acquired?

A week later my mother flew to Lima on board *Air Force One*. Her plane and a second Air Force jet carried nine tons of supplies, all raised by private donations. Consuelo Velasco, the wife of the president, was waiting at the airport in Lima to greet Mrs. Nixon. The next morning, the relief supplies were loaded into a C-135 cargo plane, which took Pat Nixon, Peru's First Lady, and members of the American press 170 miles deep into the snow-covered Andes where no jets could land on the dirt runway. Because the cargo plane was not equipped for passengers, Mrs. Velasco was strapped into the copilot's seat, and Mother sat, without a seat belt, on a chrome-and-plastic kitchen chair that had been bolted hurriedly to the floor of the plane.

Mother's interpreter, General Vernon Walters, who twelve years before had accompanied my parents on their journey to Lima and faced death with them in Caracas, described the last minutes of the flight.

When I saw the dirt air strip on which we were to land at the bottom of a deep valley at Anta, I could not believe that they would bring the first ladies of the United States and Peru into such a hazardous strip. It was short, un-surfaced and located at about nine thousand feet altitude with gigantic mountains towering many thousands of feet higher on both sides of the narrow valley. Neither Mrs. Nixon nor Mrs. Velasco seemed concerned. I was.

Walters later told members of the press corps covering Mrs. Nixon that she should have received combat pay.

From the landing camp, they flew in a Marine Corps helicopter to tour the areas of the worst destruction, areas the Peruvians were calling the Valley of Death. For five hours the two First Ladies walked through rubble. The destruction reminded one of the older reporters, a veteran of World War II, of bombed Italy at the end of the war. Men, women, and children crowded around to see the First Ladies. Many villagers had bandages around their heads because of injuries sustained when the heavy beamed roofs of their adobe homes collapsed. Yet they told my mother that they wanted their villages rebuilt on the same ground. In her years of diplomatic travel, Mother had visited combat hospitals, a leper colony, and the often impoverished institutions for the homeless. But she had never encountered such utter misery. Her response was to hug the Peruvians who gathered around her.

That evening, President Velasco hosted a dinner in honor of Señora Nixon. It was the first time the revolutionary government chose to entertain at the Presidential Palace, a building so opulent with its gold-inlaid balcony and ceilings that it reminded my mother of the Kremlin. Twenty-one months before, when Velasco took power, he had begun seizing U.S.-owned sugar plantations and oil fields. Simultaneously, he had sought closer ties with the Soviet Union. On the eve of Mother's departure for Peru, the Washington *Post* had editorialized that because of Velasco the First Lady's mission was "likely to be fraught with political complications and difficulties."

But Velasco, by the end of Mrs. Nixon's first day in his country, had been won by reports of her efforts. She had not made political comments, focusing instead on the tragedy, and trying to alleviate the suffering for a few hours. The president had heard also that Mrs. Nixon prior to a taped interview with CBS had asked the correspondent not to mention the strained relations between the United States and Peru.

The mission to Peru was a success. The Velasco government awarded Mrs. Nixon the signal honor of the Grand Cross of the Order of the Sun, the oldest decoration in the Americas. The Soviet Union was concerned enough about the effectiveness of her trip to dispatch sixty planeloads of goods. Most significantly, a month later, on July 28, Velasco in his Independence Day speech expressed appreciation for foreign help in the aftermath of the earthquake and spoke particularly of "U.S. solidarity with Peru as signified by the special visit of Mrs. Nixon."

For my mother, the trip had been a natural response to an acute human need. Associated Press correspondent Fran Lewin saw it as something more, predicting the trip was "a turning point for Pat Nixon." She noted that none of the former "activist" First Ladies—Mesdames Roosevelt, Kennedy, or Johnson—"ever tried such a person-to-person mercy mission of human concern and diplomatic side effects."

In Washington on July 16, my mother resumed her diplomatic role again, but her activities were far different from the journey to Peru and of greater media interest. Twenty-one-year-old Prince Charles Philip Arthur George, Prince of Wales and heir to the throne of Great Britain, and his nineteen-year-old sister, Princess Anne, were invited to visit Washington for the first time. Brother and sister had just completed an official eleven-day tour of Canada, and by the time their jet landed at Andrews Air Force Base, Princess Anne was feeling the strain of an exhausting tour spent in the shadow of her brother.

Before leaving for Peru, my mother had made most of the arrangements for the royal visit, with special attention to the ball Tricia and I were hosting in honor of the prince and princess. Through United States Ambassador Walter Annenberg, the queen had made a sentimental request: Could her children be quartered in the Queen's Room and the Lincoln Bedroom, which she and Prince Philip had occupied on their visit to Washington in 1957? The answer, of course, was yes, although Mother was concerned about the prince's comfort. Because foreign visitors usually stay at Blair House, she had not yet had a state guest sleep in the Lincoln Bedroom. Would the prince be able to relax in the museumlike room with its copy of the Gettysburg Address in Lincoln's hand on the desk, and the slick, black horsehair-covered chairs and sofa, all from the Lincoln era? Not even the eight-foot-one-inch-long bed with its ornately carved wooden headboard was inviting. The legend is that when Mary Todd Lincoln purchased the bed for the White House guest-room suite, the President thought it was too grand. Unfortunately, the mattress felt as if it were from the Lincoln era also. For months, until corrected by the curator, I had informed all visitors that the mattress was filled with straw, because that is what it felt like to me. But there simply was not enough time to order a new mattress before Charles's visit.

Across the hall from the Lincoln Bedroom was the guest suite known since the Eisenhower Administration as the Queen's Room. Elizabeth II and three other queens had stayed there during the 1950s. Mother ordered the heavy oak sliding doors that separated the two guest suites and the East Hall from the rest of the second-floor living quarters to be kept closed during the royal visit so that Anne and Charles would have as much privacy as possible in their makeshift East Hall "living room."

Unfortunately, not all of the news coverage of their visit was friendly. Apparently neither Prince Charles nor Princess Anne had been briefed on what to expect in the way of press attention while in the United States and seemed surprised by the persistence and informality of the White House press corps. When their black limousine arrived on the South Grounds Thursday afternoon, there were swarms of eager press representatives behind the roped-off area usually set up during the visits of foreign dignitaries. They heard Princess Anne comment to Mother as she stepped from the car, looking more grown-up than nineteen because of her three-quarter-length white gloves and picture hat with its tall crown, "Why so much press?" Prince Charles proved immediately that he was a skilled diplomat and made friends for his country during the visit. He took in stride the jostling for photographs and the shouted questions. But when Princess Anne, perhaps less prepared for the media onslaught, was asked the first evening of her visit how she was enjoying the Lincoln Memorial, she responded firmly, "I do not give interviews." Thinking the question had been misunderstood, the reporter repeated it. Again Anne said, "I do not talk to the press."

During a tour of the United States Capitol the next day, when elderly Speaker John McCormack took Anne's elbow to point out a feature of the beautiful domed ceiling, she instinctively jerked out of his grasp. Her action was captured by a television camera and was shown several times that night on the news. David and I also had been taken by the arm that morning. While in the Senate Chambers, South Carolina's Strom Thurmond had gently propelled us, my elbow in his right hand, David's in his left, a few paces away from the Capitol historian, who was explaining the lore of the room to the royal guests. In his persuasive southern drawl, the senator asked us to "take a message to your daddy"—a lot of people didn't like what was happening on busing.

In the fall of 1970, David reported to Officers Candidate School (OCS) in Rhode Island to begin training for his three-year navy duty. During senior year, a group of David's Amherst classmates and my Smith friends had joined us in our Northampton apartment to watch anxiously the first annual military lottery drawing. With a possible 365 numbers, when David's birthday drew a 30, we knew for certain he would be drafted. He decided then he would go forward with his preliminary plans to enlist in the United States Navy.

During his four months at OCS, I lived at the White House and worked toward my master's degree in elementary education at nearby Catholic University of America. David and I wrote to each other daily. While he was adjusting to the 5 A.M. three-mile runs and unfamiliar subjects like engineering and celestial navigation, I was adjusting to life in the White House. Most of my letters were written on note-pad paper, each page stamped "The White House" in dark blue. Beneath that exalted address, I began one letter, "I'm sitting here in my study and I can't think of anything new or exciting to tell you about...I really don't have too much contact with anyone outside of my daily round of classes and teaching." I went on to describe some of the intricacies of White House living.

> There are so many privileges here at the White House that one is never sure whether or not one should use them. For example, just what does it cost and what does it involve for the Signal Corps to show a TV interview or program which they have taped on closed circuit TV? I get the impression that the staff uses the privilege all the time but I am wary of doing so because I don't know what such a request involves. It's like that with a lot of things around here. (The movie services, for example.) Anyway, I mention the TV tapings because I wanted to see the "Today Show" interview with Rose. I missed the actual broadcast this morning because I went to John Burroughs elementary school to "observe." Helen Smith, Mother's press assistant, said we could watch the interview at our convenience. So Mother, Tricia and I are going to watch it at dinnertime.

By 1970, with instant communications throughout the world, news was a big business, and the public knew most everything about the President, his Administration, and his family. A small mirror that belonged to George Washington hangs in the second-floor vestibule that opens on to the elevator. It reminded me constantly of the long history associated with the White House and of how very little we know about the early Presidents. Even thirty years before, a reporter would never have dreamed of asking the very approachable Eleanor Roosevelt at a tea what she thought of the morality of her husband's attempt to pack the Supreme Court, or, later, about the war policy of fire-bombing Dresden. But my mother, Tricia, and I found that the correspondents assigned to the White House were interested in our comments on every subject. Before a state dinner, at the end of a reception, at a "photo opportunity," in a receiving line, at every turn, we were questioned on the topic of the day. In November of 1970 I wrote to David at OCS: "I hate interviews. You never sound like yourself—everything is somehow distorted. I also feel inadequate. What do I have to say in an interview? Here we go, same old women's lib, campus unrest, drugs questions."

At twenty-two years of age I did not relish being quoted constantly as a "young person" in or out of touch, according to the view of the writer, with my generation. In retrospect, I should have taken more cues from my mother, who deftly turned aside many political and personal questions. Indeed, because she was concerned that a casual quip could be misunderstood, the news media saw only a fraction of the kidding and good humor Mother displayed in unguarded moments.

As the 1970 congressional elections approached, she refused to deviate from her lifelong policy that only the candidate can speak for himself on the issues. Although some criticized her for her "blandness," other writers felt her avoidance of controversial subjects made her more effective in her appeals to a cross section of Americans. In the opinion of a reporter for Reno's *Nevada State Journal* who spent a day following "this seemingly tireless lady" as she campaigned for a Republican governor and senator from Nevada that fall, Mrs. Nixon provided "a lesson in politics as handled by a real pro." She spoke briefly at a Reno airport welcoming ceremony, telling the crowd she was happy to be "home again in Nevada." She greeted campaign workers at the headquarters of the senatorial candidate. Then she drove to the capital of the state, Carson City, for a luncheon for state employees and made a "very brief" speech telling the one thousand or more assembled of the need for good government in Nevada and in Washington. At a reception at the governor's mansion she shook hands with "an amiable mob of children." Finally, she returned to Reno and held a brief press conference. When asked whether wives of public figures should "speak their minds," she answered, "It's a decision they have to make. They should know the facts before they speak out," explaining, "I don't speak on political issues because I don't have all the necessary background." In the same breath, however, she added, "It is important for wives to campaign. Unless you are willing to work for good government, then you won't have it."

The Reno correspondent noted that at the end of Mrs. Nixon's long day she sat alone in the back seat of her car during the drive to the airport because, as some Washington reporters explained, "She said she needs a few minutes to herself." But she was not alone in the car. In the front seat were two Secret Service agents. At the end of a busy day of campaigning, Pat Nixon could not slip out for a brisk, mind-clearing walk or swim in a hotel pool or even go down to a hotel lobby to get a paperback without being shadowed. Secret Service protection also meant no reservations to make, no check-out procedures, no transportation arrangements . . . and no spontaneity.

My father was the member of the family who most enjoyed the White House. As he stepped off the elevator for dinner, the family could expect to hear a jaunty two-note whistle. He was upbeat and wanted us to be also. In four months of daily letters to David in Newport, I made only one reference to strain. On November 23, 1970, I wrote, "I didn't see Daddy last night [after an evening class]. Mother said he seemed worried and harassed. They had a nice dinner together last night, however, in the Lincoln Sitting Room."

Family dinner was special to my father, in fact, sometimes the only relaxing part of his day. All fall, winter, and spring, and occasionally in the summer as well, a fire burned in the family dining room, softly illuminating the Revolutionary War soldiers marching across the walls. The eighteenth-century paper had been chosen by Jacqueline Kennedy. If he had time, my father would shower before dinner and put on a fresh shirt. I never saw him at the White House table without a tie, or my mother in slacks. They revered the President's home. Even until our last day in the White House, my parents had a "pinch me" attitude about the mansion and its history. At dinner, my father would exclaim for the hundredth time over the beauty of the sparkling chandelier and comment on the china. The service plates were systematically rotated by the butlers, so we would have Rutherford B. Hayes's boars or elks for one meal and the Eisenhower gold sunburst for another. Without fail, my father would become excited whenever the Wilson service plates were used. These plates, with cream-white centers surrounded by a wide band of deep cobalt-blue and a narrow outer band of raised gold, were his favorite and my mother's also. "Pat, aren't these beautiful? These really are the nicest, aren't they? We should choose something similar for china when we leave." Mother would smile and agree.

My father was exuberant in his eagerness for visitors to enjoy the White House. In the Oval Office he liked to show children the silver cigar case on his desk which played "Hail to the Chief," and to point out the magnificent bas-relief Presidential Seal in the domed ceiling. He kept several desk drawers filled with pens, Presidential Seal pins for female guests, golf balls stamped "The President," and cuff links and tie clasps, and delighted in passing out the mementos.

When my parents knew that friends had visited Tricia and me, they would question us closely on whether or not we had given them a tour. What did they enjoy seeing most? Had we gone up to the Solarium for a view of the Ellipse? David's and my college friends were in and out of the third floor of the White House, and my parents' attitude was the more the merrier.

My mother also loved young children, who usually felt at ease with the First Lady. Helen Smith used to call Mother "the Pied Piper." She had a playful nature and understood children. When Lucy Winchester's five-year-old daughter mentioned to a White House policeman that she wanted a pet, he brought her three frogs and two toads. The day the creatures took up residence in the bathtub of the White House's social secretary's apartment, Lucy confided to Mother that she did not know how to take care of them.

Mother explained that frogs eat flies. Lucy panicked. "We don't have any flies in our apartment." But the White House, as in the case of most old homes, had a generous share of cluster flies, which traditionally live on the second floor. Mother always kept a flyswatter on the shelf of her sitting-room closet. She had a deadly sure swing. In the next few weeks, until Lucy's daughter took the frogs and toads to live with her grandmother in Kentucky, Mother supplied the Winchesters with flies sent in paper cups and envelopes through the interoffice mail.

Mother's staff often experienced her instinct for mothering. Staff Director Connie Stuart remembers the evening that she and her husband were due at an embassy dinner. As she was hurriedly dressing in her office for the party, the zipper of her dress ripped out. Near tears, Connie called her husband to say he should go on to the party without her. Charles Stuart suggested Connie ask Mrs. Nixon for help. When Connie protested, "I can't call Mrs. Nixon about this," Charles countered, "I'll call her." He did, and Mother's response was immediate: "Send Connie right up here and I'll fix her up." Mother quickly enlisted Fina Sanchez's help, and while Fina sewed Connie into her dress, Mother fixed Connie's hair and found an evening wrap. In Connie's words, "She dressed me up like I was going to the prom!"

Although Mother's White House schedule was the most demanding of her life, she dropped everything if Tricia or I needed her. Longtime Storer Broadcasting correspondent Fay Gillis Wells recalls, "You could feel the love in your mother's voice every time she talked about you and Tricia." Fay remembers also that once, just before a radio interview, Mother had confided that political life had not always been easy for her children. She told Fay about an incident at the beach after the 1952 convention. Tricia was digging in the sand with her shovel and bucket. Mother and I were nearby under a beach umbrella. Suddenly a woman walked up to Tricia and spat out, "I hate your father." Perhaps because Tricia and I as children had the added pressure of growing up in the public eye, Mother always wanted us to have the reassurance that she was standing in the wings to help if we needed her.

In late January 1970, when Tricia developed the measles while in Key Biscayne, Mother immediately rearranged her schedule and flew to Florida to sit for three days with Tricia in a darkened room. In 1974 when I underwent emergency surgery in Indianapolis, Mother was in the air within an hour of getting the news. At the White House if either Tricia or I was seriously ill, Mother would make us comfortable in Tricia's sitting room, which had twin beds, and stay with us through the night if necessary. During the day, we would often move down the hall to her bedroom so that while she worked in her adjacent sitting room she could easily attend to our needs if we called. As had been true throughout her married life, her family's needs came first.

In September, my parents left on an eight-day trip to Europe. Forty-eight hours before the departure, *The New York Times* carried a photograph of the President conferring with Yugoslav ambassador Bogdan Crnobrnja about his forthcoming meeting with President Tito. Also identified in the photograph was a then still fairly new face in Washington, "Henry A. Kissinger, a Presidential Adviser." Below the photograph was the news story "Wanted for Nixon Visit to Ireland: One Millhouse." American Embassy officials in Dublin had been "scouring the Irish countryside for distant cousins..."

The embassy had no difficulty contacting Ryan relatives in Ballinrobe, County Mayo, to meet with Mrs. Nixon, much to my mother's private discomfort when she discovered the search was already in progress. On our trip to Ireland in 1964, Tricia and I had decided that although our mother was proud of her Irish heritage she did not think of herself as Irish or German but as an American. We had sensed no nostalgia about returning to the family sod. Now, she was concerned about the artificiality of a public family reunion with distant cousins she had never met. As it turned out, the luncheon with thirty Ryan relatives at nineteenth-century Ashford Castle on October 4 was a happy occasion. Before sitting down to lunch, Mother had been able to talk personally with quite a few of the cousins. When ninety-six-year-old John Fahey showed the former Pat Ryan around the ancient burial ground containing the gray stone markers of their common ancestors, the old man's eyes glistened with tears of excitement. Mother protectively put an arm around his shoulder and said, "You're spry and mighty nice, Mr. Fahey."

The visit with relatives in Ireland was not the first time Mrs. Nixon and her staff had been consulted too late to make significant changes. Only seven weeks before the trip to Europe, Connie Stuart had sent Bob Haldeman a memorandum claiming that "the spirit of détente and cooperation between the President's staff and Mrs. Nixon's staff seems to be sagging a bit... in the planning of trips." Connie complained that her staff often was not informed of trips until the "eleventh hour," making preparations for a separate schedule for Mrs. Nixon very difficult. My mother was frequently exasperated by the indifference she encountered in Haldeman and some of his aides, but she had spent so many years around power that she took with a grain of salt how it changed people. I noted, however, that she always was careful not to reveal her dissatisfaction to her own staff. She despised pettiness and wanted a united front at the White House. For the infrequent times my mother decided she had had enough with a decision emanating from the West Wing, she would wait until my father and Haldeman were meeting alone together—flights on *Air Force One* were ideal—and then raise her objections with both.

It was Bob Haldeman who had felt thirty-three-year-old Connie Stuart would be a good addition to Mrs. Nixon's staff because she had a communications background. By 1970 television had become the main source of news information for a growing number of Americans. The White House increasingly focused on how and at what length the Administration was covered by television news. Connie Stuart's office routinely prepared memos such as a February 11 report on the "Impact of Mrs. Nixon's trip to Indianapolis and Chicago." Mrs. Nixon had toured a power plant and a strip mine in order to demonstrate her concern for the environment, while her husband met with state and federal leaders. Appended to the report was a final page entitled "Summary of TV Coverage of Mrs. Nixon in Chicago and Indianapolis." In Chicago, for example, ABC had given Mrs. Nixon five and a half minutes of coverage, split between the 5 P.M., 6 P.M., and 10 P.M. news shows. Connie Stuart continued to provide such memos on press coverage to the West Wing because both she and Mrs. Nixon knew that former advertising executive Bob Haldeman understood that kind of language.

Despite the last-minute planning for the First Lady's part in the 1970 European trip, her itinerary was full and, if one consults the local news accounts, successful. In Belgrade she held a press reception, and one of the Yugoslav reporters wrote:

> Pat Nixon, surrounded with a dozen of ours and four American lady corre-spondents who accompany her on the current trip, did not accept the role of only answering the questions. She started asking us questions too . . . We spon-taneously exchanged data covering the question how many women have Par-liament seats in her country and ours, and we agreed that it is still a small number. . . .

Another Yugoslav writer concluded her story: "When the tea party with Mrs. Nixon was over I wondered whether I was talking with the wife of a politician or with a woman who is herself a politician. I again remembered the words of Dwight Eisenhower: 'The Nixons are a team.'"

My parents spent a day touring with President Josip Broz Tito, one of the last of the major World War II leaders still in office, and his wife. Among the sites they visited was Tito's birthplace, a small cottage where he pointed out to his guests the mahogany cradle he had been rocked in and the rifle he had used to protect the family vineyards. Jovanka Tito, a smiling, broad, muscular woman, liked Pat Nixon, and three times that day she enveloped her in a bone-crushing bear hug. The third time, Helen Smith happened to be standing near the two First Ladies when Mrs. Tito threw her arms open in a by-now-familiar gesture and started toward Mrs. Nixon. For just an instant, Helen detected the slightest glimmer of panic in Mother's eyes, just before she "went under"; then, her head crushed against Mrs. Tito's, the First Lady looked at Helen, smiled, and winked.

My father's cousin, novelist Jessamyn West, was part of the press entourage covering the busy trip to Europe and had an interview with the First Lady during the long flight home. She later wrote penetratingly in *McCall's* magazine that Pat Nixon's "face is a private face by structure, by its owner's temperament, by her punishing and cruel experience as a girl, by reason of thirty years of political exposure." Being First Lady made my mother one of the most visible women in the world. She performed her job with aplomb and grace, all the while tenaciously resisting encroachments into her private world.

Ten months before the 1970 off-year elections, my father held a meeting in the State Dining Room with the Republican legislative leaders and their wives to discuss campaign strategy. It was Christmastime and House Minority Leader Gerald Ford told him gratefully, "Thanks for inviting wives. It's nice to be together some few hours during the holidays." As the issues were discussed, it was apparent that permissiveness on crime and on violent protest was what most concerned Americans and probably still would in November. Ford pointed to the tragedy of "eighteen crime bills in five different committees. Not one reported out." Nor had there been any congressional action on more than sixty major reforms proposed by the Administration, including legislation on government reorganization, the environment, welfare reform, and national health insurance.

As my father planned for the elections, the social issue of permissiveness was at the forefront of the campaign, with Vice President Spiro Agnew leading the effort to make the Democrats either accept or reject the radicals who were bent on disrupting society. Then in the last three weeks of the campaign my father undertook a blitz on behalf of candidates in twenty-two states. On October 29, at the Municipal Auditorium in San Jose, California, the President addressed five thousand supporters of Senator George Murphy, who was seeking re-election. Governor Ronald Reagan went to the podium first to deliver the traditional warm-up speech. But this was no ordinary rally. In the words of White House speech writer William Safire:

> . . . even before the President came on, the sound of a battering ram was heard. The hall was actually, not figuratively, besieged; the demonstrators outside envisioned it as a drum to beat upon; the staff, after a few nervous self-assurances about this kind of thing only helped our cause, began to worry about getting out safely with the President. The people in that hall, ourselves included, were at once defiant and fearful, a state which is at the least a tribute to the success of the mob's intended intimidation. The Secret Service men, who always had seemed too numerous and too officious before, now seemed to us like a too-small band of too-mortal men.

Before the rally ended, the police had pushed the crowd of about two thousand frenzied antiwar protesters away from the doors so that the President, Governor Reagan, and Senator Murphy could get into the presidential limousine. Just as the demonstrators surged toward the President's car, the agent driving gunned the engine and the limousine shot out of range. But a demonstrator jumped in front of the follow-up car, and the Secret Service driver had to slam on the brakes. Immediately behind was the control car in which Bob Haldeman and Steve Bull were riding. While the follow-up car dodged the protester and roared away, the control car stalled and the motorcade of press and staff chartered Greyhound buses came to a standstill. Some of the demonstrators appeared to be high on drugs. Steve Bull saw one young protester with a baseball bat swing wildly at his car, and miss. For a few very long minutes the mob surrounded the motorcade, screaming obscenities and throwing eggs and rocks, some "the size of a potato," as *Time* magazine reported. Bill Safire was in the staff bus with Rose Woods, and when the first rocks came smashing against the bus, she said, "Just like Caracas," and shouted for everyone to lie down in the aisle. As Safire remembers: "I, like a jerk, kept looking out the window. When a rock slammed into the window on the opposite side of the bus, I was showered with glass splinters, but with my face turned away, I was unhurt...." Finally, the control car started up and the motorcade left the mob behind.

But the effects of the San Jose incident were profound. A mob attack on a President had never happened before. Yet many of the reporters who had been on the buses were loath to write about it, fearful that the White House would "exploit" the incident and use it as more campaign ammunition. When two skeptical reporters demanded to look at the President's dented car, Ron Ziegler arranged for the Secret Service to allow them to do so. *Life* magazine proceeded to distort the facts and declared that Ziegler's act of having the press view the car was going to extraordinary lengths to gain sympathy from the incident at San Jose.

Two days after the incident in San Jose, my father told a noontime crowd in a hangar at Sky Harbor Airport in Phoenix, "As long as I am President, no band of violent thugs is going to keep me from going out and speaking with the American people whenever they want to hear me and wherever I want to go." He continued:

"Law and order" are not code words for racism or repression. "Law and order" are code words for freedom from fear in America. This new attitude means that parents must exercise their responsibility for moral guidance. It means that college administrators and college faculties must stop caving in to the demands of a radical few. It means that moderate students must take a position that says to the violent: "Hit the books or hit the road."

On Election Day, November 3, the Republicans gained two seats in the Senate and lost nine seats in the House, a strong showing in an off-year election with unemployment on the rise. But the GOP lost eleven governorships. Ignoring the significance of the congressional results and focusing on the loss of the statehouses, some of the media in post-election analyses declared a Nixon setback and that the President's chances to be re-elected had been severely diminished.

As the turbulent year ended, we spent our second Christmas in the White House. It was a subdued time but much happier than the somber Thanksgiving dinner the month before when my parents had as their guests one hundred servicemen and -women from the three nearby military hospitals who were unable to be with their own families during the holiday. Mother seemed haunted by those she had greeted who were in wheelchairs and on crutches, and spoke of the dinner for weeks afterward.

But it was difficult for anyone not to have his spirits lifted at Christmastime in the White House. Mother had exuberantly overseen the decoration of the mansion, and the calendar was full with parties for Congress, the Cabinet, the diplomatic corps, the White House staff, the volunteers who helped with both my parents' correspondence, the Secret Service, and friends and family. Large evergreen wreaths, each laden with red berries and pinecones, and with a red candle in the center, were hung in the sixteen windows facing Pennsylvania Avenue. Red candles or bulbs were placed in the chandeliers; a nineteen-foot tree stood in the Blue Room (workmen had to take down the chandelier to fit it in the room); and a nearly irresistible-to-the-touch gingerbread house was in the State Dining Room. In the East Room, seven-foot-high poinsettia "trees" were created by mounting seventy-five or more plants on pyramid-shaped scaffolds. Upstairs, Mother, Tricia, and I had fun putting the finishing touches on our family tree. We hung the special ornaments we had had for years, including a lopsided paper Christmas tree Tricia had made in kindergarten.

That Christmas the White House was open for my mother's "candlelight tours." Because she wanted as many as possible to see the White House in all its Christmas glory and realized few working people could take advantage of the daytime tours, Mother arranged for the house to be open several nights during Christmas week. Fires burned in the Red, Green, and Blue rooms, and the chandeliers and wall sconces were turned so low they appeared to be candles. Rotating ensembles from the Army, Navy, and Air Force played Christmas carols in the Grand Foyer. The atmosphere was magical. Some visitors stopped to sing carols, others even danced around the foyer before they exited down the North Portico steps. The candlelight tours were held every Christmas thereafter.

In the midst of the busy schedule, Mother and Louise Johnson stole some time together for an afternoon of Christmas shopping. It was a treat for my mother to be in a store. Because of her busy schedule she did almost all of her clothes buying through a personal shopper, who several times a year assembled a large selection of dresses to choose from in the privacy of a New

York hotel room. My mother also loved to buy unusual gifts and found it frustrating that on her trips abroad there was rarely time even to window-shop. If there were a few free hours, the security restrictions usually made any deviations from the official schedule impossible. In Rome, a few months before, when a free hour appeared on the schedule, Mother had suggested to Helen Smith that they shop on the famous Via Veneto. But Italian security sent word through the Secret Service that they were uncomfortable with such an expedition.

This Christmas at the top of Mother's list was a gift for Dick. At a favorite jeweler's on Connecticut Avenue, Mother chose rich-blue lapis lazuli cuff links, and Louise selected a similar pair for Rog. Then on the spur of the moment, Mother suggested to Louise that they walk farther down the block to the Elizabeth Arden Salon, where Mother had her hair done weekly. Judy McGohan, the manager of the fourth floor, was very surprised when the first-floor receptionist telephoned to alert her that "Mrs. Alexander" (the name Judy used to book Mrs. Nixon) was on her way up. When Mother and Louise stepped off the elevator, they were alone. "Where's your shadow?" Judy asked. "We shook him," said a smiling and delighted Mrs. Alexander. (Actually, two agents were waiting on the first floor.) Impulsively, Mother suggested to Louise that they show Judy the gifts they had selected for their husbands. Louise blanched a bit, since the packages were beautifully wrapped, but that did not stop Mother. She was like a child in her excitement, knowing for certain that her husband would like the gift. Three days before Christmas, the newspapers got wind of the cuff links and printed what Mrs. Nixon was giving the President, but, as Mother laughingly told Judy McGohan later, her gift was still a surprise "because Dick never reads the women's pages."

Three Nixons and three Eisenhowers—my parents and sister, Mamie Eisenhower, David, and I—gathered around the table in the Red Room on Christmas Day. David was home on Christmas leave from Officers Candidate School, his hair only one-tenth of an inch longer than when he had been scalped two months before. There was a blazing fire on the hearth, and no other light but candles. Outside the White House was softly glowing also.

Shortly after the inauguration, my mother had received several letters from visitors to Washington who wanted to know why the White House, a national monument, was not lighted the way the city's other landmarks, the Lincoln and Jefferson memorials and the Washington Monument, were. She began to question it herself and to remember the many times as the wife of a congressman, senator, and Vice President she had enjoyed driving friends and constituents past the White House, but always trying to do so in daylight.

That fall she began work on the lighting of the White House. She decided to fund the effort by using some of the profits from the inauguration, which traditionally are designated for use by the First Lady on any project she chooses. National Park Service engineers spent months studying diagrams of the house and grounds and submitted various plans for illumination which Mother studied. Great care was taken that the lighting be subtle but still reveal the architectural beauty of the President's house.

In August 1970, when my parents returned to Washington from a trip, as their helicopter neared the mansion, suddenly hundreds of carefully concealed lights on the White House grounds were switched on. The softly glowing mansion was a breathtaking sight from the air. Mother had not told my father that the project was completed, wanting him to be surprised. He was elated. Excited, he ordered the pilot to circle once, twice, a third time. Mother beamed with pleasure.

On November 25, at a small ceremony, Patricia Nixon pressed a button to light the White House officially as the Marine Band played "America the Beautiful." Ever since that evening, the White House has been illuminated after dusk and a lighted flag has flown by presidential proclamation, day and night. It was an exhilarating moment for my mother midpoint in the first Nixon Administration.

CHAPTER 24

1971
"The World's Hardest Job"

On January 23, presidential aide Alexander P. Butterfield sent a memo to Mrs. Nixon:

> The President wanted the following paragraph brought to your attention. It appeared in today's news summary.
>
> > Actress Mercedes McCambridge, appearing on the Dick Cavett show Wednesday evening, opened with a flood of compliments for Mrs. Nixon. Acknowledging the commendation [for her fight against alcoholism] she received at the White House, she said, "Everyone thinks Mrs. Nixon is rather cool, dignified and reserved. But it was the most amazing thing; she walked into the library and said, 'Hi.' She is really vivacious. She has a piquancy about her, and she does her job so extremely well." She makes one feel "so at ease... so comfortable." She "absolutely sparkles" and has a "brightness" about her... to which Dick Cavett said, "Yes, and the world's hardest job."

Nineteen seventy had not been an easy year. Mother had lost enough weight to arouse some press comments about it. We convinced her to go to Bethesda Naval Hospital for a checkup at the same time my father went for his annual physical. The doctors gave her a 100 percent bill of health. It was fortunate she was strong because 1971 did not augur well for the Nixon Administration. My father would later write that the initial months of 1971 were the lowest point of his first term and that he questioned whether he even would be nominated for re-election in 1972. As Congress still showed no sign of acting on dozens of Administration proposals, the war continued to dominate national news—and the Administration's agenda. For example, in his State of the Union address at the start of the year, my father had announced the start of a War on Cancer with a $100 million grant to HEW for research. At the time, the effort to conquer cancer was applauded, but news of the grant for research could not begin to be measured against the controversy surrounding the war and its staggering cost. In fact, many other programs that affected Americans in every walk of life had to take a backseat to the war. An interesting footnote is that fourteen years after the cancer initiative, when my father was asked by an ABC television interviewer what he would like to be remembered for, his answer was not the predictable China initiative or the arms agreements with the Soviets, but rather the fight against cancer, the disease that has caused so much suffering.

A low point in 1971, although it was not recognized as such then, was my father's decision in February to install a voice-activated tape-recording system. He had removed Lyndon Johnson's system when he first came into office in January 1969. John Kennedy also had secretly taped some of his office conversations and phone calls; and both Franklin Roosevelt and Dwight Eisenhower recorded some of their meetings and telephone exchanges. Later, in explaining the rationale for his taping system, my father wrote that the existence of the tapes was never meant to be made public. He planned to consult the tapes for whatever books or memoirs he might write. Because he "did not want to have to calculate whom or what or when" he would tape, a system was installed that was voice-activated. Recording devices were put not only in the Oval Office, the Cabinet Room, and my father's EOB office but also on the phones in those offices as well as on the office phone at Camp David and the Lincoln Sitting Room where my father spent so much time.

Once the decision was made to tape, my father seemed to forget that the system existed, accepting it "as part of the surroundings," as he expressed it. Only a handful of people, and no one in the family, was aware of the taping system.

It was not a well-thought-through decision. After the Presidency, assuming my father was re-elected and served out his entire term, he would have had six years of taped conversations and telephone calls to sort through, a monumental task. Only part of the material would be of historical value. In addition, my father's indirect way of dealing with people, his reluctance with most associates to let off steam and tell someone instantly when he was disappointed, meant that he vented much of his frustration in the privacy of the Oval Office to a handful of trusted aides. His manner of reaching a decision was as circuitous as his way of dealing with his White House associates. He routinely drew out others, encouraging them to expound views different from his own by indicating that he might share their ideas. Thus, at times he appeared indecisive and vacillating, as the tapes would demonstrate to his detriment during Watergate.

Yet when the decision to tape was made, my father was not in the mood to weigh the full consequences of a taping system. He was a beleaguered wartime President, and it made sense to him to protect himself from revisionist historians by taping, as Lyndon Johnson had done a few years before. Under the heading "Should We Have War Crimes Trials?" *The New York Times Book Review* would devote most of its March 28, 1971, issue to an unprecedented mass review of thirty-three books by authors against the war in Vietnam. The reviewer, Neil Sheehan, wrote, "If you credit as factual only a fraction of the information [in the thirty-three books] about what happened in Vietnam... then the leaders of the United States for the last six years at least, including the incumbent President, Richard Nixon, may be guilty of war crimes." Interestingly, Sheehan's six-year time span excluded John Kennedy, who had set America on the course of intervention by sending seventeen thousand combat troops to serve with the South Vietnamese Army and whose Administration had been the architect of the coup that led to President Diem's assassination.

One result of the feeling in the White House of being besieged was my mother's decision to have Connie Stuart hold twice weekly briefings for the correspondents who covered the First Family. Connie had argued that increasingly the press seemed dissatisfied with the White House's written releases on activities; reporters wanted to ask questions directly. In addition, the East Wing press corps in 1971 was still female, the West Wing was primarily male, with the notable exceptions of the UPI and AP correspondents, who crossed the lines. My mother respected the newswomen as professionals and concurred with Connie's view that the briefings would give them more of an opportunity in their reporting.

Shortly after Connie Stuart started the briefings in 1970, it became as common as brushing one's teeth to hear reporters ask questions ranging from what Mrs. Nixon's views were on an important issue to what the Nixons were giving each other for Valentine's Day to the trivia of even more personal details. *Time* magazine reported that Connie Stuart

... works twelve-hour days at her $30,000 a year job, without the tranquilizers used by Madames Carpenter and Vander Heuvel [the two press secretaries who preceded Connie], and unlike her West Wing counterpart, Ron Ziegler, Connie attempts to answer all questions, though she does not hesitate, with a theatrical roll of her eyes, to show her disapproval of certain queries.

The compensations for Connie Stuart in her job were occasions like the gathering of seventy-five members of the Adams family who met with Mother in late February to present to the White House portraits of John Quincy Adams and his wife, Louisa, both painted by Gilbert Stuart. The family spokesman, John Quincy Adams, the great-great-grandson of the sixth President, and great-great-great-grandson of John Adams, our second President, formally presented the portraits to my mother, remarking that they had "been in the family for a hundred and fifty years... while we treasure them—and we always will—they belong here, together, in this house, and in the public gaze that neither of them enjoyed, for all Americans to see."

A few weeks earlier, Jacqueline Kennedy Onassis, the most publicized First Lady of the twentieth century, had visited the White House for the first time since her husband's assassination seven years before. By late January 1971, the official Kennedy portraits, painted by Aaron Shikler at the request of Jacqueline Onassis, were ready to be hung in the White House. My mother, anxious to give proper honor to the portraits, personally wrote Mrs. Onassis to inquire what her wishes for a ceremony were. She in turn asked her friend and former White House press secretary Nancy Tuckerman to hand deliver a letter to Mother. It read in part:

As you know, the thought of returning to the White House is difficult for me. I really do not have the courage to go through an official ceremony, and bring the children back to the only home they both knew with their father under such traumatic conditions. With the press and everything, things I try to avoid in their little lives, I know the experience would be hard on them and not leave them with the memories of the White House I would like them to have.

Jacqueline Onassis then suggested a private viewing of the portraits to be arranged at a time convenient to my mother. Mother asked Nancy Tuckerman if she would mind placing a call to Mrs. Onassis right then to discuss dates; exactly one week later, accompanied by her children, ten-year-old John and thirteen-year-old Caroline, Jacqueline Kennedy Onassis returned to the White House.

My mother was determined that the visit be as private and as happy as possible. Only four members of the White House staff who would be directly involved in the visit were informed and they were sworn to strict secrecy. No one in either the East Wing or West Wing press offices was briefed. My mother, Tricia, and I were waiting at the second-floor elevator when the three visitors arrived. Jacqueline Onassis wore a simple but elegant long-sleeved black dress, a contrast to Caroline's school skirt and sweater. Since I did not remember meeting the then Miss Bouvier as a child, I found myself comparing the woman to the thousands of photographs I had seen. Her face with its large, wide-set eyes and pale skin framed by dark hair was exactly like the photographs, but she was larger boned and more athletic than her photos revealed.

We went immediately to the ground floor to see her portrait, an ethereal, romantic study with her head turned dreamily to the unknown. Although the children liked the portrait, they were discerning; both commented on the hands, noting that their mother's did not resemble the unnaturally elongated, slender fingers the artist had painted.

When we went to the Grand Hall to see the portrait of John Kennedy, Mrs. Onassis said nothing except to thank Mother for displaying it so prominently. Mother, Tricia, and I had not been looking forward to this moment because we wondered how the children would react. The President's head was sunk deeply on his chest, his arms crossed, conveying dejection more than the sense of tragedy that the artist perhaps intended. Caroline and John stood briefly in front of the portrait, told their mother they liked it, and then turned expectantly to us, their eyes full of excitement, as if to ask what was next on the tour.

Tricia and I took Caroline and John to the Solarium for a view of Washington at night, with Pasha and Vicky and my father's two-year-old setter, King Timahoe, racing along beside us. Mother and Mrs. Onassis quietly toured the state rooms. Mrs. Onassis was subdued, seeming to absorb the changes. Several times she commented that she liked what had been done. When my father joined us for dinner, her mood changed again and she became, as he recorded later in his diary, "very bright and talkative."

What I remember most about the evening was the visit to the Oval Office after dinner so that the children could see where their father had worked and made many of the decisions of his Administration. One of the most famous photographs of the Kennedy Presidency is of John, Jr., not yet three years old, peeking out from underneath his father's desk. In the Oval Office, my father was able to show him where he had played. It seemed to Tricia and me to be a private moment. Instinctively, we did not go inside but waited on the walkway outside the office.

The letters that the Kennedy children wrote the next day were bursting with memories. My father had taken John and Caroline to see the Lincoln Bedroom after dinner and told them the legend that anyone who sat on Lincoln's bed and made a wish had the wish come true. John wrote that his wish that he have good luck in school had indeed come true, and he added, "I really loved the dogs, they were so funny. As soon as I came home my dogs kept on sniffing me."

Caroline Kennedy's letter was so full of superlatives that in a postscript she gracefully teased herself: "All I seem to be saying is so nice, fantastic, thank you, but it is all I can say." Her mother in her letter thanked my parents for their kindness and wrote feelingly, "The day I always dreaded turned out to be one of the most precious ones I have spent with my children."

Hardworking UPI correspondent Helen Thomas, who prided herself on her thorough reporting of White House news, was the only reporter who got wind shortly before the visit that Jackie was coming. When she reached Helen

Smith in the East Wing and asked her about the visit, the latter said honestly she knew nothing about it. Then Helen Smith made a quick call to the usher's office and learned that Mrs. Onassis would indeed be arriving soon. Immediately she called Helen Thomas back: Would she be willing to keep the story off the wires if she could be guaranteed an exclusive once Mrs. Onassis and the children left Washington?

The next day when Mother saw Helen Thomas at a reception she admitted she was unhappy that the news of Jackie's visit had leaked. In her memoirs, Helen Thomas wrote, "I delivered a brief lecture on what news is. 'Mrs. Nixon,' I said, 'there is no such thing as a leak. There is legitimate news which governments or people want to suppress. But news, fortunately, does not always break at what you think is the proper time, and it cannot be manacled or programmed.'" Although Helen and my mother were friends, that was one subject upon which they would never completely agree.

My mother may not always have liked the way those in the media who covered the East Wing wrote about events, but she had known many of these reporters since vice-presidential days and admired the stamina and competitiveness they displayed in keeping pace with presidential news. Mother also understood the importance of trying to respond promptly to reporters' queries. "Your mother was always reachable," Helen Smith told me. "Many times I called her at ten or eleven at night when the press wanted to know her reaction to something." Even though Connie Stuart's briefings sometimes generated more trivial news than Mother wished, she continued the sessions because she understood some of the pressures the journalists were under from their editors to get to the heart of every story.

Mother also never lost sight of the reporters as individuals and oftentimes was able to put herself in their shoes. Fay Wells told me that on the trip to Rome in 1970, when my father spent the night with the Sixth Fleet on an aircraft carrier, a group of reporters covering the trip, noting that Mrs. Nixon had nothing official on her schedule, decided to go out for dinner. Fay remembers that they "had a gay time seeing Rome at night. In the morning we learned your mother had stayed in her room and had spaghetti because she knew that if she went to a restaurant, the press would have to spend the evening in a corridor 'covering' the event." Fay continued, "I was flabbergasted. I'd never heard of a First Lady doing something like that."

Several days before Mother's fifty-ninth birthday, my father held an unusual interview with nine newswomen in the Oval Office. His purpose was to praise his wife, and his words of tribute were the kind of birthday gift that only someone in public life can give. He told the reporters that although the First Lady had strong opinions, she believed that the President and his wife should not publicly disagree on policy issues. And he expressed what it meant to have her support.

Sometimes the question is how is the man going to feel when he alone has got to sit there and make a real tough decision. Does he have around him people who are standing with him, people that are strong, people who aren't throwing up their hands about what they heard on television that night, the lousy column or the terrible cartoon . . . somebody who brings serenity, calmness or strength into the room. That makes a great difference.

When asked his birthday wish for the woman he had fallen in love with and had once called his Irish Gypsy, he responded: "A walk on the beach . . . with her hair flying . . . and no photographers."

The focus of public attention that St. Patrick's eve, however, was not on my mother, or even on the guest of honor, Irish prime minister John Lynch, at the state dinner that night. All eyes were on Tricia wearing a white satin gown with a deep flounce of ostrich feathers on the hem. For months, Tricia had been denying—with my mother, father, David, and I faithfully following the party line—rumors of an engagement to Ed Cox, but the rumors were put to rest that night with the official announcement of her engagement. She and Ed had been in and out of, but mostly in, love for a long time. They had first met at Tricia's senior-year school dance in 1963. Both were romantic and idealistic, and both were intelligent, opinionated, and strong-willed. At times they disagreed over politics. After graduating from Princeton University, Ed spent the summer of 1968 working for consumer activist Ralph Nader, while Tricia campaigned for my father.

By the summer of 1970, they were sure they wanted to marry. At the dance for Prince Charles, Tricia, sensitive to a few silly press reports of a "romance" with the prince, requested through the British Embassy a bend in protocol; Prince Charles would invite the second hostess of the evening, Mrs. David Eisenhower, for the first dance at the ball that July night.

In November of 1970, Ed formally asked my father for permission to marry his daughter. While Ed contended with second-year law exams at Harvard University, Tricia and Mother planned the wedding for June 12. It was unbelievably complicated. Sixteen hundred members of the news media had requested White House credentials to cover the ceremony and were vying for details and any scraps of information that would make their stories more appealing than their rivals'.

By the eve of the wedding, everyone was slightly worn-down by details, such as the protocol of who would go through the receiving line first, the Chief Justice of the Supreme Court or the Speaker of the House? Mamie Eisenhower finally did. Would the youngest bridesmaid, ten-year-old Beth Nixon, faint during the ceremony as she had during the rehearsal? Would the "pool" reporters (a small group that reported back to their colleagues) covering the reception edge out the guests to witness the toss of the bouquet, the first dance, or the cake cutting? Would the weather reports threatening rain make it impossible for Tricia and Ed to be married in the Rose Garden?

That night, after the traditional rehearsal dinner hosted by Ed's parents, Anne and Howard Cox, my mother sat up visiting with Mamie Eisenhower, who was spending the night in the Queen's Room. Mamie knew that in two days I planned to fly to Athens, Greece, to meet David's ship, the guided-missile cruiser *Albany*, which was on a six-month deployment in the Mediterranean. She knew that while David was abroad, coming into foreign ports infrequently and only for a few days at a time, I planned to live with my parents rather than "follow the ship." She told Mother that she hoped I would go with David whenever I could and live with him wherever he was stationed. "I've regretted all my life—and I regret it even more now that I'm alone—that I didn't go with Ike more often."

A few hours later, at ten minutes past midnight, the day of Tricia's wedding, my father wrote her a brief note ending with one of his favorite phrases.

Dear Tricia—Well today is the day you begin a long and exciting journey—
    I want you to know how proud I have been of you through the years—some of them pretty difficult for you I'm sure.
    The years ahead will be happy ones because you will make them so. Your strength of character will see you through whatever comes—
    You have made the right choice and I am sure Eddie and you will look back on this time and be able to say—"The day indeed was splendid"—

                                Love
                                Daddy

By daybreak, the sky was a forbidding lead-gray, and it drizzled intermittently all day. By the time the guests began arriving at three o'clock for the four o'clock ceremony, Tricia and I were almost comically taking turns pacing in front of the beautiful arching windows of the West Hall overlooking the Rose Garden. Below us two rows of topiary rose trees, their bases a mass of feathery flowers, formed an exquisite passageway to the altar. The altar was sheltered beneath an iron gazebo entirely covered by hundreds of delicate white flowers. Military aides hurried to and fro, first removing chairs, then bringing them back and wiping them with cloths, only to remove them again.

While the flowers grew dewy from the gentle misting of rain, our nerves were fraying. At four o'clock there were several hurried telephone calls between Tricia and my father, who had taken refuge from the nervous preparations in his EOB office. Mother realized that Tricia had to be the one to make the decision on whether or not to move the ceremony inside. She found it uncomfortably tense to watch us pace and decided to go downstairs to wait for the cue to enter the garden—or the East Room—as mother of the bride. Finally, at four-fifteen my father received an Air Force weather report which predicted that at four-thirty there would be a fifteen-minute clearing in the Washington area. He signaled the ushers to start seating the guests as rapidly as possible, thus blithely canceling the painstaking, protocol-conscious seating plan.

Seven minutes later, to the sound of Bach's "Jesu Joy of Man's Desiring," my father escorted his firstborn from the Blue Room of the White House down the wisteria-twined stairs of the South Portico and along the path that led to the Rose Garden. There was a slight breeze and Tricia's many-tiered veil, held in place by a pearl-encrusted lace Juliet cap, fluttered gently. Not until Ed had softly kissed his bride on the cheek did the raindrops begin to fall again.

The reception was joyous and lively, and all the pre-wedding tension disappeared once the music and dancing began. It was one of the first times my parents had danced in the White House. Adele Rogers remembers that there was pure delight on their faces. When one of the groomsmen cut in, my father proceeded to ask several others to dance. He was enjoying himself. Dancing at his daughter's wedding was outside the realm of his self-imposed ban on public dancing that he had tried to follow during his congressional and vice-presidential years, relaxed completely when we lived in New York, then reinstated during the 1968 campaign. But on June 12, Pat and Dick Nixon danced—and danced some more!

When Tricia and Ed left for their honeymoon, they broke with White House tradition and did not try for an elaborate escape. Eleanor Wilson, after her marriage to William McAdoo, in 1914, had arranged for decoy cars at the four gates of the White House and successfully escaped undetected in a fifth car. Both Lynda Robb and Luci Nugent had shared with Tricia the secret escape plans they used to elude reporters assigned to follow them to their honeymoon destinations. But Tricia decided she wanted to leave still dressed in her wedding gown with family and friends pelting her and Ed with rice. And so she and Ed said goodbye on the North Portico, or, as Tricia liked to call it, "the back door."

After the last guest left, my mother and I and Priscilla Kidder, who had designed both Tricia's and my wedding gowns, walked through every room on the ground and first floors to thank the staff. Already they were at work dismantling the tables, gathering champagne glasses, and removing the masses of flowers that Mother had requested be sent to Washington-area hospitals and homes for the elderly. Most of these men and women had worked since dawn preparing for the four o'clock ceremony. Now Mother embraced some in heartfelt thanks.

Before the wedding, Mother had told Rex Scouten, the cheif usher, that she did not want the staff to have to prepare dinner for the family after the ceremony. Instead, we ate wedding hors d'oeuvres on the Truman Balcony.

We were joined by Bebe Rebozo, Priscilla Kidder, and her husband, Jim. Moonlight bathed the white wrought-iron table. The air was soft and warm. We spoke only of the wedding, wanting to savor until the last hour Tricia and Ed's day.

During coffee, however, my father got up from the table and walked over to one of the chairs at the far end of the balcony. He sat there lost in thought. Priscilla remembers how Mother looked at him, and the concern in her eyes. She realized at that moment that the President, even on the day of his daughter's wedding, had a great deal on his mind.

The next morning the newspapers were full of wedding stories. *The New York Times*, which carried a photograph of my father and Tricia in the Rose Garden and a lengthy article, also ran a news-breaking story, "Vietnam Archive: Pentagon Study Traces Three Decades of Growing U.S. Involvement." Although the *Times* did not mention it in their article, all the materials in the seven-thousand-page study, which included CIA, State Department, Defense Department, and White House documents, were still classified Secret and Top Secret. For several months the *Times* had had in its possession this study of the war in Vietnam, covering the period from the end of World War II through 1968, ordered by Johnson's secretary of defense, Robert McNamara, but it had released the documents just as a resolution requiring withdrawal of all American troops from Vietnam by the end of the year was due to come before the Senate for a vote. Not only was publication apparently timed to help antiwar critics but also, in the opinion of Johnson's secretary of state, Dean Rusk, the documents would be valuable to the Soviet Union and to the North Vietnamese.

Secretary of Defense Melvin Laird advised my father that probably 95 percent of the documents could be safely declassified, but the Administration worried about the crucial 1 to 5 percent that, among other things, might provide clues that could help crack secret U.S. codes and electronic intelligence capabilities, or expose SEATO's contingency war plans. The CIA was concerned about the safety of past and current informants active in Southeast Asia who might be exposed by the documents. Finally, Sir Robert Thompson, a student of the war in Vietnam, had written two months before that the major factor now influencing the course of the war was psychological; America was not failing on the battlefield, but dissent at home was fortifying the North Vietnamese to thwart the talks in Paris. Significantly, nine days after the "Pentagon Papers" were published, the Senate voted its first resolution establishing a timetable for the pullout of all U.S. troops from Vietnam.

Daniel Ellsberg, who had turned the study over to the *Times*, also had in his possession four volumes of recent diplomatic exchanges. Had he during his work at the Defense Department and later at the Rand Corporation copied other classified documents as well? When Ellsberg began appearing on talk shows and radio programs, thus popularizing his subversive act, my father ordered his staff to try to find out what other secrets he might reveal.

The Pentagon Papers episode certainly was not the first time during the Nixon Administration that documents affecting the security of our nation and the lives of the Americans fighting in Vietnam had been leaked. Especially in the first year, serious security breaches had occurred. According to a CIA report, in 1969 there had been forty-five newspaper stories based primarily on secret National Security Council deliberations. But the purloining of the Pentagon Papers was a breach on an unprecedented scale. My father feared other disgruntled officials might follow Ellsberg's example, thus opening a floodgate of leaks that could embarrass the Administration in its clandestine dealings with North Vietnam and China.

Less than a month later, John Ehrlichman chose "Bud" Krogh, who had been doing an outstanding job in the Administration's War on Drugs but who ironically had no investigative training, to head up a team of three whose assignment was to prod the Defense and State departments to investigate their key staff members. The group was also to investigate on its own. Only six days later, *The New York Times* ran a front-page story on the fallback negotiating position that the United States would take at the SALT talks in Helsinki, just twenty-four hours way. This new leak was a great spur to Krogh and to the other members of "the plumbers," the name they jokingly called themselves because their mission was to plug leaks.

Over Labor Day weekend in 1971, Krogh's "plumbers" broke into the office of Daniel Ellsberg's psychiatrist, hoping to find information that would reveal Ellsberg's intentions and whether or not he was part of a conspiracy. It was a fruitless raid and by late September the group started to close up operations. The desperation of this attempt to stop leaks had been escalated in part by events in May and June. The June 22 Senate vote on a Vietnam timetable meant the clock was beginning to run down on U.S. leverage to exert diplomatic pressure on the North. Most significantly, on May 3 the radicals in the antiwar Mayday movement attempted their declared goal of shutting down the federal government.

By the end of April, 200,000 demonstrators had arrived in Washington. Early on the morning of May 3, tens of thousands of the militants were out on the streets. Following the organizers' 135-page manual, they choked traffic; formed human chains across key intersections; dragged signposts, parked cars, anything movable into the streets; uncovered manholes; threw rocks and bottles at passing motorists; slashed tires; and smashed windows. Police Chief Jerry Wilson mobilized his 5,100-man force and suspended all normal field arrest procedures in order to deal with the rampaging demonstrators and clear the streets. The police succeeded; fire engines and ambulances were able to operate, and most people got to work that morning. In the White House, the

Second Lady Pat Nixon wearing a gown made from material she received on her 1953 trip to the Philippines.

Tricia and I were thrilled to attend the 1957 Inaugural Ball, but it was a late evening for an eight-year-old.

In 1957 we moved to the Wesley Heights section of Washington. This became Mother's favorite of all the houses we owned.

▶ The Nixons attended Ghana's Independence celebration in March 1957. They are shown here with tribal chief Nan Osae Djan II, whom Pat Nixon would meet again fifteen years later when she was First Lady.

▼ Because the Vice President had no official residence, my parents usually entertained in hotels. This 1957 luncheon for Queen Elizabeth and Prince Philip, however, was held in the old Supreme Court chambers.

The reports of our parents' narrow escape from the stones and clubs of a Communist-led mob in Caracas, Venezuela, in 1958 were frightening, and their homecoming was unforgettable.

As President of the Senate Ladies for eight years, Mother, far left, center, met the wives every Tuesday to roll bandages for the Red Cross.

When Madame Khrushchev visited Washington in 1959, Mother was a constant companion.

Greeting my parents as they return from the Soviet Union, also in 1959. For Mother, the most difficult part of political life was having to leave Tricia and me during foreign and campaign trips.

In July 1960, Richard Nixon became the Republican nominee for President of the United States.

During the hard-fought campaign, my parents traveled to all fifty states of the Union.

On the campaign trail my mother held dozens of coffees and teas with the Women's Press Corps.

My father conceding defeat, election night 1960. My mother will always wonder if his concession speech at 12:15 A.M. influenced the outcome of the closest election since Harrison-Cleveland in 1888.

▲ With misgivings my mother agreed to the 1962 race for Governor of California, which ended in defeat and my father's famed "last press conference."

When Tricia graduated from Finch College in 1968, Mother received an honorary Doctor of Laws degree.

▼ Six years after his "last press conference," my father, just declared winner over Hubert Humphrey, greets supporters at the Waldorf-Astoria in New York, November 6, 1968.

Heavily guarded now by Secret Service, my parents, David and I chat with Dr. Norman Vincent Peale, who would marry us twenty-nine days before the Inauguration.

With Manolo and Fina Sanchez on December 22, 1968.

Lady Bird Johnson and soon-to-retire Chief Usher J.B. West show floor plans of the White House to the incoming First Lady.

On Inauguration Day 1969, when Chief Justice Earl Warren administered
the oath of office, Mother held the Nixon family Bibles, as she had in 1953
and 1957.

Working closely together, Mother and curator Clement Conger (shown here in
the Green Room with the recently acquired portrait of Mrs. John Quincy
Adams) added more than five hundred pieces of early American furniture and
art to the White House collection.

Left
Director of Press Relations
Helen McCain Smith.

White House Social Secretary
Lucy Winchester.

The war in Vietnam dominated the
Nixon years. On a trip to South
Vietnam in 1969, my father visited
troops while my mother went to an
evacuation hospital.

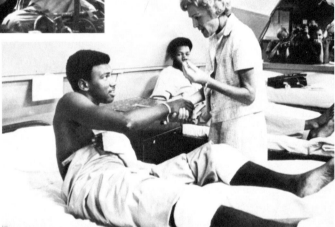

Unable to attend our college graduation because of antiwar protests, David and
I celebrated at Camp David on June 6, 1970. Flanking my father are Mamie
and Barbara Eisenhower, and my mother is seated between Milton and John
Eisenhower.

▲ Britain's Prince Charles and Princess Anne join my parents on the White House balcony during their 1970 visit.

◄ As First Lady, Pat Nixon encouraged volunteerism and community self-help. Here she is, on a visit to Oregon, riding in a Conestoga wagon.

Climbing over the rubble in the Peruvian mountain village of Yungar after the devastating earthquake in May 1970.

Tricia and her husband, Ed Cox, leave the White House following their Rose Garden wedding, June 12, 1971.

Mother looks so pleased at the November 25, 1970, ceremony for the completion of her efforts to light the exterior of the White House and its fountains for the first time.

In January 1972, Pat Nixon represented her husband at the inauguration of William Tolbert of Liberia. Here she is in the inaugural procession. (Right) Dancers wrap her in traditional lappa cloth.

Flanked by her sons-in-law as she arrives at Key Biscayne, the First Lady laughs with longtime family friend Bebe Rebozo.

▼ *Peking, 1972. A visit to the pandas.*

With Premier Chou En-lai at the welcoming banquet in the Great Hall of the People.

On the beach at San Clemente before my parents' hectic and fateful last campaign was launched.

As Jimmy Stewart, Senator Robert Dole and Governor Ronald Reagan look on, Pat Nixon receives an ovation at the end of the film about her life shown to the delegates at the 1972 Republican National Convention.

▲ Campaigning in Mamaroneck, N.Y.

▶ On a campaign trip to Hawaii in 1972, the First Lady takes part in an island game.

As Watergate charges
escalated in 1974,
hecklers turned out for
Presidential appearances.

On a trip to the Middle
East to ease Arab-Israeli
tensions in June 1974, the
Nixons pose with Egypt's
President Anwar Sadat
and his wife in front of
the Great Pyramid.

On her last official trip abroad, in 1974, Pat Nixon waves from a castle in the
Crimea.

The last family picture—taken in the solarium the night before my father's resignation speech.

An emotional farewell to the White House staff.

The Fords escort the Nixons to a waiting helicopter to begin the trip to San Clemente.

Mother poses with Gwen King, her former Director of Correspondence, at the entrance of La Casa Pacífica, in 1975.

Mother, Tricia and I arrive at Long Beach Memorial Hospital to visit my father, critically ill following emergency surgery to treat his phlebitis.

Honors: Mother dedicates the Patricia Nixon Elementary School in her old hometown; the Pat Nixon Park now honors her girlhood home.

Mother leaving the hospital following her stroke in July 1976.

Mother's White House portrait by Henriette Wyeth Hurd.

The greatest joys of the retirement years are the grandchildren; from left, Alex Eisenhower, Christopher Cox and Jennie Eisenhower; Melanie Eisenhower reading with "Ma," December 1985.

First Lady went ahead with her luncheon for wives of the 92nd Congress, and the President carried out his schedule.

Mother, in fact, had been determined that the demonstrators not disrupt her day. Since May 3 fell on a Monday, the day Connie Stuart routinely briefed reporters, she invited Connie to spend Sunday night at the White House. "We are not going to buckle to these people," Mother told Connie. Connie remembers waking up at 5:30 A.M. and looking out the window of one of the small guest rooms on the third floor. "It was like war. The buses were drawn up around the White House. Smoke was in the air. I kept hearing what sounded like cherry bombs going off. Around nine A.M. I checked in with your mother, and by ten A.M. I was briefing reporters in the East Wing Theater."

Among the most depressing moments of my father's Presidency were those spent inside the White House during massive demonstrations in 1969, in 1970, and in 1971. The day before the Mayday protest, additional security was brought into the White House. Mamie Eisenhower joined Mother, Tricia, and me for Sunday lunch in the family dining room. My father had visited briefly with Mamie and was already working in his EOB office when one of the guards accidentally dropped a canister of tear gas below the partially open dining-room window, sending all of us fleeing in tears from the room. It was just a fleeting moment of discomfort for us. What caused the lasting, unsettling discomfort was the awareness of the thousands of Americans, most of them young, who were alienated because of a bitter, divisive war.

Tragically, many in the antiwar movement were so blinded by what they saw as the wrong of America aiding the South that they refused to recognize the North as a ruthless and brutal enemy who crushed all opposition. Some of the antiwar leaders actually favored the outright victory of the Communist North, and met with their representatives in Paris even as the U.S. government struggled with both public and private peace negotiations. In 1972 representatives of the peace movement would travel to North Vietnam as honored guests and be invited to meet with POWs. Those POWs who refused to meet with them suffered purgatory. Navy Commander John McCain, now serving in Congress, was placed in a five-foot-long, three-foot-wide stone wall cell for five months because he refused to meet with the peace delegation.

After Mayday, the peace movement began to lose steam. But although the crisis of the demonstrations eased, the war was on my father's mind day and night. Often it intruded into rare unscheduled free evenings. Six months after Mayday, on November 19, 1971, when Bebe was in Washington for a visit, my father suggested that as a gesture to the Cambodians we attend the one-night-only performance of the Khmer Dancers at the Kennedy Center. Lon Nol, leader of Cambodia's first pro-Western government in recent years, had survived in office for eighteen months. The President of the United States attending a performance by the famed Cambodian dance troupe would be interpreted as a friendly, gracious gesture, and yet still not upset the delicate balance the Cambodians were determined to maintain so that the North Vietnamese would have no pretext to invade an "American puppet" country.

My father's suggestion to go to the Kennedy Center within an hour and a half was, to say the least, unexpected. But Mother immediately understood his purpose and gamely agreed. She quickly went through her closet and let me borrow one of her evening gowns. We arrived at the theater for the 8 P.M. performance still slightly sluggish after a large dinner preceded by cocktails, which my parents never indulged in on a "working night." Waiting for us in the presidential box were the Cambodian ambassador and his wife, who sat in the front row with my parents. Bebe, David, whose ship had returned from a Mediterranean deployment, and I, and Bill Codus, now assistant chief of protocol, sat behind them.

The lights dimmed, the curtain opened, and the dance began. Or did it? Although the performers demonstrated admirable grace and control, they moved only one part of their body at a time, and so slowly that the execution was barely perceptible. The music was atonal with no discernible rhythm. As the performance continued, each minute longer than the next, I noticed that Mother's head bobbed once or twice. Never had I seen her lose control in a public situation, but, clearly, she was fighting falling asleep. Next to me, Bebe was staring unblinkingly at the stage, fighting with every ounce of energy to keep awake. Bill Codus leaned over and whispered, "Did anyone warn you about Cambodian dancing?" Bebe, not turning his head, responded, "Yes." "Who?" Bill inquired. Bebe, suppressing a big grin, replied, "The President." On a stifling hot night in Phnom Penh in 1953, my parents, as guests of King Sihanouk, had watched a performance of Cambodian dancing until almost 1 A.M.

Increasingly in 1971, the family visited the presidential retreat in Maryland's Catoctin Mountains, called Shangri-La in FDR's day, but rechristened Camp David by Dwight Eisenhower in 1953 in honor of his grandson. On our first visit to Camp David after the inauguration, I was with my mother and father in their limousine when we passed the front gate and saw a large, rustic wooden sign that read "Camp Three." My father cheerfully asked the camp commander if it would be possible to find the old sign. I do not know if they were able to locate the original sign or not, but by sundown, the words "Camp David" once more were hoisted at the front gate.

I once asked my mother what she liked about Camp David. Her answer was immediate: "I was starved for exercise." In the Catoctin Mountains she tried to make up for the days or weeks she was confined in the White House. All day we walked and bowled and swam and walked some more. Even in light rain or on bitter cold days, we were outdoors.

My parents were freer at Camp David than anywhere else. Because the

134-acre camp was a fortress of security, encircled by high-voltage electric fences topped by barbed wire and guarded by marines, it was not necessary for the Secret Service to trail the family so closely. Also, since the Secret Service agents remained inside their small cabin guard posts adjacent to the terrace and the swimming pool, it was easier to pretend that there were no guards within shouting distance.

Mother so disliked the security at Key Biscayne that frequently she did not accompany my father on his trips there. Guards sat in straight-backed striped beach chairs on either side of and in between our two modest-sized houses on Biscayne Bay and got into the water with us whenever we swam with my father. Because the yards in front of the houses were small (both lots were no more than one hundred feet by two hundred feet), one had to speak softly or the guards could not help but hear the conversations. Adjacent to the helipad installed soon after my father's inauguration, the Secret Service had built a two-story headquarters from which the agents could survey all that went on in the yards below. Security was also very tight at San Clemente, where Mother worried that the Secret Service had installed security lights too profusely and at no small expense. The effect they created was somewhat like the "mood" lighting at a resort hotel. Nor was it restful at San Clemente to see and hear the change of agents every hour as they moved from one post to another around the house.

At Camp David my mother could more easily forget security restrictions. She was so busy getting exercise that she also was less aware of how restless my father was. In December of 1968, Bob Haldeman had laughingly bemoaned "the boss's" vacationing habits.

> What do we do with him? [he had asked Bill Safire]. He knows he needs to relax, so he comes down to Florida. He likes to swim, so he swims for ten minutes. Then that's over. He doesn't paint, he doesn't horseback ride, he doesn't have a hobby. His best relaxation is talking shop, but he knows he should not be doing that, because that doesn't seem to be relaxing. So what do we do with him? It's a problem.

At San Clemente, Key Biscayne, and particularly at Camp David, my father talked a lot of shop. Office hours follow modern Presidents wherever they go. In Aspen Lodge, my father conferred with staff and visitors in a small study where Mother had placed a replica of his favorite brown easy chair and ottoman, these covered in a blue raw silk. Anyone meeting with the President could get to his study by walking in the front door, thus perhaps surprising the First Lady as she read, or the visitor could go first to the kitchen, from which a military aide or one of the Filipino stewards on duty would discreetly alert Mrs. Nixon and then escort the visitor to the study. The kitchen, only about ten feet by sixteen feet, was always hot and overflowing with people who more often than not had to step over the sleeping figures of King Timahoe, Vicky and Pasha. Two navy cooks and a steward, plus the military aide, the camp commander, and often the White House photographer, Ollie Atkins, routinely spent much of the day in the kitchen. Manolo, who loved to get others to laugh, would answer the phone: "This is Aspen kitchen; I am Manolo. It is also the photo office, the aide's office, and the kennel."

One thing my father enjoyed was the movies that were shown frequently after dinner at Camp David. Mother often preferred to read in her room; reading was still her most favored way to relax. She rarely watched television and did not have a TV set in her White House sitting room or bedroom. But if the movie was an old favorite or a musical, she might be persuaded to watch. If neither Tricia nor I was at Camp David and Bebe Rebozo was visiting, often he would be tapped to choose the film from a list provided by White House electrician Paul Fischer, who doubled as the projectionist. Once, shortly after film code ratings were instituted, Bebe selected *Hammersmith Is Out*, with Elizabeth Taylor and Richard Burton. Both my father and Bebe were surprised by the profanity and sex, especially Bebe, since he thought the R stood for "regular." But no matter how poor the choice was, my father was optimistic to the end. Periodically, he would look around the room to assure himself no one had tiptoed out and to comment encouragingly, "It will get better." More often than not, Bebe would fall asleep, but even this was to be overlooked because recognition of his sleeping would be a tacit admission that the movie was a bomb.

On August 17, my mother went in three days from Virginia to Michigan to Minnesota to Oregon to California, where she crossed the border to Mexico. Her mission was to transfer unused federal land to state and local governments for recreational use. One of the twenty reporters who traveled with her, Marian Christy of the Boston *Globe*, wrote:

> Pat Nixon doesn't look it—but she's overworked and underpaid. The early morning scene at Virginia [the first stop of the three-day trip] is the same at every other dedication ceremony. Babies crying. Jets flying overhead. Ants that bite crawling on legs. Bees buzzing. Mosquitos having a field day. Temperatures soaring. High humidity. So this is glamor?

Two years before, my father had walked south on the beach in front of our house in San Clemente. The wide expanse of sparkling clean sand was deserted, peopleless because the beach was the property of the gigantic marine base, Camp Pendleton, which adjoined my parents' property. It was then that he ordered an inquiry into the use of all federal land. The result was the Legacy of Parks program, which eventually turned fifty thousand federal acres into parklands, benefiting all fifty states.

On that first Legacy of Parks trip, Mother presided as a $3.75 million, six-thousand-foot oceanfront military tract was turned over to the state of California at Border Field. During the ceremony, hundreds of Mexicans stood behind a barbed-wire fence separating Mexico and the United States. When it was my mother's turn to speak, she asked that the barbed-wire fence be cut because there was no need for a fence that "separates the people of two such friendly nations." At the conclusion of the ceremony, she ignored the whispered protests of her Secret Service agents and crossed over the border, her entourage behind her. The two peoples, many of the Mexicans barefooted, the Californians in cool, brightly colored summer clothes, mingled. Some of the tiniest children wanted a good look at the First Lady. When ABC correspondent Virginia Sherwood picked up one of the youngsters and turned to find Mrs. Nixon, she too was holding a child. As she laughingly clasped hands and signed autographs, enjoying the moment, Pat Nixon was particularly aware on that day of the power and symbolism of being First Lady.

In September, during an informal conversation with some newswomen while en route to Newport News, Virginia, to dedicate a nuclear-powered guided-missile frigate, the *California*, my mother made an uncharacteristically bold political statement: she wanted to see a woman appointed to the Supreme Court. "Don't you worry; I'm talking it up... If we can't get a woman on the Supreme Court this time, there'll be a next time." Partially because of Mother's urging, my father did instruct Attorney General John Mitchell to submit a list of qualified women, but a month later he appointed two men, Lewis Powell and William Rehnquist, to fill the vacancies. He had found that potential women nominees who had enough experience as judges or lawyers did not meet his standards for strict construction of the Constitution, necessary to balance the liberals on the court.

Mother was keenly disappointed that a woman was not chosen. She had spoken out because she felt so strongly that women in 1971 needed the recognition that a female member of the Supreme Court would bring them. She was also annoyed that her advice, offered publicly, had gone unheeded. Because David rarely had seen his mother-in-law in anything but a supportive, encouraging role, he remembers well October 21, the day the new Supreme Court choices were announced. During dinner, Mother strongly stated that one of the nominees should have been a woman and gave her reasons. My father, with exaggerated weariness, finally cut off the conversation: "We tried to do the best we could, Pat."

My mother believed totally in the capabilities of women. It was something she never questioned. In her own life she had supported herself, obtained jobs, and accomplished what she set out to do. For sixteen unbroken years, until Tricia's birth, in 1946, and the start of political life, Patricia Ryan Nixon had been in the work force. My mother publicly stated her support for the Equal Rights Amendment, which had been endorsed by the Republican Platform in 1968. In 1972 she urged that the amendment be endorsed again at the convention. Although my father raised objections that the amendment would create a judicial Pandora's box, he agreed with her argument that it was time to formally recognize that women in employment and other areas deserved equal treatment with men.

The Administration was attempting to be at the forefront of equal job opportunity. On April 22, 1971, Barbara Hackman Franklin had been appointed staff assistant to the President with the responsibility of developing a bank of names of qualified women. It was the first time a member of a President's staff had been given the job of bringing more women into the government. One year later, the number of women in policy-making positions in the federal government paying $28,000 and up had tripled, and more than one thousand women had been brought into middle-management positions previously held by men.

In small symbolic ways also, the White House tried to give equal opportunities to women. In November of 1970, with Mother's enthusiastic endorsement, five female military social aides took their places beside their male counterparts for the first time at White House social functions. The social aides' responsibilities were to make guests feel welcome, answer questions about the house's art and history, and help with the flow of guests from the receiving line to dinner, and later to the East Room for entertainment. The only instruction the women received that differed from the men's was that there was no need for them to ask guests to dance but, if they were invited to dance, to enjoy themselves!

As the first term passed midpoint, a frequent question posed by reporters was "Why does Mrs. Nixon spend so much time on her mail?" The implication was that her time could be put to better use. Even my father used to worry about the amount of time Mother devoted to her mail. Every week, an average of one to two thousand letters arrived for Pat Nixon (the number always rose to around four thousand after an appearance on television or a foreign trip), and, without fail, my mother read nearly every letter and tried to see that everyone received a response. Many times she spent four or five hours a day on mail, usually working in the evening after dinner. No First Lady had received this volume of weekly mail before.

There were many reasons people wrote, but the chief one was that the word filtered down to Americans across the country that Pat Nixon cared and was listening. Gwen King, whose job it was to oversee the drafting of responses, told me,

Your mother had acute sensitivity to the pulse of the people. I was told when I first took the job in February of 1969 not to send Mrs. Nixon controversial mail, but I thought your mother did not want to be shielded so I sent it up.

There was a constancy about her. She was going to do a good job on her correspondence because this was the people.

Gwen King and her hardworking staff were able, in Mrs. Nixon's name, to help hundreds of people by referring them to the correct government agency or by doing some sleuthing themselves. When a woman wrote that her mother, an immigrant from Italy, had the dream of becoming an American citizen before she died, but that she could not read or write, Gwen and her staff found out that since the woman had been in America for more than twenty-five years, the literacy regulation could be waived. An impoverished young girl wrote Mrs. Nixon and confided she had been caught shoplifting and had been unable since then to get a job. An impersonal letter expressing "concern" was attached to the girl's letter and then placed in one of the bulging brown folders of mail destined for the small wooden table for messages outside Mrs. Nixon's bedroom. When my mother got to the letter, she wrote across the top, "Gwen, this is fine but it doesn't really help her, does it?" Rewritten, the letter referred the girl to a Civil Service rehabilitation program for first-time offenders, and eventually she was employed. One more person had been helped.

Gwen discovered that Mrs. Nixon was approachable and without pretense. When Gwen used the phrase "the President and I" in one of her first drafts, my mother penned her a note, "In future, please do not use 'the President'— sounds too high and mighty!" On one occasion, Gwen sent her a memo indicating she would "weed out the cards and messages" from a box of photographs that needed to be signed. Mrs. Nixon responded, "Please don't do extra work—just send."

So many of the letters encouraged my mother. A waitress in Indianapolis wrote: "I would like to tell you I'm so proud and honored to have you, Mrs. Nixon, as our First Lady for our country.... There is so much feeling in my heart, I can't put it into words." Others amused her. A ten-year-old girl from Churchville, New York, suggested, "You probably think I'm crazy but I and some other people would like you to run for President.... Enclosed are campaign posters if you run..." Some letters appealed to her idealism. For the library of the city of Cerritos, she wrote, "Believe, work, achieve—then share with others so that the seemingly impossible dreams will come true."

From time to time my mother set aside letters to save in her "special file." Among them was a letter from a fifth grader in Elmont, New York, who sent Mrs. Nixon a copy of her school composition entitled "I am the wife of President Nixon."

To me being the President's wife is very difficult. All you do is go to dinner parties. You also have to get your hair set daily and buy many clothes. When I wear my mink stole everyone says "Oh how stunning." Everytime I make a speech I get a sore throat. When I go traveling with my husband we have to stand up for hours and my feet are killing me. My back aches from sleeping in so many different hotels. When I'm in bed trying to rest I hear the body guards standing outside my door. I wish I could be an ordinary housewife and wear sneakers and blue jeans. This is what it is really like to be a President's wife.

In my mother's response she reassured the young writer of the "special joy and privilege" of being the wife of the President. After signing the letter, my mother attached a note to it for her director of correspondence: "I have kept her letter. She hits the spot!"

The letters from Americans in every part of the country, in all circumstances of life, meant a great deal to my mother. They gave her personal contact with people. Because of her respect for those who wrote and her keen sense of duty as First Lady, she rejected the use of an "autopen" and personally signed all letters, even the thousands of autograph cards. In addition, my mother found that working on her mail enabled her to maintain control over at least one part of her daily life in the White House, which so often was subject to an official schedule and overtaken by the latest domestic or world crisis.

My mother highly valued her independence, and throughout the Presidency she tried to remain as self-sufficient as possible. Judy McGohan told me she will never forget one conversation with Mother just before a hair appointment. The First Lady had been on time as always. "We set our clocks by Mrs. Nixon," Judy explained, "she was never late." When Judy offered to help Mother undress and hang up her clothes, Mother responded, "Oh, no thank you, Judy. I have to keep doing things for myself. I tell my girls that if you become dependent on others and let them do everything for you, you soon become ugly." "I'll always remember she used the word 'ugly,'" Judy commented. "Mrs. Nixon never wanted anything special. Not once did she call Rita [her hairdresser] out of the salon and leave me with angry customers. If she needed her hair done before her weekly appointment, Rita went to the White House before eight-thirty A.M. or after work."

Of course in the White House my mother was waited upon at meals, a seamstress was on call, fresh flowers were available daily, and much more. That was the reality of the President's home. But, even in little ways, Mother kept doing for herself. For example, she washed her own nightgowns and personal laundry, always dressed herself for any event, did her own packing and unpacking. As often as she could, she tried to break through the artificiality and cushioning that surrounds a First Lady, whether by responding to her mail or always being ready with a handshake and warm words of greeting.

One of the last state visitors in 1971 was Prime Minister Indira Gandhi, who came to Washington at the end of a busy week: President Tito of Yugoslavia and Prime Minister William McMahon of Australia had been entertained in the preceding six days. When my parents had visited India in 1953 and Mrs. Gandhi was the young official hostess for her father, Prime Minister Jawaharlal Nehru, she was raven-haired and charming, rather than the gray, imposing woman of 1971. Yet even as a young woman in the shadow of an exacting father, Mrs. Gandhi had been coolly self-possessed. She had hosted a luncheon for Mother to meet some prominent Indian women, and she thoughtfully and carefully briefed Mrs. Nixon on the work of each. My mother and Indira Gandhi found in 1953 they had ties in common. Both had demanding public roles as hostesses, both were mothers of young children with prime responsibility for their upbringing, since Mrs. Gandhi was separated and my father was so busy. Both women were controlled and articulate. But by 1971 their paths had diverged. My mother was still at the center of power yet with no desire for power herself. Indira Gandhi was a leader in her own right, willing and capable of fighting for power to govern sprawling India.

Mrs. Gandhi's mission to Washington was to assure a skeptical White House that her country had no intention of exploiting primarily Hindu East Pakistan's demand for independence from Moslem West Pakistan. But only a month after the visit to Washington, the Indian Army, armed with Soviet weapons and fortified by tacit Soviet support, invaded East Pakistan during the civil war raging there. Indian troops joined the Bengali rebels in fighting Pakistani president Yahya Khan's troops. There also was fighting along the West Pakistani border, and United States intelligence reported that Mrs. Gandhi and her Cabinet had discussed plans to invade the West. A series of secret messages between the President and Brezhnev ensued, the United States urgently calling for an immediate settlement of the war. In large part because of subsequent Soviet pressure on the Gandhi government, the Indians and Pakistanis agreed to a cease-fire on the western front on December 17 and Yahya Khan recognized East Pakistan as an independent state.

Three days before the cease-fire was to go into effect, the Nixon Administration had been shaken by columnist Jack Anderson's publication of verbatim excerpts of minutes from Kissinger's meeting on the India-Pakistan crisis with the Washington Special Action Group (WSAG), composed of representatives of the State and Defense departments and of the CIA and NSC. The minutes revealed that Kissinger clearly had indicated a presidential "tilt" toward Pakistan, which was at variance with the neutral public position of the Administration on the war. To my father, this breach of national security was "intolerable," and he again assigned Bud Krogh and David Young, formerly on Kissinger's staff, to investigate.

They pinpointed a young navy yeoman assigned to the staff of Rear Admiral Robert O. Welander, who was responsible for liaison between the Joint Chiefs of Staff and the National Security Council. The yeoman was immediately transferred and kept under surveillance until it was determined that he no longer was leaking sensitive documents. The Anderson story, coming so soon on the heels of the Pentagon Papers, contributed to the feeling of vulnerability in the White House and the determination to prevent future breaches of security, especially those that might jeopardize secret negotiations with China and North Vietnam.

At the end of November, my mother took part in a traditional White House ceremony held each Thanksgiving, the formal presentation of a turkey to the President and his family by the Turkey Growers Association. Some sixty years before, a turkey that had been delivered to the Teddy Roosevelts escaped its pen, and Roosevelt's young children chased the fowl all over the grounds, waving hatchets, while the President laughed uproariously. The next day the Roosevelt family was reproached by the newspapers for its cruelty to animals.

At a ceremony in the Rose Garden in 1970, a forty-five-pound turkey had flapped its wings wildly and snapped at the President. Not surprisingly, early in 1971 Lucy Winchester was told by the President's schedulers that Mrs. Nixon should accept the bird that November. It was not the first time the buck had been passed for an institutionalized First Family event. Only that spring, Mother had managed to avoid the annual Easter Egg Roll, usually a running, yelling free-for-all on the South Lawn for hundreds of children, their parents in tow. When Mother received a memo in March from Mike Farrell, who had succeeded John Davies as head of the Visitors Office, asking which member of the family would be greeting the children at the event, she responded, "We drew straws and Tricia lost!"

Nobody lost when the First Lady met the Turkey Growers Association representative. Lucy had made careful arrangements. The day of the ceremony, she remembers, "the poor turkey was so tranquilized that it could hardly hold its head up. Your mother and I avoided looking at each other because we knew we would start to laugh." When Mother was asked by a reporter if the Nixons planned to eat the plump thirty-five-pound white California turkey on Thanksgiving Day, she responded, "No, I'm going to grant him a reprieve." Lucy Winchester did in fact arrange to send the bird to the Oxon Hill Children's Farm. That week, one of the reporters who had heard the First Lady claim that the turkey would not end up on the dinner table went out to Oxon Hill to see if the story was true. He found that the White House had not misled him; the now sprightly turkey was thriving in its new surroundings.

Christmas 1971 was a happy but busy time, with the annual parties for the children of diplomats, the press corps, the Cabinet, the White House staff, and volunteers. One party stood out from the rest. Four anonymous donors made it possible for sixty boys and girls from the Junior School for the Blind in Los Angeles, which mother had visited two and a half years before on the Vest Pockets of Volunteerism trip, to accept at last her invitation to travel the breadth of America to the White House. In 1969, the children joyously had sung for the First Lady "Climb Every Mountain," from *The Sound of Music*. Now they sang it for us in the White House, their voices filling the East Room. After cookies and punch we took them upstairs to the Lincoln Bedroom and laughingly tried to see how many could pile onto the bed. One of the girls told Mother, "I'm on cloud ninety. Do you know about nine? Well, I'm way above that. I'd be on cloud nine hundred if I could stand that altitude."

We were a family of six for the first time that Christmas because of Ed and Tricia's marriage. On Christmas Eve, we had an early dinner and then sat in the West Hall to open the presents under our family tree. King Timahoe, Pasha, and Vicky gleefully tore into the doggy stockings my father had asked Manolo to purchase. David, gently needling his father-in-law's penchant for indulging the dogs, presented him with a recording of "Jingle Bells" "sung" by dogs barking.

When my father went to the Lincoln Sitting Room late that evening, he dictated a diary note: "I think it is one of the best Christmases we have ever had . . . the discussion at dinner was very spirited and I regret that over previous years we have not had more such discussions like this one on such occasions."

The subject that night was the role of women. David and I had just read Betty Friedan's *The Feminine Mystique*, a thoughtful analysis of women's place in society prior to and at the onset of the feminist movement. My father was intrigued and asked for a copy as a belated Christmas gift. Tricia had commented that unless it was absolutely necessary, she felt children five years and younger should not be sent to day-care centers. My father recorded, "Pat made the point that her greatest regret was leaving Tricia so often [because of the House and Senate campaigns] during those one to five years."

The next day David's and Ed's families joined us for Christmas dinner in the State Dining Room, Mamie Eisenhower at one end of the long table, my father at the other. Afterward it was football time, thanks to the NFL's scheduling a game on Christmas Day. My father suggested that the men get comfortable and take their suit coats off. He went into his bedroom and came back with three smoking jackets, one of them an eye-boggling light blue with navy-blue elephants prancing on the back and front. My father announced he would wear the maroon jacket. Howard Cox quickly selected a conservative black velvet; and John Eisenhower, at six feet two inches, a good three inches taller than my father, gamely covered himself with elephants.

During half time we all went out to the kitchen and helped ourselves to cold turkey with cranberry sauce and more pumpkin and mincemeat pie, since Mother had arranged for the White House staff to go home after the noon meal. Later, we watched the just-released film *Nicholas and Alexandra*. As we went downstairs to the theater, Mother promised to join us shortly, but at the conclusion, she was not there. We found her waiting for us in the West Hall where she listened to a report on the movie and then escorted the various family members to their rooms—Mamie, as always, to the pink Queen's Room, John and Barbara Eisenhower and Ed's sister to the third floor with David and me, and the Howard Coxes to the Lincoln Bedroom where almost one hundred years ago Abraham Lincoln had worked through the Christmas holidays on the Emancipation Proclamation, which freed the slaves on New Year's Day in 1863.

Mother had chosen to spend the precious two hours of the movie quietly in her room. In one week she was to embark on a historic trip to Africa. Ahead also lay the journeys to the People's Republic of China and the Soviet Union. My mother needed some time alone to study, organize, and most important, prepare mentally not only for the trip but also for her eleventh major campaign. Although she had no way of knowing it then, the campaign of 1972 was destined to be perhaps the most fateful of all for our family.

CHAPTER 25

1972
"Vive Madame Nixon"

O ver the Christmas holidays, Helene Drown telephoned Mother for a long chat about the African trip beginning on New Year's Day. Mother was in an ebullient mood, teasing Helene, "As a gift this time, how about some ivory so we can both have a set of false teeth in our old age?" Since she was scheduled to have private meetings with the leaders of Liberia, Ghana, and the Ivory Coast, the State Department had prepared talking points on African and international issues, including Rhodesia, South Africa, the future of U.S. economic assistance programs, and the forthcoming presidential trip to Peking in February: "The President does not expect that the Peking trip will lead to normal diplomatic relations with the People's Republic of China. The purpose of this trip is, simply, to reduce tension."

Mother's primary mission in West Africa was to attend the inauguration of the new president of Liberia, which had been founded in 1822 by freed American slaves. The new president, a fifty-eight-year-old Baptist minister, was the grandson of a South Carolina slave. On January 3, in a small Baptist church, America's First Lady joined several hundred other official guests to witness William Tolbert take the oath of office. The two African presidents who attended the ceremony, Félix Houphouët-Boigny of the Ivory Coast and Moktar Ould Daddah of Mauritania, fanned themselves with the inaugural programs in order to get a breath of air in the more than one-hundred-degree heat. My mother could not help but notice that White House marine military aide Jack Brennan's white dress uniform was soaked through long before the new president stood to deliver his forty-minute inaugural address.

The next day, on the top floor of the eight-story Presidential Palace, there were inaugural celebrations, including tribal dancing by bare-breasted women who moved to the music of hollowed log drums and their own ankle shells. At the end of one of the dances, some of the women presented Mother with several yards of traditional bright-blue lappa cloth. Immediately she began wrapping the material around her waist. The delighted Africans took over and soon Mrs. Nixon was completely draped, a turban on her head. The news photo of Mrs. Nixon in African dress was published around the world. In Washington, my father, Tricia, and I were avidly following Mother's trip. Two days after her arrival in Liberia, my father cabled from Washington: "Excellent coverage of your arrival in Liberia and other activities. The TV coverage, particularly by CBS, was outstanding. Everybody here believes sending you on the trip was a ten-strike..."

A highlight of the visit to Ghana was my mother's trip from Accra into the hills of Aburi to renew a friendship with Nana Osae Djan II, a tribal chief whom she and my father had met in 1957 when they represented the United States at the nation's independence celebration. With Mrs. Nixon by his side, the chief declared that their friendship was now such that "not even a lion could break [it]." Though the years had greatly aged the chief and he could no longer see, my mother found he was still a man of presence as he sat on a red-carpeted dais, dressed in a flowing multicolored gown, a gold crown on his head.

On her last day in Ghana, the American First Lady addressed the National Assembly. The legislators, sounding like their counterparts in the British Parliament, welcomed Mother with cheers, cries of "Hear, hear," and party slogans. In her remarks, she acknowledged the lively reception with the comment, "Your assembly is a little bit different from ours. There [in Washington] they don't have half as much fun."

In the Ivory Coast, the last stop on her trip, a half million people greeted America's First Lady with cries of "Vive Madame Nixon." She flew home on January 9, my father's fifty-ninth birthday. He was very proud of her work in Africa. Late that evening, he recorded in his diary:

... too many times our trips abroad deal with hard problems and not enough of the far more important personal warmth and symbolism which means so much. This is true in all of the underdeveloped countries and particularly true in Latin America, Africa and also, I believe, in parts of Asia...

The amazing thing is that Pat came back looking just as fresh as a daisy despite an enormously difficult, taxing schedule. She had press conferences in each country, had had conversations with the presidents and then carried it all off with unbelievable skill. As Julie put it, what came through was love of the people of the countries she visited for her, and, on her part, love for them.

The trip to Africa, in combination with the visit to Peru, convinced my father that although throughout the years of their public trips together Mother had been an invaluable asset, she was even more effective when on a schedule of her own. He had genuine admiration for her diplomatic skill, and years later, in a 1985 memorandum to me, would reflect that

> in her travels in this country, in her acting as hostess for hundreds of dinners during the Vice Presidential and Presidential years, and her trips accompanying me or on her own, even our critics agreed that she never set a foot wrong. This did not happen by accident. It is simply a reflection of a highly intelligent person who did her homework and had the good judgment to say what was correct and to avoid mistakes.

In the aftermath of the African trip, some members of the press corps began to change their preset views concerning Mrs. Nixon. Pat Gates, who had left Mother's staff to work for the United States Information Service and who was part of the press entourage on the trip, remembers expecially how the London correspondents for *Time* and *Newsweek*, who had been sent to Africa to cover the First Lady, reacted to Mrs. Nixon as a diplomat. They particularly were surprised by her ability and ease in responding to the toasts of the heads of state at the welcoming banquets and her handling of the press conferences. "Is she always like this?" they asked Pat. "We never expected her to be this way."

There had been only one sour note. The *New York Times* correspondent William Borders, in summing up the African trip, quoted a "high-ranking American in one of the countries she visited" as stating that Mrs. Nixon's presence was politically motivated and that "the President thinks this will help him get black votes, and the word went out that hers was to be the only white face in all the pictures."

Secretary of State William Rogers was distressed enough by the story to cable the American ambassadors in Liberia, Ghana, and the Ivory Coast to see if they had any information on the validity of the remarks of the "high-ranking American," who the *Times* stated was "well involved in part of the planning." Their responses were interesting. From the embassy in Abidjan, Ivory Coast, the ambassador reported:

> There were frequently occasions when white faces were photographed with her—e.g., my wife and I and members of my staff (included in numerous

events), local French citizens such as the French Ambassador (as Dean of the Diplomatic Corps) and the French director of the Bingerville orphanage which Mrs. Nixon visited and finally members of Mrs. Nixon's staff itself. At no time was I under any impression that white persons were excluded from pictures, much less under instructions to stay out of the way.

And the ambassador in Ghana cabled Rogers: "Allegation that word went out that Mrs. Nixon should be the only white face in pictures would have been foolish in first place and impossible in second. . . ."

As was her custom, Mother arranged for the gifts presented on the trip to be displayed on the ground floor of the White House so that visitors could see them. She also selected a few of the more unusual items to be shown during an interview about the trip she had agreed to do with Barbara Walters. Instead she found herself answering a potpourri of tough political questions on Vietnam, abortion, protesters, and the new title "Ms." Only at the very end did Walters ask about the African trip.

The turn the interview took frustrated Mother but did not surprise her. She respected Walters' position as one of the few female pioneers in television journalism and recognized that she had to be as forceful—and newsworthy— as her colleagues. But the session reinforced her inclination not to give television interviews. She just did not feel comfortable discussing political issues. During Mother's trip the next month to China and to the Soviet Union three months later, television would be her best friend without her having to give one interview. By minutely covering Mrs. Nixon's activity, television enabled the American people for the first time to follow a First Lady almost step by step as she carried out a diplomatic assignment.

In a revealing diary entry my father dictated on January 17, several days after the Walters interview, he commented:

> Pat looked extremely tired. For the first time she is showing the wear and tear of the African trip. She was very put out that in her talk with Ehrlichman today, and also she said in any conversations she had had with Haldeman, that neither had mentioned the African trip. I have a hunch that some of her staff had planted this idea with her, and I told her that Haldeman, in particular, had spoken of the fact that there had been nothing which had been done during the course of the Administration which had received more universal approval than her trip. She said well, at least, they should tell me.

Smart, tough Charles Colson, whom since 1971 my father had consulted as a key political adviser, and who my father believed could help him take the message of the Administration's accomplishments to the people as no one else could, prepared a glowing seven-page assessment of the First Lady's journey with dozens of quotations from editorials and newspapers across the country. On the first page of his memorandum to the President, Colson wrote:

> As you know we have tried for three years to project "color" about you, to portray the human side of the President... Mrs. Nixon has now broken through where we have failed. She has come across as a warm, charming, graceful, concerned, articulate, and most importantly, a very human person. People, men and women—identify with her—and in return with you.

Mother took Colson's "discovery" of her potential with a grain of salt. She sent a copy of the memo to Helene Drown and penciled at the top, "Copy— For your eyes only. Thought you'd be amused at late recognition!"

No matter how bemused my mother may have felt about the attitude toward her among some of the President's staff, there was one person who never underestimated her appeal to "the people": the President. He could be schoolboyishly proud, as he was in late January when he recorded in his diary: "Pat's pictures in the *Ladies' Home Journal* had arrived and it was truly the best she has ever had. She looked like a young model in her twenties, and every picture was really a knockout."

As the 1972 campaign got under way, many were asking how much longer the fabric of American life could stand the turmoil in Vietnam. My father had become more convinced as each month passed that no settlement in Vietnam would work that did not involve both the Chinese and the Soviets. Five years earlier, private citizen Richard Nixon had written in *Foreign Affairs* magazine of the importance of establishing diplomatic relations between the People's Republic of China, the world's most populous nation, with more than 800 million people, and the United States of America, the world's most powerful country. "We simply cannot afford to leave China forever outside the family of nations, there to nurture its fantasies, cherish its hates and threaten its neighbors." Throughout the first two years of his Presidency, he made overtures to Peking. Only a month after taking the oath of office, he discussed the rapprochement with de Gaulle in Paris. In October of 1970, he pointedly told an interviewer from *Time* magazine, "If there's anything I want to do before I die, it is to go to China. If I don't, I want my children to."

For two years, with the quiet diplomatic assistance of Pakistan and to a lesser extent of Romania, he explored the possibility of an exchange of views, and even a visit to the People's Republic by the American President. On July 9, 1971, Henry Kissinger met secretly in Peking with Chou En-lai. Less than a week later, on July 15, my father announced in a dramatic three-and-a-half-minute statement that he would visit China early the next year.

On February 17, 1972, the presidential party left the White House en route to Peking. In order to be present at the small farewell ceremony on the South Lawn, I had flown up to Washington from Atlantic Beach, Florida, where David's ship, the *Albany*, was stationed. The next day, I wrote David, who was on sea maneuvers in the Caribbean, "The difficult part about yesterday [the departure] was seeing how harassed and tired Mother looked. She has really aged! She told me she was sick to her stomach on Saturday and Sunday. It must have been nerves. She has so much to do for the trip."

"The trip" was not just another trip. Intense world interest would follow my parents in Peking, Hangchow, and Shanghai. For a quarter of a century, only a handful of Westerners had penetrated behind the "bamboo curtain" of Communist China. In fact, even before the break in diplomatic relations between America and China, the vastness of China had defied outsiders to know it well. One American President and his wife, Herbert and Lou Henry Hoover, probably were more familiar with the country than most Americans. In 1899, Hoover's work as an engineer took him and his bride to China to live for several years. Thirty years later, Lou Henry Hoover spoke Chinese sotto voce to her husband when she wanted to talk to him privately while in White House receiving lines.

Now, in 1972, America acted as if it were rediscovering the vast nation. Henry Kissinger's secret trip to Peking had been code named Polo, for Marco Polo, the thirteenth-century Venetian explorer who traveled to China. News interest was such that the three networks arranged daily satellite broadcasts so that Americans could follow the week-long visit to the country that Mao Tse-tung claimed he had transformed into a classless society where peasant and scholar worked harmoniously side by side in the fields.

My mother realized she would be in a highly sensitive position in China. Mao had taught his people that they must remain strong to face the enemy, America. As the wife of an "imperialist running dog," as the Chinese colorfully labeled Western politicians, Mrs. Nixon was therefore the personification of all the "bourgeois" customs and manners of dressing that the puritanical Maoist society disdained. Would there be awkward political encounters as well? The Chinese had not confirmed what they would allow her to do, whom she would be able to visit, or which officials would accompany her. She studied the State Department briefings and last-minute, scanty biographical material on some of the Chinese leaders, and she learned a few Chinese phrases phonetically, as she had done with other languages for dozens of trips abroad in past years. But her final schedule remained a mystery.

The arrival in Peking on February 21, 1972, was somber, as befitted the tenseness surrounding my father's effort to end an era of discord. On the cold, windswept expanse of gray asphalt runway, the only splashes of vivid color were the bright-red banners of Mao's revolutionary slogans, the small red stars that adorned the military caps of the honor guard, and the deep flag-red of my mother's coat. Fifteen minutes before *Air Force One* taxied to a halt, the soldiers had marched in formation onto the runway, singing a 1930s ballad of the Red Army, "The Three Rules of Discipline and the Eight Points of Attention." Now they silently stood at rigid attention as my father, accompanied by the slight figure of Chou En-lai, passed in review. The presidential party was driven immediately into Peking in Russian-made cars with every window curtained except the driver's front view. As the motorcade hurried along, Mother had the distinct feeling that most of the city was unaware of the American visit. Its streets, as wide as Paris's Champs Élysées, were deserted except for a few bicycles and military vehicles.

Daily the press corps, which was barred from the diplomatic talks, focused on the First Lady. Via satellite television, millions of people saw China through Pat Nixon's eyes. With her, they admired the pigs and produce at the forty-thousand-person Evergreen People's Commune; witnessed acupuncture treatments; toured the Peking Zoo and the Summer Palace; and visited the kitchen of the Peking Hotel where a hundred and fifty chefs were kept busy. The camera recorded Mrs. Nixon watching in fascination as a very young chef deftly transformed a turnip into a white chrysanthemum and then picked up a green pepper and quickly sculpted a praying mantis to perch on top.

Chicago Today editorialized on February 24:

We are starting to wonder whether future historians, commenting on President and Mrs. Nixon's visit to China, won't take the view that the President talked business and politics with Chinese leaders while his wife did the important work.

Mrs. Nixon's presence in Peking and her unfailingly warm, gracious conduct are accomplishing something that official discussions, important as they are, cannot do. She is establishing direct and friendly contact with the Chinese people on a normal human level; the level where children and families and food and service and health are the most important things. As, indeed, they are.

Few in Washington had doubted that the President's trip to China genuinely would be history in the making, and competition had been fierce to get assigned to cover the journey. After protracted negotiations with the Chinese, the number allowed grew to eighty and, one week before the trip began, finally to eighty-seven. The lucky eighty-seven were chosen by the White House from more than two thousand applications.

The number of White House aides was kept at a minimum also. Mother decided she would take no one from her East Wing staff to assist her, but two weeks before departure, at my father's urging, she telephoned her hairdresser, Rita de Santis, from the Elizabeth Arden Salon, and asked her to join the traveling party. On so many of their political and diplomatic trips, my father had seen Mother washing her hair at midnight or later. Now, for the first time, she would have a hairdresser with her who could quickly revive her hair between events. Rita also would be the contact between the First Lady and the President's staff and run errands if need be. Most of all, Rita would be a familiar face in an unfamiliar land, someone with whom Mother could enjoy the lighter moments and converse with in makeshift sign language in her guest suite, expertly bugged by the Chinese. For months afterward, they would laugh whenever they remembered the showerless guesthouse. In order for Rita to shampoo "Mrs. N's" hair, the First Lady had had to kneel at the top of a three-step stool and bend over double for her head to reach the faucets of the deep, old-fashioned four-legged bathtub.

For my mother, the most memorable event of the trip was meeting Chou En-lai. Clearly Chou was in charge of even the minor arrangements for the Nixon visit. His jet-black eyes observed every detail. The morning after the nine-course welcoming banquet, Chou mused aloud to my mother about each dish that had been served and remarked he must be certain nothing was repeated in Hangchow. At the end of a busy day culminating in a bitingly cold, windswept tour of the Great Wall, the premier arranged for my parents to ride back to the city together, knowing that it would be a relief for them to dispense with diplomatic small talk at least for an hour. At one of the banquets, Mother and Chou discussed her visit to the Peking Zoo to see the giant pandas. When Mother picked up the cylindrical container of Panda Cigarettes in front of her place at the table, with its drawing of two cuddly pandas gamboling on a background of bright-pink paper, she remarked, "Aren't they cute? I love them." The premier replied, "I'll give you some." "Cigarettes?" Mother queried. "No," he answered, "pandas."

In time, two giant pandas were sent to the Washington National Zoo. The official gift from the United States was a pair of North American musk oxen, a three-hundred-pound female, Malilda, and her hundred-pound brother, Milton, which the Chinese had requested for their Peking Zoo. On paper, it was a fair exchange, but when David and I visited the Peking Zoo four years later, the drab, mangy oxen were no match for the charming white-faced pandas. At the rock-strewn panda pit, hundreds of Chinese, four deep, ringed the pit for a look at the playful animals. A five-minute walk away, no one was in front of the musk-oxen cage.

In Shanghai on the last day of the trip, China and America issued a joint communiqué in which they pledged that neither nation would "seek hegemony in the Asia Pacific region and each is opposed to efforts by any other country or group of countries to establish such hegemony." As my father wrote in his *Memoirs*, that provision "unmistakably made it clear that we both would oppose efforts by the U.S.S.R. or any other major power to dominate Asia." The communiqué signaled a new era in relations between the U.S. and the P.R.C. and, by implication, the isolation of North Vietnam from China. The days in China were, as my father declared when he delivered his final toast in Shanghai, "the week that changed the world."

The trip had been mind-expanding, exhilarating, and totally exhausting, yet one of the first things Mother did within hours of the return home was to telephone Julie Robinson, whose three young children had all come down with mumps the day of the departure for China. Mother frequently queried Julie, a recent widow, about her children and their activities, whether the new housekeeper was working out, or if another had arrived. Years later Julie told me, "With everything your mother had on her mind, it was clear she wanted to know about those children."

On March 30, 1972, on the heels of my father's January announcement that 70,000 more American troops would be withdrawn from Vietnam over the next three months, 120,000 North Vietnamese troops rolled across the internationally recognized neutral Demilitarized Zone in a massive assault on South Vietnam. It was an attack characterized by savage, indiscriminate killing of thousands of civilians, particularly at Anloc and Quang Tri, and the execution of any South Vietnamese suspected of even the slightest official contact with the Thieu government.

From the onset, it was apparent that the invasion was a potential disaster for the Administration. First, there was a chance that the North Vietnamese troops might break through the South's defenses and capture the prize, Saigon. Equally disturbing was the prospect that since the Soviet Union was supplying the North Vietnamese with most of their weapons, the summit planned in Moscow in May could not possibly take place if the Soviet-armed North was on its way to a military victory, endangering the lives of the American soldiers still in the South.

Eleven days after the start of the North's offensive, as fighting raged over South Vietnamese territory, my father had an opportunity at a State Department signing ceremony for an international convention banning biological warfare to apply subtle but pointed pressure on the Soviets. Just before leaving the auditorium, he told Ambassador Anatoly Dobrynin, who had listened attentively to the President's speech, in which he stated that no nation should directly or indirectly encourage aggression, that Mother was most appreciative of Madame Dobrynin's recent invitation to discuss the schedule for the forthcoming visit to Moscow. Dobrynin took the hint and within a few hours he was on the telephone with Henry Kissinger, suggesting that his wife meet with Mrs. Nixon at the White House the next day.

That evening at dinner my father explained to Mother that he had a special mission for her. "The Russians are acting badly," she remembers him saying. "We've got to shake them up." He asked her to tell Madame Dobrynin how much she was looking forward to seeing Russia again, and then to add it was a pity that what was happening in Vietnam might force a cancellation of the visit.

The tea the next day with intelligent, blond Irini Dobrynina, who had met her husband prior to World War II when they both were engineering students working in an airplane factory, never appeared on the First Lady's official schedule. After a perfunctory discussion about some of the places Mrs. Nixon had visited on her last trip to Russia and about Moscow in the spring, Mother mentioned that she did hope nothing would happen to prevent the next visit from taking place. Madame Dobrynin squeezed Mother's hand and nodded vigorously, saying, "Oh, yes, yes." As Mother remembers, "She went right home and told her husband about our meeting, and he immediately called Kissinger and assured him that the Soviets were in favor of the visit."

Yet during the strained days that followed, as the Soviets refused to pressure Hanoi to de-escalate or negotiate, it was far from certain that their desire to pursue the détente my father had initiated in 1969 outweighed their interest in Vietnam. Kissinger's May 2 meeting with the North Vietnamese was a complete failure. They refused to discuss any of the negotiating points, and the deadlock seemed hopeless this time. Since the North was gaining precious time on the battlefield, my father had to face the possibility that all of South Vietnam would fall to the Communists, whereupon, as he recalled in 1978, his one recourse then would have been to impose a naval blockade until the release of American POWs.

For days my parents had been living with uncertainty. Then on Friday, May 5, my father went to Camp David to prepare a speech announcing a bold course of action that he hoped would convince the North Vietnamese and the Soviet Union of American resolve in helping the South retain its independence: he would order the mining of Haiphong Harbor and the escalation of bombings of military targets in the Hanoi-Haiphong area.

Of my father's many gambles for peace in Vietnam, this was perhaps the riskiest. It was conceivable that the Soviets might cancel the summit; some members of his own Cabinet would be unable to support him in the decision; and critics of the war surely would charge escalation. When Lyndon Johnson left office in 1969, he told my father that all of the bombing halts he had ordered in Vietnam were a mistake. Yet my father had inherited Johnson's final halt, as well as strong public sentiment to negotiate rather than fight the war. Without a doubt, he was jeopardizing his re-election six months hence. In his diary, my father wrote:

Pat came up very late Friday night. I had just come back from Birch [a cabin at Camp David] where I had been working on the speech. I saw the light on in Pat's room, and when I went in, she got up and came over, and put her arms around me, and said, "Don't worry about anything."

On Monday, May 8, my parents were back at the White House, Mother to fulfill her schedule, which included the annual Ladies of the Senate luncheon and a meeting with the mayor of Monrovia, Liberia, and my father to preside over a three-hour National Security Council meeting in which he informed the members that he would go forward with the decision to mine Haiphong Harbor.

As in times past before an important speech, the family did not see him before he went on television. His diary entry for May 8 details the last-minute rush.

> ... Getting this speech ready was virtually a photo finish. I did not get my copy until 5:00. I marked it up; went over and got a haircut at 5:30; came back and had my regular wheat germ at 6:00; then spent an hour between 6:30–7:30 going over the text; jogging in place and then took a long, cold shower; went over and did the Legislative Leaders [formally informed the leaders of the Senate and House of his decision] and then went on.

At 9 P.M., he began speaking. The heart of his message was that "there is only one way to stop the killing. That is to keep the weapons of war out of the hands of the international outlaws of North Vietnam." He described the measures the United States would now take in mining the harbor and delivering air and naval strikes against military targets in the North. Then he presented a new peace proposal, which would become the basis of the final settlement achieved eight and a half months later.

After the red camera light went off, my father said good night to the crew and walked over to the house, where Mother, Tricia, and I were waiting for him. When we heard the elevator, we turned off the television. Already the commentators were unanimously agreeing that with this announcement the summit would in all likelihood be canceled. ABC correspondent Tom Jarriel called the decision a move that invited "direct confrontation" between the two superpowers. NBC's John Chancellor stated: "The U.S.S.R. will have to react." And CBS's Marvin Kalb concluded that the Nixon decision put the summit "very, very much in jeopardy."

Yet there was no immediate Soviet retaliation and, despite the alarm of the commentators, the White House was deluged with telegrams praising the President's action. Two days after the speech, my parents dined on the *Sequoia* and my father recorded in his diary: "Pat spoke on the *Sequoia*, on Wednesday night, of the need for more speeches to be made on television and for more appearances to be made because people have to have reassurances that what they hear in the media is not the truth..."

For several more weeks the trip, scheduled for May 22, hung in the balance. My parents spent much of the time at Camp David, where my father waited for news from Kissinger and the embassies about further Soviet reaction. Throughout, the Soviets loyally denounced American actions against North Vietnam, but stopped short of ruling out the summit and terminating the steps toward détente already in motion. Finally, the Soviet state-controlled news agency began a soft-sell campaign to explain the extraordinary occurrence of a meeting between the American "aggressor" and the Kremlin.

When *Air Force One* touched down in Moscow on May 22, my father and Secretary General Brezhnev commenced long, intense discussions on arms limitations and Vietnam; and my mother, with her own independent schedule, began a round of activity that *Time* magazine would summarize as "Pat Nixon's role—serious, significant."

Mother had never been more heavily guarded than on this trip. Wherever she went, the KGB agents, some of them burly women, formed a human shield around her and would not budge an inch. They made the American press's job of covering the First Lady's activities extremely difficult. Repeatedly, the Soviet agents pushed the newsmen and -women aside. Finally, in the beauty of Moscow's subway, with its crystal chandeliers and its frescoes, the Soviets and the Americans jostled one another openly and almost came to blows. When the subway ride ended, many, including my mother, were badly bruised.

The fracas was worse at Moscow's famous department store, GUM, where the Soviet police tightened their ring around their charge, preventing the by now protesting and shouting American journalists from getting near enough to hear the conversation between the First Lady and her hostess, Mrs. Gromyko, the wife of the Soviet foreign minister. The security at GUM seemed particularly excessive to Bill Codus, since the Soviets had allowed no more than a hundred people in the enormous store and had halted traffic around the building for several blocks. A week before when Bill visited GUM, it had been teeming with thousands of shoppers.

At GUM's ice cream counter, reporter Saul Pett of the Associated Press was tackled by a heavyset security guard. Mother saved him from being slapped up against a wall by calling out, "He's with me. Leave him alone." Trying hard to keep up the appearance of a relaxed Saturday-afternoon shopper enjoying a vanilla ice cream cone, the First Lady motioned to Saul Pett to join her inside the tight ring of security. In a playful gesture, she gave him a bite of ice cream. Later that day he sent her a note.

Dear Mrs. Nixon,
    I just wanted to express my gratitude to you for being so nice to me during phase I and phase II of the biggest, noisiest floating crap game in town. You've been a heckuva good sport and the ice cream was especially good.

Saul Pett—AP

The newsmen and -women privately called their ordeal "the Battle of Red Square." In tribute to the First Lady, who survived it all with a smile on her face, they later presented Mother with a pair of miniature boxing gloves.

The same afternoon that my mother and the American press corps fought their way through GUM, my father held more meetings with Brezhnev on arms limitations. For two more days the talks were deadlocked. Throughout the suspenseful period of negotiating, Mother carried on her schedule as if the talks were proceeding effortlessly. Most of her time was spent in the company of Madame Brezhnev. Unlike her overpowering husband, with his barrel chest and his dark eyes dramatically framed by black bushy eyebrows, Madame Brezhnev was softly rounded and extremely shy. She rarely made public appearances and now found herself the costar in one of the major world news events of the year. As the wives of the leaders of the two most powerful nations walked arm in arm throughout Moscow, talking and laughing, my mother occasionally patted Madame Brezhnev's hand reassuringly. It was not long before Mrs. Brezhnev was calling Mrs. Nixon "sister."

The Soviets were anxious to meet every need of their American guests. When my father unexpectedly went to Brezhnev's dacha, Mother requested a "light" meal in the guest suite for herself, Rose Woods, and Rita de Santis. Surrounded by the splendor of the mammoth chandeliers, Persian rugs, and large decorative urns, all from the days of the czars, the three Americans were served a fish course, soup course, meat course, dessert, and fruit. Communicating about matters as simple as an egg could be complicated. When the First Lady ordered a hard-boiled egg for breakfast, Manolo, without the First Lady's knowledge, sent eggs back to the kitchen eight times because they were soft-boiled. Finally, time ran out. Mrs. Nixon never got her egg for breakfast. She ate caviar on brown bread instead. The delicacy was available with each meal and seemingly in limitless supply. Only later would Mother learn from Empress Farah of Iran that the Russian waters were so polluted the Soviets were buying caviar from Iran and then recanning it in their own tins.

My father arranged for his favorite Filipino chef, de la Cruz, who cooked meals at Camp David or when we traveled to San Clemente or Key Biscayne, to come to Moscow and prepare the return banquet for the Soviet hosts. At the dinner, Mother was seated next to the unsmiling former Soviet premier Aleksei Kosygin, whom my father would describe in a diary note as "really all business, a very cool customer with very little outward warmth." Maria I. Soukhanov, a Voice of America broadcaster who was serving as Mother's interpreter, translated and kept a record of the conversation. It gives a flavor of the low-key, diplomatic style of my mother, and a flavor of what conversation on formal occasions with a formidable dinner partner is like.

... Mr. Kosygin asked how many women we have in the U.S. Congress. Mrs. Nixon replied: One Senator and five in the House of Representatives. Mr.

Kosygin interrupted, stating that women careerists in the U.S. are arrogant, ambitious, merciless, whereas in the Soviet Union, women deputies, who make up one third of the total number, are serious, studious, and reasonable officials. Mrs. Nixon pointed out that most American women have not previously had great political aspirations and consequently there was a small percentage of women in the U.S. Congress. Mr. Kosygin said Soviet women deputies are astute and relatively unemotional in their jobs, which he found quite a contrast to American women careerists. Back to some women reporters he had observed, Mr. Kosygin continued, they are like *"Kamennye meshki,"* translated literally as "rock bags." Mrs. Nixon said, however, that the American reporters do their job as they see fit; they present diversified points of view.

Mr. Kosygin launched into a discussion as to the mercantile [commercially oriented] character of Americans. He said that when he is confronted with malicious people, and he places many correspondents in this category, he either leaves the scene or responds reciprocally with arrogance and determination. Good people, on the other hand, produce a completely different effect. Their goodness influences others, he said. Mrs. Nixon continued for a while on the good versus the bad. Mrs. Nixon said she absolutely agreed with his last statement: she wished there would be more feelings of benevolence, good will, and friendliness among all the peoples of the world.

Mrs. Nixon later mentioned her compassion for the Russian people who suffered greatly during the last world war, especially for Leningraders, who died and perished during the blockade—Mr. Kosygin said he was there, and it was a dreadful experience.

Right after dessert, before my parents could even escort the Brezhnevs into the living room for entertainment by pianist Van Cliburn, Brezhnev suddenly departed, his entire male entourage behind him. A flustered group of Soviet wives was left behind to hear Van Cliburn. My parents learned later that Brezhnev had left hurriedly because he had last-minute details to attend to prior to the 11 A.M. signing of the Antiballistic Missile (ABM) Treaty and the Interim Agreement, the latter establishing a temporary freeze on the production of missiles. The signing was the culmination of the trip and something my mother did not want to miss, even though the Russians had indicated that no wives were invited to the ceremony. When she told my father she wanted to attend anyway, he suggested she wait until all the officials had entered and then slip in quietly and stand behind one of the pillars. She did, and thus was a silent witness to the moment that they had worked for while in Moscow, just as she had been part of the weeks of agony before it was sure that the summit would ever take place.

The trip to Moscow, coming so closely on the heels of the visit to the People's Republic of China, enabled millions of Americans at home to watch on television a natural, approachable woman who was earnest in her desire to meet others and extend the hand of friendship. In turn, more people than ever before began to write Mrs. Nixon. The letters came from a cross section of Americans of all ages, from every state, and writing for many different reasons. One of the letters was from a young serviceman who wrote on June 3, just days after the return from Moscow.

Dear Mrs. Nixon:
   I am only twenty years old and I have been in the Air Force for only eighteen months. When I first came in, I was like most young people who were protesting everything there was to protest about, but now since I have been overseas serving my tour here in Japan, I get a closer look at the world. I just finished a thirty day tour in Korea . . . I saw starving children and people who just didn't care for life because they looked as if they had no future or anything to live for like us Americans. Mrs. Nixon, I am from the south in the United States, and there are many poor people there, but nothing compared to what I saw in Korea.
   Mrs. Nixon, when I left Korea last week, I went to church here at Yakota AFB and got down on my knees to thank God for my country and to protect it always. . . . Give my regards to your husband on his well accomplished mission to Moscow, Russia. I was very proud to know that he is doing everything possible to bring peace to the world, because it certainly needs it.

   Back in the United States, it was apparent that although world politics was changing, American politics was much the same, and my father found himself engaged in his last campaign, one that was destined to be his most successful and his most troubled. Two weeks after the summit, he spent the weekend at the small Bahamian island, Grand Cay, owned by our good friend Bob Abplanalp, and in Key Biscayne. When he read the Miami *Herald* on Sunday morning, June 18, one of the minor front-page stories was "Miamians Held in D.C. Try to Bug Demo Headquarters." It was a small item, placed below the more important news of the continuing withdrawal of troops from Vietnam.
   My mother barely noted the news about the break-in at the headquarters of the Democratic National Committee in the Watergate apartment complex. Her attention as June ended was on the long political campaign ahead. In her heart, I think my mother would have been relieved if miraculously the need for campaigning in 1972 had been obliterated. But she never considered asking my father not to run in 1972. To my mother, McGovern's election was unthinkable. She felt that his ideas were radical and half formed, especially in the foreign policy area. He advocated a massive, unilateral paring of the American defense budget by $30 billion, which would include cutting the Air Force budget in half. He called for unconditional amnesty for draft dodgers and for an immediate withdrawal of our troops from Vietnam, stating that we would have to rely on the good faith of the North Vietnamese to release our prisoners of war.
   Another reason my mother never raised with my father the subject of bowing out of political life was that she was enormously proud of the record the Administration had achieved despite the drain of the war. Real earnings were

up, and federal taxes on citizens had been cut by $22 billion. The crime rate, which had skyrocketed in the sixties by 122 percent, had risen only 1 percent in 1972. My mother wanted to see congressional action on the crucially important welfare reform, health care, and environmental proposals. Most significant was the fight to break a forty-year trend and disperse power away from Washington with the federal revenue-sharing program of no-strings-attached funds to the states and struggling inner cities.

Like Mother, Tricia and I were proud of our father's Presidency but, also like her, longed for a private life. Although we said nothing to our father, he sensed our ambivalence about the public spotlight. In July, when my parents flew to California to rest and watch the Democratic Convention, my father dictated for his diary:

> Both Julie and Tricia separately told me that while they would like to come out here that they felt their place was with their husbands, and I totally agreed. It would be a great comfort to have them here at this time, but we cannot impose upon them in this way when their personal lives at this time are going to have to take a great beating as we go into the next campaign.

At times it seemed that McGovern conducted his campaign as if he realized he had no chance of winning. Many of his political statements and announcements reflected little forethought. Before he was even selected as the Democratic nominee, he announced his Cabinet selections if he were elected President. On April 3 my father had recorded in his diary Mother's reaction: "Pat observed she couldn't see how anyone would vote for McGovern because he had been so foolish to name his Cabinet," thereby foreclosing the flexibility that a serious presidential candidate must have. In June, McGovern started easing his way out of his promise that as President he would give every American a $1,000 welfare allotment, which the Department of Health, Education and Welfare had estimated would cost $50 billion.

Then in August, after McGovern had abandoned his running mate, Senator Thomas Eagleton of Missouri, because of adverse publicity over revelations that he had been hospitalized for depression three times between 1960 and 1966 and twice undergone shock treatment, other Democrats began to smell defeat in November. Senators Edward Kennedy, Edmund Muskie, Abraham Ribicoff, and Hubert Humphrey, Democratic National Committee chairman Larry O'Brien, and Florida governor Reubin Askew turned down McGovern's invitation to run with him for President.

By contrast, the Republican Convention, which began on August 21, offered the country the spectacle of a party that was as united as the Democrats had been in disarray. Nixon Youth had been active in all my father's campaigns, but they were especially important in 1972, and on Election Day, my father would receive 52 percent of the youth vote. Throughout the first term, the Administration had tried to make the point that the young who demonstrated against the war did not represent all youth. The Nixon White House deliberately had hired record numbers of aides thirty years and younger. Tricia and I planned to be out on the campaign trail as we had been in 1968. We knew it was inevitable that we would be compared to those demonstrating, and that some would charge that the White House was manipulating us. But while we were uncomfortable with how coverage of our activities might be used to contrast us to the protesters, it was no secret that we disagreed with the demonstrators—and that we were determined to help our parents.

The family had helicoptered from Key Biscayne to the convention hall for the nomination speech. As the helicopter touched down it stirred up waves of tear gas that had drifted from outside the hall where police were trying to control the angry crowd of antiwar protesters who were making it as difficult as possible for the delegates to get in and out. Our eyes burned as soon as the heavy doors of *Marine One* were pushed aside.

In his acceptance speech my father promised to work for a more peaceful world. He told of his May visit to Leningrad where as many as a million Russians had died during the Nazi siege of the city. He and Mother had been taken to a small museum at the cemetery where the victims are buried and been shown the diary of a twelve-year-old girl, Tanya. In her diary, Tanya starkly recorded the deaths of each member of her family: Zhenya in December, Grannie in January; then Lekow; Uncle Vasya; Uncle Lyosha; and Mama in May. Her last entry, written shortly before her own death from starvation, read: "All are dead. Only Tanya is left." He then asked his "fellow Americans to join in ... achieving a hope that mankind has had since the beginning of civilization. Let us build a peace that our children and all the children of the world can enjoy for generations to come."

My father felt that his address did not have the emotional impact he had anticipated. Mother sensed his disappointment, as is evident in his diary dictation the day after the nomination.

... Going back on the helicopter I was so tired that I was probably more quiet than I had intended to be because Pat, the next morning, told me about a call she had had from Barbara Eisenhower [David's mother] where Barbara said the speech sent chills up her back and she thought it was the best I had ever made. Pat said that she had the feeling the night before that I had seemed to be somewhat depressed, which actually was the case. . . .

So often my mother was in the role of sustainer. Daily she saw the tremendous demands of the Presidency. On April 18, as my father wrestled with the crisis caused by the North Vietnamese attack across the DMZ, he had recorded in his diary:

Pat said that she didn't know how I was able to take all the pressures that she knew I had. There is no question in that her criticisms from time to time are not intended to hurt, and that she usually does understand the problems that we have.

In the new term, with Congress likely to remain in Democratic hands, my father would need emotional support, and he was depending on my mother. On different occasions he told Tricia and me that certainly in the world of politics he often had found the women to be stronger than the men. He felt it was true in his own marriage. He recalled that in all of their political battles, once they were committed, Mother had urged fighting to the end, most notably during the fund crisis, when she would not even listen to the idea of resigning, and on election night 1960, when she opposed his conceding too soon.

My father once wrote that politics is poetry. For him it had a cadence, precision, and beauty that did not allow for many disruptions. He liked to work through a buffer, like Bob Haldeman, who shielded him from petty annoyances and subjects he did not feel he should be spending his time on. My mother was more aware than anyone of the time pressures her husband was facing daily, and she tried to avoid bringing up what she referred to as the "unpleasant subjects." When she did make suggestions, frequently they nettled, because often by the time she was aware of what was being planned, it was too late to make changes. For example, when Mother previewed the short film biography of her life that had been made for the convention, she asked also if she could see the film prepared about my father, because she had heard that it was not very good. In fact, as my father conceded in a 1975 memo, it was "lousy." But in 1972, with the convention only two and a half weeks away, and the possibility of making a new film almost nil, he had recorded in his diary, "Needless to say, I don't intend to look at mine and I'm going to see that some way we avoid her seeing it too." Yet he genuinely appreciated a suggestion that could easily be incorporated, as when on the night before his acceptance speech Mother had pointed out that the stage backdrop at the convention was blue and, as my father dictated in his diary, "that it might be necessary to change the suit. Reagan had picked a white coat for that reason."

Throughout the election year, my father was aware of the effectiveness of the family's campaigning. From previous campaigns, he knew that Mother had her own strong following. His analysis of the family's appeal was borne out the day after the election when James Reston of *The New York Times* wrote in a commentary: "It would be difficult to overestimate the political influence of the Nixon family in this campaign." In August my father had recorded in his diary:

I am going to hit Haldeman hard on it tomorrow and see to it that the Price shop [Raymond Price headed up the speech writing at the White House] does a better job in preparing material for Pat and the girls, and Ed, in the days ahead. It just seems that they won't really buckle down and get something done unless they think that they are doing it for me, which is a grievous error.

Although my parents campaigned in tandem in 1972, Mother also had her own schedule of appearances. When she agreed to Connie Stuart's suggestion of a preconvention press conference, she was nervous about the encounter. Indeed, tough questions on abortion, day care, and, inevitably, the Vietnam War were asked at the session. One reporter raised Jane Fonda's charge, which she had voiced in a Hanoi radio broadcast and later at a press conference in Paris, that dikes had been "bombed on purpose" by United States planes. Barely controlling her anger, Mother denied the Fonda allegation and added, "I think she should have been in Hanoi asking them to stop their aggression. Then there wouldn't be any conflict." Rose Mary Woods sent a memo to my father the morning after the press conference.

> Sarah McClendon [a reporter in Washington since Franklin Roosevelt's day] called because she wanted to be sure the President would get this message:
> Mrs. Nixon was superb at her press conference yesterday. They asked her everything they could think of and she handled it all perfectly! Mrs. McClendon said . . . that Mrs. Nixon outdid anyone she has ever seen, men or women. The only question she didn't ask was about who bugged the Democratic headquarters . . . and the only reason she didn't ask that was she couldn't figure out how to do it.

My father passed on to my mother Sarah McClendon's comments on the press conference and noted in his diary, "The only problem is that she goes through such agony in preparing it that I hate to have her take on the assignments."

When my mother left for a six-day solo trip in mid-September, I wrote David, whose ship was on a six-month deployment in the Mediterranean: "Poor Mom was so nervous this morning, according to Tricia . . . Six-day trip, with lots of speaking. *It is* difficult." Meeting and talking to people one on one was a pleasure. What Mother still found difficult was a schedule that called for lots of public speaking, which seemed inevitable in a campaign year. She explained to Connie Stuart several times:

> Connie, I used to be a teacher, head of the pep squad, in lots of plays, and I was quite used to speaking and performing in public. But when Dick entered politics, we decided there would be only one public spokesman in the family. During the House, Senate, and vice-presidential days I didn't give speeches. Now here I am being asked to do more and more, and I'm just not comfortable with it.

Connie remembers that Mother excelled at the short extemporaneous talks when she listened to what the others said and then "got up and spoke from the heart." But the situation that called for "prepared remarks" was a strain for her.

Even after many years of campaigning, Mother was not immune to another election-year pressure—being observed so closely. Campaigning as First Lady was, in the words of Mother's press aide Penny Adams, "like having another layer of skin at all times," because, in addition to her Secret Service agents, the highly competitive AP and UPI correspondents walked with her almost step by step, "hanging on every word or sneeze." On October 26, I wrote David:

> The campaign is really wearing Mom and Tricia down (they didn't have a trip to Barcelona) [I had just met David when the *Albany* was in port in Spain for five days]. They both are thin and haggard and McGovern is getting meaner and playing dirtier every day.

McGovern had called the bugging of the Democratic headquarters "the kind of thing you expect under a person like Hitler." Two more times he would compare the President to Hitler, and he stridently called my father "a bungling, bugging burglar." With a landslide building and the public unwilling to support McGovern's extreme positions, his attacks became more personal. The week before the election he would declare, "The main issue of this whole campaign is Richard M. Nixon." His running mate, Sargent Shriver, shrilly accused the President of being a "psychiatric case" and "Tricky Dicky" who spent most of his time "figuring out ways to keep America number one in the power to kill and destroy people abroad."

Many Democrats who disliked the thought of a McGovern victory but who did not want it to be publicly known that they were supporting a Republican contributed heavily and anonymously to the Nixon campaign before April 7, 1972, when anonymous contributions became illegal. But McGovern fanned the issue of these so-called "secret" contributions, and in September the Washington *Post* began printing leaks from unnamed sources on congressional staffs claiming illegal use of campaign funds. The Nixon campaign clearly was setting a record in campaign contributions. Although a Republican victory was almost 100 percent certain, it was the size of the victory that concerned my father, who reasoned that the larger the win the stronger his Administration would be to face postelection challenges. This attitude accounted for the no-holds-barred campaign to overwhelm McGovern and the Democrats.

It was impossible not to have misgivings about the future. The reports of corruption had triggered my mother on October 16 to telephone Helene Drown, who noted Pat's brief comment, "If I were in charge of the campaign I wouldn't be running it the way it is being run." In 1978 when I asked my mother about that comment, she told me that it worried her that more and more power seemed vested in the handful of men around my father and that he had so little direct involvement in the campaign. The Committee to Re-elect the President staff was huge—an empire unto itself. My father was more insulated from his Cabinet and the majority of his staff in the 1972 campaign than ever before. "I think I made a mistake protecting Daddy too much and in giving in too much," she explained, "but I knew he was busy, the war was hanging over us..."

Helene's notes about Mother's phone call continue with Pat's description of a visit to Rochester, and another to Chicago, where she shared a platform with Mayor Richard Daley.

> When I arrived it was like a boxing match—first he took one step towards me and then I took one—all his henchmen were around him—finally I just bounced over and it was okay. All the candidates walked with us in the parade ... Daley was friendly. He joked and told me to give his regards to my husband and that he has great admiration for him. When we were on the stands, some of Daley's henchmen came up and right in front of him said that Daley had given them permission to split their votes on election day ... So if I can believe anything, at least they're not going to try to steal votes from us like they always have ... I told Dick about this ... Thought that I had really made a mark— then [two days later] there was Daley on the front page with McGovern.

What my mother did not bother to mention to Helene was the other event on her schedule. When she visited a city, she routinely undertook three or four events, and Chicago was no exception. Following the parade with Mayor Daley, Mother had attended a tea in her honor and shaken hands for more than two hours with "nearly 4,000 Republican women," according to the Chicago *Daily News*; two thousand more women had had to be turned away. The Secret Service and advance men who were with her in Chicago still marvel at the stamina she showed that day, and several mentioned it to me when I was researching the campaign.

In Helene's recollection of the phone call from Pat, she had noted also:

> Pat very disturbed about Watergate stories—says that Dick says that there is nothing to it—had talked with Rose Mary today and she said that she supposed that she [Rose] would be next on the list ... Pat said that "I suppose that every day they will come up with some new name and some new story—if it were the Democrats we were yelling about, the press would cry smear, etc."

A few days before, the Washington *Post* had alleged that the White House was involved in a "massive campaign of espionage and spying." The story was a gross exaggeration, although it was true that Dwight Chapin, my father's appointments secretary, had hired a college friend, Donald Segretti, a young attorney and Vietnam veteran, to serve as the Republicans' answer to Dick Tuck. For years, Tuck had been carrying out what the press termed "pranks" against Republican candidates, at times, as in 1964, under the auspices of the Democratic National Committee, which employed him as a "researcher." An example of Tuck's "pranks" was his hiring pregnant black women to picket my father's hotel at the 1968 convention. The women carried Republican campaign signs reading "Nixon's the one." Segretti had organized similar tricks, but his actions went far beyond the "prank" category when he sent out official-looking letters from different Democratic campaign offices asserting that two of the Democratic candidates had records of sexual impropriety and that another suffered from mental instability.

The corruption accusations were damaging, but what my mother disliked most and found difficult to abide was the Democrats' theme of warmongering and indifference to ending the fighting in Vietnam. The war had cast a pall over the full four years of the Nixon Administration. No one wanted to see the troops come home more than my parents.

As usual, antiwar demonstrators were active during the campaign, but they usually left my mother's large, friendly crowds alone. An exception was a dinner in Boston on November 1 when, as the Associated Press reported: "Several thousand antiwar demonstrators smashed windows, burned a car and clashed with riot-equipped police outside a Republican fund raising dinner attended by Pat Nixon tonight." Mother had entered and left the hotel by a side entrance, but there was an unmistakable atmosphere of unease in the dining room that night as thousands of demonstrators waited outside the hotel.

There were other reports of violence during the campaign. By Election Day, Nixon headquarters in Texas, Ohio, Minnesota, Arizona, and California had been either bombed, burned, or broken into and their literature destroyed. I was in Phoenix on the night of September 27, and was scheduled to visit the Republican headquarters in the morning. A small delegation of Republican leaders quietly called on me in my hotel room the next morning to tell me the headquarters had been burned to the ground by arsonists. It was an un-smiling, strained group.

Because of the violence, the demonstrations, and, most of all, the fear of an assassination attempt, Secret Service protection during the campaign was unparalleled in the history of the agency. On May 15, Alabama governor George Wallace, campaigning in Maryland for the Democratic presidential primary vote, had been severely wounded by Arthur Bremer. The assailant's diary revealed he had also stalked my father when he visited Canada. In the wake of the Wallace shooting, *The New York Times* had editorialized that because of the violence in the country perhaps the candidates should not hold outdoor rallies, and should campaign instead through television or at closely controlled gatherings.

By October 17, my father was exasperated by the tightness of the Secret Service protection. He recorded in his diary:

We still have an almost impossible problem with regard to the Secret Service. They surrounded me so tightly that I have to work out in future stops . . . that there can at least be some impression that I am meeting people directly without being completely hemmed in. But, of course, they are petrified at the possibility of another one of the Wallace incidents, but I don't think that their actions in this way will make any difference at all. If somebody is going to make an attack he will be able to do so even though they are surrounding me.

My mother did not dwell on the possibility of an assassination attempt either, and she too found the tight web of security oppressive. I felt elated when I discovered a way to relieve some of the campaign tension. Mother and I started to go for walks on Roosevelt Island, a small tract of wild, wooded land along the Potomac River only a ten-minute drive from the White House. Since it was impossible to walk on the White House grounds without being in view of the tourists who stood at the fence most hours of the day, we found the island a haven. Very few people used this memorial to Teddy Roosevelt, although it was open to the public daily and had adequate parking facilities. Sometimes during a thirty- or forty-minute walk, my mother and I and our Secret Service agents, who tried to keep at least ten yards behind us, would not meet anyone else.

During the last two days of the campaign, my parents traveled together to Illinois, Oklahoma, Rhode Island, North Carolina, and New Mexico. The final stop was California, home. At a large rally in Ontario, not far from where my parents' first campaign had begun, my father spoke for the last time as a candidate for public office.

On Election Day, November 7, my parents voted at Concordia Elementary School in San Clemente and then flew back to Washington. Tricia and Ed had voted in New York; David, who had taken leave to fly home for the election, and I voted in Gettysburg. We were all together for dinner in the White House at six-thirty. Only an hour later, the first substantive returns were available. It was indisputable now. My father was going to win by millions of votes. He lost only the District of Columbia and one state in the Union, Massachusetts. In the morning, *The New York Times* would point out that the election was "a spectacular personal victory for Richard Nixon ten years to a day and almost to the hour after his humiliating defeat by Pat Brown in the 1962 election for the Governorship of California."

A great many hopes were invested in the 1972 election. My father had told the crowd at Ontario that he sensed the start of a new unity in America. No longer was it so deeply divided, no longer "West against the East, the North against the South... let me tell you, wherever you go across America, this nation is getting together." A new coalition of voters who had never been on the Republican side before—Catholics, labor-union families, and voters with a grade-school education—had helped re-elect my father overwhelmingly.

We in the family all seemed to be in different rooms on the second and third floors of the White House during most of election night. My father, who had lost the cap on one of his front teeth shortly after dinner, had emergency dental work done on it, and spent the rest of the evening in the Lincoln Sitting Room listening to *Victory at Sea* and light classical music. David and Ed went back and forth from the West Wing to the Lincoln Sitting Room to give him reports from his staff. Mother, Tricia, and I were in and out of one another's rooms, talking on the phone with friends, meeting with Ed and David in the hall, and periodically going down to see my father. It was for us an evening of mixed emotions. There was the first jubilant moment when the family realized that my father had won the second-largest landslide in American history. There was also a sense of relief that the people had rejected George McGovern's radical beliefs. But the moments of elation were tempered. It had been an ugly campaign at times, and the prospect of four more years in the public eye, four more years of being guarded, was sobering.

For my father, the political man, his re-election should have been a night of triumph, but he also felt a tinge of melancholy, although the family only sensed it at the time. A few days after the election, he confided to his diary that although "I had determined before this election evening to make it as memorable a one as possible for everybody concerned... I was not as upbeat as I should have been." In his *Memoirs* he reflected on the possible reasons: Watergate and the fact that despite his personal victory Republicans had not gained control of Congress, the war in Vietnam as yet unresolved, and, perhaps as well, that it was his last campaign.

The victory celebrations were short. Within days of the election the pressures resumed as though the election had not happened, and my father emerged running in a new campaign to bring the war to an end and to defend the peace settlement in the offing. Once again, my mother led a dual existence. On the surface was the gaiety of the Christmas season as four thousand people, many of whom had played a key role in the re-election victory, were entertained at the White House. Mother's calendar for December shows that from the seventh through the twenty-second, including Saturdays and Sundays, she had an event every day. But beneath the holiday mood of the parties was the reality that for the fourth Christmas of the Nixon Presidency the war in Vietnam was the center of another controversy.

Shortly before the election, there had been much speculation about a peace settlement. On October 26, I had written David:

I guess you have heard that a peace settlement is near. I wish I could have talked to Daddy about it today but I didn't want to bother him as his schedule was full, plus he left for Kentucky at 5:15. All I can say is that the news of a settlement really *bothers* me. I just remember how I felt when Johnson called the bombing halt a few days before the election in '68.

By October 5, the North Vietnamese apparently had come to the conclusion that since there was no chance McGovern could win, they might get a better war settlement from Nixon before the election than after. On the twenty-first, the North Vietnamese indicated they agreed to the U.S. position: an immediate cease-fire; the withdrawal of U.S. forces within sixty days; the unconditional release of the POWs; closing the border sanctuaries in Cambodia and Laos; and the creation of two bodies to verify compliance by both sides. But now President Thieu refused to agree to the proposed settlement, despite his realization that if negotiations remained deadlocked, Congress, when it reconvened in January, planned to cut off all appropriations for the aid and defense of South Vietnam regardless of whether or not the fighting had ceased. Thieu wanted an agreement that established the DMZ as a "secure border" and specifically called for the withdrawal of North Vietnamese troops from the South.

The election came and went and there was no settlement. By December 13, Kissinger's negotiations with the North Vietnamese in Paris were stalemated hopelessly. He suggested a recess until after Christmas, and my father recorded grimly in his diary, "This day, December 13, is really one of the toughest days we have had during the Administration." He felt he had but one alternative left: to show the North Vietnamese that America would no longer tolerate the stalemate.

On December 14, my father gave the order to prepare to commence a reseeding of the mines in Haiphong Harbor and to resume the B-52 bombing strikes against military installations in Hanoi-Haiphong. Beginning on December 18, for eleven long days, with the exception of Christmas itself, the bombs fell. On the afternoon of December 28, the North Vietnamese indicated they would resume "serious" negotiations in Paris; Le Duc Tho and Henry Kissinger would meet in Paris on January 8.

The strategy to bring the North to the negotiating table had worked, but the roar of criticism for what some in the media called the "Christmas bombing" all but blasted my parents out of Key Biscayne, where they flew on December 23 to spend Christmas. From many press reports that December, Americans got the impression that Hanoi was being gutted and civilians deliberately killed. Outraged editorials were published from coast to coast: the Boston *Globe* headlined: "The Rain of Death Continues"; and the St. Louis *Post-Dispatch*: "New Madness in Vietnam"; and CBS declared the United States "has embarked on a large-scale terror bombing." Actually, the precision bombing resulted in between thirteen hundred and sixteen hundred casualties, by North Vietnam's own count at the time. And our pilots exposed themselves to greater risks because of the orders to strike specific military targets and avoid collateral damage to population areas. On February 5, columnist Richard Wilson chronicled some of the charges that were leveled at the President during the bombing: "war by tantrum," "dishonorable strategy," "maddened tyrant," "senseless terror."

During this period of uproar, my father was silent. He explained in his *Memoirs* why he did not try to rally the American public with a speech like the one delivered November 3, 1969: if the President had announced he was resuming the bombing to get the Communists to the negotiating table, the fanatical North would never have capitulated and agreed to an ultimatum that caused it to lose face. But because there was no rhetoric, the North, once convinced of the President's resolve, took the final steps toward signing the Paris Agreement on Ending the War and Restoring Peace in Vietnam.

From the day my father arrived in Florida, he was tense and preoccupied, constantly on the telephone to receive reports and give instructions. It had been that way for weeks. Henry Kissinger had become increasingly frustrated by the intransigence of the North Vietnamese negotiators, and he had begun to question his own usefulness in the negotiations. At night, after dinner, Mother would hear my father on the telephone with Kissinger: "Henry, you've got to stay on the job, you can't quit until I give the word." She told me later that the intricacies of those negotiations and what she saw my father go through made her wary of second-guessing or questioning his decisions in the months ahead. Only one person could know all the facts and all the pressures that were being brought to bear. That is why as Watergate unfolded, she was reluctant to probe. Her husband had handled the big problems well in the past; he could handle this one.

It was my parents' first Christmas without either Tricia or me at home. Tricia and Ed were on a trip to Europe, which they had planned since Ed's graduation from Harvard Law School in June and had delayed until after the campaign. They met David and me in Athens where David's ship, the *Albany*, was in port for the holidays. On Christmas morning when Mother suggested opening the gifts, my father mumbled something about "later." Neither really had the heart for the family ritual. The packages were taken back to Washington, still wrapped. Before retiring Christmas evening, my father noted in his diary a rare recognition of his own loneliness.

It is inevitable that not only the President but the First Lady become more and more lonely individuals in a sense who have to depend on fewer and fewer people who can give them a lift when they need it, even though ironically there are millions more who know them and would help if they could just be given the chance to do so. It is a question not of too many friends but really too few—one of the inevitable consequences of this position.

As this Christmas Day ends I am grateful for... all of those who basically are our family at a time the girls are so far away.

When Tricia and I returned home, we were anxious to break the tension both my parents were under as the final peace negotiations commenced. We decided to give my father a surprise party on January 9, his sixtieth birthday. Mother helped us make up a small guest list of twenty or so friends, including Roger and Louise Johnson, Bebe Rebozo, Bob and Josie Abplanalp, and Paul and Miriam Keyes; they were asked to bring only funny gifts.

Earlier in the week my father had told Mother that he did not think they should plan any celebration this year. The furor over the December bombing was still fresh and the North Vietnamese had not yet agreed to the U.S. terms. But the afternoon of January 9, my father got a wire from Kissinger indicating a major breakthrough in the negotiations. He elatedly returned to the White House to tell my mother the news. Then he added wistfully that it was too bad some sort of birthday had not been planned.

Mother kept mum and that night my father was totally surprised. In order to maintain the fiction that nothing special was being planned, the table in the second-floor dining room was set with places for just the immediate family. When we gathered for dinner, Tricia suggested casually that it might be fun to try something new, cocktails in the Red Room.

A fire was blazing on the hearth in the Red Room when we entered. My father's mouth dropped in astonishment when the door from the Blue Room opened and his friends sauntered in. Bob Abplanalp presented the President with a wooden plaque bearing a replica of the state of Massachusetts and of the District of Columbia, McGovern's only wins, with the legend "For the man who has almost everything." Mother had noticed that during the Christmas and New Year's football games my father had laughed each time he saw the TV commercial for a brand-new device, a hair-styling brush for men. So she presented him with one. My gift was a framed "Berry's World" cartoon that gently tweaked Bob Haldeman's careful monitoring of who saw the President: my father is seated behind his desk in the Oval Office, facing a guest in an armchair opposite him. The guest is none other than his red setter, sitting up very tall. The caption read, "Well it's nice that Bob Haldeman let you come for a visit, even if it is only for a few minutes, King Timahoe."

The White House staff had placed a long table in the Blue Room. It was beautifully set with the Woodrow Wilson service plates gleaming in the light cast by four candelabra. Before the cake was served, my father asked Manolo to bring in King Timahoe, Vicky, and Pasha for a special treat of steak tidbits.

There was much good humor in the spirited toasting. Bebe delivered a straight-faced tribute to a "fine person, a wonderful guy who is doing great things—let's drink to Bob Abplanalp." In his responding toast, my father thanked his friends for coming. His next words were deeply felt. He mentioned

David being overseas with his ship and then spoke of all the men serving their country around the world. "Let's drink a toast to the men in the armed forces. God bless them and we'll prove that they were right." I recorded in the diary I kept sporadically that month that my father "didn't say a word about Vietnam or about the decisions he was having to make at that point or that it had been a tense, hard week . . . just that he was so proud of the men who were serving and that he was trying to do what was best for them."

After dinner we went to the White House theater to see the film classic *The Maltese Falcon* with Humphrey Bogart. The lights dimmed, the melo-dramatic overture began, and the movie credits were flashed on the screen. Suddenly there was a break in the film, and seemingly out of nowhere, TV comedians Dan Rowan and Dick Martin were on the screen singing "Happy Birthday" and exchanging quips.

DAN: Our President is sixty years old today.
DICK: George McGovern is sixty years old?
DAN: George McGovern is not our President.
DICK: Sure, you can tell me that, but how are you going to break it to the Washington *Post*?

For ten minutes the gags kept coming in a hilarious birthday skit arranged by Paul Keyes. Paul remembers that as *The Maltese Falcon* resumed, Mother squeezed his arm and whispered, "Thank you for doing this for Dick. Thank you so much!"

On January 15 all bombing and mining of North Vietnam was stopped. My father recorded in his diary:

I had Henry call Pat and give her a rundown on affairs shortly after the announcement. Henry said that the four years he had known Mrs. Nixon he had never heard her sound so elated—that she was enormously pleased.

Julie just wanted to call. She was bubbly and upbeat and she and her mother, who was apparently in the room with her, were very proud of what had happened. I began to answer by indicating that the stopping of the bombing I suppose was pretty popular and all that sort of thing. She said, no, that isn't what she meant. She and her mother were proud of the fact that I had gone ahead and done what was right.

I too made a diary note about the phone call: "His voice sounded so tired and old when he said, 'Well, we don't know what will happen. We don't know if it will work out.'"

For six more days, it was not certain whether President Thieu would join the United States and North Vietnam in signing the peace settlement. As my father wrote later in his 1985 study of the war, *No More Vietnams*, Thieu was concerned, and justly so as it turned out, that the Communists would use the cease-fire to quietly build up their shipments of troops and supplies. In a letter to Thieu on January 16, my father reassured him that the U.S. would "react strongly in the event the agreement is violated," and on January 21, Thieu announced he would accept the peace terms.

Sadly, on January 22, only hours before the formal initialing of the peace accord that had eluded him as President, Lyndon Baines Johnson died of a heart attack. Only a month before, on December 26, American flags had flown at half-staff for Harry S Truman. The contrast between the two deaths was poignant. Truman had lived a full life, not only in age, eighty-eight years, but also in terms of recognition for his accomplishments. When my parents flew to Independence to pay their respects to Mrs. Truman, they visited her in the Victorian house where she and her husband had enjoyed their retirement. In the living room with the President's piano and a large portrait of daughter Margaret, they sensed sadness but acceptance. But Lyndon Baines Johnson's last years had not been easy ones. At the 1968 and 1972 Democratic Conventions, he had been a nonperson in the party he had helped build since coming to Congress in 1937 as a supporter of FDR's New Deal. The war in Vietnam had gutted his Presidency and curtailed his plans for a Great Society.

As soon as my father received word of President Johnson's death, he telephoned Lady Bird Johnson at the LBJ Ranch. Mother was in the room when the call was placed, but she did not speak, because, as my father recorded in his diary that evening, she had told him, "I'm just no good on the telephone." She never would master her dread of the emotional encounter with one who is bereaved. Lady Bird Johnson's voice was serene. She would continue to be disciplined and controlled throughout the state funeral when a half smile never left her face. On January 24, as my parents escorted her to the Rotunda of the Capitol where her husband's body lay in state, she was composed enough to reminisce about the number of times she had waited for Lyndon at the door of the Senate.

Large crowds of people lined the streets of Washington on the cold but brilliantly sunny day of the last tribute to Lyndon Johnson. Luci's husband, Pat Nugent, who, like the President's other son-in-law, Charles Robb, had served in Vietnam, quietly told my father, "Thank you for peace."

The day before, January 23, the representatives of North Vietnam and the United States initialed the peace agreement. On January 27, the twelve-year-long American involvement in the war in Vietnam would officially end. *Newsweek* magazine, in its February 5 issue, described the treaty as "at times vague and confusing," yet embodying a "masterly set of compromises that finally made peace possible." Accompanying the story was a somber portfolio of photographs, the sole caption: "A war without winners."

My father briefly addressed the nation the night of January 23 to announce the cease-fire. Then he went immediately over to the house, where Mother,

Tricia, Ed, and I were waiting for him in the Solarium. Within minutes, Henry Kissinger telephoned to congratulate my father on the conclusion of the four years of unceasing effort to end the fighting in Vietnam. He found that the President, instead of savoring the moment, already had his mind on the task awaiting him in the morning, briefing the congressional leaders. Then:

> Mrs. Nixon took the phone to congratulate me. It took stout hearts to see it through, she said. What a gallant lady she had been. With pain and stoicism, she had suffered the calumny and hatred that seemed to follow her husband. Unlike the President, she was not capable of the fantasy life in which romantic imaginings embellished the often self-inflicted daily disappointments. She was totally without illusions and totally insistent on facing her trials in solitude. Her dignity never wavered. And if she seemed remote, who could know what fires had had to be banked in her stern existence. She made no claims on anyone; her fortitude had been awesome and not a little inspiring because one sensed that it had been wrested from an essential gentleness.

The "peace with honor" had not been achieved easily. It had taken a toll on the nation and on its thirty-seventh President. Mother had been the first one to reach my father when he walked into the room. She silently embraced him. As I watched them, I felt her gesture said it all: it signified relief, sadness for what had gone before, and a desire to shield her husband from what might lie ahead.

CHAPTER 26

1973
"Fight, Fight, Fight"

The second Nixon inauguration had taken place three days before the announcement of a January 27 cease-fire in Vietnam. Speaking from the east front of the Capitol, my father began his brief address with the words: "When we met here four years ago, America was bleak in spirit, depressed by the prospect of seemingly endless war abroad and of destructive conflict at home. As we meet here today, we stand at the threshold of a new era of peace in the world." He had told the family while he was working on the speech that he wanted it to "lift people." Now on that cold January day he promised that his Administration would try to achieve a peace that would endure, and spoke earnestly of the nation having to "answer to God, to history, and to our conscience for the way in which we use these years."

After the ceremonies at the Capitol, we began the parade down Pennsylvania Avenue toward the White House and the reviewing stand. Antiwar demonstrators were on the scene as they had been for most presidential events during the past four years. Suddenly the Secret Service raised the windows of the convertible Mamie Eisenhower and I were riding in several cars behind my parents. David had been unable to take leave from his ship for the inauguration, and Mamie, as she impishly told all, was "playing David." She had been waving exuberantly to the crowd, urging me to join her in using not just my gloved hand, but my entire arm. She looked surprised when the windows went up and the car started to gain speed. I guessed that we were nearing the corner where most of the demonstrators had massed. The agents had received a radio message that the presidential limousine had just been showered with eggs and debris. Both my parents had refused to sit down, and remained standing in the open air. But the Secret Service was not going to take any more chances than it needed to with the other cars in the procession.

As in 1969, many Nixon, Milhous, and Ryan family members had traveled East for the inaugural festivities of concerts, receptions, and balls. My father's eighty-year-old aunt, Jane Beeson, who had been one of his piano teachers and who still had twenty students come to her Lindsay, California, home weekly, wrote "Dear Pat" a thank-you note on January 25.

> ... I want to tell you how wonderful you have been through the years in your loving care and sympathetic understanding of Richard, at all times and under varying circumstances a perfect complement to him in every way. I appreciate it so much as I have felt so proud of his accomplishments, ability and dedication, and know what an important role you have played to encourage him. Harold [her late husband] used to say "Pat takes first prize in making one feel her interest in each one individually, regardless of station in life, influence or financial status." You make each one feel his or her importance.
>
> Do hope you both get rested—you looked tired and still had hard things to go through ... Lovingly and prayerfully,
>
> Aunt Jane

At the outset of his second term, my father declared war on waste in the bureaucracy. On Mother's copy of *The Weekly Compilation of Presidential Documents* for March 5, 1973, she underlined a passage from the President's message to Congress on human resources and urged Tricia and me to read it.

> During the middle and late 1960s ... state and local governments and the private sector were elbowed aside ... literally hundreds of new programs were established on the assumption that even the most complex problems could be quickly solved by throwing enough Federal dollars at them ... The American people deserve better than this. They deserve compassion that works—not simply compassion that means well. They deserve programs that say yes to human need by saying no to paternalism, social exploitation and waste.

Mother picked out that passage in the long message because she believed in the goals of the new budget, described by columnist Joseph Kraft as taking "the breath away. It moves to impose on our whole society his belief in the work ethic."

My father challenged the Democratic-controlled Congress to cut spending and to establish projected spending limits for the next two years. But the Administration's effort to tame the bureaucracy and to treat the President's budget as a ceiling on congressional spending was not welcomed by the majority of Democrats in Congress who feared the President might succeed in shaping his New Majority into a potent political force. House Majority Leader Tip O'Neill would boast later to writer Jimmy Breslin that by January 1973 he knew he wanted Nixon to be impeached.

On January 11, only eight days after Congress reconvened, the Senate Democratic Caucus had voted unanimously to investigate Watergate and Republican 1972 election misdeeds. Compounding matters, morale in the Administration had not been high since the morning after the election when my father stunned his Cabinet and White House aides, who had worked hard for his election, by calling for the resignation of every noncareer government employee in the executive branch. "Most of the resignations would not be accepted: my action was meant to be symbolic of a completely new beginning," my father wrote in his *Memoirs*, conceding in retrospect that his decision was a "mistake." But at the time, he was only mildly aware of rumblings of discontent. Insulated at Camp David, where he spent eighteen days out of the first month following the election, he devoted much of his time to meetings with forty old and new appointees, who were shuttled to the mountain retreat by helicopter.

My mother was also surprised and unhappy about the request for resignations. What disturbed her more, however, was the growing tendency of my father to depend upon one man, Bob Haldeman, to gather information and to relay orders. Much of the sensitivity and thoughtfulness we saw in my father was squeezed out by the time Haldeman, overworked and with far too many details to attend to everything himself, parceled out the orders to his young aides. Increasingly, loyalty was demanded of all, not judgment.

By the time of the second inauguration, most of my father's original band of aides and supporters had little contact with "the boss." My father wanted Bob Haldeman to be the sole conduit to him, and Haldeman seemed to want that even more. As early as my father's first week as President, Rose Woods had confided to Bebe Rebozo that Haldeman had issued Executive Office Building rather than White House passes to Pat Buchanan and Ray Price, certainly two of my father's closest aides and political friends. A mistake or a deliberate action? Rose had not said anything to my father, explaining to Bebe that "the boss" felt criticisms of Haldeman were motivated by jealousy. But Bebe went immediately to my father, who asked that Price and Buchanan be given unlimited access to the White House.

My father had come to depend mightily on Bob Haldeman, and he did not want to hear criticism of his chief of staff, who worked hours as long as his own. So he closed his eyes to Haldeman's occasional overstepping as he went about accomplishing what the President wanted.

After the election, one of my father's meetings at Camp David was with communications chief Herb Klein. My father was disappointed that Herb had not been more aggressive in his dealings with the media and hoped he would adhere to a statement he had made that fall that he would be leaving the White House sometime early in the second term. But Herb also was a good friend, one my father did not want to hurt in the process of a changeover. On the cold January day that Herb Klein helicoptered to Camp David, marine military aide Jack Brennan was on duty to announce those summoned to the President's study in Aspen Lodge. In that small, intimate room with its two dark-blue chairs, side table with my father's pipe rack on it, and simple tabletop desk, conversations were conducted at close range, face-to-face. When Herb Klein's meeting with the President went past the allotted time, Brennan crisply knocked on the door and entered to announce that Governor Nelson Rockefeller had arrived for his appointment. He could see that the President was agitated. When Klein left a few minutes later, the President still did not signal Brennan to escort Rockefeller into the study. Brennan waited another five minutes and then knocked again on the office door. He could hear the President on the phone talking angrily to Bob Haldeman: "You told me Herb *wanted* to leave..."

I was at Camp David during part of the transition period. One evening my father mentioned casually that Mike Farrell, who for two years had skillfully run the Office of White House Visitors, was leaving the White House and an old political friend would be taking his place. I immediately called Mike to say how much I would miss him and what a fine job he had done. He was astounded and did not know how to respond since it was the first he had heard that he was leaving. When I told my mother about the conversation with Mike, she was upset by the idea of his being replaced and immediately asked my father what the story was. We sat next to him on the white sofa in front of the fire in Aspen Lodge and listened as he telephoned Haldeman. It was obvious that my father had wanted a place found for the political friend and had assumed Haldeman would surgically take care of the matter without ruffling feathers. Now, from hearing only my father's end of the conversation, we surmised that Bob was assuring the President it was all a misunderstanding and that Mike had indeed indicated he wanted to leave. At this point my father was annoyed by the whole episode. As he hung up, he informed us it was all a mix-up; Mike would remain. Then he quickly put the episode out of his mind, chalking it up to a lack of communication.

It was not so easy, however, for the family to forget that my father seemed unconcerned about the amount of manipulation going on in order to achieve his requests. When the new *Air Force One* was completed, my father recorded in his diary entry for February 14:

I was concerned by the fact that the plane had a poor configuration and frankly Julie had raised it with me, and David had as well, and also the point was made by Bebe... It's this kind of thing... in which the Secret Service can't even tilt their chairs back and there's a huge amount of space in the staff area that gives Haldeman a very frankly bad image with the staff and there's no need for him to do so.

On the same day, my father also recorded another eye-opening criticism of Haldeman, this time in connection with the new building program at Camp David. A large staff lodge had been constructed across from the badly termite infested "old Laurel." My mother and Bebe, knowing that words of criticism would not be as effective with my father as a firsthand view, decided he should see all of new Laurel. Bebe and my father walked over to the "cabin." When they entered the huge living area with its cathedral ceiling and large picture windows looking out over the fairyland of trees, Bebe told the President that the dozen or so dining tables were reserved for senior staff only. Then he led him to a small room, as my father recorded in his diary, "just crowded to over-flowing with the doctors, military aides and helicopter pilots." Haldeman had given orders that only top staff were to eat in the main dining area because of the sensitive conversations that might take place, but he had neglected to be sure that the junior staff dining area was adequate.

The isolation of the President in the White House is not so much self-imposed as it is imposed by others and by the nature of the office itself. The ushers, military aides, and key staff members all try to insure that the President's energy is reserved for the big decisions; to spare him the petty details of life; to fulfill as quickly as possible his requests, small and large. His family is similarly isolated by East Wing staff and are oddly unaware of most of the rumors that sweep through Washington and give a unique flavor to the city. When my father left office, I continued to live in Washington and was amazed by the amount of Washington gossip about the White House staff, everything from who was having an affair with whom to who had the President's ear, to the purported significance of the geography of staff offices and access to official cars and how such things demonstrated the pecking order within the Administration.

In my father's case, presidential isolation had increased because under the pressures of the war he had preferred to work through two or three key staff members. My mother was more aware of the isolation within the self-contained city that is the White House. She constantly looked for ways to simplify her own staff operation and thus have more control over it, as well as to help contain expenses. She insisted on a tightly run East Wing office and scaled-down advance and support help on trips. Bill Codus, who did more advance work for her on foreign trips than anyone else, told me, "The thing I admired so much about your mother was that she was so concerned about costs. Repeatedly she told me, 'Go with a small group, Bill,' or 'Why do you need so many with you?'" Bill did travel with just one aide, and the Secret Service sent its own representative. Occasionally, the First Lady's office sent someone also, but Mother seemed embarrassed by the size of even this modest advance party.

When Connie Stuart left the First Lady's staff shortly after the inauguration for a job in a government agency, which would give her more time with her husband, my mother decided not to hire a new staff director. Press assistant Helen Smith, who was popular with the correspondents who covered the East Wing, would handle all press duties now, and Mother would have more direct dealings with her staff.

Another member of my mother's staff, Coral Schmidt, who had helped primarily with trip arrangements, was also leaving and Mother decided not to replace her either. When Coral came to say goodbye, my mother revealed that she was aware there were still some who rumbled that Mrs. Nixon did not have one main "First Lady project." After their talk, Coral wrote:

Dear Mrs. Nixon,
During our conversation on Tuesday, you asked me two questions which I have given further thought to and would like to share with you. One was whether or not I could think of a slogan or phrase for a special project that you are associated with. Mrs. Nixon, you care about people. You do not need a special project or a catchy slogan...

You so selflessly and patiently give of your time to recognize people by congratulating them for their achievements and reaching out to them when they are in need. Your response to all those letters, your willingness to sign every autograph (sometimes even on the gum wrappers) and your shaking that last hand are proofs that you care deeply for everyone.

You have sown seeds of promise for our country. You expect the very best from everyone and consequently people strive to measure up.

Through interests and activity and a pet project one can endeavor to beautify the environment, upgrade education and improve the standard of living. But a special project does not heal the broken heart, eliminate hatred, loneliness and suffering—*it takes love*. And you care about our most precious resource—people. This is the gift you have given to our country...

That spring, with the war no longer the focus of attention, slowly, steadily the word "Watergate" began to dominate the news as my mother fulfilled a full calendar of events: state dinners for Britain's Edward Heath, King Hussein of Jordan, and Golda Meir of Israel; the annual dinner for the governors and their wives; teas for the National Center for Voluntary Action, the Chamber of Commerce, and Hadassah, among others.

As always, Mother's St. Patrick's Day birthday was a red-letter date on the White House calendar. Each year something special was planned, although nothing could top the first year in the White House when my father, Tricia, and I succeeded in surprising her with a birthday party with more than one hundred friends. On March 17, 1973, after the Irish ambassador to the United States had made his traditional call on the President and the First Lady in the Oval Office to present a gift of shamrocks, Mother, as was her custom, sent the shamrocks neatly packaged in a plastic bag to the East Wing desk of Susan Porter, who delighted in her Irish heritage.

Early that morning on his way to the Oval Office, my father had admired footman (the archaic title for the men who assisted the White House ushers) Freddie Mayfield's wide, kelly-green bow tie. Impulsively, he asked Freddie if he would mind trading neckwear for the evening. At 8 P.M. when the President greeted his guests at an evening of entertainment with country-and-western singer Merle Haggard, he was smiling broadly, Freddie's green tie at his neck. The First Lady was also "wearing the green." After the entertainment, my parents received guests in the Blue Room and encouraged all to go upstairs to see the Lincoln Bedroom and the Queen's Room, which were opened that evening as a special treat. "This house is yours tonight—you help pay the rent," my father joked with the guests. "We can't offer you moonshine or Irish whiskey—but we've got California champagne, so watch out!" It was one of the last relatively carefree evenings of the Nixon Presidency before the full force of Watergate struck.

On February 5 a resolution was introduced in the Senate to establish a Select Committee on Presidential Campaign Activities, and Senator Sam Ervin of North Carolina was chosen by Mike Mansfield to chair what became known as the Watergate Committee. The FBI had been investigating the break-in at the Watergate for more than six months. At a presidential press conference two days before the St. Patrick's Day party, my father answered numerous questions on Watergate. He repeated several times what he had no reason to believe was untrue: that no one in the White House had been involved in the break-in. The next day, however, March 16, and again on March 17, my father talked with thirty-four-year-old John Dean, the White House legal counsel, whom he had asked to "ride herd" on the Watergate matter. Throughout March, Dean had assured the President that there was no Watergate evidence against Chapin, Colson, or Haldeman. But now more facts were emerging in the Watergate mosaic, and the technicality of no White House *knowledge* of the break-in had become almost irrelevant in the light of White House actions *after* the break-in and attempt to bug the Democrats' headquarters. On the seventeenth, Dean told the President about the burglary of the office of Daniel Ellsberg's psychiatrist. It was explosive news, because two of those involved in the burglary—Howard Hunt and Gordon Liddy—had been caught at the break-in at the Watergate. Since Hunt and Liddy had worked for John Ehrlichman, that meant they were linked to the White House, not just to the Committee to Re-elect the President.

On March 21, my father again met with John Dean, who stated that the White House was now being blackmailed and "people are going to start perjuring themselves very quickly . . . to protect other people and the like." Haldeman, Ehrlichman, Mitchell, and himself, Dean continued, were all involved in the decision to finance attorneys' fees for the men arrested at the Watergate. The money came from a $350,000 White House cash fund from the 1972 election; the money was kept in a Washington bank and was at Bob Haldeman's disposal. Now it seemed Howard Hunt was asking for more money, and he was accompanying his request by a threat to destroy John Ehrlichman.

In the intervening months since the June break-in, my father, his principal aides, Bob Haldeman and John Ehrlichman, as well as legal counsel, John Dean, had been hoping that the problem would go away, rather than trying to get to the bottom of it. Consequently, by the time of the March 21 meeting, each man was looking at the matter from his own perspective. Bob Haldeman was worried that Jeb Magruder, deputy director of the Committee to Re-elect the President, might falsely accuse him of having known about the break-in beforehand, almost oblivious to the greater danger that he had approved large attorneys' fees and payments to the defendants. John Dean still had not explained how deeply involved he was in the efforts to "contain" the problem. And John Ehrlichman seemed to be the least familiar with the facts of who had known about the bugging and how it all affected him.

As my father tried to sort out the convoluted details of Watergate, we in the family could sense that something was terribly wrong. Over Easter weekend in Key Biscayne, my father was more tense and uncommunicative than I ever remembered him. Easter morning, when the Filipino stewards had laid out the Sunday newspapers on the glass-topped dining-room table as usual, the Washington *Post* carried four different front-page stories on Watergate.

During that stay in Key Biscayne, Mother was solicitous toward my father, but he had withdrawn into his own world and away from the family. She remembers thinking at the time how silly it was to be in the Florida sunshine, supposedly there for a rest, and to feel tension in the air so thick that it was almost unbearable. She spent most of her time reading in a lounge chair beneath several palms, a small oasis of escape in our yard. Once or twice I lured her for a walk along the quarter mile of sand in front of our house and the others on Bay Lane. At Mother's suggestion, the agents carried fins and snorkel gear so that they would appear less conspicuous.

In an interview a few weeks after our return to Washington, I told Bill Safire, who had left the White House staff in January and was now a *New York Times* columnist, about the trip to Florida and how different the evolving Watergate crisis was from other difficult times in the past.

The other times he'd [my father] call us, but this time we'd call him to say hello...he didn't try to cheer Mother up, and that was very rare. In Key Biscayne, around 5 in the afternoon he'd go for a swim, and come back not saying anything, and after dinner he was feeling low. You know how Mother is, always thinking of other people, she wanted him to know that we were with him all the way, but he was just closed off.

I felt he wasn't giving her enough credit for having such confidence in him, so during a movie I sat next to him and said, "Mother's trying so hard to make things right, and you don't realize it. It's hard for her too." He just said, "I guess so," and all through the movie I felt horrible that I had blurted that out, he didn't need any more burdens from us, but then after it was over he turned to me and said, "You're right, it's hard for her too. I'll try." And he did.

My comments to Safire are a pale rendering of the alarm I felt when I saw my father so deeply troubled, and Mother equally troubled because she felt helpless. She had long ago come to understand that my father did not want his family to be involved in his political decisions. He liked to tackle problems by turning them over and over again in his mind until they became digested and resolved. It was a solitary process, and because both my parents were very private people, their relationship was a delicate, polite one that did not allow for much second-guessing.

We later learned that in Florida my father had been wrestling with a cruel decision: whether to ask for the resignations of his two most trusted and valued aides, Bob Haldeman and John Ehrlichman. Since April 19, John Dean and his lawyers, in a push for immunity, had begun leaking a barrage of damaging reports that the President's closest aides were responsible for the break-in at the Watergate and the subsequent cover-up. By April 27 the public outcry for the resignations of Haldeman and Ehrlichman had become insistent. I can remember that Friday evening when my father helicoptered to Camp David. Since Easter, his tenseness and fewer hours at home had been a signal to the family that he wanted to keep us at arm's length from the Watergate mess. We had no idea that once at Camp David he planned formally to accept his aides' resignations, to be announced on Monday. That announcement would be the signal that Watergate was more than an episode and that the second Nixon Administration, only three months old, was fighting for survival.

David, who had just been released from the Navy, and I were staying at the White House for a few weeks. Friday night we waited until my mother had gone to bed so as not to worry her and then stayed up until dawn with Tricia, who had come down from New York. Although the family rarely injected itself into decisions, this time we discussed which one of us should go to Camp David and encourage my father in making what inevitably would be a painful break with Haldeman and Ehrlichman.

At 8 A.M. Saturday, Tricia was driven by the Secret Service to the fogged-in camp. My father seemed glad she had come, quietly listened to her, and then asked if she would stay with him for the rest of the day. But Tricia knew it would be better if she went back to Washington. Shortly before 11 A.M., she was winding her way down the mountain and my father was steeling himself for the face-to-face meetings on Sunday afternoon with first Haldeman, then Ehrlichman.

As my father grappled with a problem whose dimensions no one fully understood yet, he lived through one of the longest weekends of his Presidency. The decisions he made that weekend marked a point of no return. In retrospect, he was harshly self-critical about asking Haldeman and Ehrlichman to resign.

> They deserved the best possible chance to save themselves, and in asking them to leave I had ensured that they would never be able to prove that their motives had been innocent. I had done what I felt was necessary, but not what I believed was right. I had always prided myself on the fact that I stood by people who were down. Now I had sacrificed, for myself, two people to whom I owed so much.

When Haldeman and Ehrlichman's car disappeared along the curving road that takes one away from Aspen Lodge, my father felt very much alone. In time, Ron Ziegler would help fill Haldeman's role as a sounding board. But for the present, there was a terrible void mixed with a premonition that despite the break with Haldeman and Ehrlichman, it would not be possible to avoid deeper Watergate involvement.

Ray Price was at Camp David that weekend, helping my father write the speech that would announce his aides' departures and address the Watergate issue in an effort to put it behind him. On Monday afternoon when Ray came over to the study in Aspen to work on the speech, he found the President "emotionally ravaged, his hands unsteady, anguish written in every one of the deepened lines of his face." Point-blank he asked Ray: Should I resign as well? Ray was surprised, but his answer was instant: No; he had a responsibility to do the job he had been elected to do. Only he could complete the "structure of peace." Vice President Agnew, for all of his good qualities, would not be able to carry on the diplomatic initiatives that showed so much promise for a troubled world.

Maybe my father was half hoping Ray would tell him that he should renounce the Presidency. When he did not, the task of the speech had to be met. The next day, April 30, when he delivered his nationally televised broadcast, my father's hope was that in announcing the resignations of his two closest aides the public would, as he stated in his *Memoirs*, "become impatient with Watergate and exert pressure on Congress and the media to move on to something else..." Certainly the aim of his speech was to close the subject of Watergate with the departures of Haldeman and Ehrlichman and the firing of John Dean. What he did not say in the speech was that he still did not know the full details of Watergate or how deeply involved all the key players were. Nor did he say that for more than a month he had cast about for some way to protect his friends and political associates and to minimize the damage to the Presidency and his Administration. What he failed to provide, as he wrote five years after that bitter April night, was

> an accounting of my role ... explanations of how a President of the United States could so incompetently allow himself to get in such a situation. That was what people really wanted to know, and that was what my April 30 speech and all the other public statements I made about Watergate while I was President failed to tell them.

Mother, Tricia, Rose, Bebe, and David watched the speech together in the West Hall. I watched in a motel room in Orlando, Florida, where in the morning I was scheduled to meet with Girl Scouts. When the last words were spoken and the camera moved away from the close-up of my father's face, I realized something was wrong.

My feelings of foreboding were confirmed minutes later when I called the White House and asked to speak to my father. Because there had been so many controversial speeches in the first four years of his Presidency, a family custom had evolved of telephoning my father after a major address. But when the telephone rang in the West Hall that night, to my surprise Mother answered. She told me my father had gone down to the Lincoln Sitting Room and was not taking calls. Until late that night, for the first time, Mother, Tricia, David, and Rose took all the incoming calls from friends who offered words of support.

I did not learn until later the sequence of events when my father came upstairs immediately after the address. The family had embraced him, then he had turned and started walking toward his bedroom. The phone rang and Mother picked it up, and so, unlike the others, she was not close enough to hear him say brokenly, his back to them all, "I hope I don't wake up in the morning."

My father was not able to conceal totally his anguish in the days ahead. Mother's reaction was to rally in a superhuman effort to encourage him in every way. For her there could be no criticism and no revelation of the despair she may have felt; only support for the goals and achievements of the Nixon Presidency that she believed in so deeply. There was no doubt in her mind that Watergate was a political witch-hunt, and that my father would withstand it. For the next fifteen months, in the face of blow after blow, she was steadfast. Never before or since has she shown so much strength.

Throughout the first weeks of May, my father tried to set his sights on the important work left for him to do, especially in the field of foreign affairs.

John Volpe, our ambassador to Italy, had sent him a message from Pope Paul VI after a meeting with the pope at the Vatican.

> His Holiness said that history will record that you have done more than anyone else to capture world respect as an effective peacemaker during the last four years... he told me that he simply can't understand how Americans writing in the American press can so brutally tear down their own country and its institutions. He is confident, however, that you will be able to pass through this difficult period and continue your fine work for world peace. The Holy Father said he will offer his prayers and a mass for your intentions.

On May 24, however, the day of the gala White House dinner in honor of the returning prisoners of war, men my father respected and wanted to be accorded thanks from the country they had served so well, he questioned again whether he should continue to serve as President.

The 591 men who came home from Vietnam were an extraordinarily courageous group. Some had been held captive as long as eight years, and many had been tortured and kept for months—even years—in solitary confinement. Opponents of the war closed their eyes to the few reports that trickled out of Hanoi about the barbaric treatment of American POWs. They wanted to believe that the Vietcong and the North Vietnamese were humane, dedicated revolutionaries. In August 1969, members of the antiwar movement had been able to obtain the release of two POWs. When the peace activists praised the Communists' treatment of the captives, one of the newly freed prisoners spoke out in a hospital press conference.

> I don't think solitary confinement, forced statements, living in a cage for three years, being put in straps, not being allowed to sleep or eat, removal of fingernails, being hung from the ceiling, having an infected arm almost lost without medical treatment, being dragged along the ground with a broken leg, and not allowing exchange of mail for prisoners is humane.

In 1972 Ted Kennedy arranged for Ramsey Clark to testify before the Senate about his recent trip to North Vietnam and the excellent health he had found the POWs in when he visited a camp in Hanoi. Clark, who was attorney general under Lyndon Johnson, had told reporters that the men he saw had health "better than mine, and I am a healthy man." In truth, the men were malnourished and many had endured both physical and mental torture. But in February 1973, the returning POWs revealed little if any bitterness for what they had been through.

As the former POWs, almost all painfully thin and feeble, disembarked from the military transports that had brought them home, Mother was one of millions of Americans who were glued to the television to witness the scene.

One after another, the men offered simple, heartfelt, and often eloquent words of faith in God, in their country, and in the loved ones who had waited for them. Captain Jeremiah Denton had these words to say: "We are honored to have had the opportunity to serve our country under difficult circumstances. We are profoundly grateful to our Commander in Chief, and to our nation for this day. God bless America." A few days later at Travis Air Force Base, San Francisco, Captain James Stockdale, limping visibly, his left arm immobile from injuries, recited Greek poetry to express himself. "'Nothing is so sweet as' to return from sea and listen to the raindrops on the rooftops of home,'" adding, "We're home. America, America, God shed his grace on thee." In time, Stockdale would receive the Congressional Medal of Honor because "he deliberately inflicted a near-mortal wound to his person in order to convince his captors of his willingness to give up his life rather than capitulate."

When Sammy Davis, Jr., performed at "An Evening at the White House" on March 3, he had suggested to my parents that the POWs be honored by some of America's finest entertainers. They immediately liked the idea, but Mother insisted that a White House dinner be given as well. All honor was due these men. Already my parents had tried to express a fraction of the joy they felt at having the men back. Thirty-three years before, my father had given Mother her first orchid corsage on their wedding day. Now, they sentimentally purchased more than six hundred corsages for the mothers and wives to wear as they greeted the returning POWs. It was their personal gift. But the dinner would express the entire nation's gratitude.

On May 24, my parents hosted the POWs and their families at the largest dinner ever given at the White House. A huge tent was erected on the South Lawn and my parents opened all the rooms on the state floor and even the family quarters so that the men and women could see the Queen's Room, the Lincoln Bedroom, and the living area where the President and his family relaxed. There was the electricity of excitement in the air at 1600 Pennsylvania Avenue that evening. Lucy Winchester was standing with a group of guests when one of the men introduced his wife to an old friend. Another returned prisoner who was near them heard the wife's name, wheeled around suddenly, and asked tensely of his fellow POW, "Are you————?" They then realized that they had had adjoining cells for several years during their confinement. Through a code of tapping on the wall, each had told the other about their wives and families, their hopes and fears. Now they shook hands for the first time.

It was an emotional evening for every person who sat under the rain-drenched tent. In a voice gravelly with age, yet strong in spirit, Irving Berlin led all of us in singing "God Bless America," which he had written originally for Kate Smith during the Depression. When the colors were brought in, Air

Force Lieutenant John Dramesi held aloft the tiny flag he had made secretly in prison from bits of underwear, blanket, and a string from a Red Cross package.

Air Force Brigadier General John Flynn, a prisoner for five and a half years, spoke on behalf of the POWs. He told my father what the decision to bomb had meant to the men in prison. "We knew you were in a very lonely position. The decision was contested, but I would like to also report to you that when we heard heavy bombs impacting in Hanoi, we started to go and pack our bags, because we knew we were going home, and we were going home with honor."

It was 12:30 A.M. when my parents said good night and went upstairs. Below, there was the sound of music and laughter and animated voices, which would last until 4 A.M., when the last couples left the dance floor. Around 1 A.M. the telephone rang in David's and my bedroom on the third floor. My father asked if I could come down to the Lincoln Sitting Room; he already had telephoned Tricia. When I arrived he was still in his evening clothes, smoking a pipe and looking into the fire. The glow from the logs was the only light in the room. My father seemed drained, as if the emotion of the evening had been too much for him. Tricia recorded in her diary later: "He called Paul Keyes and thanked him for arranging the entertainment. They joked for a few minutes, but it was almost painful for us to see how sad Daddy's face looked despite the laughter in his voice."

After he said good night to Paul, no one broke the silence for a few moments. Then my father looked at us and said, "Do you think I should resign?"

Almost in unison, Tricia and I started talking. "No, why should you? . . . The country needs you. . . . What can you be thinking of?" After we finished talking, he just smiled slightly. Gently, he thanked us for coming down and talking to him. Numbly, Tricia and I said good night. Out in the hallway we looked at each other, and then, without speaking, we took double steps up the back stairway to the third floor to talk. But, really, there was little to say, and Tricia ended her diary entry for that night with the words: "And so the evening concluded—an evening representing a great historical and personal achievement for Daddy, marred by a great personal tragedy. I could not help but think how man lives in the hope of perfection but lives in the reality of imperfection in himself and in those around him."

Once before, almost three weeks earlier at Camp David, my father had spoken to us of resignation. Would it be better for the country, my father asked, would the wounds heal faster, if he resigned? He spoke lightly, gingerly broaching the subject with the family. Despite his studied casualness, our response was a chorus of noes. What had he done that would warrant resignation? And because Mother particularly had urged fighting, perhaps that is why he did not raise the subject with her the night of the POW dinner.

Now Tricia and I wondered if he would ask us periodically about resigning.

But in the next fourteen months, he never mentioned the subject again until August 2, 1974, when the decision to resign already had been forced upon him.

On June 18 the second U.S.–Soviet summit officially began. The Senate Watergate Committee had agreed to a White House request to postpone for one week John Dean's testimony so that it would not coincide with Brezhnev's visit to Washington.

Throughout his stay in the United States, the secretary general was in an expansive mood, fervid in his assurances that great progress would be made during the talks. Within hours of the first meeting in the Oval Office, he announced that he had already invited the President to a summit the next year in Moscow. Later that day, Brezhnev and my father flew to California on *Air Force One*; my mother with Madame Andrei Gromyko and Madame Dobrynin followed on a second plane. Madame Brezhnev had not accompanied her husband, and the secretary general, who boasted to my parents that he soon would become a grandfather, had no inhibitions about flirting with most of the American women he encountered during his visit.

During the stay in California, my mother was more aware of Brezhnev's boyish personality than of what she called his "rough and tough" side which had been so evident in Moscow the spring before. The secretary general had insisted upon staying at La Casa Pacifica despite the efforts of our government officials to convince the Russians that there were far more spacious and adequate quarters at Camp Pendleton, an easy helicopter ride from San Clemente. Brezhnev had rejected the Pendleton suggestion, perhaps because of a desire to emphasize the nature of the friendship between the American President and himself. My mother was left with no choice but to place Brezhnev in either Tricia's room or mine, the only two guest rooms in the house.

Leonid Brezhnev therefore was ensconced in Tricia's feminine room, with its fragile white wicker furniture and walls papered in bold pink, blue, and lavender flowers. His guards were housed in my room, adjacent to Tricia's, and additional security was crowded into the patio, which forms the center of the Spanish-style house. Because Tricia's room and my mother's both open on to a narrow hallway, Mother was aware of the secretary general's activities throughout his visit.

When the final arrangements were being made for the visit to San Clemente, the Russians had requested a trailer. It was parked on the Coast Guard grounds adjoining La Casa Pacifica and housed the stewardesses who had flown on the Soviet aircraft to the United States. These women were at the beck and call of the secretary general. Brezhnev's entourage did not bother to try to conceal the trailer arrangements. Certainly they assumed that if Brezhnev was not being tapped, he was being closely watched. Surveillance is a way of life in the Soviet Union and, in fact, is a highly developed art. For example, when in Russia, Henry Kissinger's aides used a manual typewriter for sensitive documents because of a well-grounded suspicion that the "telemetry" of an electric typewriter could be read by the Soviets.

The day had begun with a poolside reception attended by dozens of Hollywood stars, followed by a small dinner for ten in the dining room at La Casa Pacifica. Brezhnev had then napped for an hour. Refreshed, he sent word to Henry Kissinger that he wanted to continue the discussion that had begun earlier in the day. My mother said later that Brezhnev was clever in requesting the midnight session, since he was rested and knew that my father, who rarely napped, would be at a disadvantage physically. Indeed, the President was tired from the long day and was already in his pajamas when a Secret Service agent knocked on his door to inform him that Kissinger had sent word that Brezhnev wanted to talk.

For the next three hours the men conferred in my father's study. Like all the rooms he chose for working and thinking, the study was small and tucked away, its fireplace and bookshelves framed by small hand-painted Mexican tiles. During the at times emotional talk, which centered on the Middle East, Brezhnev adamantly insisted that the Israelis bow to Arab demands, including the withdrawal of Israel's forces from all occupied territories. In other words, he was asking the United States to abandon Israel to a Middle East settlement based on Arab terms. Repeatedly, my father countered that any imposed settlement was doomed to fail and that the vital point was to get the Arabs and the Israelis to begin talking to each other. The next morning, when Brezhnev and my father signed the joint communiqué, in the short section devoted to the Middle East it is apparent that nothing was resolved. A terse sentence summed up the status quo: "Each of the parties set forth its position on this problem."

The communiqué, however, did contain positive agreements on trade, transportation, agriculture, oceanic exploration, and the peaceful use of atomic energy. Summit II had further drawn the U.S. and U.S.S.R. into a partnership of cooperation, with the promise that the talks set for 1974 would bring more progress in limiting nuclear weapons.

After the communiqué was signed, Brezhnev and my father made some remarks in front of La Casa Pacifica. It was a bright, sunny day. The American and Soviet flags were flying from the flagpole a dozen yards from the front door. Various officials were lined up to say goodbye to Brezhnev. Already the drivers had started the engines of the cars. Suddenly Brezhnev said to my mother, "Can't we step inside for a moment? I want to bid you a personal farewell." He walked with my parents through the patio, back to the living room. His aide followed hurriedly behind, carrying two boxes. When the boxes were opened, my parents found shirts that the peasants wear in Brezhnev's native Kiev, an unabashedly sentimental gift. Mother saw that there were tears in the secretary general's eyes.

• • •

With Leonid Brezhnev's return to Moscow on June 25 came the storm. That day, as John Dean began his testimony before the Senate Watergate Committee, the House of Representatives voted in favor of a Senate bill that immediately cut off the funds for bombing Communist sanctuaries in Cambodia and forbade all direct and indirect military operations in Indochina. The cutoff, in my father's words, denied the United States "the means to enforce the Vietnam peace agreement."

Since the cease-fire, the Communists had violated the peace accords—barely noted in the American press—by moving seventy thousand troops and eighteen thousand trucks down the Ho Chi Minh Trail. The White House closely followed what was happening but took no retaliatory actions in February and March. The major restraint then on my father was the fear that the release of the POWs might be jeopardized. He did not act in April or May either, unaware that it was his last chance to prevent the shipment of troops and matériel into South Vietnam. He wrote in retrospect that American restraint that spring was "a major mistake."

My mother had witnessed my father's struggle to end the war on an honorable basis, so that South Vietnam would be able to remain an independent entity. Now, with Congress's decision to cut off funds for combat activity in Indochina, South Vietnam's future was in jeopardy. She had also just spent a week as part of the summit meeting where the world's two most powerful nations had attempted to resolve differences. Yet the significance of those two events, the summit and the congressional action on Indochina, was lost in the media blitz of John Dean's testimony. For five days, from opening to closing gavel at day's end, the three television networks broadcast Dean's slow, dispassionate recitation of his version of the "cover-up," and millions of Americans watched mesmerized. Helene Drown in California remembered a remarkable quote from the First Lady. "The hearings," Mother told Helene, were "just like a snake about to devour people."

For eight months, Dean claimed, the President had conspired with him to obstruct justice. Dean testified that on September 15, 1972, and on February 28, 1973, he had discussed the cover-up with my father. Yet, as the White House tape of the September 15 conversation shows, Dean did not, as he claimed, tell the President that Watergate might "unravel" or that he had assisted in "keeping it out of the White House." In fact, Dean had said the opposite: "I think I can say that fifty-four days from now [Election Day] that not a thing will come crashing down to our surprise." When Dean testified about the March 21 conversation between himself and the President, he asserted, "I certainly told the President everything I knew at that point in time." But the tape of the conversation disproves Dean's statement, which implied he had informed the President of the promises of clemency for the Watergate burglars, of his own involvement in convincing Jeb Magruder to perjure himself, or that he had destroyed evidence from Howard Hunt's safe. In this way John Dean skillfully shaded the truth about his own role in the cover-up and magnified the extent of the President's knowledge and involvement.

During Dean's testimony, my father kept focusing on the discrepancies in his statements, failing to recognize, as he conceded later in his *Memoirs*, that "it no longer made any difference that not all of Dean's testimony was accurate. It only mattered if *any* of his testimony was accurate." And Dean in his account of the March 21 meeting was more accurate than my father, who, from the time of his first address to the nation on Watergate, had implied that he had acted like a prosecutor in the case.

Because Dean's defense was based on the premise that he was a subordinate and thus a victim of a corrupt White House, he portrayed every political act of the Administration in the most sinister light. Dean's portrait of the Nixon White House as a place peopled by cynics without goals or vision was as damaging as his testimony about the President's role. Among the most titillating revelations from Dean were the "enemies lists." Dean produced a memo, composed by himself, on "dealing with our political enemies." In addition to a list of twenty prime political opponents, whom Dean recommended that the Administration target, were several lists of names running into the hundreds, which were to be referred to in determining who received White House jobs and invitations. In his book, *With Nixon*, Ray Price points out that when he learned from Dean's testimony of the existence of the lists, he called them "Dean's enemies lists," because "after all, it was Dean who proposed the unused plan to 'screw our enemies,' and Dean who collected the lists in his filing cabinet."

The Joint Congressional Committee on Internal Revenue Taxation, headed by two Democrats, Wilbur Mills of Arkansas and Russell Long of Louisiana, undertook a meticulous investigation of how the IRS handled the tax audits of every one of the people on the lists. In its report it concluded that there was no evidence the audits were more harsh than for any other individual, and "indeed, if anything, the opposite is true. Several individuals on the list appeared to pose collection problems for the IRS." But that report was a mere belated postscript to the staggering amount of publicity accorded Dean's revelation.

How did names get on Dean's lists? Some for obvious reasons: the names of "Democratic contributors of $25,000 or more in the 1968 campaign"; eleven members "involved with the 1972 National Committee for the Impeachment of the President." But there were other names on the lists for which there was no apparent reason. In October, four months after Dean's testimony, Mother would pose for photographs with the Muscular Dystrophy poster child. Two days later, the famous pioneering heart surgeon Dr. Michael DeBakey, who had been at the photograph session, wrote a gracious letter of tribute, not unlike many others Mother received, but the letter coming from whom it did, and at the time it did, was significant. Michael DeBakey's name inexplicably had been on one of Dean's "enemies lists." But DeBakey, realizing that my parents had nothing to do with the lists, was gracious and generous enough to offer the hand of friendship.

For thirty-two more days after Dean testified, more than 325 television hours, the Ervin Committee probed the Nixon Administration. In unprecedented executive branch cooperation with Congress, my father waived executive privilege so that his White House aides could testify. Some 155 witnesses were called. Bernard Levin, political columnist for the London *Times*, called the committee an "inquisition . . . Men are having their reputations destroyed in full view of millions; worse, men who may shortly have to face a criminal trial are having their cases literally prejudged, without any of the safeguards of true legal proceedings." As ABC correspondent Howard K. Smith pointed out, Chairman Sam Ervin did not do "anything at all to discipline those demonstrations by a small biased audience in the hearing room, magnified by television. It's wild applause for him, it's loud groans of dislike and hatred for the witness." Ervin would be a folk hero by the end of the sessions, and, as Smith observed, his record of "lifelong opposition to extend civil rights to Black Americans" was forgotten.

Among the other senators who were to be the judges of the Nixon "campaign practices" was Herman Talmadge, who had made headlines in 1954 as a white supremacist for his promotion of a state constitutional amendment giving Georgia the power to convert its public schools into a private system in order to maintain segregation. In 1979 he would be formally denounced by the Senate for mishandling his office and campaign finances. Ervin, Talmadge, and Democrat Daniel Inouye of Hawaii seven times had voted to limit, or were announced as favoring limitations on, the 1964 congressional investigation of Lyndon Johnson's close friend Bobby Baker, who ran a high-level influence-peddling business that allegedly involved dozens of important political and business people as well as the White House. The potentially explosive investigation had been contained only because Congress was controlled by the Democrats. In 1974, only one year after Inouye had sat through weeks of grilling Nixon officials on campaign ethics, his campaign organization would accept an illegal contribution from the American Ship Building Company and receive a suspended sentence. And as revealed by *The Wall Street Journal* in late June 1973, dummy committees allegedly were used in the 1970 campaign of another senator on the committee, Democrat Joseph Montoya of New Mexico, in order to launder the sources of as much as $100,000 in contributions. When the charge was aired, Montoya's spokesmen denied it.

Mother had been in political life for more than two decades, but even she was amazed by the double standard and the complete lack of perspective as the Watergate hearings ground on all summer. Although she did not have the heart to watch more than a half hour at a time, toward the end she watched all of the testimony of Pat Buchanan, called before the committee to testify on Republican "dirty tricks." His testimony came on the heels of three days of leaks from the committee that set him up as the architect of dirty tricks. But Pat turned the tables by delivering a feisty counterattack in which he documented with facts and figures how the Democrats had, in effect, written the book on dirty tricks in American politics. When the committee asked Buchanan just how far he would go in political tactics, his reply was "anything that is not immoral, unethical, illegal or unprecedented in previous Democratic campaigns." Unfortunately, by the time Buchanan appeared, only one network was covering the hearings.

Elated by reports of Pat's appearance, my father invited him to stop by the White House immediately following his testimony. At 6:30 P.M., my parents were waiting for him in the West Hall. As soon as she saw Pat, Mother gave him a brief hug and whirled him around in a little dance. It was a brief dance and a brief moment of victory. Twenty-four hours later, Pat Buchanan's testimony had been relegated to a one-day wonder as the spotlight again was on alleged Nixon Administration hard-ball politics, espionage, abuse of power, and the Watergate cover-up.

In the course of his testimony, Buchanan had pointed out that the Democrats' dirty trickster, Dick Tuck, was on the McGovern payroll at the '72 Republican Convention. But Tuck was never called before the committee because the Democratic majority insisted on focusing solely on 1972 political abuses and decided not to ask him to testify on the grounds that most of his "tricks" were perpetrated before the 1972 campaign. The committee withheld a memo from William C. Sullivan, the former FBI number-three man, who volunteered to testify on previous political intelligence operations. A few years later, when some of these details became known, antiwar activist professor Noam Chomsky would declare that the FBI operations under Kennedy and Johnson were "incomparably more serious than anything charged in the congressional Articles of Impeachment or any other denunciations of Nixon."

Indeed, more than once that summer Mother asked me why no one considered the vote fraud of the 1960 campaign a "cover-up." Why was no one outraged that Lyndon Johnson had bugged the Nixon 1968 campaign plane? Why was Bobby Kennedy's use of all available government power to "get" Jimmy Hoffa, who was squandering Teamster Union pension benefits, not denounced by those who now accused an ad hoc group called "the plumbers" of trying to "get" Daniel Ellsberg, who had just leaked seven thousand pages of classified government documents? And why, as William Safire put it, did "the incredible similarity of the devotion of Gordon Liddy and Daniel Ellsberg to a 'higher law' lead one to lionization and the other to incarceration"? Adlai Stevenson's workers had bugged John Kennedy at the Democratic Convention in 1956. The peacetime Kennedy Administration had tapped more individuals, well over one hundred, than the wartime Nixon Administration. The Ervin Committee knew about Lyndon Johnson's wiretaps of Robert Kennedy, Martin Luther King, and other black leaders at the Democratic Convention. Also well known in Washington was the fact that Bobby Kennedy had authorized phone taps on Martin Luther King. But silence prevailed.

My mother began putting aside various news-summary items that summer for the record: Franklin Roosevelt's son John commenting to columnist Bob Considine: "Hell, my father just about invented bugging. He had them spread all over, and thought nothing of it." The FBI under Roosevelt had systematically investigated major figures, among them Charles Lindbergh and those who opposed Lend-Lease and our entry into World War II. She saved as well a Russell Kirk column that pointed out:

> When Jack Anderson published the contents of secret documents purloined from a Senatorial Committee investigating Watergate, certain of my columnar colleagues actually praised his action. One must assume that while it is wicked to invade the Democratic Campaign Headquarters, it's virtuous to steal Congressional papers. Everything depends on what office has been burglarized.

Not surprisingly, Mother believed Watergate was a political battle, pure and simple. As the steady blizzard of new facts and rumors surfaced, she knew that inevitably the men and women covering the Presidency would begin to see all their stories through the lens of Watergate. Already by midsummer, there were signs.

The Watergate hearings climaxed on July 16 when former Haldeman aide Alexander Butterfield was called by the Senate Watergate Committee and revealed that the President had a taping system. Partisan reaction was swift and categorical. Speaker Carl Albert called it "an outrage, almost beyond belief." When White House lawyer Fred Buzhardt confirmed the existence of the system and compared it to the one that Johnson had, LBJ aide Joseph Califano charged "an outrageous smear" and asserted that there had been "absolutely no secret wiring in the place." Apparently he was unaware that Johnson himself had shown my father and Bob Haldeman the system in December of 1968, shortly before leaving office. Johnson had even tape-recorded all incoming and outgoing telephone conversations on board *Air Force One.* My father had ordered that sophisticated monitoring system removed from the plane. When the curator of the Kennedy Library, Dave Powers, was asked if there were tapes there, or any Kennedy tapes for that matter, he said no. Shortly thereafter, however, the library admitted the existence of 125 tapes and 68 Dictabelt recordings of various meetings and telephone conversations.

Immediately, the Senate Watergate Committee and Archibald Cox, the special prosecutor demanded by Congress and named by Attorney General Elliot Richardson in May, requested the tapes. My father opposed relinquishing the tapes on several grounds. While nothing said to the President in the Oval Office was meant to be kept secret from him, much that was discussed should not be spread across the public record. To my father, an equally significant reason for holding on to the tapes was the conviction that the Presidency, as an independent branch of the government, should not be forced to surrender documents to Congress. The courts had never ordered the House of Representatives to give up records from its files; nor should the President be required to do so now.

At the time of the uproar over the discovery of the taping system, my father was in no condition to make important decisions. He lay in Bethesda Naval Hospital with a painful case of viral pneumonia and a fever of one hundred and two degrees. It was his first major illness in the four and half years of his Presidency. Because of the pain and his difficulty in breathing, he could not sleep and seemed almost delirious with fever and worry. The second morning of his hospitalization, when Mother picked me up at David's and my new home in Bethesda to drive to the hospital, uncharacteristically she was wearing sunglasses. She was very quiet in the car, and I remember how she protectively put her hand on top of mine.

My mother saw immediately that unlimited access to the President's private, candid conversations spelled disaster. She told me later that she felt the tapes should have been destroyed. But at the hospital she said nothing about the tapes, relying on an even stronger instinct: her implicit faith in her husband. She would not worry him by more probing, especially when he was ill—and vulnerable. She tried in the next few days to think of little ways to comfort him. For instance, the artworks on the walls of his hospital bedroom were drab, and so she supervised the hanging of a few paintings from our New York apartment, which since 1969 had been in storage on the third floor of the White House.

It was during the hospitalization that my father passed up his best and last opportunity to destroy the tape recordings. In early June he had listened to some of the tapes for the first time and decided, as he wrote later, that

> they were a mixed bag as far as I was concerned . . . but I recognized that they indisputably disproved Dean's basic charge that I had conspired with him in an obstruction of justice over an eight-month period. . . .
>
> If I had indeed been the knowing Watergate conspirator that I was charged as being, I would have recognized in 1973 that the tapes contained conversations that would be fatally damaging. I would have seen that if I were to survive, they would have to be destroyed.

As he lay in the hospital, as troubled as any time I could remember seeing him, his instincts were to fight still for his honor and for his reputation. To destroy the tapes would give an impression of guilt. Yet, when on August 28 Judge John Sirica ruled that the President must surrender nine requested tapes to the special prosecutor and my father appealed the decision on the grounds of executive privilege, many Americans assumed his reluctance to hand over the tapes was an admission of guilt, and few were willing to accept arguments that executive privilege, as my father believed, "stands at the very heart of a strong Presidency," or to consider that Sirica's decision had marked the first time in the history of the United States that a court purported to compel the President to surrender personal documents.

In the midst of the tape controversy, the Administration was dealt a blow that, coming as it did on top of the Watergate charges, could not have been more unfortunate. On August 1, Vice President Agnew had been informed by Attorney General Richardson that he was being investigated by federal prosecutors for accepting bribes and kickbacks in return for granting state contracts while he was Baltimore county executive and governor of Maryland. For the next eight weeks, as the Justice Department gathered copious testimony against Agnew, the Vice President repeatedly declared his innocence, insisting that the investigation against him was political. And, as Agnew emphasized in the meetings he had with my father during that period, political contributions by contractors were commonplace in perhaps as many as three-quarters of the states. The Vice President declared that the monies he had received were campaign contributions and that the contractors chosen for jobs were all first-rate.

For weeks, my parents and the many supporters of the Vice President kept hoping that Agnew's unconditional avowals of innocence were true. My parents sympathized with Ted and Judy Agnew as they endured the steady flow of leaks and probing stories. But sadly, by September 25, it was clear to my parents that the Vice President would probably have to resign. On that day, Henry Petersen, who headed the Justice Department's Criminal Division and whom my father had asked to examine independently the Agnew case because he did not fully trust the Richardson-headed probe, reported that beyond any doubt Agnew would be found guilty. For two more weeks, the public was fed tidbits about the Vice President's case. Then, on October 9, Agnew gave up. He had negotiated a plea bargain with the Justice Department and pleaded *nolo contendere* to a single count of income tax evasion. When he resigned his office the next day, October 10, I recall how troubled both my parents were, Mother telling me, "It's so sad for him—and for the country."

When my father traveled to Camp David on October 11, he had recommendations for a successor to Agnew from more than four hundred Republican leaders, members of Congress, the Cabinet, and his presidential staff. Congress would have to approve the choice, and the Democrats had made it clear they wanted a "caretaker" Vice President who would have no ambitions beyond 1976. Republican Minority Leader Gerald Ford was the man most preferred by members of Congress. The knowledge that longtime friend Ford would probably be confirmed was the President's overriding reason for selecting him over the other leading contenders: John Connally, Nelson Rockefeller, and Ronald Reagan. At nine o'clock Friday night, October 12, at a televised ceremony in the East Room, my father named Gerald R. Ford as his choice to fill the Vice Presidency.

Afterward my father ate a late dinner in the West Hall while Mother, David, and I visited with him. We were abruptly interrupted when Chief of Staff General Alexander Haig, who had replaced Bob Haldeman, arrived to inform my father of an urgent message from the Soviet Union about the crisis in the Middle East, a crisis that had begun six days before when Syria and Egypt attacked Israel. On October 9, my father had made the decision to resupply the embattled Israelis with military equipment. Now the Soviets, although they themselves had undertaken massive airlifts of an estimated seven hundred tons of weapons and matériel daily to Egypt and Syria, made it clear they did not look lightly on the prospect of American supplies being shipped to Israel the next morning. But my father ignored the veiled threat and ordered the aid to continue. Within days, the Israelis were receiving a thousand tons a day.

The Middle East crisis came at a time when the country was still reeling from the resignation of the Vice President. My father knew also that his decision to help Israel defend itself might cause the Arabs to react by cutting off oil supplies. And there was one more matter very much on his mind: on the morning of October 12 he had received news that the Court of Appeals had ruled 5-2 against the President in the special prosecutor's suit for the nine tapes. The court had stated that although unlimited access to presidential materials would cripple the Presidency, it disagreed that only a President could decide what material was or was not privileged. It was inevitable now that Special Prosecutor Archibald Cox would demand more and more tapes.

Since the Harvard law professor had been sworn in on May 24, with his close friend Ted Kennedy as one of his guests at the ceremony, Cox and his staff of eighty had expanded the scope of the investigation day by day. It now included the purchase of our San Clemente home, the ITT antitrust case, government wiretapping, Bebe Rebozo, the "plumbers," and the handling of demonstrators at rallies. My mother was particularly upset by the unabashed partisanship of Cox's prosecutors. Seven of the eleven prosecutors he had hired had worked or campaigned for either John, Robert, or Ted Kennedy; one had been a special assistant to Ramsey Clark; another a speech writer for Sargent Shriver.

On August 8, 1973, *The Wall Street Journal* had summed up what seemed to be the intentions not only of Cox but also of the Senate Watergate Committee:

The President's critics are starting to worry that they may not be able to pin the coverup on him after all. So they point to the spending on his homes. If that starts to slip away, they point to the ITT anti-trust case. If that falters, on to the Cambodian bombing, and so on and on. So impeach Nixon, they suggest, regardless of a specific culpability on Watergate. Impeach him, indeed regardless of a specific culpability on any of these successive charges.

In a defiant mood, my father decided to ask the respected, long-term Democratic senator from Mississippi, John Stennis, a former judge, to listen to the tapes, verify line by line the accuracy of the third-person White House summaries, and decide whether any omissions of irrelevant or national security materials were valid. This procedure would assure him of evenhanded treatment without completely abandoning the time-honored practice of not relinquishing presidential control over materials. "The Stennis compromise" was accepted in principle by the Ervin Committee and on October 19 the President announced it.

But the next day Cox called a press conference to declare he was going ahead with his request for tapes. Cox was openly defying a presidential directive; instead of resigning in protest against the Stennis plan, he was challenging the President to fire him, knowing that Richardson would leave with him, since the latter had given his word to the Senate that he would not fire the special prosecutor. My father's response came at 8:22 that night when Ron Ziegler announced in the White House briefing room that the President, through Solicitor General Robert Bork, had fired Special Prosecutor Archibald Cox. Ziegler also announced that Elliot Richardson and Deputy Attorney General William Ruckelshaus, who felt bound by Richardson's pledge of no limits to the investigation, had resigned and that the special prosecutor's office would be abolished and its functions returned to the Justice Department.

Immediately, television networks broke into their regular programming to present specials. The outcry over the decision, which the media christened "the Saturday night massacre," was intense, and within seventy-two hours of firing Cox, my father felt sufficient pressure to reverse his position and agreed to provide Judge John Sirica with the subpoenaed tapes. Eight days later, a new special prosecutor, Houston Democrat Leon Jaworski, was named. As Ray Price described it in *With Nixon*, the President had "his back against the wall" since Ford's confirmation was being held hostage and twenty-one impeachment resolutions were under discussion in Congress.

Another consideration throughout the crisis was the threat that the Soviets, sure now that the President was in a weakened position, would exploit the turmoil in the Middle East, where the Arabs for the first time since their attack began losing on the battlefield. On October 19, Brezhnev, as yet unsure how far to go on behalf of the Arabs, suggested that Kissinger come to Moscow for immediate talks. When Kissinger arrived, he carried a sternly worded presidential request to the Soviets to begin peace efforts forthwith. But, as my father wrote in his *Memoirs*, he

> purposely mitigated the hard language in the text with a handwritten note extending personal regards from Pat and me to him and Mrs. Brezhnev. Brezhnev, I knew, would understand what this mixture conveyed: if he was willing to get behind a serious peace effort, I would not consider that the Soviet airlift had affected our personal relationship or deflected the course of détente.

From Moscow came a quick reply from Brezhnev professing his desire for a cease-fire and adding his own handwritten postscript: "Mrs. Brezhnev is grateful for the regards and in turn joins me in sending our best personal regards to Mrs. Nixon and to you."

Then, on October 22, two days after Cox was fired, and shortly after the Arabs and Israelis agreed to a U.N. cease-fire, Israel charged the Egyptians with violating the terms and resumed fighting. My parents were at Camp David and from there Mother called Helene. She remembers that Pat was so incensed, she was "fighting mad." Helene noted that "Pat said that Dick, after he fired Cox, had asked Richardson not to resign until after the Israel-Arab war had been settled, that negotiations were so serious now [Henry Kissinger was then in Moscow] and Richardson refused to wait. Dick was furious and so was I..." My mother had also told Helene that she was in the room and "had heard Dick on the hot line with the Russians and Israelis; that the cease-fire was such a tremendous thing. Here he is trying to settle a war and all this stuff is going on."

On October 24, after further conversations between the President and Brezhnev, a second Middle East cease-fire went into effect. But only hours later, Secretary General Brezhnev sent warning messages to the President that the Israelis were breaking the agreement. Although the United States knew this was not true, Brezhnev persisted in arguing that the U.S.S.R. and the U.S. should send military units to Egypt. When Brezhnev warned that if the U.S. did not join the U.S.S.R. in a jointly sponsored action, the Soviet Union might move on its own, my father viewed the message as "a scarcely veiled threat of unilateral Soviet intervention."

An emergency meeting was called at 11 P.M. in the White House Situation Room attended by Kissinger, Haig, Secretary of Defense James Schlesinger, the head of the Joint Chiefs of Staff, Admiral Moorer, and CIA Director William Colby. They unanimously recommended to the President that all American conventional and nuclear forces be put on military alert. My father gave the order and accompanied it by a personal message to Brezhnev calling for "harmony" and "cool heads" and rejecting unilateral action. He had already sent Egypt's president Anwar Sadat a message warning, "Should the two great nuclear powers be called upon to provide forces, it would introduce an extremely dangerous potential for direct great-power rivalry in the area."

The Mideast alert was effective. At 7:15 A.M. on October 25, Sadat informed the President that the American position was now clear and that he would ask the United Nations to provide an international peace-keeping force. Thirteen days later, on November 7, 1973, the United States and Egypt resumed diplomatic relations after six years of estrangement. What Brezhnev had resisted, greater American influence in the area, had come to pass.

Golda Meir would write the postscript in her autobiography, published two years later: "I am still sure that President Nixon ordered the U.S. alert on October 24, 1973, because, détente or no détente, he was not about to give in to Soviet blackmail. It was, I think, a dangerous decision, a courageous decision and a correct decision." But it was not viewed as such by the American press at the time. Only an hour after the arrival of Sadat's message, as my father briefed congressional leaders on the alert, Henry Kissinger held a press conference and was dismayed by the skepticism he encountered as he explained what had transpired between Brezhnev and the President. Bitingly he told the press:

> It is a symptom of what is happening to our country that it could even be suggested that the United States would alert its forces for domestic reasons [allegedly to divert from Watergate] . . . It is up to you ladies and gentlemen to determine whether this is the moment to try to create a crisis of confidence in the field of foreign policy . . .

My father's anger over the questions that Kissinger had been subjected to erupted at a press conference the next day. He had been asked by CBS for his thoughts on the impeachment movement. There was an audible gasp from the assembled press corps as the President snapped, "I have never heard or seen such outrageous, vicious, distorted reporting in twenty-seven years of public life. . . . I can assure you that whatever shocks gentlemen of the press may have, or others, political people, these shocks will not affect me in doing my job."

Mother and I watched the conference together, wondering how there could be so much animosity in the room between the elected President of the United States and the men and women whose job it was to report his actions to the American people. When my father lashed out at the reporters, we winced, and if we, family who loved him and understood why he spoke, winced, we could only begin to imagine what the reactions of people sitting in their living rooms across the country must have been.

Where would it all end? For six months now, the charges had mounted as the Ervin Committee and the special prosecutor had investigated the Nixon Administration; and the media, fed by leaks and rumors from the committee, its staffs, and even from grand juries, had reported every charge. As humiliating as it was that my father's decision in a matter of life and death could be questioned, it was no more humiliating or excessive than the leaks and rumors since May of Nixon's private gain from public office. By now, the stories ranged from Ervin Committee "sources" informing a California newspaper on May 13 that my father may have used a million dollars in campaign funds to buy San Clemente, to Jack Anderson's story of cash-filled Swiss bank accounts, and even to *Newsweek*'s contention that Tricia may have improperly filed her income tax returns because of my father's manipulation of family property. Nor could the charges be ignored; they were paving the way to the threat of impeachment or to my father's forced resignation.

My father had responded immediately to the rumors about the financing of San Clemente and Key Biscayne by ordering an audit, which cost him personally twenty-five thousand dollars, of the purchase of both. Despite the audit, which was made public on the twenty-seventh of August, false stories continued to be reported. They included ABC's charge that my father had a million-dollar "secret private investment portfolio" and the allegation that Howard Hughes had helped him buy San Clemente. Then, for the third time in my parents' lives, a civil servant in the IRS unlawfully leaked their income tax returns to the media.

By the end of November, my father had reached the conclusion that the only way to quell the ugly rumblings that the President had paid too little tax on his income was to allow the Joint Congressional Committee on Internal Revenue Taxation to review his tax returns. He also ordered the General Services Administration (GSA) to make public the amount of government money that had been spent on San Clemente, the two houses in Key Biscayne, Bob Abplanalp's home in the Bahamas, and on security for Tricia and me at our homes. On August 6, the GSA totals were announced: $1.1 million, all but $13,400 of it specifically requested by the Secret Service, had been spent on security for the houses and surrounding grounds; $2.5 million on the security and construction of the office complexes and security for government property near the houses; $6.1 million for presidential communications equipment and support, 60 percent of which would be recovered at the end of the Nixon Presidency; and $211,000 more on Secret Service equipment, 90 percent of which would be reclaimed by the government at the end of the Nixon term. The next morning, however, the headlines in the nation's two most influential newspapers, *The New York Times* and the Washington *Post*, were, respectively: "$10 Million Spent at Nixon Houses" and "$10 Million Spent on Nixon Homes." The immediate impression for readers was that the money had been spent on the homes themselves. For months afterward, as the $10 million figure was cited repeatedly, all but forgotten was that the vast majority of the money had been spent on security and communications, and only 2 percent on the houses themselves.

The costs of presidential security when totaled up came as a shock to the public—and to us in the family. The process had begun with John Kennedy's assassination. As *The Wall Street Journal* pointed out, "In the wake of that tragedy Congress passed laws calling for open-ended spending on presidential security. The great bulk of the questioned spending [on San Clemente and Key Biscayne] was clearly pursuant to the hang-the-cost intent of those laws or simply to provide the necessarily elaborate communications."

Routine Secret Service requests went directly to the GSA; my parents were almost never consulted. A minor example was the decision to erect a six-foot-high aluminum picket fence around our home in Key Biscayne in order to keep out tourists as well as would-be assassins. It would later be decided by a congressional inquiry that my parents should have shared the cost of the security fence with the government because a chain fence would have been cheaper. Rex Scouten, who began in the Usher's Office in the Kennedy Administration and has continued helping run the executive mansion through the terms of six Presidents, told me once, "The President has all the problems in the world to live with; our job was not to add to them." That was his attitude and the attitude of the staff around him; it was also the attitude of the Secret Service and the GSA, whose job it was to secure the President's home quickly, efficiently, and without making waves. Knowing the President and the First Lady were far too busy to be bothered with details, people constantly would come to Rex with requests: "The President says..." or "The First Lady wants..." "In the end," Rex told me, "you just had to be the judge yourself of whether or not it was something the President or your mother really wanted."

My mother was heartsick with the stories about $10 million being spent on the Nixons' homes. She came to believe that nothing hastened the turning of public opinion against the Nixon Presidency more than the suggestion of profiting at the taxpayers' expense. Long after people had forgotten the details of Dean's testimony, "the Saturday night massacre," or the Mideast alert, she believed they would remember the huge government expenditures.

There was an element of truth to the charges that the expenditures had been excessive, and there was no denying that the Nixons' life-style had benefited from the by-now routine presidential perks. Indeed, during the first term, Mother occasionally had questioned some of the elaborate support procedures afforded modern Presidents, and throughout she had been told that the President must have communications and security support, that other Presidents had had it, and that was the way it was.

Congressman Jack Brooks of Texas used his chairmanship of the House Government Operations Subcommittee to wring more out of the $10 million story. But before proceeding with the inquiry, the partisan Brooks made sure that full accessibility to the Johnson records was not available (mainly because the Department of Defense rather than the GSA had handled most of the expenditures, which included installing a runway at the LBJ Ranch and air-conditioning the huge airport hangar where Johnson occasionally held press conferences). Nor were the Kennedy records on security expenditures at his five regular vacation spots available, because, as Kennedy's naval aide testified to the subcommittee, he "accidentally" had dropped the records overboard while his ship was either somewhere near Europe or in the Philippines.

The final subcommittee report was issued in May of 1974, in plenty of time for the impeachment hearings. During a six-month investigation, the Brooks subcommittee, by adding everything that had been spent over five years at San Clemente and Key Biscayne, including maintenance and equipment costs for the offices, the salaries of those in the army communications units, and all security and support costs, came up with the figure of $17 million. They even included the value of the Army Signal Corps' worldwide communications equipment, which would, of course, leave San Clemente at the end of my father's term.

From March, when the story was first leaked, until my father's resignation five months later, and after the resignation as well, the phrase "$17 million in improvements on Nixon homes" was repeated and repeated. The three Republicans on the subcommittee refused to sign the report, Congressman John Buchanan branding it "absolutely untrue" and claiming that the subcommittee's investigation had "degenerated into the worst political witch-hunt I've seen in all my time on the Hill. . . . It was one of the grossest political smears I had ever seen."

Another blow to the Nixon White House came on October 30, 1973, when the White House announced that two of the nine subpoenaed conversations ordered turned over to the special prosecutor had never existed. My father's aide Fred Buzhardt had informed Judge Sirica on the thirtieth that one subpoenaed conversation, a phone call to John Mitchell, was made from a telephone in the family quarters, which had no recording equipment on it. The second conversation, with John Dean on the evening of April 15 in the Executive Office Building, had not been recorded because the Secret Service, which monitored the taping system, had not anticipated that my father, who rarely used the EOB office on Sunday, would spend all day in conversation there. He was speaking to Attorney General Richard Kleindienst at 1:15 on Sunday afternoon when the reel of tape came to an end, running out in midsentence. The media treated the two *nonexistent* tapes as "missing tapes." The idea of two "missing tapes" caused Senator Edward Brooke of Massachusetts to be the first Republican in Congress to urge the resignation of the President.

Within three weeks, there was more news about the tapes—the now infamous "eighteen-and-one-half-minute gap." Rose Mary Woods had been given the task of transcribing the subpoenaed tapes, very difficult work because the voice-activated system was primitive, to say the least. Often when two or more spoke at the same time, their words were all but indecipherable. If a person had a high- or low-pitched voice, or spoke with his head up or down, this affected whether the words were distinct or indistinct. On October 1, the day Rose was transcribing the June 20, 1972, conversation between Bob Haldeman and my father, the Secret Service had provided her with a new Uher 5000 machine. Until then, she had always used a Sony. While working on the tape, she was interrupted by a five-minute phone call. When she went back to the machine, she discovered a shrill buzzing sound and eighteen and one-half minutes of the tape missing. Rose Woods stated later that she thought she could have inadvertently erased five minutes during the phone call, but she could not account for the full eighteen and one-half minutes.

The sensation that followed the revelation that there were eighteen and one-half minutes missing from one of the subpoenaed tapes caused the matter to be turned over to a grand jury and a panel of court-appointed experts approved by the White House. The experts, however, had their expertise in the theory of acoustics, not in the use of tape recorders. In January, they issued a report that the buzzing sounds had been put on the tape "in the process of erasing and rerecording at least five, and perhaps as many as nine, separate and contiguous segments." The findings would be challenged by *Science* magazine in a little-noted rebuttal of the report. Based on their own two-month study, *Science* stated that the experts never examined whether or not the erasures could have been made accidentally by a malfunction in the machine. *Science* pointed out that the court experts had tested their hypothesis by using only one machine, a Sony, not a Uher 5000. In addition, one of the court-appointed experts had testified that in examining the machine Rose used, he and his colleagues "of necessity had to open up the interior . . . and tighten down several screws and quite conceivably . . . may have tightened a ground connection to a point where it was making more firm contact than previously." They had found a defective transistor and replaced it, throwing the defective one away. When Rose's attorney, Charles Rhyne, asked the expert, "So in effect you obliterated the evidence which anyone else would need to test your conclusions, did you not?" the expert had responded, "Yes, in large part." Another who challenged the experts' report was a former general, Allan D. Bell, head of Dekor Counterintelligence and Security. After extensive testing of the Uher, Bell concluded that the erase-head marks could have been caused by fluctuating current and a defective transistor.

One of the most painful times for the family in the aftermath of the eighteen-and-one-half-minute "gap" was the ordeal that Rose Mary Woods underwent when she testified before a court hearing and the grand jury. Each morning before she left to give testimony, Rose would pray, "Mom and Dad, you have to get me through this." Underneath the high-necked dresses that she usually wore was a cross that had belonged to her mother, and on the fourth finger of her left hand, a rosary ring. She did not discuss any of her appearances with my parents. In fact, she instructed her right-hand aide, Marge Acker, who shared her office in the White House, that if the President buzzed for her to just say she was out on an errand. Of course, there were times when my father knew for certain that Rose was testifying, but on other occasions Marge would just say, in as matter-of-fact and casual voice as she could, that Rose had had to go out. On July 17, 1974, Jaworski informed Rose Mary Woods's attorney that no case had been developed against her, but no public announcement of this fact was ever made.

According to Russ Braley, in his study of the editorial policy of *The New York Times*, its index for 1973 had under the "Watergate" heading ninety pages of fine print; "at a minimum estimate, the *Times* published three million words on Watergate in 1973, or 30 books of 100,000 words each." Across the country, newspapers and television gave massive coverage to the investigations by the Ervin Committee and four other congressional committees, the FBI, the General Accounting Office, and grand juries in Los Angeles, New York, Florida, and Texas. Daily the family did not know what charge or development the morning news would bring. Nor did my father. As apparent as it was to us close to my father, it was apparent to Americans at large that the President was being buffeted by charges, rumors, and revelations. The Presidency is a strong institution, but the Nixon Watergate staff of ten members working full time was no match for Special Prosecutor Leon Jaworski's staff of eighty, the Ervin Committee staff of ninety-two, the courts, and the resources of the adversarial press. With critical story after critical story, how did one take the President's case to the people? How could one answer every charge? As the Watergate stress increased daily and with no relief in sight, I wrote across the top of the October 26 page in my calendar: "Fight, fight, fight."

Throughout this period, my mother kept going, almost as if the White House had not become embattled. Ten days before the April 30 speech, in the midst of the tension before the full fury of Watergate began, she had hosted the first tour of the White House grounds. Never before had the public been permitted to wander through the Rose Garden, adjacent to the President's office, and the Jacqueline Kennedy Garden, on the east side of the mansion. Visitors could stop and smell the flowers and be within a few feet of the colonnades flanking the Oval Office. Special booklets were provided so they could locate the trees planted by twenty-five Presidents, including Chester Arthur's graceful, flowering Japanese maple; the magnolia replanted from Andrew Jackson's estate, which my parents enjoyed looking at winter and summer from their bedroom windows; and the red oak chosen by Dwight Eisenhower.

My father's enthusiasm for the gardens had given Mother the inspiration for the tours. Each succeeding year my parents spent in the White House, no one was more excited about the changing beauty in the gardens than he. Breathlessly, he would step off the elevator at dinnertime to announce that the crocuses were up, or that the fall planting of multicolored mums had just been completed.

The spring of 1973 the Rose Garden was again a breathtaking sight. Dozens of bright-red tulips were massed beneath the soft billows of pale-pink flowers on the crab-apple trees. The tour was enthusiastically received by the public. Mother decided to make it a semiannual event, in fall and spring. The tours continue to this day, and Rex Scouten told me recently, "I don't know of anything in the White House that pleases people more." The wonder of a small, exquisite green park in the midst of a busy city, and the sense of history one feels walking the "backyard" trod by every American President except George Washington, make the garden tours unique.

Mike Farrell, who had coordinated all of the preparations for the tour of the gardens, continued to be amazed by the First Lady's knowledge of the different groups that wrote to his Office of White House Visitors, wanting to be received by Mrs. Nixon. "She had an encyclopedic knowledge of organizations," he told me. "She always knew which groups she should see." Her schedule remained full—ground breaking for a new building at Gallaudet College, a school for the deaf, the Women's Advisory Commission on Aviation. The difference now was that there were fewer trips outside of Washington, since my father, deeply entangled in trying to answer the myriad of questions on Watergate and non-Watergate investigations, found himself more and more tied to the White House.

The busy schedule was a relief for my mother. She could not overtly fight the charges, but she could—and would—carry on. Getting as much exercise as possible was a relief also. Physical activity had always helped her meet the pressures of the White House. Shortly before the second inauguration, I had written David overseas that my mother and I had vowed to "walk outside each day or go *crazy.*" On busy days when it was not possible to get to Roosevelt Island before it closed at dusk, we began to walk after dinner in downtown Washington. The streets were usually deserted, because the area near the White House was a favorite spot for muggers. It was not dangerous, however, if one was protected by the Secret Service. My mother wore a scarf, and after our first successful outing, when no one had noticed us, we both felt jubilant, almost free. We could walk at night now, rather than walk "on display" around the south grounds of the White House.

Under the Watergate pressure, my parents seemed to find some relaxation in spending time with David and me and our young friends, particularly Cynthia and Bob Milligan, both recent graduates of George Washington University law school, where David was a first-year law student. The family also began to count more and more on the brief hours away from the White House, and on moments when we could pretend, at least for a while, that Secret Service agents were not within a shadow's distance of us. I wrote to a friend that I had decided riding in one of the large black limousines of the presidential fleet of cars, something I always had avoided because the car drew attention, was a good idea because the glass partition between the front and back seats could be closed and provided "a little touch of freedom." In other words, one could have a personal conversation during a long drive, since the agents in the front seat could not hear voices through the glass. My father had discovered the same advantage to the limousines, and he began to go for afternoon drives with Bebe, General Haig, and others. In the climate of Watergate, the press decided that these drives, which the President insisted not be announced, so that he would not be trailed by the media, were very odd, even a sign of mental instability.

My father himself inadvertently had fueled the instability speculation in late August when he flew to New Orleans to speak at the convention of the Veterans of Foreign Wars. During the flight, the Secret Service informed my parents that it had enough evidence of an assassination plot to compel the cancellation of the planned motorcade into the city. My father had been counting on the large, friendly crowds expected along the route to give a much-needed boost in the aftermath of the long weeks of Watergate testimony. His frustration built as he was driven a back way into downtown New Orleans. At the Convention Center, as he was going into the holding area where he would gather his thoughts a few minutes before going on stage, he saw that Ron Ziegler, accompanied by a large contingent of White House press, was about to follow him. He lost his temper completely and shoved Ron in the back. The shove was accompanied by unmistakable instructions to take the reporters to the room that had been set aside for them. Although my father apologized to Ron that day, some reporters seized on the incident as a sign of severe stress. CBS News showed the President pushing Ziegler not once, but twice—in slow motion.

Because my father's will to fight and to survive was a major factor in the unfolding Watergate drama, the press was scrutinizing his actions as if he were beneath a magnifying glass. Presidential press aide Jerry Warren was asked if the President was using drugs, or seeing a psychiatrist, and whether or not he still believed in prayer. The drinking rumors were the most persistent, perhaps because it seemed he *was* drinking a little more than he ever had before, but at dinnertime, when he was trying to unwind. He still adhered to his self-imposed code of no alcohol on nights he was attending receptions or dinners, nor did he drink during the day. Nonetheless, the drinking rumors multiplied.

Other rumors about the President's behavior under stress were rife in the White House press room. There was even one story that he was wearing makeup to disguise an illness. When I heard that, I remembered with a shudder the first time I read a makeup charge: *Women's Wear Daily* had concluded their coverage of my wedding with a sarcastic, brazen lie, "And Daddy was wearing more makeup than Julie."

Mother was with my father at McCoy Air Force Base, near Orlando, Florida, on November 17 as they "worked the fence," shaking hands with those who had come out to meet their airplane. When my father patted Master Sergeant Edward Kleizo on the cheek, a gesture he frequently used among the family, *The Wall Street Journal* reported that the President had slapped the man, and the story was carried widely. There was analysis about the purported tension that had precipitated such an "incident"—even though Kleizo himself stated that he was not slapped. "I was affectionately tapped on the cheek," he said, adding, "I consider the President's gesture the greatest honor that I've ever had."

While some journalists were finding signs of erratic behavior in unannounced car rides, others were giving weight to the predawn phone calls and charges by Martha Mitchell. Suggestions that she might be an unstable person and therefore not the best source on Watergate were dismissed as part of the grand scheme of the "cover-up."

Watergate illuminated the tragedy of Martha Mitchell, but her life was in disarray long before the break-in at the Democratic National Committee headquarters in June of 1972. Since my mother had first met Mrs. John Mitchell in 1966 she had watched with dismay her disintegration, unable to prevent it in any way. At the first dinner party in the Mitchells' home shortly after John Mitchell became a partner of the Nixon, Mudge, Rose, Guthrie, and Alexander law firm, Martha was intoxicated, dinner was late, and the evening was a loss. But Mother did not place much emphasis on one evening, thinking it might have been an off night for Martha. However, drunken phone calls followed, with Martha scolding, "After all, our husbands are partners now and we should have lunch together more often." When my father urged John Mitchell to come to Washington as his attorney general, he declined, declaring he had no desire to leave corporate law for the White House, and admitting that he was concerned about how his wife would adjust to the nation's capital. She had just been released from the hospital where she had been treated for alcoholism and hysterical depression. My father prevailed by arguing with Mitchell that he needed him, the country needed him, and that Washington would be a challenge for Martha and lift her out of her problems.

But, tragically, John Mitchell was right. Martha's life in Washington became her undoing. Her personality craved attention, and yet when she received it, she could not handle it. In the immediate weeks after the first inauguration, Martha telephoned my mother two or three times a day for advice on what invitations to accept, what to wear, and to complain that Mother's staff members were being short with her. She requested an appointment with Mother and then proceeded to demand that my mother's press secretary, Gerry Vander Heuvel, be fired immediately. In July of 1969 Martha had again been hospitalized. Then, in November of 1970, newspapers reported Martha's charge that "Connie [Stuart, Mother's staff director] is trying to get rid of me, to kill me, because I announced to the press that I called her at five A.M." She had called Mrs. Stuart to "get her attention" because she allegedly was not delivering messages to Mrs. Nixon.

After only a few months in Washington, it was apparent Martha needed someone to arrange her schedule as well as to give her advice. Haldeman suggested that a staff person for Martha be assigned to the First Lady's East Wing office. Mother protested firmly, "No. It just can't be in my office. I have tried to help Martha, but she will not listen to advice and I cannot take the responsibility." Throughout the first term, Martha's behavior remained erratic, and her drinking a nightmare to her family.

Martha's outlandish comments and unpredictable phone calls were manna to the Washington press corps. During the first term, it seemed to Mother as if both John Mitchell and the President were enjoying the media's reporting of Martha's colorful comments on the topics of the day. Mother was frequently the voice of reality, pointing out to my father that the press attention was not cute and that Martha did not realize some were making fun of her.

John Mitchell, with his tough image of fearless decision maker and his wartime service in the riskiest branch of the navy, patrol torpedo boats (one of his lieutenants was John F. Kennedy), became increasingly distraught as the southern belle he had married disintegrated. By the time of the 1972 campaign, he was spending less and less time on attention to details. Even in the middle of high-level meetings, Mitchell, as Bob Haldeman recalls, would abruptly excuse himself if he received word from home that Martha or his young daughter Marty needed him, or that his wife's companion-secretary had had to leave and Martha was alone. When my father was interviewed by David Frost in 1977, he raised eyebrows by stating that because John Mitchell was so preoccupied and distraught by his wife's condition, something as stupid and nonproductive as bugging the Democratic National Committee headquarters had occurred. But that was his opinion then and it is now.

After the Watergate break-in, the press prominently reported Martha's accusations. In one phone call to UPI's Helen Thomas, she claimed, "If my husband knew anything about the Watergate break-in, Mr. Nixon also knew about it." Martha claimed also that she had read a 1972 campaign book planning the Watergate break-in and bugging, written by the President and Bob Haldeman. Though the tapes would reveal that neither my father nor Haldeman knew anything about the planning of Watergate, all of Martha's accusations at the time were widely reported.

Finally in September of 1973, Mitchell gave up and the couple separated, their only child choosing to remain with her father. As Martha lived out her final years, alone and troubled, relying on both alcohol and pills, her position as a prime symbol of Watergate victims became enshrined, one of the most vivid and yet incomplete images to come out of the entire Watergate story.

By Christmas 1973, all of us in the family were discouraged and frankly overwhelmed by the repeated blows of Watergate. David and I spent Christmas Eve and morning with his family in Pennsylvania and then drove to Washington in time for Christmas dinner at the White House. I had been fighting the flu and by late afternoon had to go to bed with a fever. At six o'clock, my parents, Tricia, Ed, and David gathered in the West Hall. They were joined by Rose Woods and Cynthia and Bob Milligan. Since Cynthia was expecting her first child in early February, the Milligans could not fly home to Nebraska to be with their families for the holidays. My parents adopted them for the day.

At first Mother was more quiet than usual, perhaps remembering Christmas the year before when they lived through the last gasp of the war in Vietnam. But as the evening progressed, she rallied, trying to cheer my father, who was also subdued. Rose had brought over from her office a gift that had just arrived from Clement Stone, a close and thoughtful friend, who had been among the first men to support my father financially in his bid for the Presidency in 1968. His present was a box of a half-dozen silk ties. My father held up each tie to be admired, then passed them out to David, Ed, and Bob Milligan.

While Cindy and Bob quietly opened some packages Mother had wrapped for the new baby, my father made several Christmas phone calls. Despite the Watergate difficulties, and no matter what his mood, he had not abandoned his practice of placing weekly phone calls to the small- and big-town heroes and heroines across the country. The names for suggested phone calls came from dozens of different staff members but primarily from the speech and correspondence sections. The calls to firemen who had been commended for heroism or to a young achiever were one way my father kept in touch with at least a small cross section of America. With the war's end, this Christmas was the first since he had come into office when he had not placed calls to some of the next of kin of the men who had been killed in Vietnam.

As my parents and their guests enjoyed a turkey dinner in the Red Room, my father became nostalgic. He told Cindy and Bob about his first Christmas at Duke University Law School. He and only one other student in the school could not afford to go home for Christmas and a professor had invited them to his house for Christmas dinner. My father said he had never forgotten that kindness. The conversation became more nostalgic, especially about his foreign policy triumphs—the trip to China, the meetings with Mao and Brezhnev, the conversations with Golda Meir at the time of the Yom Kippur War and the military alert.

After dinner my parents came up to my room on the third floor. Both were distressed that I was sick. All I could think of was how sorry I was, because I knew that they were convinced my illness was due to the pressures of the last few months. In the darkened room, Mother sat in a small armchair at one end of the bed, my father in a straight-backed chair at the other. He told me he felt he had to get away from Washington and that he intended to fly to San Clemente on a commercial airplane so that there would be no criticism of the use of fuel for a vacation trip.

When he told his Secret Service agents what he wanted to do, they protested that it was too grave a risk. Hijackings, though fewer than in 1969 and 1970, were still a threat. Most important, they pointed out, the President would not have the worldwide communications he needed in case of an emergency. But my father was in a defiant mood over criticisms of presidential travel. He knew too that people were at the end of their patience with the long lines in the cold for gasoline, no sales of gasoline on Sundays, and repeated calls for car pools and lower heating temperatures. It was of little comfort to Americans that winter of 1973 to be reminded that in 1971 the Nixon Administration had been the first in history to issue a presidential message on the burgeoning energy problems—and that Congress had not acted on the proposals. In April 1973, my father had sent Congress five major new energy program requests; then, in September, he again urged Congress to pass several energy bills. Yet by Christmas, Congress still had passed only one major energy bill, the Alaska pipeline.

Tricia and Ed accompanied my parents to San Clemente. The flight was the most strained Tricia ever remembers. No one was physically uncomfortable, but the curiosity among the fellow first-class passengers was so intense that for five and a half hours most of the eyes in the cabin were glued on the family, even during the movie.

The weather in California was unusually cold. Small electric heaters were moved from the living room to the dining room to the bedrooms as the day progressed. My parents had hoped for relief from the cold of Washington, and relief from worry about what lay ahead. But it was not to be. It was almost certain that within a few months the House Judiciary Committee, with twenty-one of its thirty-eight members Democrats, would vote impeachment. The pro-impeachment forces were formidable. The American Civil Liberties Union had produced a fifty-six-page book that described how to swiftly and surely bring about impeachment. The AFL-CIO, which in past elections had supported nineteen of the twenty-one Democrats on the committee, started a nationwide campaign, distributing leaflets entitled "Nineteen Points for Impeachment," and within a few weeks it had distributed four million pamphlets. Public opinion was steadily shifting against my father. Walter Cronkite, perhaps the most respected television journalist, was asked at a public meeting whether or not he would "walk the streets of San Clemente" and conduct a post-presidential interview with Nixon once he left office as he had with Dwight

Eisenhower and Lyndon Johnson. Cronkite answered the question by cracking, "San Clemente or San Quentin?" Then he quickly amended: "That's wrong. I am an objective newsman."

On a cold afternoon the last day of December, Bebe and my father talked in the living room at San Clemente, a gray Pacific below them. Point-blank, my father asked his oldest and closest friend whether or not he should resign. Significantly, Mother was not in the room. He knew what her reaction would be: give not an inch, fight. But Bebe might have a different view. Since July he had been hounded by the Ervin Committee about a $100,000 Nixon campaign contribution that representatives of Howard Hughes had offered in 1970 and he had accepted and kept in a safe-deposit box in the Key Biscayne Bank. The contribution was intended for the 1972 campaign, but when a well-publicized internal fight began in 1970 for control of the Hughes empire, Bebe, remembering the press furor in 1960 and 1962 over the Hughes loan to Don Nixon, decided to hold on to the contribution until after the election, when it could be used to pay off campaign deficits or for the upcoming 1974 congressional races. But Bebe returned the money to the Hughes organization in 1973 when the IRS began investigating the billionaire's holdings, and he knew he would be questioned about the contribution. He had the serial numbers of each bill recorded by his attorney and the agent in charge of the FBI locally, and the numbers on the bills confirmed that the money all had been printed before Rebozo received the contribution and had all been issued through California and Nevada banks, thus evidence for his contention that he had left the money unused in the safe-deposit box until he returned it to the Hughes empire.

The Ervin Committee, however, was convinced that the money had been used illegally. Staff members interviewed Bebe on four separate occasions, exhaustively questioned his family and business friends, and subpoenaed all of his business records for the previous six years and all of the records of anyone he had done business with during the same period. They even interviewed everyone to whom he had written a check during that six-year period, and grilled him on five hundred telephone numbers, which they obtained from anyone even remotely connected with the Administration, scattered throughout all fifty states and with no identity or date provided.

Leaks from the Ervin Committee provided the media with seemingly limitless stories on the supposed use of the Hughes money and on Bebe's alleged wheeling and dealing. Bebe, who for years had given unstintingly of his time and money to the Boys Club of America, the Kiwanis, and other service organizations, now saw his reputation damaged. His bank's business had fallen off because of the all-too-frequent camera crew stakeouts. As we in the family watched Bebe endure the harassment, the attack on him was like attacking one of us.

But Bebe's undaunted reaction to the idea of my father's resigning was an immediate "No, you can't. You have to fight." Then he changed the subject, acting as if my father had not really been serious. That night my father picked up the tortoiseshell-bound note pad Mother had given him, and which he kept by his bedside, dated it, noted the time, 1:15 A.M., and wrote: "The basic question is: Do I fight all out or do I now begin the long process to prepare for a change, meaning, in effect, resignation?" Then he continued:

The *answer—fight*. Fight because if I am forced to resign the press will become a much too dominant force in the nation, not only in this administration but for years to come. Fight because resignation would set a precedent and result in a permanent and very destructive change in our whole constitutional system. Fight because resignation could lead to a collapse of our foreign policy initiatives.

And on January 5, at 5 A.M., he made these notes:

Above all else: Dignity, command, faith, head high, no fear, building a new spirit, drive, act like a President, act like a winner. Opponents are savage destroyers, haters. Time to use full power of the President to fight overwhelming forces arrayed against us.

1974
The Last Year

*T*he winter and spring of 1974, with gas prices at an all-time high, and still the long, frustrating lines at service stations—the fruits of the Arab oil embargo—my parents curtailed their trips to Camp David. Instead, they began visiting David and me at least twice a week at the white-brick house in Bethesda, Maryland, which we were renting from Bebe Rebozo. Although Washington real estate was a good investment for Bebe, he bought the house primarily so that we could provide my parents with another place to relax away from the White House. Our home on Armat Drive was only twenty-five minutes by car from the White House, and until David and I moved into an apartment in downtown Washington in June, it provided another world. We had been attracted to the house because of its privacy. It was set on an acre of unusually tranquil and beautiful yard. Dozens of pink, white, and red azaleas bloomed that harrowing spring. Birds flew among the flowers and shrubs, and two of them, a cardinal and a blue jay, became almost like pets. As soon as my parents arrived at the house, usually around 6:30 P.M., the birds appeared outside the glassed-in porch where we always sat. They chattered and called to us as they preened.

David remembers the evenings as dreamlike. Not only were there no food preparations, since my parents brought dinner ready made from the White House, but also the conversation was far removed from what was on everyone's

mind, Watergate. My father always first lit the fire. While we sat in front of
it, Mother would try to divert him by pointing out what was coming into
bloom. Many evenings my father reminisced about the car and train trips he
and Mother had taken during their courtship and early married years. He
wistfully talked about planning a train trip in late spring, or perhaps a summer
train ride across America. As he spoke of the past and of the future, ignoring
the present, he steadfastly was trying to sustain a lifelong philosophy of not
giving in to defeat.

On January 30, 1974, my father delivered his last State of the Union address.
He concentrated on the tasks that lay ahead: a lasting peace in the Middle
East; meeting the energy crisis; enacting the Administration's health insurance
program; economic measures to bring prices down; and continuing efforts to
make the states more responsive to local needs. There was no mention of
Watergate in the official text, but as he neared the end of his address he spoke
extemporaneously to the congressmen, many of whom had been his House
and Senate colleagues in years past. One year of the Watergate investigation
was enough, he declared, adding, "I have no intention whatever of ever walking
away from the job that the people elected me to do for the people of the
United States." The Nixon loyalists among the congressmen stood and wildly
applauded while their colleagues remained seated.

As Watergate ground on, Congress concentrated on the impeachment inquiry, passing only half the number of bills it had during the same time span
a year before. Slowly, steadily a consensus in favor of impeachment was
growing. It had been reported in December that two-thirds of the members
of the Judiciary Committee agreed that one did not even have to violate the
law to commit an impeachable offense. In fact, the committee could not
decide on a definition of impeachment. Finally, it was determined that each
member would make up his own mind as the proceedings progressed. Clearly,
the impeachment proceedings were shaping up as a political battle devoid of
clear-cut legal standards. The depressing reality was that the impeachment
motions placed Congress in the position of weighing and then ratifying or
rejecting dozens of disclosures of well-established but questionable practices.
In fact, even my father's supporters would have difficulty endorsing as a standard for future Presidents some of the measures taken by the wartime Nixon
Administration, no matter how justifiable at the time.

The House Judiciary Committee never tried to assess Nixon in light of his
predecessors. In the opinion of Democrat Ray Thorton of Arkansas, it was
the right course to judge Nixon in a vacuum since "only the Constitution is
the proper standard for presidential conduct." Given that criterion, most of
our wartime Presidents might have been impeached. Lincoln, a wartime
President like Richard Nixon, spent millions of unauthorized dollars, bypassed
Congress to institute his own code of laws for the Union's army and navy,

extended his war powers to free the slaves, and even suspended the right of habeas corpus for anyone tried by court-martial or in a military prison. He decreed that all persons "discouraging enlistments, resisting military drafts, or ... guilty of any disloyal practice" would be subject to military law. Lincoln did not live to confront the impeachment inquiry directed at his Administration through his successor, Andrew Johnson.

Franklin Roosevelt, considered another strong President, was responsible for a famous violation of individual rights by ordering after Pearl Harbor the mass roundup and imprisonment of 110,000 Japanese-Americans simply because of their ancestry. Roosevelt did not survive his fourth term and, in death, escaped the recriminations aimed at him through his successor, Truman. In 1962, John F. Kennedy's peacetime manipulation of the news at the time of the Cuban missile crisis was defended by *The New York Times's* James Reston, who quoted Assistant Secretary of Defense Arthur Sylvester's statement that lying is part of the government's arsenal. "The reflex action of the press is to howl like a scalded dog every time it catches the government tinkering with the truth," Reston wrote, "but ... it is palpable nonsense to talk about these distortions as being unprecedented. . . ."

Increasingly, friends tried to stay in touch with Mother to let her know that they were supportive. Those who knew her well did not make direct references to the Watergate miasma. On January 28, Mamie Eisenhower wrote from her Gettysburg farm:

> Pat Dear—
> This is not an engraved invitation but I would love to have you come up here when the President goes away—you could rest, walk, read, and gossip with me—now please everything would be on the QT. What fun we would have—have told Julie and David they could come too—come a running—
>
> Love,
> Mamie E.

The subject of Watergate had become entwined in all the First Lady's public events. The morning Mamie wrote, my mother had hosted a reception at the White House for the annual meeting of the Religious Broadcasters of America. The questions from reporters revealed their interest in the President's state of mind. The UPI story, printed nationwide, reported:

> Asked by reporters to comment on reports Mr. Nixon has not been sleeping well lately, her [Mrs. Nixon's] eyes flashed and she said: "He doesn't sleep long but he sleeps well." Sometimes his sleep is "interrupted by telephone calls," she added.
> Did he get up in the middle of the night to play the piano?
> He plays "before he goes to bed," Mrs. Nixon responded. Then thrusting

up an arm with her fist clenched, she said: "He is in great health, and I love him dearly and I have great faith."

When a group of the women who came through the receiving line mentioned their faith in the President and that they were praying for him, she had asked them pointedly to "pray for the press" also. Immediately a reporter asked, "Does the press need prayers?" Mother had answered, "We all do. Who doesn't?"

Mother was increasingly frustrated because her events were being either ignored or viewed solely from a Watergate angle. On February 11, she called Helene Drown to admit that the parade of receptions and meetings now seemed endless to her: "My schedule isn't doing a darn thing to help." She described how excited, but ultimately disappointed, she had been ten days before when she met with Indian potters from New Mexico. Their traditional pottery work had been in danger of dying out until a civic-minded group financed a revival. The Pueblo Indians and their sponsors who flew to Washington to meet with the First Lady were justifiably proud of the rebirth of the artwork, and were upset when the Washington *Post* made no mention of the reception. One of the sponsors later called Lucy Winchester to inform her that she had reached the *Post* reporter who attended the reception to ask, "Why the silence?" She had been told, "I'm sorry, but the newspaper sent me to cover the mood of the family, not the event." As Mother commented ruefully, "In other words, it doesn't matter what we're doing—the press is just looking for cracks."

Part of my mother's frustration stemmed from the fact that she was a doer and now there seemed to be little she could do. On January 14, she had talked at length to Helene and Jack Drown about getting some kind of television ad programming going that would counteract the negative stories. When they succeeded in getting the ads on the air, Mother said, they would celebrate with the old bottle of sherry the Drowns had given the Nixons after the first election to Congress. Helene and Jack had predicted then that someday they would crack it over the mantel of the White House.

The ad campaign never got off the ground, and in the weeks ahead, the troubles mounted, yet Mother's mood remained one of resolve, not despair or immobility. To her, these many months of Watergate were but another political battle, albeit the greatest of her life.

On March 1, John Mitchell, Bob Haldeman, John Ehrlichman, Chuck Colson, and three members of the Committee to Re-elect the President were indicted on charges of conspiracy and, with the exception of one of the members of the committee, with obstruction of justice as well. Six days later, Ehrlichman, Colson, and Liddy were indicted for the break-in at Daniel Ellsberg's psychiatrist's office. Tragically, they were destined to be tried in Washington, where a recent poll indicated that 84 percent of the residents questioned thought that the men were guilty. Washington also was the only place in the United States other than Massachusetts that had voted over-whelmingly against Nixon in 1972. Yet when the defendants' lawyers asked for a change of venue, it was denied. All the indicted would serve prison sentences.

Washington had been rife with rumors of the indictments for weeks. As David attended law classes he had daily contact with professors and students whose colleagues or friends were on the various congressional investigative staffs, the special prosecutor's staff, or the Senate Watergate Committee. To him, earlier than the rest of us, the situation looked irretrievable. He became increasingly quiet at family gatherings. In early February he wrote my father:

> Julie has undoubtedly mentioned my low spirits this past week. In a nutshell, nothing in my life prepared me for the thunder clap of criminal charges pressed against people I know and respect and essentially on grounds growing out of dedication to your cause. . . .
>
> I never accepted that life could be so unfair and it's unquestionably just the beginning. I spent the better part of this week wrestling with my feelings on the situation. I hope I haven't been misunderstood. Last night I discovered an appropriate thought, "There is no despair so absolute as that which comes with the first moment of our first great sorrow when we have not yet known what it is to have suffered and be healed, to have despaired and recovered hope." The quote was from George Eliot, of course. I wondered when it was you experienced your "despair so absolute"—14 years ago, 1 year ago—ours may have been last week. But the point of the passage and of your experience is hope. Under these circumstances hope means determination. We are happy with any part of redeeming the work you have done for America and we aren't alone either, come what may.

In response, my father wrote on February 3:

> Dear David,
>   Your note which I read when I got up this morning gave me a much needed lift. It was eloquent, thoughtful and above all *right*. . . . Julie and you have been a great comfort to us during this past year. We only regret that you both had to suffer with us one blow followed by another. . .
>   God bless you both—keep the faith—
>
>   RN

Ten days after the March 1 indictments, Mother flew to South America to attend the inaugurations of the presidents of Venezuela and Brazil. It was to be the last solo foreign trip of her public life. In both nations, she was hailed. The Brazilian inaugural ceremonies were delayed for six minutes because of the ovation that greeted America's First Lady, the only standing ovation accorded a foreign representative. From Caracas, where fifteen years and ten months before she had faced angry mobs, the American ambassador cabled this report: "Subject: the extraordinary success of Mrs. Nixon's official visit." He described how when the First Lady emerged from the Congress building at the close of the inauguration of President Pérez

> there was a tremendous ovation from the crowd; and when I had the honor of escorting the First Lady to the military parade yesterday, the throng in the grandstands rose to its feet and everyone heartily applauded. These manifestations of friendship were genuine and at times we almost had a fear that Mrs. Nixon's popularity would overshadow that of the new president and his first lady.

Along the crowded motorcade route to the ceremonies, Helen Smith remembers, "People were trying to touch her, touch the car, touch anything. They so admired her and her courage in returning."

She flew back to America on March 16, her sixty-second birthday. It was arranged that her plane stop in Nashville so that she could join my father for the opening of the new Grand Ole Opry. A huge, jubilant crowd of country-and-western devotees had packed the Opry theater to hear all their favorites. At one point in the program, an upright piano was wheeled out onto the stage and my father played "Happy Birthday" while the audience enthusiastically sang along. When the music ended, Mother got up from her chair and walked toward my father, her arms outstretched in delight and thanks. But he was already turning toward the center of the stage, gesturing to the master of ceremonies that he had interrupted the program long enough and that it could proceed.

Some of the more cynical correspondents covering the evening, however, interpreted the President's action as a sign of odd indifference to his wife rather than as mixed signals between two people. Others now speculated openly about the fact that since my parents rarely kissed in public, there was a coldness. But my parents are very private people and no amount of gossip was going to alter their public restraint. Connie Stuart told me that she often saw my parents "in receiving lines holding hands, but only until someone came along. Holding hands was a private moment for them, and when the moment wasn't private anymore, they resumed their public roles." Now, in the ugly climate of Watergate, dissection of the Nixon marriage was considered fair game by some.

In the opinion of ABC's Virginia Sherwood, the great majority of reporters always try to be fair, but they are intensely competitive and have to go after a story, even if it means relying at times on rumors and flimsy sources. She wrote a radio commentary about how difficult it was for many of the news people who covered Mother in the White House "to ask the hard questions

... knowing they must be asked," adding, "I am torn with sympathy for this lovely, courageous lady... and the need to do my job." Her closing words were about an impromptu birthday party for Mother on the flight from Brasília to Nashville and of how she picked up a glass to drink a toast "to the lady who stands with grace and courage amidst the Watergate rubble."

Three days after Mother's trip to South America, Senator James Buckley of New York became the first of my father's conservative supporters to call for his resignation. He claimed that a televised trial in the Senate "would become a twentieth-century Roman Colosseum, as the performers are thrown to the electronic lions." A week later *Newsweek* magazine reported as the leading item on its "Periscope" page that the morning after the statement, Buckley's office received a telephone call from the White House: "The message from one of Mr. Nixon's aides: any further requests for White House tours for Buckley constituents, a routine courtesy normally granted to Senators within hours, would be subject to a thirty-day delay." As soon as Mike Farrell read *Newsweek*, he sent Mother a copy of the magazine with a memorandum attached: "I just wanted to assure you that this is not true... interestingly, Senator Buckley's office has also indicated they did not receive such a telephone call from the White House. They are so informing the press—as we are."

But the false item was part of an all-too-familiar pattern of trivial accusations—and major ones, such as NBC's report that Dick Moore, who had been on the Nixon staff since the 1968 campaign, had been named as an unindicted co-conspirator in the Watergate case. The report was totally false, yet Moore was unable to get a retraction. Watergate had become a story out of control, the umbrella for dozens of charges and investigations. The special prosecutor's and the Senate Judiciary Committee's inquiries ranged from military actions in Cambodia to the price of ground beef as set by the Cost of Living Council to whether the President should pay for his dogs using aisle space on *Air Force One*.

The Watergate umbrella extended as well to the highly publicized Vesco trial in New York where former attorney general John Mitchell and former secretary of commerce Maurice Stans were accused of allowing a $200,000 campaign contribution from wealthy financier Robert Vesco (accepted before Vesco began the thievery that had made him a notorious figure by 1974) to influence a Securities and Exchange Commission investigation. The spectacle of two of the President's former Cabinet officers on trial for seventy days at times almost overshadowed other Watergate news. The reports from the trial during March and April were that Stans and Mitchell were in deep trouble and that John Dean's testimony against them had been effective. But on April 28, when Mitchell and Stans were acquitted, it was apparent that the jurors had believed them rather than John Dean, who had admitted in court that he hoped his testimony against the two men would result in a lessening of his sentence for Watergate crimes. But Stans's and Mitchell's exonerations came too late to stop the momentum that was moving toward the White House.

On April 3, headlines across the nation announced that my parents would have to pay $400,000 in back taxes because their gift of some 600,000 vice-presidential papers, a donation similar to those made a few years earlier by Lyndon Johnson and Hubert Humphrey, had been disallowed. Although the documents had been delivered to the National Archives four months before the July 25, 1969, deadline whereby Congress had discontinued deductions for public papers, the lawyers who had prepared my parents' income tax returns had not completed the proper paper work in time and had proceeded to backdate the deed for the gift. Although the gift had been in possession of the U.S. government since March 1969, the Joint Congressional Committee on Internal Revenue Taxation staff decided the President had not made a legally proper gift. But the GSA, which was in possession of the papers, decided he had and refused to return the documents. My father, who had declared he would not contest the findings of the committee, thus paid fully *and* lost the papers.

The avalanche of news stories on the taxes continued to be negative. It was decided my parents should have paid full capital-gains tax on the sale of their New York apartment because, the staff contended, the White House was the Nixons' principal residence. In the opinion of Senator Carl Curtis of Nebraska, who was a member of the Joint Committee, the staff's finding "bordered on the absurd. The White House is a public building; its occupant does not even own the furniture." The committee staff also decided that my father would have to reimburse the government for air fare when Mother, Tricia, and I had flown on *Air Force One* not in official capacities. No other President had been required to do so. And it was concluded that the President took an improper deduction when he claimed his study in Key Biscayne as an office since theoretically the government could have built him one there.

For Mother, the thousands of words written about the income taxes were particularly painful, since she had opposed my father's decision to release the confidential information contained in five years of tax returns. No political figure in American history had ever made such a disclosure before. She had predicted that the data on the taxes would not kill the vicious rumors of illegal funds to buy San Clemente or of the alleged secret bank accounts. Rather, she had argued, those who made the charges would begin to focus—as indeed they did—on the President's large deductions, implying that he should not have taken advantage of the tax deductions available. She had acquiesced only because my father was so determined to kill the false stories already circulating—and because they had no other options left.

The cumulative effect of charges raised and left dangling, and of grand jury, prosecutor's office, and congressional committee leaks, which were more often than not labeled by the press as "highly damaging," had taken its toll. By April

13, a Harris poll found that 43 percent of the public now favored impeachment as opposed to 41 percent against. A climate had been created in which the public easily could believe the worst of its President. All around us, hundreds of people—White House aides and Committee to Re-elect the President officials, campaign contributors and fund raisers, secretaries and clerks—were caught up in the prosecutory fervor and were subjected to questioning, publicity, and sometimes harassment. In my calendar book for May 12, in which I rarely did more than jot down the time of meetings or of phone calls to be made, I wrote, "Rose said, on Sunday, 'If there is a hell on earth, we are living through it now.'" The feeling of helplessness about the tide engulfing the Administration and the never-ending leaks was almost unbearable. Pat Buchanan had expressed the frustration well when he called a press conference during the Watergate hearings to denounce yet another Ervin Committee leak to the Washington *Post*, this time one of his memos:

> Charles Colson was convicted and faces possible disbarment and possible imprisonment for leaking derogatory information about an individual [Ellsberg] under indictment. It seems to me there is no ethical difference, and I doubt there is any legal difference, between that felony and what the nameless, faceless character assassins on the House Judiciary Committee are doing today.... Who is doing the systematic leaking, why they are doing it, seems to me to be a news story, a major news story, news that the American people have a right to know.

But that story was never told. The leaks were what fed the Watergate engine.

Franklin B. Smith, editorial writer for Vermont's Burlington *Free Press*, was one of an articulate but overshadowed group of journalists who stood back from the Watergate story and took stock of the often sensational, frantic reporting. As early as June 1973, he wrote:

> The Watergate "disclosures" ... have long since reached the ludicrous. This week, for example, *Newsweek* magazine "reported" that ousted White House counsel John Dean told investigators that President Nixon was "personally aware" of dairy industry contributions in 1971, totaling more than $300,000, and that he knew the funds were "intended to influence the government." Good grief, folks! Big Labor contributed more than $60 million to Hubert Humphrey's 1968 Presidential campaign, and do you suppose Humphrey knew that perhaps a penny or two of the $60 million were "intended to influence the government" if he were elected?!

Mother stopped reading the newspapers that spring. Instead, she kept abreast of what was happening by studying the news summary still prepared daily by a team of researchers who worked out of the Executive Office Building. It simply was easier to confront the blows by reading the news in normal type rather than in the two-or-more-inch-high headlines. Like Mother, I found it difficult to get up in the morning and look at the newspapers. It became a wry joke between David and me that as soon as he sat down with his first of several cups of coffee to read the paper from cover to cover, I would ask, "Did anything horrible happen today?"

Still, I tried to keep informed. Since September of 1973 I had worked as an assistant editor at the Curtis Publishing Company, which published *The Saturday Evening Post, Holiday*, and four children's magazines. I spent two days a week in Indianapolis, where Curtis was headquartered, but in any spare time I continued to travel across the country as I had during the 1972 campaign, primarily on behalf of health care, the environment, and educational programs for the young and the elderly. After the election, the tremendous number of invitations had not lessened and I tried to accept as many as I could. Between the summers of 1972 and 1973, I made more than 150 trips. When the questions in May 1973 started to be more on Watergate than on the purpose of my visits, I did not dodge them. I believed in the programs I was involved with, was proud, for example, that the Administration was responsible for the nation's first environmental program, and was not going to stop my activities because of Watergate. Although I never gave a speech on Watergate or embarked on any kind of "campaign," the news I now generated was almost all Watergate-related. Finally, by the spring of 1974, I had to face the fact that my presence at a Conference on Cancer and Human Values might make a difference to those attending it, but the next day the only news would be Julie's response to questions on the latest Watergate issue.

Throughout these difficult months Tricia came from New York as often as she could to be with my parents. Although articulate and effective when she made appearances—her television tour of the family quarters of the White House with Mike Wallace in 1970 had been highly praised—she was never happy with a public role. Consequently, in contrast to Tricia's infrequent appearances and Mother's reluctance at hers to get entangled in Watergate questions, my activities took on added significance in the eyes of the media, and I found myself in the unwanted and unsought role of the one "unafraid to speak out on Watergate." None of us was afraid.

My mother was the one who most encouraged my appearances. The message of countless of her letters, many of which she would bundle into brown manila envelopes at the end of an evening of signing and set aside for me, was "thank you for sending your daughter" or "we hope Julie will continue to fight." But my father never asked me to be out front. As I look back on it now, I remember more than once at dinner when he asked me, his voice full of concern, "You don't have any trips scheduled this week, do you, Julie?" perhaps anticipating that some new disclosure or new leak was about to be made public. He never discussed strategy with us, if indeed he had a plan. In fact, we never sat down as a family to talk about Watergate. It was a story with an obscure beginning, no definable middle, no end in sight; an unfolding drama to which the public, our family, and the President himself reacted to daily. In his *Memoirs*, my father wrote:

I did not want Julie to take the brunt of the Watergate questioning but she could not bear the fact there did not seem to be anyone else who would speak out for me. Whenever I suggested that she not become so involved, she always replied, "But, Daddy, we have to fight."

By March, the House Judiciary Committee had received the materials originally provided the special prosecutor: nineteen presidential tapes and more than seven hundred documents. But before the committee even had listened to the tapes and studied the documents, it requested forty more tapes. Although it was now clear the committee was on a fishing expedition (in a few weeks it would request 142 more), my father knew he had to comply with its requests or be held in contempt and then surely impeached. With his lawyers, he decided to supply the committee with verbatim transcripts of the tapes, omitting only those passages unrelated to Watergate and what Ron Ziegler referred to as "expletives deleted." What became known as the Blue Book, because it was bound in a blue cover, was released to the public on April 29. The transcripts proved conclusively that Dean had lied when he said he had discussed the cover-up with the President over a period of months. But the transcripts undermined my father's assertion that he had "acted like a prosecutor" when informed by Dean of the cover-up.

The greatest story from the release of the Blue Book, however, was the reaction in Congress and the press to the "moral tone" of the conversations: the mention of hush money, the President's indecisiveness, and the plethora of "expletives deleted." As my father wrote in his *Memoirs*, "The American myth that Presidents are always presidential, that they sit in the Oval Office talking in lofty and quotable phrases..." was shaken by the transcripts. In addition, the tapes cover just thirty-three hours out of more than forty-six thousand in office. Because the subject of the transcripts was Watergate, all else that was going on in the Administration—the efforts to end the war in Vietnam, the Middle East peace initiatives, the SALT agreement with the Soviets, all the domestic problems being tackled—was unrepresented.

The Richard Nixon on tapes was not the Richard Nixon the family saw every day. Not only did my father avoid profanity in the family circle (aside from an occasional goddamn) but also the man on the tapes, so completely oblivious to being recorded as he talked to his alter egos, seemed to be unaware of any manipulation or that his aides were more in control of the situation at times than he was.

My mother's greatest regret in the aftermath of Watergate was that my father did not consult her about the tapes before their existence became common knowledge. She would have urged that they be destroyed forthwith. How could any individual survive a public reading of private conversations? she asked; the petty along with the generous comments, the cutthroat and the forgiving, the wavering and the self-assurance that make up uninhibited, natural exchanges with friends or family or associates. She chafed as the theme of an unfit President continued to build.

In the last eight months of the Nixon Administration, badly crippled as it was, there was one final signal foreign policy achievement: the start of a dialogue between Israel and its Arab neighbors. In January, Henry Kissinger, as personal envoy of the President of the United States, had ferried back and forth between Israel and Egypt to work out mutually agreed upon withdrawals of troops. Then followed the more difficult, and some felt impossible, task of encouraging Israel and Syria, the bitterest enemies in the Middle East since the birth of Israel almost twenty-six years before, to agree to troop disengagement.

On May 29, after Kissinger had spent thirty-two days in extremely effective "shuttle diplomacy," a disengagement agreement was reached. My father rapidly made the decision to meet personally with the heads of state in the Middle East, hoping that if the leaders committed themselves publicly to coexistence, the fragile peace might endure. Egypt's president Anwar Sadat, increasingly a voice of moderation among his Arab neighbors, had told columnist Henry J. Taylor in March that he was concerned about the Watergate attacks on the President, who was the mediator amidst all the Middle East divisiveness. "I need time," Sadat had said. "I wonder if I'm going to have it. I need six months. You know what I would like to do? I would like to come to Washington and fight for President Nixon."

On June 10, my parents left an already warm, flower-filled Washington en route to Salzburg, Austria, where they would spend a day before traveling on to Cairo the next day. In Salzburg my father was troubled by phlebitis, his first major flare-up since his 1964 business trip to Japan. He had dinner that evening with Mother and Rose and showed them his left leg. Although it was red and very swollen, almost twice the size of the right, he reassured them that the assistant White House physician, Dr. William Lukash, had looked at it and decided that the swelling of the vein probably was the aftermath of inflammation and that he was not in great danger now of a clot breaking loose into the bloodstream. Lukash recommended warm towel compresses as often as possible and no standing for long periods. Throughout dinner, my father kept his foot elevated on an ottoman. He swore Mother and Rose to secrecy, convinced the trip was far too important to have anyone know about the swelling.

Later it would be written that he had a death wish and risked his life needlessly. His doctors, however, apparently did not feel a great urgency about the leg, because it was not until a month later, on July 8, that my father was fitted in his Executive Office Building study for an elastic stocking, ordered in the name of Secret Service agent Stuart Knight. And my father had assumed all along that the problem would eventually go away, just as it had after his bout in 1964.

In Salzburg my father managed to keep his leg condition out of the news. But another story beyond his control dominated the headlines. Upon Henry Kissinger's return to the United States from the Middle East, he had been infuriated by the spate of press stories that reported leaks from the House Judiciary Committee implying he had not been honest about the 1969 national security wiretaps he had authorized. In Salzburg he unexpectedly called a press conference, explained at length his testimony on wiretaps, and then proceeded to declare to the reporters in attendance that he would not tolerate his "public honor" being an issue and would resign if his "character and credibility" continued to be assailed. His threat generally quieted those who had been attacking him.

One of Kissinger's closest friends in the media, Joseph Alsop, defended him by pointing out that he, Alsop, had been subjected to three wiretaps, all pre-Nixon, and that "in short, the servants of the Nixon Administration are plainly being judged by different tests than those that prevailed in happier times." And another journalist friend, Joseph Kraft, wrote, "While he may have lied, the untruths are matters of little consequence when weighed against his service to the state." In other words, Kraft deemed Henry Kissinger indispensable, which by implication raised a question: Was the President indispensable?

The reception on June 12 in Cairo was beyond anything my parents or the other seasoned travelers in the presidential party had anticipated. Henry Kissinger, in reflecting in his memoir *Years of Upheaval* on Anwar Sadat's bold policy of accommodation with the Israelis, wrote that both Sadat and Nixon "were determined to make peace and the people of Egypt seemed rapturous at the thought of it." On the seven-mile drive from the airport, people were lined along the road a hundred deep. Most were unable to see much of the motorcade, let alone the two Presidents riding side by side in an open convertible. But they demonstrated their approval with thunderous cheers and clapping. Between six and seven million Egyptians greeted "Nix-son" at some point during the two-and-a-half-day visit.

Toward the end of a three-hour train ride in an old Victorian coach from Cairo to the city of Alexandria, Steve Bull, Rose Woods, and Dr. Lukash were sitting together in the dining car when Lukash was summoned to the rear of the train to attend to the President. Steve Bull remembers that Lukash left hurriedly. The President had not been himself in Salzburg, Steve reflected; he was definitely cranky.

From Egypt my parents flew to Jidda, Saudi Arabia, to meet with King

Faisal, whose massive financial aid to both Syria and Egypt made him a powerful presence in the Middle East. During the flight, some of my father's aides joked with Mother, half seriously, that the Saudis would not allow her to disembark. The Moslem view of women as inferior was still alive and strong.

Mother had met Faisal in 1957 at the first-anniversary celebration of the independence of Morocco. He was then foreign minister and would later depose his brother to become king. She remembered Minister Faisal on that occasion because, although it is not the custom for Moslems to show deference to women, he had bowed to her and waved her ahead of him when the guests were being seated. He surprised her again as he greeted *Air Force One* by indicating that she was to be included in the ceremonial welcoming tea at his palace.

In the evening, while the king hosted an all-male banquet in honor of the President of the United States, Faisal's Turkish-born queen hosted a dinner for Mother. The king's dinner was held in the guest palace where my parents were housed. It was an opulent, beautiful building, which the queen had designed, but which her husband had refused to move into because he felt it was too overpowering a sign of his vast wealth. Mother's bedroom was so large that it was lighted by six chandeliers. It was air-conditioned to what Mother guessed was a frigid fifty degrees. She later confided to Bill Codus with a smile that she spent the night huddled under all the bedding in the marble bathtub, the warmest spot in the suite. *

My mother found the queen's dinner, which she hosted in her own palace, to be the most interesting evening of the trip. The Secret Service agents, much to their chagrin, had not been allowed into the queen's palace. Even when they protested that they must at least check the rooms, they had been turned down. Nor was Bill Codus allowed to escort the First Lady past the entrance door. Bill remembers bidding Mrs. Nixon adieu and seeing the completely black-clad queen at the top of the grand staircase with heavily veiled ladies-in-waiting at her side.

The Saudi women Mother met that night frankly acknowledged that they realized that in the United States their husbands were criticized for not allowing them freedom. But, they asserted, they would live no other way. Their husbands spoiled them. They traveled abroad a great deal where they did not have to wear veils and robes. Shopping in Paris was a favorite occupation. In

---

*As with many of the personal details in this book, I did not learn about the bathtub from Mother. She has always been circumspect about conversations or experiences that occurred when she was "on the job" as First Lady. When Bill Codus told me the story and I asked Mother for more details, her reaction was "Oh, you don't want to mention that! It might hurt the Saudis."

fact, that evening each of the women was wearing a beautiful Parisian ball gown. The queen herself was continental and witty, a woman of modern ideas, yet of ancient and royal restraints. At eleven o'clock the next morning, when she came to pay a call on my mother, she arrived covered head to foot by a black robe and veil, under which she was wearing a beautiful aqua-and-yellow full-length gown and a panoply of jewels that set off her reddish-blond hair and gray eyes.

In fanatically anti-Jewish Syria, no American flag had flown in the nation for seven years as President Assad strengthened his ties to the Soviet Union. But on June 15 when *Air Force One* landed in Damascus, Assad dispelled any doubts about the nature of Syria's welcome, declaring in his toast that evening, "Let us open a new page and begin a new phase in the relations between our two countries." At the welcoming banquet, which featured an entire roasted lamb with an apple in its mouth, a genial Assad kept urging the First Lady to sample everything. My father recorded in his diary later that Mother had noticed Assad "had a flat head in the back which she said was probably because he hadn't been turned when he was a baby." In the morning, at the departure ceremony, Assad dramatically punctuated the significance of the visit by kissing my father on both cheeks, the highest compliment that could be paid.

Before returning to the United States on June 19, the presidential party visited Israel and Jordan. Back in Washington, my mother was more excited than I had seen her in a long time. To think, she told me, that Egypt, Syria, Jordan, and Saudi Arabia might begin to regard Israel in a way that could lead to reduced tensions—and to meaningful negotiations. She was proud of my father's role, and although she had only six days to prepare for the trip to Moscow for Summit III, the euphoria of the history-making journey to the Middle East buoyed her.

Frankly, I did not see how she or anyone else in the presidential party had the physical strength to embark on another journey so soon. Mother did admit to Helene when they talked by phone twenty-four hours after the return home that although still elated she had never been more bone tired. The schedule had been tight, and my father's phlebitis was aggravated by the rigors of the trip. He had been unable to elevate his leg as much as the doctors wanted; there simply had not been the opportunity. Consequently, when he left for the Soviet Union, his leg was still painful and swollen, and now it was no longer a secret that he was suffering from phlebitis. Just before flying to Brussels, the first stop of the trip for ceremonies marking the twenty-fifth anniversary of NATO, the news media filed stories about the vein-inflammation episode in the Middle East.

There were several differences between the journey to Moscow in 1974 and the one two years before, the "historic first," as my father liked to call it. By

1974 the pro-détente sentiment in the United States had lost ground: liberals objected to Soviet treatment of dissidents and Jews; and conservatives and many in the military establishment flatly opposed the SALT II goals of limiting offensive nuclear weapons and of a nuclear test ban treaty. Brezhnev was well aware of the growing anti-détente sentiment and that the President had been gravely weakened by Watergate. If Nixon did not survive impeachment, would his successor honor the much-heralded détente, or would Brezhnev find himself out on a limb with the anti-American forces in his own government?

The first day of formal talks produced a stalemate on a nuclear test ban, with the Soviets still refusing to agree to on-the-ground verifying procedures, which the United States insisted were crucial. The session was adjourned for a late-afternoon flight to Brezhnev's dacha in the Crimea. Since my parents had entertained the secretary general at their "country estate," he had insisted on reciprocating. The invitation, however, had given some gray hairs to members of the American advance team that had preceded my parents to Russia a month earlier to make the arrangements. The problem was that the dacha was located in Yalta. It would never do for the American President to negotiate with the Soviets in Yalta, where Franklin Roosevelt, then a very ill man, had met with Churchill and Stalin in 1945 to decide the fate of Eastern Europe. The American planners and their Russian counterparts came up with a solution: since Brezhnev's dacha was not technically in downtown Yalta, but rather in an outlying neighborhood called Oreanda, this suburb of Yalta would be rechristened as the town of Oreanda. Soon, freshly painted signposts blossomed along the road giving the distance to "Oreanda." When the President and the First Lady arrived in the Crimea, the Soviets discreetly skirted downtown Yalta entirely during the drive to the villa set in the hills overlooking the Black Sea.

After a night's rest in Oreanda, my father, Kissinger, and members of their staffs held talks with the Soviets at Brezhnev's cabana, a small building built into the rocks with the sea below. The negotiations were long and difficult; and while both sides agreed to restrictions of ABMs and limits on environmental warfare, neither side could agree to specific limitations of MIRV (multiple independently targetable re-entry vehicles) construction. At the end of the exhausting discussions, my father joined Mother for a quiet dinner on the balcony of the guesthouse. My father recorded in his diary:

> As we looked out at the sea, there was a three-quarter moon. Pat said that since she was a very little girl, when she looked at the moon, she didn't see a man in the moon or an old lady in the moon—always the American flag. This, of course, was years before anybody ever thought of a man actually being on the moon or an American flag being there.
>
> She pointed it out to me and, sure enough, I could see an American flag in the moon. Of course, you can see in the moon whatever you want to see.

My parents returned to Washington on July 3, and within two days of the summit, attention shifted back with a force to Watergate as the House Judiciary Committee began releasing its *Statement of Information*, a thirty-eight-volume compilation, much of it masses of material on lower levels of the Watergate conspiracy that were totally irrelevant to the impeachment of the President. But the sheer size of the volumes was impressive and generated headlines. The committee's activities had cost the government more than a million dollars and, according to a February Associated Press report, the committee's staff numbered more than ninety, thirty-nine of them attorneys. Simultaneously, the Ervin Committee began to leak and then release charges from its supposedly confidential Watergate report. On June 27, Peter Rodino, chairman of the House Judiciary Committee, had told some reporters from the Los Angeles *Times* and ABC that all the Democratic members were planning to vote for impeachment. When the story appeared in print, Rodino denied in the House that he had made the comment, but the reporters who had been present reaffirmed that their stories were accurate. Apparently, the Democrats already had made up their minds, even though no witnesses had been heard and a defense not made yet.

On July 12, my parents flew to San Clemente with Tricia and Ed. One week later, on July 19, the members of the House Judiciary Committee and Americans across the country who listened on television heard the committee counsel, John Doar, deliver an intense, skillful argument for impeachment. That evening my father recorded in his diary: "I intend to live the next week without dying the death of a thousand cuts. This has been my philosophy throughout my political life. Cowards die a thousand deaths, brave men die only once."

On July 27, while my father swam at the Red Beach, south of San Clemente, the Judiciary Committee voted 27–11 to approve the first article of impeachment: that the President had obstructed the investigation of the Watergate case. That night, after dinner, the first President in 106 years to be faced with impeachment went to his study and reflected on the day in his diary:

> I remember that Tricia said as we came back from the beach that her mother was really a wonderful woman. And I said, yes. She has been through a lot through the twenty-five years we have been in and out of politics. Both at home and abroad she has always conducted herself with masterful poise and dignity. But, God, how she could have gone through what she does, I simply don't know.

On the morning of July 28 my parents flew to Washington. Helene Drown returned with them for a visit. She would be in the White House for six days as the Judiciary Committee voted 28–10 for Article II, which charged that the President had abused the power of his office, and 21–17 for Article III, the charge that he had refused to comply with Judiciary Committee subpoenas. Article II was so broadly drawn that some described it as the "Christmas tree" article with something for everyone. It made no distinction between legal and illegal acts, holding the President to a higher standard than the criminal law. The dissenting minority on the committee wrote: "It is a far-reaching and dangerous proposition that conduct *which is in violation of no known law*, but which is considered by a temporary majority of the Congress to be improper because undertaken for political purposes, can constitute grounds for impeachment."

Helene remembers those six days as a busy time for my mother, and that she deliberately kept the television set off. She was working with Clem Conger on decorating the Garden Room, on the ground floor, the first room that the public visitors saw, and on the second-floor East Hall. Also, a major redecoration of the Queen's Room was under way. Mother showed Helene the circa 1950 furniture that soon would be replaced by nineteenth-century American antiques.

She was excited that Clem Conger finally had succeeded in finding a nineteenth-century Oriental rug large enough for the State Dining Room. One morning, then again in the afternoon and evening, Mother and Helene went downstairs to check the color of the rug in the different light so that the new draperies could be coordinated effectively. They walked on Roosevelt Island, played gin rummy, listened to records in the Solarium, and, as always, Mother spent time on her mail. Thousands of letters were pouring into the White House from people who did not want the President to resign. Each response, signed "Pat Nixon" in indelible blue ink, had to be carefully set aside until dry. Helene helped with the task of gathering the papers once they were dry and putting them back in folders.

Mother's sense of duty never deserted her. During the most stressful periods of Watergate or even when she had just returned from a trip, if a staff member sent a note or request to Mrs. Nixon, a response was awaiting her the next morning. Patti Matson, who was Helen Smith's chief assistant during the last two years of the Nixon Presidency, told me, "Your mother was always a professional. She took being First Lady seriously in the sense that she understood the pedestal the American people place their First Ladies on. I never got the impression that she put herself on the pedestal in personal terms, but rather that she knew what being First Lady meant to others."

Throughout her visit, Helene witnessed the ordeal my mother was going through yet never saw her lose her sense of humor. She laughed as she told Helene that when reporters began asking her about Watergate, "I just pretend I don't hear them. The next thing I know there will be the report that I'm getting deaf!" Then, in earnestness, she added, "But they are not going to get anything out of me. I won't let an offhand comment become a Watergate story." At one point, Mother admitted to Helene that she was frustrated by her amorphous position vis-à-vis the media. "No matter what I do I can't win. If I give the press all the tidbits about people and issues, they would say I was talking too much. And if I give them nothing, they accuse me of having no opinions or being capable only of small talk."

"The mood in the White House was tense," Helene recalls. "Your mother seemed to want to be distracted. She was *not* going to give in to the whole mess. But she was worried about the morale of her staff, and the President's staff, and she was worried about you and Tricia. She had to hold things together for all of you."

Although I did not see it at the time, Mother was indeed the one holding it all together. In the pre-Watergate years she had seemed fragile. We had worried about her and wanted to protect her. Now she was the strongest of all. Only to Helene did she admit her anguish. "Dick has done so much for the country. Why is this happening?" She was in awe of what my father was trying to accomplish in his Presidency. Helene told me frankly:

> Your father never had a better admirer. At times she would tell me she was "angry" or "furious" about a decision, but always, overriding it all, was a tremendous respect for him about the little things and the big. She said so many times to me that I can almost repeat it verbatim, "He always knows the right thing to say," because she herself found public speaking difficult. Most of all, she had respect for the enormous problems he was dealing with.

On July 30, the House Judiciary Committee voted down the final two articles: Article IV, the secret bombing of the Communist sanctuaries in Cambodia, and Article V, on personal finances. But it was a foregone conclusion that the House would vote for impeachment when it reconvened on August 19. My father could either resign or he could undergo a trial in the Senate, which would probably last six months.

On August 2 Helene left for home. When she came into the First Lady's small study-dressing room to say goodbye, Mother looked up and said, "I hate to see you go." Helene told me: "For a moment, she looked more worn and fragile than I had ever seen her, as if a little puff of wind could have blown her away. And she looked forlorn. She had always been a doer and now there was nothing she could do." On the drive to Dulles Airport, Helene wept silently in the backseat of the White House car.

A few hours before Helene boarded her flight for California, I had a private talk with my father in his EOB office. He had removed his suit jacket and slipped into one of his soft cashmere smoking jackets. Now from the comfort of his favorite easy chair, he told me in a low, steady voice that he had no support left, that he would have to resign. He did not elaborate and it was obvious that he had much to do and others waiting to see him. But the finality in his voice meant that this, at last, was the end.

My heart racing, I hurried across East Executive Avenue in the hot, hazy air, and then entered the coolness of the ground floor of the West Wing, its walls covered with blown-up pictures of my parents' recent trips to the Soviet Union and the Middle East. The minute I burst through the door of my third-floor bedroom, I picked up the phone and asked the White House operator to try to reach David at law school. When the message was handed to David in the middle of class, all eyes were on him as he silently read the piece of paper: "Please call your wife." He knew instantly that resignation was near. As soon as class ended, he returned my call. When I heard his voice I started to cry and asked him if he could meet me at the White House at lunchtime.

Only then did I go downstairs to see my mother. I felt as if my heart would break. I could hardly bear to tell her the fight was over, just as my father could not. More than any of us, she had been so indomitable; so sure that the cause was right; so convinced that resignation was wrong. She was in her bedroom, which Lady Bird Johnson had decorated, and which Mother, in her practical and saving way, had not changed. As a result, the room was never a reflection of her. Now she stood near the door, as if she had been waiting for something to happen or for someone with news. I told her immediately that Daddy felt he had to resign. A look of alarm spread across her face and she asked, "But why?"

I answered something like, "He has to for his own good or he'll be impeached."

Her mouth began to tremble. We embraced for a moment, our arms around each other very lightly, barely touching, knowing that if we drew any closer we would both break down and not let go. When I stood back I saw that Mother had tears in her eyes. For me, those tears that were shed so briefly were perhaps the saddest moment of the last days in the White House.

As inarticulate as I had been about my father's decision, my words had conveyed the irrevocableness of the situation. At noon, when Mother knew the maids would be gone from the laundry and storage area, she went upstairs and found boxes. Quietly, she began the process of packing important papers and belongings in her room and my father's.

I learned later that Mother attended to one other matter that morning. On July 31, she had looked at several designs submitted by the Lenox Company for the Nixon White House china, including a beautiful cobalt-blue plate with gold fluted edges. Now she telephoned Clem Conger: "I won't explain, Clem, but don't go ahead with the porcelain. Call it off." He remembers her voice had wavered slightly as she spoke.

They had worked closely together and accomplished much for the White House, and now she was leaving. Six days later, the night of the resignation speech, Clem Conger would type a brief note from his ground-floor office, which had once been Abigail Adams's kitchen.

Dear Mrs. Nixon:

I just wanted you to know that we all love you, the President, Julie and Tricia . . . I have great admiration for the great things the President has accomplished. It has been the greatest privilege of my lifetime to have been associated with you in our wonderful work in improving the White House history. It is all thanks to you and your inspiration as well as to the President's great interest in making the White House the most beautiful and most important house in the country. Be sure to let us hear from you from time to time . . . Very sincerely, Clem.

I had telephoned Tricia immediately after I tried to reach David at law school. She recorded in her diary: "Julie called, very down this morning. She informed me that Daddy had had a talk with her that was serious but she hesitated to elaborate over the phone. Immediately I said I was coming right down." Tricia arrived by shuttle from New York in a few hours. We talked briefly in my bedroom, then Tricia took the elevator to the Lincoln Sitting Room to see my father. The moment he had dreaded, confronting the family with the reasons he must resign, had arrived.

On July 24 the Supreme Court had ruled unanimously that my father hand over to the special prosecutor the sixty-four new tapes he had requested. Among the tapes was one for June 23, 1972. Now my father began to describe concisely and clearly the content to Tricia. On the tape, he and Haldeman had discussed having the CIA limit the FBI investigation of the break-in at the Watergate— for political reasons, rather than the national security reasons he had claimed in his public statements on Watergate.

Because the tape revealed that my father's first reaction was to try to protect his aides and his campaign and to minimize the incident, the Republican Minority members, who had argued that in the mountain of Doar material there was no evidence that the President had obstructed justice, were now confronted with evidence. Whether in fact he had committed an obstruction of justice was debatable, but he would now surely be charged with committing an impeachable offense.

One by one we joined my father in the Lincoln Sitting Room. Bebe had flown up from Florida the day before. He stood near the fire now, close to Tricia. Mother sat with her back to the windows, facing my father, who was sunk in his brown chair, with his legs elevated on the ottoman. David and I were together on the only sofa in the room. My father called General Haig and asked him to send over four transcripts of the tape. Soon Manolo arrived with the copies. David and I took one and went down the hall so that we could be alone to read it. Tricia and Ed, who had arrived from New York minutes before, went in the opposite direction with their copy. Bebe left the room also, as dejected as I had ever seen him; for once he did not try to cheer others. Mother remained with my father, the fire on the hearth crackling companionably. I sensed in her a rocklike solidarity with my father and a fierce protectiveness. I am not sure she even looked at the transcript. She remembers that he told her, "I don't know what I'm going to do, but I know you will all stand behind me."

When we came back, we gave our opinions. Tricia and I were adamantly opposed to his resigning, and Ed was also opposed. David's response was to encourage my father to do what he thought was best. My father launched into the reasons for resignation: It was wrong for the country to have a weak President. His support was gone. What if the Soviets attempted something? They had gone almost to the brink of war in the Middle East dispute. Through all this Mother listened intently.

After he had spoken we sat wordlessly for a few minutes in the comfortable, tucked-away room, illuminated now only by firelight. My father was the first to break the silence. "Was it worth it?" he asked, looking around the room.

When we heard those words, our minds traveled back to the 1968 campaign when candidate Nixon had spoken in his stump speech of the "high adventure" of political life and of his belief that to be engaged in battle mattered more than whether one won or lost. In turn, each of us in the small sitting room assured my father that it had been worth it and Mother spoke of fighting on. Then we said good night. For another hour or more he smoked his pipe in front of the fire thinking over his decision. As he wrote in his *Memoirs*:

> My family's courage moved me deeply. They had been through so much already, and still they wanted to see the struggle through to the end. Pat, who had let the others do most of the talking in our meeting, told me that now, as always before, she was for fighting to the finish.
>
> I decided that instead of resigning on Monday night, I would release the June 23 tape and see the reaction to it. . . .

The family went together to Camp David the next afternoon, but I remember almost nothing of that Saturday night and Sunday morning. We were simply biding time, waiting for the next blow.

Monday, August 5, the transcript of the June 23 tape was released to the public. My father asked if Rose, David, Tricia, and I (Ed had to return to his law firm in New York) would join Mother and him for dinner on the *Sequoia*. I do not think anyone in the family, with the exception of my father, ever thoroughly enjoyed the rather public rides on the *Sequoia*, but we recognized they were relaxing for him. Being on the *Sequoia* was like bobbing along in a glass bottle. The boat moved at a snail's pace, with no particular destination and under full view of escort Coast Guard speedboats. Now, in August of 1974, a flotilla of press accompanied us also. Reporters and photographers were posted as well at every bridge. We were the subject of a deathwatch.

But that night we all pretended we were alone on the river. We talked about films and teased Rose about her skirmishes with insistent callers. It was obvious that my father did not want to talk about the telephone report he was waiting for, a report that would tell him whether or not he still had congressional support in the wake of the release of the tape. After dinner, he went below and lay down in one of the staterooms. I remember thinking that it was odd he did that and mentioned it to my mother. She explained then for the first time that his left leg had been bothering him a great deal since the trip to the Middle East and the Soviet Union and that the doctors had asked him to elevate it as much as possible. The news startled me. I had seen stories about a limp in the newspapers in June but dismissed them as exaggerated, especially since my parents had not mentioned any problem to me. They both apparently had resolved not to let health become part of the Watergate deluge, but now I was worried.

While my father rested below, Rose Woods called Al Haig to get the congressional reaction. Mother, Tricia, David, and I sat in one corner of the *Sequoia's* living room as Rose spoke in a low voice on the phone across the room. Then she went below to report. When my father came upstairs to disembark, he did not mention the phone call or Rose's findings.

By the next afternoon, it was public knowledge that if my father decided to fight impeachment, he would now assuredly face conviction in a Senate trial. His congressional aide, Bill Timmons, reported that there were only seven senators he could count on for sure. He called Rose into his office that afternoon and asked her to tell the family that resignation was inevitable.

Al Haig and Ron Ziegler met with the President in his EOB office soon after Rose left on her mission. He would resign Thursday night. The words spoken, he turned to the windows, with the view of the White House across the street. Ziegler remembers that the President said, more to himself than to them, his eyes still on the White House, "Well, I screwed it up good, real good, didn't I?"

I think I know what my mother's reaction would have been to those words: No! Unacceptable! I heard her say many times during the crisis and long after that in the same situation, and with the same pressures and fear of political consequences to the election campaign, and with the loyalties my father felt toward friends and political associates, she could understand the route he had taken of closing his eyes and hoping someone would make it all go away. "I would have done the same thing," she told me.

Given a chance, my mother would have been willing to see the fight through to the end, to narrow the charges instead of accepting the blanket indictment that resignation would imply. But she knew her husband well. He was not one to give up easily either, and so when Rose delivered her message, Mother knew the struggle was over. Rose, her voice choked with emotion, explained that the resignation would be announced Thursday night. The way we could help most now, she continued, was not to challenge what my father knew he must do.

Later that afternoon, Rita de Santis came to comb Mother's hair. As she finished, she called out in her cheery voice, "See you tomorrow." Mother just hugged Rita. Tears stood in her eyes. Rita knew then what was happening. Throughout all the difficulties, Rita remembers, "Even at the times when things were the most unfair, I never saw Mrs. N. in a bad mood. She never shouted either. Sometimes I think she should have shouted and screamed. But she was always very considerate and tried to be cheerful. Once in a while she would be a little quiet."

All day the White House was deluged with telephone calls. Helen Smith and Lucy Winchester reported to Mother periodically throughout the day, feeling it was their duty to deliver the urgent pleas from people who begged, "Don't give up." Friends were sending messages also. From Gettysburg, Mamie Eisenhower wrote:

> Dearest "Pat,"
>   I only want to say I'm thinking of you today—always you will have my warm affection as will your husband President Nixon—
>
> > Your friend, Mamie Eisenhower.

Gwen King had sent Mother a thick folder of letters of support that morning. Mother telephoned later and said briefly that she preferred that Gwen simply file the letters and responses. She would send them down with the usher. When old, gray-haired Mr. Jefferson, the kindly dispatcher whose job it was to fold and seal the First Lady's correspondence, opened the returned folder, he looked stricken: the letters were unsigned! Some of the staff gathered around. Gwen recalls, "We all began to hold our breath."

David's parents were in Washington for a visit. After dinner with them at our apartment, I slipped over to the White House to leave a note on my father's pillow. I knew it would be too painful to confront him face-to-face with my plea, but I still was convinced he was being stampeded and that events were moving too fast. Repeatedly he had said in public statements and to us privately that resignation would set a dangerous precedent for the Presidency. I knew he still believed that. When my father went to bed at 2 A.M., after working out some thoughts for his resignation speech, he found my note.

> August 6

> Dear Daddy
>   I love you. Whatever you do I will support. I am very proud of you.

Please wait a week or even ten days before you make this decision. Go through the fire a little longer. You are so strong! I love you.

Julie

Millions support you.

In the morning, Ed and Tricia, and later Ed and David, went over to talk to my father in the EOB. In the anteroom of the office, my father's long political career passed before one's eyes. Cartoons dating from his first term in Congress hung chronologically on two large walls. A five-foot-high embroidery of the Presidential Seal, with the legend "God Bless America, Land that I love," was proudly displayed next to the door to the office. Each stitch, according to seventy-eight-year-old Mrs. L. D. Perry, who had completed it for my father in 1970, represented "something good about America."

Inside the office itself was the same blend of the political and the personal: on my father's desk, side by side lay the paperweight of a red setter like King, which he had purchased for Mother during their courtship, and a wooden gavel used during the '68 convention. On the wall opposite hung a lacquered painting in deep reds and burnt orange given to him during his visit to Hanoi in 1953. On a shelf behind my father's desk was a photograph of him with his Duke Law School class, and one as a young Vice President with Winston Churchill.

My mother had decorated the room in warm red and cream colors. Now my father sat in his red-and-beige easy chair, a duplicate of the one in the Lincoln Sitting Room, as Tricia, and later his two sons-in-law, asked him whether he was convinced that resigning was the course he should take. They wanted reassurance before the decision was made public that he felt what he was doing was best for him and for the country.

The first draft of his resignation speech was already on my father's desk. Attached to it was a note from Ray Price, who had been at my father's side since March 1, 1967, when it looked as if Richard Nixon might try the long shot for the Presidency. Ray wrote that resignation had become "a sad but necessary decision in the circumstances. But I do hope you'll leave office as proud of your accomplishments here as I am proud to have been associated with you, and to have been and remain a friend. God bless you; and He will."

My father had one last painful meeting that day before he joined the family for dinner in the Solarium. The Republican leadership, Senators Barry Goldwater and Hugh Scott and Representative John Rhodes, paid a formal call to say that there was very little support left, even among Republicans. The brief meeting was actually a formality, since the men were expressing something my father already knew.

An hour later, the family and Rose gathered in the Solarium for the last family dinner in the White House. As my father entered the room, despite his fatigue and inner turmoil, he etched into his memory every detail of the scene that greeted him.

> Pat was sitting up straight on the edge of the couch. She held her head at the slightly higher angle that is her only visible sign of tension, even to those who know her. As I walked in, she came over and threw her arms around me and kissed me. She said, "We're all very proud of you, Daddy." Tricia was on the couch, with Ed sitting on the arm next to her. Julie sat in one of the bright yellow armchairs, tears standing in her eyes. David stood beside the chair with his hand on her shoulder. Rose, who was as close to us as family, sat on a large ottoman next to my yellow easy chair. I said, "No man who ever lived had a more wonderful family than I have."

The White House butlers placed trays in front of each of us and departed. In the last year of the Administration we had frequently eaten from trays in order to be able to talk more freely than when served formally. Tonight, we spoke only of light things. My father asked Manolo to bring up the dogs and we laughed as they played and begged for food.

There was an unexpected knock at the door. It was Ollie Atkins, the official White House photographer. Ollie was known for his ready smile. Now he was sporting one of his widest grins I had ever seen. He acted as if it were a routine assignment to come up and take a picture. I could see from Mother's expression that she was upset. Softly, she explained to Ollie that no one really felt much like posing. But my father interrupted. He had requested the picture, he explained, "for history." To ease the tension, Tricia got up and suggested that we all just stand together and link arms, as we had for one of our favorite family portraits taken in 1971 in front of the Christmas tree in the Blue Room. Quickly, we got into place: Ed and Tricia, my father, Mother next to him, David and I. I tried to hide partially behind Mother, because tears were in my eyes and I didn't want them to be recorded in the photograph. After Ollie had snapped a few frames and thanked us all, I threw my arms around my father and he held me close. In the family photograph, it is very difficult to tell that I am crying. But my mother hates that picture, and when it was being considered for inclusion in my father's memoirs, she told me why: "Our hearts were breaking and there we are smiling."

The next evening, August 8, at 9 P.M., the thirty-seventh President spoke for the thirty-seventh and last time from the Oval Office. Tricia had told Rose that the family wanted to be with my father during the address, not on camera but in the same room. But he felt he could not get through the talk if we were only a few feet away. Numbly, we sat together in the West Hall where we had watched most of my father's speeches throughout his Presidency. My father was composed and his voice strong as he explained that because he no longer had adequate political support in Congress, he could not justify seeing the constitutional process through to its conclusion. With the disappearance of his congressional base, "I now believe that the constitutional purpose has been served, and there is no longer a need for the process to be prolonged." He would resign, effective at noon the next day.

The last part of his address was about the new beginnings that had been made toward peace among nations. But the challenges that remained were great.

> Around the world—in Asia, in Africa, in Latin America, in the Middle East— there are millions of people who live in terrible poverty, even starvation. We must keep as our goal turning away from production for war and expanding production for peace so that people everywhere on this Earth can at last look forward in their children's time, if not in our own time, to having the necessities for a decent life.

In his Inaugural Address five and one-half years before, he had pledged to work for peace. Now he told the American people:

> I have done my very best in all the days since to be true to that pledge. As a result of these efforts, I am confident that the world is a safer place today, not only for the people of America, but for the people of all nations, and that all of our children have a better chance than before of living in peace rather than dying in war.
>
> This, more than anything, is what I hoped to achieve when I sought the presidency. This, more than anything, is what I hope will be my legacy to you, to our country, as I leave the presidency.

I think we were all completely drained of emotion by the time he had spoken the last words. No one said anything. Then the telephone next to the chair where my father always sat rang. I went over and picked up the receiver. The operator, without the customary announcement of who it was, had connected me directly to Bebe. He was sobbing. No words came. Through my own tears I asked: "Wasn't it a great speech? How did he do it?" Then abruptly, Tricia told me to say goodbye because our father was on his way over from the office and we wanted to be downstairs in time to meet him.

Mother did not sleep that night. As quietly as she could, she continued the enormous task of trying to sort out what should be sent to storage and what would be needed in San Clemente. That day she had met with Rex Scouten and gone over lists of our belongings: the boxes of briefing books, photo albums, and memorabilia; personal items and books, some of them from the vice-presidential years; furniture from the New York apartment; the racks of winter and evening clothes on the third floor. Throughout the night as Mother worked, below her, on the state floor, Rex Scouten and a small army of men labored to set up chairs and to lay television cables in the East Room where my father would say farewell to his staff, and on the south grounds where Gerald Ford would escort him to a helicopter for the first leg of the journey back to California. Mother and Rex, who had first met twenty years before when Rex traveled the globe with her as a Secret Service agent, did not say goodbye to each other in the morning. There was too much love and respect on both sides to say it all in one word: "Goodbye."

David and I were up throughout the night as well. For several hours after we got back to our apartment on Virginia Avenue where we had moved in June, there were telephone calls from friends who wanted to reach my parents or us with their messages of love and support. In the remaining hours until dawn, we simply could not sleep. At 8 A.M., Cindy and Bob Milligan, who had never been far away throughout the ordeal, dropped by our apartment. Cindy's excuse was that she needed to bring my laundry. In the last tense, busy month, she had taken my laundry home with her to McLean, Virginia, several times a week so that I would not have to use the public machines in our apartment building. When I saw Cindy and Bob at the door, I said, not thinking, "Why, we really don't need the laundry today." Cindy gave me a big hug and reassured me that it was no trouble since she was on her way to her law office a few blocks away and Bob was going to his job at the Commerce Department. I learned later that after saying goodbye they had turned around and driven home. They had just wanted to be sure that we were all right.

By nine-fifteen, the White House household staff was waiting quietly in the West Hall to say farewell. Mother came out of her room wearing a crisp pink-and-white cotton dress, her dark sunglasses the only sign that anything was out of the ordinary. I did not trust my emotions enough to express thanks and say goodbye to these men and women who had become friends, and so I stood at the far end of the hall and watched my mother and father shake hands and exchange words with each. My father even talked with the butlers about the latest baseball news. Then, with heartfelt thanks, he told them what a magnificent job they had done in serving the family and the many visitors to the White House since 1969.

Steve Bull appeared at the threshold of the West Hall. It was time to go downstairs. The Cabinet and the White House Staff were waiting in the East Room to hear the final words of farewell. We all crowded onto the elevator. There was so little room we could barely turn around. Steve, his face to the elevator door, began describing in a calm voice where we would stand on the platform and where the television cameras would be positioned. With the words "television cameras," Mother and Tricia became very upset. There was anguish in Mother's voice when she said, "Oh, Dick, you can't have it televised." She was to the end a private person, and she felt instinctively that my father's painful words of thanks and farewell to his staff were between him and those in the East Room. But it was too late to make any changes.

I was fighting for control, and I could tell from Mother's and Tricia's irregular breathing that they were fighting equally hard. Somewhere in the back of her mind, Tricia had tucked away a friend's formula for suppressing sobs: take three deep breaths, she commanded us. We did and it helped.

The elevator door opened and we turned the corner to the Grand Hall. Ahead were the open double doors to the East Room, a mere white blaze of light. Inside, the gold-and-white chairs filled the room and people were standing shoulder to shoulder along the wall. In a resonant voice, marine aide Jack Brennan announced, "Ladies and gentlemen, the President of the United States of America and Mrs. Nixon. Mr. and Mrs. Edward Cox. Mr. and Mrs. David Eisenhower." We walked into a thunder of applause, following one another blindly down the aisle, Steve Bull leading the procession. Our destination was the raised platform where name tags designated our positions. My father stood in the center, David and I were a few feet away on one side; Mother, Tricia, and Ed on the other side were also separated from my father by several feet. Those few feet between his tag and ours, insignificant on any other day, created a feeling of great physical separation.

For just a moment, I permitted myself to glance over at Mother. I saw that she was not wearing her dark glasses, but now held them in her hand. She had moved away from her tag closer to Tricia and Ed. She told me later that as the East Room resounded with sustained applause, she had started to look at the faces in the audience. Many had worked during the 1968 campaign and had fought for the Administration programs ever since, even through the last bitter months. They were among the ones whom my father would write later, "I had let down so badly." Some would share the exile in San Clemente, among them Ken Khachigian, who had come to the Administration in 1970 as a young law school graduate. His loyalty in the spring of 1974 would cause friends to post on his office door the words of Lieutenant Onodo, the Japanese soldier found in the rain forest twenty-five years after the defeat of Japan: "I did not surrender because no one gave the order." When Mother saw that many in the room were weeping, she quickly turned her eyes back to the podium.

Gradually the clapping subsided. In the hush my father began to speak. He thanked his Administration colleagues for "the sacrifice all of you have made to serve in government..." And he spoke from the heart about his heritage, of his parents, Frank and Hannah Nixon. Several times his voice cracked with emotion, and we, his family standing with him, ached with him.

Finally, he read an excerpt from the diary of young Theodore Roosevelt written after his first wife's death: "And when my heart's dearest died the light went from my life forever." But Teddy Roosevelt had gone on, my father continued,

> and he not only became President, but, as an ex-President, he served his country always in the arena, tempestuous, strong, sometimes wrong, sometimes right, but he was a man. And as I leave, let me say, this is an example I think all of

us should remember . . . We think that when someone dear to us dies, we think that when we lose an election, we think that when we suffer a defeat, that all has ended. We think, as Teddy Roosevelt said, that the light had left his life forever.

Not true. It is only a beginning, always. The young must know it; the old must know it. It must always sustain us, because the greatness comes not when things go always good for you, but the greatness comes and you are really tested when you take some knocks, some disappointments, when sadness comes, because only if you have been in the deepest valley can you ever know how magnificent it is to be on the highest mountain.

I saw it written later that it was "odd" my father mentioned his parents but not his wife in those farewell remarks. But that would have been asking too much of any man. We were standing so close to my father that he could reach out and touch us if he wanted. When he spoke the words "when sadness comes," much of the regret he felt at that moment, yet left unspoken, was that he had let his family down.

Within fifteen minutes it was all over and we were walking quickly out of the East Room. People were clapping wildly and many were crying openly. Jerry and Betty Ford had not been in the East Room. Already they were symbols of a new Administration, apart, waiting for my parents on the floor below in the Diplomatic Reception Room to escort them out of the White House, down the red carpet flanked by the color guard at attention, and to the waiting *Marine One* helicopter.

Four abreast, the Nixons and the Fords walked across the South Lawn. There was a firm handshake between the thirty-seventh and the thirty-eighth Presidents. A quick kiss for Pat from Betty and Gerald Ford. The goodbyes to David and me, who were remaining behind in Washington. My father was the last to board the helicopter. He paused beneath the arched doorway and waved broadly a final time.

On board, everyone took his accustomed seat: my parents in the oversized chairs facing each other at the big window; Tricia and Ed on the couch opposite them; at the back, Ron Ziegler, Walter Tkach, Steve Bull, Jack Brennan, Manolo and Fina Sanchez with their bird. It was very quiet. Jack Brennan felt a "terrible emotion" in all. In the pilot's seat, Gene Boyer, who had flown *Marine One* since 1969 and had taken Mother over the Peruvian Andes, was crying silently.

At Andrews Air Force Base, where Richard and Patricia Nixon had departed so many times before on their missions abroad—their first trip around the world in 1953, China in 1972, the Middle East in 1974—they boarded the presidential jet for their last flight. There were no crowds at Andrews, but Bill Codus was there, along with Roger and Louise Johnson, who had been present for the start and the end of almost all the vice-presidential journeys. The friends embraced silently.

At twelve noon, as *Air Force One* cruised over Missouri, my father ceased to be President. Mother sat alone in her small, private compartment, which had room for no more than her bunk, desk, and one chair. Next door to her, my father was sunk into the padded swivel chair of his cabin office. Though separated only by three paces and a sliding partition, the two exchanged no words then. Both were totally drained, content for a few hours to live in a state of suspended reality. Neither watched Gerald Ford, with Mrs. Ford holding the Bible, take the oath of office from Chief Justice Warren Burger. Nor did they hear him speak to the nation:

> Our long national nightmare is over. . . . In the beginning, I asked you to pray for me. Before closing, I ask again your prayers for Richard Nixon and for his family. May our former President, who brought peace to millions, find it for himself.

A half hour before the airplane was due to land at El Toro Marine Base, one of the stewards knocked first on my father's door and then on my mother's to say that a large crowd, later estimated to be five thousand, was waiting for them. But the idea of facing yet another group was overwhelming to my parents. As *Air Force One* approached the runway, it glided over a snaking mile of cars bumper to bumper still trying to crowd onto the base. Among those who already waited behind the fences at the runway were strangers and friends alike. Paul Keyes was there, knowing that the Nixons would have no way of finding his face in the crowd but wanting to be present. The night before, my father had tried to reach him by telephone. It was one of the dozen or more calls he made after the resignation speech until the early-morning hours, and to each valued friend, he repeated the same words: "I hope I haven't let you down."

When the airplane doors opened, my parents saw that many in the crowd below them were holding small American flags; others were crying openly. My father went to the fence and began shaking hands. At one end of the crowd, someone started singing "God Bless America." Slowly, steadily, the song was taken up by more voices. Then my father heard someone call out, "Whittier's still for you, Dick," and for a sharp, poignant moment he was back at the Benson Hotel in Portland in 1952 when Tom Bewley and Tom Riley had flown up from Whittier to reassure him that the town was still behind him as he fought for his political life. He had not planned to talk to the crowd, but merely to wave farewell and board the helicopter for the trip to San Clemente. But that shouted comment changed his mind. With Mother by his side, he thanked all those who had come, telling them feelingly that he would continue to fight for what he believed in and for "the cause of peace and freedom."

A camouflage-brown Marine Huey helicopter, the kind that had seen duty in Vietnam, was waiting at the edge of the runway. My parents walked briskly, hands waved high in greeting, smiles on their faces, eyes partially shut against the intense glare of the sun on the asphalt runway. With Tricia and Ed, they boarded the Huey for the fifteen-minute flight to San Clemente. When it landed at the Coast Guard station adjoining La Casa Pacifica, Secret Service agent Bill Hudson, who had headed my mother's detail in the past two years and become a friend, was among the guards waiting. He remembers: "Both your parents had smiles on their faces as they got off the helicopter. They were always like that, smiling graciously no matter what they felt inside." They waved to the small crowd that had gathered and then got immediately into the golf cart for the three-minute drive to the residence. They were home.

Part IV

1976-1986

CHAPTER 28

A Solitary Person

For a few days, the resignation speech seemed to have brought the healing my father hoped that it would. My parents were even tempted to believe that the worst was behind them. But in the weeks ahead, my father would devote untold hours to dealing with some twenty lawsuits, many of them purely harassing actions, and a dozen more judicial procedures or congressional inquiries. His legal fees would reach more than $1 million within four years. The House of Representatives would pass a bill seizing all of the Nixon papers and tapes, making him the only President in history to be denied control over his presidential documents. The American Bar Association would adopt a resolution condemning the former President; and the Special Prosecutor's Office, instead of closing shop, would continue its pursuit of its special target: the President's friend, Bebe Rebozo.

In the end Bebe would be investigated for sixteen months by not only the Watergate Special Prosecutor's Office, but also by the Senate Watergate Committee, the Internal Revenue Service, the Government Accounting Office, and the Miami district attorney, costing the taxpayers an estimated $2 to $3 million. Yet Leon Jaworski's comment on January 9, 1975, that his staff could find no evidence of wrongdoing was a small news item not carried by all newspapers, and no mention of Rebozo's innocence was made on television at all. The Special Prosecutor's formal report ten months later stating there was no evidence to warrant charges against Bebe Rebozo was also a one-day story.* In the eyes of millions who had heard repeated charges on television and read them in the news, Rebozo appeared guilty and remained so. All those long months, my parents churned inwardly as they watched Bebe try to deal with pressures they were powerless to ease.

Just four months before the resignation, on April 8, at the height of the Watergate stories, Clare Boothe Luce had written an open letter to *Time* magazine:

> No President of the U.S. except Lincoln (in retrospect, now to be considered another impeachable character) has ever been more savaged by the press than Nixon. . . . And he has shown that he can take it and take it and take it, with cool and courage. But few journalists—none on *Time*—have even the sportsmanship, no less the journalistic objectivity to report that whatever Nixon is or is not, he is one helluva gutsy fighter.

But in the aftermath of the resignation, my father had little fight left. He had written in 1962 in *Six Crises* that the greatest danger comes not during the battle but afterward. It was true of him in the fall of 1974.

Mother was a sustaining force. Pat and Shelley Scarney Buchanan flew out from Washington to spend Labor Day with my parents. Shelley remembers that they gathered at the pool before dinner and that Rose Woods joined them there. "It was a warm and balmy evening. Your father was very quiet. He did not seem well, but your mother was in some of the best spirits I have ever seen her. You would never have guessed anything was wrong. She carried the evening."

In reality, her life then could not have been much bleaker. Tricia and Ed, who had used his yearly three-week vacation time in order to ease the transition to San Clemente, had returned to New York, leaving a void for my parents. David and I were also three thousand miles away in Washington where David was in his second year of law school. Mother faced the unpacking alone, the prelude to the task of creating a new life in the wake of an enforced and clouded retirement. And, within a week of the evening with the Buchanans, she had to endure the beginning of a series of illnesses for my father, as well as what she has called "the saddest day of my life."

My parents spent the weekend of September 7 and 8 at Sunnylands, the magnificent Palm Springs estate of their friends Lee and Walter Annenberg. In the warmth of the desert and the seclusion of the lush green acres of the private golf course that surrounds the Annenberg home, my parents heard the

---

*The Special Prosecutor's report was made public in fact only after Common Cause, thinking Rebozo had been shown favoritism, sued for disclosure under the Freedom of Information Act.

news of Gerald Ford's announcement from the White House that he had pardoned former President Richard Nixon "for all offenses against the United States that he, Richard Nixon, has committed or may have committed or taken part in during the period from January 20, 1969, through August 9, 1974." A few days before, when my father learned that Ford was at the point of issuing a pardon, he had met with his attorney, Jack Miller, to discuss whether or not he should accept it. The idea of a pardon was abhorrent to him because he realized it would tend to convey an admission of guilt he did not feel. And, by accepting the pardon, while it would make him immune from prosecution, he would forgo forever any chance of narrowing the charges against him. But Miller argued cogently that in no circumstances would he be able to get a fair trial with an impartial jury in the immediate future, or perhaps ever.

Since resignation day, my father had called me in Washington daily without fail, usually in the morning. But on September 8, when I learned for the first time, along with the public, about the pardon, I did not hear from him and my own phone call was not returned. When I finally reached my mother in the early evening, she was obviously upset and uncommunicative. I asked her how my father was and she answered abruptly, "He told me, 'This is the most humiliating day of my life.'" Months later she would explain that it was for her the saddest day. In her eyes, my father had done nothing to require a pardon and his acceptance of it would imply surrender to his enemies.

The night of September 8, my father had a stabbing pain in his lower abdomen on the left side. In June, during his trip to the Middle East when the swelling and discomfort in his left leg were so severe, he had been warned by both Doctors Walter Tkach and William Lukash that pain in the abdominal area might indicate that the clot in his leg was moving toward his lungs— with potentially fatal consequences. At Tkach's urging, my father was examined by Dr. John Lungren, chief of staff at Long Beach Memorial Hospital, who had been caring for my parents off and on ever since first volunteering as a doctor on the campaign train in 1952. He discovered significant swelling in the left leg extending up to the thigh and recommended hospitalization. For two weeks, my father resisted while Mother seemed strangely unaware of the gravity of untreated phlebitis. During our frequent phone calls, she mentioned only once casually that my father had "the same problem" with his leg he had had in June. Jack Lungren finally prevailed and my father entered Memorial Hospital on September 23. Tests revealed a clot, which apparently had broken off in his left leg and traveled to a lung. Heparin treatment—a slow drip of anticoagulant to shrink the clot—was begun immediately. It was a torturous process. For five days, my father could not sleep because of the pain, the flashing light on the heparin apparatus, and its never-ending beep tone.

His only relief was Mother's visits. The Secret Service drove her the hour and fifteen minutes from San Clemente to Long Beach every day, usually arriving in time for supper. Most evenings my parents ate McDonald's hamburgers, and together they discovered the five o'clock reruns of the TV western *Bonanza*, which they were seeing for the first time.

On October 4, my father was allowed to come home. Awaiting him were a motorized hospital bed ordered by the doctors, long rest periods with his leg elevated, and a strict regimen of anticoagulant drugs. Awaiting him also were ugly news stories and cartoons that questioned whether his illness was a fabrication that had freed him from appearing at the Washington trial of his former aides Bob Haldeman, John Ehrlichman, and John Mitchell. The small, familiar cartoon figure of Puck the Penguin says sardonically, "Somebody tell him he has the wrong foot up."

Mother found it was almost more than she could bear to see her husband so changed physically and so discouraged. For two weeks, he spent most of the day in bed, permitted to come into the living room only at dinnertime, eating from a TV tray placed to the side of his elevated left leg. On October 23, Jack Lungren came to San Clemente to check on the leg. He was alarmed that despite the anticoagulant drugs there was a new swelling. Immediately, he made arrangements to readmit my father to Long Beach for more heparin treatments. On October 28, my father was still in the hospital when his doctors found a new, large clot higher in his left leg. They ordered emergency surgery for 5:30 the next morning. They had wanted, in fact, to operate immediately but did not feel that my father was strong enough physically to face the surgery without a night's rest. And too, there was the family to prepare. Mother had already returned for the night to San Clemente by the time the diagnosis was made. Jack Lungren reached her there. A few minutes later, he telephoned Tricia in New York and me in Washington. It was near midnight, Eastern time.

Bebe Rebozo and Bob Abplanalp were informed of the operation as well. Bob had a premonition that it would not go smoothly. At 3 A.M. he called, urging that I accept his offer to pick up Tricia and me at dawn and fly us to California in his airplane. I tried to explain to Bob that Mother, through Jack Lungren, had suggested that we wait a few days before we came West, believing that my father would most need our visit during the slow convalescence.

When my father was wheeled out of the recovery room at 7 A.M., Mother was waiting for him. She sat next to his bed, feeding him little chips of ice with a spoon. He kept whispering "water" and his eyelids fluttered uncontrollably. He was so deadly white that Mother began to feel uneasy. At 8 A.M. she telephoned first Tricia, and then me, asking us to come to California on the first convenient flight. She did not tell us that she was frightened, only that she now felt my father would want us to be there.

Only two hours later, while propped up on the edge of his bed, flanked by his navy corpsman, Bob Dunn, and a nurse, my father fainted suddenly and almost fell to the floor. Dunn and the nurse rolled him back onto the bed, the nurse slapping his face several times, urgently repeating, "Richard, wake up, Richard!" Later he would dimly remember her voice calling him by the name few but his mother ever used.

Two doors away, in a hospital bedroom where she waited with Rose Woods, Mother heard over the public-address system: "Emergency operating unit to seventh floor." There was only one patient on the new seventh floor—her husband. She immediately went down the corridor and saw six people around his bed with lifesaving equipment. There was nothing she could do. Stunned, she turned and walked back to her room.

For three desperate hours, while my father was unconscious and in cardio-vascular shock, the team of doctors tried to stabilize his blood pressure, which had dropped to sixty over zero because of unexpected, massive internal bleed-ing. At midpoint in the struggle, Jack Lungren came into Mother's room, squeezed her hand, and spoke the only truthful words of comfort he could muster. "Well, Pat, we're just doing all we can."

Half an hour before my flight landed in Los Angeles, a stewardess slipped into the seat next to me and said, "Julie, I'm so sorry." Bewildered, I asked, "What do you mean?" "Why, I thought you knew," she explained, "your father is in critical condition." She had heard the news about my father's sudden bleeding via the pilot's radio.

Helene and Jack Drown met my plane and drove me to the hospital. When Mother first saw me, for a moment her eyes glistened with tears, and then they were gone. She was composed as she described what had happened during the hours I was in the air, but she did not try to hide the gravity of my father's condition.

When Tricia arrived, Jack Lungren permitted us to go in to see my father "just for one minute." Through the maze of tubes in his throat and nose, and the wires attached to his chest, arms and legs, my father murmured, "You're here." And his fingers moved slightly, a bare whisper of a gesture of reaching toward Mother, Tricia, and me. Bebe and Bob Abplanalp arrived later that night, but Bob was too upset to go into the room even for the permitted one-minute visit.

For two days my father, only semiconscious, remained in mortal danger, and during that time Mother, Tricia, and I spent every waking hour at the hospital and the nights at the Drowns' home, since they lived only a half hour from Long Beach. Coincidentally, Gerald Ford was in Los Angeles on October 31 on a campaign trip on behalf of the 1974 Republican congressional can-didates. For twenty-four hours prior to his arrival in California, there was much speculation about whether or not he would visit my father. Some contended that the President would not jeopardize the congressional races by associating himself so vividly with Nixon and thus Watergate; others speculated that it would not be right if he failed to see an old friend fighting for his life.

At 10 P.M. on October 31, Ford telephoned Mother, not long after we had returned to the Drowns' for the night. Helene, Jack, Tricia, and I were with her in Jack's study and overheard her end of the conversation. We anticipated that the President would be relieved if the phone call could substitute for a visit, because less than one-half hour before, Dr. Lukash, who had stayed on as Ford's physician and was traveling with him on the visit to Los Angeles, had telephoned Mother to say that in addition to a very tight schedule, the presidential staff was concerned about "security problems." Mother simply had pointed out that the Secret Service was already protecting the hospital and, further, that her husband was the only patient in the brand-new wing of the seventh floor. When the President came on the telephone, he asked her, "Would a visit help?" Mother answered unhesitatingly, "I can't think of anything that would help Dick more."

The next morning at ten o'clock, President Ford walked into the room where we were waiting and embraced first Mother, then Tricia and me. Twenty feet away, Bob Dunn and two maintenance men worked feverishly, trying to open the door to my father's critical-care-unit room, which had locked accidentally just as the President was arriving at the hospital. For fifteen minutes they tried everything, even unscrewing the glass panels. Finally they had to saw through the bolted lock and remove the door entirely. All the while, my father faintly grinned at them. Two days before his operation, he had warned Dunn that the door locked. When the three men finally burst through the threshold, he said slowly and with great effort, but with an unmistakable teasing tone in his voice, "See, I told you the door didn't work."

While the President visited for a few minutes with my father, we tried to make small talk with Ford's chief aide, Bob Hartmann, whose bleary eyes bespoke the campaign pressures. As soon as the President left, we went into my father's room. He seemed overcome by Gerald Ford's gesture and was pensively quiet. For all of us it had been an emotionally difficult visit, an in-flesh confrontation with the realities of August.

The disastrous election results for Republicans four days later deeply depressed my father. Among the defeated were four members of the House Judiciary Committee who had voted against impeachment—Charles Sandman of New Jersey, David Dennis of Indiana, Wiley Mayne of Iowa, and Joseph Maraziti of New Jersey. In a normal atmosphere, they probably would have won re-election. As my parents looked around them, they saw many other innocent men whose lives were in disarray because of their association with or support of the Nixon Administration. In July, John Connally had been indicted at the instigation of the Watergate special prosecutor on charges of accepting two illegal $5,000 contributions from the Associated Milk Producers. The key witness against Connally was a highly questionable individual who had an indictment pending for misappropriating $825,000 from a San Antonio savings and loan association. Only because of the climate of the times was

Connally, a distinguished former secretary of the treasury, three-time governor of Texas, and secretary of the navy, even on trial, given the flimsiness of a case based on a dubious informant. He would be acquitted by a jury nine months later, but his chances for the Presidency in 1976 were over.

Perhaps the most thoroughly investigated figure during Watergate, other than the President himself, was Maurice Stans, who was pursued for almost three years by the Special Prosecutor's Office. At the end of Stans's nightmare, the Watergate Special Prosecutor's Office conceded that although it could find no significant conflict in anything Stans had told investigators, it would indict him unless he pled guilty to five technical, nonwillful violations. Stans thus became the first political fund raiser to be sentenced for the unintentional offense of neglect to report contributions that were sent back to the donors.

As the election receded, Mother, for once Pollyannaish, denied the severity of Watergate's effect on the results, but, despite her reassuring words, she and my father realized that he was the unspoken, and more often spoken, primary issue of the campaign. His supporters in the House were good men. They had not deserved to be part of the purge.

Before being discharged from the hospital on November 14, twelve pounds underweight, weak, and ill, my father made some decisions about his future. One of them was to sell the television rights to his memoirs to the British producer–TV personality David Frost. The Frost agreement, to be interviewed for twenty-six hours, with no say in the final editing to six and a half hours of TV viewing, was made because Frost's was the only bid received. My father was faced with the cold fact of mounting legal fees with no end in sight. Since becoming Vice President in 1953, he had never taken an honorarium from public speaking and to this day does not charge for speaking or transportation when he gives an address. Nor did he feel comfortable with the idea of being paid to serve on boards. His income, apart from a generous government pension, would have to come from his *Memoirs* and other books.

Frost would discover when he tried to market the interviews that none of the three networks or major advertising agencies would touch the project. Then, as Frost tried to obtain financing, *The New York Times* demanded in an editorial that Frost reveal the "personnel of the 'international consortium' that is to be Mr. Nixon's financial angel." With potential backers apparently intimidated by the *Times*'s editorial and the mood of the press in general to a project that would give Nixon a voice, Frost was forced to fly to London and arrange short-term money to cover his production expenses until he was able to put together a group of independent stations.

Christmas 1974 was the lowest point in my father's life. For Mother, it was the time to remain stoically strong, no matter what she felt inside. 'In the hospital she had sat by his bed hour after hour, not tiring him with much conversation, telling me later, "He liked to know I was there." Mother fully realized how feeble he was, and she was quite aware that it would be many weeks or months before he could begin to resume any kind of normal life.

Gardening became my Mother's salvation. Many days she worked side by side with our gardener seven hours or more. She greatly simplified the care of the acre and a half immediately around the house, removing the rose garden on the north side and replacing it with a colorful ground cover of purple gazanias and pink and white geraniums. That first year in San Clemente, Mother went through four pairs of heavy canvas garden gloves. Mother's gardening pleased my father. He told her again and again how beautiful everything looked. Her efforts were comforting to him in another sense as well. Several years later he told me about a scene he remembered vividly from a movie he saw when he was in college: a German woman in moments of great stress got down on her knees and scrubbed the floor. My father realized that for Mother the garden provided the same release.

But that Christmas there was no release for my father. His blood pressure was checked three times a day. Since he was bedridden, unable to walk more than a few yards at a time, memories were his most constant companion. Perhaps during that long winter he questioned whether he should have resigned earlier. As he began work on his *Memoirs*, he would describe John Foster Dulles as a man who "recognized the fundamental truth a public man must never forget—that he loses his usefulness when he, rather than his policy, becomes the issue. In this respect Foster Dulles was perhaps the most con-scientious public man I have ever known." It was a revealing and poignant comment.

The one point in the day during which my father seemed to be able to partially forget and to brighten slightly was dinnertime, when he and Mother ate from trays in front of a roaring fire in the living room. They enjoyed the scent of the eucalyptus-leaf kindling prepared by Manolo; the drama of the first high-leaping flames, then the steady, comforting burn; and finally, the red-hot stumps of logs that warmed my father, who always felt cold now because of his blood-thinning medicine and the damp sea air.

On Christmas Eve, Tricia and Ed, David and I linked arms with my parents in front of the tall, full pine Mother had decorated before our arrival. Manolo took a snapshot of us with a borrowed Instamatic. We are all smiling broadly, grateful to be together. But it was not a happy time. Suddenly my father was old and Mother was weighed down by many concerns. And, though we did not realize it fully then, each of us was concentrating on surviving each day, not on living.

I remember one particularly cold night shortly before New Year's. I was on my way over to my father's office to pick up a book. A Secret Service agent on temporary duty at San Clemente came out of the guard gazebo a few yards from our house. He said in a thick southern accent, "I just want you to tell your parents we care about them. All my friends back home feel the same way. It just isn't right the way you folks don't see anyone—are all holed up. It just isn't right."

With the new year, slowly yet unmistakably my father regained his health. As he felt better physically, he renewed some of his fighting spirit. In late February he began going to the office for several hours a day, and by March he could take a walk without his blood pressure rising sharply.

Both my parents had always lived self-regulated and disciplined lives, and in retirement, their routine was something to count on and a means to mark time. They awakened early in the morning, Mother often making herself lie in bed until her clock read six-thirty. My father was in his office by seven-thirty or eight. Mother put his old brown velvet chair, with the ottoman for his feet, in one corner. It had traveled far—from the New York apartment to the Lincoln Sitting Room at the White House and then to San Clemente. In that chair, my father began dictating his *Memoirs*. It was a time when perhaps the best therapy would have been concentrating on the future, but his self-appointed job was to analyze and record his past. Most of all he had to try to sort out the Watergate labyrinth of unanswered questions.

During that year of convalescence, Mother spoke to me often by telephone of her admiration for the way my father was weathering all that came, enduring even the humiliation of having to be examined by a team of three doctors dispatched by Judge Sirica from Washington with orders to determine whether he really was too ill to testify in court. He and Mother agonized as fifteen members of his White House staff and re-election committee began their prison terms. One morning, as my father breakfasted from a tray in the living room with his eyes on the sea below, Mother, her own despair near the surface, could not resist saying, "Dick, I don't know how you keep going." He answered, "I just get up in the morning to confound my enemies."

My father may well have asked Mother the same question: "How do you survive?" Tricia and I saw that they both survived because when my father felt defeated, Mother upheld him, and when she was spiritless, he rallied to comfort her. We never saw them give in to despair at the same time. It was a lesson of how two people can sustain each other in a marriage. The gestures were small—my mother leaving a fragrant gardenia from the bush by the front door on my father's pillow; he encouraging her to eat more at dinner, to try the "delicious squash from the garden"—and their efforts made the difference between a bleak existence and a better one.

The small triumphs of the day were discussed at dinnertime: Mother reporting the progress of weeding the circle in front of the house; my father with news of an exchange of letters with one of his favorite sports figures. The adventures of our three dogs were a major source of humor in conversation. Mother even relaxed her ironclad rule about dogs making themselves comfortable on living-room furniture.

When Louise and Roger Johnson spent a weekend at La Casa Pacifica in the late spring, Louise told me, "I felt a closeness between your parents, a camaraderie." Around four o'clock, my father came home from the office and the friends got ready for a swim, followed by cocktails and dinner on trays. Mother told Louise that their usual evening routine often did include a short swim, recommended by my father's doctors, but always early enough so that as they ate dinner they could see *Bonanza*.

Many old friends wanted to come to San Clemente to say hello. But because my father tired so easily, and because both he and Mother were too sapped by all that had happened to feel like entertaining, there were only a few guests in 1975. One of them was film star Jimmy Cagney. He had telephoned our mutual friend Paul Keyes and said, "You know, young fellow, I was driving back from San Diego and I drove by the dear man's house [La Casa Pacifica is directly off an exit of the San Diego freeway] and I thought it would be nice if I could go in and pay my respects. Do you think you could arrange it?" The three men had luncheon in the dining room, my father making a rare departure from his usual glass of skim milk, RyKrisp crackers, and cottage cheese with pineapple. He enjoyed beef Stroganoff with the others and served the last bottle of red wine given him by Winston Churchill in 1958. The men lingered long at the table, speaking of Churchill, Chou, Mao, and Brezhnev.

When it was time to leave, my father escorted his friends to the door. Cagney stood at ramrod attention and, as he vigorously shook my father's hand, spoke his mind: "Well, Mr. President, thanks to you there are no American boys dying anywhere in the world. There are no American boys fighting anywhere. Thanks to you, we are talking to China and we have an understanding with Russia."

Paul Keyes listened to Cagney and then heard what my father said in response. Those words seemed to Paul a better explanation of what Watergate was all about than any others: "Yes, Jimmy," my father said, "we did all the big things right and we screwed up the goddamned little things."

With the end of public life, my mother relished her newly gained freedom. She did not feel she ever had to give another press interview—and to this day she has not. Although she could not maintain close ties with all her White House associates, she spoke frequently by telephone to Lucy Winchester, and to Gwen King, who had done so much to help her communicate with the public who wrote her. Gwen, in fact, was one of the few staff members Mother contacted in the immediate aftermath of the resignation. Four days after my parents arrived in San Clemente, Mother had called Gwen to make sure she received all her messages.

A year later, Gwen visited San Clemente. Mother picked her up at the airport in San Diego, and that evening they sat at the dining-room table with my father and talked until after 10 P.M. It was windy during the night, and by morning dozens of palm fronds littered the roof and ground. Mother enlisted Gwen in helping her gather them, even sending her friend up to the roof, teasing "because you're the lightest," to throw the branches down.

Helene Drown was Mother's most frequent overnight guest, and once my father was feeling better, Jack Drown would accompany her to San Clemente to watch televised football or baseball games with him while the ladies played gin rummy for a penny a point. Mother enjoyed spending a day or two at the Drowns' as well. During one of Helene's visits to San Clemente, she and Mother decided to drive to Tijuana, just across the Mexican border. Perhaps because no one expected to see the former First Lady in town that day, she was unrecognized. Uninhibited, the two went into dozens of shops, each of which claimed to have a better bargain than the preceding. Before going home, they posed Tijuana-tourist-style in a donkey cart, Helene wearing a sombrero reading "I love" to complement my mother's "Mexico."

At the end of May 1975, Mother went "home" to Artesia, now known as Cerritos, for the dedication of the Patricia Nixon Elementary School. I was mystified why, after refusing hundreds of invitations, she had agreed to the one in Cerritos. Her life there was a distant memory, and I knew she had little sentimental feeling about it, especially since the town was no longer the farming community of her youth. When I asked her about her decision, she explained how my father had pleaded, "You just have to go, Pat." She told me, "I went for him."

In her remarks that day to the schoolchildren and to the old and new residents, she said, "I'm proud to have the school carry my name. I always thought that only those who have gone had schools named after them. I am happy to tell you," she smiled, "that I'm not gone—I mean not really gone."

In our apartment in Washington, David and I heard her comments as we watched a short news clip about the dedication. When we turned the television off, David told me that he thought he understood what Mother was saying. The resignation in many ways was like a death or an assassination. One got the feeling that everyone had died and been carried away. But Mother was asserting, in essence, that her life, and my father's, had not ended.

For Pat Nixon, the day in Cerritos was a rare excursion from her carefully controlled private world in San Clemente and, in fact, her only solo public appearance in the five and a half years in California. Her chosen world was creating a home. She took pride in making each room pleasing to the eye, placing small arrangements of cut flowers mixed with wild flowers throughout the house. She delighted in experimenting with the seasonal blooms, occasionally even using unusual weeds in her arrangements. Artichoke stalks gone to seed made a dramatically beautiful dining-table centerpiece, and partially opened azaleas and geraniums looked like rosebuds.

When she was not gardening, she was reading, averaging five books a week. She read current fiction, biography, and, when she ran out of new material, reread Jane Austen, Ernest Hemingway, Thomas Wolfe, Somerset Maugham, Pearl Buck, and others. Her favorite books were the historical novels by the prolific writer Taylor Caldwell, who crammed her stories with rich details on the eras she wrote about, be they Biblical times, ancient Greece, or nineteenth-century America. What my mother found intriguing was that Taylor Caldwell believed in international plots, and to this day my mother's perception of Watergate is that it was partly an international scheme, or, at the very least, that double agents were involved. Like many others, she had questioned from the beginning the suspicious circumstances surrounding the apprehension of the burglars. Was it a setup? Was the CIA involved? How deeply was Howard Hughes or his organization involved?

Mother sought out Taylor Caldwell's novels primarily because they were wonderful avenues of escape from the inevitable discussions of "what might have been," which even the most well-meaning friends could not resist. She, and my father as well, avoided reading any of the books on the Nixon years, favorable or unfavorable. Increasingly, Pat Nixon was becoming a solitary person, happy with her individual pursuits and her private world of family and home.

Yet, always intruding into the life she created at San Clemente was the reality of the larger existence outside—politics, world affairs, and, everlastingly, Watergate. In April 1975, both she and my father were very depressed by the news of the fall of South Vietnam. Ever since Congress had reduced by one-half military and economic aid to South Vietnam in 1974 and cut it another third in 1975, the South had no chance of surviving a Soviet-supplied invasion from the North. The War Powers Resolution passed in November 1973 effectively denied the President the ability to enforce the Paris agreements, and Ford was powerless when the North poured more than 100,000 troops into the South and the U.S.S.R. stepped up its delivery of weapons and supplies. "When that happened," my father wrote later, "Vietnam finally fell to the same kind of large-scale conventional assault we successfully repelled in Korea."

Twenty million Vietnamese were now consigned to the fate of submitting to Communist rule, losing their lives, or trying to escape. Today we know that since the Thieu government fell, the Communists have killed more than 500,000 Vietnamese. Another million, the courageous "boat people," risked their lives to flee, and it is estimated that half of them, perhaps as many as 600,000, were drowned at sea.

Two months after the fall of Vietnam, my father testified in his office for two days before a special grand jury. Most of the questions were about Bebe Rebozo and campaign contributions. I called Mother a few weeks before the testimony, during the time my father was under intense pressure as he prepared to answer questions about numerous events three years before, and asked her when she was going to use the airplane ticket to Washington I had sent her as a Mother's Day gift. She answered, "Why don't you come out here?" When I explained that I did not want to leave home while David was cramming for second-year law school exams, she rejoined with a rare and heartbreaking comment that revealed the despair she felt that Watergate would never be behind them: "You have only one person to take care of there but two broken people here."

"A Shoulder to Everyone—But Whose Shoulder Does She Lean On?"

My parents' inaccessibility to the public in the months following the resignation only heightened the extraordinary curiosity about the Nixons. When they left in February 1976 on their first extended trip since the Presidency, an unofficial eight-day visit to the People's Republic of China at the invitation of Mao Tse-tung, two dozen American journalists followed them every step of the way. But the constant press scrutiny marred Mother's enjoyment at seeing China for the second time, as did the stories published back in the United States that speculated the Nixon visit had been timed to hurt Ford in his February 24 New Hampshire presidential primary battle against challenger Ronald Reagan. Actually, my parents undertook the trip in order to be in China on the anniversary of their historic visit in 1972.

The growing fund of knowledge that spring about "abuses" by others than Nixon, and especially the Senate Intelligence Committee's report several months before the trip to China, which revealed the misuse of the CIA and the FBI under all Presidents since Franklin Delano Roosevelt, prompted outspoken Washington *Post* columnist Nicholas von Hoffman (who twelve days before the resignation had declared, "The President is like a dead mouse on the American family kitchen floor . . . we've got to get that decomposing political corpse out of the White House . . .") to comment:

In the months since his departure, his [Nixon's] defense looks better and better. Half a dozen Congressional committees have brought forth columns of information all adducing that the break-ins, the tapping, snooping, and harassment have been routine government activities for a generation at least.

Von Hoffman also wrote: "These past three years, Nixon has had a worse press than Stalin at the height of the Cold War. The only name for it is hysterical contagion . . . to the very end, Nixon contended that he conducted the office in much the same fashion as his predecessors, and he was right."

The greatest cover-up of all in the opinion of William Safire in his *New York Times* column was

. . . the suppression of the truth about Democratic precedents to Watergate . . . the reason for the deliberate suppression of evidence in 1974, for the lackadaisical reportage then of what we see now, was the fear that a false claim that "everybody did it" might make it impossible to hound Mr. Nixon out of office . . . And as each new abuse of power finally dribbles out we can ask ourselves: "Why now?" "Why not two years ago?"

When the Senate Intelligence Committee was formed in 1975, Senator Frank Church had stated that "the American people are entitled to know what their government has done—the good and the bad, the right and the wrong." But by early summer 1975, he had decided not to hold open hearings on the CIA's involvement in plots to assassinate foreign leaders, claiming that he did not want to "hold up the whole sordid story and telecast it to every corner of the world." A preliminary look at the files had revealed that government plotting against foreign leaders had peaked dramatically not under Nixon or Johnson, but Kennedy.

Also making news was Washington *Post* editor Benjamin Bradlee's admiring memoir of his friend John Kennedy, in which he told of a telephone call from Mayor Richard Daley of Chicago to Kennedy on election night, 1960: "Mr. President . . . with a little bit of luck and the help of a few close friends, you're going to carry Illinois." As William Buckley pointed out in a column on Bradlee's book: "Nixon's close friends went to jail. Kennedy's keep getting re-elected mayor of Chicago."

When I spoke to my mother by telephone about the Buckley column and others in which the political double standard was revealed, she told me, her voice a hollow monotone, that she frankly did not have the heart to read them. "What's the use? It isn't going to change anything." Indeed, as the conservative journalists got in their licks, their liberal counterparts seemed determined to portray Nixon in the last months of his Administration as neurotic and capable of every conceivable abuse of political power. Wide coverage was given to Henry Kissinger's remarks at a dinner party in Canada in October when he told his table partner, not realizing that a microphone was recording his words, that my father was "a very old man."

Throughout the Presidency, Mother had always liked and respected Kissinger, and he was extremely cordial to her, but she was guarded when around him. She had no illusions that the Nixon-Kissinger relationship was anything more than a marriage of convenience. They hailed from different perspectives; Kissinger had been a Humphrey supporter and was a longtime associate of Nelson Rockefeller. It was the crisis of the war in Vietnam that had brought Nixon and Kissinger together. Mother had known all along the day would come when the two men would go their separate ways, and the parting was public now.

At the turn of the year came the release of the highly successful film *All the President's Men,* based on the book by Carl Bernstein and Bob Woodward, who had broken the Watergate story. By 1976, the two were at the forefront of a new breed of writers who do not hesitate to wed fact with rumor. With the publication of their second book, *The Final Days,* about the last months of the Nixon White House, Woodward and Bernstein created a sensation by implying that my father had been dangerously unbalanced. Dozens of people had their minds read, usually without the benefit of quotation marks. The authors claimed to have interviewed 394 people, yet did not name them. They claimed every story in their book was true because nothing was included unless confirmed by two or more sources. What this means, in the words of Ray Price, is that "if two people have heard the same rumor, [the writers] weave a story around it, wrap it in manufactured detail and sprinkle it with quotation marks, and present the story as fact." John Osborne, known by readers of the *New Republic* as an unbending critic of the Nixon Administration, declared the book to be "on the whole the worst job of nationally noted reporting that I've observed during forty-nine years in the business."

The authors purported to have the inside story on Mrs. Nixon as well as the President, writing that she "was becoming more and more reclusive and drinking heavily." For Mother, the most unbearable part of the book was the analysis of her marriage as loveless. When excerpts from the book were first published, David, the only member of the family who agreed to be interviewed by one of the authors, was questioned by the Washington *Post* about some of his comments. Unfortunately, the *Post* so distorted his response that he felt compelled to issue a public statement a few days later.

One week ago a reporter of *The Washington Post* asked me to respond to portions of *The Final Days* which indicate the Nixon marriage had been unhappy and so on. I denied that the Nixon marriage was unhappy and added that such was a general characterization of that relationship which would require forty-five minutes to rebut, forty-five minutes the reporter and I did not have. The

Saturday *Post* carried my reaction as stating the unhappy marriage portion of *The Final Days* was indeed "a general characterization" of the Nixon marriage. The reporter had begun the conversation by telling me how much pride he takes in quoting people accurately.

The Nixon family is a close family. The love and respect of each for all is a beautiful thing. Beating the bushes for evidence to the contrary may conform with a pre-disposed conclusion about Mr. Nixon and his "inhumanity" but in my view it is the lowest aspect of this obsessional hatred for Mr. Nixon and is inexcusable.

Unfortunately, apart from an article in *U.S. News & World Report*, David's protest was barely noted. Nationwide, AP and UPI ran small items but failed to quote the key paragraphs printed above.

For three months, from April through June, the publicity blitz on the book was staggering. The Book-of-the-Month Club made *The Final Days* its main selection; *Newsweek* magazine, owned by the two journalists' employer, the Washington *Post*, ran two lengthy installments, the first time the magazine had ever published excerpts from a book; *Saturday Night Live*, a popular late-night television program, portrayed my mother as a drunken slob.

My father's cousin Jessamyn West was also on a book tour in late May and wrote me of her distress about *The Final Days*: "I suppose, or at least I hope, that long experience in political life has somewhat armored Richard and Pat for this really obscene attack of the last few months." But in reality, it was a time of inward rage for my family. As my parents had learned during the fund crisis in 1952, the chances of proving malice in a libel suit are slim at best. In 1976 there was a further consideration against legal action: their ability to withstand—emotionally and physically—the long months of a public trial.

At the end of June, David, who had just graduated from George Washington University Law School, and I arrived at San Clemente for a month's visit. On July 3 we attended a Bicentennial party organized in my parents' honor by some of the men and women who had supported them since 1946. The party in Newport Beach was their first formal public event together since China. My parents stayed late greeting old friends and signing autographs and did not arrive home until 1 A.M.

Three days later, on July 7, my mother suffered a stroke. It had been a traumatic day. In the morning she had read part of *The Final Days*, which, despite my father's protests, she had finally borrowed from one of the secretaries in his office. Even as she read, uppermost in her mind was the news he had shared with her just before leaving for work at 8 A.M.: that the next day the big story would be of his disbarment from the practice of law. Despite all my father's efforts in the previous months to have his resignation accepted, the New York State Bar had gone ahead with a full and expensive disbarment proceeding, presumably in the hope of humiliating the former President.

Since Manolo and Fina Sanchez were in Spain on a month's vacation, my mother had spent most of the afternoon housecleaning. When she sat down on a chaise longue on the patio around four o'clock, the late-afternoon sun was warm and soothing to her face. But the rest of her body felt heavy and spent. She was so exhausted she did not think she could ever get up again. Shortly before five o'clock, however, she forced herself up from the chaise, and, stumbling slightly as she walked, managed to get to her room, undress, and change for a predinner swim with my father, David, and me. She spent most of the time on the steps in the shallow end, but since she occasionally did that, we noticed nothing out of the ordinary. During dinner, she said little and ate only a few bites of the meal I had prepared and then went to her bedroom.

She remembers that she could hardly walk. But she had no idea that she was having a stroke, nor did any of us guess that something was wrong. When I went to her room an hour later to see if she wanted to watch the televised White House dinner in honor of Queen Elizabeth, she was lying on her bed, fully clothed, sound asleep. I thought it was odd, but the room was dark and I assumed that she had simply been extremely tired and would undress later.

In the middle of the night, Mother woke up and felt she should wash her hair, as we were planning to have dinner with Charles and Connie Stuart, her former staff director, at a restaurant the next day. But she found she was so fatigued she could barely move. She managed to get her nightgown on and fell back into bed. In the morning, shortly before seven o'clock, Mother went out to the kitchen to get my father's coffee ready. She had trouble with her left hand when she tried to open a new can of coffee, and when my father came in a few minutes later, he found her struggling with the top of his grapefruit juice bottle.

He noticed immediately that the left corner of her mouth was drooping and that her speech was slightly slurred. He guessed then that she had had a stroke. Not wanting to frighten her, he said nothing. Quickly, he drank his juice and a few sips of coffee, and then told Mother he was going over to the office.

Instead, he rapidly walked through the inner courtyard and knocked on my bedroom door, calling, "Julie, Julie." His voice was so low that David did not awaken, but I could tell by the tone that something was wrong. I opened the door and he beckoned for me to follow him down the corridor toward the front door. As we rapidly walked along, he said, "I think your mommy's had a stroke." It was 7:30 A.M.

He asked me to go into the kitchen and try to convince Mother that the weakness she felt in her left side was not normal and that she should get into bed. By eight-ten, he was able to reach Jack Lungren, describe the symptoms, and, at Lungren's request, call for a doctor from nearby Camp Pendleton. Despite Mother's objections, the chief of medicine from Pendleton examined her at ten and told her that she had had a "tiny stroke." Then the doctor and I went outside into the courtyard for a private conversation. He stated that Mother would need to be hospitalized in order to determine how much damage she had suffered from the stroke and, more important, to observe her in the next crucial twenty-four hours as the stroke ran its course. As we stood on the patio talking, the sun was already hot and brilliant. Next to us the sound of the soft splash of water from the fountain of Mexican tiles was soothing; birds and butterflies darted among hanging baskets and beds of flowers. It was beautiful and unreal. A few feet away, Mother lay in a shuttered, dark room while David tried to talk lightheartedly to her about anything but illness.

Fifteen minutes later, after a conversation in his office with the doctor, my father ordered an ambulance and came over to the house to tell Mother gently but firmly that they would be going to the hospital. She protested, claiming that she was just tired and that all she needed was rest. But, despite the brave words, she was frightened. When the Camp Pendleton doctor took her blood pressure it was markedly elevated—175 over 110.

Mother herself packed a small suitcase, and when the ambulance arrived for the trip to Long Beach Memorial Hospital, she climbed independently onto the stretcher table in the van. My father and I rode with her the forty dreary miles of freeway that stretches between San Clemente and Long Beach, the same trip she had made so many times almost two years ago to visit him. The spires of taco and burger stands and the gas station signs loomed above the stretches of tract housing. Mother kept her eyes closed throughout most of the trip. There was very little conversation. Each of us was wrapped in his own thoughts, including Secret Service agent Bill Hudson, who sat in the front seat next to the ambulance driver. Just as all of Mother's friends would feel as soon as they heard the news, Bill was stunned by what had happened.

Tricia, with her little gray poodle, Pooh, under her arm, was in the air en route to California from New York within an hour and fifteen minutes of hearing from my father that Mother had had a stroke. When she landed in Los Angeles, she saw a large headline, "Pat Stricken." To see the words in print was a shock to her. It was just as well that she had not heard the statement of Mother's neurologist, Dr. John Mosier, who told the press that evening that Mrs. Nixon's stroke was only 35 to 50 percent completed. "I think she will walk," Mosier said. "She may not walk normally. If the stroke doesn't get any worse, she's not going to die. If it gets worse, well, people do die from strokes."

Mother was sitting up when Tricia entered the room. One of her eyes was open, the other shut. Slurring her words, she told her daughter, "Oh, Dolly, what a pretty dress." When Tricia bent to kiss her, Mother apologized that she could not hug her in return because her left side was not functioning.

Tricia blurted out, "I'm so sorry you had to have the spinal tap," the culmination of three hours of tests she had just undergone. Mother answered Tricia, for once not belittling pain, "Oh, honey, it really did hurt."

Tricia and I spent the night at the Drowns' in order to be closer to the hospital. When Tricia remarked to Helene, "Mother doesn't seem depressed," Helene responded truthfully, "Of course she's depressed." She had seen the head nurse of intensive care, the vibrant, confident woman who had cared for my father twenty months before, go into Mother's room, and heard Mother say slurringly, "Connie, I'm beat. I'm through." But to my father, to Tricia and to me, and even to Helene, she was magnificently brave.

At San Clemente that night, Diane Sawyer, who was part of a research team of three assisting my father with his *Memoirs*, stayed late to answer the telephones. On her list of callers, which included Bebe Rebozo, Ambassador Huang-Chen of the People's Republic of China's Liaison Office, Dr. Henry Kissinger, and John B. Connally, there was the name Clark Wanger. Next to his name, Diane had recorded:

> Just a private citizen. Spent entire evening trying to get a number to call, finally did at two A.M. EST. Sent a wire, too, but felt somehow that wasn't enough to express how he and his family feel. They are simply part of what RN used to call the silent majority. The people still out there who believe in him, still do. Wanted to wish speedy recovery. Wants nothing in return... said "this will mean nothing to RN, but I just want him to know that there are so many who are sorry, so many who love..."

In the next week an average of six thousand messages and fifty bouquets of flowers arrived daily at the hospital. Despite the shock and all-encompassing fatigue of the stroke, Mother checked each day to see if the flowers had been distributed to other patients and the hospital staff. Thousands of more letters and telegrams were sent to San Clemente. In the end, more than a quarter of a million pieces of mail were received.

Those first weeks my father was numb. I doubt he was even aware—or refused to recognize—the magnitude of what had happened. He concentrated on things: the mail, the telegrams, the flowers, the news reports, what Mother needed at the hospital, and what Tricia and I were eating and whether or not we were getting enough sleep.

From the very first day he established a ritual for his daily morning visit with Mother: he would come into her room very upbeat, kiss her on the cheek, and then say immediately, "Well, let me feel your grip." Mother, who could barely lift her hand from where it lay inert, a heavy weight by her body, each day gritted her teeth and tried determinedly to grasp his fingers, and each day she grew stronger.

Then he would sit in a chair by her bed and read some of the telegrams, letters, and editorials he had selected to bring with him that day. One of the wires he read was from New York City's Taxi Drivers Local Union No. 3036: "You can't keep a good woman down. Best wishes for a speedy and complete recovery. We all love you dearly. Please get well quickly." The Young Democrats of Rock Island County (Illinois) wired: "May the charm and grace you showed us as First Lady return very soon as we take this moment to offer our prayers and best wishes. Our best regards to President Nixon and your family as well."

Mother listened to the messages we read her but most of them washed over her. Even after fifteen minutes of visiting, we could tell she was exhausted. But when she was home and had a chance to reread some of the letters and editorials, I am sure that the outpouring of concern from so many she had never met strengthened her in her determination to get well.

It took character to fight back from the physical and emotional devastation of the stroke. Her therapy exercises were her own private battle. She wanted no sympathy and no witnesses to the struggle, not even Tricia and me, until she sensed how desperately we needed to see her progress. So she would do the steeple for us—the laborious process of joining the stricken fingers of her left hand with those of her right. At the end, her forehead would be dotted with perspiration. She told us later that another exercise, climbing the three steps in the therapy room, was "the hardest thing I have ever done physically."

At her own request, she saw few visitors. Jack and Helene Drown came, as did their daughter Maureen. One morning she asked me if her Secret Service agent Bill Hudson was on duty, and he stopped by the room for a few minutes. Tom Ryan came; Tom's visit, which Tricia and I had surprised Mother with, was difficult for her because it meant so much. When he walked in, the first words he spoke in his slow, soft voice were "Hi, Babe." Throughout the short visit, he stood at the foot of the bed and reassuringly from time to time squeezed his sister's toes beneath the white bed sheet. Neither said much, and Mother's emotions were very close to the surface.

Through sheer grit, she made rapid progress during her two-week hospitalization. She pushed herself. On July 13, only six days after the stroke, my father arranged an "All Star" baseball picnic in order to watch the American League battle the National League in their annual game. Diane Sawyer and Frank Gannon, the latter my father's chief assistant on his *Memoirs*, prepared a hollowed-out watermelon filled with my mother's favorite fruits to go with the fried chicken we brought from home. The television was set up in the therapy room, and Mother, leaning heavily on my father, walked unsteadily and slowly the few feet from her room in order to join us. By the time she reached her chair, she was panting. But she sat there, fatigue on her face, her neck slack—and as proud as she could be that she had made it to the All Star party.

Jack Drown, who joined us for the party, David, and my father were yelling uninhibitedly when Dr. Lungren came into the room on his evening rounds. He was not happy with the sight of his patient at the All Star picnic, but he grinned as he said, "This is insanity. I can't believe this. When are you going to get back into bed?" Mother was all smiles.

After Mother's release from the hospital, in some ways the months recuperating at home were harder than the two weeks at Long Beach. The stroke had been a blow, one that neither she nor any of us could quite believe. Only seven months before, at Christmastime, her blood pressure had been normal when it was taken during one of my father's daily checks. Since Bebe Rebozo, who had a history of high blood pressure, was visiting, my father teasingly suggested a contest between him and Mother, knowing that Bebe would lose. He did lose that morning, since Mother's blood pressure had registered a normal 140 over 82.

Yet sometime during the succeeding months, her blood pressure skyrocketed. Few human beings could have withstood almost two years of harassment, culminating in the publication of *The Final Days*, which my father would publicly pinpoint as the precipitator of the stroke. Mother's doctors, in response to reporters' questions about the possible causes of the stroke, had stated that stress could well have been a contributing factor. Too, there was much truth in what David told an interviewer in 1973: "I . . . worry about her because she never lets any of us know what troubles her. She is a shoulder to everyone—but whose shoulder does she lean on?"

When Mother came home, her greatest fear was that she would be a burden. A private, twenty-four-hour nurse was hired for the first weeks, because she did not want Tricia and me to have the responsibility of caring for her. When we both returned East in mid-August, Mother faced long months of convalescence. Inevitably there were many hours for introspection. My mother blamed no one but herself for the stroke, telling me, "I'm so angry with myself—getting ill." Not once did she question "Why did this happen to me?" But during a visit with her in October, three and a half months after she was stricken, she also admitted that she was discouraged that her recovery was slower than she wished. We were walking the two hundred yards from our house to the gateway of the Coast Guard grounds where I was going to spend the afternoon in my father's office working on *Special People*, a book of profiles of six public people. We stopped at the turnoff point where I would head to the office and Mother return home. When I suggested that she come with me to say hello to the dozen or so volunteers who came daily to open the mounds of mail that had arrived for her, she answered that she just did not have the energy to see people or to do things: "I've had it. I'm beat."

It was a nightmare for me to hear those words, which I knew she had spoken only once before, to her nurse on the day after the stroke. I realized that just moving was an effort and that the clumsiness of her slight limp was debilitating and disheartening. I knew also that most stroke patients do go through a period of depression. But I was upset because I felt there was more behind those words—a feeling of being battered, and of questioning whether or not she would ever be healed.

A few days later, as we sat together on the patio, side by side on chaise longues, she told me more about how she felt. My father was a few feet away in the living room, separated from us by glass double doors, watching a sports program on television. Through these many months she had remained fiercely protective of him, rejecting all criticism, even from old friend Ray Price, who wrote in *With Nixon* that my father had a light side and a dark side. As she spoke, Mother turned her face toward my father, her eyes on the back of his head. "Watergate is the only crisis that ever got me down. I guess it did because every day there were more ugly stories and there still are. It is just constant. And I know I will never live to see the vindication."

She paused and then said, "The thing that's so sad is that I don't think there's a man living who has more noble qualities, who is as kind and thoughtful and unselfish. He's always thinking about the country and not himself. Well, there just isn't anything small about him in any way."

Mother had not yet been released from the hospital when the Democrats held their 1976 presidential convention in New York. The men they nominated were the former governor of Georgia, Jimmy Carter, and as his running mate, Senator Walter Mondale of Minnesota. Carter announced publicly that he would not make an issue of Watergate, but Mondale's convention speech was a scathing attack on Ford's pardon of my father.

When the Republicans met a month later in Kansas City, Watergate was also an issue, albeit a silent one. My father had quietly informed Mary Louise Smith, the national chairwoman, that he would not be attending the convention. But some Republicans and most in the news media proceeded to make an issue out of the fact that he was not there. The only reference to him in the platform—a tribute to his China policy—was removed in committee. Ford ran a campaign in which he carefully referred to his record of two years of achievement. The previous five and a half Nixon years were taboo. Ironically, by dissociating himself so carefully from the Nixon record on foreign and domestic policy, Ford seemed only to heighten the significance of Watergate. When he was narrowly defeated by Carter in November, my father felt a sadness, and, as he told me in 1979, "a great sense of responsibility for Ford's loss."

With the new Administration, Nixon was less the issue. He was still a major news item, however. When a Dr. Abrahamsen, a Manhattan psychiatrist who had never met my father, wrote a psychohistory in which he concluded that in Richard Nixon's diligent mashing of potatoes for his mother, "the extent and intensity of this activity might suggest that this potato mashing was a form of aggression against an inanimate object which was a substitute for people," the book was widely quoted and discussed. More outrageous was a New York *Post* columnist's report on an alleged scene in the yet unpublished memoirs of Bob Haldeman: Richard Nixon in the Oval Office stripping off his clothes, sitting down naked behind his desk, and asking Haldeman, "Now what's on the agenda?" Although Haldeman called reporters from Lompoc Prison, where he was serving eighteen months for his part in Watergate, to tell them the story was totally false, it became an immediate national sensation and remained the subject of jokes.

One of the greatest difficulties of the postresignation years for my parents and those who shared their life in San Clemente was that it was futile to try to answer all the erroneous stories and charges. My father's office policy became and has remained one of "no response" to almost all press inquiries. But on rare occasions, incensed staff members were able to convince my father to permit a reply, as when his chief aide, Jack Brennan, wrote a "Letter to the Editor" of *U.S. News & World Report* denying the relatively insignificant item that the Nixon office, using taxpayers' money, had bought five color televisions in 1978.

Loie Grant, who has been a friend of the family since 1950, when she first worked for my father, and who along with Jack Brennan ran the retirement office, helped my parents through the upheavals of the postresignation years. When bad news came, she was always a calming, reassuring presence, carrying on as if nothing had happened. Yet, whenever I looked closely at her face, I could always detect any pain, for she loved my parents as if they were her own family, and when they felt distress, it was in her eyes as well.

One day in Loie's office, I noticed a five-by-seven-inch note card tacked to a shelf above her cluttered desk. On the card in her handwriting was a verse from "The Ballad of Sir Andrew Barton":

"I am hurt,"
Sir Andrew Barton said.
"I am hurt but I am
Not slain!
I will lie me down and
Bleed awhile—
Then I'll rise and
Fight again!"

CHAPTER 30

"Onward and Upward"

My mother had a phrase that she used countless times to end conversations with her White House staff members throughout my father's Presidency: "Onward and upward." She continued to repeat the phrase whenever former staff people called her in San Clemente, always speaking the words with spirit, sometimes with a laugh in her voice, sometimes a more wry tone, and occasionally a touch of defiance.

As in the White House, the light, cheerful sound of music came from Mother's room at La Casa Pacifica most hours of the day. She told me once that she wondered what she would do if she did not have her radio. Music transported her to another world, the world of the composer, which she told Jessamyn West in a 1970 interview was the career she would choose if she had her life to live over again.

When the students of the Patricia Nixon Elementary School in Cerritos returned to classes for the school year 1977–1978, they found a surprise awaiting them: a wishing well made of hand-painted tiles. Six months before, when my father had suggested to Mother that they give the school a gift, she immediately thought of a wishing well. On one side of the brightly colored well is a small plaque that states, "May all your good wishes come true." For, despite all the blows of life, Patricia Nixon is still a romantic and a dreamer of dreams.

Before Christmas, one of those dreams—a grandchild someday—came true. David and I learned that our first child would be born in August. When I lightheartedly asked my mother what she would like the baby to call her, she answered quickly, "Pat... then it won't make me feel so old."

Gradually, Mother was growing stronger, her footing more sure as she walked. Apart from a slight limp, my father, Tricia, and I could detect only one major sign of her illness, something that she could not conceal, the daily blood pressure readings. When something stressful happened, her blood pressure zoomed. What we did not realize was that she suffered numbing, demonic pain in her left hand and shoulder. Because she thought the pain was arthritic and therefore could not be helped, she mentioned the discomfort only a few times in passing. The cause of the pain was inadequate therapy, and as Mother's muscles atrophied, her joints grew stiffer and stiffer. Finally, she could no longer zip or button her clothes or pick up small items with her left hand. Not until she had another checkup and began a new program of therapy, primarily turning a large wheel that was set up in the inner courtyard of the house, did she begin to get relief. And it was only then that she admitted that many nights she had been unable to sleep because of pain.

She was well enough that summer of 1978 to attend two parties at La Casa Pacifica, one a fund raiser for Orange County Republicans at which longtime friend John Wayne bent low over her outstretched hand and, in a courtly gesture, kissed it. He told reporters afterward: "I was with the ex-President when he was a winner, and a loser, and a winner again." The other party marked the publication of my father's *Memoirs*. When he gave Mother, Tricia, and me the first three copies of the book, having had them specially shipped from the plant in Chicago, he urged us to start at the beginning and read through to the end. He realized, of course, that the temptation would be to start at the Watergate section. In fact, Mother did go to Watergate the first day. But when I saw her the next morning, she admitted she was back at the beginning of the book because she felt sick after seeing how much, at least a fourth of the 1,090 pages, had been devoted to Watergate. She told me, "He'll never get any credit for anything he says on the subject anyway. I wanted him to just state frankly that he didn't know, that no one knows, the full story of Watergate."

On August 15, Jennie Elizabeth Eisenhower was born at San Clemente General Hospital. Mother told me that she cried when she read the two-page handwritten letter my father wrote the day after his first grandchild arrived. In part he said:

In the years ahead you will have many happy moments. But in life you must expect some disappointments and sadness. At such times you will always be sustained by the fact that so many people love you very much... We all look forward to the excitement of watching you grow up into a lovely young lady.

Your Great Grandfather, President Eisenhower, had the great gift of being able to light up a room with his smile. My fondest wish, which I know will come true, is that you will have that same gift.

Whatever you do, wherever you go, and whatever you become, we shall always be proud of you—RN

One of the four bedrooms at San Clemente was transformed. The honey-colored crib that Helene Drown had used thirty-five years before for her first child was placed in one corner; a baby buggy stood against the wall by the door; and a changing table and diaper pail were put in the dressing alcove: Jennie's room.

When David and I left Jennie overnight with "Ma" and "Ba" for the first time, there was a small skirmish over whose room she would sleep in. My father, with a straight face, offered, "Pat, you take King and I'll take Jennie." Mother just laughed; some bargain. The setter, then nine years old, had to get up twice at night, whereas Jennie slept through until 6 A.M. For Mother, caring for the big, lumbering red setter was almost like having another child on her hands, particularly after Manolo and Fina Sanchez retired and returned to live in Spain shortly after Jennie's birth.

Among the visitors as 1979 began were Rose Mary Woods and Clare Boothe Luce. Later, Mrs. Luce told me that when Mother brought her a breakfast tray she complimented her that she could detect no visible signs of the stroke. The intensity of Mother's response surprised her: "Yes, but I *did* have a stroke. You don't know the struggle I had getting back the use of this hand. I couldn't put blocks into square holes or do any of the other simple exercises. I began to feel I was a baby all over again, and then I knew that unless I had the will to conquer this thing I would never get the full use again."

The struggle to recover from the stroke was worth it if for no other reason than to be able to lift her grandchildren. On March 14, two days before Mother's sixty-seventh birthday, Christopher Nixon Cox was born at New York Hospital. Mother had flown to New York to keep Tricia company that last week before the baby was due. She and Ed's mother waited together in the hospital during the cesarean delivery. Around 3 A.M., Anne Cox said, "Pat, I think that baby's about to be born." They took the elevator to the floor above, and when they stepped off, they heard the first cries of their grandson. When Christopher was christened a few months later, and friends of the family gathered at Tricia's apartment for the occasion, Mother would tell Adele Rogers not once but twice, "This is what life is all about, children and grandchildren, isn't it, Adele?"

In February 1980, Mother's desire to see all her grandchildren more often became a reality. On the ninth of that month, five and a half years to the day since my parents left the White House and arrived in San Clemente, they moved back East. Their eagerness to be near their children and grandchildren—David and I had moved a month earlier to a Philadelphia suburb—was not the only reason for leaving California. In the past twelve months both increasingly had felt isolated at La Casa Pacifica. San Clemente is a two-hour drive from Los Angeles and an hour and a half from San Diego, not a convenient stopover for friends, or, for that matter, foreign visitors. All of us in the family had been aware for quite some time that my father was anxious to lead a more active life and be able to meet more easily with old colleagues from Washington and abroad. But when my parents first discussed a move to New York City, I was surprised by the sureness of my mother's desire as well to make a major change. She told me, "We're just dying here slowly."

Their new four-story East Side town house on 65th Street in Manhattan, only seven blocks from Tricia, Ed, and Christopher, was a radical change from San Clemente. In place of an acre and a half of rustling palms and cypress trees and blooming flowers, they now had a fifteen-by-twenty-foot walled patio dominated by Christopher and Jennie's rubber wading pool, their sandbox, and a large stack of firewood for the town house's six fireplaces. As the months in New York passed, Tricia and I felt relieved that the transition to Manhattan was going so smoothly. My parents, after shoring up their physical and mental strength during the sojourn in San Clemente, looked upon New York as a fresh adventure. Once more, as in the sixties, but at a much slower pace for Mother, they enjoyed an occasional museum visit or play, and the restaurants and shopping.

But despite their affinity for the city, by the fall of 1981 my parents began to yearn again for the privacy and freedom of their own backyard. In October 1981 they moved to Saddle River, New Jersey, a fifty-minute commute to Manhattan, so that they could combine the best of both worlds. At his office near Wall Street, where he has written four books on world leaders and foreign affairs, my father meets with a steady stream of political and international figures. Mother leads a more restricted life because of the poor health that has hospitalized her in recent years four times due to pneumonia, bronchitis, and a small stroke in 1983. Her attitude toward these illnesses is the same as it has been since she was a young girl: ignore the discomfort and don't give in. She delays until the last minute taking medicine or even calling the doctor and is stoic about not complaining. In fact, it is like pulling teeth to get her to admit when we talk by phone that she does not feel well. During one of her hospitalizations for pneumonia, I told her how relieved I was that she finally had gotten some help after at least a week of being ill. Her response made it clear she felt calling the doctor was more like a surrender: "I've fought it a long time," she told me.

In 1984 she decided to decline the Secret Service protection afforded our former First Ladies. Since she had limited contacts with outsiders because of her health, in her view the government expense of twenty-four-hour security was unwarranted. A year later my father declined security as well. The annual budget for protecting former Presidents Carter, Ford, and Nixon, their wives, and Lady Bird Johnson is approximately $25 million, of which the Nixon detail cost around $3 million. Since the move to New Jersey, my father had become increasingly uncomfortable with the amount of money being spent on his protection. Tricia and I grew accustomed to him raising the Secret Service subject with us every few months. Finally, in mid-1985, with Mother's concurrence, he announced he would provide for his own security.

Mother's world today revolves around her passion for reading and her home. Although her health prevents her from gardening as much as she would like, she still draws immeasurable sustenance from nature. I remember so well Mother's remark in October 1983 when David and I traveled to Saddle River for our son Alex's third birthday. She was reading by her second-story window. Occasionally she would pause and look out at the treetops. With a smile of pleasure she commented to me, "Julie, even though it is fall and the flowers are almost gone, it is still so beautiful. The leaves make a garden in the sky."

My parents adore their four grandchildren. It is not uncommon to receive a phone call from my father's secretary announcing, "The President is on the phone," not for Julie or David, but for Jennie, Alex, or Melanie. And Mother, despite her uncertain health, is a willing playmate for hours of imaginary games. Jennie's enduring favorites are "shoe store," in which *all* of Grand-mother's shoes are lined up in the bedroom, and "circus," a lively game as Ma and Jennie and Alex alternate as ringmaster, performers, and audience. Christopher and Ma spend hours on plans for an Amusement Park for Dogs. She believes that children should be allowed to be children and grow up slowly, "the old-fashioned way." The grandchildren love her because she really listens to them, laughs with them, and shares their dreams.

During the last months in San Clemente, Mother very reluctantly posed for her White House portrait, having resisted five years of periodic letters and phone calls from Clem Conger, who had remained at the White House as curator, reminding her and my father that already President and Mrs. Ford's portraits hung in the mansion. I told her I hoped she would do it for Tricia and me and for our children. At one point I even argued, "Mother, don't give those who would be happy if Daddy's and your portraits never hung in the White House a victory by default." Her response was matter-of-fact: "Why not? They won, didn't they?"

When she finally agreed to the portrait sitting, she reminded me more than once during the sessions, "I am only doing this for Tricia and you." Each morning at nine she put on the lace gown she had worn with such plea-sure in Africa and at the White House and went to the sunny breakfast room in La Casa Pacifica to pose for Henriette Wyeth Hurd, the noted painter from a family of artists—her brother is Andrew Wyeth; her father, the illustrator N. C. Wyeth; and her husband, Peter Hurd. For four hours without a break, Henriette painted. Her small, quick form, agile despite seventy years, darted first to the canvas with a dab of paint, then to the window to check the light, then closer to her subject, back to the canvas; the cycle repeated again and again until the strokes took form. When the painting was completed, Mother would call it "artistically beautiful," but insist that the mouth was not hers—"it makes me look too sad."

Henriette Wyeth is a keen observer, and for her, painting a portrait "is the exciting pursuit of the truth . . . and pretty agonizing sometimes." After spending five weeks with Mother while working on the painting, her word portrait of Pat Nixon is illuminating and perceptive as well.

> Your mother has gained a certain detachment in her life. She is careful. She is one who appreciates delicacy. In conversations she is not afraid—she has great strength—but she feels her way. With some subjects, her answer is a question mark and rejection is thought over later.
>
> She has such bravery, and a charming sense of humor about herself . . . She once said of Washington, of Watergate, "it was completely terrible." But that was a great concession to even allude to the troubles.
>
> She loves beauty and the care of things and caring for others. The care of their lives means a tremendous amount to her. A home to your mother is like playing a piano, a painting. She can arrange things so they give beauty. She makes a theater of her own and takes an aesthetic delight in her house. She can't do it with life itself but the house is something she has control over.
>
> She's a perfectionist the way she moves. The way she puts the plates down at lunch so that the design immediately meets your eye; the little bouquets of flowers—they are a great comfort to her. While she posed for me, there were times I could tell she wanted to be outside picking off the dead things. "Things in the garden," Henriette laughed, "were going to hell without her."

Henriette told me that in choosing the colors for the painting "I could not deal in sweet pastels." She wanted some darkness. That is why she incorporated into the painting the black-brown of the simple straight-backed chair Mother sat in when she posed. There is a single flower in the lower-right corner of the portrait, a white hibiscus plucked from a bush outside Mother's bedroom window. The hibiscus, with its deep scarlet center, glows white and luminous against the gray and green earth tones of the background of the painting. In Henriette Wyeth's words, "The spring flower is produced in the roots and manure of the earth." What she succeeds in conveying in her painting is that Patricia Nixon is also of the earth and yet glowing and apart. When artist Jamie Wyeth, Henriette's nephew, saw the portrait for the first time, he stood in front of it for a full thirty minutes studying a woman dressed in a gown more blue than gray, her neck encircled by graceful curving rows of pearls, which reflected pink and gold glints from the light. It was the face, however, that mesmerized him. Later, he called his aunt and spoke of the "nobility and poignance" and especially of the "haunting expression in her eyes."

Henriette had told me:

> Above the high bridge of a nose that is almost Greek, your mother has eyes that are like no one else's. The eyes reveal an unusual spirit. They are the eyes of a sixteen-year-old girl—an expression of great sweetness. And, in that expression, occasionally the doors close and the lights go out. For there is a wistfulness in your mother's beauty, which is what one finds in all great beauties. Always the feeling of something beyond—a desire for the unattainable. She has maintained a kind of fragile beauty about her life. When she looked out the window at the hummingbirds, I liked the expression then in her eyes best. She still believes despite injustices.

During their courtship, my father was drawn to the wistful quality in young Patricia Ryan, this woman of dreams of whom he wrote in 1939, "You have the finest ideals of anyone I have ever known." He was drawn also to "the vagabond within you that makes you want to go far places and see great things." Together they traveled far, but by a turn of fate, most of their journey was taken in the public eye. Although my mother continued to believe intensely in the causes that kept the Nixons in public life, the political road was not easy for one who had always valued her privacy and independence. At the center of an ever-widening life involving world travel and leaders, campaigns and political controversies, she continued to have her feet firmly planted on the ground. Always she was aware of what writer Anne Morrow Lindbergh has defined as "the uniqueness of each member of the family; the spontaneity of now; the vividness of here . . . the essence of life itself." Today, Patricia Ryan Nixon cherishes the privacy of her retirement years and the family times that have been among the happiest of her life.

Interviews

*P*enny Adams; Mary Bragg; Jack Brennan; Herbert Brownell; Patrick Buchanan; Shelley Scarney Buchanan; Mrs. Wiley T. Buchanan; Marian Budlong; Steve Bull; Jack Carley; William Codus; Virginia Shugart Counts; Dorothy Cox; Tricia Nixon Cox; Kay Cunningham; John Davies; Rita de Santis; Helene Drown; Jack Drown; Robert Dunn; Barbara Thompson Eisenhower; Mamie Doud Eisenhower; Susan Eisenhower; Michael Farrell; Carol Finch; Robert Finch; Margaret Fuller; Loie Gaunt; Anne Davis Griffin; Bryce Harlow; Beatrice Counsel Hawkins; Patrick Hillings; Marion Hodge; Mrs. Bob Hope; William Hudson; General James "Don" Hughes; Henriette Wyeth Hurd; Louise Johnson; Paul Keyes; Priscilla Kidder; Gwen King; Clare Boothe Luce; Pat Gates Lynch; Betty MacKinnon; Patti Matson; Earl Mazo; Judy McGohan; Cynthia Hardin Milligan; Pat Mosbacher; Bessie Newton; Clara Jane Nixon; Donald Nixon; Edward Nixon; Maureen Drown Nunn; Ann Duggan Oestreicher; Charles G. "Bebe" Rebozo; Neva Bender Renter; Julie Robinson; Charles Rochner; Mrs. William P. Rogers; Susan Porter Rose; Alice Martin Rosenberger; Eva Ruinys; Dorothy Ryan; Thomas Ryan; William Ryan; Rex Scouten; Jack Sherwood; Virginia Sherwood; Helen Smith; Kathleen Stans; Mrs. Herbert Stein; Connie Stuart; Loretta Stuart; Ned Sullivan; Margaret O'Grady Theriault; Dr. Walter Tkach; Jo Rockwell Tobin; Fay Gillis Wells; Lucy Winchester; Rose Mary Woods; Ron Ziegler.

Index

ABC, 215, 247, 264, 275–76, 300, 307, 321, 339, 377, 386, 404, 415
Abplanalp, Bob, 343, 355, 386, 434, 435
Abplanalp, Josie, 355
Abrahamsen, David, 453–54
Acheson, Dean, 275
Acker, Marge, 121, 390
Adams, Abigail, 260
Adams, Duque, and Hazeltine, 204
Adams, Earl, 203
Adams, John, 130, 309
Adams, John Quincy, 205, 309
Adams, John Quincy (great-great-grandson), 309
Adams, Louisa, 309
Adams, Penny, 284, 348
Adams, Sherman, 179
Adenauer, Konrad, 170
Afghanistan, 141
AFL-CIO (American Federation of Labor–Congress of Industrial Organizations), 396
Africa trip of 1957, 166–67
Agnew, Judy, 381
Agnew, Spiro, 276–77, 301, 368, 381
Ahearn, Monsignor, 219
Air Force, U.S., 343

Air Force One, 291, 299, 340, 362–63, 379, 405, 406, 412, 429
airplane hijackings, 282, 396
Alaska pipeline, 396
Albany guided-missile cruiser, 313, 334, 354
Albert, Carl, 379
Alcorn, Meade, 179
All the President's Men (Bernstein and Woodward), 446
Alsop, Joseph, 411
American Association of Nurserymen, 275
American Bar Association, 431
American Civil Liberties Union, 396
American Foreign Service, 283
American Ship Building Company, 377
Amherst College, 259, 290, 291
Anderson, Jack, 127, 325–26, 386
Andrews, Bert, 101, 125, 127
Anne, Princess of England, 293–94
Annenberg, Lee, 432
Annenberg, Walter, 293, 432
anti-American sentiment, 172
Antiballistic Missile (ABM) Treaty, 342
anti-Vietnam War movement, 235
    Cambodian incursion and, 285, 287
    on campuses, 280–82

anti-Vietnam War movement (*cont.*)
  Communist victory favored by, 317
  in elections of 1968, 244, 245
  in elections of 1972, 350
  at Inauguration of 1969, 252
  at Inauguration of 1973, 359–60
  Kent State killings and, 287–90
  Mayday movement in, 316–17
  during Park visit, 272
  POWs and, 370
  at San Jose, 301–2
  Vietnam Moratorium in, 274–75, 277
Apollo 11, 272
Appalachian Fireside Crafts, 284
Arab-Israeli War of 1973, 382, 383–84
Arab oil embargo, 399
Argentina, 172
Armstrong, Neil, 268
Army, U.S., 149
Army Signal Corps, 388
Asia goodwill grip of 1953, 135–44
  Communist specter witnessed in, 138–140
  demonstrations during, 139–40
Askew, Reubin, 344
Assad, Hafiz al-, 413
Associated Milk Producers, 436
Associated Press, 116, 159, 266, 293, 308, 340, 348, 350, 415, 447
Atkins, Ollie, 320, 424
Australia, 136
Austria, 161, 410–11

Baker, Bobby, 377
Bao Dai, 139
Bassett, Jim, 180
Baxter, Frank, 42–43
Bay Lane houses, Key Biscayne, Fla., 249, 258, 319, 386–88
Beale, Betty, 178
Becker, Elizabeth, 286–87
Becky Sharp, 46
Beers, Mr. and Mrs., 35–36
Beeson, Jane, 360
Bell, Allan D., 389
Bender, Matthew, 19
Ben-Gurion, David, 170
Bentley, Elizabeth, 99
Berlin, Irving, 24, 371
Bernstein, Carl, 446
biological warfare convention, 337
Birmingham *Post*, 181
Black Panthers, 274, 277, 282

blacks, 193, 231, 284–85
Block, Herbert, 99
Blue Book, 409
boat people, Vietnamese, 442
Boddy, Manchester, 107
Bolivia, 172, 275
bombings and bomb threats, 274, 282
Bonanza, 434, 440
Book-of-the-Month Club, 447
Borders, William, 331
Bork, Robert, 383
Borman, Frank, 268
Boston *Globe*, 320, 353
Boyer, Gene, 428
Boys Club of America, 397
Bradlee, Benjamin, 445
Bragg, Mary, 22
Braley, Russ, 390
Brazil, 172, 403–4
Breckinridge, John C., 201
Bremer, Arthur, 350
Brennan, Jack, 330, 362, 428, 454
Breslin, Jimmy, 361
Brezhnev, Leonid, 325
  in Middle East negotiations, 384–85
  at San Clemente, 373–74
  in summit of 1972, 340, 341, 342
  in Summit III, 414
Brezhnev, Madame, 341
Broder, David, 274–75, 280
Broken Dishes, 35
Brooke, Edward, 388
Brooks, Jack, 387–88
Brown, Pat, 206, 209, 211, 212, 213
Brownell, Herbert, 115, 128
Buchanan, John, 388
Buchanan, Pat, 227, 238, 239, 240, 276, 291, 361, 378, 407, 432
Buchanan, Ruth, 181, 185, 188
Buchanan, Wiley, 181, 188
Buckley, James, 405
Buckley, William F., Jr., 445
Bulgaria, 96
Bull, Steve, 282, 411, 426, 427, 428
Bullitt, William, 225
Bullock's Wilshire, Los Angeles, Calif., 47–48
Burger, Warren, 267, 286, 429
Burlington *Free Press*, 407
Burlington Zephyr, 74
Burma, 139–40, 142
Burnight, Ralph, 30
Burns, James MacGregor, 155
Burton, Richard, 320

Butterfield, Alexander P., 306, 379
Buzhardt, Fred, 379, 388

Cabinet, U.S.:
   Education Committee of, 285
   under Eisenhower, 155–56, 157
   under Nixon, 361
Cagney, Jimmy, 440
Caldwell, Taylor, 442
Califano, Joseph, 379
California guided-missile frigate, 321
Cambodia, 138, 291, 317–18, 375
   incursion into, 285–87
Camp David, 188, 318–20, 362, 363
campus unrest, 274, 280–82, 290
Canada, 293
cancer research, 307
Cape Porpoise, Maine, 76
Carley, Jack, 210, 212, 245
Carlson, Joel, 278
Carnegie Endowment for International
   Peace, 99
Carter, Amy, 267
Carter, Jimmy, 453
Catholics, 109, 193–94
Catholic Sisters of Charity, 36–37
Catholic University of America, 295
Cavers, David, 73
CBS, 196, 213, 275–76, 293, 339, 353,
   385, 392
Ceauşescu, Nicolae, 271
Central American goodwill trip of 1955,
   153–54
Chambers, Esther, 102
Chambers, Whittaker, 99–102, 205
Chancellor, John, 339
Chapin, Dwight, 236, 247
Chapin School, 219, 222, 226
Charles, Prince of Wales, 293–94, 312
Checkers speech, 118–27
Chicago Daily News, 114, 349
Chicago Today, 335
Chicago Tribune, 122
Chile, 172
China, People's Republic of, 135, 271,
   326, 329, 332, 333–37, 444
Chomsky, Noam, 378
Chotiner, Murray, 92, 114–15, 119, 120,
   124, 151, 215
Chou En-lai, 333, 335, 336
Christian Science Monitor, 111, 143
Christy, Marian, 320
Church, Frank, 445
Churchill, Winston, 230, 423

CIA (Central Intelligence Agency), 174,
   315, 316, 419, 444, 445
CIO (Congress of Industrial
   Organizations), 91
Citizens for Eisenhower, 120
civil rights, 193, 221, 231
Clark, Ramsey, 370, 382
Cleaver, Eldridge, 282
Cleveland Plain Dealer, 193
Cliburn, Van, 342
Codus, Bill, 268, 318, 340, 363–64, 412,
   428
Colby, William, 384
Cold War, 114
Collier's, 145
Colombia, 174
Colson, Charles, 332–33, 402–3, 407
Columbia State, 193
Commission on the Status of Women,
   265
Committee of 100, 85, 86, 89
Committee on the Preservation of the
   White House, 262
Committee to Re-elect the President, 349,
   366, 402, 407
Communist Party, U.S., 99–101, 149
Communists:
   in Asia, 138–39
   in Burma, 139–40, 142
   in CIO PAC, 91
   as election issue, 107, 116, 128
   in Europe, 96
   HUAC investigation of, 95
   McCarthy investigations and, 149–50
   in South America, 172
Community Receptions, 209–10
Conference on Cancer and Human
   Values, 408
Conger, Clement, 263–64, 416, 418–19,
   459
Congress, U.S.:
   Captive Nations resolution of, 183
   energy program bills in, 396
   impeachment proceedings in, 396,
      400–401, 406–7, 409, 415–16, 417,
      421, 423, 424–25
   Joint Committee on Internal Revenue
      Taxation, 376, 386, 406
   Nixon Administration's reform proposals
      in, 301, 307
   Nixon's relations with, 360–61
   Vietnam War and, 353, 375, 442
   see also House of Representatives, U.S.;
      Senate, U.S.; Watergate Committee

Congressional Quarterly, 88
Congressional Record, 88
Congressional Wives Club, 94
Congress '66 committee, 224
Connally, John, 382, 436–37, 450
Considine, Bob, 379
Cooke, Terence Cardinal, 267
Coolidge, Calvin, 130
Copeland, Vern, 269
COSVN (Central Office of South
    Vietnam), 287
Cotton, Hamilton, 271
Counts, Carol, 146
Counts, Curtis, 61
Coward, Grace, 25, 26, 29
Cox, Anne, 313, 457
Cox, Archibald, 380, 382–83
Cox, Christopher Nixon, 457, 458, 459
Cox, Dorothy, 95–96, 105
Cox, Ed, 218, 312–15, 351, 352, 419,
    420, 423
Cox, Howard, 313, 327–28
Cox, Patricia Nixon (Tricia):
    at Beverly Hills home, 204–5, 215
    birth of, 87
    child born to, 457
    in college, 222
    dating problems of, 256
    Dwight Eisenhower and, 256–57
    during Eisenhower's campaign, 117,
        123
    in elections of 1952, 117
    in elections of 1956, 161
    in elections of 1960, 188–89, 195–99
    in elections of 1968, 227–28, 234,
        236, 241–42, 256
    on European trip, 217
    during family holidays, 354, 355
    during father's illness, 434, 435, 436,
        438
    at Forest Lane house, 168–70
    in gubernatorial campaign, 206–7,
        209, 212–14, 216
    in high school, 203–4
    at Inauguration of 1957, 162–64
    at Inauguration of 1969, 251–54
    as infant, 87–88, 93, 95, 96, 97, 98,
        102
    during Kennedy family visit, 310
    on Kennedy Inauguration, 201
    marriage of, 312–15
    during mother's illness, 449–50, 456
    in New York, 218–20
    during Park visit, 272
    during Presidency, 255–57, 260
    in resignation decision, 419, 420, 423
    at San Clemente home, 271–72
    during Senate campaign, 109–10, 111
    at Sidwell Friends school, 170
    South American incidents and, 173,
        177–78
    during Vice Presidency, 131–32, 134,
        135–36, 138, 146–47, 148, 150,
        151, 168
    during Watergate investigation, 367–68,
        369, 372, 386, 395, 396, 408
    during White House farewells, 426–27,
        428, 430
crime rate, 231, 344
Crnobrnja, Bogdan, 299
Cronkite, Walter, 396–97
Cuban missile crisis, 211–12, 401
Curtis, Carl, 406
Curtis Publishing Company, 408
Czechoslovakia, 96

Daddah, Moktar Ould, 329–30
Daily Worker, 108
Daley, Richard, 246, 247, 349, 445
Dark Tower, The (Woollcott and
    Kaufman), 55, 56, 57
Davies, John, 264
Davis, Bette, 35
Davis, Sammy, Jr., 371
Dawes, Charles G., 130
Day, Roy, 89, 255
Dean, John, 365, 366, 367, 368, 373,
    375–77, 388, 405, 409
DeBakey, Michael, 376–77
defense budget, 343
Defense Department, U.S., 315–16, 388
de Gaulle, Charles, 170, 333
Dekor Counterintelligence and Security,
    389
Democratic National Committee, 350
Democratic National Conventions:
    of 1956, 160
    of 1960, 188
    of 1968, 243–44
    of 1976, 453
Democratic Party, 22
    in California gubernatorial race, 206,
        209
    in elections of 1954, 150–51
    in elections of 1956, 160, 161
    in elections of 1958, 179
    in elections of 1972, 348, 350
    political tricks used by, 350, 378–79

Dennis, David, 436
Denton, Jeremiah, 371
Depression, Great, 35
de Santis, Rita, 335–36, 341, 422
desegregation, 284–85
Detroit Free Press, 187
Dewey, Thomas E., 85, 98, 99, 120, 122, 179, 219
Díaz Ordaz, Gustavo, 272–73
Diem, Ngo Dinh, 308
Dietrich, Marlene, 48
Dillon, Douglas, 201
Dirksen, Everett, 198
Dixon, George, 160
Doar, John, 415
Dobrynin, Anatoly, 337
Dobrynin, Irini, 337–38, 373
Donovan, Robert, 268–69
Douglas, Helen Gahagan, 105, 107–8, 118
Downey, Sheridan, 104, 107
Doyle, Sarah Jackson, 261
Dramesi, John, 372
Drown, Bruce, 109
Drown, Helene Colesie, 119, 171, 214, 441, 450, 451
  background of, 71
  in elections of 1960, 196, 197, 199
  in elections of 1968, 231–32, 246
  in elections of 1972, 348, 349
  on European trip, 217
  in Hawaii, 112
  during impeachment proceedings, 415–417
  at Republican Convention of 1952, 114, 115, 117
  in Senate campaign, 108–9
  during Watergate investigation, 375, 384, 402
  in Whittier, 71–72
Drown, Jack, 125, 158, 214, 402, 441, 451, 452
  in elections of 1968, 231, 246
  on European trip, 217
  in Hawaii, 112
  Richard Nixon's relations with, 71, 420
  in Senate campaign, 108
Drown, Larry, 109
Drown, Maureen, 217–18, 451
Drummond, Roscoe, 107, 220
Dudman, Richard, 286–87
Duke, Francis Vincent, 37–38, 41, 44
Dulles, John Foster, 157, 438
Dump Nixon movement, 156–58, 180

Dunn, Bob, 434–35, 436
Dworshak, Henry, 154

Eagleton, Thomas, 344
East Ely White Pine News, 18
Economist, 286
Ecuador, 173–74
Edson, Peter, 118
Efron, Edith, 276
Egypt, 217, 382, 384, 385, 410, 411
Ehrlichman, John:
  in elections of 1968, 245
  in Watergate, 366, 367–68, 402–3, 434
Eight Girls in a Boat, 39
Eisenhower, Alex, 459
Eisenhower, Anne, 163
Eisenhower, Barbara, 257, 328
Eisenhower, David, 163, 229–30, 232–233, 253, 351, 352, 446–47
  on Albany cruiser, 313, 334, 354
  antiwar protests and, 291
  courtship and marriage of, 229–30, 232–33, 257–60
  in elections of 1968, 236–39, 242, 246, 247, 256
  in Navy, 294–95
  in OCS, 294–95
  in postresignation years, 447, 448, 449, 452
  in resignation decision, 418, 419, 420, 423
  during Watergate investigation, 367, 369, 391–92, 395, 399–400, 403
Eisenhower, Dwight D., 132, 135, 177–178, 205, 252, 307, 318
  Adams' resignation requested by, 179
  Dump Nixon movement and, 156–58
  elections of 1954 and, 150, 151
  in elections of 1956, 159–60
  in elections of 1960, 192, 194, 200
  in elections of 1968, 236–37, 242, 248–49
  heart attacks of, 154–55, 237
  at Inauguration of 1957, 162–63
  McCarthy and, 149–50
  Nixon campaign fund charges and, 120, 122, 124, 125, 127
  in Palm Springs, 207–8
  at Republican Convention of 1952, 114–16
  at state dinners, 147
  stroke suffered by, 171
  Tricia Nixon and, 256–57

Eisenhower, Jennie Elizabeth, 456–57,
458, 459
Eisenhower, John, 199, 290–91, 327–28
Eisenhower, Julie Nixon:
at Bethesda home, 399
at Beverly Hills home, 204–5, 215
birth of, 98
children of, 456, 459
courtship and marriage of, 229–30,
232–33, 257–60
at Curtis Publishing, 408
in elections of 1952, 117–18
in elections of 1956, 161
in elections of 1960, 188–89, 195–99
in elections of 1968, 227–28, 234,
241–42, 256
in elections of 1972, 345, 347, 350
on European trip, 217
during family holidays, 354, 355–56
during father's illness, 434, 435, 436,
438
at Forest Lane house, 168–70
in gubernatorial campaign, 209, 212–
214
in high school, 224–25
at Inauguration of 1957, 162–64
at Inauguration of 1969, 251–54
on Kennebunkport vacation, 76
during Kennedy family visit, 309–10
media coverage of, 295–96
during mother's illness, 447–49, 452–
453, 456
in New York, 218–20
during parents' retirement, 442–43
during Park visit, 272
on Republican Convention of 1964,
220–21
in resignation decision, 417–23
during second-term transition period,
362
Secret Service protection for, 282, 290
during Senate campaign, 109–10
at Sidwell Friends school, 170
at Smith College, 225–26, 229–30,
242, 259–60, 290, 291
South American incidents and, 173,
177–78
at Tricia Nixon's wedding, 312–14
during Vice Presidency, 131–32, 134,
135–36, 138, 146–47, 148, 150,
151, 168
during Watergate investigation, 366–67,
369, 372, 380, 381, 385, 386, 390,
391, 395–96, 406, 407–8

during White House farewells, 426–27,
428
as White House guide, 264
Eisenhower, Mamie, 116, 232, 258
during Eisenhower Presidency, 161–62,
254
in elections of 1952, 125–26
in elections of 1960, 194–95
in elections of 1968, 237, 248–49
during Nixon Presidency, 252, 278,
290–91, 312, 313, 317, 328, 359–
360, 422
in Palm Springs, 207–8
during Watergate investigations, 401
Eisenhower, Mary Jean, 162
Eisenhower, Melanie, 459
Eisenhower, Milton, 181, 290
Eisenhower, Susan, 278, 290–91
elections of 1946, 85–92
"house meetings" in, 89
issues in, 91
"Pat and Dick" team launched in, 88–
89
volunteer workers in, 89
elections of 1950, 104–10
campaign schedule in, 105–7
Catholicism issue in, 109
Red-baiting in, 107–8
elections of 1952:
campaign fund issue in, 118–27
Communist issue in, 116, 128
Vice Presidency nomination in, 114–
117
elections of 1954, 149–51
elections of 1956, 156–61
campaign issues in, 160
Dump Nixon movement in, 156–58
elections of 1958, 178–80
elections of 1960, 188–200
Catholicism issue in, 193–94
civil rights issue in, 193
Nixon-Kennedy debates in, 191–92
vote fraud allegations in, 198, 200
elections of 1962, 205–14
elections of 1964, 220–22
elections of 1966, 228, 230
elections of 1968, 235–49
preliminary campaign for, 230–31
primary campaigns in, 236–40
Secret Service protection in, 241–42
Vietnam War issue in, 238, 239, 244–
246
volunteer workers in, 243
elections of 1970, 296

gubernatorial results in, 302–3
premissiveness issue in, 301
elections of 1972, 343–52
 campaign funds issue in, 348
 corruption charges in, 349–50
 Democratic platform in, 344
 violence in, 350
elections of 1974, 435, 436–37
elections of 1976, 453
Elizabeth II, Queen of England, 136, 169, 170, 180–81, 222, 293, 294
Ellsberg, Daniel, 315–16, 365, 402
Ely, Nevada, 17–18
Emerson, Tom, 75
energy program, 396
equal job opportunity, 322
Equal Rights Amendment, 321–22
Erskine, Helen, 145
Ervin, Sam, 365, 377
Ervin Committee, *see* Watergate Committee
Everts, P. J., 146
Excelsior High School, 28–31, 49
Excelsior Life, 30
executive privilege, 381, 382
Executive Protective Service, 264

Fahey, John, 299
Fair Campaign Practices Committee, 193
Faisal, King of Saudi Arabia, 411–12
Farah, Empress of Iran, 341
Farrell, Mike, 326, 362, 391, 405
FBI (Federal Bureau of Investigation), 274, 365, 378, 379, 419, 444
Felknor, Bruce L., 193
Felps, Curl J., 80
Feminine Mystique, The (Friedan), 327
Final Days, The (Bernstein and Woodward), 446–47, 452
Finch, Bob, 192, 197, 201, 207
Finch, Carol, 207, 225, 249
Finch College, 222
Finkelstein, Louis, 267
Fischer, Paul, 320
Flukus, Sergeant, 167
Flynn, John, 372
Fonda, Jane, 347
Ford, Betty, 428, 429
Ford, Gerald, 215, 301, 382, 383, 428, 429, 433, 435–36, 442, 444, 453
Foreign Affairs, 333
Forest Lane home, Washington, D.C., 168
France, 20, 96, 138

Franklin, Barbara Hackman, 322
Frick Collection, 225
Friedan, Betty, 327
Frost, David, 394, 437
Fuller, Bill, 155
Fuller, George, 146, 155, 163–64
Fuller, Margaret, 121, 134, 146, 155, 168
Fullerton Junior College, 34, 39

Gallaudet College, 391
Gandhi, Indira, 324–25
Gannon, Frank, 451
Garbo, Greta, 48
Garment, Len, 242
Gates, Pat, 269, 270, 331
Gaunt, Loie, 162, 173, 454
Gaynor, Janet, 46
George Washington University, 391–92
German Democratic Republic (East Germany), 96
Germany, Federal Republic of (West Germany), 228
Germany, Imperial, 20
Germany, Nazi, 72, 75
Getty, Jean Paul, 228
Ghana, 166, 167, 329–32
Gibson, Dunn, and Crutcher, 121
Ginsberg, David, 73
Glaser, Vera, 243
Glass Menagerie, The (Williams), 225
Goldfine, Bernard, 179
Goldwater, Barry, 205, 220–21, 222, 423
Gortikov, George, 30
Graham, Billy, 247, 250, 267, 280
Grand Ole Opry, 404
Great Britain, 20, 72, 96, 228, 268
Great Society programs, 231, 244
Greece, 96, 108
Green Book, 133–34
Green Island, 80
Gregory, Dick, 277
Gromyko, Madame, 340, 373
GSA (General Services Administration), 386–87, 388, 406
GUM department store, 340–41

Hadley Republican Women's Club, 229
Hagerty, Jim, 154, 158
Haggard, Merle, 365
Haig, Alexander, 382, 384, 419, 421
Halberstadt, Kate, *see* Ryan, Kate Halberstadt
Haldeman, H. R. (Bob), 272–73, 288, 299, 300, 302, 394, 454

Haldeman, H. R. (Bob) (*cont.*)
  in elections of 1968, 240–41, 246
  as gubernatorial campaign manager, 210
  on Nixon's vacation habits, 319
  as staff conduit, 361–63
  in Watergate, 365, 366, 367–68, 389, 402–3, 434
Haldeman, Jo, 249
Hall, Leonard, 157, 179, 205
Hammersmith Is Out, 320
Harlow, Bryce, 194
Harris, Lou, 246
Harrison, Benjamin, 265
Harrison, Beth, 57
Harris polls, 406–7
Hartmann, Bob, 162, 176, 436
Haskell, Doc, 25, 26
Hawkins, Beatrice Counsel, 51, 197, 208–9
Hayden, Tom, 274
Hearst, Alicia, 155
Hearst, Austine, 163
Hearst, William Randolph, 163
Heath, Edward, 228, 364
Herter, Chris, Jr., 135
Herter, Christian, 94, 96, 158
Herter Committee, 96–97
Hess, Stephen, 126
HEW (Health, Education and Welfare Department), 307, 344
Hilliard, David, 277
Hillings, Pat, 118–19, 121, 122–23, 124
Hiss, Alger, 98–102, 215
Historical Research Foundation, 276
Hitler, Adolf, 72, 348
Hoffa, Jimmy, 211
Holiday, 408
Hoover, Herbert, 69, 205, 334
Hoover, J. Edgar, 205
Hoover, Lou Henry, 334
Horace Mann Public School, 146, 161, 170
Horkan, George, 290–91
Houphouët-Boigny, Félix, 329–30
House of Representatives, U.S.:
  Education and Labor Committee of, 95
  Government Operations Subcommittee, 387–88
  Judiciary Committee of, 396, 400–401, 409, 411, 415–16, 417
  Un-American Activities Committee of, 95–96, 99, 100
Hudson, Bill, 430, 449, 451

Hughes, Betty, 199
Hughes, Howard, 386, 397
Hughes, James (Don), 166, 167, 282
  in elections of 1960, 195, 196, 199
  on South American trip, 174, 175, 176, 177
Hughes Tool Company, 198, 211
Humane Society, 168
Humphrey, Hubert H., 194, 243, 244–246, 247, 248, 250, 259, 344, 406, 446
Hungary, 96, 161, 163
Hunt, Howard, 365–66, 376
Huntington Central Oil Company, 19
Hurd, Henriette Wyeth, 459–61
Hurd, Peter, 460
Hussein Ibn Talal, King of Jordan, 364

impeachment proceedings, 396
  Articles in, 415–16, 417
  and erosion of Nixon's congressional support, 423, 424–25
  lack of legal standards in, 400
  public opinion on, 406–7
Inaugurations:
  of 1953, 130–32
  of 1957, 162–64
  of 1969, 250–54
  of 1973, 359–60
Independent Voters of South Pasadena, 90
India, 141–43, 268, 324–25
Indonesia, 136, 143–44, 268
Inouye, Daniel, 377
INS News Service, 136
International Brotherhood of Teamsters, 211
Iran, 136, 137–38
Ireland, 299
Iron Curtain, 271
IRS (Internal Revenue Service), 386, 397
Israel, 228, 374, 382, 384, 410
Italy, 75, 96
ITT antitrust case, 382
Ivory Coast, 329, 330, 331–32

Jack Paar Show, The, 212
Japan, 75, 136
Japanese-Americans, 401
Jarriel, Tom, 339
Javits, Jacob, 220
Jaworski, Leon, 383, 390, 431
John Birch Society, 206, 208
Johnson, Andrew, 401
Johnson, Lady Bird, 229, 250, 251, 260–

261, 262, 266, 357
Johnson, Louise, 94, 98, 146, 155, 168,
    264, 303, 304, 355, 428–29, 440
  on Bahamas trip, 203
  in England, 221–22
Johnson, Lyndon B., 131–32, 188, 193,
    282, 307, 308, 388, 406
  death of, 357
  on Democratic Convention of 1968,
    243–44
  demonstrations against, 235
  in elections of 1964, 221, 222
  elections of 1968 and, 238, 239, 241
  Great Society programs under, 231
  Kennedy aides and, 260–61
  at Nixon's Inauguration, 250–51
  Vietnam War and, 228–29, 231, 245–
    246, 338
  wiretaps and bugs used by, 378, 379
Johnson, Roger, 94, 98, 146, 155, 203,
    355, 428–29, 440
Johnston, Mrs. Vic, 168
Joint Chiefs of Staff, 165, 287
Jones, Edward Vason, 263
Jordan, 228
Jorgensen, Frank, 104
Juárez de Oporta, Aurora, 275
Junior School for the Blind, Los Angeles,
    326–27
Justice Department, U.S., 101, 193, 381,
    383
J. Walter Thompson, 210

Kalb, Marvin, 339
Kanady, Johnson, 122
Kaufman, George, 55
Keating, Kenneth, 212
Kefauver, David, 117
Kefauver, Estes, 161
Kennedy, Caroline, 255, 309–10
Kennedy, Edward M., 344, 370, 382
Kennedy, Jacqueline, see Onassis,
    Jacqueline Kennedy
Kennedy, John, Jr., 309–10
Kennedy, John F., 103, 129, 188, 307,
    308, 378–79, 382, 387, 388, 401,
    445
  assassination of, 219, 221
  in Cuban missile crisis, 211–12
  in elections of 1960, 190–98, 200
Kennedy, Robert F., 193, 194, 238, 239
    241, 378, 379, 382
Kent State University, 287
Keogh, James, 100

Key Biscayne, Florida, 148, 226, 249
Keyes, Miriam, 355
Keyes, Paul, 204, 212, 355, 356, 429,
    440
KGB agents, 340
Khachigian, Ken, 427
Khmer Dancers, 317–18
Khrushchev, Nikita, 170, 181–85, 189
Khrushchev, Nina, 181, 183, 184–85
Kidder, Priscilla, 247, 314, 315
King, Charles Bird, 261
King, Coretta Scott, 167
King, Gretchen, 82
King, Gwen, 322–23, 422, 440–41
King, Martin Luther, Jr., 167, 193, 239,
    290, 379
Kirk, Russell, 379
Kissinger, Henry A., 91, 270, 299, 374,
    414, 446, 450
  China policy and, 333, 334
  in India-Pakistan crisis, 325
  in Middle East negotiations, 384, 385,
    410, 411
  in Vietnam peace talks, 337, 338, 340,
    353, 354, 355, 358
  wiretaps authorized by, 411
Kiwanis Club, 56, 397
Klein, Herb, 199, 207, 213, 362
Klein, Marge, 199
Kleindienst, Richard, 388
Kleizo, Edward, 393
Knebel, Fletcher, 193
Knight, Stuart, 411
Koch, Alice, 68
Korea, 135, 136, 139
Koslov, N. T., 183
Kosygin, Aleksei, 341–42
Kraft, Joseph, 360, 411
Krogh, Egil (Bud), 288, 316, 325

LaBerge, Dominic, 31, 32
Ladies' Home Journal, 187, 207, 333
Ladies of the Senate, 187–88
La Follette, Bob, 22
Laird, Melvin, 315
Landers, Ann, 53
Lang, Walter, 204
Laos, 138
Latrobe, Benjamin, 262
League of Women Voters, 85
Le Duc Tho, 353
Legacy of Parks Program, 320–21
Lenox Company, 418
Levin, Bernard, 377

Lewin, Fran, 293
Lewis, Hobart, 240
Liberia, 166–67, 329–30, 331
Libya, 167
Liddy, G. Gordon, 365–66, 402–3
Life, 80, 151, 302
Lincoln, Abraham, 201, 328, 400–401
Lincoln, Mary Todd, 293
Lindbergh, Anne Morrow, 461
Lindbergh, Charles, 379
Lindsay, John, 220
Lippiatt, Jean, 51–52
Lisagor, Peter, 153–54, 167
Lodge, Henry Cabot, 129
Long, Russell, 376
Long Beach *Independent Press Telegram*, 109, 123
Longworth, Alice Roosevelt, 113, 152, 157, 168
Lon Nol, 285, 317
Look, 127
Los Angeles *Times*, 44, 105–6, 162, 180, 415
Luce, Clare Boothe, 115, 432, 457
Lukash, William, 410, 411, 433, 436
Lungren, John, 433, 434, 435, 448–49, 452
Lynch, John, 312

McAdoo, William, 314
MacArthur, Douglas, 205
McCain, John, 317
McCall's, 300–301
McCarthy, Eugene, 238, 241, 242, 259
McCarthy, Joe, 149–50
McClendon, Sarah, 347
McCormack, John, 294
McGohan, Judy, 304, 324
McGovern, George, 343, 344, 348, 352
McKinley, William, 113
MacKinnon, Betty, 103–4, 128
MacKinnon, George, 103–4, 128
MacKinnon, Kitty, 103, 104
McMahon, William, 325
McNamara, Robert, 315
Madison, Dolley, 263
Magruder, Jeb, 366, 375–76
Making of the President 1960, The (White), 192
Maltese Falcon, The, 356
Mansfield, Mike, 365
Mao Tse-tung, 444
Maraziti, Joseph, 436
Marcantonio, Vito, 107, 108

Marine One helicopter, 428
Markel, Hazel, 187
Marshall, George C., 96, 149
Marshall Plan, 97
Martin, Dick, 356
Martin, Joe, 95, 96, 116
Martin, John Bartlow, 122
Martin, Virginia, 104–5
Matson, Patti, 416
Mauritania, 329
Mayfield, Freddie, 365
Mayne, Wiley, 436
Mazo, Earl, 126, 166, 200, 204
media:
advocacy journalism in, 275–77
in California gubernatorial race, 213
"domestic martyrdom" theme in, 187
in elections of 1968, 243
First Family briefings for, 308
First Lady "project" promoted by, 254, 266
income tax stories reported in, 406
Nixon marriage as portrayed by, 404, 446–47
Pat Nixon's relations with, 145–46, 187, 254, 266, 276, 277, 296, 299–300, 308, 311, 332
during Prince Charles's visit, 294
at Soviet-U.S. summit of 1972, 340–41
Watergate coverage in, 375, 383, 385–387, 390, 392–93, 401–2, 404–5, 407–8, 445–46
White House correspondents in, 295–296, 308, 310–11
White House reports on, 299–300
Meir, Golda, 364, 385, 395
Memoirs (Nixon), 92, 102, 108, 122, 126, 151, 155, 156, 179, 188, 201–2, 206, 211, 213, 215–16, 275, 336, 352, 354, 361, 368, 376, 384, 409, 420, 437, 438, 439, 451, 456
Mexican-Americans, 52–53
Mexico, 69–70, 225, 320–21
Meyers, Mabel, 35
Miami *Herald*, 148, 343
Middle East communiqué, 374
Mikoyan, Anastas I., 182, 183, 184
Miller, Jack, 433
Milligan, Bob, 391–92, 395, 426
Milligan, Cynthia, 391–92, 395, 426
Mills, Wilbur, 376
Mitchell, John, 233, 246, 247, 321, 366, 388, 393–95, 405–6, 434
Mitchell, Martha, 233, 393–95

Miyakawa, Marjorie, 30
Mondale, Walter, 453
Montgomery, Ruth, 189
Montoya, Joseph, 377
Moonglow goodwill trip, 268–71
Moore, Dick, 405
Morocco, 412
Mosbacher, Pat, 269
Mosier, John, 449
Moslems, 412
Moynihan, Daniel Patrick, 284–85
Mudge, Stern, Baldwin, and Todd, 216
Murphy, George, 301
Murray, Jim, 128
Muskie, Edmund, 344

Nader, Ralph, 312
National Archives, 406
National Center for Voluntary Action, 364
National Day of Protest (May 9, 1970),
    287–90
National Mobilization Committee to End
    the War in Vietnam, 244
National Park Service, 304–5
National Security Council, 155–56, 166,
    316, 339
National Student Association, 287
National Symphony Drive, 146
NATO (North Atlantic Treaty
    Organization), 114
Navy, U.S., 75–85, 295
NBC, 122, 258, 275–76, 339, 405
Nehru, Jawaharlal, 325
Nelson, Drusilla, 154
Nevada State Journal, 296
New Deal, 86, 91
New Republic, 446
Newsweek, 91, 150, 160, 180, 256, 331,
    357, 386, 405, 447
Newton, Bessie, 146, 196, 226
New York, 276
New York, N.Y., Nixons' home in, 216–
    217
New Yorker, 156
New York Herald Tribune, 101, 119, 166,
    200
New York Post, 118, 178, 454
New York State Bar Association, 216,
    447–48
New York Times, 181, 236, 275, 280,
    281, 283, 299, 315, 316, 331, 346,
    350, 351, 366, 386, 390, 401, 437,
    445
New York Times Book Review, 308

New York Times-Herald, 117
New York Times Magazine, 281
New Zealand, 136
Ngo Dinh Diem, 308
Nicaragua, 174
Nixon, Arthur, 57
Nixon, Beth, 312
Nixon, Don, 69, 131, 198, 211, 397
Nixon, Ed, 60, 62, 86–87
Nixon, Frank, 56, 61, 62, 66, 68, 86, 93,
    111, 113, 116
  death of, 158–59
  illness of, 97
  Pennsylvania farm purchased by, 94
Nixon, Hannah, 57, 62–63, 66, 68, 78,
    86, 88, 94, 111, 155, 191, 198
  campaign fund issue and, 121, 126
  death of, 232
  illness of, 97, 98
  as Tricia Nixon's caretaker, 87
Nixon, Harold, 57, 63
Nixon, Julie, see Eisenhower, Julie Nixon
Nixon, Mudge, Rose, Guthrie and
    Alexander, 216, 222, 393
Nixon, Patricia:
  on Asia trip (1953), 135–44
  as avid reader, 442–43
  back injury of, 171
  birthday party for (1973), 365
  on campus tour, 280–81
  as Catholic, 109
  childhood of, 17–27
  on China trip, 333–37
  Christmas preparations by (1970),
    303–4
  in college, 34, 42–49
  Community Receptions initiated by,
    209–10
  courtship of, 54–66
  discipline techniques of, 169
  in Dobrynin meeting, 337–38
  on European official tour (1970), 299–
    301
  on European vacations, 221–22, 227–
    228
  family needs placed first by, 298
  father's illness and, 32–33
  First Lady projects of, 265–67, 364
  as gardener, 23, 438
  as grandparent, 456–58, 459
  in high school, 28–31, 32
  homes decorated by, 111, 168–69, 271
  during honeymoon and early marriage,
    70–73

Nixon, Patricia (*cont.*)
  as hospital worker, 36–39
  in husband's decision to run for
    governor, 205–7
  at Irish family gathering, 299
  on Legacy of Parks trip, 320–21
  libel suit urged by, 127
  mail answered by, 322–24, 416
  in Manhattan (1963), 218–19
  marriage of, 66–70
  media's relations with, 145–46, 187,
    254, 266, 276, 277, 296, 299–300,
    308, 311, 332
  meticulousness of, 210
  modesty of, 263–64
  on Moonglow goodwill trip, 268–71
  mother's illness and, 25–27
  name changed by, 34, 36
  at Nixon, Mudge law office, 222
  official entertaining by, 283–84
  official portrait of, 459–61
  official schedule for, 265–66
  personal diplomacy emphasized by, 254
  on Peruvian earthquake trip, 291–93
  philosophy of, 243
  in plays and movies, 29–30, 35, 39–
    40, 46–47, 54–55, 57
  political disillusionment of, 204
  in presidential race decision (1968),
    230, 231–32, 234, 235–36
  press conferences held by, 347–48
  during Prince Charles's visit, 293–94
  privacy preserved by, 238, 300–301
  retirement life of, 439–40
  self-sufficiency of, 324
  separate First Lady campaign for (1960),
    189–90
  staff for, 265, 299, 363–64
  stroke suffered by, 447–53
  as teacher, 48–55, 70–71
  on Venezuela/Brazil inaugurations trip,
    403–4
  volunteerism emphasized by, 266–67,
    280–81
  wardrobe of, 186–87
  during wartime separations, 75–83
  on West Africa tour (1971), 329–31
  White House decorated by, 260–64,
    416
  as women's rights advocate, 321–22
  young children loved by, 297–98
Nixon, Richard M.:
  background of, 56–57
  back taxes paid by, 406
  birthday party for (1973), 355–56
  Cabinet and aide resignations requested
    by, 361–62
  courtship of, 54–66
  disbarment of, 447–48
  as freshman Congressman, 93–97
  as grandparent, 457, 459
  during honeymoon and early marriage,
    70–73
  impeachment proceedings and, 396,
    400–401, 409, 415–16, 417, 421,
    423, 424–25
  Inaugurations of, 250–54, 359–60
  isolation of, 363
  knee injury of, 190–91
  legal fees incurred by, 431
  marriage of, 66–70
  media's relations with, 275–77, 385
  mental instability rumors about, 392–
    393
  in Navy, 75–85
  pardoning of, 432–33
  phlebitis suffered by, 222–23, 410–11,
    413, 433–37
  pneumonia suffered by, 380–81
  and release of Watergate tapes, 419–20
  as Republican fundraiser, 111–12, 224
  resignation of, 368, 372–73, 397–98,
    415–30
  resignation address of, 423, 424–25
  retirement life of, 439–40
  as solitary figure, 367
  surgery performed on, 434–37
  tape recording system installed by, 307
  vacation habits of, 319–20
  vice-presidential staff of, 132–33
  White House enjoyed by, 296–97
  White House farewells of, 425–30
  Whittier law practice of, 51, 56
  wife's support for, 345–46
  see also specific topics
Nixon, Tricia, *see* Cox, Patricia Nixon
Nixon Doctrine, 269
Nixon for Governor Committee, 209
Nixon Special, 118–19
Nixon Youth, 344–45
Nkrumah, Kwame, 167
No More Vietnams (Nixon), 356–57
Nordquist, Kay, 44–45
North American Newspaper Alliance, 243
Northampton *Hampshire Gazette*, 290
November Vietnam Mobilization (New
    Mobe), 277
nuclear disarmament, 181, 374

nuclear test ban treaty, 414
Nugent, Luci Johnson, 251, 314
Nugent, Pat, 357

O'Brien, Larry, 344
Officers Candidate School (OCS), 294–95
O'Grady, Margaret Mary, 52, 58, 60, 63, 77
Ohio State University, 282
oil embargo, 399
Onassis, Jacqueline Kennedy, 117, 219, 297, 309–11
  in elections of 1960, 190, 196
  White House decorated by, 260–61, 262, 264, 297
  at White House in 1971, 309–11
O'Neill, Thomas P. (Tip), 361
OPA (Office of Price Administration), 73, 74, 75, 78
Osborne, John, 446
Oxon Hill Children's Farm, 326

Pakistan, 137, 268, 325, 333
Panama, 154
Panama Canal Zone, 72–73
Paraguay, 172
Paramount, 39–40
Paris peace talks, 353–58
Park, Chung Hee, 272
Parker Herbex, 46
Pat Nixon Park, 273
Patricia Nixon Elementary School, 441
Patton, George, 86
Pat Week, 189–90
Paul VI, Pope, 370
Peale, Norman Vincent, 257, 267
Pearl Harbor, 75, 401
Pearson, Drew, 127, 198
Peking Zoo, 336
Pendergast, Mae Belle, 209
Pennsylvania Academy of Fine Arts, 263
Pentagon Papers, 315–16, 326
Perdue, Bill, 71
Perry, Herman, 85, 86
Perry, L. D., 423
Peru, 172–73, 291–93
Petersen, Henry, 381
Pett, Saul, 340
Philippines, 268
Pidgeon, Walter, 48
"plumbers," 316
Poland, 72, 96, 184
political intelligence operations, 350, 378–79

Porter, Susan, 283–84, 365
Powell, Lewis, 321
Powers, David, 379
POWs, in Vietnam War, 317, 338, 353, 370–72, 375
Price, Ray, 361, 368, 376, 383, 423, 446, 453
Price Waterhouse, 120, 121
Progressive Party, 22
Pueblo Indian artwork, 402
Punch, 180

Quakers, 50–51, 62–63, 76

race riots, 235, 239, 284–85
Radford, Arthur W., 165
Radio Free Europe, 184
Raine, Louise, 23–24, 25, 26, 273
Raine, Myrtle, 23–24, 25, 26, 273
Raine, Oliver, 31–32
Rand Corporation, 315–16
Reader's Digest, 82, 240
Reagan, Ronald, 242, 273, 301, 382, 444
Rebozo, Charles G. (Bebe), 158, 318, 319, 452
  background of, 148
  confidences maintained by, 148–49
  in elections of 1968, 230–31, 236
  as family friend, 148–49, 259, 290–91, 315, 320, 355, 399, 434, 435
  Hughes's campaign contribution and, 397
  investigations of, 431–32, 442
  at Key Biscayne, 148–49, 226
  on Mexico trip, 225
  in resignation decision, 397–98, 419–420, 425
  Watergate investigation and, 361, 363, 369, 397–98
Red Cross, 75
Rehnquist, William, 321
Religious Broadcasters of America, 401
Renter, Marc, 54
Republican National Committee, 111–12
  in elections of 1960, 192
  women's division of, 189–90
Republican National Conventions:
  of 1948, 98–99
  of 1952, 113–17
  of 1956, 158–59
  of 1960, 188
  of 1964, 220–21
  of 1968, 242–43

Republican National Conventions (*cont.*)
  of 1972, 344–45, 346
  of 1976, 453
Republican Party:
  in elections of 1958, 178–79
  in elections of 1964, 222
  John Birch wing of, 206, 208–9
  McCarthy and, 149, 150
  voter coalition in, 352
Reston, James, 346, 401
Rhodes, John, 423
Rhodesia, 329
Rhyne, Charles, 389
Ribicoff, Abraham, 344
Richardson, Bobby, 267
Richardson, Elliot, 380, 381, 383, 384
Robb, Charles, 357
Robb, Lynda Bird, 251, 253, 255, 314
Robinson, Julie, 283, 337
Rochner, Chuck, 241
Rockefeller, Nelson, 216, 217, 220, 239,
  242, 362, 382, 446
Rockwell, Annie, 32, 35–36, 67
Rockwell, Jo, 36, 75
Rodino, Peter, 415
Rogers, Adele, 154, 199, 266, 272, 314,
  457
Rogers, Tony, 154
Rogers, William, 119, 120, 122–23, 127,
  154, 331, 332
Romania, 96, 268, 271, 333
Romney, George, 221, 237
Roosevelt, Eleanor, 38, 270
Roosevelt, Franklin D., 38–39, 91, 131,
  271, 307, 379, 401
Roosevelt, John, 379
Roosevelt, Theodore, 69, 113, 130, 326,
  351, 427–28
Rosenberg, Ethel, 149
Rosenberg, Julius, 149
Rotary Club, 56
Rovere, Richard, 156
Rowan, Dan, 356
Ruckelshaus, William, 383
Rusk, Dean, 315
Ryan, Bill, 35, 67, 76, 87, 253
  childhood of, 17–27
  in college, 39, 40, 41, 43, 46, 49
  in high school, 29, 31, 32–33
  on Kennedy-Nixon debate, 191
Ryan, Dorothy, 87
Ryan, Kate Halberstadt, 18–27, 228
Ryan, Kate (Sister Thomas Anna), 36–38,
  40, 43–44, 47, 49, 67

Ryan, Mamie, 44
Ryan, Neva, 18, 20, 21, 24, 54, 67, 69,
  117
Ryan, Thelma Catherine, *see* Nixon,
  Patricia
Ryan, Tom, 67, 87, 205, 232, 273, 451
  childhood of, 18–27
  in college, 39, 40, 41, 43, 46, 49
  in high school, 29, 31, 32–33
  at Inauguration of 1953, 131, 132
Ryan, Will, 17–27, 31–33

Sadat, Anwar, 385, 410, 411
Saddle River, N.J., Nixons' home in,
  458–59
Safire, William, 91, 301, 302, 366, 367,
  378, 445
St. Louis *Glove-Democrat*, 227
St. Louis *Post-Dispatch*, 287, 353
SALT, 316, 414
Sanchez, Fina, 208, 239, 248, 298, 428,
  457
Sanchez, Manolo, 208, 239, 248, 258,
  320, 341, 428, 438, 457
San Clemente, Calif., Nixons' home in,
  271–72, 319, 373, 386–88
Sandman, Charles, 436
Saturday Evening Post, 51–52, 408
Saturday Night Live, 447
Saudi Arabia, 411–13
Sawyer, Diane, 450, 451
Scarney, Shelley, 227, 233, 240, 432
Schlesinger, James, 384
Schmidt, Coral, 364
school busing, 284–85, 294
Schulz, Robert, 257
Science, 389
Scotland, 221–22
Scott, Hugh, 423
Scouten, Rex, 137–38, 142–43, 314,
  387, 391, 425–26
Scranton, William, 221
Sebald, William, 140
Secret Service:
  at Camp David, 319
  in elections of 1968, 241–42, 249
  in elections of 1972, 350–51
  equipment requested by, 386, 387
  at Inauguration of 1973, 359–60
  in Johnson Presidency, 235, 241
  for Nixon as Vice President, 174, 175,
    176, 197–98
  in Nixon Presidency, 255, 258, 259,
    269, 270, 281, 282, 288–89, 296

after Nixon's resignation, 433–34, 436, 438
for past Presidents, 458–59
protection law coverage under, 131
on South American trip, 174, 175, 176
for Vice Presidents, 131, 132–33
in Watergate period, 391, 392, 396
White House taping system monitored by, 388, 389
Securities and Exchange Commission, 179, 405
security breaches, 315–16, 325–26
Segretti, Donald, 349–50
Senate, U.S., 316
Foreign Relations Committee of, 133
Intelligence Committee of, 444, 445
see also Watergate Committee
Senate Democratic Caucus, 361
Sequoia, 339, 420–21
Sevareid, Eric, 212
Shaw, George Bernard, 266
Sheehan, Neil, 308
Shell, Joe, 206, 208–9
Sherwood, Jack, 132, 148
on Asia trip, 137, 139–40, 141, 142
on 1960 presidential campaign, 198–99
on Rebozo, 148
on South American trip, 172–74
on Soviet trip, 183, 184
during Vice Presidency, 131, 165
Sherwood, Virginia, 264, 321, 404–5
Shikler, Aaron, 309
Shriver, Sargent, 348, 382
Shugart, Virginia, 45–46, 55, 58, 61, 63, 69, 146
Shultz, George, 291
Sidwell Friends school, 170
Silent Majority, 275
Sirica, John, 381, 383, 439
Six Crises (Nixon), 101, 154, 172, 204, 240, 432
Small Town Girl, 46
Smathers, George, 148
Smith, Al, 85
Smith, Dana, 118, 127
Smith, Ely, 17
Smith, Franklin B., 407
Smith, Helen, 297, 300, 304, 310–11, 364, 404, 422
Smith, Howard K., 215, 377
Smith, Mary Louise, 453
Smith College, 225–26, 229–30, 242, 259–60, 290, 291
Snyder, Howard, 194

Socialist Party, 91
Society of Friends (Quakers), 50–51, 62–63, 76
Sophian, 259
Soroptimists, 275
Soukhanov, Maria I., 341
South Africa, 329
South American goodwill trip, 172–78
South Pacific Air Transport Command (SCAT), 79
Soviet Union, 99, 293, 332
American National Exhibition in, 181–182
Arab-Israeli War and, 382, 383–84
in Cuban missile crisis, 211–12
Nixon's 1959 visit to, 181–84
in summit talks, 340–43, 374, 413–14
Vietnam War and, 337–38, 339–40, 442
Special People, 452
Sputnik, 179
Stalin, Joseph, 99
Stanford, Neil, 143
Stanford University, 282
Stans, Kathleen, 218–19, 267
Stans, Maurice, 218–19, 224, 230, 405–6, 437
Stassen, Harold, 98–99, 158
State Advisory Committees, 285
State Department, U.S., 100, 137, 149, 177, 265, 315, 316, 334
state gifts, 265
Statement of Information (House Judiciary Committee), 415
state visits and dinners, 147, 169–70, 272–73, 364
steel strike of 1959, 278
Steinem, Gloria, 276
Stennis, Coy, 133
Stennis, John, 383
Stevenson, Adlai, 122, 123, 150–51, 160, 378–79
Stewart, Jimmy, 85
Stockdale, James, 371
Stone, Clement, 395
Storer Broadcasting, 298
Stouffer, David, 49
Stout, Bill, 213
Stripling, Robert, 100, 101
Stuart, Charles, 298, 448
Stuart, Connie, 298, 299–300, 308–9, 311, 317, 347, 348, 364, 394, 404, 448
Stuart, Gilbert, 263, 309

Stuart, Loretta, 94–95, 171, 193–94
Students for a Democratic Society (SDS), 245, 274
Suez Canal crisis, 163
Suharto, Madame, 268
Sukarno, Gunter, 143–44
Sukarno, Madame, 143–44
Sulky, Tom, 68
Sullivan, Ned, 216, 217, 219, 236
Sullivan, William C., 378
Superior Oil, 221
Supreme Court, U.S., 285, 321, 419
Sylvester, Arthur, 401
Syria, 382, 410, 413

Taft, Robert, 98, 114
Taft, William Howard, 18, 69
Talmadge, Herman, 377
taxes, federal, 344
Taxi Drivers Local Union No. 3036, New York, N.Y., 451
Taylor, Elizabeth, 320
Taylor, Henry, J., 410
Taylor, Robert, 46
Tet offensive, 236
Thailand, 268, 269
Thieu, Madame, 270
Thieu, Nguyen Van, 269, 270, 353, 356–357
Thimmesch, Nick, 263
Thomas, Helen, 254, 310–11, 394
Thomas, Madeline, 30–31
Thompson, Llewellyn, 182
Thompson, Robert, 315
Thorton, Ray, 400
Thurmond, Strom, 294
Tilden Street home, Washington, D.C., 147
Time, 91, 95, 99, 102, 128, 153, 186, 215, 254, 281, 284, 302, 331, 333, 340, 432
Times (London), 180, 377
Timmons, Bill, 421
Tito, Jovanka, 300
Tito, Marshal (Josip Broz), 299, 300, 324–25
Tkach, Walter, 190, 290–91, 428, 433
Tobey, Lillian, 187–88
Tolbert, William, 329
Truesdale Estates home, Beverly Hills, Calif., 204
Truman, Harry S., 91, 98, 99, 128, 131, 357
Truman, Margaret, 257

Tuck, Dick, 350, 378
Tuckerman, Nancy, 309
Tulane University, 227
Turkey, 108
Turkey Growers Association, 326
TV Guide, 276
Twentieth Century-Fox, 43, 49
20–30 Club, 56

Ulua, 72–73
United Nations, 384, 385
Universal Studios, 43
University of Wisconsin, 282
UPI (United Press International), 100, 254, 308, 310, 348, 394, 401–2, 447
Urban Service Corps, 256
Uruguay, 172
USC (University of Southern California), 33, 41, 42
U.S. News & World Report, 137, 266, 283, 447, 454
U Thant, 139

Van Buren, Martin, 156
Vander Heuvel, Gerry, 269, 394
Vanocur, Sander, 192
Velasco, Consuelo, 291–92
Velasco Alvarado, Juan, 292–93
Venezuela, 174–78, 403–4
Vesco, Robert, 405
Vest Pockets of Volunteerism, 266
Veterans of Foreign Wars, 392
Vice Presidency, office of, 113, 130
  car assigned to, 132, 133
  protocol for, 133–34, 147
  salary and expenses for, 169
  staff for, 132–33, 165
Victor, Sally, 184–85
Vietcong, 287
Vietnam, 135, 138–39
Vietnam, North, 274, 317, 326, 442
Vietnam, South, 268, 269–70, 275, 375, 442
Vietnam Moratoriums, 274–75, 277
Vietnam War, 231, 235, 236, 259, 260
  Cambodia incursion in, 285–87
  Christmas bombing in, 353–54
  DMZ crossed in, 337
  as election issue in 1968, 238, 239, 244–46
  elections of 1972 and, 347, 350, 352–353
  Haiphong Harbor mined in, 338–39

peace accords violated in, 375
peace talks in, 337, 338, 340, 353–58
Pentagon Papers on, 315–16, 326
POWs in, 317, 338, 353, 370–72, 375
presidential agenda dominated by, 307
Soviet Union and, 337–38, 339–40
U.S. troops withdrawn in, 269, 285
Vietnamization policy in, 269
war crimes issue in, 308
see also anti-Vietnam War movement
Volpe, John, 370
volunteerism, 266–67, 280–81
von Hoffman, Nicholas, 444–45
Voorhis, Jerry, 85, 86, 88, 90–92, 95, 215

Wallace, George, 350
Wallace, Mike, 408
Wall Street Journal, 377, 383, 387, 393
Walters, Barbara, 332
Walters, Vernon, 173, 174, 175, 176, 292
Wanger, Clark, 450
Wardlaw, Mr. and Mrs. John, 163
War on Cancer, 307
War on Drugs, 316
War Powers Resolution (1973), 442
Warren, Earl, 251
Warren, Mrs. Earl, 117
Warren, Jerry, 392
Washington Daily News, 153–54, 186
Washington National Zoo, 336
Washington Post, 99, 119, 159, 193, 252,
    274–75, 280, 281, 286–87, 292,
    348, 349, 366, 386, 402, 407, 444–
    445, 446–47
Washington Special Action Group
    (WSAG), 325
Washington Star, 130–31, 170, 201
Watergate, 90
  as election issue in 1972, 348
  family position on, 408–9
  impeachment proceedings and, 396,
    400–401, 409, 415–16, 417, 421,
    423, 424–25
  Martha Mitchell and, 394
  Pat Nixon's reaction to, 90, 343, 354
  Richard Nixon's resignation and, 368,
    372–73, 397–98, 415–30
  Richard Nixon's speech on, 368–69
Watergate Committee, 98, 365–98
  Dean's testimony before, 375–77
  double standard in, 377–79
  "enemies list" before, 376–77
  indictments following from, 402–3

"missing" tapes and "gaps" issue before,
    388
private gain issues before, 386–88
Stennis compromise accepted by, 383
tape transcripts in, 409–10
taping system revealed in, 379–81
witnesses called by, 377
Watergate Special Prosecutor's Office,
    431–32, 437
Watt, R. G., 42, 44, 46–47, 48
Watts, Phil, 135
Wayne, John, 456
Weather Underground, 274, 282
Weekly Compilation of Presidential
    Documents, The, 360
Welander, Robert O., 325–26
Wells, Fay Gillis, 298, 311
West, Jessamyn, 300–301, 447, 455
Western White House (San Clemente
    home), 271–72, 319, 373, 386–88
White, Theodore, 192, 244
White House, 260–68
  antiques in, 263
  at Christmas, 303
  difficulties of living in, 255, 278
  gardens of, 390–91
  isolation of President in, 363
  Jacqueline Kennedy's decoration of,
    260–61, 262, 264, 297
  lighting of, 304–5
  Pat Nixon's decoration of, 260–64, 416
  Richard Nixon's enjoyment of, 296–97
  special tours of, 264–65
  staff for, 265
  tape recording system in, 307–8
  telephone and TV systems in, 261
  tourists in, 255, 278
  worship services at, 267–68
White House Easter Egg Roll, 326
White House Visitors Office, 264, 391
Whitney, John Hay, 169
Whittier, Calif, 50–51
Whittier, John Greenleaf, 50
Whittier College, 50–51
Whittier Community Players, 54–55
Whittier Daily News, 86, 155, 273
Whittier Review, 57
Whittier Union High School, 48–49, 51,
    55, 70–71
Wicker, Tom, 283
Williams, Tennessee, 225
Willkie, Wendell, 85
Wilson, Eleanor, 314
Wilson, Jerry, 316

Wilson, Richard, 127, 354
Wilson, Woodrow, 18, 20
Winchester, Lucy, 267–68, 272–73,
    297–98, 326, 371, 402, 422, 440
Wingert, Bewley and Nixon, 56, 73
With Nixon (Price), 376, 383, 453
Witness (Chambers), 101
Women's Advisory Commission on
    Aviation, 391
women's rights, 321–22
Women's Wear Daily, 281, 393
Woodbury College, 33
Woods, Rose Mary, 159, 169, 285, 341,
    411, 457
  on Asia trip, 135
  background of, 110
  in elections of 1952, 121, 124
  in elections of 1960, 191, 198, 199,
    201
  in elections of 1968, 227, 240
  in gubernatorial campaign, 207
  as Herter Committee bookkeeper, 97
  in New York, 220
  Pat Nixon's relationship with, 110–11
  after resignation, 432, 435

  in resignation decision, 420, 421–22,
    423
  on South American trip, 176
  on staffing needs, 165–66
  Watergate investigation and, 361, 369,
    389–90
Woodward, Bob, 446
Woollcott, Alexander, 55
World War I, 20
World War II, 72, 75–83
Worley, Chandler, P., 80
Wray, Marsha Elliott, 28–29
Wyeth, Andrew, 459–60
Wyeth, Jamie, 460–61
Wyeth, N. C., 459–60

Yahya Khan, Agha Muhammad, 325
Years of Upheaval (Kissinger), 411
Young, David, 325
Young Democrats of Rock Island County,
    451
Yugoslavia, 299, 300

Ziegler, Ron, 248, 302, 368, 383, 392,
    409, 421, 428

PICTURE CREDITS

Author's collection: 1–15, 17–21, 23–28, 30–33, 37, 38, 42, 49, 55, 68, 97, 103, 104
A.P. (Billy) Bell/Nixon Volunteers: 29
Del Ankers Photographers: 52
Mr. and Mrs. Jack Drown: 34, 41
Engstead: 43
Hessler Studio: 50
Los Angeles Times: 16
New York Times: 65
San Francisco News: 22
UPI: 35, 36, 39, 40, 51, 56, 58, 59, 61, 62, 66, 67, 69, 72–75, 81, 82, 85, 86, 89, 91, 95, 96, 98–101
Hank Walker, *Life Magazine*, c 1960 Time Inc.: 63
White House: 45, 46, 57, 70, 71, 76–80, 83, 84, 87, 88, 90, 92–94, 102
Wide World: 44, 47, 48, 53, 54, 60, 64

The author expresses appreciation to Vincent Virga, photography editor, for his perceptive and expert assistance.